# THE CLINICAL PRACTICE OF CHINESE MEDICINE

# THE CLINICAL PRACTICE OF CHINESE MEDICINE

Lonny S. Jarrett

*The cover depicts Yijing hexagrams 23 on the left and 24 on the right. Hexagram 23, "splitting apart," represents the accumulation of mundane* yin *and the process by which authentic nature is eroded. Hexagram 24, "the return," symbolizes the return of* yang *as our guiding spiritual influence and the basis of authentic self. Side by side, these hexagrams represent two gates, the gate of death (23) and the gate of life (24). Positioned in front of these two gates, we are reminded that every action we take and word we speak has one of two consequences and results in either perpetuating, or dispelling, suffering and ignorance. The choice is always ours.*

---


*Published by Spirit Path Press, PO Box 1093, Stockbridge, MA 01262*
*http://www.spiritpathpress.com*
*Email: Lonny@nourishingdestiny.com*

*Library of Congress Catalog Card Number: 2003096297*
*ISBN Number: 0-9669916-1-3*

*Book Design by Ruth Kolbert*
*Composition by Toni Kenny, Elements of Design*



*Printed and bound in the United States.*

---

DISCLAIMER

*This book is designed to provide information on the covered subject matter. It is sold with the understanding that the material herein is scholarly in nature and that any clinical application is the sole responsibilty of the practitioner. Readers should consult a licensed herbalist before making use of any plant for medical purposes.*

*Every effort has been made to make this text as accurate as possible. However, there may be errors in content or that are typographical in nature. The author and Spirit Path Press have neither liability nor responsibility to any entity or any person with respect to any loss, injury, or damage caused, directly or indirectly, by the information contained in this book.*

*If you do not agree to the above, you may return this book to the publisher for a full refund.*

*To the Revolution*

# CONTENTS

# FOREWORD

> Yi, the legendary master archer, can teach you how to shoot, but he cannot make you hit the bull's-eye. Wang Liang, the famous warrior, can teach you how to handle a battle cart, but he cannot prevent you from toppling over. In the same vein, the essential details of the art of medicine can be communicated through words, but their inner meaning cannot be fully transmitted through the medium of language; they can be expressed through the rationale of numbers, but they cannot be fully understood through this rationale alone. When faced with the unlimited potential of life's changes, therefore, one must ultimately rely on the truth that flows from one's own heart rather than on the rigid adherence to orthodox principles—otherwise loss will be certain.
>
> – *From Fang Xiaoru (Ming dynasty),*
> *"The Physician in Touch with the Source"*

Lonny Jarrett has written another book in his unmistakable style. In *The Clinical Practice of Chinese Medicine,* he continues the message that Oriental medicine is not merely a technique, but an art that draws near when its core begins to resonate with the heart and spirit of the approaching student. He invokes respect for the ancient source of the medicine, including the five-element lineage of his teacher J. R. Worsley, and correlates them to more recent philosophical trends favored by modern TCM, but it is the writing between the lines that carries the main pronouncement of this work: at a certain stage in every practitioner's development, similar to a calligraphy student who is eventually done imitating the brush strokes of his predecessors, there is the need to soar and arrive at the heart of one's own medicine.

While providing a tremendous amount of clinical information that is immediately applicable in a practicable realm, *The Clinical Practice of Chinese Medicine* primarily transmits this message. In a sense, this work must be read as the autobiography of a master practitioner who shows us his roots, his growth process, and the amalgamation of Chinese medicine with everything he is, thinks, and knows—all in the spirit of inspiring us to do the same. Drawing us into the author's world, which includes the *Daodejing,* the Yellow Emperor's Classic of Medicine, J. R. Worsley, Don Beck, Andrew Cohen, and Ken Wilber, this work empowers each one of us to recognize and awaken our own mastership. It thus continues a silver thread of inspirational writing that goes back to the sages of Chinese medicine themselves. The Ming dynasty scholar Sun Zhixiong once stated, "Medicine is a combination of fixed principles and their flexible usage that makes them come alive in the magic of the moment. The former transmits the truth of the ages, while the latter follows the subtle dynamics of time. Both of them need to be adhered to." His famous contemporary Sun Yikui, in a tableau entitled "A Biography of Six Masters," took this message even further.

> A physician becomes perfect in the waves of change. Adherence to rigid principles will only create stagnation. Every wanderer on the path of medicine necessarily looks to the laws of nature expounded by the masters of old, but when the moment of action arrives, s/he must receive the transmission of the heart and become enlightened to the atmosphere of the moment when the sages first recognized these laws—almost as if one was creating these laws oneself, over and over again.

The Song dynasty literatus Guo Yong, finally, pointed out in his "Supplementation of What Has Been Lost from the Shanghan Lun" that one must be both academician and shaman alike when aspiring to become a master practitioner of Chinese medicine:

> Zhang Zhongjing's art stems from academic learning, while Hua Tuo's was the gift of enlightenment. When the heart awakens, the waves of change become maneuverable—this way of practicing is unique and may appear strange to others, and only a few may be able to follow the likes

> of Hua Tuo when studying his techniques. Realistically, therefore, academic instruction needs to begin with those essential details that can be a standard for generations of physicians. The archetype for this style of transmission is, of course, Zhang Zhongjing. His way within the Dao of medicine is the way of the constant. Hua Tuo, on the other hand, exemplifies the way of change that puts the constant to use.

While the field of Oriental medicine seems to be heading more and more toward a state of domination by standardized textbooks, standardized tests, and a standardized pantheon of Chinese medicine heroes, this book shows us how much life, creativity, passion, and intuition lies in the vast depths of our growing profession, and models how these rather personal sparks combine rather naturally with the data of the classical traditions to cast the cultivational path of the healer. Personally, it makes me extremely happy that the field of Oriental medicine has matured to produce a Lonny Jarrett. It reflects well on all of us.

HEINER FRUEHAUF
*Chair, Department of Classical Chinese Medicine*
*National College of Naturopathic Medicine*
*Portland, Oregon*
March 2003

# PREFACE

This book is divided into five parts that correspond to different aspects of clinical practice. Part I focuses on treatment paradigms that help level the playing field as a first therapeutic step in order to lay a foundation for subsequent constitutional and ongoing treatment. In Part II, I present different categories of acupuncture points and their clinical implications. In Part III, I consider treatment planning and how to prioritize the material already presented in the context of clinical practice. I also suggest how to offer therapeutic suggestions effectively and the importance of metaphor as medicine in restoring conscious awareness. I then examine the nature of acupuncture point function as an evolving inquiry. In Part IV, I discuss the inner nature of all the acupuncture points on the twelve main meridians as well as my rationale for combining points. Finally, Part V addresses the cognitive styles in the practice of Chinese medicine. Here I create a context for understanding the types of consciousness that have impacted the practice of Chinese medicine throughout its history up to the present.

## *Part I*

A general principle in Chinese medicine is to clear stagnation prior to tonifying deficiencies. There is no greater source of stagnation in life than having lost the authentic self. Hence Part I focuses on treatments to clear shock that separates heart from mind and thus rectify the heart/kidney axis. In this way the primordial influence of original nature as the guiding force in our lives can be restored. Without first creating such a framework of functional harmony, it is unlikely that subsequent treatment will promote healing in a way consistent with the core values elaborated in *Nourishing Destiny*. Therefore, in Chapter 1, I discuss the physiology of shock and the importance of recognizing it and clearing it early in treatment. I also review my previous work and sum up my current orientation toward the clinical practice of Chinese medicine.

The subsequent chapters in Part I review treatment protocols that form the core of my approach to resolving shock and setting the stage for ongoing constitutional treatment aimed at healing the fundamental divisions within us that maintain our false sense of a separate self. Most of the paradigms reviewed here are utilized extensively in the lineage of J. R. Worsley, and here I discuss my understanding of them arrived at in the context of my own studies and clinical practice.

In Chapter 2, I examine "evil *qi*" *(xieqi)* or aggressive energy (AE) and its role in obscuring authentic self. I address the nature and etiology of AE and provide detailed instructions on how to clear its presence. I find this to be one of the most generally applicable and profound treatments for removing the pathological *qi* that fuels habituated thought and behavior.

In Chapter 3, I talk about the phenomenon of possession, its historical context, and modern clinical relevance. I discuss possession as a phenomenon that obscures both the authentic self and egoic personality and from the perspective that ego itself is a type of possession which clouds the reality of who we truly are. When it is indicated, the treatment of possession must take precedence over other methods because that which possesses will deny the benefits of all other treatment as long as it maintains dominion over the patient.

Chapter 4 presents the husband/wife (H/W) imbalance in its clinical context. The presence of the H/W suggests a patient is highly vulnerable to serious illness and that *yin* and *yang* are at a terminal point of separation. This is a state that is almost always arrived at through suppression of the evolutionary impulse as it manifests in the alignment of human will with the will of heaven. The philosophical context of this imbalance was discussed at length in Chapter 7 of *Nourishing Destiny*. Here I review some of this material while providing the detailed protocol of how to clear this block.

Chapter 5 considers the flow of *qi* in the twelve main meridians and how its disruption can manifest as exit/entry (E/E) blocks that have broad clinical implications. If the functional apparatus of the twelve main channels is not intact, treating points on the channels will often not have the desired result. Because of their global implications, clearing even one E/E block has the potential to relieve a wide range of dysfunctional expressions.

In Chapter 6, I continue the theme of E/E points by discussing the implications of such blockage when it occurs between the conception (CV) and governor vessels (GV). An E/E block between these two extraordinary channels can effectively starve our entire being by denying us connection to our primordial sources of *yin* (CV) and *yang* (GV). Such a blockage can result from physical trauma, but it more often occurs as a result of suppression that arises as we react unconsciously to a perceived betrayal of intimacy.

Chapter 7 examines the akabane imbalance. The presence of this block indicates that the flow of *qi* is disrupted between the left and right halves of a paired meridian. Like E/E blocks, akabane imbalances must be corrected at the beginning of treatment in order to ensure the functional integrity of the meridian system as a whole.

Chapter 8 considers the role of centering the umbilical pulse in order to establish functional integrity of the center early in treatment. This is a gentle technique that has both diagnostic and therapeutic value and can often be utilized during the physical exam portion of the initial intake.

In Chapter 9, I present a simple point protocol I have developed for quieting the mind when patients are so agitated they cannot relax enough to assimilate healing. This method can be useful when a patient is so identified with thought that the mind will not lower its defenses enough to allow the patient to introspect or contemplate.

In Chapter 10, I address my use of Chinese herbal medicine for establishing functional balance early in treatment. Formulas are presented for stabilizing the pulse, clearing blood stagnation, calming the spirit, opening the sensory orifices, clearing E/E blocks, treating possession, and clearing pathogens.

Lastly, in Chapter 11, I discuss other blocks that can prevent ongoing treatment from being successful. These include detrimental lifestyle choices that perpetuate pathology that is too strong for treatment alone to overcome. The likely presence of these blocks can be noted during the intake and addressed early in treatment. These blocks must also be considered if treatment is not progressing despite having cleared all imbalances according to the methods presented in earlier chapters.

## *Part II*

Part II elaborates the point paradigms that are useful in long-term constitutional treatment. Here I outline the fundamental categories as they occur to me in my clinical practice.

In Chapter 12, I discuss the sixty-five element points as they form the basis of the five-element tradition of acupuncture. I review the five-element model as a context for understanding the broad uses of this most important point category. I then examine the diverse application of these points in both diagnosis and treatment. I present five-element point protocols beginning with standard four-needle technique and transfers of *qi* as well as several paradigms of using five-element points I have cultivated in my clinical practice. I include a methodology to help you understand the rationale for point selection in the five-element tradition and to help cultivate your ability to think synthetically.

Chapter 13 focuses on the source points and their importance in bringing treatments under the guiding influence of nature. These points provide access to a primordial source of *qi* that can renew life and touch, to some degree, every aspect of functioning inherent in the other points on a given channel.

Chapter 14 presents *luo* points (junction points) from several perspectives. I discuss their traditional roles of uniting paired meridians, joining the bilateral halves of each channel, and venting pathogenic *qi* to the exterior. I also review their role in helping direct awareness relatively internally or externally in life.

Chapter 15 presents the *xi*-cleft points and their importance in moving stagnation in the officials.[1] I discuss how to combine them with *luo* points to clear pathological mental states that result from the compounding of emotions due to excessive engagement with one's feelings.

Chapter 16 presents the *mu* points and their use in both diagnosis as well as treatment. I address both their functions of moving stagnation and of tonifying the true *yin* of an official.

In Chapter 17, I present the *shu* points, which constitute strong reserves of *qi* for each official. I consider the fundamental relationships between each inner and outer *shu* point and the corresponding governor vessel point at the same anatomical level.

Chapter 18 discusses the concept of spirit points, their properties, and when they are appropriate in treatment. The "heavenly window" points are a special class of spirit points, presented in Chapter 19. I examine the inner workings of the window points and why they can be so strong in revitalizing the spirit and revealing the authentic self.

Chapter 20 presents the meeting points and their role in integrating any given treatment by providing a functional connection between the other points chosen. One meeting point can serve as the focal point that unites a complex treatment into a single intention. The brevity of this chapter does not diminish the importance of understanding how to utilize this important point category.

## *Part III*

Part III is a transitional section that forms a type of pivot between the application sections presented earlier and the discussion of individual acupuncture point functions that constitute Part IV.

In Chapter 21, I discuss my approach to treatment planning, which includes both a discussion of how I prioritize the clearing methods presented in Part I as well as how I initiate constitutional treatment in a patient utilizing some of the point categories covered in Part II. I also offer advice so practitioners from other traditions may begin to incorporate the material thus far presented into clinical practice.

In Chapter 22, I present the suggestive process in treatment and the importance of metaphor in restoring conscious awareness. People make themselves sick by personalizing thoughts and feelings as myths created in their native tongue. Chinese medicine provides a rich metaphorical language in its physiological concepts, as well as in the names of the herbs and acupuncture points that can be used in both diagnosis and treatment. Here I provide some general rules to help guide the process of communication in clinical practice.

In Chapter 23, I talk about my orientation toward acupuncture point function. This discussion sets the stage for my elaboration in Part IV of the individual natures of each of the acupuncture points on the twelve main channels.

## *Part IV*

Part IV contains thirteen chapters. The first twelve (Chapters 24–35) cover the inner functions of all the points on the twelve main meridians in the order of *qi* circulation, beginning with the heart and ending with the spleen official. In these chapters I present the main and alternate names and Chinese characters for each point, which are later referenced in a separate index to the appropriate lesson in Weiger's etymological text and *Mathews' Chinese-English Dictionary* to help you with your own research.

In Chapter 36, I elaborate how I combine points to empower specific virtues in a patient. Detailed analysis of many point combinations will empower you to comprehend this aspect of treatment and further develop it for yourself.

### *Part V*

Chapter 37 discusses the cognitive styles present in the practice of Chinese medicine. I elaborate the differences between the five-element and eight-principle systems and conclude they are complementary in nature and exist implicitly within each other. The five-element system relates relatively more to treating the innate constitution, whereas the eight-principle system, as it forms the core of modern Traditional Chinese Medicine (TCM), is relatively more useful for treating the acquired constitution.[2] I examine the reasons for the predominance of the eight-principle system of thought in the world today and conclude that, unless the natural hierarchy that exists between the two methods and their associated cognitive styles is restored, Chinese medicine will fail to be relevant in the face of the challenges we face as a species. I finish by considering the different stages in the evolution of human consciousness, according to Spiral Dynamics, as they have impacted the development of our medicine up to the present time.

### *The Appendixes*

Appendix A offers the new practitioner some advice in practice building and management cultivated from my own clinical experience. Appendix B discusses the various needle techniques I employ when treating patients. Appendix C provides tables of the various meeting points as elaborated in Chapter 20. Finally, Appendix D lists resources.

### *Conventions in the Text*

All transliterations of Chinese in this text are written in pinyin, a system for romanizing Chinese ideograms. For the sake of consistency, I have changed all source material, including direct quotes, to pinyin. This is essentially a work on human nature, and therefore I have written the text to be as gender neutral as possible.

## *NOTES*

1. For a discussion of the officials, see *Nourishing Destiny* (hereafter *ND*), Chapter 10.
2. In this text I use the term *TCM* to denote the state-run medical system in modern China, as formulated under the auspices of Marxism, as well as its Western derivatives.

# ACKNOWLEDGMENTS

First and foremost, I would like express my deep gratitude to Andrew Cohen for awakening me to the absolute purpose of life itself. I'd also like to thank my family—Emilie, Anjelica, and Zev, the moon, the stars, and the sun—for their love and patience.

Because this is a clinical text, I must acknowledge my patients, who are my true teachers of Chinese medicine. It continues to be an honor and a privilege to serve you. I am indebted to those who extended the great kindness to me of healing. Special thanks to Lauren Conway, Lauren Henning, and Brinn Quell, who have helped teach me the meaning of strength and character. I'd also like to thank my students, who strive to receive what I try to transmit. I must also acknowledge Dr. J. R. Worsley for his role in helping to preserve the spiritual practice of Chinese medicine.

I'm so appreciative of the time Heiner Fruehauf took to critically read my text. His enlightened perspective on Chinese medicine is a beacon of light that should inspire all who study this art. Great thanks also to Livia Kohn. I consider her many translations and commentaries on Daoist spiritual practice to be the best and most beautiful available. I am so pleased to have the opportunity in this text to introduce the writing of Thea

Elijah. Her inspired perspective promises to bring a new depth of insight to Chinese herbal medicine.

I'd like to thank Dorrit Reznick at the Academy for Five Element Acupuncture in Hallandale, Florida, and Bob Duggan and the other faculty at the TAI-Sophia Institute in Laurel, Maryland. Both schools offer a profound opportunity to learn the spirit of the five-element tradition as discussed in my writing.

I'm very grateful to Kelly D. Welch for helping cross-reference the point names to the reference texts, for fact checking, and for his thoughtful reading of the book. Special thanks to Will Wadsworth for his loyalty, friendship, and insight. I'd also like to thank Jeffrey Yuen for his beautiful calligraphy and for reviewing parts of the text, David LoPriore for his calligraphy and comments on the text, and Sharon Smith for taking the time to review Part I.

Finally, I'm indebted to my outstanding production team: Toni Kenny (composition), Ruth Kolbert (design), and Anne Lesser (editorial), who care as much about their art as I do. And thanks to Tom Huston for creating the tables of the meeting points.

# INTRODUCTION

"I would change nothing in my life if it meant not being here now." These words, when spoken freely, without a waver in the voice or blink of the eye, suggest we have arrived at a place of healing. They imply that we now understand how every trauma we have suffered in our lives has played its role in bringing us back to ourselves. These words can only be spoken sincerely when we have fully grasped that life has damaged no part of our original nature, and, despite our tribulations, we have returned home to remember who we are, why we are here, and what we are supposed to be doing about it. I offer this book to further the efforts of those committed to these ideals in healing.

In my first text, *Nourishing Destiny: The Inner Tradition of Chinese Medicine,* I examined the theoretical foundations of Chinese medicine as an art/science focused on empowering the manifestation of life's purpose. That book concentrates on the historical and theoretical underpinnings of a specific lineage of thought and relatively less on the practical application of clinical techniques to achieve the desired goals therapeutically.

In this book, I elaborate an approach toward clinical practice that will help you administer treatment in a way consistent with the values inherent in *Nourishing Destiny.* I recommend you read my first book and become familiar with its principles before trying the treatments described here. Although this book focuses largely on the application of acupuncture point paradigms, I do include some material on Chinese herbal medicine.

The notion of what constitutes a specific tradition of practice is a complex issue. Individual traditions of Chinese medicine are a composite of several traditions and reflect the ongoing synthesis of material by each practitioner as well as that assimilated by his or her lineage of teachers. Practitioners who identify themselves with the lineage of J. R. Worsley, for example, consider themselves and are identified as five-element practitioners. Although the material presented in Part I comprises a significant part of that tradition, much of it has nothing to with the five-element model. Rather, it represents several diagnostic and treatment paradigms assimilated by Dr. Worsley that are necessary to consider before approaching constitutional treatment in the five-element paradigm. My own clinical experience and study of Chinese medicine has led me to integrate additional methods and ways of knowing into the tradition of practice I relate here.

I remember Ted Kaptchuk describing why in China when a recently fabricated clay pot is represented as an antique, the seller may not be considered unscrupulous. For that pot may be made from the same materials and methods and by the same family that has made such clay pots for generations. It is not the actual pot that is the antique, but the spirit and the intention received through the form of the vessel.[1] Similarly, what I would identify as the tradition associated with J. R. Worsley is based relatively more on identifying a certain spirit of practice and overall orientation toward healing, as opposed to the idea that such a collection of techniques was ever actually practiced historically.

As I did in *Nourishing Destiny,* I have acknowledged historical sources while also relating to the material in a spontaneous way from my own experience in clinical practice. The information here conveys as accurately as possible my approach to treatment. My intention is not to convey the specific methods or recommendations of any other person's thinking or school's curriculum.

In *Nourishing Destiny,* I made the distinction that Western medicine excels at critical care and lifesaving intervention, and Chinese medicine excels at preventive and chronic care.[2] Yet Chinese medicine does, in fact, save life. To live a hundred years and die ignorant is a terrible tragedy. In restoring a patient's memory of original nature and purpose, we have saved life in perhaps an even greater sense than is possible with critical care medicine. For surgery and medication may save the form of a life, but Chinese medicine can resurrect its purpose. Therefore we must approach the return of spirit as the guiding force in an individual's life with the same seriousness and sense of urgency as we would approach any lifesaving intervention. And we must approach the study and cultivation of our art with the highest sense of purpose and discipline. It is my hope that this text furthers these goals.

## *NOTES*

1. See Larre and de la Vallee, 1985, p. 55.
2. *ND*, p. 446.

# PART I

# SETTING THE FOUNDATION

# INTRODUCTION

*The masses, in their frantic creeping about, thirst only after riches and honors. They may well be called walking corpses.*
– GE HONG[1]

A general rule in many traditions of Chinese medicine is the importance of moving stagnation concurrent with or before using methods that tonify. For if we tonify without clearing stagnation, we run the risk of worsening the condition we are trying to treat.[2] If a stove's smokestack is clogged, for example, stoking the flames can only lead to disaster. Many traditions conceive of stagnation in thermodynamic terms and talk of moving stagnant *qi*, blood, or heat or clearing external pathogens such as wind, damp, or cold. There is no more significant or fundamental stagnation in life, however, than what comes from having forgotten our true self.

In conducting a diagnosis, I can basically pose three questions to a patient that are of clinical significance: "Who are you?", "Why are you here?", and "What are you doing about it?" There is ultimately no correct answer to these questions, but there is a correct way of answering. Either the patient is on a path of inquiry into self and life or the patient is not. I do not ask these questions explicitly, of course, but they are implied as I note the quality of the patient's response to every question as well as how his or her answers agree with clinical reality as gleaned by my diagnostic tools.

In the absence of compelling evidence to the contrary, my basic assumption in treating all new patients is that they arrive at my practice in various states of shock. Unless an acute condition threatens the loss of life or function, the initial stage of all treatment involves clearing shock and restoring the memory of original self that lies buried under life's traumas. Clearing shock requires all the therapeutic tools at my disposal including metaphor, acupuncture, and herbal medicine. This stage of treatment thus moves stagnation before it tonifies.

I apply the acupuncture paradigms discussed in Part I in the context of either clearing the therapeutic field before initiating constitutional treatment in a new patient or in addressing these blocks if they arise during ongoing treatment. These protocols derive from the lineage of J. R. Worsley, who learned them in various places and unified them into his own tradition of practice.[3] I present my understanding of them here as they occur within my own orientation. As I said in the Preface, do not take any of the ideas presented here as reflecting any other person's view other than my own regarding the theory or application of these methods. Although I relate here what works for me in my own practice, I have referenced the protocol sections of these chapters to Sharon Smith's *The Five Element Acupuncture Handbook*, which offers a good description and summary of how these protocols are taught at the TAI-Sophia Institute (TAIS) in Maryland.[4]

Dr. Worsley's tradition as he formulated it did not include the practice of Chinese herbal medicine. As his tradition has grown in the United States, many of his students have gone on to include the practice of Chinese herbs in the spirit of his orientation toward healing. After presenting several acupuncture paradigms for clearing and stabilizing the therapeutic field, I discuss the application of some Chinese herbal formulas in clearing shock as I utilize them in my practice.[5]

## *NOTES*

1. Ware, 1966, p. 76.
2. This same notion is expressed nicely by Zhang Congzheng in the *Rumen Shiqin* (c. 1228): "[Physicians who] consider a supplementing [therapy] for persons who have been affected by evil [influence] accumulations [already] are followers of Gun who drowned in the great flood [because he applied the wrong method to drain it]," *Rumen Shiqin*, Chapter 2, quoted in Unschuld, 1988, p. 216. For a discussion of Emperor Yu and how he quelled the flood by leading the excess waters to the sea, see *ND*, pp. 16–20.
3. The influences of J. R. Worsley's tradition of practice are well covered in Eckman, 1996.
4. Smith, 1998.
5. I learned herbs in my studies with both Ted Kaptchuk and Leon Hammer as well as through my own research. Since 1986, Thea Elijah has been my main inspiration in the study of herbal medicine.

# I

# THE NATURE OF SHOCK

*The way to transcend karma lies in the proper use of the mind and will. The oneness of all life is a truth that can be fully realized only when false notions of a separate self, whose destiny can be considered apart from the whole, are forever annihilated.*

– *Li Junfan*[1]

IT IS A MATTER OF FATE THAT EACH OF US WILL LOSE ORIGINAL nature and forget ourselves early in life. Whether we wake up to rediscover the lost self or die ignorant is a matter of our choice to either turn away from or embrace destiny. In Chapter 6 and 7 of *Nourishing Destiny,* I discuss the human journey through life and the progression of losing and possibly regaining original nature. I suggest you review that material now because it will help you create a context for this discussion. Here I elaborate the basic physiology of this model as it pertains to separation of the five elements and loss of integrity in the heart/kidney axis due to shock.

Essentially, each of the five-element constitutional types is conceived with a virtue that is to be manifested in the world during life. This virtue is stored in *jing* and corresponds to the function of the *yin* official in each elemental pair. Each of the five elements also possesses a spirit that is relatively *yang* in nature compared to the *yin* of the potential virtue. This spirit falls relatively under the purview of the *yang* officials and overlaps with what Westerners call *mind.* See depictions of these relationships in Figures 1.1 (pp. 6–7) and 1.2 (p. 12).

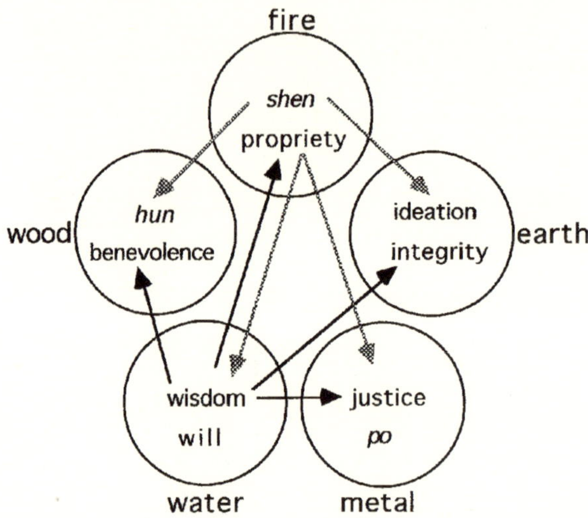


*Figure 1.1a*

SPIRIT AND VIRTUE: THE HEART/KIDNEY AXIS

*The* shen *rises out of the kidney* jing *and ascends to its throne in the palace of the heart. The* shen *then radiates to each of the other elements just as the emperor is present in each of his ministers. Hence the heart provides* shen *to each of the other* yin *officials. This relationship is shown by the dotted arrows. The kidney provides* jing, *which is the basis of virtue in life, to each of the other* yin *officials. This relationship is shown by the solid arrows. The heart/kidney axis is the only direct line of communication between heart* shen *and kidney* jing. *The alignment of this axis matches our alignment to the poles of heaven and earth, and its integrity is vital to our ability to manifest destiny in life.*

The heart/kidney axis is the foundational axis of alignment between the spirit and potential virtue of each human being. It is the interpenetration of the *shen* and *jing* through this axis that allows us to know ourselves through introspection and permits our original natures to flourish in the world. Whereas the conception and governor vessels align us to the cosmological poles of heaven and earth, the heart/kidney axis aligns all functions to these poles as they exist within us. The functional integrity of this axis is maintained by *zhengqi,* the "upright *qi*" that Porkert states is the very basis of immunity.[2] When the heart/kidney axis is compromised, we become vulnerable to functional imbalances such as aggressive energy, possession, or the husband/wife imbalance. Eventually such functional blocks and imbalances become embodied as illness.

The axis between the spirit and virtue of each element is a microcosm of the heart/kidney axis. The integrity of each minor axis within each element and the integrity of the heart/kidney axis are reciprocally related to each other. Any shock in life that compromises the heart/kidney axis will

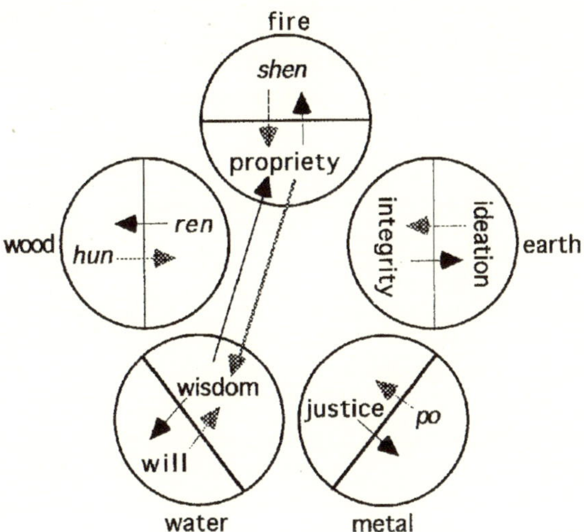


*Figure 1.1b*

SPIRIT AND VIRTUE: THE HEART/KIDNEY AXIS

*The heart/kidney axis is replicated within each pair of* yin *and* yang *officials as the* shen *and* jing *of each pair of officials interact. The relative nature of* shen *is* yang, *and the relative nature of* jing *is* yin. *The radiance of each element's spirit may be likened to the workings of the mind in probing our depths and in conveying our virtue to the outside world. Inasmuch as this is so, we may associate the* shen *of each element with the mental-level functioning of the* yang *official in each elemental pair. The* jing, *which is the basis of each element's virtue, is associated with the* yin *official in each pair. It is the action of each* yang *official in focusing the* shen *on the* jing *that allows us to manifest our specific elemental virtue in life.*

disrupt the interpenetration of spirit and virtue within a given element as predicted by the patient's constitutional dynamics. Any shock that affects the interpenetration of the *yin* and *yang* officials that comprises a specific element will, through resonance, compromise the integrity of the heart/kidney axis itself.

Hence in initial treatment we must focus on restoring the heart/kidney axis as the internal pillar that supports evolution and life. We can accomplish this by removing specific impediments to the interpenetration of *jing* and *shen,* such as possession or the presence of aggressive energy, or by stabilizing the heart so it may begin once again to focus internally on *jing*. In fact, you can think of all the protocols covered in Part I as clearing the therapeutic field by empowering the reintegration of the heart/kidney axis.

The physiological dynamics of shock can be explained in the following way. At the moment of receiving the primary shock in life that initiates our loss of original nature, functional dynamics are disrupted to a degree that they cannot be spontaneously recovered according to the normal

 *THE AUTHENTIC NATURE OF SPIRIT* 

The cycling of the five elements represents life's endless process of transformation on planet earth. This process is represented as being cyclical because the ancient Chinese had no knowledge of evolution. The five-element cycle can be taken to represent the relativity of all conditioned phenomena. Hence each season repeats as an endless cycle of weather, thought, and feeling. External syndrome patterns arise when we personalize the weather, and internal syndromes arise when we personalize our thoughts and feelings. Each of the sixty element points can be thought of as representing a specific nuance of weather (external circumstance), thought, and feeling that typify a fixed constitutional position in life. Stuck habitually in this cycle of *samsara,*[3] the conditioned mind sees only its own perspective, which colors all of life's experience. In this regard the five-element cycle is a cycle of ignorance to be transcended. The absolute position in this model is represented by the axis (*taiji*) between heaven and earth around which the elements spin. This straight line represents the perspective of the authentic self as it arises out of its ground of being to join the two cosmic poles. The notion of this straight line is present as the stroke for heaven (一) as it unites the heart (心) and mind (目) in the character *de* (德) denoting both original nature and virtue. Similarly, the absolute perspective is represented by the heart/kidney axis as it mediates the interpenetration of *jing* and *shen* that is our foundation of liberation from the fears and desires of the ego. *Zhenqi* (真氣) can be translated as "authentic *qi*." As such it is the *qi* of destiny fulfilled and is equivalent to the will of the authentic self to manifest only that which is straight (*yang*, virtue, wholesomeness) in life.

Historically, the Chinese had no concept of a unified soul. Like all things, spirit was differentiated according to its elemental quality, and each of the elements was thought of as having its own spirit. From the absolute perspective, however, all five spirits are blended into one and the authentic self is the basis of all spiritual expression. From this perspective, spirit can be understood to be that aspect of ourselves that is never touched by life. It is fully formed within at conception and, throughout life, is always ready to be expressed as absolute virtue the moment we choose to identify with it. Therefore, when I discuss treating at an illness at a spirit level we must understand that it is never the spirit itself that is sick or in need of healing. From this perspective all notions discussed in this text, such as "scattered *shen*," "wandering *hun*," or possession, must be understood to represent distortions of the mind as it is conditioned by ego.

checks and balances of the *sheng* and *ke* cycle. Congruent with receiving this shock, *qi,* of the specific elemental quality associated with our constitutional type, floods through our being. The emotion associated with our constitutional type streams into consciousness and is forever paired with our pain of losing original nature.

At this precise instant of childhood, we do something we have never done in the face of all previous stresses in life: we generate a belief about our own nature and the nature of life itself so we can cope with what appears to us as unbearable pain. The specific belief we create, however, does not conform to reality. Rather it serves only to turn our minds away from distress in a way that gives birth to the created self. Now our mind turns outward into the world, looking for the source of our pain externally instead of looking inside to the truth contained in *jing.* Thus the integrity of the heart/kidney axis is compromised as *shen* fails to penetrate *jing.* Disordered beliefs about life and self obscure communication between the *yin* and *yang* officials of the constitutional element as health slowly erodes (see Figure 1.2, p. 12).

The created self, or ego, is essentially a defensive mechanism that thrives on our personalization of our thoughts and feelings. Eventually true self, based on the natural spontaneity *(ziran)* of *dao,* is wholly forgotten as we identify our thoughts and feelings as constituting who we are. Because the created self is born in a moment of trauma, the operational assumption of our lives, to the extent they are predicated on ego, is of there being a fundamental problem and conflict at the root of existence itself. This conflict is then projected continually throughout life in a way determined by constitutional dynamics. The nature of the false self is that it will usurp all resources available in order to maintain its possession of a person. Hence all endeavors born of ego are ultimately unfulfilling as we are driven to work excessively both emotionally and physically, ultimately to deplete our reserves of *jing, qi* and *shen.*[4]

With their minds turned externally, children's coping mechanisms distort their innate virtues into talents that help them survive in the world. For example, benevolence, a virtue associated with the wood element, becomes distorted into decisiveness. Hence the wood constitution learns to argue well but, failing to embrace the virtue of benevolence, becomes excessively concerned with being right to the point of being belligerent and judgmental when confronted with any perceived injustice. Over time such distortions tend to become embodied as illness.

The created false self permeates every aspect of who we are as if we were looking at life through a window with a tint on it. The color and quality of this tint corresponds to the elemental associations of our constitutional type. From the perspective of looking through this window, all of life is colored with our dysfunction. However, to borrow a metaphor from Daoism, we do have a choice to take one step toward the central axis *(taiji)* around which the elements spin and align ourselves with the absolute.[5] From the absolute perspective, the conditioned five elements are a cycle of ignorance and delusion perpetuated by the personalization of thoughts and feelings internally, and the external circumstances of life as symbolized by the weather.[6]

When we have embraced the absolute perspective, the ego is only one degree of life's circle and we immediately experience 359 degrees of freedom. The ego, thoughts, and feelings are still present, but they no longer play a significant role in motivating speech or behavior. From this perspective we can see through our stories and the workings of our minds. Now the metabolic resources that sustained the false self are harnessed for the sake of the whole.

The primary virtue of the center, corresponding to the earth element, is integrity (*xin:*信), which emerges as that ultimate stagnation of false self is cleared from every aspect of our being. When earth (integrity and intention) properly controls water (will and fear), fear will cease to overwhelm the opening of the heart as compassion and intuition are restored.

In rectifying the heart/kidney axis and restoring the integrity of the constitutional element, the dysfunctional *qi* that supports the existence of the created self dissipates. Eventually destiny reasserts its primal urge to manifest as we stop identifying with the thoughts and emotions that fuel the dysfunctional stories we generated as children or young adults in order to survive. In this way our acquired talents may better reflect virtue as innate purpose once again flows freely into the world. With destiny fulfilled, all virtues become one as we can be viewed from any direction and no deviation is found in our hearts. In fact, this is the very definition of virtue (*de:*德) itself.[7]

As the influence of the created self diminishes, the natural hierarchy inherent in the *sheng* and *ke* cycles emerges to become the predominant force in guiding physiological relationships. Now all the officials, and especially the constitutional official, perform their functions for *the sake of the whole* rather than to support their own narcissistic agendas based on habitual reaction to the arising of thought and the presence of feeling.

---

## *A Global and Evolutionary Perspective*[8]

Fifteen billion years ago there was an explosion and something came from nothing. This no-thing is the eternal ground of being that gives rise to the phenomenal universe. The outward momentum of this explosion is the force behind evolution itself. Up until our own moment of original trauma, we too live in a state of nonarising. However, it is fate that we must lose ourselves and, in response to some shock in life that constitutes our own personal "big bang," a new pathological momentum is generated as the ego is born and our life diverges from its ground of being in *dao*.

As adults we may realize the assumptions we made at the age of four no longer serve us at forty-four and that our compensations no longer protect us but are, in fact, gradually killing us. It is in this moment of insight we may understand that nothing ever happened, that the "big bang" was an illusion of our own construction, and we are exactly who we need to be to change now. Similarly, the time has come for the human race as a whole to realize the ego has outlived its usefulness as the primary source of motivation for human behavior.

The ego, or created self, is a vestigial aspect of mind that no longer contributes any significant function to our individual survival or to the survival of the species. The appendix may have, at one time, performed an important physiological function for human beings. Now it merely collects and sublimates toxicity until it cannot contain any more, at which point it ruptures. In such cases, death from toxemia occurs rather quickly in the absence of intervention. Similarly, the ego may well have conferred a selective advantage when we first crawled out of the primordial ooze. Now, however, with nearly six billion egos on earth, it is increasingly clear that greed, narcissism, and self-interest threaten human existence itself.

Humanity is at a turning point.[9] This turning point requires us to choose between the death of the species or the death of the human ego, or collective created self, as the next step in human evolution. For only if humanity can see itself as one with all of creation, and only if our primary motivation as individuals becomes for the sake of the whole, will we humans survive to fulfill the promise of our collective destiny on planet earth.

The clock is ticking, and the time this evolutionary step must be taken is now. For the ego thrives on time alone. Born in our moment of unbearable pain, the ego derives its momentum from our past. It lives fueled by all our erroneous interpretations of our life experience strung together to prove to our imagined selves that we are who we think we are and that life is how we think it is. The ego also thrives on the notion of some imagined future that will afford us the time to change. This notion, that life will at some point be better, allows us to "work on" our issues without actually ever dropping them.[10] The clock is ticking, and the time to change is now.

Acupuncture provides a perfect momentary stimulus to instantly align a patient's *qi* with the absolute to provide a memory of original nature untouched by life experience. However, that experience must be properly nurtured and cared for by the patient or we will only ever help him become relatively more functional. If the patient's own will is not focused on freedom as his primary goal, we will only ever use the five-element system to continually chase his excess and deficiencies around the *sheng* cycle, effectively keeping him in a state of ignorance *(samsara)*.

Every action has one of two consequences: it either perpetuates or dispels ignorance. To harmonize a patient's *qi* and return him home with his ego in control is no different than treating a battered woman and sending her back to an abusive husband. The ultimate goal of treatment is never a relative improvement, but rather an absolute alignment of the heart/kidney axis with the evolutionary momentum of *dao* itself. The ability to initiate such a change does not depend on any level of technical knowledge regarding healing; rather, it is born solely of the practitioner's alignment with the absolute and the desire to be free and engender freedom *more than anything else.*[11]

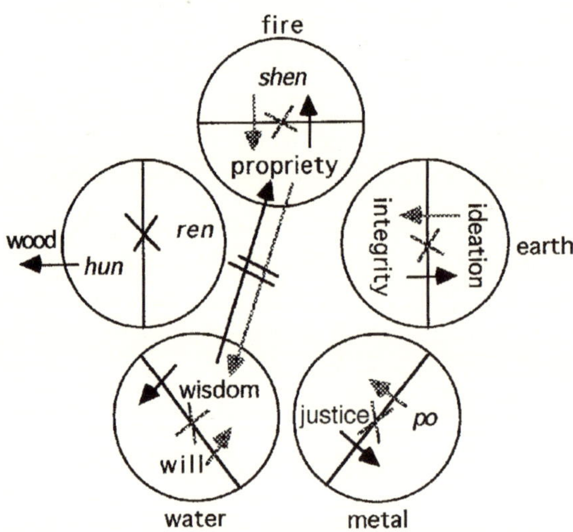


*Figure 1.2*

THE EFFECT OF SHOCK ON THE HEART/KIDNEY AXIS

*This figure depicts the physiological consequences of shock as it disrupts the heart/kidney axis and the integrated function of the five elements in a wood constitutional type. An initial shock has caused the wood element to disrupt communication between its spirit (*hun*) and virtue (*ren*). The aspect of mind associated with the wood element (vision, decisiveness) turns out into the world and away from the potential virtue of benevolence (*ren*) presided over by the* yin *official and stored in* jing*. Along with this shock, the heart/kidney axis is disrupted and the interpenetration of all* yin *and* yang *officials is eroded as the checks and balances of the* sheng *and* ke *cycle are compromised.*

In the following sections, I explain several treatment paradigms that help clear blocks and restore the integrity of the heart/kidney axis in order to lay a solid foundation for long-term treatment. It must be clear at the outset that I view the goal of all healing relative to diminishing the influence of the false self and the emergence of a new being, one that embraces an enlightened perspective on life, not out of self-interest but for the sake of the whole.[12]

---

## *Conclusions*

Here is a summary of my previous work and current orientation toward the material contained in this book:

**I.** Loss of True Self

a. A shock occurs early in life.
b. A constitutional thought (I am this way and life is this way) and emotion is born to which the false self becomes attached to and identified with.
c. A momentum is generated that gives rise to the created self and grows it through a lifetime of accumulated ignorance as we become increasingly separated from reality as based in *dao*.
d. An ignorant death for self and species is the result unless we each make the choice to wake up.

**II.** The Purpose and Method of Constitutional Medicine

a. The constitutional official is "egotistically" usurping all resources to perpetuate its own function while it gradually depletes and undermines the functioning of the whole.
b. Identify the element that is constitutional. This is the element that is most attached to the thought and feeling that sustains the momentum of the created self.
c. Treat the acquired constitution using the eight-principle model and the innate constitution using the five-element model to undermine the momentum of the false self.
d. Educate the patient regarding how symptoms are a manifestation of having a dysfunctional relationship to thoughts and feelings. Help the patient make a connection between what he complains about and his disordered beliefs and behaviors.
e. Act and speak from an absolute perspective in life.

**III.** The Result

a. Having no attachment to either thought or feelings and not identifying them as self.

b. The subjugation of the created self (ego) and the embracing of an enlightened perspective.
c. The spontaneous arising of natural hierarchy as the evolutionary impulse is liberated in the human heart and mind.
d. Vastly more *qi* available to the whole system as it is no longer being usurped by the false self.
e. Lack of self-concern emerges as one's life becomes now for the sake of the whole.

IV. The Big Picture
a. The operating assumption is that there is no time left.[13]
b. The collective ego and false self of humanity is destroying the prospect of human life on earth.
c. The only hope for humanity is letting go of self-interest through a massive ego death/suicide and each of us working for the sake of the whole precisely as predicted by the holographic nature of the five-element model.[14]
d. We practitioners of Chinese medicine have the tools and knowledge to help restore *dao* as the guiding force in human evolution.
e. We cannot take this final step with our patients unless we taste the fruit of the promise of our medicine ourselves.

V. The Premise
a. The enlightened perspective is available now.
b. There are no excuses, and nothing lies in the way to fulfilling our individual and collective destiny, which are one and the same.
c. The first step lies in setting the will *(zhi)* on wanting to be free more than anything else.

## *Questions*

1. If ego did not play a significant role in motivating human behavior,
   a. What would be the relevance of the five-element and eight-principle models of Chinese medicine?
   b. What would be the relevance of psychotherapy?
2. What is in the way of you embracing an enlightened perspective now?
3. Have you set your will to want freedom more than anything else?
4. If you were to obtain an enlightened perspective, what would be in it for you?
   a. Patients come to us with a stated goal of wanting to heal, yet how many really want to accomplish this goal "more than anything else"?
   b. How much of the patient's metabolic resource actually goes into denial of his stated goal of healing?

5. To what degree do we want our patients to receive the potential benefit of our medicine "more than anything else"?
   a. If this is what we truly want for them, could we ever compromise in the pursuit of this goal?
   b. Could we ever be satisfied that patients might only become relatively more functional as a result of treatment?
6. Which is most important, for the practitioner or the patient to have his will fixed on the desired result of treatment?

## *NOTES*

1. Li Junfan (Bruce Lee), 1979, p. 7.
2. Porkert, 1982, p. 172. Note the functional relationship of *zhengqi* to *zhenqi* (authentic *qi*) in empowering immunity see Porkert, p. 171.
3. The Sanskrit term *samsara* denotes the state of being lost in illusion and ignorance. The Chinese characters for *samsara* are *sheng* (生) and *si* (死), denoting life and death, respectively. Hence one caught in a state of *samsara* is trapped in an endless cycle of death and rebirth. The *sheng* (相生序) cycle, denoting the endless transformation of the five elements into each other, in one sense depicts this predicament. The *sheng* cycle is a continual cycle of habitual identification with thought and feeling to the degree the elements are conditioned by ego.
4. For a discussion of the emotions and thoughts associated with each constitutional type, see *ND*, Chapter 10.
5. This discussion represents, in part, an extension of my own ideas based on the writings and teachings of Andrew Cohen, teacher of "Impersonal Evolutionary Enlightenment" and author of many texts as well as founding editor of the magazine *What Is Enlightenment?* His work is available on the Web at Andrewcohen.org or by calling 1-800-376-3210.
6. The presence of external pathogens such as wind, cold, and damp or the "weather" can be viewed as the embodiment of ignorance *(samsara).*
7. For a discussion of the etymology of the character *de*, see *ND*, p. 45.
8. This discussion is based in large part on the work of Andrew Cohen. See note 5.
9. For a review of the turning point and its relevance, see *ND*, Chapter 7.
10. If you have been in clinical practice awhile, you cannot help but be struck by how much resistance most patients have to actually changing in order to further their stated goal of getting better. In fact, we might say that "everyone wants to get better but no one wants to change." For a discussion of the role that waiting plays in perpetuating the suffering born of created self, see Cohen, 2001, pp. 62–64.
11. See note 5.
12. The concept of this "new being" is discussed by Andrew Cohen as part of his teaching model (see Andrewcohen.org). If we look intently at the model of the *sheng* and *ke* cycle in Figure 12.1, it may be clear we are looking at the depiction of a fully functional and integrated living entity that can simultaneously describe both self and culture as a whole.
13. For a discussion of time and its relationship to insight, see my discussion of GV-10 and GV-11 in *ND*, pp. 349–351.
14. For a discussion of the holographic nature of the five-element model, see *ND*, pp. 130–135.

# 2

# AGGRESSIVE ENERGY

*When* yin *and* yang *divide, the five elements become disordered. The five elements, metal, wood, water, fire, and earth, represent the five* qi.[1] *The five elements of early heaven create each other following the* sheng *cycle. These five elements fuse to form a unified* qi. *From them issue forth the five virtues* (de*) of benevolence, righteousness, propriety, wisdom, and integrity. The five elements of later heaven overcome (*ke*) one another following the* ke *cycle. This manifests as the five rebels of joy, anger, grief, happiness, and desire.*

*When the five elements are united, the five virtues are present and* yin *and* yang *form a chaotic unity. Once the five elements divide, the distinguishing spirit (*shishen*) gradually arises, and the encrustation of the senses gradually takes place; truth flees and the false becomes established. Now, even the state of the child is lost.*

– *Liu Yiming*[2]

IN A STATE OF FUNCTIONAL BALANCE, THE FIVE ELEMENTS produce and limit each other effortlessly according to the checks and balances of the *sheng* and *ke* cycles. When shock stops *qi* from flowing in its natural progression around the *sheng* cycle, it tends to become fixed in its expression in a way congruent with constitutional dynamics. Now, instead of regulating each other harmoniously, the elements begin to overcontrol each other dysfunctionally across the *ke* cycle. Pernicious *qi* that travels along the *ke* cycle to injure organ function is termed *aggressive energy* (AE).[3] Such *qi* can form the basis of serious pathology such as cancer, heart disease, mental illness, and other degenerative conditions.[4] Further, AE can distance us sufficiently from original nature that we are unable to manifest virtue in any realm of function.

I test for the presence of AE and drain it if necessary as the first treatment on almost all new patients. If a patient has AE, its presence must be cleared first before doing other treatments that transfer *qi* from one official to another. Otherwise you run the risk of merely aiding the spread of this noxious influence and perpetuating illness. Clearing AE can have such a profoundly positive effect across such a broad spectrum of dysfunctional expression that I consider it one of the single most important point protocols I have at my disposal.[5] Also, because the needles do not penetrate deeply, this gentle technique helps relax patients who are new to this type of treatment.

---

## *What Is Aggressive Energy?*

Porkert has identified several types of pathological *qi* in the literature of Chinese medicine that may provide a historical basis for the notion of AE.[6] These include *keqi* (客氣), *siqi* (死氣), *liqi* (戾氣), *duqi* (毒氣), and *xieqi* (邪氣). Of these, Eckman states that *xieqi* (literally, "evil *qi*") constitutes the historical basis for AE.[7] He attributes the transmission of the AE treatment itself to J. R. Worsley by the French acupuncturist Jacques Lavier.[8] Eckman notes that Li Dongyuan (1180–1251 C.E.) recommends a protocol similar to the draining of AE. Li recommended treating the back *shu* points of the *zang (yin)* organs for any condition resulting from the penetration of any acquired evil *qi* secondary to an internal deficiency of central *qi*. He referred to this as a *yin* disease affecting the *zang* that was located in the *yang* or back. Li considered his approach to be grounded in the theory of the *Shanghan Lun* (200 C.E.).

Aggressive energy is either contracted externally by exposure to a pathogen or generated internally. In its external etiology, AE can be contracted from exposure to pathogens in the environment or from exposure to another person who has AE. The external pathogens are cold (water), wind (wood), heat and fire (fire), damp (earth), dry (metal), and trauma. The presence of AE after such an exposure can not be entirely explained by the pathogen alone. Not everyone who is exposed to a pathogen contracts it, and not everyone who contracts a pathogen develops AE even when the ensuing illness is severe. Hence the specific nature of the patient's internal vulnerability to such a negative influence is central in determining if AE will be generated. Recognizing this, Li Dongyuan emphasized the role of central *qi* deficiency as a contributing factor to our vulnerability to external invasion. From a practical standpoint, discerning the etiology of a patient's AE is not crucial because the treatment and expected result is the same regardless of its origin. Knowing the relative contribution of internal and external factors to this "infection," however, can aid both in prognosis and in directing the patient to make lifestyle changes if AE repeatedly emerges as a clinical issue.

We can think of externally contracted AE in two ways. It is either the result of a fulminating influence that attaches itself to a pathogen or it is generated by the specific interaction of the pathogen with the person. These two possibilities are not mutually exclusive because there is always an interaction between the quality of any given pathogen and the quality of the substrate it is interacting with. Tainted food, water, air, or drugs can all transmit AE to people. Aggressive energy can also be contracted in places or in interactions with people that are experienced as "unclean." Hence I have seen people contract AE after visiting prostitutes, smelling urine in the New York City subways, or witnessing an assault.

None of these specific experiences, however, have any particular elemental pathogen associated with them. But they can all fall under the nonspecific heading of trauma, which is why I mentioned shock as key in the etiology of AE earlier. The influence that initiates the onset of AE in this way appears to be karmic in nature. That is to say, I see it as often congruent with a life lesson to be learned by the patient and with some internal vulnerability within the patient based primarily on a disordered aspect of mind that clouds the spirit. There seems to be in each case a dissonance created between what was experienced and the patient's ability to assimilate what happened with his or her spiritual nature. It is this very conflict that I believe is in evidence when the presence of AE is detected as a quality of vibration on the pulse.

The relationship of the AE to a specific pathogen is similar to the relationship between sarcasm and humor inasmuch as sarcasm can be said to ride on the back of humor. The initial humor in a comment can open our vulnerability to receive a person's bitterness and resentment that is present as sarcasm. In essence, the sarcasm taints the quality of the joke being made. When we are open, we may be particularly vulnerable to the pathological *qi* that resides in certain situations or in the toxic emotional states of others. In fact, I once experienced this phenomenon quite clearly myself. I spent the last week of my acupuncture training studying with Father Claude Larre and Elisabeth Rochat. I was very excited to be graduating and realizing my dream of becoming a practitioner of Chinese medicine. I was also thrilled to spend time with two people I admired as inspired thinkers and for their embodiment of the deeper aspects of Chinese medicine as a living art.

The class required my full attention because of the relatively poor English and strong French accents of the teachers. This bothered me not one bit as it sharpened my focus on not just the words but the expression of these two living masters. Upon returning from a break, I opened the door to enter the lecture hall, and another student who was leaving looked directly at me and said, "Why the hell can't they get us teachers who can speak English?!" I felt her anger and resentment pierce right through me, and by that night I was so on edge I couldn't concentrate or sleep. The next day I sat through a one hour and forty-five minute AE drain and, upon its completion, immediately felt as clear and happy as I had before the negative interaction of the previous day. In retrospect, the student's comment had brought up, in one moment, all my internalized conflict that had been suppressed during years of schooling. Her resentment drew my sublimated anger to the surface to create a strong cognitive dissonance I was unable to let go of, with a massive amount of AE generated as a result.

When internally generated, I consider AE to constitute the most superficial form of *qi* that propagates habitual functioning of the mind as it is mediated by the nervous system. In turn, the mind itself may generate AE as it dwells on negative interpretations of our life experience. Liu Yiming refers to the *qi* of later heaven *(houtianqi)* as the acquired mundane influence that obscures our capacity to know original nature within and truth without. We can think of aggressive energy as a type of mundanity that taints healthy *qi*. This mundanity is generated at the edge where our negative interpretations of life conflict with the true nature of reality as we engage with it. Aggressive energy is both generated by, and perpetuates, the cognitive dissonance that arises when we are exposed to external situations or take actions in the world that are in direct conflict with our reason for being. Later on, I discuss this etiology further in relationship to pathological emotional states.

The mind is the most rapidly transmitted and frequently changing aspect of our being. Subjected to input from within (the spirit) and without (life events), the activity of the mind continually fluctuates trying to balance and integrate these two influences. The presence of AE indicates that a patient is habituated and being run by the superficial functioning of the mind and is relatively less attuned to heaven's will externally or the intention of his or her own heart. Such a person is often described by others as having an "edge" and not being able to relax or introspect.

Dr. John Shen designated the nervous system as corresponding to the outermost level of *qi* and therefore associated it with the *taiyang* level in his four-systems theory.[9] The bladder is the longest meridian in the body and runs parallel to the afferent and efferent nerve roots for the entire length of the spine. The nervous system as the embodiment of mind is accessible through the bladder *shu* points. In this regard, note that the Chinese characters for nervous system are *shenjing* (神精), or literally, "wires that transmit spirit." Hence AE is drained through superficial needling of the bladder *yinshu* points. The *yinshu* points provide access to deep reserves of *qi* for each official. This is in keeping with the function of the bladder official, which is to store reserves. By needling only superficially during the AE drain, we are, in effect, clearing negative influences from the surface of each official's available pool of reserves. If this is not done and the AE is allowed to fulminate, it will tend to pollute and erode the core functions of the affected officials and their associated organ systems.

To summarize, AE is a fulminating pernicious influence that is either contracted externally or generated internally. Externally, it is an opportunistic influence that attaches itself to pathogens to gain entry based on some internal vulnerability. Internally, AE is generated by the cognitive dissonance induced in the mind as our spiritual purpose in life conflicts with our actions and life experiences.

## *Assessing the Presence of AE*

We may discern the likelihood that a patient's functioning is compromised by AE according to a variety of signs. The presence of AE is suggested by a preponderance of toxic emotional states. These emotions result from the mind projecting the source of its pain outward rather than resolving the inner issues on which the suffering is based. Hence the emotions stagnate to cause internal "friction" and heat, with the result that they fulminate and become toxic. Such attitudes and behaviors represent the emotional and spiritual equivalent of chronic infection.

In my clinical experience, I have identified five emotional states that represent the toxic counterparts of the otherwise healthy emotions already identified in the practice of Chinese medicine. These toxic emotions both result from, as well as perpetuate, extreme habitual reaction to the presence of otherwise healthy emotional states. As discussed previously, each of the elements is associated with the presence of a given emotion. The healthy and toxic emotions are listed in Figure 2.1.

| Element | Emotion | Toxic Emotion | Behavior | Display | Experience |
|---|---|---|---|---|---|
| Water | Fear | Paranoia | Secrecy | Intimidating | Impotency |
| Wood | Anger | Resentment | Passive Aggression | Seething | Injustice |
| Fire | Joy | Bitterness | Lying | Sarcastic/Teasing | Betrayal |
| Earth | Sympathy | Disgust | Ingratiation | Complaining | Abandonment |
| Metal | Grief | Disdain | Pontification | Snide | Insult |

*Figure 2.1*
TOXIC EMOTIONS

*In health, individuals are able to feel each emotion without habitually reacting to its presence. Healthy water constitutional types feel fear in the appropriate context and do not unconsciously react to the presence of that emotion in self or in another. Fear does not dictate their actions in the world. When we habitually respond to the presence of a given emotion with that same emotion itself, over time the emotions feed on each other and transform into their toxic counterparts. Therefore, fear of fear becomes paranoia, anger over our anger becomes resentment, sadness as a reaction to our sadness becomes bitterness, needing sympathy because we have so much sympathy leads to disgust, and grief over our grief leads to disdain.*

Each of these pathological emotional states is associated with a deviant type of behavior as well as an outward display of the toxic emotional state. Here I present examples for each of the elements.

Reacting to the presence of the emotion fear with fear itself, the paranoid person projects distrust externally and is therefore secretive. Lying by omission, secretive people manipulate personal relationships by never quite revealing their intentions. They use their hidden resources in an attempt to overwhelm and intimidate others with their pathological will.

Angry over "being made" to feel the emotion anger, resentful people act passive aggressively. They avoid direct confrontation and manipulate their world by trapping others into compliance with their plans and decisions. The suppression of anger leads to mounting internal pressure, which manifests as seething.

Having lost the joy of relationships, those with a dysfunctional fire element may become brokenhearted and bitter. Bitterness over perceived betrayal may lead to lying as they wear a false face in the world and are no longer able to trust enough to let another close. Sarcasm and teasing are the resulting forms of communication that may serve to prevent others from becoming too close. Both behaviors indicate that the essence of the heart is not being communicated clearly to the outside world.

Out of a reaction to feeling sympathy, those with a dysfunctional earth element tend to be ingratiating, catering to others' needs endlessly.

Excessive sympathy leads to the craving of sympathy for the terrible plight of having to take care of everything and everyone. They become disgusted, having "had it up to here" (pointing to St-9), literally not being able to swallow. They communicate disgust by constantly complaining about the neediness of others.

Those possessing a dysfunctional metal element may react to the presence of the emotion grief with grief itself. Possessing the unique ability to find the fatal flaw in everything, metal types may come to disdain what is regarded as lowly. Talking down to everyone, metal types pontificate to the unworthy. What is impure within the self is expressed outwardly as being snide.

These toxic emotional states all result from the compounding of emotions upon themselves. Such states may all be felt in the *yang* complementary positions of the pulse as tight, biting, and often slippery qualities.[10] These very same qualities often indicate the presence of an acute infection. However, when they are present chronically, they may indicate that, like an infection, the emotions themselves have become toxic. Often such emotional states indicate the presence of AE. Aggressive energy may also present initially as a smooth vibration superficially on the pulse and eventually as a rougher and deeper vibration as it penetrates more deeply into inner realms of function and illness becomes more physically manifest.

When sitting with a patient who has AE, we can be struck with an edginess that makes it difficult for the patient's mind to turn inward and introspect. The patient has difficulty relaxing and "letting go" on the treatment table because of the habitual tendency of the mind to engage outwardly and avoid the inner conflict that arises from addressing emotionally challenging material. AE may also present as a constant mental vigilance as the mind attends nervously to every aspect of the patient's environment that could possibly be invasive. This shows up as a superficial tightening on the whole pulse or the positions of affected organs as the mind and nervous system work overtime driven by AE and its associated pathological emotions. After treatment I expect the entire pulse to exhibit less tension over its entire course with less tightness superficially, an overall increase in volume, and diminished vibration at all depths.

When AE is present, patients often manifest symptoms across the *ke* cycle, indicating that one element is pathologically overcontrolling the other. For example, a patient might display simultaneously excessive anger, a sour taste in the mouth, bloating after eating, and sugar cravings. In this scenario, wood may be said to be overcontrolling the earth element across the *ke* cycle. Similarly a patient may display habitual fear regarding intimacy. This pattern speaks to a pathological relationship between water and fire across the *ke* cycle. The qualities suggesting the presence of AE on the pulse are also expected to be found in *ke* cycle relationships pertaining to the officials.

Note that many people, including those who do not have AE, show constitutional patterns that involve *ke* cycle relationships. For example, a person's constitutional pattern may involve the relative balance between the metal and wood elements. This pattern is only suggestive of the presence of AE to the degree the *ke* cycle relationships are dysfunctional and are manifesting in a way that mesh with the presentations described here.

---

## Yin *and* Yang *Organs*

Often AE evidences as tight and biting qualities having noticeable vibration on pulse positions that correspond to the *yang* officials. This is because the *yang* official represents the functional aspect of mind for each elemental pair.[11] In this regard I have found treating the *luo* and *xi*-cleft points of the *yang* official to be an excellent way of supplementing the AE treatment and of preventing the occurrence of AE over time (see Figure 2.2). The *luo* points can vent mundane *qi* to the outside world and thereby deflate the internal pressure that feeds habitual nature. With this tension removed, the habit may be broken long enough for patients to gain perspective on their situation and to stop making it worse by perpetuating it with negative thoughts and behaviors. Of course, combining the *xi*-cleft with the *luo* point can help eliminate latent pathogens as well that may be contributing to the generation of AE. I utilize this technique after AE has been drained and during the course of treatment when AE is not yet present to prevent the accrual of internal emotional toxicity.

| Meridian | *Luo* Point Number and Name | *Xi*-cleft Point Number and Name |
|---|---|---|
| Bladder | 58 fly and scatter | 63 golden gate |
| Gallbladder | 37 bright and clear | 36 outer mound |
| Small intestine | 7 upright branch | 6 nourishing the old |
| Three heater | 5 outer frontier gate | 7 assembly of ancestors |
| Stomach | 40 abundant splendor | 34 beam mound |
| Large intestine | 6 side passage | 7 warm current |

*Figure 2.2*

LUO AND *XI*-CLEFT POINTS ON THE *YANG* MERIDIANS

*Think of the* luo *points on the* yang *meridians as pressure valves that help vent functional consequences of self-perpetuating emotional states trapped in the interior. Note that the names of these points all impart a sense of clearing stagnation and opening to the exterior. The* xi-cleft *points help move the stagnation on which these dysfunctional emotional states are based.*

The *xi*-cleft points on the *yang* meridians may be used to help move the stagnation that supports the pathological expression of the emotional states discussed here. Each element is prone to a certain type of stagnation that can fester and contribute to the presence of AE (see Figure 2.1). Once stagnation is moved, the *luo* points on the *yang* meridians can be particularly useful for draining pernicious *qi* to the exterior.

---

## *Addictions*

Draining AE is one of the single most effective first interventions when treating anyone for an addiction. To some degree, I believe Chinese medicine is primarily effective through its ability to break habits. These may be physical habits such as muscle spasms, gross-level habits such as drug addictions, or more subtle habits such as false concepts of self that sustain the ego structure and the acquired mundane nature.

Aggressive energy is one of the greatest sources of input into the habitual behaviors that fuel addictions. Addictions are based in large part on escaping from some underlying painful truth that the addiction helps suppress from entering consciousness. The addiction itself represents a conflict between who an individual really is and how he or she is behaving in the world. In every instance, addictions are compensatory behaviors that enable us dysfunctionally to avoid cultivating virtue and taking responsibility for our own suffering.

All addictions initially offer an enticement, but over time they erode the virtue that their given bait is meant to attract. For example, marijuana initially offers the user creativity and expanded vision. Over time, however, the virtues of planning, decision making, and growth associated with the liver are eroded to the point that the user is happy to just sit around and smoke pot while accomplishing nothing at all.[12] For a chart of other addictive substances and how they erode virtue, see Figure 2.3.

Clearing AE can help take the force out of addictive behavior long enough for the patient to catch a glimpse of what life is like without it. After years of not being able to stop for more than one day at a time, I have seen patients stop smoking three packs of cigarettes a day until their next treatment five days later after merely one AE drain. Draining AE may afford the patient enough clarity to experience self without the addiction. In this way the memory of original nature can be restored long enough for its influence to begin and reestablish itself. By removing the toxic edge that drives the mind, nervous system, and repetitive behavior, addiction may be broken long enough that subsequent treatments can really take hold to promote the spontaneous function synonymous with health.[13]

## *Interpretation of Findings*

If present, AE tends to manifest as a dark red circle, or erythema, on the skin around the acupuncture needle in the *shu* point corresponding to the affected organ (see Figure 2.4, p. 28).[14] The needles are generally retained until the redness disappears, indicating the AE has been drained successfully (see Photo 2.1, p. 26). To ensure that a reading of AE is accurate, I place a test needle in each *jiao* as a type of control. Some patients have very reactive skin and develop a red erythema anywhere their skin is touched. If a patient has a positive test for AE, the reaction around the needles placed in actual points will probably be substantially larger and darker than any reaction seen around the test needle (see Photo 2.2, p. 27). After needles have been retained for five minutes and no reaction occurs, you may assume AE is not present and remove the needles. It is likely the patient will feel relatively relaxed, and treatment can then progress to whatever next step you deem necessary.

Note which points turn red and their organ correspondences. From the patient's reaction we may discern where the AE began and how it has progressed over time. For example, if a patient evidences AE on Bl-18 (liver), Bl-20 (spleen), and Bl-23 (kidney), we can deduce from the direction of the *ke* cycle that the AE originated on the liver, traveled to the spleen, and then entered the kidney. The seriousness of AE is indicated by the number of "legs" affected along the *ke* cycle. In the example just given, two legs (liver to spleen and spleen to kidney) were involved. If three legs are involved, the patient is likely highly vulnerable to, or suffering

| **Element** | **Drug** | **Promises** | **Erodes** |
|---|---|---|---|
| Water | Heroin | No pain | Will to live |
| | Coffee | Energy | Kidney *yin* and *yang* |
| *User becomes exhausted* | | | |
| Wood | Marijuana | Creativity | Liver yang |
| *User becomes bored and boring* | | | |
| Fire | Sex | Connection | Intimacy |
| *Sex becomes a way of avoiding intimacy* | | | |
| Earth | Sugar | Satiation | Contentment |
| *User is hungry all the time* | | | |
| Metal | Tobacco | No emptiness | Receptivity |
| *Lungs become frail* | | | |

*Figure 2.3*
THE IRONY OF ADDICTION

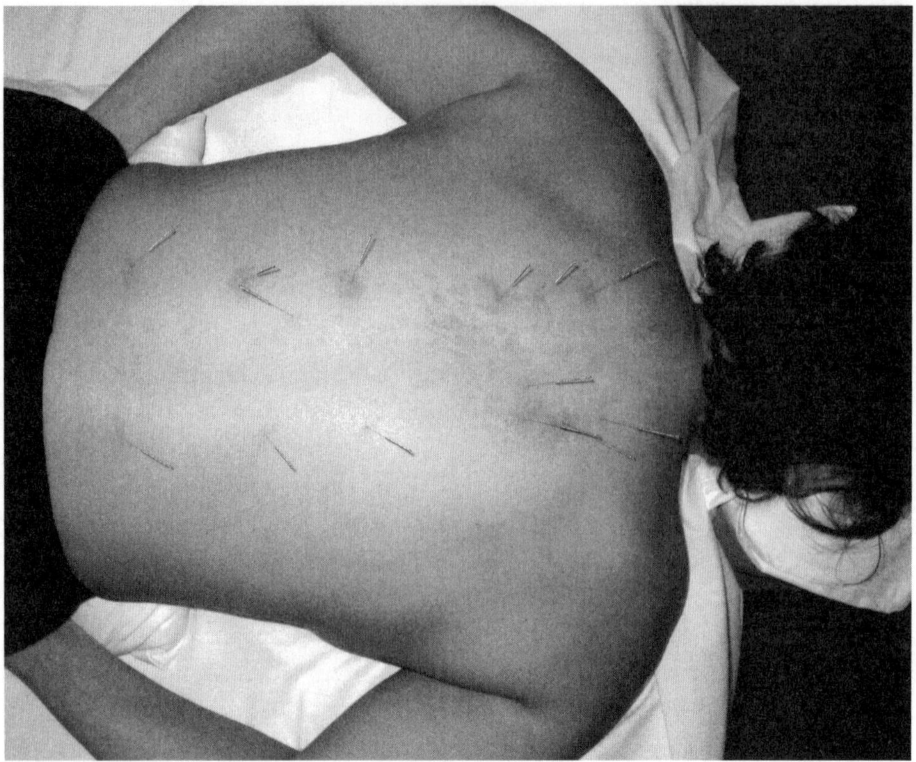

*Photo 2.1*

from, serious illness. We may also assess the seriousness of AE by noting the time it takes to drain and if it tends to reoccur.

If a patient tests positive for the presence of AE, retest that patient on the subsequent visit. This will help ensure that AE has been substantively cleared. If the patient does evidence AE on the second draining, it is likely this will clear relatively quickly and therefore prove not to be as deep. It is also likely that the patient's reaction will not be as strong as it was to the initial treatment. For example, if during the first clinical session a patient shows the presence of AE and it takes 45 minutes to clear, it is likely that on the subsequent treatment it will clear in 5 to 10 minutes.

If a patient does evidence the strong presence of AE, it may return at a future date. After all, once we have manifested any condition, our inherent susceptibility to it is implied. If a patient who has been generally progressing well in treatment arrives at an appointment in an edgy state and displays the signs of AE, treat it immediately. Taking the time to test for the presence of AE if you suspect it is time well invested, for no other treatment holds the potential to be as beneficial, and, if AE is allowed to progress, it will disrupt function at increasingly deep levels. Some patients evidence AE repeatedly over many years and it never seems to leave, even after repeated treatments. I generally take this as a sign that either the patient is being continually

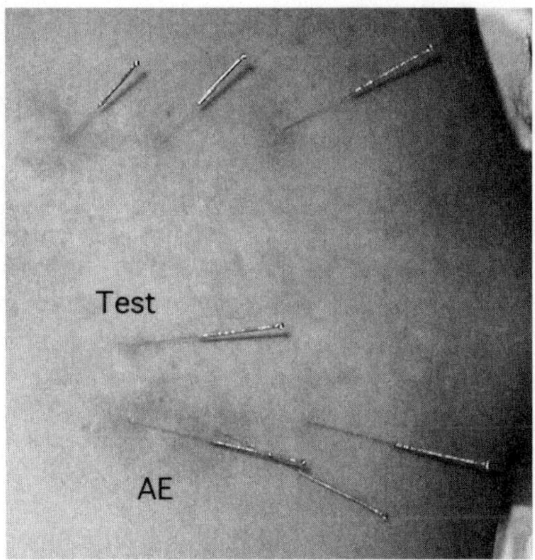


*Photo 2.2*

exposed to a harmful situation such as pollution or abuse or that a serious internal degenerative process is occurring. Either way, such a patient is highly vulnerable to the manifestation of disease.

REMINDERS

1. It can take up to two hours for AE to drain during an initial treatment session. Make sure the patient has scheduled sufficient time for the treatment.
2. Because of the potential duration of the treatment, patients should empty their bladder before the session.
3. Be sure to check in on the patient occasionally. If this is the first session, it is best that he or she does not feel alone.
4. Because reactions to the treatment can be very powerful, make sure the patient has scheduled sufficient time after the session to assimilate the treatment. Schedule all first treatments for patients so they do not have to go right to work or to another obligation.
5. If erythema appears unilaterally on a given point or points, indicating a positive response to the AE test, check to make sure the contralateral needles are located properly.

---

## *Treatment Method*

The presence of AE is drained through superficial needling of the bladder *yinshu* points. These points are found on the inner bladder line halfway between the center of the spine and the inner edge of the scapula (see

Figure 2.4). There are two methods for positioning patients to receive this treatment. In the first (see Photo 2.3), the patient may sit straight up in a chair with back straight while the needles are being placed. After the needles are inserted the patient may lean forward against the table in a relaxed position. In the second method, which I prefer, the patient lies face down on the treatment table. While needles are being inserted, the patient should have arms straight back (see Photo 2.1) so the relationship of the points to anatomical landmarks such as the spine and scapula are not distorted. After the needles are in place, the patient may hang arms off the table or place them in any other comfortable position.

When draining AE, I merely place an insertion tube directly over each point and tap the needle into the skin, exerting no extra force to push the needle any deeper. Needles are placed directly into the point and are not slanted either with, or against, the flow of *qi* in the bladder meridian as is done when tonifying or sedating. One-inch needles inserted correctly should lean toward the floor rather than penetrating deeply enough to remain perpendicular to the patient's body. Do not think of the draining of AE in this way as actually treating the *shu* points that are needled. Rather, take the paradigm as a whole and think of it on its own terms as a treatment unto itself. Points are needled from top to bottom and right to left. The heart *shu* (Bl-15) is generally tested for the presence of AE after

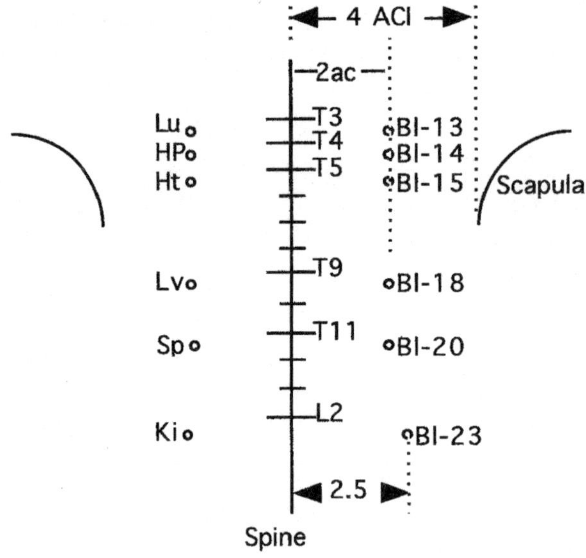


*Figure 2.4*
THE *YINSHU* POINTS

*The* yinshu *points are found at 2 aci (anatomical Chinese inch), halfway between the center of the spine and the medial edge of the scapula. The kidney* shu, *Bl-23, is found at 2.5 aci lateral to the spine.*

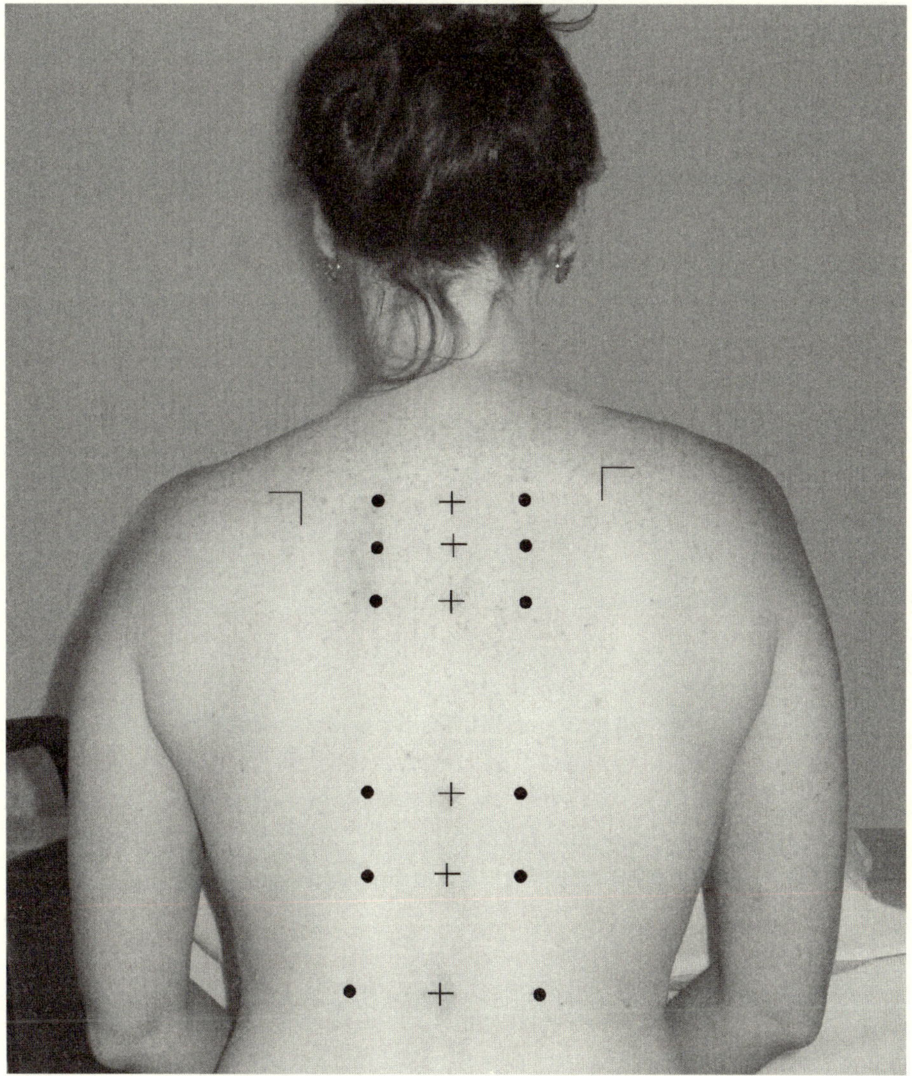

*Photo 2.3*

all the other organs have been cleared. This allows us to approach the emperor reverently and can provide a gentler experience for the patient.

PROTOCOL

1. Have patient empty bladder because the treatment can take some time.
2. Position patient comfortably either sitting facing the treatment table or lying face down with arms behind. If this second option is chosen, the use of a face cradle will help make the patient more comfortable and keep the points in proper relationship to the spine because the patient's head will not be turned.
3. Insert needles superficially into the *yinshu* points. Treat the heart

*shu*, Bl-15, after you have tested or drained the others. You can do this in the same session or at the next appointment.

4. Insert one test needle in each *jiao* immediately after needling the *shu* points of that *jiao*.
5. After five minutes, note the patient's response.
6. Even if there is no indication of the presence of AE, I often leave the needles in for ten minutes to gently relax the patient.
7. If the patient tests positively, retain the needles until the skin is clear, which will constitute the entire first treatment. If there is no indication of AE, remove the needles and progress with treatment as you judge appropriate.
8. If you have detected and drained AE, recheck it on the subsequent visit.

---

## *Treatment Reactions*

Reactions to having AE successfully cleared range on a continuum of exhaustion to elation. Individuals whose minds have habitually propelled them to work past what their inner resources are capable of supporting tend to feel exhausted after treatment. With the dysfunctional *qi* that supports their flight from self now abated, the person's entire system can finally allow him or her to relax. I have had patients report to me that after AE is drained they went home and slept for sixteen hours straight.

In contrast, patients whose minds have kept them functioning habitually at a decreased level often feel euphoric after an AE treatment. Emotions such as bitterness and resentment may have obscured their true nature to the point that they have wholly forgotten what it feels like to be content, happy, or relaxed. With AE cleared, the true self may shine through as if the sun has returned after a long winter. Between these two extremes, patients tend to feel generally relaxed and relatively more balanced. Anxiety tends to diminish and the patient feels a sense of "my old self returning."

In terms of a patient's symptomatology, there is virtually no degree of positive change that is too much to expect from a successful AE drain. In *Nourishing Destiny*, I discuss the case of a man who experienced excruciating pain from polyneuropathy for many years. Reread that case study in conjunction with this chapter because it so well illustrates the possibilities for healing inherent in this simple protocol.[15] After only one treatment for AE, all of his pain associated with the neuropathy disappeared and returned only years later just prior to his death from lung cancer.

From relatively spirit-level imbalances such as depression to relatively physical manifestations such as hip degeneration, patients may attain speedy and long-lasting relief from both pain and suffering once AE is cleared. Of course, things tend to feel better long before they are better, and both ongoing treatment and appropriate lifestyle changes are important if healing is to be complete.

---

## *Counseling on the Possible Effects of the Treatment*

It is important to know how to talk to patients about the specific treatment we are performing. Especially during the first treatment, patients are curious about what is happening and you must use empowering language. The quality of the initial intake creates the context for the ongoing therapeutic relationship between patient and practitioner. Additionally, a patient's positive experiences with initial clearing treatments such as AE will form the basis of their impressions of Chinese medicine and set the foundation for their own path of healing.

Take care when describing the intention of any treatment to tailor your metaphors to the needs of the specific patient. It is not useful for either patient or practitioner to have a fixed concept of what any particular treatment is useful for, how it works, or what results might be accomplished. The most pressing impact that clinical experience imparts to the open mind of the healer is that anything is possible given the correct therapeutic action at the right moment.

In light of these considerations, you might discuss the AE treatment in several general ways. The notion of "draining toxicity" is not necessarily empowering to patients. Using a word such as *toxicity* may unconsciously influence the patient to think of himself or herself negatively. However, a patient's primary complaint may in fact be of feeling toxic or of having been exposed to toxins. For such a patient, the reassurance that treatment can help resolve such influences may be beneficial.

I often let patients know that this treatment should be generally relaxing and help to "take the edge off." I might add that they may feel less run by their emotions and more effortlessly at rest in life. On other occasions I say the treatment helps equilibrate the organ systems so aspects of self that are overworking might relax and aspects that have not been carrying their functional load might have more facility to work harder. This statement can subtly influence patients to consider the ways they have been working too hard as well as the areas of life they have not attended to sufficiently.

## *Contraindications*

I generally consider draining AE to be a gentle and effective first treatment across a broad spectrum of clinical cases. However, the use of this paradigm may be tempered in some special circumstances. In cases of severe degenerative illnesses, patients can become so ill that, in fact, their only available *qi* is AE. In such a scenario, a patient's pathology may be the only thing sustaining him or her. In this case, do not drain AE for long periods of time. Rather, drain it a little bit at a time, perhaps for no longer than fifteen minutes in each treatment session. To drain AE excessively in people so debilitated might leave them depleted of their last reserve of *qi* and actually accelerate the progression of their illness. This consideration can apply to people debilitated by either cancer or AIDS, for example.

## *Other Considerations*

The relationship of clinical reality to theory is an interesting one and overlapping at best. I have found cases in which I am convinced AE has been drained yet little or no redness has appeared around the needle. I have also had cases, usually when patients are quite sick, in which I am convinced AE is present yet the treatment effects no change by any parameter I can assess. In this instance, I believe other factors of the illness cause the patient to hold on to the pathology and make it impossible for the pernicious *qi* to leave. Sometimes this can be true when such tainted *qi* represents the patient's sole reserve, as in patients with AIDS or cancer. Aggressive energy may also fail to drain if the patient suffers from possession.

Sometimes redness can appear around the needles and it does not represent the presence of AE but rather a local histamine reaction in the skin due to the presence of the needles. It has been suggested that the practitioner not leave the room during the AE treatment particularly during the patient's first treatment session.[16] I disagree with this assessment and find a patient's time to reflect and experience the treatment on his or her own terms is imperative. Of course, check in regularly to be sure the patient is comfortable and feels attended to.

## *Integrating the AE Treatment into Clinical Practice*

Practitioners from other traditions who do not diagnose or treat AE might benefit greatly from integrating this protocol into their clinical practice. My suggestion is to begin utilizing this procedure as the first treatment on all new patients for several months. This will be sufficient time to assess whether your patients and practice are benefiting from including the AE protocol as a clinical tool. Do not include other points or prescribe any herbs during this session so you can assess the results of the AE drain on its merits alone.

## JAYNE
### ANXIETY AND A NERVOUS HEART

*Constitution: Fire*

Jayne is a 28-year-old woman who came to me in crisis relating to her divorce. During the intake Jayne cried often and could not focus very well on our discussion. Her husband was trying to get custody of her children, and her court date was approaching in only a week. She had been referred by her psychotherapist because she was experiencing panic attacks, constant chest pain, and an all-pervasive anxiety. Jayne was at the point of considering the use of antidepressants, and her therapist hoped to avoid this because they often slow progress in therapy by sublimating psychologically challenging material. During the interview, Jayne complained of frequent urinary tract infections typified by burning urination.

***Findings***

Jayne's pulses were tight bilaterally with a fine vibration throughout the *qi* depth of the entire pulse. This finding indicated agitation of Jayne's heart spirit. Her left distal position was very tight, particularly in the area that corresponds to the heart protector official.[17] This suggests both a state of heart *yin* deficiency and of fear constricting her heart. Lastly, Jayne's tongue had a heart crack down the center with a very reddened tip, suggesting the heart official was a constitutional issue for her and heat was trapped in that organ. The presence of this heat suggests a possible etiology for her bladder infections as heat from her heart vents through the small intestine to disturb her bladder function.

***Treatment***

After conducting the intake, I assured Jayne that Chinese medicine was totally capable of addressing her concerns. Because of the acute nature of her distress, I decided to test for and drain AE during the first session. The AE drain evidenced a strong positive reaction on the upper *yinshu* points corresponding to the lung, heart protector, and heart officials. The treatment lasted for thirty-five minutes until all traces of red had vanished from the area around the needles.

After removing the needles I asked Jayne how she felt, and she responded warmly that she was at peace for the first time in many months. I used this opportunity to reinforce the suggestion that she would receive help with treatment and that true self is never really very far away no matter how far removed we might feel in the moment. Jayne returned the following week and reported that her court date had been delayed but she now knew she could handle the divorce. She exhibited far less anxiety and was resolved that she would not lose custody of her children. Her resolution was subsequently borne out.

### SARAH
#### AE AND HYPERTENSION

*Constitution: Metal*

Sarah was a 59-year-old woman who had recently been diagnosed with hypertension. Previously she had an episode of high blood pressure in her early 40s but this had cleared up with meditation. Her current pressures were as high as 170/95, and her physician had given her three months to try alternative methods before putting her on medication.

Sarah was concerned about her age and whether she was still attractive to her husband. Her sexual drive was low and she worried constantly about losing him, even though they had been married thirty years, and she was sure they had a loving relationship. In fact, many of Sarah's worries centered around her value to her husband, her family, and her work. In general, Sarah appeared agitated and quite unable to relax comfortably. But she responded well to emotional warmth and caring and would settle down and become quiet when I gave her positive reinforcement in any way. During these quiet moments, Sarah smiled brightly and had a twinkle in her eye.

Sarah's pulses were bilaterally tight and pounding, indicating a state of *yin* deficiency that is typical of women in this age group. Her pulses also exhibited a uniform cotton quality that indicated the presence of both sadness and resignation. She experienced pounding headaches along the gallbladder channel rising from Gb-20 through Gb-1.

*Analysis*

Sarah's constitution was clearly metal as evidenced by her CSOE (color, sound, odor, and emotion). I interpreted her insecurities to be based on lack of self-worth, a virtue I associate with the metal element. Her constant worry suggested the involvement of the earth element, and her symptoms of headache involved the gallbladder channel. These *ke* cycle relationships (metal, wood, earth) along with her agitation suggested the presence of AE as a contributing factor to her hypertension. Therefore I drained AE during the first treatment session, finding a positive reaction for its presence on all points tested. Needles were retained for an hour and fifteen minutes until her back was clear.

***Outcome***

Sarah arrived for her next session a week later both relaxed and smiling. Her systolic and diastolic pressures had both dropped during the week by 10 points to an average of 160/85. Within several treatments, Sarah's blood pressure dropped to an acceptable range of 130/70 to 140/80 on average. She maintained this range with bimonthly treatment and a low dose of Chinese herbs for seven months.

However, after going on a so-called vacation to visit her family over the Christmas holidays, Sarah returned in crisis. Her blood pressure had returned to its highest readings since the beginning of treatment. Apparently the trip had been quite stressful and had involved several family fights. After two follow-up acupuncture sessions and an increase of her herb dosage, the elevated pressures had not subsided. In the third session, I retested for the presence of AE to find it again on her lung, heart protector, and liver *shu* points. After draining AE again for an hour Sarah got off the table to say, "I feel like my old self again." Her pressure was once again in an acceptable range and has stayed there now again for several months.

## *NOTES*

1. Cleary writes that the five *qi* are "sense, essence, vitality, spirit, and energy." Liu Yiming, however, in the edition I have translated, does not define them.
2. From Liu Yiming, *Symbolic Language: Breaking Open Doubt*. Liu explains the hidden symbolism of Chinese alchemical writing. He enumerates seven stages each of losing original nature, returning to it, and becoming a sage. Written in the early 1800s, Liu's work is of deep significance in understanding the spiritual and psychological aspects of Chinese physiology and the inner tradition of healing in Chinese medicine. This work has been translated into English (see Cleary, 1986a). I discuss Liu's work at length in *ND*, Chapters 6 and 7.
3. In my writing I have avoided the use of the English word *energy* as a translation for the Chinese character *qi*. See *ND*, pp. 301–302, for my thoughts on this matter. However, here I retain the usage because this protocol is widely known as the "aggressive energy," or "AE" treatment.
4. This concept can be traced to the 53rd and 54th difficult issue in the *Nanjing* (see Unschuld, 1986, pp. 485–494).
5. I consider the AE treatment to be one of J. R. Worsley's most significant contributions to the practice of Chinese medicine. In order, these are (1) the notion of constitutional type, or "causative factor" as he calls it, (2) the notion that acupuncture points have deep emotional and spiritual aspects of function, (3) the AE treatment, and (4) the point protocol for treating possession.

6. Porkert, 1982, pp. 170–173.
7. Eckman, 1996, p. 113.
8. Eckman, 1996. Lavier taught a two-week class on acupuncture in London in 1948 where both J. R. Worsley and Peter Van Buren received their initial introduction to the art.
9. For a discussion of Dr. Shen's four-system theory, see Hammer, 1990, Chapter 14. The *Shanghan Lun* specifies six levels of the progression of cold-induced illness from exterior to interior. From the exterior inward these are the *taiyang, yangming, shaoyang, taiyin, shaoyin,* and *jueyin*. These stages are paired with the six channel pairs of small intestine/bladder, stomach/large intestine, gallbladder/three heater, spleen/lung, heart/kidney, and liver/heart protector, respectively. The *taiyang* is the outermost channel and thus associated with the function of the nervous system.
10. This is my observation. The positions I refer to are those of the Shen/Hammer system. See Hammer, 2001.
11. See *ND*, pp. 169–172.
12. Note that tetrahydrocannabinol (THC) is a very cold herb and effectively freezes the liver, thus undermining the function of liver *yang*. Frequent pot smoking (five days a week or more for five years or more, depending of course on a patient's innate endowment of liver *yang*) can result in an empty liver pulse. This finding indicates that the liver's primordial source of *yin* and *yang* are separating in a way that leaves the liver highly vulnerable to serious illness.
13. For a discussion of health and illness from the perspective of spontaneity and habit, see *ND*, pp. 316–317.
14. Erythema is defined by the *American Heritage Dictionary* as "Redness of the skin caused by dilatation and congestion of the capillaries, often a sign of inflammation or infection." It is interesting to note that I have talked about AE as if it were an infection, and, in fact, the presence of erythema on the skin when draining it suggests it is reasonable to think of it in this way.
15. *ND*, pp. 254–255.
16. Smith, 1998, p. 56. Smith also notes that patients who are treated sitting up should not be left alone because of the possibility of fainting during treatment. In eighteen years I've never seen this happen, but the possibility does suggest that treating patients while they are lying down might be the best option.
17. This position for the heart protector official according to the Shen/Hammer system of pulse diagnosis.

# 3

# POSSESSION

*Things are not strange in and of themselves. They must wait for me before they can be strange. The strange lies within me. It is not that things are strange.*
– GUO PU[1]

THE DISCUSSION OF POSSESSION IS A PARTICULARLY DELICATE topic. As Chinese medicine becomes assimilated into mainstream Western culture, the discussion of demons and possession is considered impolitic. Traditional concepts such as possession appear to be at odds with the notion of having Chinese medicine accepted as a modern science of the human condition. Further, some practitioners are apt to mystify themselves in the face of such a discussion and amplify it into the realm of new age fantasy. By attributing intentionality and causality to the phenomenon known as possession, they create stories about past lives, deeds, and psychospiritual issues that fail to empower the patient.

Nevertheless, learning to recognize and treat possession is essential for the practitioner who is holistically oriented. I have found that clearing possession is the single most profound treatment at my disposal for restoring the memory of original nature to a patient. In fact, treating and clearing possession must take precedence over all other concerns if its presence is suspected.[2] For if a person is not in possession of himself or herself, no further treatment can ever do more than just manage symptoms. Here I examine the notion of possession and the important role it can play in modern clinical practice.

## *The Historical Basis of Possession*

> *Cinnabar tastes sweet and is slightly cold, it cures the hundred diseases of the body and the five* zang. *It nourishes the* jingshen, *makes the* hun *and* po *peaceful and benefits the* qi. *It brightens the eyes and kills demons and injurious ghosts. If you take it for a long time you can communicate with the spiritual brightness (*tong shenming*) and you will not grow old.*
>
> – *Shennong Bencao Jing*[3]

The concept that disincarnate spirits could cause illness dates back as early as the Shang dynasty. Demonology existed as a major branch of Chinese medicine in the distant past and has evolved along with the rest of Chinese medicine up until the present. Historically, the causes of illness in Chinese medicine were attributed to either the internal (anxiety, fear, anger, sorrow, worry, and grief) or external (cold, wind, heat, fire, damp, dry, and trauma) demons. Prior to the introduction of Western religious ideology, the Chinese had no concept of a unified soul. Rather, they considered the body to be animated by a number of spirits *(zhi, hun, shen, ling, yi, po)* that derived from different sources, served different functions during life, and returned to different places after death. In fact, according to the traditional Chinese view, human life itself could be seen as a type of spiritual possession.

Many of the great medical texts included discussions of possession, and Sun Simiao wrote extensively on the use of acupuncture, herbal medicine, and even calligraphy to treat possession. The great physician Li Shizhen (1519–1593) ended his *Material Medica* (*Bencao Gangmu*) with a discussion of such curiosities as the metamorphosis of humans into animals or minerals, the birth from humans of nonhuman offspring, and of humans born from nonhuman parents. He ends his work entreating those of learning to study "human changes that fall outside of constant principle" and not to simply reject "the boundless transformations of the universe past and present."[4] As the Chinese state formulated medicine according to the constructs of Marxism, such discussions were banished from the medical literature. Of course, the communists were faced with helping bring China into the modern world. In attempting to formulate Chinese medicine according to the principles of dialectical materialism and Western scientific principles, however, much of the spiritual basis of the medicine was lost. The notion of possession is contained in several characters relevant to the practice of Chinese medicine. In fact, the character *yi* (醫), meaning "medicine," has an etymological derivation related to the concept of possession. Unschuld notes that during the final centuries of the Chou empire, attempts were made to combat demons with the same measures that had already proven effective in human battles. Several times a year, exorcists would race shrieking through the city streets, entering courtyards and homes and thrusting their spears into the air in an attempt to expel the evil influences.[5] Unschuld has suggested that acupuncture as a system of applying needles to the body may have derived directly from practices aimed at driving demons away. He suggests that, "just as one attempted to kill invisible spirits responsible for all kinds of public problems by stabbing with swords and lances into the corners of streets, yards and houses, the belief that demons took refuge in the organism, causing various illnesses there, may very well have suggested the pricking of various body parts with lances and swords of a minor scale, that is, with needles."[6] The oldest character for medicine (毉) had at its bottom the character *wu,* denoting two women dancing.[7] These women were shamans, and the etymology of the character suggests that Chinese medicine and the practice of acupuncture specifically evolved from the shaman's role in protecting the sick from evil influences.

The character *gui* (鬼) depicts the head of a ghost or demon floating in the air.[8] On the lower right we see a hook (冂), which symbolizes the

### *Medicine:* Yi 醫

In the upper left hand of the character *yi* is the character *shi* (矢), depicting an arrow fixed in a human body. The abstract meaning is of an action that has come to its end and is irrevocable, as when an arrow is fixed in its target.[9] The character *ji* (医) depicts a person so afflicted within a house and suggests a sudden sickness as if one had been struck by a dart. *Ji* also depicts a quiver (匚) used for holding arrows (矢). The character *shu* (殳), in the upper right, depicts the hand (又) making a jerky motion (几). Taking the upper left and right characters together, the newly formed character *yi* depicts a hand taking an arrow out of a quiver in order to shoot.[10] The bottom half of the character is *yu* (酉), which depicts an ancient vase used for making and keeping herbal decoctions. Taking all components together yields the character *yi* and denotes medicine as it was practiced by the ancient sages who sent arrows against the evil influences that cause sickness and gave the sick elixirs to revive them. Hence the character for medicine contains the notion of piercing the skin with arrows similar to piercing the air with lances to chase away the demons.[11]

effectiveness of the demon in ensnaring those that are to be possessed. The *gui* are disincarnate entities that live in the ether between heaven and earth. When such spirits incarnate they become either *hun* or *po,* the spirits associated with the liver and lungs, respectively.

The character *hun* (魂) is composed of the character *yun* (云) on the left, signifying clouds, and *gui* (鬼) on the right. The ascent of the *hun* is fueled by the three Daoist treasures, the *jing*, *qi*, and *shen,* which empower the evolution of the human spirit toward heaven as denoted by the image of the clouds. Upon death the *hun* ascends to heaven through the top of the head at GV-20 where it reports to the spirits that preside over destiny the degree to which each of us have fulfilled our life's purpose. The character *po* (魄) consists of the character *bai* (白) on the left, meaning white, and *gui* on the right. White is the color of metal, and the *po* is the *shen* (spirit) associated with the lungs. Whereas the character for *hun* includes the image of clouds *(yun)* that exist in heaven to signify the ascension of spirit, the character *po* depicts the color white, the color of bones that lie buried within the earth. Upon death the *po* descends through the anus and returns to the earth as fertilizer for the next incarnation. I consider the *hun* as it ascends to heaven to represent the highest of light and virtue that we have cultivated in life. I think of the *po* as it returns to earth as representing the mundane influences and issues we have not mastered in life.

The evil *gui* may be considered in contrast to beneficent *ling* and *shen* spirits. *Ling* denotes the aspect of spirit that watches over and protects the deceased's family after death. *Shen* denotes the spirit of those who have cultivated virtue and are buried with ceremony. The *shen* stay within their coffins after death as propriety would dictate. In comparison, the *gui* are wandering earthbound spirits that create mischief if they are not venerated by their descendants. Hungry *gui* are said to steal the offerings off of other more meritorious people's graves. It is the *gui* that are thought to take advantage of a vulnerable person through the mechanism of possession.

Girardot states that all *shen,* because they are *yang* in nature, are the natural enemies of the *gui* who are *yin* in nature. He tells us the ancient Chinese considered *yang* and *yin* to be engaged in an eternal struggle and that the worship of spirits had no higher purpose than that of inducing them to protect humanity against evil, or, by descending among men, to drive demons away by virtue of the enlightened spirits' intimidating presence.[12]

A homophone for *gui* (鬼), the dead, is the character *gui* (歸), meaning "to return." Hence the dead (*guiti:*歸體) are those who have returned back to the earth and "into the mysterious workings of things."Another homophone of the character *gui,* referring to demons, is *gui* (詭), meaning odd or strange. In the quote that begins this chapter, Guo Pu suggests that all things have a rational basis and the strangeness of any apparent phenomena lies within the human failure to comprehend it and not inherently within the nature of the phenomena itself. Any conception regarding the nature of the clinical state referred to as possession is subject to social, political, and economic considerations. Certainly it is fascinating to study and speculate about the traditional Chinese notions of possession. Ultimately I have no definitive opinion about the precise nature of what we diagnose and treat when we address this phenomenon clinically. I do know that there is far more on heaven and earth than is dreamt of in the modern scientific explanation of the human condition. I also know that regardless of the true nature of what we call possession, practically speaking, those of us intent on helping our patients profoundly must learn to identify and treat it successfully.

## *Vulnerability to Possession*

Any condition we are capable of manifesting must find its basis within us as karmic and genetic potential. Possession occurs when a patient is highly vulnerable to dysfunctional influences that reside either internally or externally. Such a high degree of vulnerability occurs when immunity is compromised because of poor living habits or receiving a shock of sufficient magnitude that the core of one's being is compromised.

Vulnerability to the external demons is heightened during exposure to extreme environmental conditions. I have seen patients return from trips to the desert or from hiking in the bitter cold who have become possessed as severe conditions weakened their immunity. I have also known patients to suffer possession after living in dark and damp basements. Patients who experience severe emotional trauma such as physical or sexual abuse may become possessed during the trauma itself. Here the patient's own spirit *(hun, shen)* tends to disassociate as a defensive mechanism to help insulate the person from the experience of trauma. The moment the patient loses consciousness and goes into shock, an opportunistic influence may take hold from within or from without. Such a detrimental influence can continue to motivate behavior and obscure open awareness, making it difficult for innate spiritual disposition to reassert its purpose in governing life.

## *Possession and Ego*

At conception the moon, stars, and sun shine to install original nature within us as *jing, qi,* and *shen.* These primordial influences are the basis of the authentic self, fueling our continual evolution as inborn potential is transformed into virtue. The authentic self is aligned with the absolute and represents that aspect of who we are that is untouched by life experience. It is that aspect of self that exists prior to the arising of feeling or the presence of thought. It is the commitment to act in life from the absolute perspective of the authentic self that constitutes the single-minded devotion of the sage.

The false self, or ego, is born of pain and suffering. Its existence is based on a momentum of dysfunctional *qi* established and propagated by the mind's personalization of thoughts and feelings. If we pay attention, we can discern that thoughts and feelings are a by-product of neural functioning and bear no relevance to the absolute nature of our life's purpose. To the degree we personalize them, thoughts and feelings are no more than a residue of our past obscuring our experience of the present in order to sustain our false concept of who we are and how life is.

The ego, as a vestigial part of self, is now present developmentally in most every human being. What is typically thought of as "possession" is the presence of "something else" that obscures both personality as well as original nature. However, I have come to believe the ego itself may be considered a form of possession to the degree it plays a role in motivating behavior. In fact, I have come to use the protocols discussed here to clear the possession of false self and diminish its momentum in dominating the patient's concept of who she is. The larger and more forceful the ego in dominating a person's behavior, the earlier in treatment I prioritize addressing possession.

Transcendence of ego is the goal of many spiritual paths. However, I have seen patients become possessed when engaging in activities that dissolve the "protective" mechanisms and boundaries associated with ego structure. It appears that many teachers and techniques offer an experience of transcendence but fail to reestablish the *zhenqi* and rectify the heart/kidney axis. The only true medicine is consciousness, and if the authentic self is not restored as the guiding force in life, merely lowering the boundaries of the ego can actually lower immunity.[13]

Such false paths can include psychedelic drug use, spiritual retreats involving prolonged meditation, being present during trance channeling, and so-called therapeutic regimens in which altered states of consciousness are induced through rigorous breathing. Often during these experiences people may feel very open, yet in letting down their normal defenses negative influences have an opportunity to take hold of them if they are susceptible. This is particularly true when a teacher guiding such practices has attained the level to lead students to an altered state but has not cultivated absolute integrity himself. Hence purity of motive and integrity of action are essential in both teacher and student if the potential positive results of the relationship are to be realized.

To sum up the preceding, from the absolute perspective of the authentic self, what passes for sanity in this world is as disturbed and crazy as mental illness appears to the average person. And, from the absolute perspective of the authentic self, the expression of ego in this world appears to be as clear a form of possession as the presence of evil might appear to the average person.

---

## *Diagnosing Possession*

Although we may speculate endlessly about the exact nature of the clinical state diagnosed as possession, what is important is being able to recognize, diagnose, and treat such cases effectively. Practically speaking, I find that patients who are possessed are so stuck in one form of emotional expression (the internal devils), there is no room for any spontaneity or subtlety of expression. In this case, morbid infatuation with their own thoughts and feelings has thoroughly obscured their heart's light. This is equally true if an environmental pathogen (the external devils) has so clouded the natural expression of a patient's being. In the average person who has lost self, it never seems as though original nature is very far away. With such a person I can generally find the light within that is struggling to rise and assert its positive influence. In people who are possessed, there appears to be only darkness, and I am often unable to make contact with any sane or clear influences at the patient's core. Another way of stating this is to say that in cases of possession ego, as the substantial basis of stagnation in humanity, is thoroughly dominating and obscuring the authentic self.

Possession often appears on the pulse as qualities that indicate internal chaos throughout the patient's being. These include several of the *sanmai* or *qi*-wild pulses that indicate *yin* and *yang* are reaching a terminal stage of separation within the organ systems.[14] The pulse most suggestive of possession is one in which rate, rhythm, amplitude, and intensity are changing continually on the entire pulse. A pulse in which all positions show constantly changing qualities can also be indicative of possession.

Listening to the patient's language can provide cues regarding the possibility of possession. A patient who states, "I feel as though something has latched on to me" or "I just don't feel like myself" suggests that you should consider a treatment for clearing possession.

## *Eye Contact and the Sensory Orifices*

*[A] thousand illuminations, myriad illuminations, are all two illuminations, inward illumination and outward illumination, which in totality are one illumination; therefore it is called fire.*

– *YIJING*[15]

A hallmark of possession is your inability to make and sustain eye contact with the patient. The nature of possession may obscure the expression of individual purpose to the degree that you have a strong sense in assessing the patient that "no one is home." Such a diagnosis is typical in, but not limited to, cases of mental illness and severe depression. The clarity of light in a patient's eyes and quality of eye contact reflects the degree of integration between the fire implanted within by heaven at conception with reality as illuminated by heaven in each moment. This interaction between inner and outer illumination is mediated by the sensory orifices, which include the eyes, ears, nose, and mouth. These seven holes in the head correspond in number to the stars in the Big Dipper, the central administration of human destiny.[16] The inner clarity of the heart orifice itself depends on and is reflected in the functioning of these outer orifices. The sensory orifices represent the interface between the patient's inner being and her interaction with the external world.

The proper functioning of *mingmen* ("gate of destiny") preserves the integrity of the relationships that constitute health. A chief function of *mingmen* is to regulate the interpenetration of early heaven (genetics) and later heaven (life). In receiving life through the senses, reality (what is) must be channeled directly into the gate of destiny in a way that is uncolored by the mind's interpretation of events. The interpretations of the habitually conditioned mind may be likened to chemical food additives that are not congruent with true self and obscure the positive influence of original nature contained in *jing, qi,* and *shen.* The sensory orifices are windows into the world, and it is essential that they convey reality accurately to our interior. Drawing conclusions about who we are and how life is, based on our inner experience, is the primary internal cause of stagnation in human beings.

To the degree that life is colored by our mind's interpretation, we will be unable to manifest our seed of potential accurately. Hence the phrase "unblocks the orifices" as applied to an herb or acupuncture point function can be interpreted as indicating that a given herb or point empowers the accurate perception of reality. In the *Neijing Suwen,* the term *mingmen* is used to refer to the eyes, which suggests a reciprocal relationship between the function of Bl-1 (*jingming,* "eyes bright") and the fires of *mingmen*. When reality is accurately perceived via the sensory orifices (of which the eyes are representative), the fires of destiny are fueled and burn brightly. In turn, the clarity of heaven's intent is evidenced in the brightness of one's eyes (and acuity of one's senses in general). The lack of eye contact that typifies possession is evidence that true nature has been obscured and the stagnation exists between the sensory orifices and the heart. The phenomenon of possession is clearly such a stagnation that must be attended to expediently if ongoing treatment is to have any meaningful degree of success.

In severe instances, the obfuscation of the sensory orifices can present as coma, epilepsy, and mental illness. However, these are extreme examples of loss of consciousness, which, according to my earlier definition, can be present on quite subtle levels including states that can be described as constituting ignorance. Initially, in my practice, I only recognized possession as an extreme phenomenon and treated it only in people with a severely clouded spirit. Often these people would have a biomedical diagnosis corresponding to mental illness. Over time, I have learned to differentiate increasingly fine shades of the phenomenon known as possession. Now I find these protocols effective in cases where the patient's access to the spiritual influence of true self is more subtly obscured by ego.

---

## *The Thirteen Ghost Points of* Sun Simiao

Sun Simiao (590–682 C.E.), perhaps the most venerated historical figure in Chinese medicine, mentioned in his *Thousand Ducat Formulas* the thirteen acupuncture points he considered particularly effective for treating possession. The thirteen acupuncture points bear such revealing names as "ghost camp," "ghost heart," "ghost path," "ghost bed," and "ghost hall. " Unschuld suggests that the needles used to penetrate a "ghost heart" in the treatment of an individual were analogous to the spears used by the exorcists at the time of Confucius (551–479 B.C.E.), when shamans ran through the streets stabbing spears in the air in order to free the citizens from the threat of evil spirits.[17]

The ghost points are used in modern times for the treatment of manic disorders and epilepsy. We must remember that the definitions of all illness are culturally determined. It is easy in retrospect to understand how people in Sun Simiao's time could have perceived mental illness and seizure disorders as possession by spirits. What is perhaps not so easy to

*The Thirteen Ghost Points*

| | | |
|---|---|---|
| • GV-26 | *Guigong* | Ghost Palace |
| • GV-16 | *Guizhen* | Ghost Pillow |
| • GV-23 | *Guitang* | Ghost Hall |
| • CV-24 | *Guishi* | Ghost Market |
| • Lu-11 | *Guixin* | Ghost Faith |
| • LI-11 | *Guitui* | Ghost Leg |
| • St-6 | *Guichuang* | Ghost's Bed |
| • Sp-1 | *Guilei* | Ghost Fortress |
| • HP-7 | *Guixin* | Ghost Heart |
| • HP-8 | *Guicu* | Ghost Cave |
| • Bl-62 | *Guilu* | Ghost Path |
| • Extrapoint | *Guifeng* | Ghost Seal |
| • Extrapoint | *Guicang* | Ghost Store |

was also known as *Yumentou* (extra point) in women and *Yinxiafeng* (extra point) in men, both points more or less corresponding to *Huiyin,* CV-1.

see are the limits of current so-called scientific myths about the neurochemical genesis of such dysfunction. From the point of view of Chinese medicine as a largely nonmaterialistic science, it is still a spirit clouded by ego that forms the basis of and motivates even these neural and chemical pathologies.

I have never found Sun's protocol to be effective. Its complexity and the number of points involved make it less appealing than the two protocols given for treating possession here that I find work reliably. I have listed Sun's thirteen ghost points here for those who are interested.[18]

---

## *The Internal and External Dragons*

As with all diagnoses, determining if a patient is afflicted with the internal or external demons is a matter of both intuition and prior clinical experience. You may note if a patient has been exposed to extreme environmental conditions or to severe emotional stress. As you gain expertise it may be sufficient to treat only the internal or external dragon points, depending on your assessment of the nature of the possession. However, for the beginning practitioner, I advise the use of both protocols to assure an effective treatment.

The internal dragon points: the "master" point between CV-14 and CV-15, St-25, St-32, St-41
The external dragon points: GV-20, Bl-11, Bl-23, Bl-61

### *The Points*

The seven internal dragons comprise a "master" point on the conception vessel between CV-14 and CV-15, which is palpated for, and three bilateral points, adding up to seven points.[19] Similarly, the external dragons include GV-20 and three pairs of bilaterally needled points.

### *Some Thoughts on the Points*

Think of the dragon point treatment as a single unified approach in which the sum is greater than the whole of its parts. However, just as we can think of an herbal formula as having its own function, we can also break it down to its constituent herbs to analyze individual contributions to its overall effectiveness. The following analysis represents my own speculation on the point functions that contribute to the efficacy of the protocol for possession. However, only the treatment as a whole works effectively to clear possession, and it must be taken on its own merits.

### *The Internal Dragons*

Chen Shiduo, author of the *Shishi Milu,* argued that madness is the result of mucus being produced in the heart.[20] Mucus or phlegm that "obscures" the orifice of the heart represents those acquired influences that are not congruent with true self and therefore suppress original nature. A heart so smothered may generate heat that disturbs the spirit *(shen)* producing symptoms such as agitation and/or depression. These symptoms today might be diagnosed as mental illness. The notion of phlegm obscuring the heart orifice is synonymous with ignorance and delusion. Such phlegm is the embodiment of our inability to fulfill our heart's desires in life in a way that leads to contentment. Failing to pursue what would be truly satisfying because it seems unattainable, the hungry heart seeks to satiate its desires through the stomach. The stomach in turn finds sources of nourishment that are not congruent with true self, and the result is phlegm.

Chen felt it was too dangerous to dissipate the flame of the heart directly. He suggested instead that strengthening the earth would diminish excessive fire, because the fire element would not have to work as hard to produce earth. The decrease of heart function, combined with the increase function of the spleen (which transforms mucus), would result in decreased mucus production, and the symptoms of madness would therefore subside.

This notion could explain the selection of the points in the internal devils treatment. Considering this orientation we can see that the internal dragon points consist of one point to calm the heart (CV-15) and three points that treat the earth element. St-25 is effective for sedating stomach fire and helps the stomach digest and transform phlegm. St-32 helps nourish the earth element. Lastly, St-41, as the fire point on the stomach meridian, helps sedate the excessive presence of fire within the earth.

---

## *The External Dragons*

The six-division model explains how invasions by wind/cold proceed from the exterior to interior levels of the human being. The outermost level of defense in the meridian system is the *taiyang* stage, consisting of the bladder and small intestine meridians. We may note that three of the points that comprise the external dragons are on the bladder meridian associated with the *taiyang* stage in the six-division model of cold-induced illness. The *taiyang* constitutes the first stage of defense against attack by external wind/cold pathogens.

Note that fear is the emotion associated with the water element, and the lack of eye contact that typifies possession is often accompanied by a wide-eyed stare, suggesting the patient is frozen with terror. In this regard, I have always been interested in the inclusion of Bl-61, a key point on one of the eight extra meridians *(yangqiaomai)*, in the protocol. It occurs to me that Bl-61 may affect the *yangqiaomai* in a way that helps dissipate existential terror frozen in the patient's depths. Hence an alternate name for Bl-61 is *anxie,* or "quieting of evil."

The inner functions of GV-20 have been discussed at length in *Nourishing Destiny.*[21] Located at the apex of the head, GV-20 represents the North Star as the universal center embodied within human beings. At the pinnacle of the governor vessel, GV-20 aligns a patient toward the central axis of heaven and unites all her spiritual influences toward heaven, restoring clarity and clearing consciousness.

TREATMENT PROTOCOL

1. Needles are inserted straight in, top to bottom, right to left, with a slight counterclockwise (dispersing) rotation until *qi* is felt.
2. Needles are retained until the pulse changes and possession is cleared. Generally I find 15 to 30 minutes is sufficient time.
3. Needles are removed in the same order they were inserted.
4. If the patient is *qi* or *yang* deficient, each needle may be tonified as it is removed (rotate clockwise and obtain *qi*). In this case, remove the needles left to right.
5. If there is no change as assessed by pulse diagnosis and the patient's demeanor, tonify the points top to bottom and left to right, removing them in order of insertion.
6. Both IDs and EDs can be done in the same treatment if the patient is strong enough.
7. After a successful clearing of possession, test for and drain AE either in the same session or the following session.

---

## *Considerations*

In general, begin by treating the internal dragon points. Needle these points from top to bottom and right to left. Place needles using a straight insertion perpendicularly to the meridian, and turn them approximately one turn counterclockwise until you feel *qi* in order to sedate the points. You must feel *qi* at all points for the protocol to be effective.

If, after leaving sufficient time (about 15 minutes), you do not find the treatment effective, recheck the needle placement assuring that *qi* is available at all points of insertion. If *qi* has been obtained, try tonifying the points with one clockwise turn on each needle in order to obtain *qi*. If the treatment is still not effective, attempt the complementary treatment, which, in this case, would be to treat the external dragon points in the same manner.

Some practitioners suggest that a window be left opened in the room while treating for possession, with the idea that any evil *qi* that has left the body might find its way out of the room. In New England in the winter I do not open the windows much and feel confident in saying that departing *gui* must have found their way out by other means because I have never to my knowledge picked up such an influence from a patient. Nevertheless, practitioners are theoretically vulnerable to such invasions, and so take care to have good health and strong boundaries when working with patients at these deep levels.

## Ancillary Treatments

After clearing possession, it is imperative to reinforce the strength of the patient's constitution so it can be reestablished in exerting its influence of governing life in a healthy fashion. I find that treating H-7 ("spirit gate") as well as the source point on the patient's constitutional meridian is generally effective in affirming the patient's possession of self.

A patient who has suffered possession is inherently vulnerable to the condition returning. As with any treatment, educate patients about their vulnerability and help remove them from contexts in their life that may expose them to severe environmental conditions or to abusive relationships.

It is highly recommended that a patient who has had a possession cleared return shortly after for a follow-up visit to reinforce the *zhenqi* and decrease vulnerability. Possible follow-up treatment are many and varied, and it is up to you to determine what are the best means of supporting the patient. Whenever possession has been cleared, it is best to check for and drain any AE that might be present.

There is another point combination that I have found to be very strong in either clearing possession outright or for reinforcing the dragon points after they have been done.[22] The point combination of Ki-6 (the master point of *yinqiaomai)* coupled with Ki-27 (the highest point on the kidney meridian) is superior for channeling the course of the kidney meridian and resolving existential fear that emanates from the depths of self. This is an excellent treatment for people who wake with night terrors or who are in shock from near death experiences.

## Reactions to Treatment

I can think of no other single treatment that has the potential in only one session to so dramatically change a patient's life for the better. I recall one patient who had been through many rounds of electroshock therapy. She exhibited a severe *qi*-wild condition on all pulse positions with constant change in all assessible parameters. Within moments of placing the last needle when treating the internal dragon points, the pulse stabilized completely to the point of not missing a beat. Such a dramatic change indicated the heart had instantly reasserted its authority to rule. Similarly I have seen symptoms as diverse as crippling back pain, seizures, migraine headaches, and panic attacks all disappear permanently after clearing possession.

I have also seen some patients being treated for possession display signs such as rolling eyes and a thrashing tongue that we might associate with a Hollywood-style possession. To a person, however, these were patients who somehow had it in their head they were possessed and I was treating them for the condition with their knowledge of what was being done. We can never discount the effect of popular culture or the human capacity to mystify itself when addressing an issue such as possession. Still, I find this to be a real phenomenon, whatever its nature, that must be taken seriously by the modern clinician who aspires to practice medicine with both depth and breadth.

Upon clearing possession the patient may experience sensations such as emotions or smells associated with the place and time of the possession. Also, memories of traumatic events may reemerge that have been suppressed by the possession. Less dramatic and more frequently encountered reactions to the dragon treatment are typified by the patient feeling deeply relaxed with an increased sense of clarity. Often immediately after the treatment or during the follow-up session, the patient will report "feeling my old self again." These words, of course, are the best clinical sign that the foundation for true healing has been put in place.

---

## *Discussing the Treatment*

I do not make a big deal to patients about treating possession for two reasons. First, the modern patient may not have a context for understanding the concept, and second, I do not want to raise any defensive mechanisms that might interfere with the treatment's effectiveness. I do not advise telling patients you are going to treat them for possession at their next treatment. Detrimental influences of the sort that possess a person have a vested interest in keeping their adopted home. A patient so advised may not return for treatment. There have been occasions when I have decided in the week after a patient's last session to treat him or her for possession, only to never hear from the patient again.

Generally I just inform patients that the treatment will help to "put them back in charge" or help free them from "negative influences." After needling the points I often advise patients to relax and focus on their heart as the governing influence in their life. Occasionally I tell patients that I have needled seven dragon points and they may think of these dragons as protective influences that watch over them like sentinels and illuminate their depths to eradicate destructive influences.

---

## *Herbs for Treating Possession*

Several types of herbal formulas are helpful in clearing possession. For resolving external cases of possession, formulas that resolve chronic wind/cold/damp can be effective.[23] We can think of these external pathogens as the embodied representations of that which has entered us in life that is not congruent with true self. These pathogens can obscure the sensory orifices in a way that separates heart and mind and propagates delusion.

For treating internal demons, aromatic formulas that open the sensory orifices and formulas that move congealed blood can be effective. The fragrance of aromatic herbs may help break accumulations of phlegm and dampness that occlude the heart orifice and obscure the accurate perception of reality.

We can think of congealed blood as representing the body's attempt to sublimate emotional traumas that are too threatening to assimilate consciously.[24] Eventually, suppression can lead to the influence of original nature being so obscured that we become vulnerable to possession. Herbs and formulas that move blood and resolve congealedness can initiate a movement back into consciousness of material that has been suppressed. As patients receive support to cope with their trauma, the demons that plague them may be let go of more expediently.

I have also found Guizhi Tang (Cinnamon Twig Soup) to be an excellent formula for treating possession in women who have suffered the trauma of sexual abuse. This formula harmonizes the relationship between nutritive *(ying)* and defensive *(wei) qi*. In health, the *weiqi* surrounds the body and protects it from harmful influences. We can conceive of one aspect of *weiqi* as a type of fire that burns away impurities before they have a chance to make contact with the body. *Yingqi* represents a combination of the most refined essences acquired through breath and alimentation. In health, *yingqi* is contained and circulates within the vessels to sustain the functioning of the officials.

In cases of abuse, the *weiqi* may collapse in the face of assault while the *yingqi* spills, as it were, to the outside. Such spilling may be apparent by constant crying, neediness, flushing, and heart palpitations, and feelings of being exposed. Here the patient's feelings of vulnerability are based on the collapse of the defensive *qi*, leaving the inner self *(yingqi)* no longer contained. Now the patient is available to others in a way that leaves her feeling taken advantage of. This conjures the image of hungry ghosts feeding from her to steal essence and *qi*. Meanwhile the *weiqi* has collapsed and retreated to the inside rather than protecting the outside. Think of troops in the periphery of the country having been defeated and rushing back toward the interior to defend the capital. Such a retreat can allow a pernicious influence to inhabit and reside in the interior. In fact, some people who have been sexually abused do impart a sense of having retained some essential part of the mind or spirit of the perpetrator that possesses them.

By reharmonizing the *ying* and the *wei,* Guizhi Tang can push the defensive *qi* back out to the exterior while holding and strengthening the *yingqi* in the interior. This can help push out undesirable influences while fortifying the defensive mechanisms that help keep them from reentering.

## JILL[25]

***Complaint:*** *Chronic schizophrenia*
***Diagnosis:*** *Possession*
***Constitution:*** *Spleen with wood invading earth*

Jill was a 28-year-old woman who had been suffering from schizophrenia for twelve years. Although attractive, her face was overly thin, corresponding to an inability to digest a wide range of foods. In fact, she ate very little and was unable or unwilling to take the time to nurture herself. Jill had left a highly dysfunctional home as a teenager and spent several years taking drugs and living in the streets of Chicago. During that time she had witnessed several horrible events, which she would never discuss explicitly but alluded to throughout the course of early treatment. Jill was a single mother of a 12-year-old son from whom she felt estranged because she had "been crazy during his entire life." She worked on an organic farm, driving herself hard to put in long days in every type of inclement weather. Although the hard work was ultimately depleting her, she only felt safe and whole when she was in the fields with her plants.

Jill's main symptoms were her inability to eat and her tendency to feel merged with anything in her environment that made a mechanical sound. When she came for treatment I would have to turn the space heater and lamps off in my office because any sound would distract her. She would often sit on the floor of the office while we talked because she felt overly confined in chairs. At the time of the initial consultation, she had been on antipsychotic drugs including lithium for ten years and was told by her physicians that she would never be able to get off them.

Despite the severity of Jill's symptoms and the clear presence of possession, I strongly believed in her capacity to heal from the moment I first met her. Although completely obscured from her own awareness, I was able to find a light trying to assert itself in Jill that I believed could be cultivated.[26] Although this light was nearly completely obscured by her illness and her mind was wholly chaotic, I could sense its presence deeper in her spirit. Here was a woman possessed whose spirit was fighting to emerge. I informed her during the first session of my complete confidence that she would heal. Although she tried her best to test this confidence for the first two years of treatment, I never wavered in asserting that I could see her light and she would indeed heal.

### *Clinical Findings*

Jill was unable to make eye contact with me and sat on the floor during the initial portion of each treatment and stared at the wall while we talked. This total inability to make eye contact strongly confirmed my diagnosis of possession.

Her tongue was pale with a red tip indicating blood deficiency and heat trapped in her heart. A heart line on the center of her tongue with phlegm in it indicated obfuscation of the heart orifice. Her pulse was bilaterally thin at all depths with a rough vibration on the entire organ depth of the pulse. The thinness of the entire pulse suggested blood deficiency. The rough vibration in the depths of the pulse suggested severe heart *qi* agitation. This finding suggested it was likely she had been present during a terrible event such as a rape or murder.

I see this profound level of agitation when it occurs deep in the pulse as signifying that the patient's mind cannot reconcile some event or action in life with his or her spiritual purpose for having incarnated. The specific nature of this event was never revealed to me during treatment, although its existence was generally confirmed. Lastly of note was the finding of a spinning bean pulse at her left middle position. I interpret this pulse to suggest a state of existential terror.

### *Treatment*

After the intake I elaborated to Jill my belief that we each have a destiny and that, although her journey had been painful, it would eventually bring her to a place of peace and balance. As I spoke, she sat on the floor and stared quietly away into a corner of the room.

I treated Jill for over three years. For the first year she came every week and for the second every other week. By the third year, treatments varied from once every three weeks to monthly. The initial stage of treatment involved helping take her out of shock and restore her spirit as the governing influence in her life. Therefore the very first treatment consisted of the internal and the external dragon points. The response to this treatment was simultaneously subtle and powerful.

Upon taking her pulses after treating the internal dragon points, the deep vibration I previously felt was greatly diminished. Further, the spinning bean quality was entirely absent. Jill suggested on follow-up the next week that she was not aware of any significant difference other than feeling a bit more relaxed the evening of the session. However, upon leaving the first session, something occurred that signaled to me that deep healing had been initiated. Walking to the door of my office, Jill turned to me and, for just a moment, she smiled and made direct eye contact with me. At this time she stated, "It is only your belief in destiny that gives me hope." She then immediately turned to leave.

I knew from this moment of eye contact, and the light that emerged in her eyes and smile for just that instant, that she had reconnected to the light in her core. Now it would merely be a matter of cultivating that light until it became the predominant influence in her life. Over the next few years, I treated the dragon points several times with each of those sessions revealing a new clarity in her depth. Intermediate treatments involved the cultivation of *qi* and blood and ultimately *zhenqi,* that force that holds us humans upright between heaven and earth. To this end the treatment of GV-20 in conjunction with Ki-1 played an important role in her healing.

***Outcome***

During a treatment session three and a half years later, Jill revealed to me that she had taken herself off all medications and had been free of them for six months. She had not wanted to tell me until she was sure she was free of them for good. She has now been living free of medication for eight years and has been able to hold a regular job. She has married again and has a 3-year-old baby girl she loves dearly.

Six years after I had finished treating Jill, I received a letter from her that I quote from here.

> *I wonder if you ever knew*
> *what comfort*
> *you and your Chinese medicine brought to my life,*
> *to my heart?*
> *How could I ever thank you*
> *for all that you taught me?*
> *For all that you believed I could be*
> *I truly*
> *have*
> *peace and joy*
>
> – *Jill*

## *Questions*

Historically, Chinese medicine explained certain types of psychospiritual and behavioral dysfunctions as due to possession. In modern times, these dysfunctions are often diagnosed as mental illness and are attributed to neurochemical imbalances affecting the central nervous system.

a. Which explanation is correct?

b. What proof do you have for your choice?

c. To what degree is each explanation socially and culturally determined?

d. Because brain chemistry and experience change simultaneously, is it possible to attribute causality to the relationship between the two?

e. Is consciousness a secondary by-product of physiology?

f. Does spirit motivate matter?

g. Discuss ego as a form of possession.

## *NOTES*

1. In Zeitlin, 1993, p. 18. Guo Pu (272–324 C.E.) wrote an influential neo-Daoist preface to the *Class of Mountains and Oceans (Shanhaijing).*
2. Of course, treating bleeding or other critical conditions that threaten imminent loss of life or function always takes precedence.
3. *Shennong Bencao Jing.* Cinnabar is the first herb discussed in the *Bencao Jing.* This passage can be read to imply that it enables us to be in contact with (*tong*) the emanations of our own heart (*shenming*) and/or the heart of heaven.
4. See Zeitlin, 1993, p. 4. Zeitlin does a wonderful job discussing the classical Chinese discourse on the things considered strange.
5. Unschuld, 1985, p. 37.
6. Ibid., p. 96.
7. See Lu and Needham, 1980, p. 78. The character *wu* (巫) was changed to that of *yu* (醫) depicting a vessel holding an herbal infusion by the Han dynasty, suggesting perhaps the elevation of medicine to more of a science and the importance that herbal remedies played at that time. The character *wu* is an important component of the character *ling* (靈), denoting spiritual potency and the ability to perform ritual effectively (see *ND*, p. 53).
8. Wieger, 1965, p. 112.
9. Wieger, 1965, lesson 131, p. 300. See also lesson 22d, p. 65, and phonetic 51, p. 408.
10. Ibid., phonetic 618, p. 524.
11. Unschuld, 1985, p. 37.
12. Girardot, 1983, p. 250.
13. The ego can only express itself ironically and, in a very real sense, the compensation that is slowly killing us can often be what is keeping us alive. Hence I have often seen people give up drinking or smoking or make some other dramatic change relatively late in life, only to receive a terminal diagnosis shortly thereafter. In this regard, note my observation that in people with degenerative illness it is best not to drain AE for too long because it may be the only *qi* they have sustaining them.
14. Hammer, 2001, pp. 128–135.
15. Cleary, 1986, p. 126.
16. For a discussion of the Big Dipper, see *ND*, p. 50. In the Chinese enumeration of being, the number seven corresponds to the loss and return of original nature. There are seven stars in the Big Dipper, seven holes in the head, seven external pathogens, and Ki-7 governs the return of *yang* and the new light on the winter solstice.
17. Unschuld, 1985, p. 45.

18. Deadman and Al-Khafaji tells us that historically there has been ambiguity concerning the ghost points. Some authorities thought that *guixin* was in fact *taiyuan* (Lu-9) rather than *daling* (P-7), and that *guilu* was either *jianshi* (P-5)or even *laogong* (P-8) rather than Bl-62. These authors also state that Gao Wu's alternative list of these points in the *Glorious Anthology of Acupuncture and Moxibustion* included *shenting* (GV-24), *ruzhong* (St-17), *yanglingquan* (Gb-34), and *xingj*ian (Lv-2) and omitted *shenmai* (Bl-62), *shangxing* (GV-23), *quchi* (LI 11), and *yumentou/yinxiafeng.* Deadman and Al-Khafaji, 2000.
19. The term *master* here refers to the notion that the point is a nonchannel point included in the knowledge of the master practitioner. There is not an implication that this point rules the treatment. Note that the seven dragon points correspond in number to the sensory orifices.
20. Unschuld, 1985, p. 222.
21. See *ND*, pp. 347–348.
22. This treatment was taught to me by a student of Kiiko Matsumoto, who attributed it to her, although in another context.
23. Note that the herb formula Chuanxiong Chatiao Wan (Ligusticum and Green Tea) can be efficacious in this regard. This formula is presented by Thea Elijah in Chapter 10.
24. For a discussion of blood in Chinese medicine, see *ND*, Chapter 11.
25. To do Jill's case study justice, I would have to write fifty pages. Here I only attend to the main details central to diagnosing and treating her possession.
26. I have stated earlier that possession tends to be characterized by the inability to find a "sane" light at the patient's core. In Jill's case, however, I was able to contact this light clearly. However, it took years before she was able to perceive it clearly and believe in it as I did.

# 4

# THE HUSBAND/WIFE IMBALANCE

THE INTEGRITY OF LIFE DEPENDS ON THE BALANCED functioning of the twelve officials, or organ systems. The constitutional foundation supporting this function is the interpenetration of our original endowment of *yin* and *yang*, which constitutes the *yuanqi*. The *yuanqi* is the seed of true nature that heaven plants deep within at the moment of conception. We must nurture the potential of this seed to fulfill our life's purpose. In the course of living, however, our true nature is forgotten as mundane consciousness and accumulated habitual behaviors extinguish the fire of heaven's intent. By receiving our personal name, self-awareness dawns and original nature is lost. Gaining self-awareness forms the original crack in our balanced functioning and paves the way for the separation of *yin* and *yang*. When we lose touch with our true natures, the result is the creation of a false self based on our erroneous interpretations of life experience. This leads to the unbalanced functioning of the five elements—water, wood, fire, earth, metal—bringing us, ultimately, to death.

The separation of *yin* and *yang* is both predictable and treatable using the diagnostics and therapeutics of Chinese medicine. The condition is evident on the pulse and is known in the five-element tradition as the husband/wife (H/W) imbalance. The presence of this imbalance suggests vulnerability to serious and perhaps imminent illness.

In Chapter 7 of *Nourishing Destiny*, I discuss at length the separation of *yin* and *yang* as it appears in Chinese creation mythology, the *Yijing*, the spiritual alchemy of *mingmen*, and in Chinese physiology. To understand the theoretical background of the husband/wife imbalance, review this material first. Here I examine this imbalance as it is specifically relevant to clinical practice.

## *The Law of Husband and Wife*

*He who comprehends the greater destiny becomes himself a part of it. He who comprehends the lesser destiny resigns himself to the inevitable.*
– ZHUANGZI[1]

In the five-element tradition, the separation of *yin* and *yang* as it occurs on the pulse is called the husband/wife imbalance. The "law of husband and wife" may be summarized as follows.

When *yin* and *yang* are in relative harmony, the pulses on the left hand (the husband, *yang*) are stronger in quantity than the pulses on the right hand (the wife, *yin*).

The functional movement of the left-hand pulses involves drawing the stored genetic potential out of water and manifesting it in the world. We may liken this to a tree (wood, spring, *qi*) sending down its roots to draw on earthly reserves (water, winter, *jing*) and channeling them in growth toward the sun (fire, summer, *shen*). This movement corresponds to the ascension of the *hun* spirit to heaven. The right-hand pulses correspond to the second half of the year when the expression of life returns back into empowering the potential of the seed. Late summer (earth) and fall (metal) correspond to the time of the harvest and the digestion and integration of life. This movement corresponds to the descent of the *po* spirit as it returns back to the universal pole of earth (see Figure 4.1, p. 60).

Each element on the left half of the cycle governs a virtue that propels the ascension of the *sheng* cycle as we evolve. The kidney governs our will to assert our original natures in the world and manifest destiny. The liver governs aspiration as we draw on will and tap its potential to channel our resources toward heaven. Fire governs the opening of the flower and the joy and illumination that results as the light in our depths (kidney fire) joins the light in heaven (heart fire). The H/W imbalance is generated

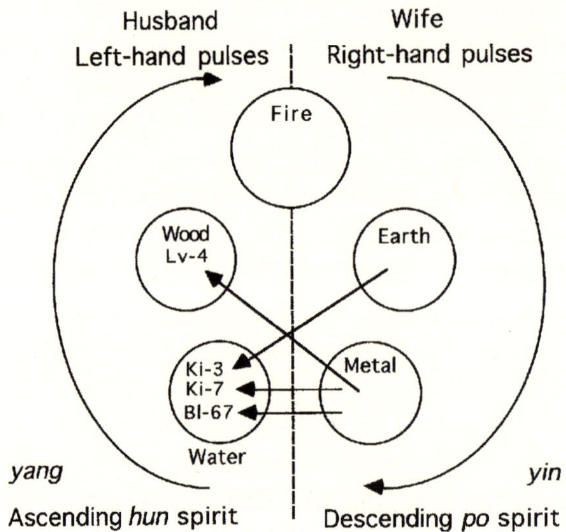


*Figure 4.1*
THE HUSBAND/WIFE IMBALANCE

*The dotted line indicates the juncture at which the pulses separate in a husband/wife imbalance. Ki-7 is the key point for assisting in breaking the husband/wife imbalance and reestablishing the functional link between metal and water. The name of Ki-7, "returning current," recalls the function of the point in aiding the connection of metal to water and thereby supporting the return of original nature. Bl-67 tonifies water by drawing on a relative excess in the metal element. Ki-3 tonifies water by drawing on a relative excess in the earth element. And Lv-4 tonifies wood by drawing on a relative excess in the metal element. Together these four points—Ki-3, Ki-7, Bl-67, and Lv-4—help revive upward movement on the left half of the* sheng *cycle by reviving the water and wood elements' virtues of will and aspiration.*

when our virtues of will, aspiration, and illumination are smothered by resignation to life's circumstances, hence Zhuangzi's statement earlier.

The pulses of the left hand correspond fundamentally to the quality of function of the organ systems themselves, which finds its basis in the constitutional strength of kidney *yin, yang,* and *jing*. The right-hand pulses correspond to the digestive system. If the pulses on the right hand are significantly stronger in quantity, and better in quality, than the left-hand pulses, we may surmise that the actual functioning of the organ systems has collapsed. This collapse suggests the resources of *jing*, *qi*, and *shen* have been severely depleted and are compromised as guiding influences in life. In this case, the digestive system is compensating and overworking in order to extract the maximum amount of essence from food and air so it may support the continued functioning of the organism. The collapse of the organ system corresponds to the compromised function of *mingmen,* which plays a key role in guarding the inherited constitution.

If the functioning of the digestive system, which guards the acquired constitution, also collapses, serious pathology cannot be far off. In this scenario, all pulse positions evidence a superficial pounding. However, there is no depth to the entire pulse, indicating the pounding felt is the patient's final store of *yangqi* dispersing. This "empty" pulse is indicative of an extreme "*qi*-wild" condition in which *yin* and *yang* are at their terminal point of separation. With the true *yin* (the *yuanyin* as imparted by heaven at conception) exhausted, the patient's *yang* floats to the top of the pulse. Now we are truly knocking at the "door of death" as the functional dynamics of the pulse exactly replicates the image of hexagram 23 in the *Yijing.*[2] This pattern generally is evidenced later in time than the classic husband/wife imbalance just described. It indicates that the functions supporting the digestive system have collapsed so they may no longer compensate for the failure of the organ system.

---

## *The Dynamics of the H/W Block*

*When the "wife" follows the "husband,"*
*water and fire balance each other.*
– *Liu Yiming*[3]

The initial separation of *yin* and *yang* begins when the child or young adult forgets true nature and begins to create an imagined self out of his or her interpretations of life's events. This separation signals an alienation from true self on the most fundamental level. Continued separation from self is based on the individual's self-concept constructed from erroneous interpretations of life's experiences. Over time, as this crack in the individual's constitutional foundation widens, serious illness manifests in all spheres of function. The functional basis of this illness is a lifetime of false beliefs and interpretations.

The presence of the husband/wife imbalance shows we have been brought to the very brink of destruction. However, habitual delusion is only one possible path to arrive there. A person may have congenitally poor kidney *qi* and therefore be prone to this imbalance from birth. Further, a severe physical trauma may so deplete the kidney that a husband/wife imbalance manifests. These last two scenarios could be described as being beyond the control of the individual and resting with the will of heaven. Even so, the concept of *karma* still places the responsibility for appropriate action on the patient. By the time an individual has an H/W imbalance, *yin* and *yang* are fast approaching the terminal point of separation. Precursors of this imbalance in an individual's life are separation from the very sources of life's vitality. Two such sources that have major impact on the overall condition of health are relationship to family and relationship to work.

Patients showing an H/W imbalance tend to feel trapped in a situation that is harmful and appears to be outside of their control. Often the very basis of personal identity and self-esteem is derived from this harmful work or personal relationship, but in order to leave the situation, they would have to kill their fundamental source of ego identification. Rather than endure the emotional pain associated with such an extreme step, individuals habitually suppress their inner drive for self-expression as it is empowered by the spirit of the kidney (*zhi,* willpower). Eventually the will of the kidneys to manifest destiny collapses under the weight of acquired conditioning and suppression and the left side of the pulse collapses with it.

With heaven's will for us defeated, growth is no longer channeled into evolution but into pathological change at the cellular level, forming the organic basis for serious illness. In this scenario, the practitioner expects to see a fundamental tearing apart on deep functional levels that corresponds to the separation of the primordial *yin* and *yang*. Self-destructive tendencies can often be seen in other areas of the patient's life as he is unconsciously driven toward death. This may manifest in a tendency to cut or burn oneself, to addictive behaviors, or to "accidentally" harming oneself in more serious ways.

For example, I have often seen people suffering from a H/W block involved in automobile accidents.[4] Each moment of life, we are faced with a choice between renewing our vitality through authentic action or avoiding reality and increasing our burden of mundane *yin* that eventually kills us. This choice is represented metaphorically by *Yijing* hexagrams 23 and 24, named the "door of death" and "gate of birth," respectively.[5] We must affirm that, regardless of the nature of our thoughts or feelings, all our actions are volitional, and the path to our present circumstances in life has been tread deliberately, one step at a time. In choosing a path of healing, we as adults must bear responsibility for the consequences of every action taken in our lives as well as for the consequences of everything that has ever happened to us.[6] In this way the past can be put in the past, and, choosing now the gate of birth, vitality can be renewed.

If a person lives long enough with a husband/wife imbalance and continues to function habitually, an extreme "*qi*-wild" (*sanmai*:散脈) pattern may appear on the pulse; now *yin* and *yang* are at their terminal point of separation.[7] In addition to the symptoms already described, the patient may evidence both extreme fatigue and an all-pervasive anxiety that emanates from the conscious or unconscious knowing that life is slipping away.[8] Thus the husband/wife imbalance is a clinically useful distinction with both diagnostic and therapeutic implications.

We may go along through life habitually driven, turning our back on destiny and continually choosing the easy way out in the face of life's challenges. If we proceed in this way, the separation of *yin* and *yang* will ultimately manifest on our pulse, signaling gross imbalance throughout our being. By this time we are either involved with or soon headed for serious, life-threatening symptomatology. Here we are truly at a crossroads that may spell the difference between life and death.

---

## *Discussion*

*Though the grease burns out of the torch, the fire passes on,*
*and no one knows where it ends.*
– *Zhuangzi*[9]

Heaven does all it can to nurture the unique seed it has planted within each of us. However, heaven's only vested interest is that this unique aspect of *dao* be expressed in the world. Ultimately heaven will sacrifice the individual before it sacrifices its own expression of spontaneous self-becoming. Heaven does not care who does the expressing of its will just so long as its will is expressed. Hence there are two ways of returning.

The first involves returning to the root in life represented by the *yuanqi* and manifesting the will of heaven as it is stored there. Here we continually establish the connection between metal and water, which allows for a perpetual return and "coming into being." However, if we turn our back on destiny and the link between metal and water is broken, we perish, returning instead back into the "mysterious workings" of the eternal *dao*.

In treatment, there are times when the separation of *yin* and *yang* progresses past the point that medicine can restore physical health. However, even then, it is still possible to restore to the patient the consciousness of original nature so destiny may be fulfilled. I find that Ki-7 can still play a crucial role at this point and help a patient make peace with dying and return gracefully "back into the mysterious workings of things." Hence an alternate name for Ki-7 is *waiming* (外命), meaning "beyond destiny."[10] This name indicates that, if illness now has its own life and has gone further than even the fulfillment of destiny or medicine can resolve, Ki-7 may still help patients in their transition to death as their "current" "returns" back home to the primal *dao*.

Ultimately, healing must be concerned with the evolution of the individual rather than solely with his survival—the domain of modern medicine. As practitioners of the inner tradition, we are always assisting patients in their return to original nature. When heaven wills this as a renewal of life, we assist in the furthering of that life. When the connection between metal and water separates and the condition has gone beyond what nature can restore, we still assist patients in their return, back to the greater origin of life, which is heaven. The *Book of Liehzi* reminds us, "Dying is the virtue in us going to its destination. The men of old called a dead man 'a man who has gone back.' Saying that the dead have gone back they implied that the living are travelers. The traveler who forgets to go back is a man who mistakes his home."[11]

---

## *Treatment*

> *If one knows about white and preserves the black, then divine clarity comes of itself. The white is the metal essence, the black is the basis of water.*
>
> – *ZAN DONGJI*[12]

The essential nature of the husband/wife imbalance is that the separation of the *yuanqi* and compromised function of *mingmen* has led to a failure of the *sheng* cycle to make the all-important transition between the metal and water element. Hence the basic principle in treating the husband/wife imbalance is to restore the connection between the organ functions represented by the right and left pulses. Of particular importance is aiding the transition from the metal to the water element along the *sheng* cycle.

The primary strategy is to choose points that tonify the wood and water elements by drawing *qi* from the right half of the cycle to the left half. Ki-7 and Bl-67 are the primary tonification points that establish the link between metal and water. The secondary tonification point Ki-3 draws *qi* from earth to tonify water, and the secondary tonification point Lv-4 draws *qi* from metal to tonify the wood element. These four points constitute the primary strategy used to break the husband/wife imbalance. Generally, I repeat these points until the patient returns for treatment with a sustained kidney pulse. If this protocol does not break the H/W block, you can consider other treatments (reviewed later in the protocol section).

In my experience, Ki-1 and Bl-1 needled together in the same session have proved valuable in breaking a husband/wife imbalance.[13] Ki-1 is the source of all power in the kidney meridian and when tonified has the function of helping restore collapsed *yang*. The function of restoring collapsed *yang* specifically calls to mind the transition between hexagram 23, "splitting apart," and 24, "return."[14] Bl-1, located at the medial canthus and named "eyes bright," aids in stimulating the spontaneous interaction between early and later heaven. For the eyes receive life (later heaven) and channel it down into the fire of *mingmen*, where it meets the *yuanqi* (early heaven). In a given individual, any point done at precisely the right moment may help restore the memory of original nature necessary for restoring health. Generally, however, when trying to break this particular habitual pattern, choose only points that tonify the left-hand pulses or sedate the right-hand pulses.

Lastly, if the pulses of both hands have collapsed and the patient evidences the *qi*-wild pattern described earlier, you must choose a different therapeutic strategy. The *yin* of the whole being must be tonified in order to root the *yang*. CV-1, named "meeting of *yin*," represents the source of *yin* in the human being. GV-20, named "hundred meetings," is the gathering point of the *yangqi*. These two points together represent the central axis of heaven and earth as it occurs in the human being. Treating them together can help restore balance of the primordial *yin* and *yang* and help realign a patient to these dual poles of universal function. Treating CV-1 and GV-1 together, as discussed in Chapter 6, can also be helpful in this regard.

## *Considerations*

Do not view the H/W block as a technical problem that can be solved by applying medical treatment. If we adopt this attitude, we run the risk of merely enabling the patient to remain in an unlivable situation where he may be subjected to further harm. We must identify the source of the H/W and educate the patient about the beliefs and behaviors that give rise to it. If the H/W is being perpetuated by abuse, it is necessary to help the patient extricate himself from the ongoing source of the threat. Consider educating patients about the sources of input to their imbalances a standard part of every treatment protocol.

In two scenarios the pulse can lead us to misdiagnose an H/W block. The first instance involves patients who have from birth for constitutional reasons an abnormally deep and feeble left-hand pulse. On the one hand, these people can benefit from long-term tonification to support the functional processes governed by the left-hand pulses. On the other hand, it is unlikely any amount of treatment will yield a significant change in the underlying pulse pattern. I know of at least one person who has had such a pulse pattern for the seventeen years we have been friends, despite having been treated by a variety of practitioners over that time. Although treatment has helped improve her health, the basic H/W pattern on her pulse has never changed.

The second scenario that can lead to the misdiagnosis of an H/W block involves the presence of a *fanguan* (反關脈) pulse on the left wrist.[15] In this case, the left artery runs anomalously on the back side of the wrist. When this occurs, no information found at either the regular or anomalous position is reliable in pulse diagnosis. Often there will be a deep and feeble pulse present in the normal location, but this is not the radial artery and does not suggest the presence of an H/W block. I have seen more than a few cases in which patients have come to me for treatment, after other practitioners had spent years trying to break a misdiagnosed H/W imbalance on them, only for me to find a *fanguan* pulse. In most cases the patient with the *fanguan* pulse will appear far more healthy by all other diagnostic parameters than the presence of an H/W would predict. Therefore I suggest that whenever you suspect a H/W, take a moment to be sure you are truly feeling the radial artery in its proper position.

## *Reactions to Treatment*

As the block between metal and water is cleared, the patient should feel a renewed vitality and commitment to life. With the will to live restored, the patient should evidence a new striving toward goals and the attendant joy that comes with accomplishing them. In every way possible patients should feel reconnected back to the source of life and purpose that lies in their depths. As such healing is nurtured, we can feel confident that patients have stepped back from the brink and remain optimistic that they can avoid whatever serious potential illness might have befallen them had *yin* and *yang* continued to separate.

## *Treatment Protocol*

The general treatment strategy in breaking the H/W block is to transfer *qi* from the right half of the *sheng* cycle to the left half. In this way the will of the kidney and the inherited constitution can be revived using the relative excess of *qi* available from the acquired constitution.

1. Educate patients about the source of the H/W in their life and the beliefs and behaviors that perpetuate it. If the etiology of the imbalance is ongoing, support patients to extricate themselves from the source of the threat.

2. Before proceeding to break the block using techniques that transfer *qi*, check for the presence of AE and drain it if you detect it. Otherwise, we run the risk of spreading the AE to officials that may have been previously unaffected.
3. Transfer from metal to water to initiate the return of *yang* back to the root of life. In essence, Ki-7 empowers the conception of self by bringing the metal element into functional contact with the water element.
   a. Tonify Ki-7 and Bl-67.
4. Transfer from earth to water by tonifying Ki-3. As the earth point within water, Ki-3 supplements the inherited constitution (water) with the strength of the acquired constitution (earth). As the channel's source point, Ki-3 provides access to fundamental reserves of *yin* and *yang*.
   a. Tonify Ki-3.
5. Transfer from metal to wood by needling Lv-4. Strengthening the presence of metal within wood can empower wood to "let go" and move on in life.
   a. Tonify Lv-4.
6. After steps 3, 4, and 5, I always take the pulses to ascertain if the H/W has been broken. As soon as I detect a significant increase in volume on the left half of the pulse, I stop treating and allow the patient to rest. If, after 10 to 15 minutes I return to find the treatment has held, I occasionally tonify Ht-7, the source point on the heart channel. This helps restore the rule of the emperor and direct the *qi* back up the *sheng* cycle toward fire. Note that, in this regard, some feel it is imperative to treat Ht-7 and SI-4 after breaking the H/W. I have not found this to be the case.

---

## *Ancillary Methods*

If the H/W is not broken with the protocol just described, you may try several other methods. These first four options are listed in the order they are recommended by TAIS. Please note that in my own practice I have found option 5 possibly followed by option 2 to suffice and have never had to try the others. I include option 1, 3, and 4 for the sake of completion only.

1. Sedate the source points of the relatively excess officials on the right side of the pulse and tonify the source points on the relatively deficient officials found on the left side of the pulse.

| SEDATE | TONIFY |
|---|---|
| Lu-9 | Ki-3 |
| LI-4 | Bl-64 |
| St-42 | Lv-3 |
| Sp-3 | Gb-40 |

2. Tonify the kidney and liver *shu* points. These two points provide a strong reserve of *qi* to strengthen these officials and revive the functions on the left half of the *ke* cycle. The kidney *shu* revives the virtue of potency, and the liver *shu* revives the virtue of aspiration.
   a. Tonify Bl-23 and Bl-18
3. Sedate the *shu* points of lung and spleen and tonify the *shu* points of liver and kidney. This is a stronger treatment than number 2 and diminishes the capacity of the strong side to overcontrol and suppress the weak side of the pulse. Here needles are retained in Bl-13 and Bl-20 until you feel the pulse diminish on the right side. Then tonify Bl-23 and Bl-18.
   a. Sedate Bl-13 and Bl-20.
   b. Tonify Bl-18 and Bl-23.
4. Sedate all the *yinshu* points on the officials of the right hand and tonify all the *yinshu* points on the officials of the left hand. This is a stronger treatment than number 3 because we are sedating the heart protector and tonifying the heart. These two officials were omitted from treatment number 3 because these points strongly affect heart function and are approached only as a last resort.
   a. Sedate Bl-13, Bl-14, and Bl-20.
   b. Tonify Bl-18, Bl-15, and Bl-23.
5. Tonify Ki-1 and Bl-1. Both these points are the first on their respective meridians and provide access to the source of *yin* and water as discussed earlier.
   a. Tonify Ki-1 and Bl-1.
6. Use the four-needle technique presented in Chapter 12 to tonify the kidney and liver if necessary.
   To tonify the kidney using the four-needle technique:
   a. Tonify Ki-7 and Lu-8.
   b. Sedate Ki-3 and Sp-3.
   To tonify the liver using the four-needle technique:
   a. Tonify Ki-10 and Lv-8.
   b. Sedate Lv-4 and Lu-8.

---

## *Herbal Treatment*

In treating the H/W imbalance with Chinese herbs, you must take more into consideration in terms of pulse diagnosis and overall assessment than merely the presence of the basic pattern described here. Generally, herbal treatment involves reestablishing movement on the left half of the *sheng* cycle. The formula Zuogui Wan (Restore the Left Pill) can be efficacious here as can Liuwei Dihuang Wan (Rehmannia Six) or Bawei Dihuang Wan (Rehmannia Eight Formula). To each of these I add the herb Wuweizi (Schizandra) to strengthen the connection between metal and water. Of course you must consider whether the patient's digestion can tolerate *yin* tonics. I have also found the formula Renshen Gejie San (Ginseng and Gecko) to be effective in reestablishing this connection and helping break the H/W imbalance.

## JULIE

***Constitution:*** *Wood/fire*
***Diagnosis:*** *H/W imbalance*

Julie was a 38-year-old woman who approached me seeking treatment for depression and fatigue. She felt trapped in a marriage and was not confident about supporting herself or her children. Several times throughout the interview she cried tears of frustration, but these never lasted long because she didn't appear to have enough energy to sustain the effort. She revealed that when she was younger, her father, an alcoholic, had hit her when he was drunk. Her father had died of liver cancer at the age of 54 when she was 21. Her husband, whose business was in trouble, was now drinking regularly and had been losing his temper with increasing frequency. Julie lived in constant fear that eventually he would hit her.

Julie had painted as a hobby but had stopped after becoming depressed. Occasional efforts to begin painting again were fruitless, and she couldn't find the necessary motivation or joy to sustain the activity. She commented, "I wasn't really that good anyway." Julie sighed softly throughout the interview and seemed hopeless that anything could or would change for her.

### *Pulse and Tongue*

Julie's pulse evidenced the classic pattern of the H/W imbalance. The right side of her pulse was tense and pounding, indicating stagnation of both *qi* and heat. The entire left side was both deep and feeble and suggested depletion of *qi*, blood, *yang*, and *jing*. Julie's tongue was peeled with a red tip, indicating *yin* deficiency in the kidneys and heat trapped in her heart.

### *Interpretation*

The dynamics that initiated Julie's H/W wife imbalance likely started when she was young. One of the difficulties of having an alcoholic parent is that the young child does not receive appropriate feedback about behavior. Rather than relate to the child on the merits of his or her own words or actions, the parent's emotional state is run instead by his or her relationship to the addiction. Julie learned very young to be quiet. There was no point in initiating anything because her father would likely strike down her best laid plans in a drunken rage.

Often adults choose a partner in life so they can work out unresolved issues from childhood. Julie's husband was not an alcoholic when she married him, but she failed to recognize many of the same attributes he shared with her father such as a quick temper and his tendency to try to control her. Painting had been her creative outlet, and her negative self-appraisal suggested a lack of vision regarding her work that I felt was really quite good. Stopping painting suggested that her liver's virtue of creativity and aspiration had collapsed at the same time as the onset of her exhaustion and depression. Likely the development of the H/W pattern on her pulse occurred at about this time as well, although there is no way to verify that clinically.

Her weak sighing suggested her liver was trying to raise *qi* in an effort to sustain growth and life, but she lacked the vitality to push ahead and was largely resigned to her circumstances. The symptoms of exhaustion and depression matched her CSOE, all of which suggested she was wood constitutionally and her wood had stopped striving along with the collapse of her will. Her father's and husband's alcoholism and her father's death from liver cancer all suggested that issues regarding the wood element were of a karmic nature. The lesson of wood, self-esteem, was a virtue she would have to master in this life if she was ever to heal. Her father's cancer at such a young age, along with the presence of the H/W block on her pulse, raised the concern of her own serious illness, possibly imminent.

### *Treatment*

During the initial intake, I pointed out the themes related to the wood element as they ran through Julie's life. Chief among these was the issue of how she had learned to cope as a young girl by disappearing and never asserting herself. Although this had served the function of protecting her then when she was young and defenseless, it was contributing dysfunctionally to her illness now as an adult. Now, in fact, she could change her life situation by standing up for herself. It was quite challenging for Julie to hear my assertions. She still believed in her husband and could not bear to break up her family. I explained that standing up for herself would not necessarily do this, but that if she did not, she would likely become ill, which would certainly be of no benefit to her children. Rather than believe in her husband she could believe in herself and know that any action taken to make herself healthier and stronger would be of benefit to the family as a whole. She was able to embrace this long-term vision, and when she left the intake session, she shook my hand and stated she would at least try.

The basic treatment H/W protocol did break the imbalance, but it returned occasionally if Julie overextended herself or had a fight with her husband. Therefore it was necessary to use several of the supplemental methods discussed earlier to revive the left half of the *ke* cycle. In Julie's case it took six months to break her H/W imbalance to the point that it did not return. During this time I prescribed the formula Qiju Dihuang Wan (Lycii, Chrysanthemum, and Rehmannia Formula) to tonify her liver and kidney *yin* and address the heat flaring up in her heart. To this formula I added the herb Wuweizi (Schizandra) to promote the functional connection of metal and water along the *sheng* cycle. This formula also "brightens the eyes" to strengthen both internal and external vision.

***Outcome***

I reinforced Julie's self-esteem in every treatment session and supported her taking a stand for what she believed in. As she grew stronger she eventually returned to painting. Within two weeks of breaking her H/W imbalance for good, Julie took her children and moved out of her house. She did not divorce her husband, however, but insisted he join Alcoholics Anonymous and attend family therapy with her and the children.

To her amazement he consented and, although it has been a long and tough road, her family is now back together and her husband has been sober for four years. Julie feels renewed strength and pride that she fought for what she cared about and won. Her pulses have filled out nicely on her left hand, and, although still tending toward deficiency, the severity of the H/W pattern and its attendant symptoms of depression and exhaustion have not returned.

## MARGARET

***Constitution:*** *Water*
***Diagnosis:*** *H/W Imbalance*

Margaret was a 32-year-old woman who was beginning her career as a professional actress. Margaret came to me complaining of constant exhaustion, shortness of breath, coughing, and high vulnerability to lung infections as evidenced by a recent succession of colds. She was particularly concerned because she was to debut in a musical in just three weeks.

***Findings***

An evaluation of Margaret's CSOE revealed she was a kidney constitutional type. Her pulse revealed a H/W imbalance of recent onset.[16] In Margaret's case the kidney pulse was relatively deep and feeble compared to the liver and heart pulses, which were less deep although still *qi* and *yang* deficient relative to the right side of her pulse. The pulses of the right hand were tense, slippery, and slightly pounding. Her special lung pulses were tense and slippery. Margaret's tongue was pale with teeth marks and had a thin white coat with some phlegm evident. Her cheeks evidenced a slight flush.

### *Analysis*

Margaret was stuck in a cycle of lung infections. Her vulnerability was based on deficient kidney *qi* and *yang*. Each new infection further weakened the link between her metal and water elements, and her pulses were just shy of a full-blown H/W imbalance. Her right-hand pulses suggested stagnation of *qi,* heat, and damp. And her special lung pulses suggested that stagnant *qi* and dampness in the form of phlegm were obscuring her lungs, a finding borne out by the presence of phlegm on her tongue. The flush in her checks suggested kidney *yin* deficiency.

### *Treatment*

I initially prescribed the formulas Xingsu San (Apricot Semen and Perilla) for her cough and Erchen Tang (Citrus and Pinellia) to help resolve the phlegm in her lungs.

In the first session I checked for, and drained, AE, which was present only on her lung *shu* point (Bl-13). She returned three days later feeling more clear and reported that her current cold was subsiding (no doubt because of the herbs I had prescribed). However, she was still exhausted. In this session I treated her with the typical H/W protocol of KI-3, KI-7, Bl-67, and Lv-4. Her pulses responded immediately, and I tonified Lu-1 and KI-27 to strengthen the functional connection between the kidneys and lungs and thus empower the kidney's ability to grasp *qi.*[17] The point Lu-6, the channel's *xi*-cleft point, was also added to move stagnation in the lungs that I felt inhibited the metal element's ability to generate healthy water.

Margaret returned the next week feeling much better but still not entirely back to her old energy. Her big debut was on Friday evening, only three nights away. Checking her pulse I found the kidney had improved slightly in volume but was still noticeably deficient relative to her right-side pulses. I therefore treated Bl-18 and Bl-23, the liver and kidney *shu* points, with a strong tonification technique. Margaret's entire face changed and her pulse did too. Immediately the entire left side of her pulse revived, and only the kidney pulse was still somewhat deficient with respect to the other pulses.

Long-term treatment with Margaret involved building the reserves in her kidneys as well as her immunity as governed by *weiqi.* To this end I prescribed the Health Concerns formula Astra Essence, a balanced kidney tonic that strengthens *yin* and *yang (jing)* in even proportions.[18] I also prescribed Yupingfeng San (Jade Windscreen Powder) to increase her resistance to colds.

### Outcome

Margaret literally got off the treatment table after her third treatment feeling like her old self. She performed on Friday evening in perfect form. Her H/W block never returned, and her immunity improved to the point that the following winter she experienced only one minor cold that did not progress past the initial stage of sore throat.

## NOTES

1. Morgan, p. 28.
2. See *ND*, p. 107.
3. In Cleary, 1986a, p. 34.
4. Maribeth Kaptchuk first brought this finding to my attention.
5. These hexagrams appear on the front cover of this text. Their significance is discussed in *ND*, pp. 105–109.
6. From a lecture by Andrew Cohen, January 2003.
7. The *qi*-wild pulse condition is a loss of functional contact between the *yin* and *yang* of specific organ systems indicated by a unique set of pulse qualities. If not resolved, it may lead to death. See Hammer (1990, pp. 315, 336–338).
8. The concept of "possession," as it occurs throughout several traditions of Chinese medicine, is applicable here. Often the patient will be so stuck in one form of emotional expression (the internal devils), there is no room for any spontaneity or subtlety of expression. The practitioner is unable to make contact with any sane or clear influences at the patient's core. For a further discussion, see Chapter 3.
9. Watson, 1964a, p. 49.
10. Hicks, 1985, p. 16.
11. Graham, 1990, p. 26. Girardot (1983, p. 160) points out the emphasis in Daoism is on learning to return while still alive. *Gui,* "the dead," is a homophone of *gui,* meaning "to return" or "one who has gone home."
12. Homann, 1976, p. 47.
13. The use of these points in this regard was first brought to my attention by Jonathan Klate.
14. See *ND,* p. 107.
15. The character fan can mean literally to "reverse," and the term applied to the pulse suggests the artery is displaced from its usual location.
16. If long standing, the H/W tends to present with the left side of the pulse evidencing deep and feeble/absent qualities in all locations. However, I find that often the entire left side does not collapse all at once. Frequently, the left proximal position corresponding to the kidney becomes deep and feeble first with the left middle and distal positions representing the liver and heart, respectively, eventually following suit.
17. Typically it is advised to avoid tonifying points on the right side of the *ke* cycle when attempting to break the H/W imbalance. The dictum "do what's right," however, takes precedence over all theory.

18. Ingredients of the Astra Essence Formula as listed by the Health Concerns company:

| PINYIN | ENGLISH |
|---|---|
| Danggui | Tangkuei |
| Duzhong | Eucommia bark |
| Goqizi | Lycii fruit |
| Heshouwu | Polygonum root |
| Huangqi | Astragalus root |
| Nuzhenzi | Ligustrum lucidi fruit |
| Renshen | Ginseng root, white |
| Shayuanzi | Astragalus seed |
| Shanzhuyu | Cornus fruit |
| Shudihuang | Rehmannia root, cooked |
| Tusizi | Cuscuta seed |

# 5

# EXIT/ENTRY BLOCKS

In a simplistic way, the flow of *qi* through the meridians resembles the passage of water through a series of twelve pipes. A blockage that occurs between two meridians in the sequential flow of *qi* is known as an exit/entry (E/E) block and can adversely affect the balance of the entire functional system.[1] Clearing an E/E block can have profound effects on patients' pulse, overall presentation, and experience of their condition. It is therefore often necessary to clear an E/E block before treatment at the constitutional or symptomatic level will hold. Here I discuss the theory of E/E blocks and how to treat them.

## *The Chinese Clock*

The circulation of *qi* in the twelve main meridians corresponds to the circulation of macrocosmic *qi* in the twelve terrestrial branches of Chinese phase energetics.[2] This Chinese clock, if you will, is based on the notion that each of the twelve officials has a two-hour period during which its function is most active physiologically (see Figure 5.1, p. 76). In the five-element tradition, the order of the flow of *qi* designates the heart as the first meridian. Some traditions maintain that the flow of *qi* begins with the lungs and so name the lung meridian as first in the order of the sequential flow of *qi*. The inner tradition of healing in Chinese medicine is a heart-centered tradition, and the designation of the heart official as first in the order of *qi* flow emphasizes the heart as monarch in our inner kingdom of being. Note that the Chinese characters that denote spirit, such as *shen* (神), *ling* (靈), or the physiological influence of heaven as in *yuanqi* (元氣), all begin with a single stroke depicting the number one and denoting the influence of heaven. As the son of heaven on earth, it is fitting that the heart as emperor is designated as the first official in the circulation of *qi*.

| SEQUENCE OF *QI* CIRCULATION | TIME | MERIDIAN | ENTRY POINT | EXIT POINT |
|---|---|---|---|---|
| I | *11 A.M.–1 P.M.* | *Heart (Ht.1–Ht.9)* | *Ht.1* | *Ht-9* |
| II | *1 P.M.–3 P.M.* | *Small Intestine (SI.1–SI.19)* | *SI.1* | *SI.19* |
| III | *3 P.M.–5 P.M.* | *Bladder (Bl.1–Bl.67)* | *Bl.1* | *Bl.67* |
| IV | *5 P.M.–7 P.M.* | *Kidney (Ki.1–Ki.27)* | *Ki.1* | *Ki.22*[*3]* |
| V | *7 P.M.–9 P.M.* | *Heart Protector (HP.1–HP.9)* | *HP.1* | *HP.8** |
| VI | *9 P.M.–1 P.M.* | *Three Heater (TH.1–TH.23)* | *TH.1* | *TH.22** |
| VII | *11 P.M.–1 A.M.* | *Gallbladder (Gb.1–Gb.44)* | *Gb.1* | *Gb.41** |
| VIII | *1 A.M.–3 A.M.* | *Liver (Lv.1–Lv.14)* | *Lv.1* | *Lv.14* |
| IX | *3 A.M.–5 A.M.* | *Lung (Lu.1–Lu.9)* | *Lu.1* | *Lu.7** |
| X | *5 A.M.–7 A.M.* | *Large Intestine (LI.1-LI.20)* | *LI.4** | *LI.20* |
| XI | *7 A.M.–9 A.M.* | *Stomach (St.1–St.45)* | *St.1* | *St.42** |
| XII | *9 A.M.–11 A.M.* | *Spleen (Sp.1–Sp.21)* | *Sp.1* | *Sp.21* |

*Figure 5.1*

THE CHINESE CLOCK AND THE E/E POINTS OF THE TWELVE MERIDIANS

*Note: Exit and entry points do not always correspond to the first and last points on each meridian. This discrepancy is indicated by an asterisk next to the given exit or entry point.*

---

## *Detecting an E/E Block on the Pulse*

An E/E block can be picked up on the pulses as qualitative differences between the affected meridians. When an E/E block exists between two meridians, we expect the meridian that comes first numerically in the order of *qi* circulation (hereafter referred to as the "earlier" meridian) to have a greater strength than the meridian that follows it (hereafter referred to as the "later" meridian). Further, we expect the qualities that indicate amount of *qi,* such as volume, length, width, amplitude, and intensity, will be relatively greater on the earlier meridian.[4]

This is analogous to a series of pipes where the pipes before the obstruction are full and the following pipes are relatively empty. Hence with an E/E block between liver and lung, we would expect the liver pulse to be stronger than the lung pulse because the liver is the eighth meridian and the lung is the ninth.[5] Regardless of the specific nature of the E/E block's presentation on the pulse, you will be impressed by a relatively greater amount of *qi* before the block and a relative deficiency after it.

When an E/E block occurs, generally the earlier official shows symptoms of stagnation and/or excess and the later official shows symptoms of deficiency. Hence the earlier meridians show taut to tense and/or inflated qualities on the pulse. The presence of the inflated quality indicates that *qi*, heat, or possibly blood is able to flow into these organs but becomes trapped and is not able to flow out.[6] The latter meridians, on the "other side" of the E/E block, evidence feeble/absent qualities and often flat waveforms on the pulse. The presence of the flat pulse indicates that *qi* is able to flow out of these organs but is not able to enter.

For example, similar qualities of *qi* stagnation and/or excess heat may be found on the pulses corresponding to the lungs, colon, stomach, and spleen, which are the ninth through twelfth meridians, respectively (Figure 5.2, p. 78). However, palpation of the left distal position heart pulse may show a waveform that is flat and/or feeble/absent. In this scenario, needle Sp-21 and Ht-1 to harmonize the imbalance and clear this particular E/E block.[7] Success in treating this block will be evident immediately and on later examination of the pulse. The pulse should show what I term an *equalization* of the qualities on both the earlier and later meridians involved in the particular E/E block treated. That is, there should be relatively less excess and stagnation on the earlier meridians and relatively less deficiency with a corresponding increase of *qi* on the later meridians.

### *Causes of E/E Blocks*

E/E blocks may occur for a variety of reasons. Externally, physical injury to a region may result in an E/E block, particularly if scaring is involved that restricts the flow of *qi.* A meridian injured by a surgical scar, for instance, may often show signs of either a local excess or deficiency. In a relatively strong person, traumatic injury will often generate inflated qualities on the pulse that correspond to the organ or region injured. These qualities indicate either trapped *qi*, heat, or blood. A

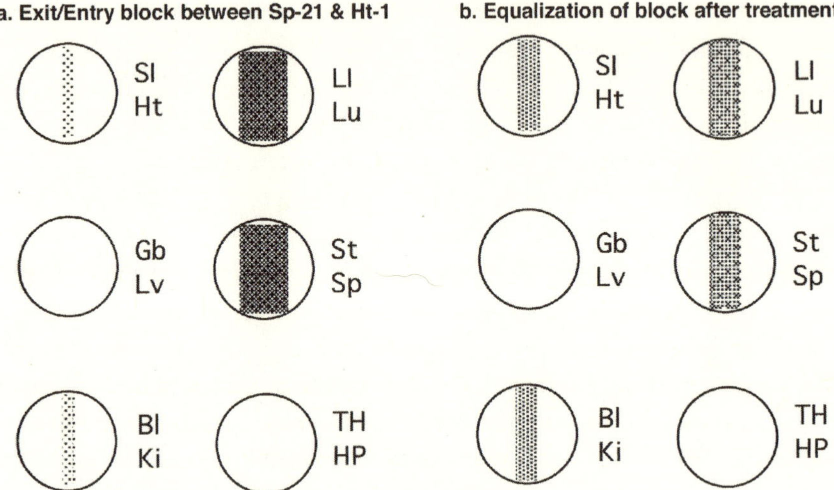


*Figure 5.2*
EXIT/ENTRY BLOCKS

*a. Here an E/E block is depicted between the spleen and heart meridian. The darkness and density of shading indicate the relative amount of stagnation and/or excess and deficiency in the involved organs. This figure depicts a relative excess on the ninth through twelfth meridians, which are the lungs, large intestine, stomach, and spleen, respectively. A relative deficiency on the first through fourth meridians represents, in order, the heart, small intestine, bladder, and kidney. The empty circles corresponding to the wood (gallbladder and liver officials) and fire (three heater and heart protector) elements indicate only that these meridians are not directly involved in this specific E/E block.*

*b. This figure represents the functional state of the pulses after the block has been cleared by treating the exit point on the spleen (Sp-21) and the entry point on the heart official (Ht-1). Now there is relatively less stagnation in the organ systems found before the block and a relative increase of* qi *in the organ systems that lie after the block. Often the involved meridians show near complete equalization after the block is successfully cleared.*

weaker person may evidence a flat quality on the pulse after the same injury. An appropriate strategy in either case may be to treat the E/E points before and/or after the affected meridian as the pulse suggests. For example, with a scar across the abdomen at Lv-13, you might needle Gb-41 (exit point of gallbladder) and Lv-1 (entry point of liver). You might also treat Lv-14 with Lu-1, the exit and entry points on their respective channels. In addition to treating local points to help the *qi* bridge the scar tissue, the E/E treatment can flush stagnancy from the affected meridian by opening the flow of *qi* at either end.

Internally, E/E blocks can arise from a constitutional predisposition or lifestyle imbalance that affects a specific aspect of physiology. For example, a person who is earth constitutionally and prone to dampness and heat may have chronic sinusitis with an attendant E/E block between LI-20 and St-1. The same imbalance might be generated in anyone who eats too much rich food. Another major cause of E/E blocks is stagnation due to emotional suppression (discussed later). I have noticed that a given patient may be prone to a specific E/E imbalance that reasserts itself periodically. The specific nature of this reoccurring block appears like an overlay on the constitutional type and often points to a specific life issue that needs to be resolved at continually more profound levels. Often a chronically reoccurring E/E imbalance is indicative of constitutional type. For example, a person who regularly presents with a block between the spleen and heart officials is likely to be either earth or fire constitutionally. Only when this block is finally cleared will the virtue associated with the constitutional type finally emerge in force.[8]

In my clinical experience, E/E blocks that occur on meridians "between" elements are encountered more frequently than blocks on meridians "within" elements. Hence we are relatively more likely to encounter an E/E block between the fire and water elements (intra-elemental) involving the small intestine and bladder officials and relatively less likely to encounter an E/E block within the water element (inter-elemental) involving the bladder and kidney officials. Such imbalances between officials within an element are very effectively treated with *luo* points. Generally, only if the *luo* point has failed to achieve balance within an elemental pair of officials would I consider using E/E points.

The intra-elemental E/E points of the *yin* meridians, located on the chest, are all related to stagnation and/or deficiency affecting the heart and/or lungs. The emotional genesis of these blocks is often associated with imbalances that stem from real or perceived betrayal of intimacy.[9] These blocks relate directly to the internal world of the heart, circulation of *qi* in the chest, and circulation in general. As these blocks occur in the domain of the heart, they tend to relate to one's inappropriate relationship to feelings. The inter-elemental E/E points of the *yang* meridians are all located on the head. E/E blocks in these meridians relate directly to stagnation of mind obscuring the spirit. Located next to the sensory orifices, these points are largely responsible for the accurate perception of reality as it occurs in later heaven. Hence the presence of these E/E blocks are often created by, and in turn contribute to, erroneous interpretation of reality as it occurs both internally (who we are) and externally (what happens to us).[10] As these blocks occur in the domain of the mind, they tend to relate to one's inappropriate relationship to thoughts. For the mind and heart to function as one, any diagnosed E/E blocks must be cleared early in the course of treatment.[11]

### *Specific E/E Blocks*

E/E blocks are not strictly local or superficial phenomena at the meridian level of function. Each of the E/E blocks has its own characteristics that emanate from and contribute to unbalanced function of the twelve officials.[12] E/E blocks are generally characterized by the functions of the two officials immediately before and after the block. However, the specific presentation of a given E/E block may be as varied as the patients who have it. The fact that any number of meridians may be involved before or after the block also adds to the variability of signs a given block may present. Note, therefore, that all earlier or later meridians that show the same qualities of stagnation, excess, and deficiency on the pulse can be equally affected by the presence of the block and its removal.

Here I discuss the natures of the six E/E blocks that occur between elements as they have appeared to me in my clinical practice. This discussion is from the perspective of the officials immediately before and after the block as well as the specific natures of the individual acupuncture points used for clearing it. Although I present certain patterns of symptomatology I have found that characterize particular E/E blocks, you must understand that a particular E/E block may be accompanied by diverse and seemingly unrelated symptomatology depending on the meridians and officials involved.[13] You can only diagnose E/E blocks reliably from the pulse and never from specific symptom patterns. As mentioned previously, it is often essential to clear the presence of a given E/E block before you can proceed effectively with other treatment.

### *The* Yin *Meridians*

Three pairs of meridians flow into each other via their E/E points across the chest area transversing the heart. Instability of the heart function and inhibition of the lung rhythm are often accompanied by E/E blocks involving these meridians. Clearing these E/E blocks can contribute to harmonizing patterns of stagnation and deficiency emanating from or affecting the upper burner. The points involved with the E/E blocks are discussed here only briefly. I suggest you supplement this reading by referring to the individual description of each point provided in Part IV.

#### *Spleen/Heart*

In the sequential flow of *qi,* spleen is the twelfth meridian and heart is the first meridian. *Qi* leaves Sp-21 and flows to the heart meridian where it enters at Ht-1. We see the nature of this E/E block in the inability to let nourishment into the deepest level of our heart. The spleen produces blood that must in turn nourish the heart. With this block, the patient's unbalanced relationship to intimacy may have affected that aspect of self receptive to nourishment. Characteristic of this pattern's symptomatology are appetite disorders such as bulimia, anorexia, oral compulsions, and heart deficiency patterns including shortness of breath, palpitations, and insomnia. All of these may be seen as a weak, yielding heart that is overpowered by the spleen's tendency toward worry and obsession.[14] Another scenario is that an unstable heart may overtax the spleen's function of providing nourishment. Here, no amount of nourishment ever appears to be enough to satisfy the hungry heart. Eating disorders may, in fact, be a result of an unnourished heart crying out for love.

Belief patterns attendant to this condition revolve around the notion that substantial nourishment is not available in life. One other assumption foundational in this imbalance is the tendency to rely on significant others for nourishment and then feel abandoned when the other feels burdened by the relationship and pulls away. This pulling away can occur on the most subtle of levels, yet patients habitually respond as if they have been abandoned. Negative affirmations and beliefs such as "I am not enough" typify this block. With our hearts literally not being fed, we may evidence a tendency toward excessive need for control and selfishness as we try without success to have our needs met. My experience suggests that often an unbalanced relationship to the mother during formative years is significant in contributing to the tendency toward this block.

---

### ❖ **Sp-21, Dabao,** Great Enveloping, Exit Point (大包)

The character *bao* reveals in its etymology the image of a fetus surrounded by the womb.[15] Sp-21 is the great *luo* point that sends collaterals branching around the entire torso and effectively surrounds each person with an enfolding, motherly embrace. The term *baoyi* (包一) in Daoism means to "embrace the one."[16] This evokes the image of the Daoist making the spiritual journey of restoring original nature *(de)* and returning back to the womb by patterning himself on the primal *dao*. The sage who is "for the belly" receives the unconditional nourishment of the mother. The inner nature of Sp-21 is to empower us to feel surrounded by unconditional nourishment in life as though still in the womb.

---

### ❖ **Ht-1, Jiquan,** Utmost Source, Entry Point (極泉)

As the first point on the heart, itself the first meridian, Ht-1 may be considered the first point in the circulation of *qi* in the twelve main meridians. Hence Ht-1 as a source *(quan)* is given the designation of utmost *(ji)* respect. As the polestar is the center of the universe and "heart of heaven," the sun the center of the solar system, and the emperor the center of the nation, so too is the heart the center of our internal being. All these centers represent the same functional influence, each having its own unique physical manifestation. Ht-1 empowers the alignment of our heart with these universal centers so we may be nourished from the primal source.

*Kidney/Pericardium*

In the sequential flow of *qi,* kidney is the fourth meridian and heart protector is the fifth meridian. *Qi* leaves Ki-22 and flows to the heart protector meridian, where it enters at HP-1. Technically, the entry point on heart protector (HP-1) is "forbidden" to needle on women and HP-2 is recommended instead. However, I have found that HP-1 is important both as an entry point and as a window to the sky for treating betrayal of intimacy. In my opinion it is quite feasible for experienced practitioners to needle this point in women with smaller sized breasts. Because of its position on the breast, male practitioners must be sensitive to issues regarding propriety and appropriate boundaries if they choose to needle this point on a woman.[17]

Congruent with this E/E block are any of a wide variety of kidney/heart patterns. Presentations may include heart palpitations, chest pain, fibrocystic breast disease or breast cancer, anxiety, insomnia, and depression. Betrayal of intimacy is a major cause of chronic E/E blocks between these two points. Hence a hallmark of this pattern's symptomatology is that it usually increases when the "threat" of intimacy is present. Our fear of intimacy may continually extinguish our heart's fire, resulting in our being emotionally cold and joyless. Too, the perceived threat of intimacy may disinhibit the heart protector's fire that blazes in its presence. In this scenario we are likely to show tendencies toward mania and hypersexuality. In this regard the habitual drive toward sex may actually be a way of avoiding real intimacy.

---

❖ **Ki-22, Bulang,** Walking on the Veranda, Exit Point (步郎)

Here the kidney meridian rises off the abdomen and up onto the rib cage. The character *lang* gives the sense of a corridor, veranda, or "upward path."[18] Through their names, the previous points on the kidney meridian Ki-18 to Ki-21, "stone border," "*yin* capital," "through the valley," and "dark gate," respectively, tell a story of a journey through darkness. The kidney meridian reaches the highlands of the rib cage and then the flow of *qi* shifts to HP-1. Kidney points that follow the exit point (Ki-23 through Ki-27) represent the deepest reserves of spiritual influences on the meridian. These points form a corridor along the rib cage similar to the animal figures found lining the spirit road (*shendao*) of the ancient imperial mausoleums.[19] In fact, the name of Ki-24, "spirit burial ground," precisely calls forth these imperial burial places. The kidney function represents the depths of self as it is present in the *yuanqi* and *jing*. This E/E combination helps us make the transition from this deep journey with its attendant fears to empowering the joys and pleasures associated with the heart protector.

---

❖ **HP-1,Tianchi,** Heavenly Pond, Entry Point (天池)

HP-1 is a "window of the sky" point and as such provides the deepest possible connection to spiritual levels of intimacy. This point can help restore our memory of our heart as a place of safety before it became burdened by life's sorrows. Further, this point can empower us to experience the world as a safe place, helping clear the effects of past pain and betrayal.

*Liver/Lung*

In the sequential flow of *qi*, liver is the eighth meridian and lung is the ninth meridian. *Qi* leaves Lv-14 and flows to the lung meridian where it enters at Lu-1. Typical of this E/E block are symptoms of liver *qi* stagnation and lung *qi* deficiency. These may include breast tenderness, sighing, gas pain, shortness of breath, and asynchronous heartbeat and breath rhythms. Here we may see symptoms across the *ke* cycle that reflect the unbalanced relationship of metal and wood. Sighing is often a sign of resignation, suggesting that stagnant liver *qi* is affecting the lungs' capacity to empower inspiration.

**Stagnation Between the Middle and Upper Burner**

The presence of an inflated pulse in the diaphragm position (between the medial and distal position pulses bilaterally) indicates stagnation of either *qi*, heat, or both in the diaphragm. The presence of this pulse can indicate trauma, lifting beyond one's capacity, or the repression of tender feelings. Here I focus on the latter. The emotional basis of the stagnation suggested by the diaphragm pulse results precisely from situations such as divorce. In the process of separating from a lover we are often compelled to repress the tender feelings felt for that person. These feelings emanate from the heart in the upper burner and "sit on top" of the feelings of anger generated by the liver in the middle burner. It is the opposing forces of the tender feelings being "shoved down" and the anger rising that causes the stagnation halfway between the middle and upper burner in the diaphragm.

One excellent treatment that may contribute to clearing this imbalance is treating the E/E combination of Lv-14 and Lu-1.[20] Lv-14, *qimen* ("gate of hope"), helps remove the stagnation caused by the suppression of anger.[21] Too, as the liver function empowers vision it may provide a larger view beyond the present difficult situation toward a brighter future. The *qi* of the liver channeled to the lungs at Lu-1 can now empower the functions of that "tender" official. Stimulating the function of Lu-1 to circulate the *qi* of the chest may help relieve the stagnation there. Further, this treatment may empower the lungs' function of grieving and processing one's tender feelings so the loss of the relationship may be processed adequately.

---

❖ **Lv-14, Qimen,** Gate of Hope, Exit Point (期門)

Lv-14 is the highest point anatomically on the liver meridian and empowers the quality of aspiration. Here, at the top of the tree (liver is the wood element), the branches reach up to touch heaven, which is represented by its connection to the lung meridian at Lu-1. Symptomatic of this E/E block is a loss of both aspiration (liver) and inspiration (lungs). The *qi* in leaving the liver meridian through the "gate of hope" helps us keep our eyes turned toward the future with optimism. Lv-14 may be useful for treating the person who cannot see the light at the end of the tunnel.

---

❖ **Lu-1, Zhongfu,** Middle Palace, Central Treasury, Entry Point (中府)

The flow of *qi* from Lv-14 to Lu-1 provides a connection between the eyes turned upward toward heaven with optimism and great vision and the inspiration of a spiritual connection with heaven. A treasure in the center of the chest is the *zhongqi*, which empowers the synchronicity of all rhythmic movements in the organism. A child often responds to early trauma and/or disappointments in life by shutting off the heart and suppressing lung rhythm. Depletion here is suggested by the presence of a caved-in chest and shoulders that are hunched forward. Characteristic of this imbalance is frustration giving way to despair as the liver *qi* stagnates. The patient can evidence an internal emptiness and loneliness because the lungs have failed to bring quality into his inner landscape or to make contact with his inner worth (the central treasure).

### *The* Yang *Meridians*

Three pairs of *yang* meridians flow into each other via their E/E points, which are all located on the head and bring *qi* through the sensory orifices. Stagnation and deficiency of *qi* affecting the mind and spirit may be cleared using these E/E point combinations as dictated by the pulse.

*Small Intestine/Bladder*

In the sequential flow of *qi,* the small intestine is the second meridian and the bladder is the third meridian. *Qi* leaves SI-19 and flows to the bladder meridian where it enters at Bl-1. Symptomatic of this E/E block is the inability to perceive or accept life accurately as it occurs in the moment. People's senses of listening and seeing tend to be so conditioned by ego that they are unable to perceive reality or respond to it authentically. Patients with this block often seem completely unable to hear accurately what others are saying. The patient's mind so colors his perception of life that his interpretation of what is said and what occurs bear no relation to reality. In fact, the patient's interpretation of what is said is often diametrically opposed to the actual communication. I have noticed that patients with this particular E/E block often immediately repeat what I say to them, presumably in an attempt to assimilate the information in a way they can take it in. Quite frequently what they repeat is noticeably different from the communication I intended. Another hallmark of this E/E imbalance is that the patient may herself have a predominant sense of not being heard. She may be convinced that others do not understand her, not realizing this is a result of her own unclear communication.

This block can be embodied as ringing in the ears, temporomandibular joint dysfunction (TMJ), chronic ear infections, headaches, and dizziness. Further, this E/E block may contribute to a wide range of bladder and urinary dysfunctions. Nervous anxiety that is generalized to all situations can present as the bladder official is cut off from the flow of *qi.*

---

❖ **SI-19, Tinggong,** Listening Palace, Exit Point (聽宮)

The function of SI-19 is archetypal of the relationship between the heart and small intestine officials. The character *ting* ("listen") is etymologically related to the character *de,* which means "virtue" and has undertones of suggesting the power of intuition. From the imagery of the character *ting* we might define the ability to "listen" as the ability to hear one's heart and the hearts of others without deviation. One who is "listening" in this way is able to know the nature of things immediately in his heart, directly bypassing the analytic faculties of his mind.[22]

---

❖ **Bl-1, Jingming,** Eyes Bright, Entry Point (睛明)

An alternate name for Bl-1, based on a different character but also pronounced *jingming,* may be translated as "radiance of essence."[23] When the fires of mingmen ("gate of destiny") burn brightly, the eyes shine with a radiance that reflects the purity of our essential nature *(jing)*. See Figure 5.3 for an explanation of this relationship.[24]

*Three Heater/Gallbladder*

In the sequential flow of *qi,* three heater is the sixth meridian and gallbladder is the seventh meridian. The *qi* leaves TH-22 and flows to the gallbladder meridian, where it enters at Gb-1. The function of the gallbladder empowers vision, and the three heater represents the external world as

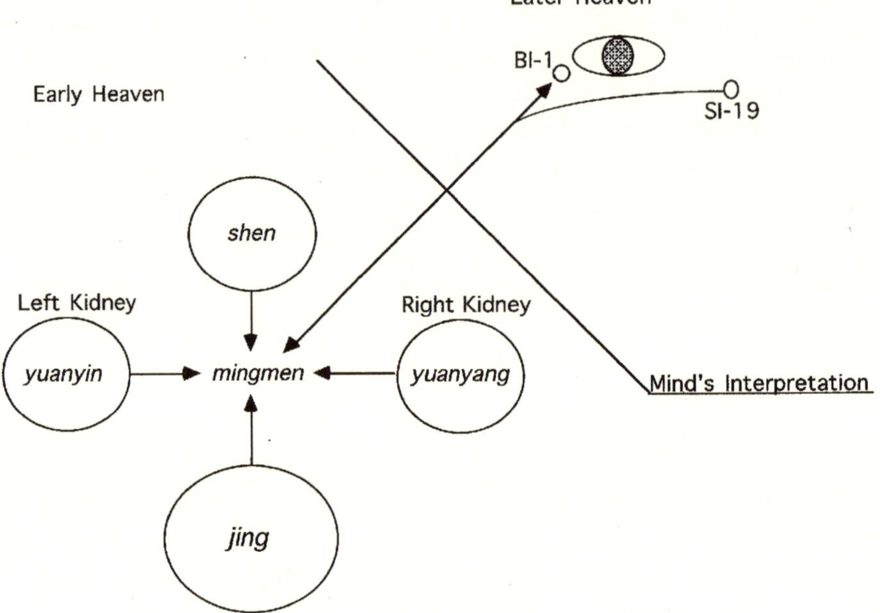


*Figure 5.3*
THE PHYSIOLOGY OF *MINGMEN*

*This figure depicts the physiology of* mingmen *as it relates to preserving the integrity of the key relationships between the* jing *and* shen, *primordial* yin *and* yang, *and early and later heaven. It is the integrity of these relationships that assures the continued interpenetration of* yin *and* yang, *which serve as the deepest foundation for health and well-being. The influence of early heaven is represented by the* jing, yuanqi, *and* shen. *Later heaven is reality as it occurs in life moment to moment. All the intra-elemental E/E points on the* yang *meridians are located on the head by the sensory orifices and play a crucial role in channeling later heaven into the fires of* mingmen *where they interact with early heaven, our genetic and karmic influences. Chief among these points are SI-19 and Bl-1. The two-way arrow between Bl-1 and* mingmen *indicates the reciprocal relationship between these related functions. Momentary reality must be transmitted directly to* mingmen *without the deviation imposed by the mind's interpretation.*[25] *When this occurs, the fires of* mingmen *are fueled, evidenced by the brightness of the eyes and acuity of hearing.*

the outer frontier.[26] The three heater as the body's thermostat maintains contact and balance between the internal and external world. This contact may be undermined by stagnation and the corresponding lack of clear vision that occurs when an E/E block is present between these two officials. One outcome of this E/E block is often a projection of our own judgments onto ourselves and the external world as a result of receiving incomplete information from the three heater's function. This can result in anger typified by bitterness, resentment, and the projection of judgment onto self and others. Presentations associated with this E/E block are migraine headaches, visual disturbances including glaucoma and cataracts, TMJ, grinding of the teeth, and clenched jaws.

---

❖ **TH-22, Heliao,** Harmony Bone, Exit Point (和髎)

As the body's thermostat, the main function of the three heater is to create harmony among the many aspects of interdependent functions that contribute to health, stability, and well-being. Both TH-22 and Gb-1 are reunion points of the gallbladder, small intestine, and three heater channels. These three *yang* meridians are prone to excesses of stagnant *qi,* heat, and fire that may cause imbalances in hearing and vision. In my clinical experience, TH-22 is a main point for harmonizing all manner of imbalances because they undermine clarity of mental function. This function is emphasized by this point's location along the horizontal axis of the head, suggesting its role in "leveling" the mind.

---

❖ **Gb-1, Tongziliao,** Orbit Bone, Entry Point (瞳子髎)

The function of Gb-1 is directly related to our quality of discernment and perspective on our own inner natures and the nature of life around us. Traditional functions ascribed to this point include draining heat and wind. Heat here is the physiological by-product of an underlying mental/emotional process based on frustration. Something has blocked our progress, and the result of the emotional work done trying to move that stagnation has caused heat. Wind is anything that moves in an unpredictable fashion. Here, we are unable to discern a clear picture of the world, which appears as an unrelated string of chaotic events. This external confusion undermines the clarity of our vision and is mirrored by the appearance of internal wind and heat.

*Large Intestine/Stomach*

In the sequential flow of *qi,* the large intestine is the tenth meridian and the stomach is the eleventh meridian. Qi leaves LI-20 and flows to the stomach meridian where it enters at St-1. The nature of this E/E block is characterized by an inability to let go of the undigested aspects of past experience. One key hallmark of this imbalance that I have noted clinically is an inability to cry. On a physical level this block may be associated with symptoms such as chronic sinusitis, candida, nasal polyps, face rash, allergies, a diminished sense of smell or taste, and a wide variety of visual or digestive symptoms.

---

❖ **LI-20, Yingxiang,** Welcome Fragrance, Exit Point (迎香)

The function of LI-20 relates to the receptive qualities of the metal element and the functional connection between the large intestine and the lung official. The sense faculty of smell is one of the most important ways in which the reality of later heaven is transmitted to the internal world. The sense of olfaction contributes in a profound way to human emotional behavior, and current scientific understanding of this phenomenon is in its infancy. In this regard, note that the olfactory nerve terminates in an area of the brain directly related to human emotion (the limbic system). Additionally, our sense of smell contributes in a large way to the way things taste. Hence LI-20 and St-1 may provide significant input into the process by which alimentation and respiration support the fires of *mingmen.* Traditional functions ascribed to this point include opening the nasal passages and dispersing wind and heat. Here, wind and heat arise from the inability to digest life properly and eliminate that which has lost its essential value.

---

❖ **St-1, Chengqi,** Receive Tears, Entry Point (承泣)

The role of the stomach is to digest and integrate life's contribution to physiological function. When emotional material has not been digested and integrated, it burdens us emotionally in much the same way as undigested food may make us feel heavy. If the large intestine is unable to let go of undigested emotional material, we may never reach the stage of grieving a traumatic loss so we can put the past in the past where it belongs. Hence St-1 may empower the receiving of tears, indicating the stuck *qi* has moved on and we are now integrating the experience and being nurtured by the highest it has to offer us. This point opens up the flow of *qi* at the source of the stomach meridian and therefore may help us flush out undigested material in all realms of being.

---

## *Conclusion*

Identification of E/E imbalances on the pulse is conceptually straightforward and easily taught to those in their initial study of pulse diagnosis. The seasoned practitioner can easily incorporate the paradigm into clinical practice. The presence of an E/E block on the pulse indicates a pattern of stagnation, excess, and deficiency in the meridian system that is important to clear before attempting deeper level treatment. In fact, if the block is not cleared, treatment may only contribute to the preexisting patterns of excess and deficiency. E/E blocks may also arise during ongoing treatment, so you must learn to identify and clear such blocks before they are expressed symptomatically or become embodied as illness. Clearing a block can activate the entire functional influence of the meridians involved by removing the stagnation in the earlier meridians, thus supplementing the later meridians' deficiency. In treating in this way, you may follow the example of Emperor Yu who quelled the floods by channeling through the mountains that blocked the raging waters from flowing onward to the sea.[27]

## Catherine

***Diagnosis:*** *E/E block between spleen and heart*
***Constitution:*** *Metal/earth*

Catherine contacted me about receiving treatment while going through a difficult divorce. Although she lived in New York City, she was willing to make the three-hour drive each way to my office to receive regular treatment. Catherine arrived for her first session impeccably groomed and wearing a black and white checkerboard dress and silver jewelry. Her voice was weak, yet she spoke in a refined way and her overall appearance was one of effortless elegance and beauty. Her skin was pale and her hair was jet black.

Her CSOE were all aligned in the metal element (white, weeping, rotten, and grief, respectively), and the theme of loss and longing ran throughout the intake. She complained of decreased appetite and noted that her weight had dropped from 115 down to 98 pounds. She was feeling weak and weepy all the time and felt like she had no strength in her center. Catherine cried often during the interview as she discussed separating from her husband of eighteen years. She was 42 and her husband was nearly 60. She also cried while recounting how her father had died when she was just 6 years old and her mother had put her in a boarding school and only visited her occasionally. Looking for a way to support herself she returned to jewelry making and was starting her own business. The jewelry she showed me was inspired and of extraordinarily fine quality.

Catherine's pulse was bilaterally thin and lacked *qi* depth. The entire pulse spread on pressure. Her right middle pulse, corresponding to the spleen, was strongest, showing the greatest volume and amplitude of any of the other pulses. Her left distal position, corresponding to the heart, was both feeble and deep. Catherine's tongue was pale and evidenced teeth marks around its perimeter.

*Interpretation*

Her CSOE and the constant presence of themes centered around loss and longing all suggested that Catherine's constitutional element was metal. Her constitutional element also expressed itself in her choice of livelihood as a jewelry maker. Metal constitutions also tend to dress in the sharp contrast of black and white or shades of gray that embody the functional dichotomy of receiving above (lungs) and letting go below (large intestine) associated with the metal element. Her own elegance and refinement, so well embodied in her jewelry, also spoke to the association of the metal element with its ability to contact essence in life.

Internally, however, Catherine had been cut off from her father early in life and grieved his loss to such an extent that she married a much older man who could, for a time, symbolize her father and fill this void within her. But as she grew spiritually in life and healed her wound, she grew further and further apart from her husband. Still, in grieving his loss, the loss of her father and all other losses in her life came present simultaneously. Her separation from her mother was tied in with diminished function of her digestive system, and thus while divorcing her husband her weakened earth element suffered as her appetite gradually diminished. The fact that she was willing to drive so far for treatment, despite my best efforts to refer her to a closer, more convenient practitioner, suggested her high degree of motivation to care for herself and therefore offered an excellent prognosis.

The thinness, depth, and spreading quality of Catherine's pulse all suggested she was both blood and *qi* deficient. The findings in her tongue also supported the diagnosis of both *qi* and blood deficiency. The increased volume on her spleen and diminished volume on her heart pulse suggested the presence of an E/E block between these two officials.

*Treatment and Outcome*

Treatment of Catherine focused on nourishing her with needles, moxa, and herbs. After checking for and clearing the presence of AE, I focused her treatment on building blood and *qi* by working on the lung, spleen, heart, and liver officials as well as *chongmai.* I directed Catherine's attention to the role that loss had played in her life and how it had affected her capacity to care for herself and become strong on her own terms.

Burning moxa on CV-8 played an important role initially in helping heal her separation from her mother.

Catherine grew gradually stronger, she seemed happier every week, and her appetite and weight began to improve. However, one week she came in and was weeping again inconsolably and told me her weight was dropping again. She felt clear about leaving her husband but felt empty and that nothing she did in life ever really had fed her heart to nourish her. It was at this point that I realized the import of the E/E block I had detected on her pulse between the spleen and heart channels.

To treat this block I had Catherine remove her shirt and bra and lie on the treatment table under a sheet. Beginning the treatment, I lifted the sheet to reveal a 3-inch-long scar directly above Sp-21 in line with the rib cage in the sixth intercostal space. In fact, this scar lay directly between Sp-21 and Ht-1. When queried, Catherine related the story of how her mother had come to visit her at the boarding school when she was about 12. When the visit was over and her mother was leaving, Catherine raced after her in tears, pleading with her not to leave. A piece of steel protruding from a wall tore right through Catherine's shirt and ripped her flesh open at this spot. The injury was so severe that Catherine bled profusely, lost consciousness, and was rushed to a hospital. Catherine cried while telling this story and noted that she hadn't thought of this incident since she was very young.

I pointed out to Catherine the poetic beauty of how metal (her constitutional type) had severed this connection between Sp-21 (her mother's embrace) and her heart. I also suggested how poignant it was that she had become a jeweler and had learned how to mold metal and transform it into something of beauty. Catherine was profoundly taken with this metaphor, and I immediately supplemented its effect by treating the E/E points of Sp-21 and Ht-1. After this session, Catherine's healing accelerated and she returned to her previous weight with her appetite fully intact. Winter prevented her from coming up to New England for treatments, but she revealed four months later that this particular treatment session had been the strongest experience of healing she had ever felt.

## *NOTES*

1. This chapter represents a synthesis of two traditions of Chinese pulse diagnosis. The first is that taught at the TAI-Sophia Institute (TAIS) in the tradition of J. R. Worsley. This tradition finds its historical basis in the Nanjing (c. 100 C.E.; Unschuld, 1986) and in Wang Shuhe's *Classic of the Pulse* (c. 280 C.E.). The second is the

Shen/Hammer tradition. See Hammer, 2001, and Dale, 1993. Please note that it is the *positions* of organ correspondence specified by the *Nanjing* system that I refer to for the purposes of detecting and assessing the treatment of E/E blocks. However, the interpretation of the specific pulse *qualities* that comprise an E/E block are drawn from the system and nomenclature of the Shen/Hammer system. The term *exit/entry* as used here comes from the TAIS and the teachings of J. R. Worsley. However, my interpretation of E/E blocks comes from my own clinical experience and research and should not be taken to reflect the teachings of TAIS. Note that the concept of E/E points has also been discussed by Omura (1982, p. 44).

2. For a discussion of phase energetics, see Porkert, 1982, p. 55.
3. As taught at TAIS, the exit point on the kidney meridian is Ki-22. In their books, Omura (1982) and Mann (1974) concur with this designation. However, other texts on acupuncture designate Ki-25 as the exit point on the meridian. Note that Ki-22 does send a collateral that unites with CV-17, the beginning of the heart protector meridian (Low, 1985, p. 60). Further, Ki-21 is the last point on *chongmai* that might make Ki-22 the logical exit point on the meridian. In writing this section I have cited Ki-22 as the exit point, which is consistent with my clinical experience.
4. The quantity of *qi* in the pulse is arrived at from the overall picture that emerges from the various qualities present. Although a given pulse may feel "stronger" than another as evidenced by greater volume or a pounding sensation, this so-called strength may be emanating from an underlying deficiency. For example, a liver pulse that is *yin* deficient (to the point of *jing* deficiency) and wiry may well feel stronger by virtue of its pounding due to deficient heat than a lung pulse that is feeble and indicates *yang* deficiency. Both sensations denote an equivalent degree of deficiency even though the *yin*-deficient liver pulse feels stronger. My use of the word *strength* relative to E/E blocks should be taken to indicate that, regardless of the varied qualities present, my overall impression is there is relatively more *qi* before the E/E block than after the block.
5. An E/E block may be determined by palpating the points involved as well. Similar to the pulse, the point and region before the block is expected to show excess and/or stagnation and the point after the block deficiency. Note that Lv-14 and Lu-1 are E/E points as well as "alarm" points felt in palpatory diagnosis.
6. An inflated pulse that is yielding indicates trapped *qi,* which is the most frequently encountered E/E block. An inflated pulse that is tense indicates heat trapped in an organ or area. This is generally due to an unresolved pathogenic factor. An inflated and very tense pulse indicates blood trapped in an organ or area due to a traumatic injury.
7. My clinical experience has yielded the following treatment protocol. Place the needle in the exit point of the earlier meridian facing the entry point of the later meridian. I retain this needle in place while I tonify the entry point of the latter meridian. Here, tonifying indicates a moderate insertion with immediate fast withdrawal upon obtaining *qi.* Note that both needles may be retained for an indefinite period of time, as per the clinician's intuition. In this case I generally retain the needles until the expected change is felt on the pulse.
8. For a discussion of constitutional type, virtue, and the inner tradition of Chinese medicine, see *ND,* Chapters 8, 9, and 10.
9. For a detailed discussion of treating betrayal of intimacy with Chinese medicine, see Jarrett, 1995a, 1995b, and 1995c.
10. Note that the herb formula Chuanxiong Chatiao Wan (Ligusticum powder, taken with green tea) can be efficacious in certain circumstances for opening the E/E blocks in the head. Thea Elijah discusses this use of the formula in Chapter 10.
11. For a discussion of the functional relationships between the heart and mind, see *ND,* pp. 169–172 and 204–210.
12. The use of the term *official* stems from Chapter 8 of the *Neijing Suwen* in which each

organ is personified as an official in charge of specific functions (see *ND,* Chapter 10). I use the concept of "official" to refer to the sum total of a given organ's sphere of influence in all levels of body/mind/spirit. In the context of this book, the term *meridian* is often used synonymously with the term *official.* The term *meridian* is also used to indicate the channels and their points through which the officials are accessed with acupuncture. In this usage, a meridian is conceived of as a relatively more superficial aspect of its corresponding official.

13. Practitioner Karen Kisslinger notes the case of a woman presenting with intractable pain in the right foot distal to Ki-1. Detecting an E/E block between the kidney and heart protector officials, Karen first treated Ki-22 and HP-2 (the alternate entry point on the heart protector meridian for women; see the description of HP-1 and HP-2 in Chapter 28). The patient reported near total relief of the condition within two days and remained pain free for the time she was followed clinically. Although this treatment helped pain in the foot, it is not appropriate to draw the conclusion that these two points treat foot pain.
14. The functional dynamic of this particular E/E block is quite similar to that of the herbal formula Guipi Tang (Restore Spleen Soup). This formula tonifies spleen *qi* and nourishes heart blood and, in my clinical experience, is similar in its effects to the combination of Sp-21 and Ht-1.
15. Wieger, 1965, p. 144.
16. Girardot, 1983, p. 63.
17. Different traditions list different points that are supposedly forbidden to treat. The reasons for many of these prohibitions is not clear. I take the forbidden points as guidelines for the beginning practitioner and in my own practice adhere to only one principle, "do what is right." For legal reasons, however, I do adhere to the standards that suggest certain points not be treated after particular stages of pregnancy.
18. Ellis, Wiseman, and Boss, 1989, p. 217.
19. The character *lang* means "corridor" as well as veranda. For a beautiful account of the imperial burial grounds, see Paludan, 1991. Also, see the photograph in Chapter 27.
20. Clearing an E/E block between Ki-22 and HP-1 may also be helpful in this regard.
21. I locate Lv-14 in the notch on the nipple line on the lower border of the rib cage. This follows the teachings of TAIS. This location differs from that of other traditions which place Gb-24 in this location. Please note that the "reversal" of the positions of Gb-24 and Lv-14 is consistent with other historic traditions of practice. See the point location chart in Unschuld, 1988, p. 204.
22. For a discussion of the virtue of listening, see *ND,* pp. 65 and 215.
23. See Porkert, 1982, p. 244.
24. This figure is expanded in *ND,* p. 80.
25. This deviation occurs, for each person, according to the associations of his or her constitutional type. See *ND,* Chapters 9 and 10.
26. The specific functions of the three heater as they relate to personal boundary and intimacy are discussed in *ND,* pp. 217–223. Note that the three heater as the outermost boundary and frontier is represented by the name of TH-5, "outer frontier gate" *(waiguan).*
27. See *ND,* pp. 16–19.

# 6

# EXIT/ENTRY BLOCKAGE OF THE CONCEPTION AND GOVERNOR VESSELS

LOCATED ALONG THE CENTRAL ANTERIOR AND POSTERIOR axis of the body, the conception vessel (CV) and governor vessel (GV) are the seas of primordial *yin* and *yang* within us. These two meridians form the axis that orients the twelve officials and their functions to the universal poles of heaven and earth. The interpenetration of *yin* and *yang* is foundational in creating the context for health and balance. Thus the conception and governor vessels must be in clear communication with each other at all times. Blockage in the flow of *qi* between these two channels can arise for a number of reasons. The ability to diagnose and clear such a block is imperative if subsequent treatment is to be effective.

## *The Nature of the Vessels*

The eight extraordinary meridians form the functional template in relation to which the physical body and all functional mechanisms develop. The emergence of these vessels during embryogenesis is based on traditional

Chinese notions of cosmology and the emergence of being *(wei)* from nonbeing *(wuwei)*.[1] Embryologically, CV and GV are the first to develop.[2]

The conception vessel is the first to emerge and form a channel for the distribution of both *yin* and *jing* throughout the fetus. These three—*yin, jing,* and the CV—represent the *dao* as undifferentiated potential and the basis for all of life's manifestations. The next vessel to emerge is the governor vessel, which forms a conduit for the influx of *shen* and *yang. Shen* and *yang* are the activating impulses that configure potential and empower its manifestation as form in the world. These three—*yang, shen,* and the GV—represent heaven as the inspirator of all creation.[3]

*Chongmai,* the penetrating vessel, is the third vessel and arises between CV and GV to govern the interpenetration of heaven (GV) and earth (CV) through the human being as it is mediated by the functions of *qi* and blood. If CV and GV are not in communication, the influence of *chongmai* suffers as deficiency of *qi* and blood become predicated on a deeper deficiency of *yin* and *yang.*

---

## *Pathology*

The CV/GV block has three basic etiologies, all of which eventually manifest as an exit/entry block between these two channels that is characterized by severe depletion of *qi,* blood, *yin, yang,* and *jing.* These three etiologies are an unresolved husband/wife (H/W) imbalance, sexual or physical abuse, or physical trauma.

If the H/W imbalance is not resolved in a timely fashion, eventually the organs of digestion represented by the right-hand pulses will no longer be able to compensate for the weakness of those on the left. In this case, the pulses of the right hand collapse and leave the patient with pulses that are bilaterally deep and feeble, indicating systemic deficiency of *yin, yang, qi,* blood, and *jing.* Here the patient's will has collapsed both at the level of spiritual evolution (the left hand) and at the level of physical survival (the right hand). In this scenario, the patient has arrived at this state of depletion through a mechanism of suppression and resignation. The H/W blocks suggests a deep tearing apart at the level of *yuanqi* due to an internalized conflict between our innate will and an irreconcilable situation in life to which we become resigned. When the situation wins this struggle, our wills collapse along with the entire left side of the pulse. This finding suggests that the *yang* within the kidneys has been suppressed to the point that it no longer powers the rise from water to wood to fire along the left side of the *sheng* cycle. Eventually the digestive system weakens, and when it too collapses we are left having exhausted our supplies of innate (kidney) and acquired (spleen) *jing*, indicating our attempts to survive in an unlivable situation have been in vain.

Sexual or physical abuse can lead us to suppress our instincts toward sexuality and intimacy. The origin points of *yin* and *yang*, CV-1 and GV-1, are located just in front and back of the sexual organs on the perineum and beneath the tailbone, respectively. The sexual impulse is a manifestation of the evolutionary impulse that is the authentic driving force of our incarnation. Suppression of sexuality, because of either our reaction to abuse or the dysfunctional dynamics inherent in the husband/wife imbalance, can also lead to a lack of communication between the conception and governor vessels. Finally, physical trauma in the area of these points or anywhere along the two vessels can ultimately result in a lack of communication between *yin* and *yang* at this fundamental level.

When the CV/GV block is present, it becomes necessary to tonify the roots of *yin* and *yang* and open up communication at their source. With such grave deficiency, merely working on the main twelve meridians will not be sufficient to promote lasting change. *Yin* and *yang* constitute the very roots of life, and if CV and GV are not in communication, the function of the officials is not resting on a firm foundation.

---

## *The Channels and Points*

We can think of the course of the conception and governor vessels as one continuous meridian that makes a figure eight as it flows through the body (see Figure 6.1). The *qi* begins to flow at CV-1 rising through the body up to CV-24. Here the *qi* exits CV-24 and descends through the core of the body, transversing the midline, down to GV-1. From GV-1 the *qi* flows up to GV-20 and then descends to GV-28 on the upper gum. At GV-28 the *qi* again exits and flows back through the core of the body, transversing the midline, to reunite with CV-1. *Yin* and *yang* are the primordial foundations of life, and their crossing through the human being provides for the infinite variety of humanity's expression. Essentially a blockage in flow between the two channels is addressed as an exit/entry block by opening the entry and exit points of both channels sequentially. Here I discuss the inner natures of the four points involved, in the order they are treated.

---

### ❖ Conception Vessel-1, *Huiyin,* Meeting of *Yin*

CV-1, named "meeting of *yin*," represents the source of *yin* in the human being. GV-1, named "long strength," is a gathering point of the *yangqi*. Treating them together can help restore the balance between the primordial

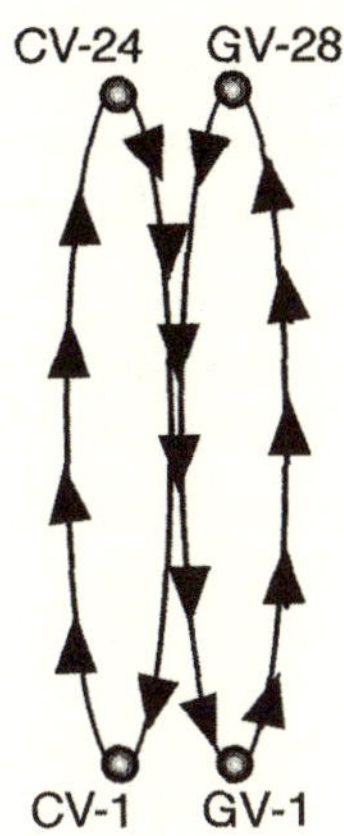


*Figure 6.1*

THE CIRCULATION OF *QI* IN THE CONCEPTION AND GOVERNOR VESSELS

Qi *flows up the front of the body along the conception vessel from the entry point at CV-1 to the exit point at CV-24.* Qi *than descends posteriorly through the core of the body to enter the governor vessel at GV-1. The* qi *then rises along GV to its exit point at GV-28, where it then descends anteriorly through the core of the body to reunite with CV-1.*

*yin* and *yang* and provide access to a fundamental reserve of these influences. An alternate name for CV-1 is *jinmen,* or "golden gate," which recalls the entrance to the kingdom of the Xiwangmu, the queen mother of the West.[4] In myth, the primordial brother and sister resurrect the human race after riding the crest of the flood through the "golden gate." Similarly, a key function of CV-1 is revival after drowning. The *Neijing* states that the conception vessel originates in the uterus and, as in myth, it is the "golden gate" which provides passageway into and out of the womb of *dao.*[5]

Hence CV-1 can be useful for treating infertility when deficiency of *yin* and blood are the fundamental issue, particularly when these deficiencies have resulted from suppression. CV-1 is also useful for aiding in conception and restoration of self when mundane influences *(yin)* have extinguished the fires of evolution synonymous with the influences of kidney *yang.*

---

### ❖ CV-24, *Chengjiang,* Receiving Fluid

The flow of *qi* leaves CV-24 to descend back down through the body to enter GV-1. Hence CV-24 is the exit point on the conception vessel meridian. At CV-24 the CV and GV meridians unite with those of the stomach and large intestine. The name of CV-24 alludes to the relationships between these organs and the importance of fluid in digestion as discussed earlier. I use CV-24 in a similar fashion to GV-28 for empowering the assimilation of food through nourishing the mouth with fluid. Note that both points are excellent for addressing issues of separation from mother and appropriate boundaries regarding nourishment in life. The mouth is that place of last physical separation from our mother upon weaning, and any unresolved issue regarding this separation can become embodied in this area. I often treat the combination of CV-24, GV-28, and St-4 in this regard.

---

### ❖ GV-1, *Changqiang,* Long Strength

As the first point on the governor vessel, GV-1 represents the root of each person's connection to *yang* in both self as well as in the universe. The name "long strength" denotes the ability of this point to empower the GV to raise *yangqi* from the root of our being all the way to the top of the head. Primordial *yang,* as invested by heaven at conception, rises through us during our lifetime as our spirit ascends fueled by the good works we do in this world. Hence the alternate name for this point, "stairway to heaven" (*shangtianti:* 上天梯), suggests the ascension of spirit governed by *yang.* The course of the governor vessel runs from the base of the spine to the top of the head at GV-20 and then descends to its exit point at GV-28. Hence the spine itself may be likened to a "stairway to heaven" (the head). Each point along the governor vessel aligns a different aspect of being to the cosmological pole of *yang* as it fuels the ascension of the human spirit toward heaven.

---

### ❖ GV-28, *Yinjiao,* Mouth Crossing

Here, at the last point on the governor vessel, the flow of *qi* exits to enter CV-1 back on the perineum. GV-28 is thus the exit point of the GV meridian and helps the *qi* to cross the mouth in making this transition. At GV-28 the governor and conception vessels intersect with the stomach channel, giving rise to the name "mouth crossing." Stimulating us to find sources of nourishment in the world congruent with our needs is one essential role played by *yang* as expressed through the stomach official. Another function of the clear *yang* is to rise digestive fluids (saliva) up to the mouth to initiate the "cooking" of food during eating. I often find this point indicated when the mouth seems contracted and dry as evidenced by many wrinkles on the lips. I believe this condition is a manifestation of the functional state of the digestive system and indicates a lack of fluid throughout. Treating GV-28 in this instance may nourish the skin and muscles around the mouth with fluid and help revitalize digestion and assimilation of nutrients as well.

## *Elaboration of the CV/GV Block*

The CV/GV block is given rise to by patients who internalize their pain and suppress their response to it. Something has happened in life that is perceived at an existential level to have compromised the foundation of who they are. I have seen this pattern frequently with people who have experienced incest. Here a family member who shares ancestral bonds has transgressed against the patient in a way that has lead to failure of *yin* and *yang* to communicate at the most fundamental levels of being. The pain of incest touches aspects of being that transcend merely this lifetime. It occurs at that level of being that ties us to the moment of conception and our ancestry.[6]

I have also seen the CV/GV block in cases of people who have had sexual relations with their spiritual teachers. We should consider this event a type of incest for, like family, spiritual teachers share a deep karmic bond with their disciples. Priests, gurus, and other spiritual teachers touch us at a level of being that is congruent with our deepest spiritual connections to our life path. If we feel compromised at this deep level of our soul journey, communication between *yin* and *yang* can also be compromised.

In essence, it is not the event of the incest or betrayal itself that initiates a CV/GV block in a causal sense. Rather it is our own reaction of retreating from and suppressing pain arising from such an event that compromises the communication of *yin* and *yang* at such a deep level. The depth of the pulse in evidence with a CV/GV block indicates the degree to which we have suppressed our innate tendency to evolve in relation to that which has hurt us. One mechanism of such suppression is holding a secret about the event that inhibits communication of it to others. Eventually, we suppress our ability to communicate down to a fundamental level of being that compromises communication between *yin* and *yang* itself.

The single largest cause of the CV/GV block is this suppression of self in the face of trauma. Each of us is conceived with an innate complement of resources to help support us in the face of life's challenges. We each have a different capacity given the same stress to deal with it effectively. A person born with a relatively weak endowment has less capacity to cope with stress than a stronger person facing challenges of the same nature. Therefore, a patient evidencing a CV/GV block need not have a trauma of the magnitude discussed here. The point is, relative to the patient's capacity to stand up in the face of life's challenges, an event has occurred that has devastated his functional capacity at the deepest level of being.

The CV/GV block may also arise from external causes in life such as physical trauma or illness, particularly if there has been significant bleeding. Profuse bleeding during childbirth or menopause can also give rise to this pattern. Here the pulse appears bilaterally deep and thin, indicating a great deficiency of both *qi* and blood. In this scenario the herbal formula Danggui Decoction to Tonify the Blood (Danggui Buxue Tang) is often the appropriate herbal formula to initiate healing.[7]

I have found it interesting that I have diagnosed severe trauma in patients from such a pulse configuration many years after the incident itself. Although the patient had been given blood transfusions at the time and would not presently be diagnosed as clinically anemic, he or she still evidenced a pulse of severe blood deficiency from the viewpoint of Chinese pulse diagnosis. This, I believe, is because the Chinese notion of blood deficiency is concerned relatively more with the nutritive content of the blood, whereas the Western medical view emphasizes the mineral (hemoglobin) content exclusively. In such cases, treating the CV/GV block has often proved valuable.

In treating the CV/GV block that arises from internal causes, we may think of the treatment as tonifying and promoting a reconnection to the very root of life. We are reopening connection to and communication between the very forces that united initially at the moment of patients' conception to place them on this earth in a body, thus giving their spirit a framework for manifesting its work in this world. Of course, we must also direct patients' consciousness toward the nature of their suppression and try to offer them tools to cope in a healthful way with the nature of the pain they have been suppressing.

Regardless of whether the etiology of the CV/GV block is internal or from external trauma, we expect that after successfully breaking the block, the overall volume and amplitude of the entire pulse will increase, indicating the primordial sources of *yin* and *yang* that empower patients at their depth have been tapped and reunited. Once the block has been broken, you must remain vigilant for the possibility of its return. I suggest regular weekly treatments for at least two months after breaking the block, emphasizing tonification of any depleted vital substances. Often, after breaking a CV/GV block, treatment of *chongmai* proves more fruitful as the existence of blood and *qi* is based on *yin* and *yang*.

---

### *Considerations and Discussion of the Treatment*

Because the key points for breaking the CV/GV block are in the area of the genitals (CV-1 and GV-1), merely being touched in this area may retrigger memories and feelings of abuse. Because the very nature of the CV/GV block often has to do with issues of sexual betrayal, you must maintain the utmost sensitivity when implementing this treatment.

In general, I think it is a wise idea for male practitioners to refer female patients to female practitioners for this treatment. Similarly a female practitioner might consider referring her male patient to a male practitioner for this one session. Certainly, to attain minimum standards of propriety, a person of the same sex as the patient should be in the room to observe the treatment. Observing this standard protects both the patient from potential abuse by unscrupulous practitioners and protects you from potential lawsuits from patients who might feel touched in an inappropriate way.

You must determine on a case-by-case basis whether to let the patient know what points you are treating at the time or if you think the patient might benefit from discussing the treatment during a prior session to provide some time to assimilate the idea of the treatment. Base your decision on the patient's relative emotional stability and the degree to which he or she can make a spontaneous decision without feeling pressured. When discussing the nature of this treatment, I often point out the connection between the patient's trauma, possible suppression in regard to the trauma, and his or her general experience of sexuality and vitality. It is then an easy leap for most patients to comprehend the possibility of being blocked in the region of the genitals and the reasonableness of receiving treatment there.

## PROTOCOL

1. Points are needled in this order with the following depths of insertion: CV-1 (10 *fen*), CV-24 (1–3 *fen*), GV-1 (3 *fen*), and GV-28 (1 *fen*).
2. Generally, due to the extreme nature of deficiency associated with this block, all points are tonified with a quick insertion and removal. However, on occasion I retain CV-1 for 5 to 10 minutes while I monitor the pulse. When the volume and amplitude of the pulse improves, I tonify the subsequent points.

## CONSIDERATIONS

1. Make sure patients are draped appropriately to minimize their feelings of being exposed and vulnerable.
2. Use gloves when working near the genitals.
3. Take pulses after each point to determine where the flow of *qi* was blocked.
4. Either refer patients of the opposite sex to a same-sex practitioner or have a person of the same sex present to observe the treatment.

## Grace and Constraint

***Complaint:*** *Tori Palatini*
***Constitution:*** *Metal/wood*

Wendy is an attractive 48-year-old woman possessing the tall thin body of a ballet dancer. She had danced professionally and toured the world with various dance troupes. Her training schedule had been rigorous and involved hours of practice and performance daily for many years. Her regimen had included four hundred sit-ups daily, and her body was both trim and toned. By the time Wendy approached me for treatment, she had given up performing a decade earlier and had become a practitioner of Chinese medicine. Her specific health concern focused on several bony outgrowths on the roof and floor of her mouth, known collectively as tori palatini (tori is from the Latin *torus,* meaning " to protrude," and palatinus refers to the palate). The largest of the growth was roughly 1 inch long, 1/8 inch wide, and protruded 1/8 of an inch down from the roof of her mouth. Other smaller growths were on the floor of her mouth.

Many of Wendy's friends had died of AIDS. Her response to this crisis was to donate blood every ten weeks for five years. Her previous acupuncturist had spent two years tonifying *chongmai* (the penetrating vessel also known as "the sea of blood") with acupuncture and moxibustion and building blood with formulas like Women's Precious (Bazhen Tang). Wendy had also been treated with large doses of Chinese herbs to disperse hardened phlegm nodules, but these did not work to diminish the size of the growths. At the time of the consultation Wendy had been recently divorced and been largely celibate for several years.

***Analysis***

My impression was that the symptom of the bony growth was so physically manifest that it was not likely treatment with Chinese medicine could remove it. At best, perhaps the progress of the condition could be slowed or stopped as the underlying functional imbalance on which it was based was resolved. Immediately upon taking Wendy's pulses I recognized the bilaterally deep and feeble/absent pulse picture I associate with an exit/entry block of the governor and conception vessel. The pulses surely were "thin" in quality and therefore blood deficient, but the depth of the deficiency went beyond this conventional interpretation. Working on *chongmai* to build blood and *qi* would certainly help Wendy function and feel better but would be unlikely to address the underlying deficiency of *yin* and *yang* on which her condition was predicated. After all, *yin* and *yang* are the primordial basis of healthy *qi* and blood. I believed that once functional contact was restored between the conception and governor vessel, work on *chongmai* and the officials would prove more fruitful.

There were several possible contributing factors to Wendy's CV/GV block. The number of sit-ups she had done over so many years may well have constrained her conception vessel in a way that prevented her *qi* from flowing smoothly through this channel. Further, excessive exercise over many years could have depleted blood and *qi* in the penetrating vessel *(chongmai)* leading to stagnation based on deficiency. Donating so much blood could also have contributed to her blood deficiency to disrupt the function of the CV. Lastly, the bony growth itself located directly behind GV-28 ("mouth crossing") could have impeded the smooth flow of *qi* from the governor to the conception vessel. However, the growth at this location could well have been contributed to by the global deficiency of *qi* and blood evidenced in the pulse diagnosis. Hence a general principle is that pathological growth tends to occur when *qi* does not flow smoothly.

Upon recognizing the CV/GV block and considering these various etiologies, I wondered if there wasn't a deeper etiological factor congruent with the blockage in these channels than merely deficiency or physical trauma. I therefore asked Wendy if she had ever been sexually abused. Her response was "No, nothing but the usual date rape. Nothing I couldn't get over." In fact, the degree of deficiency on her pulse and the substantial blockage along the channels suggested she had not in fact gotten over this trauma. Rather it seemed likely she suppressed her rape and eventually encapsulated it as the hardened mass in her mouth. Further inquiry into the nature of her subsequent relationships revealed she had only ever entered into unsatisfying relationships with men who were ultimately unavailable to her in the intimate way she so craved. Her celibacy had been largely out of resignation, believing her needs would never be met. Suppression of sexuality and the capacity for intimacy in response to abuse can be a central etiology of the CV/GV block.

### *Treatment*

Because Wendy lived far away, I recommended that she visit an acupuncturist who could execute the CV/GV treatment as well as several follow-up sessions. Wendy reported feeling the benefits of having the CV/GV block cleared for many months after the treatments. When I saw her several months later, her pulses had increased substantially in both volume and amplitude, indicating a renewed flow of blood and *qi* in the conception and governor vessels. Her health and vitality has continued to thrive. She also took the opportunity to reconsider the impact of being raped and how it had affected her beliefs regarding sexuality and intimacy.

TREATMENTS

1. CV/GV protocol.
2. Tonify Lu-8, Lu-1, Ki-7, and Ki-27 with retention of needles for 10 minutes. The intention here was to forge the link between metal and water along the *sheng* cycle.
3. Tonify Ki-1 and Bl-1 to open the origin of water and *yin* on the left side of the pulse.
4. Tonify Lu-7, LI-4, and Lu-1. This is the first purely constitutional treatment I prescribed once I ascertained that breaking the CV/GV block had indeed held for several weeks.
5. Tonify *chongmai* by treating Sp-4, HP-6, Ki-16, and CV-15 with needles, and use moxa on the Sp-4 and HP-6. Tonify *gaohuangshu* (Bl-38 [43]) with needles and moxa. Once the CV/GV block is broken, tonification of *chongmai* is more likely to be fruitful. *Gaohuangshu* is an important point for helping heal chronic exhaustion of *qi* and blood.

## *NOTES*

1. For a discussion of Chinese cosmology and its relationship to physiology, see *ND,* pp. 3–117.
2. Along with *chongmai* and *daimai.* Larre, Schatz, and Rochat de la Vallee, 1986, p. 144.
3. Continuing this cosmology, *chongmai* arises between CV and GV as the *chongqi* arises to unite heaven and earth. *Daimai* is the fourth to develop yielding volume, so the first three channels exist in three-dimensional space. In this condition the body is just a torso and resembles a chicken egg, the Daoist symbol of undifferentiated wholeness. The next four channels, *yinweimai, yangweimai, yinqiaomai,* and *yangqiaomai,* govern the attachment of the limbs to the torso and the manifestation of our potential into the world through action.
4. For a discussion of Xiwangmu, the first woman to become a Daoist immortal, see *ND,* pp. 19–21.
5. Ibid.
6. For a discussion of Chinese medicine and it role in diagnosing and treating rape, incest, and divorce, see Jarrett, 1995a and 1995b.
7. Bensky and Barolet, 1990, p. 254. For a case study where this formula played a crucial role in healing, see Jarrett, 2002, pp. 152–166.

# 7

# AKABANE IMBALANCES

THE TWELVE MAIN MERIDIANS RUN BILATERALLY THROUGH the body. In a state of functional harmony, the relative amount of *qi* on each side of a given meridian pair should be equivalent. Developed by Kobe Akabane (1895–1983), the akabane procedure helps diagnose and resolve unilateral imbalances affecting the flow of *qi* in paired meridians. During the initial stage of treatment, akabane imbalances must be resolved if constitutional treatment is to progress as expected. Further, akabane imbalances may arise during treatment. Attend to these immediately before the flow of *qi* is compromised throughout the meridian system.

From a practical standpoint, I find that most akabane imbalances correct themselves after other more serious blocks such as AE, possession, or the H/W imbalance have been rectified and constitutional treatment has been initiated. Still, this is not always the case, and ensuring the balanced flow of *qi* in the twelve main meridians is imperative in laying the foundation for effective treatment.

## *Theory*

As with other blocks, an akabane imbalance can arise from either an external or internal etiology. The external cause of an akabane imbalance involves injury that blocks the free flow of *qi* in the affected channel. Any insult that cuts through a channel's pathway can inhibit the flow of *qi* in a way that results in an akabane imbalance. This includes accidental as well as surgically induced trauma to the path of a meridian (yes, tattoos and piercings are included). A blow to the body that causes severe bruising, breaks a bone, or knocks the spine out of alignment can also initiate an akabane imbalance.

When the akabane imbalance is caused by external trauma, any of the impacted meridians are likely to be affected. Because all the meridians are functionally related, an akabane imbalance that begins in one meridian may eventually cause similar imbalances in other meridians. According to the diagnostic criteria discussed here, the meridian with the greatest imbalance is likely to be the one that suffered the initial insult and propagated the functional disturbance in the others.

An akabane imbalance can also arise from internal causes, although I believe this etiology is less frequent. The gallbladder official is prone to one-sided symptomatology that is the embodiment of the limited perspective this official tends dysfunctionally to embrace in life. I frequently find that when a patient's gallbladder is dysfunctional in this way, it can manifest as akabane imbalances in various meridians. When this is the case, the gallbladder meridian tends to evidence the greatest discrepancy between the amount of *qi* in its left and right channels. Further, clearing the imbalance in the gallbladder meridian will tend to clear all other akabane imbalances in those meridians where the balanced flow of *qi* has been compromised. Commensurate with clearing such an akabane imbalance, patients are expected to embrace a greater perspective in life, evidencing they are more in contact with *ren* (benevolence), the virtue associated with the wood element.[1]

Any time that pain or dysfunction is exclusively one sided, consider the possibility of an akabane imbalance. For example, sciatica, headaches, shoulder pain, visual disturbances, and trigeminal neuralgia can all be one sided and therefore based on an akabane imbalance. A great variety of symptoms and functional disturbances can exist as secondary compensations for an underlying akabane imbalance, however, and therefore clearing it can have wide-ranging therapeutic effects.

## *Assessment*

Testing for akabane imbalances can be part of the initial physical exam for all new patients. Noting any imbalances that are present, you may clear other more substantial blocks such as AE, possession, or the H/W imbalance and then retest the akabanes. If any appreciable imbalances are still present, treat the most severe first and test the affected meridians again. Generally, if you resolve the worst imbalance first, the others will resolve as well because they were secondary compensations for the primary imbalance.

To test for akabane imbalances, have the patient lie on the treatment table on his back. Then quickly pass a lit incense stick back and forth directly over the nail point of each toe and finger where the meridians either begin or end (see Figure 7.1a and 7.1b).[2] For readings to be accurate, take care to (1) hold the incense at the same distance from each point tested, and (2) move it back and forth across the point at the same rate.

After instructing the patient to say "warm" when she feels the heat, count the number of passes it takes the patient to report a sensation of heat. Impress on the patient that the point of the exercise is not to tolerate as much heat as possible, but merely to indicate as soon as a sensation

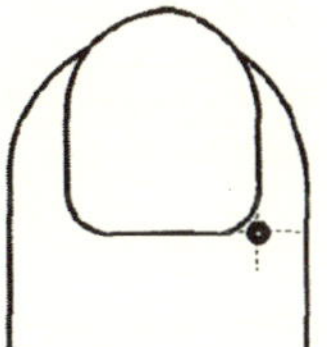

*Figure 7.1a*
THE NAIL POINT

*The nail points are found at the base of the nail where lines drawn from the base and the lateral edge of the nail overlap.*

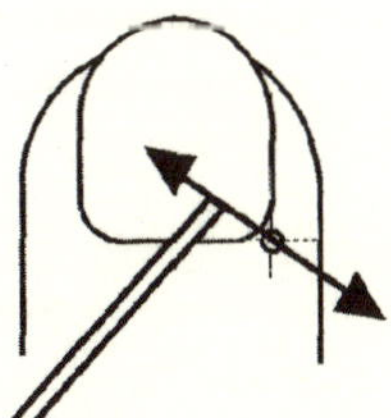

*Figure 7.1b*
TESTING AKABANES

*In the akabane text, incense is moved quickly over the point at a 45-degree angle.*

of heat is felt. Record these readings on the intake form or chart (see Figure 7.3, p. 111). Note that in many of the readings listed in Figure 7.3, the numbers are roughly equivalent. However, three of the meridians—the bladder, gallbladder, and stomach—show a discrepancy between the left and right half of each meridian pair.

In our example the patient reported feeling a sensation of heat when the incense was passed over Gb-44 on the left foot nine times. On the right side, however, the patient reported feeling heat only after twenty-six passes. Hence it took roughly three times as many passes to feel the heat on the right side as it did on the left. This indicates roughly one third as much *qi* flowing through the gallbladder meridian on the right as there is on the left. In other words, because of a deficiency of *qi* in the right-side gallbladder channel, we had to add relatively more warmth before the patient could feel it. (Warmth is analogous to *qi.* Remember a central function of *qi* is to provide warmth.) Hence the side that takes the greatest number of passes is relatively more deficient. For a ratio to be considered clinically significant, there must be at least a 30 percent difference in reading between the two sides. For example, a reading on the kidney channel of 13/10 would not be considered clinically significant, whereas a reading of 15/10 would be.

## *Treatment*

Administering the akabane treatment consists of several steps. First, test all nail points and calculate the relative balance of *qi* in each of the bilateral meridian pairs.[3] Then determine which meridian's imbalance you will correct first. The treatments I most frequently find effective in correcting the akabane imbalance are presented here in order of implementation. A more thorough protocol is listed in Figure 7.2.

Before attempting to correct the akabane imbalance with needles, always check and center the umbilical pulse first. Any left/right imbalances in the meridians may exist as a secondary compensation for the umbilical pulse having drifted off center. As a first attempt to correct an akabane imbalance with needles, tonify the *luo* point on the meridian's deficient side. For example, if the bladder meridian shows a reading of eight passes on the left and thirty on the right, tonify Bl-58 on the right side.[4] Now retest the meridians. If the bladder meridian has balanced, and the two sides now show equivalent readings, all the other imbalances should have changed as well. If you discover that only the bladder has improved and the other channels are still unbalanced, you have not found the meridian that is the root cause of the imbalance. In this instance, treat

1. Tonify the *luo* point on the deficient side.
2. Tonify the source point on the deficient side.
3. Tonify *luo* and source together on the deficient side.
4. Moxa the *luo* and source points on the deficient side.
5. Sedate the *luo* points on the excess side and tonify the *luo* point on the deficient side.
6. Tonify the *shu* point on the deficient side.
7. Sedate the *shu* point on the excess side.
8. If akabane imbalances have still not corrected, check for scars and injuries and treat them directly.
9. Consider the possibility of deeper blocks such as possession, the H/W, or AE.

*Figure 7.2*
METHOD FOR CORRECTING AKABANE IMBALANCES

the next most unbalanced meridian and continue until all channels are in relative harmony.

If the bladder meridian has not corrected itself after the first treatment of Bl-58, select the source point to tonify on the deficient side. Again retest the akabanes and note which have changed and which have not. If the akabanes still have not corrected, sedate the source and *luo* points on the excess side of the meridian. Assuming the problem has still not corrected, you can tonify the *shu* point on the deficient side. In the example here, Bl-28 on the right would be tonified. If the imbalance is still not rectified, try sedating the *shu* point on the excess side. See Figure 7.2 for a prioritized list of the different methods for correcting an akabane imbalance.

It is rare that akabane imbalances are not resolved with the procedures just outlined. In fact, I have rarely had to proceed past the second step in harmonizing an akabane imbalance. If the imbalance is not resolved after taking these measures, examine the course of the meridian for potential physical blockages such as cuts or scars. At this point you may use needles to help bring *qi* through the scar. Often tonifying the points before and after the scar on the traversed meridians is sufficient to help *qi* flow past the obstruction.

## *Considerations*

1. Do not test for akabane imbalances on the feet of patients with diabetic neuropathy. Insensitivity tends to cause erroneous readings, and it is possible to burn these patients because of their inability to perceive the stimulus.

2. Begin on the left side of each meridian first. For example, test Bl-67 on the left and then Bl-67 on the right.
3. If you cannot test the nail point for any reason, such as amputation or the presence of a cast, use the first available point on the meridian and test it bilaterally.
4. If an akabane test reveals that several meridians are unbalanced, prioritize which to correct first. The accepted order of priority is as follows:[5]
    a. Correct the imbalance if it occurs on a constitutional meridian first. For example, if a patient is earth constitutionally and six meridians show evidence of akabane imbalances, treat the ones affecting the stomach and spleen channels first if they are present. All imbalances are secondary compensations for the constitutional element and tend to respond if this underlying disharmony is resolved.
    b. Correct the imbalance in the mother element of the constitutional type. If earth is the constitutional element but does not evidence an akabane imbalance, correct any present in the fire officials as a first step.
    c. Treat the meridian with the greatest imbalance. If a meridian has suffered trauma, it may compromise functional dynamics systemically. Resolving the greatest imbalance can resolve all akabane imbalances.
    d. If a patient presents a one-sided symptom, test and correct the akabane on the affected channel. For example, a patient may complain of sciatica just down the right leg along the bladder meridian. Test the bladder, and if it shows evidence of an akabane imbalance, correct it.
    e. If a pattern of imbalance appears around the *sheng* cycle, begin with the first unbalanced meridian and correct them in order around the cycle. For example, an akabane test may reveal that the bladder, gallbladder, and small intestine are unbalanced. In this case, correct the bladder first and then recheck the akabanes. Next correct the imbalance in the gallbladder and then the small intestine if necessary.

## FRED

***Constitution:** Gallbladder*

Fred was a dentist who had recently retired from clinical practice and moved to his new home in the country. He was proud of not having "missed a day of work for illness in forty years." After moving into his new home, Fred worked enthusiastically many hours every day, often lifting weight several times beyond his capacity. While moving a large piece of furniture, Fred heard a pop and felt like a "hot poker" had been pushed into his lower spine. His biomedical diagnosis was herniated disk at L-4, with low back pain and sciatica down his right leg. His sciatic pain was focused at GV-3 and radiated down the outside of his right leg to follow the course of the gallbladder meridian.

Along with the onset of his pain, Fred began to hear a high-pitched sound in both ears. He grew increasingly depressed and resigned as his pain limited his ability to enjoy the retirement he had worked for his entire life. Fred came to me for treatment as a last resort before considering surgery and after a failed course of physical therapy and steroid injections.

Because of the clear one-sided nature of his symptomatology, I checked Fred's akabanes during the initial intake (see the results in Figure 7.3).

| Ht | SI | Bl | Ki | HP | TH | Gb | Lv | Lu | LI | St | Sp |
|---|---|---|---|---|---|---|---|---|---|---|---|
| 4/3 | 4/4 | 8/18 | 5/6 | 3/3 | 3/4 | 9/26 | 5/4 | 3/4 | 4/4 | 8/20 | 5/7 |

*Figure 7.3*
FRED'S AKABANE RESULTS

*Akabane imbalances are expressed as ratios giving the relative number of passes it takes the patient to feel heat on the left and right side of each paired channel. Here the gallbladder, bladder, and stomach channels all show akabane imbalances. The higher readings on the right suggest the flow of* qi *is deficient in the right half of these channels as compared to the left.*

It was clear from the results of this test that the channels of the gallbladder, bladder, and stomach channels all evidenced akabane imbalances. Because of Fred's resentment and resignation over his situation, I decided to first drain AE and then retest his akabanes on the subsequent treatment. Generally, I expect that an AE drain will effectively harmonize most akabane imbalances. Retesting his akabanes yielded the result that the stomach channel had corrected itself, but the gallbladder and bladder channels were still unbalanced.

Fred felt relaxed as a result of the AE drain and appeared to be much less edgy. He reported that the ringing in his ears seemed less "invasive" and the muscles in his lower back felt more relaxed. However, the pain traveling down his right leg was undiminished. There were three good reasons to choose balancing the gallbladder akabane as the first step of the follow-up session. Gallbladder was Fred's constitutional official, and its channel showed the greatest akabane imbalance. Further, the course of Fred's pain followed the course of the gallbladder channel down the right side of his leg.

I therefore chose to tonify Gb-37 unilaterally on the right side. Fred felt a strong sensation of *qi* at this point. Retesting the gallbladder and bladder channels yielded the result that both the akabane imbalances had improved, but not completely. Therefore I supplemented the treatment by tonifying Gb-40 on the right side. I let Fred rest awhile and then came back into the room to recheck the akabane imbalances. Both the bladder and gallbladder channels were now balanced, with readings of 13/12 and 15/15, respectively. At the conclusion of the session, I evoked the spirit of Gb-40, "wilderness mound," by telling Fred that I was sure his pain would resolve (I offered hope, a virtue associated with the wood element) and it could be helpful to embrace a larger perspective on his situation. After all, he had overcome other obstacles in life, and he would overcome this one.

In fact, my prediction was correct. Fred returned the next week feeling much better. His sciatica was largely gone and no longer traveled down his leg. Although he still had some pain localized in his right lower buttock (Bl-50) and lower back, this resolved over the next several treatments. For many years I treated Fred occasionally when his back acted up, but debilitating pain never recurred. Fortunately, Fred has been able to lead the active life in retirement he had worked so long and hard for.

## *NOTES*

1. For a discussion of the virtue *ren,* see *ND,* pp. 238–241.
2. Note that you may use the inner nail point of the small toe to test the kidney meridian because it is not feasible to use Ki-1 located on the ventral surface of the foot.
3. As you gain clinical experience, you may decide to test only the one or few meridians you think are imbalanced.
4. Note that often readings are higher on the bladder meridian compared to the other channels because the outer nail point of the little toe tends to become calloused and less sensitive to heat. Still, if the bladder meridian is balanced, the readings bilaterally should be virtually equivalent.
5. Note that I often find it most effective to correct the greatest imbalance first, as I discussed previously.

# 8

# THE UMBILICAL PULSE

THE *HARA* DEFINES THE PHYSICAL CENTER OF THE BODY AND, as such, is the embodied representation of the center of our being. *Hara* is the Japanese pronunciation of the Chinese character *fu* (腹), meaning "belly." A healthy center empowers grace and balance through transitions in life. The quality of the *hara* is strengthened by living life with the type of integrity (信) that nurtures, and is nurtured by, the earth element.[1]

The umbilicus provides our connection in the womb to our mothers, who ideally embody for us during gestation the unconditional nourishment of *dao*. Under the umbilicus is a pulse that can be felt by pressing in gently with four fingers (see Photo 8.1, p. 114) as the patient exhales. Think of any discrepancy in the location of this pulse as compared with the center of the umbilicus as representing the discrepancy between who a patient really is and what she is expressing in this world through word and deed. This pulse should be centered directly under the umbilicus, reflecting a global centering of *qi* in the patient's being. If you feel the umbilical pulse off center, you can gently massage it back until it is again directly underneath the navel. Note the location of the umbilical pulse on the exam sheet during the physical diagnosis portion of the intake (Figure 8.1, p. 115). Assuming you do not

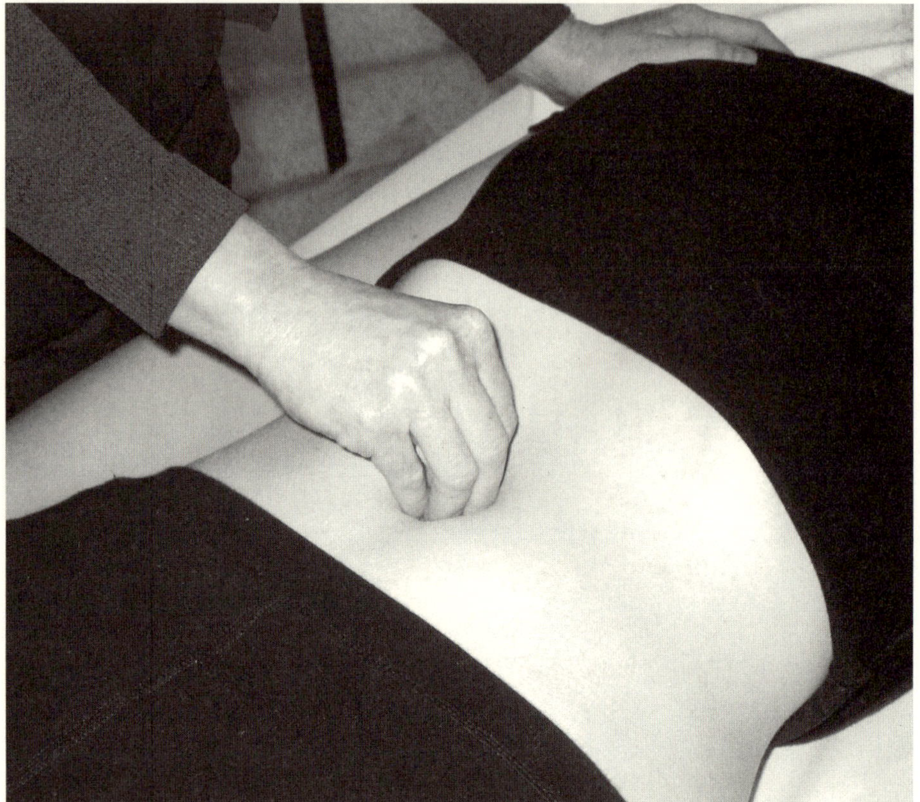

*Photo 8.1*

detect the presence of more serious blocks such as possession or aggressive energy, the centering of the umbilical pulse comprises the first alignment of the patient's *qi* before you attempt to influence it with the use of needles.

I do not consider aligning the umbilical pulse to be a major treatment but rather a good opportunity to provide some gentle human contact in a way that nourishes the center during the initial visit with the patient. If a patient in ongoing treatment reports a trauma such as a motor vehicle accident or falling on ice, I always check the umbilical pulse and center it if necessary before beginning with needles. If a patient's umbilical pulse repeatedly drifts off center, an herbal formula that tonifies *qi* to empower the holding of center, such as Buzhong Yiqi Tang (Benefit the Center Tonify the *Qi*), a strong physically centering formula, or Guipi Tang (Restore Spleen Soup), a strong emotionally centering formula, may be indicated.

The direction that the umbilical pulse deviates from center can give you information about elemental balance (see Figure 8.2, p. 116). If we take the umbilicus as the center corresponding to the earth element, the areas below and above the umbilicus correspond to the water and fire elements, respectively. And the areas to the left and right, from the

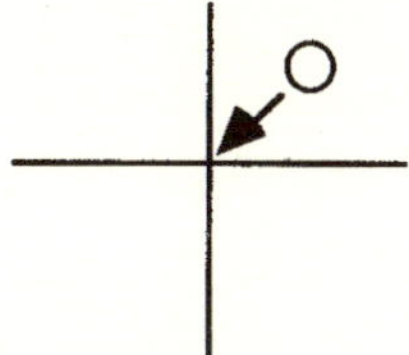

*Figure 8.1*
NOTING THE LOCATION OF THE UMBILICAL PULSE

*On the exam sheet, the location of the umbilical pulse can be referenced to a simple crosshatch where the central position denotes balance. Here I have noted the direction the pulse is off center. Treatment involves gently massaging the pulse back toward center as represented by the arrow.*

patient's perspective, correspond to the wood and metal elements, respectively. Alignment of the umbilical pulse generally leaves patients feeling relaxed and centered and can play an important role in setting the foundation for subsequent treatment. Centering the umbilical pulse is an essential first step when correcting akabane imbalances because aligning the patient's *qi* to center globally can initiate a better bilateral balance of *qi* flow in all the meridians.[2]

## MAGGIE

***Complaints:** Severe abdominal pain, lack of appetite, constipation*

Maggie was a 48-year-old woman with a master's degree in nursing. She approached me for treatment after hearing me lecture on Chinese medicine at a local hospital. At her first appointment, Maggie informed me that during the lecture she realized she was supposed to practice Chinese medicine. She felt unvalued as a visiting nurse and craved independence so she could practice in a way uncompromised by the strictures of the managed care system.

Metal constitutionally (large intestine), Maggie always arrived for treatment dressed in either black or shades of gray and with a twinkle of inspiration in her eye. Although very bright and attractive, finding a mate had alluded her, and she mentioned during nearly every session her struggles in this regard. Both grief and longing typified these discussions, and it was clear that every time she thought she had found "the one," it turned out to be not quite right. Her inspiration was slowly slipping away.

During the course of her sessions over a two-year period, Maggie came to be much less occupied with the issue of relationship. Her focus turned more toward herself and her own feelings of unworthiness relative to finding a partner. Her interest in practicing Chinese medicine went as far

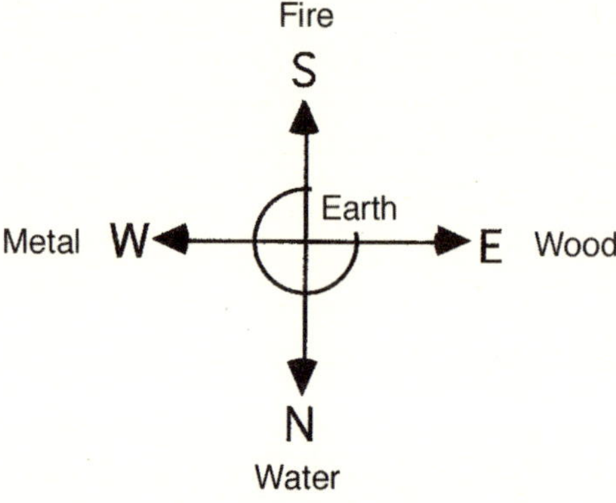


*Figure 8.2*
ELEMENTAL BALANCE

*Here the five-element map is superimposed over the umbilicus. The Chinese map assumes the holder is facing south while reading it.*

as actually applying and being accepted to school. However, as the time to make arrangements drew near, Maggie felt she couldn't let go of her friends or the area where she was living to move six hours away to attend classes. She also felt the size of the loan was too much for her to handle. Instead, she accepted a job nursing in a local retirement community. Although it didn't allow her the independence she desired as a practitioner, it did permit her to stay in the area.

During one of Maggie's treatment sessions, I noticed her pulses were even tighter than usual. The tight quality suggests to me a systemic state of *yin* deficiency when it occurs at all positions as it did on Maggie's pulse. This condition is not unusual in women who are approaching or going through menopause, but Maggie's pulses were far tighter than they had been previously. She reported feeling constipated, and after treating her I suggested she drink more water. She replied that her work schedule did not permit her the time to drink as much as she thought she should. I reinforced how important it was to take care of herself and that I thought increasing her water intake was vital.

The following week Maggie returned, and her situation had grown worse. She had had only one bowel movement in the previous five days and felt weak. Having her lie on the table I felt her umbilical pulse and was alarmed to find it a full half inch to the right (west, metal) of her navel and pounding harder than any I had ever felt on her before. I centered her pulse and treated her with acupuncture points Ki-3, St-44, St-25, and LI-2. This session relaxed Maggie greatly. However, based on the umbilical pulse finding, I insisted she go immediately to the emergency room. Maggie refused but promised to go the next day if things had not improved. I called the next morning to again insist, and Maggie agreed to go to the hospital. She was immediately put on intravenous fluids and morphine. Apparently she was suffering from a virus that had caused severe inflammation of the stomach and bowel.

In this case, taking the umbilical pulse alerted me to the severity of Maggie's condition and the need for immediate medical attention. After her recovery, Maggie returned and I rechecked her umbilical pulse and found it drifting off to the right again. I checked and centered the pulse over the next several sessions, focusing on the relationship between the stomach and large intestine officials. After about five weeks, Maggie began returning with the umbilical pulse on center, signaling to me that the condition had been resolved.

## *NOTES*

1. See *ND*, pp. 278–294.
2. See Chapter 7.

# 9

# CALMING THE MIND

VERY OFTEN PATIENTS' MINDS ARE SO LOUD AND ACTIVE, they are afforded little opportunity to listen to others or to receive any clear message from their own heart. People we might describe as always "being in their head" personalize their thoughts to such a degree that true relaxation becomes impossible. Always driven by the mind, meditation and contemplation are unobtainable. Such people exhibit very little sign of openness because any attempt by the heart to manifest its true nature is immediately controlled by the mind as soon as it is initiated. I find in these circumstances that the mind does not allow people the experience of relaxing into, or assimilating, the potential benefits of an acupuncture treatment.

In response to this phenomenon, I have developed a protocol for greatly relaxing the mind. In fact, I consider this point protocol to be almost hypnotic, effectively shutting down the dominating influence of conditioned mind so the heart can better assert its authority. In this place of "no mind," the *zhenqi* has a better chance of reasserting itself to reestablish the heart/kidney axis. Here I present this framework for selecting points to still the mind. I recommend you look up the individual points discussed in Part IV, where their functions are elaborated.

## *Protocol*

The basic procedure is to select Bl-66 with a water point on another *yang* meridian. I then pair these with a point on the head on the same *yang* meridian and with the extra point *yintang*. The points are listed in Figure 9.1.[1]

## *The Water Points*

The two most distal points on each channel, the *jing*-well and *ying*-spring points, have a special relationship to the mind and nervous system. Dr. John Shen, in his four-system model, postulated that these points are uniquely related to the nervous system.[2] The specific relationship of the channel points to the four systems has not been elaborated to my knowledge, and the orientation here is from my own experience. Generally, I find the nail points (*jing*-well) are very stimulating and literally wake people up who are suppressing something, as opposed to the goal here of "putting them to sleep" when the mind is overly active. Draining latent pathogens can initiate law of cure reactions as the exiting pathogen stimulates old patterns on its way out.[3] During such a healing crisis, the *jing*-well points can be utilized to reinforce awareness of the lesson inherent in the crisis so the issue can be resolved.[4]

In contrast, the function of the *ying*-spring points, and particularly the water points on the *yang* channels, is to quiet the agitated mind, effectively putting the patient to sleep. Here the overactivity of the mind characterizes patients' state of delusion as they are driven to constantly be alert, always paying attention to everything other than the core issue that motivates their anxiety.

| Distal | Local | GV |
|---|---|---|
| Bl-66 | Bl-2 | GV-24.5 (*Yintang*) |
| Gb-43 | Gb-4 | GV-20 |
| SI-2 | SI-19 | |
| TH-2 | TH-22 | |
| St-44 | St-8 | |
| LI-2 | LI-20 | |

*Figure 9.1*
POINTS TO QUIET THE MIND

## *Point Selection*

Dr. Shen characterized the nervous system as related to the *taiyang.* By this he meant the *qi* of the nervous system is the fastest moving and outermost *qi* of the four systems. The bladder channel is the longest channel of the body and follows the course of the sciatic nerve, which is also the longest nerve. The course of the bladder channel down the back takes it directly over the afferent and efferent innervation of the spinal cord. Anxiety and fear deplete *yin,* which in turn gives rise to patterns of disharmony that further agitate the mind and nervous system. The water points on the *yang* officials all have a cooling and quieting effect on the mind by treating the *yin* and soothing the nervous system. Bl-66, the water and horary point on the *taiyang* bladder channel, can be considered the transmitting point of water for quieting the nervous system.

In this protocol, Bl-66 is chosen as the transmitting point in combination with a receiving/water point on another *yang* channel. The other *yang* channel chosen will generally be constitutional in nature, corresponding to the specific quality of thought that is habitually driving the patient. For example, if a patient tends toward obsession (*si:*思), the pathological emotion of the earth element, I would pair Bl-66 with St-44, the water point on the stomach channel. Just as the kidneys underlie the internal syndrome patterns, fear tends to drive overthinking in the other *yang* officials.[5] By treating Bl-66 and St-44 together, we are cooling and quieting the mind in the depths and calming agitation in the nervous system to ease the spirit (*yi:* thought) of the earth element.

After choosing the two distal points, I select a local point on the head on the *yang* meridian that was paired with Bl-66. In the example just described, I would select St-8 ("head tied") as the local point. Lastly, I choose GV-24.5 *(yintang)* for its function of quieting the mind. Whereas the two eyes represent dualistic thinking, *yintang*, the "no name" point, represents the vision of the sage that rolls all dualities back into one.[6] In Daoist alchemy and meditation exercises, the point between the eyes and one inch back toward the brain is referred to as the *mingtang,* or "illuminated palace."[7] I find this point serves to effectively shut down dualistic thought and deeply relaxes the mind into a near hypnotic state. Located at the position of the "third eye," *yintang* empowers the unitary vision of unnamed *dao* that is characterized by nonarising. With the mind so quelled, the heart and intuition are better able to flower.

Figure 9.1 lists the point combinations I use most frequently to quiet the mind in the context of this protocol. Other points may be substituted or added as called for by the context of any particular treatment. On occasion I add GV-20 for its effects in centering the mind and draining the destabilizing influence of wind.

### *Technique*

I always use the thinnest possible needles (gauge 36) when treating Bl-66 and treat the point with a gentle insertion so it is not painful. Bl-66 is treated first, followed by the second *ying*-spring point, then the head point, and GV-24.5 is treated last. Needles are generally retained for 20 to 40 minutes.

## *NOTES*

1. Note that although I have presented LI-20 in this figure for the sake of completion, I rarely choose this point in this protocol because it is often too stimulating. In cases when I want to treat the large intestine official, I often treat Bl-66 and LI-2 together with just GV-24.5.
2. Shen's four systems in order of depth are the nervous, circulatory, digestive, and organ systems. These are discussed in Hammer, 1990, Chapter 14.
3. For a discussion of the law of cure, see *ND*, pp. 326–331.
4. From a lecture by Jeffrey Yuen on the divergent meridians.
5. In the *yin* officials, fear is the foundation of personalizing feelings. In the *yang* officials, fear is the basis of personalizing thoughts. From a certain perspective, water can be said to be the foundation of all internal patterns of disharmony. However, from another perspective, the heart can be considered the basis of all patterns. In my own work I emphasize the integrity of the heart/kidney axis as foundational. From one perspective, "setting the will" on wanting freedom more than anything else is the basis of the spiritual path. This orientation is discussed by the ancient philosophers such as Confucius and Mencius and by modern sages such as Andrew Cohen. From another perspective, the will (*zhi*) itself can be seen as an extension of the heart spirit (*shen*) into the depths.
6. J. R. Worsley considered *yintang* a point on the governor vessel. He has numbered it 24.5 and chosen wisely not to give it a name because naming is the very source of duality itself.
7. See my discussion of the *mingtang* in relation to Bl-39 in the point section of Part IV.

# 10

# REMOVING BLOCKS WITH CHINESE HERBS

THE NATURE OF THE SPIRITUAL JOURNEY IS THAT THE TRAVELER must remove all concepts that create deviation in the path between her heart and mind, *jing* and *shen*, and early and later heaven. Phlegm, damp, pathological heat, internal wind, stagnant *qi*, and congealed blood are the embodiments and physiological correlates of dysfunctional aspects of mind and spirit that obscure these fundamental relationships.

The first step in treatment planning is to clear imbalances that can prevent long-term healing. For example, if a patient is bleeding, the first therapeutic measure is to prevent the loss of blood. On a psychospiritual level, the first step must be to help take a patient out of shock so the primordial influences of *jing, qi,* and *shen* can reassert their authority in guiding the patient's life. Regardless of the degree of symptomatic relief provided, if a patient remains in shock and leaves treatment ignorant of true self, little has been done to promote meaningful healing in the long term. The dysfunctional *qi* that supports the created self will always find a way to distort potential virtues into pathology.

Here I review several herbal formulas I use to set the stage for healing early in treatment. I suggest acupuncture equivalents for some of these formulas with an analysis of my point selection. Stabilizing rate, rhythm, and intensity on the pulse is paramount as a first step to realignment of the heart/kidney axis and the restoration of authentic self. In this regard I discuss four formulas: Shengmai San, Yunan Baiyao, Banxia Houpo Tang, and Zhigancao Tang. These can be applied individually or in combination to quickly reinstitute a fundamental balance predicated on autonomy of the heart official early in treatment.

I then present two formulas, Meridian Passage and Women's Chamber, that can be used to treat blood stasis.[1] Such stasis often results from one's reaction to perceived betrayal and suggests the heart's capacity for intimacy has been compromised by its own defenses.

Next I review three formulas that can be appropriate when shock so disrupts the spirit that we lose our capacity to focus or rest. These formulas, Calm Spirit (modified Dingxin Wan), Bupleurum and Dragon Bones, and Schizandra Dreams, can be used for calming an agitated heart spirit, often mitigating the need for antianxiety medications.[2]

Lastly are two sections on the importance of opening the sensory orifices. The first section, which I have written, is on the herb formula Niuhuang Qingxin Wan (Cow Gallbladder Clear the Heart Pill). I discuss this formula in order to illuminate the nature of consciousness and ignorance as mediated by the heart orifice. Then Thea Elijah contributes a section on two herb formulas: Erchen Tang (Two Cured Soup) with Changpu and Chuanxiong Chatiao San (Ligusticum Powder Taken with Green Tea).[3] Thea discusses these in relationship to their application in clearing pathogens and possession and treating exit/entry (E/E) blocks with Chinese herbs.

---

## *Stabilizing the Pulse and Resolving Shock*

The heart as emperor is the foundation of insight and understanding into self and life. The constancy of the heartbeat reflects the heart's underlying commitment to momentary presence. Changes in the parameters of rate, rhythm, and intensity on the pulse can signal that the heart is struggling to rule effectively according to the principles of *wuwei.* If the emperor is not at peace while seated on the throne, there can be no harmony in the nation. The first order of business clinically, therefore, must involve stabilizing the heart to lay the foundation for the return of original nature. Specific herb formulas and acupuncture point treatments can help stabilize the pulse. However, bear in mind that any of the clearing protocols previously discussed can contribute significantly to this goal. Centering the umbilical pulse, draining AE, or clearing possession can all stabilize the pulse in and of themselves. For that matter, merely treating the source point on the constitutional meridian, or any point in the right context, can help stabilize the pulse and restore original nature.

You can use the formulas and point combinations discussed here early in treatment when stabilizing the pulse is the foremost concern or when other clearing treatments such as draining AE have not proven effective in this regard.

---

## *Shengmai San (Generate Pulse Powder)*[4]

Shengmai San (Generate Pulse Powder) is a versatile formula that can play an important role in laying the groundwork for effective treatment.[5] No clinical finding is more suggestive of shock than that of instability on the pulse. The inner use of Shengmai San (SMS) is to help regulate the pulse by stabilizing the functional relationship between the heart and lungs. This can be done early in treatment to clear the therapeutic field or later if the patient suffers an emotional shock or physical trauma that destabilizes the pulse.

You can also use Shengmai San effectively to tonify the *yin* of the heart, spleen, and lungs when *yin* becomes deficient from internal or external causes. Of course, SMS may be combined with other formulas to modify or enhance the desired effect. Here we focus on the use of SMS in creating stability on the pulse and clearing shock. I also discuss two formulas that SMS can be combined with—Pinellia and Magnolia (PM; Banxia Houpo Tang) and Yunan Baiyao (YBY)—as well as one formula that can be used in its place: Baked Licorice Soup (Zhigancao Tang).

### SHENGMAI SAN

| PINYIN | ENGLISH |
|---|---|
| Renshen | Ginseng |
| Maimendong | Ophiopogon |
| Wuweizi | Schizandra |

***Analysis***

Schizandra tonifies the lungs and, through the process of astringency, empowers a clear strong channel to promote open communication among the heart, lung, and kidney officials. By stabilizing the heart/kidney axis and engendering breath, schizandra empowers the *shen* to descend and enter the *jing*. The descent of the *shen* into the depths is empowered by the contractive force of the *po* spirit associated with the lung official.[6] By stabilizing the connection of the heart and lungs, harmony is brought to the officials of the upper *jiao*. And by strengthening the connection between the metal and water elements, schizandra empowers the conception of true self by promoting the integrity of the *sheng* cycle. Ginseng serves to tonify *qi* and empower the earth element's virtue of center within the lung and heart officials. In essence, ginseng is able to fill the channel created by schizandra with abundant *qi*. Ophiopogon helps synchronize the rhythm of the heart with the rhythm of the lungs by tonifying the *zongqi* in the center of the chest. Together these ingredients work to dispel shock, resynchronize the breath and heartbeat with the universal rhythm of *dao*, and reinstate the interaction of *jing* and *shen* through stabilization of the heart/kidney axis.

*Shock*

Children often respond to early trauma in life by shutting off their heart and suppressing their respiratory rhythm. In effect, this may be the child's only mechanism to defend against a shock of great magnitude. So isolated, a child can evidence an inner emptiness due to the lungs' loss of receptivity and inability to attract quality into her life. She may also lack self-worth and inspiration as she fails to acknowledge her own inner value.

The loss of rhythm between the heart and lungs can lead to stagnation and the eventual buildup of heat as the body tries to move the stagnation. Over time, excess heat tends to give way to deficient heat as *yin* is consumed. The individual for whom this formula is appropriate may evidence feelings of having been "burned" by life and of having lost what she valued. As a longer term intervention, SMS tonifies lung *yin* and can help soothe the pain of loss. As a constitutional lung formula, SMS can help restore the virtue of self-worth, which tends to be undermined by the primary shock that initially destabilized the pulse.

In my experience, this formula is often vital to restoring a stable foundation during the initial stages of treatment when chaos predominates the clinical picture. Indications for this formula are pulses that are intermittent, irregular, feeble/absent, and either unusually fast or too slow.

When SMS works to clear shock and stabilize the pulse, the effects can be dramatic and far reaching. Patients tend to feel centered in their hearts and experience much less anxiety. Sleep often improves as the spirit rests more comfortably in the heart. Because SMS is also a *yin* tonic, hot flashes and night sweats can also diminish. Patients often report "feeling like I have my old self back" after several weeks on the formula.

### *SMS as a* Yin *Tonic*

SMS can be used as a lung *yin* tonic for deficiency resulting from either external or internal causes. Internally, the lungs can become *yin* deficient due to excess emotional states such as grief and longing. In such a scenario the lung pulses are expected to have a tight quality similar to the thinnest string on a guitar. With *yin* deficiency the tongue is expected to be red and peeled. Deficiency from such an internal cause takes a relatively long period of time to become embodied and is a longer term therapeutic issue.

Deficiency from external causes can include dryness due to excess heat generated from fever. In such a scenario the lungs feel parched with difficulty inhaling.

### *Dosage*

In order to stabilize the pulse, I prescribe this formula in small doses (1–3 grams daily) for short periods of time (two to three weeks).[7] When prescribing for *yin* deficiency, you can give the formula indefinitely as deemed necessary in doses ranging from 1 to 3 grams three times daily. When prescribing for lung *yin* deficiency as a result of acute illness, I may double this dosage for up to two weeks.

### *Acupuncture*

I often use the following acupuncture point protocol to stabilize the pulse. I do not always use all these points together, and sometimes I substitute or add points. For example, I might utilize CV-15 instead of CV-17 or I might add Lv-3 or Lv-14 if I think *qi* stagnation is an issue. I view the following points as a core pool of points I would pick from and utilize over the first several treatments while clearing other blocks or addressing constitutional dynamics in order to stabilize the pulse early in treatment.

POINTS

| | | |
|---|---|---|
| Lu-9 | *Taiyuan* | Very Great Abyss |
| Lu-1 | *Zhongfu* | Central Treasury |
| CV-17 | *Yuaner* | Primordial Child |
| HP-4 | *Ximen* | Cleft Gate |
| Lu-6 | *Gongxi* | Palace Cleft |
| Ht-7 | *Shenmen* | Spirit Gate |

### *Analysis of Point Selection*[8]

Lu-9 is the assembly point of the pulse and as such excels in stabilizing the pulse or tonifying *qi* and *yang* when the entire pulse evidences deficiency of these influences. The name "very great abyss" suggests the point's efficacy in addressing the emptiness that can be associated with the pervasive loss and loneliness experienced when the metal element is unbalanced. As the channel's earth point, Lu-9 can empower substantiality (earth) within the void of the lungs (metal) to fill emptiness and ease longing. Earth also empowers the virtues of center and integrity to provide stability in the lungs and the upper *jiao*. As the channel's source point, Lu-9 supplies the lung official with fresh reserves of *qi* to empower receptivity and connection to the influence of heaven.

Lu-1 is the *mu* point of the lungs, and its name, "central treasury," suggests its ability to reestablish our connection to value in life. A treasure in the center of the chest is the *zongqi*, which empowers the synchronicity of all rhythmic movements in the organism. Hence Lu-1 can empower our connection to the *dao* as our ancestor and the generator of all movement. CV-17 is a reunion point among the heart, heart protector, and lung officials. By synchronizing the functions of these three officials, harmony is restored to the upper *jiao*. The name "primordial child" denotes the ability of CV-17 to reestablish the influence of the child's pure heart in guiding life unaffected by life's sorrows. HP-4 and Lu-6 are the *xi*-cleft points on their respective meridians. Both points can help move and resolve grief and sorrow resulting from loss or perceived betrayal that is embodied as stagnation in these two officials.

Ht-7 is both source and earth point on the heart meridian that works in tandem with Lu-9 to stabilize and "ground" the pulse. As the channel's earth point, Lu-9 empowers center within the heart and nurtures the upper *jiao*.

### *Combining SMS with Other Formulas*

Next I examine several formulas that you can combine with SMS early in treatment to help clear the therapeutic field and set the groundwork for lasting healing.

### *Treating Shock to the Circulatory System: Yunnan Baiyao*[9]

Yunnan Baiyao (YBY) is a remarkable formula, generally used to stop bleeding and treat blood stasis resulting from traumatic injury. Hence YBY can be considered an "intelligent" formula that can mitigate the loss of healthy blood and move congealed blood depending on the unique requirements of each patient. Although its ingredients are supposedly a Chinese state secret, it is generally believed to contain a large proportion of Tianqi (Radix Pseudoginseng). According to legend, the man who wrote this formula followed a hundred injured animals through the jungles of China and noted the herbs they ate to heal. The Chinese government forced his family to divulge the formula, but it was only partially given.[10]

As a formula used to treat trauma, YBY corresponds to the lowest level of medicines used to treat physical symptomatology. However, YBY is quite effective at treating the "bleeding" heart that is suffering both emotionally and spiritually. Further, the intelligence of the formula in distinguishing between healthy and congealed blood suggests it may actually belong to that highest class of medicine that nourishes destiny. Administration of YBY is indicated when the patient gives the impression of drowning in her own overwhelming sorrow. In fact, it may feel to you as though the patient is drowning in her own blood (sorrow). This is frequently the case in divorce when the psychic and spiritual connections between a person's heart and the heart of her lover have been torn asunder.

Another indication for this formula is when the patient likens her pain to feeling as if she had been "shot in the chest" or "stabbed in the back." For this individual, more emotional information is arising than can be processed adequately and it is overwhelming all aspects of her being. In essence, she is in shock and bleeding spiritually. As always, the first intervention medically must always be to stop the bleeding, a principle that applies equally to treatment in the psychic and spiritual realms. By mitigating shock to the heart and circulatory system,[11] YBY may help stabilize the patient and empower her to process and integrate emotional material at a more comfortable rate.

*Administration*

YBY is available in pill and powder form. Additionally, each package includes a single small red pill that acts quickly to mitigate shock. Usually, I prescribe this tiny pill only if the insult has occurred relatively recently. I generally prescribe one or two capsules or an equivalent amount of powder, three times daily, for eight days. I counsel patients to try and discern the effects of the formula so they may take it periodically thereafter as needed. Administration of YBY need not occur close to the time of the shock for it to be effective. Any imbalance evidencing an etiology of shock to the heart, heart protector, and/or the circulatory system can also be treated to good effect with this formula.

*Acupuncture*

POINTS

| | | |
|---|---|---|
| **HP-6** | *Neiguan* | Inner Frontier Gate |
| **TH-4** | *Yangchi* | *Yang* Pond |
| **CV-15** | *Shenfu* | Spirit Storehouse |
| **Bl-14** | *Juque* | Great Tower |
| **Bl-38** (43) | *Gaohuangshu* | Rich for the Vitals |
| For mania or depression add | | |
| **GV-10** | *Lingtai* | Spiritual Tower *and* |
| **GV-11** | *Shendao* | Spirit Path |

*Analysis of Point Selection*

HP-6 and TH-4 are the *luo* and source points on their respective meridians. This combination helps integrate the function of the fire officials and restore balance to the circulatory component of the pulse. CV-15 is the heart protector *mu* point and helps calm and strengthen the influence of the *shen* spirit. Bl-14 is the heart protector *shu* point, and Bl-38 (43) is on the outer line of the bladder meridian directly lateral to Bl-14. Together these points can access a deep reserve of *qi* to support the function of the heart protector. Bl-43 empowers the highest virtue of the heart protector's contribution to blood, the ability to choose intimacy from a position of strength. GV-10 and GV-11 strongly orient the heart to the governor vessel as the central axis of *yang* and heaven in the human being.[12] These points can play a significant role in calming mania associated with shock or, conversely, in helping revive the influence of the heart if one is listless and depressed.

I must point out that any points that empower the balanced function of the heart and heart protector officials can help mitigate the effects of shock associated with a broken heart. The combination discussed here is only one theoretical possibility I might choose if the context of the treatment confirms the point selection.

### *Harmonizing the Diaphragm*
### PINELLIA AND MAGNOLIA (BANXIA HOUPO TANG)

| PINYIN | ENGLISH |
|---|---|
| Banxia | Pinellia |
| Fuling | Poria |
| Houpo | Magnolia |
| Zisuye | Perillae |
| Ganjiang | Ginger |

The type of *qi* stagnation for which this formula is indicated often results from a tendency toward being ingratiating and habitually taking care of others. Each time we say "yes" to avoid conflict, we swallow the tension that would have arose if we stood up for our own interests by saying "no." In time, our inability to communicate our own needs is embodied as *qi* stagnation and dampness as our relationships cease to nourish us and are transformed into burdens.

Pinellia and Magnolia (PM) is a drying formula and well balanced by the *yin* tonifying properties of SMS. The use of PM is indicated by tense to inflated pulses in the diaphragm and distal positions of the pulse. The distal pulses can also evidence a tense and slippery quality, indicating stagnation of dampness. Liver *qi* stagnation can present as pressure and distension in the diaphragm area and chest and as tightness in the throat with difficulty swallowing ("plum pit *qi*"). This type of stagnation can be experienced as frustration, resignation, and depression as we feel as though we have hit a wall in life we cannot move past. Psychically, this wall can be the pain associated with the shock of separation from those we love. Physically, this wall is embodied as the diaphragm that separates the middle *jiao* from the upper *jiao*. The liver channel rises to its highest point at Lv-14, which is located directly over the diaphragm. Liver *qi* must find a creative way around this obstacle if its aspirations of flowing to Lu-1 are to be realized.

I consider PM a magic formula in the sense that it can just banish the pathological emotions associated with *qi* stagnation in the upper *jiao*. Upon taking this formula, pressure in the chest, tightness in the throat, frustration, sorrow, and grief can clear as quickly as if the clouds had parted to reveal the sun on a rainy day. This formula can also play an important role in clearing stagnation in the diaphragm between the middle and upper *jiaos*. Such stagnation is indicated by the presence of the diaphragm pulse as discussed in Chapter 5 and often results from the conflict between feelings of tenderness and anger that arises during painful separation from a loved one. Successful treatment is suggested by the findings that the diaphragm position on the pulse diminishes in time and the patient is better able to be present with the seemingly contradictory feelings of love and anger without habitually suppressing one or the other.

*Dosage*

When using PM to treat the conditions just discussed, I prescribe 1 to 2 grams of powder one to three times daily. When prescribing the formula for phlegm in the chest during and acute illness, I prescribe up to 6 grams three times daily.[13]

*Acupuncture*

POINTS

| | | |
|---|---|---|
| Lv-3 | *Taichong* | Supreme Rushing |
| Lv-14 | *Qimen* | Gate of Hope |
| Lu-1 | *Zhongfu* | Central Treasury |
| Lu-9 | *Taiyuan* | Very Great Abyss |
| LI-6 | *Bianli* | Side Passage |
| CV-17 | *Yuaner* | Primordial Child |

*Analysis of Point Selection*

The use of Ht-7, Lu-9, and CV-17 to stabilize the pulse has already been discussed. Lu-9, as the earth point, can empower the lungs to better digest mucus. Lv-14 and Lu-1 are the exit and entry points on their respective meridians. They help circulate the *qi* of the chest by moving stagnation in the diaphragm and chest region. As the exit point on the liver meridian, Lv-14 represents the highest branches on a tree as they aspire to heaven whose presence is symbolized by Lu-1, the entry point on the lung meridian. Lv-14 may be thought of as empowering "aspiration" and Lu-1 as empowering "inspiration." The ability to strive and receive are essential if we are to move on in life and overcome stagnation releasing burdens from the past. Lv-3 helps relieve *qi* stagnation and works with Lv-14 to open the diaphragm. LI-6, the channel's *luo* point, can help vent stagnant *qi* and heat to the exterior and empower us to let go of all that no longer serves in life.

Other points to move stagnation in the diaphragm and chest include Bl-13 *(feishu)*, Bl-14 *(jueyinshu)*, and Bl-15 *(xinshu)*, the lung, heart, and heart protector *shu* points. Bl-17 *(geshu)*, the *shu* point of the diaphragm, and Bl-18 *(ganshu)*, the liver *shu* point, can also be helpful in this regard. The other exit/entry (E/E) combinations that empower the free flow of *qi* through the chest include Sp-21/Ht-1 and Ki-22/HP-1 and can be effective as well.

### *Combining SMS with PM*

In combining PM with SMS, I adjust dosage to reflect the degree to which I think suppression or shock are playing relative roles in the pattern of disharmony. Pinellia and Magnolia addresses suppression of feelings regarding a life circumstance, whereas SMS addresses more directly one's embodiment of the original shock of the incident. I also consider the degree to which the patient is either damp or dry. Pinellia and Magnolia help resolve dampness that is the physical embodiment of grief and burden. Shengmai San can soothe dryness congruent with feelings of having lost what we valued and of having been burned by life.

### BAKED LICORICE SOUP (ZHIGANCAO TANG)

| PINYIN | ENGLISH |
| --- | --- |
| Gancao | Licorice |
| Guizhi | Cinnamon |
| Shengjiang | Ginger |
| Renshen | Ginseng |
| Ejiao | Gelatin |
| Dazao | Date |
| Maziren | Linum |
| Maimendong | Ophiopogon |
| Shudihuang | Rehmannia |

Baked Licorice Soup can be used in place of SMS in patients with a suitable presentation. Here, as with SMS, instability on the pulse is a key finding. Notice that ginseng and ophiopogon, two of the three constituents of SMS, are included in this formula. Baked Licorice Soup is a key formula for treating shock to the heart that results in instability on the pulse. It is, however, a broader formula than SMS. Here ginger and cinnamon help reinstate the heart's fire, and the presence of rehmannia balances the heart's fire by tonifying kidney *yin.*

This formula is a modified version of Cinnamon Twig Soup (Guizhi Tang), a formula useful for harmonizing the relationship of the *ying* and *wei.*[14] *Ying* is nutritive *qi* and belongs in the interior, and *wei* is defensive *qi* that defines our exterior boundary. In cases of shock that result from abuse, the natural relationship of the *ying* and *wei* can become reversed. As a result, the defensive *qi* retreats to the interior and the nutritive *qi* leaks out to the exterior. Feelings of shame and humiliation are often congruent with this disharmony as the patient tends to feel excessively exposed in life.

An interesting inclusion in this formula is the presence of gelatin (Ejiao) or ass-hide glue. Ejiao treats bleeding and can be helpful for "thin-skinned" people who are easily "cut" in life. Hence this formula can be appropriate for harmonizing the relationship between fire and metal across the *ke* cycle and restoring balance to the upper *jiao*. Baked Licorice formula is suitable for stabilizing the pulse in cases of incest, rape, or any shock to the heart where shame seems to be an important component. Note that the patient may also project her pain by shaming others. The inclusion of gelitan along with rehmannia helps tonify heart blood and moisten the upper *jiao,* thus nurturing the emperor's ability to perform ritual effectively and receive from the heavens. The patient for whom this formula is indicated will tend to exhibit a dry upper *jiao* that can be metaphorically described as a desert wasteland. Hence I generally utilize this formula in patients when I think the deeper functions of the upper kidney points are applicable.

### *Dosage*

I prescribe this formula in the range of from 2 to 3 grams, three times daily. Note that whenever treating instability on the pulse it is critical that patients are consistent in performing their ritual of taking herbs regularly and on time.

### *Acupuncture*

POINTS

| | | |
|---|---|---|
| **Ki-3** | *Yingu* | *Yin* Valley |
| **Ht-3** | *Xiaohai* | Little Sea |

| | | |
|---|---|---|
| **CV-14** | *Jueque* | Great Gate Tower |
| **Ki-23** | *Shenfeng* | Spirit Seal |
| **Ki-24** | *Lingxu* | Spirit Burial Ground |
| **Ki-25** | *Shencang* | Spirit Seal |
| **Lu-1** | *Zhongfu* | Central Treasury |
| **HP-6** | *Neiguan* | Inner Frontier Gate |
| **TH-5** | *Waiguan* | Outer Frontier Gate |

*Analysis of Point Selection*

Ki-3 as the channel's source point tonifies both kidney *yin* and *yang* in a balanced way similar to the effect of the presence of the *yin* (rehmannia and ophiopogon) and *yang* (ginger and cinnamon twig) tonics in the formula. Ki-3 can also help moderate the effects of strong spirit points such as Ki-23, Ki-24, and Ki-25. H-3 is a water point and therefore empowers the qualities of *yin* within the functional domain of the heart official. This supplements the effects of Ki-24, which tonifies *yin* in the upper *jiao* when it has become a desert. Treating Ht-3 can harmonize the relationship between the kidneys (water) and heart (fire) by empowering the receptive qualities of *yin* within the heart. CV-14 is the *mu* point of the heart official, and its name suggests the gate towers at the entrance to the dwelling of the emperor in the forbidden city.[15]

The upper kidney points, Ki-23, Ki-24, and Ki-25, are important points for balancing the *ling* and *shen* spirits, which are the *yin* and *yang* aspects of heart spirit, respectively. The functional dynamics of these points are addressed at length in my book *Nourishing Destiny*.[16] Note that these three points would rarely be needled in the same treatment. Rather I would likely treat Ki-24 to tonify heart *yin* during a given treatment and then treat Ki-23 and Ki-25 either separately or in tandem during the following sessions. Lu-1 is the *mu* point of the lungs and its function was discussed earlier.

HP-6 and TH-5 harmonize the inner and outer aspects of fire and, in so doing, help set an appropriate boundary in life between true self (the heart) and the outside world.

---

## *Resolving Betrayal, Moving Blood Stasis*

A central function of the blood is to nourish the spirit *(shen)* and to carry its influence to every part of ourselves. Congealed blood can perpetuate patterns based on separation from self by limiting our conscious access to the nature of our suffering. Herbs that stop bleeding like YBY can be used in proximity to shock or when recovering painful memories, in order to mitigate our pain in the face of such experiences. Herbs that move blood, in contrast, can be appropriate to promote its flow so painful information that has been separated out and away from consciousness can be reintegrated.

Toward this end I use several formulas early in treatment when I have evidence that blood stasis is a therapeutic issue and when I deem this stasis is perpetuating ignorance and other dysfunctional states predicated on it. Explicit signs of blood stasis can include purple lips, a purple tinge to the tongue, thickened purple vessels under the tongue, sharp stabbing pain that is fixed in location, and qualities such as choppiness or vibration on the pulse.[17]

### *Formulas*

When treating blood stasis, you must differentiate all signs and symptoms in order to arrive at the correct formula. A wide variety of formulas could be used to achieve the results I have discussed. Here I discuss only two such formulas that are readily available in tincture or pill form.

MERIDIAN PASSAGE

| PINYIN | ENGLISH |
|---|---|
| Honghua | Safflower flower |
| Zirantong | Pyrite |
| Gusuibu | Drynaria rhizome |
| Ruxiang | Frankincense |
| Moyao | Myrrh |
| Danggui | Tangkuei |
| Qinjiao | Gentiana macrophylla root |
| Niuxi | Achyranthes root |
| Chuanxiong | Cnidium |
| Baishao | White peony root |
| Qianghuo | Notopterygium root |
| Xiangfu | Cyperus rhizome |
| Gancao | Licorice root |

Meridian Passage (MP) was adapted by Ted Kaptchuk from the traditional formulas Shentong Zhuyu Tang and Moyao Xiangsheng. Think of the primary function of MP as promoting "bleeding," that is, to move and break up congealed blood.[18] This formula is ideal in cases in which the patient does not have emotional access to her pain. It is appropriate for patients exhibiting signs of blood stasis who you suspect may have issues regarding suppressed pain and betrayal. With administration of this formula, old memories often resurface. Dreams can be enhanced and often contain images of past abuse. This gradual emergence of betrayal into awareness can correspond to the dissolution of blood stasis in the form of a "psychic tumor." This tumor is formed from past pain that has been too difficult to assimilate consciously and is therefore repressed. Meridian Passage is also appropriate for patients who state that emotional material is "too painful to talk about." Patients taking this formula have reported that it makes them feel as though their pain is "able to surface effortlessly and to leave without getting stuck." One patient described feeling as though he was "coated with Teflon inside" and that his pain was leaving effortlessly "like bubbles rising to the surface."

If the formula is given for extended periods of time, it can tend to overly thin the blood. In this case the patient may report feeling "edgy" or "jumpy." Within the context of this usage, I think of the two formulas, YBY and MP, as existing on a continuum. Yunan Baiyao primarily stops bleeding and MP moves blood. If too much emotional content surfaces while taking MP, its effects can be moderated by taking one capsule of YBY. This will stop the "flow" of emotional pain within a short time and allow the patient to integrate whatever material has come up. In this way, feelings of being overwhelmed by too much emotional material may be mitigated.

*Dosage*

When treating physical pain with embodied blood stasis or congealment, I prescribe this formula in the range of 8 to 16 drops, three times daily. For treating the psychospiritual realms, I prescribe 4 to 8 drops, two to three times daily.

*Acupuncture*

POINTS

| | | |
|---|---|---|
| **HP-6** | *Neiguan* | Inner Frontier Gate |
| **TH-4** | *Yangchi* | *Yang* Pond |
| **Bl-14** | *Queshu* | Tower Gate *Shu* |
| **Bl-38 (43)** | *Gaohuangshu* | Rich for the Vitals |
| **Lv-2** | *Xingjian* | Walk Between |
| **CV-15** | *Jiuwei* | Dove Tail |

*Analysis of Point Selection*

HP-6 is the channel's *luo* point, and TH-4 is the channel's source point. Together the source and *luo* points integrate the functions of these two officials to empower their functions of warmth and connection. The warmth empowered by the heart protector is in large part based on the presence of healthy blood. Bl-14 is the heart protector's *shu* point and both tonifies and mobilizes the *qi* of that official to empower the blood with the virtue of allowing us to choose openness from a position of strength. Such openness suggests the dissolution of static blood as we reintegrate our pain in life and move on. Bl-38 (43) *(gaohuangshu)* promotes healing from long-term illness and strongly tonifies the blood of the heart protector official. Lv-2, the fire point on the liver channel, can simultaneously remove excess heat from the blood while empowering the blood (fire) with the wood element's virtue of movement and clarity. Note that I sometimes pair HP-8 with Lv-2 to strongly cool or move the blood.[19] CV-15 is the *mu* point of the conception vessel channel. Its inclusion here helps regulate the heart and calm the spirit so the experience of reintegrating trauma can proceed in a gentle way. In actuality, any point associated with the heart protector official can help break up stasis and promote healthy blood in the way described here.

## Women's Chamber

| PINYIN | ENGLISH |
|---|---|
| Sanleng | Sparganii (bur-reed) |
| Chishao | Red peony root |
| Niuxi | Achyranthes root |
| Ezhu | Zedoaria rhizome |
| Fuling | Poria |
| Guizhi | Cinnamon twig |
| Taoren | Peach kernel |
| Mudanpi | Tree peony root |
| Danshen | Salvia root |
| Yanhusuo | Corydalis rhizome |
| Xiangfu | Cyperus rhizome |
| Gancao | Licorice root |

Women's Chamber was adapted by Ted Kaptchuk from the traditional formula Guizhi Fuling Wan (Cinnamon and Poria Pill).[20] Whenever a woman reports that her period is unusually painful, I am always careful to consider the possibility that she has unresolved issues regarding either abuse or perceived betrayal.[21] Women's Chamber is a gynecological formula that moves blood in the lower *jiao*. Because it works specifically on the sexual and reproductive organs, it can be quite powerful for healing pain repressed from past betrayals that has been embodied as blood stasis in these organs. Women's Chamber is ideal for helping reintegrate issues of betrayal back into a woman's consciousness so she can process and move past them. In this way she can be empowered to choose intimacy from a position of strength instead of habitually protecting her heart inappropriately in ways that dysfunctionally limit her capacity for intimacy.

*Analysis*

We can contrast the function of salvia with that of the herb amber. Amber helps take a person back to the moment in time of her trauma. Salvia, in contrast, empowers a person to work through trauma to arrive at a new place so her heart is strong enough to once again feel and bear her pain.

*Dosage*

When treating physical pain with embodied blood stasis or congealment, I prescribe this formula in the range of 8 to 16 drops, three times daily. For treating the psychospiritual realms, I prescribe 4 to 8 drops, two to three times daily.

*Acupuncture*

POINTS

| | | |
|---|---|---|
| Sp-4 | *Gongsun* | Grandfather-Grandson |
| HP-6 | *Neiguan* | Inner Frontier Gate |
| St-29 | *Guilai* | Return |
| Lv-9 | *Yinbao* | *Yin* Wrapping |
| Lv-3 | *Taichong* | Supreme Rushing |
| Bl-38 (43) | *Gaohuangshu* | Rich for the Vitals |
| Bl-48 (53) | *Baohuang* | Womb and Heart Diaphragm |

*Analysis of Point Selection*

Acupuncture points Sp-4 and HP-6 open the *chongmai* channel and tonify blood and nourish *qi*. *Chongmai* can help revitalize the womb with new blood and help move blood stasis that is predicated on deficiency. St-29 helps warm the lower *jiao* and disperse cold congruent with stagnation of both *qi* and blood. Lv-3 eases *qi* stagnation so the *qi* can help move the blood, and Lv-9 eases *qi* constraint in the reproductive organs. Bl-38, *gaohuangshu*, empowers the heart protector's virtue of allowing us to choose openness from a position of strength. This is in part accomplished by moving stasis and building healthy blood. Lastly, Bl-48 treats the heart protector as it impacts sexual function and the reproductive organs.

---

## *Calming the Spirit*

People often initiate treatment in proximity to a traumatic event. For example, a person might begin treatment to help cope with the trauma of a rape or divorce, recovering memories of a past trauma, or just after receiving a potentially life-threatening diagnosis. In these situations the patient's mind may be so agitated that calming her enough to receive treatment must be prioritized. Of course, stabilizing the pulse can play an important role in clearing and calming the spirit. In turn, settling the spirit can contribute to stability on the pulse. I use these formulas to calm patients who are distraught in order to allow them to relax enough to receive the beneficial effects of treatment.

These formulas can often help patients avoid the use of antidepressants and sedatives that would usually be prescribed by physicians to help them cope with stress. Herbs offer the distinct advantage of not being addicting and do not, in my experience, have the negative side effects associated with drug use. When properly prescribed, herbs have the potential to empower healing by addressing underlying functional imbalances as opposed to merely disassociating patients from their pain, which appears to be the mechanism of drugs.

These formulas excel in quieting the mind early on so the patient can receive the beneficial effects of their other treatment. They can be appropriate when the patient experiences anxiety attacks and her mind races too quickly to process adequately the shock of whatever insult has affected her. Further, these types of formulas can also help improve the quality of sleep when anxiety contributes to insomnia, which in turn leads to exhaustion and leaves the patient too weak to address the challenges that confront her. Lastly, these formulas can all play a role in helping calm a patient who needs to break an addiction for treatment to progress.

Generally, I prescribe these formulas short term for anywhere from one to six weeks, by which time most patients are doing well enough that their debilitating anxiety has subsided. As is the case with formulas that move blood, a great number of formulas that calm the spirit can be used to clear the therapeutic field and create stability early in treatment or after trauma. You must differentiate each patient's signs and symptoms according to her unique situation so you can choose the correct formula. Here I discuss only three formulas that I find to be generally useful in order to demonstrate my approach.

### Calm Spirit

| Pinyin | English |
|---|---|
| Baiziren | Biota |
| Danggui | Tangkuei |
| Fushen | Poria |
| Yuanzhi | Polygala |
| Suanzaoren | Zizyphus |
| Baishao | Peony |
| Maimendong | Ophiopogon |
| Dangshen | Codonopsis |
| Hupo | Succinum (Amber) |

ENZYMES

| | |
|---|---|
| Peroxidase | Horseradish Root |
| Catalase | Aspergillus Niger |
| Amylase | Aspergillus Oryzae |
| Protease | Aspergillus Oryzae |
| Lipase | Aspergillus Oryzae |
| Taurine | |
| Magnesium | Aspartate |

Calm Spirit is a patent formula formulated by the Health Concerns company based on the traditional formula Dingxin Wan (Stabilize Heart Pill). The main function of the formula's herbal content is to tonify heart *qi* and blood. In addition to Chinese herbal content, Calm Spirit also contains a number of nutritional enzymes that both address the metabolic consequences of stress and help relieve stress, by calming the heart and nervous system. This formula played a key role in Janine's treatment (see case study later in this chapter).

*Analysis*

The herbs biota, tangkuei, zizyphus, and peony all nourish blood and *yin* to calm the heart and quiet the *shen*. Heart blood is the basis of the emperor's quiet repose on the throne. It empowers the virtue of compassion to soften the heart's need for excessive control so it may preside over our inner kingdom according to the principle of *wuwei*. As *yin* tonics, these herbs quiet the overactive *shen* and ease its tendency to consume *yin*. In biomedical terms, these *yin* tonics soothe an overwrought nervous system. Remember that the Chinese term for nervous system is *shenjing*, or "wires that transmit *shen*."

Biota seed nourishes the connection of the heart and kidney through the conception vessel by tonifying heart blood and *yin*. The kidney gently evokes the presence of the heart in the depths through receptivity and openness. When the heart fails to hear this invitation because the *shen* is agitated, biota can help quiet the heart and empower a state of repose, allowing the emperor to extend his vision into his depths.

Fushen and Yuanzhi both open the heart orifice by draining damp. In this way the emperor can perceive reality clearly in a way unobscured by confusions. Yuanzhi, "long will," helps clear the channel between the heart and kidney and allows the *shen* to contact the *jing* in a way that empowers connection to original nature. Also, as its name implies, Yuanzhi extends the heart spirit into the kidneys to empower the will. Maimendong tonifies *zhongqi* to help synchronize the beating of the heart and lungs, thus stabilizing the officials in the upper *jiao*. Maimendong also tonifies heart and lung *yin* to quiet the spirit and soften the sharpness of dry grief and sorrow. Dangshen tonifies lung and spleen *qi* and thus improves digestion and respiration so as to supply an abundance of *qi* to the heart.

Hupo, a mineral, settles the heart spirit and moves blood stasis in the heart. These dual functions address the person who is doubly removed from herself due to shock. On the one hand, the presence of blood stasis suggests that painful material has been shut off from awareness, and on the other, an unsettled spirit suggests the *shen* has been startled and, having dissociated, is not at home in the heart. By moving blood, amber can help us regain conscious awareness of our traumas that we have hardened ourselves to in the form of blood stasis. Amber can also allow the spirit to settle back into the heart when shock has caused it to wander. This is applicable to the person who has never resolved having been startled by a shock. Such a person can resemble an animal who has been injured and is wandering aimlessly. Her spirit never reenters its home in the heart because if she were to truly feel her pain she would faint from the agony of it. Instead, she becomes numb because the *shen*'s lack of presence fails to engender awareness.

Amber helps move the blood so the internally suppressed pain can be reintegrated and simultaneously settles the spirit back into the heart so we can effectively deal with our pain as the nature of our traumas reenter conscious awareness. In a sense, amber reverses time. Amber as a mineral is actually fossilized tree sap and, as a fossil, captures the moment of time in which it was formed. Amber often traps insects and, in so doing, preserves the moment of their deaths perfectly for the ages. As an herb, amber can take us back to the moment of our trauma prior to the onset of shock and pain. Because of this function, amber can stimulate law of cure reactions in promoting healing.[22, 23]

*Dosage*

I prescribe this formula in doses of from one pill daily to three pills, three times daily, depending on the intensity of the patient's anxiety levels. I find this to be a strong formula. A low dosage can work well to soothe the spirit and help a patient be less reactive to the challenges that confront her.

*Acupuncture*

POINTS

| | | |
|---|---|---|
| **Ht-7** | *Shenmen* | Spirit Gate |
| **Ki-3** | *Taixi* | Great Mountain Stream |
| **CV-15** | *Jiuwei* | Dove Tail |
| **Ear *Shenmen*** | *Shenmen* | Spirit Gate |
| **GV-24.5** | (*Yintang*) | No Name |

*Analysis of Point Selection*

As the channel's earth point, Ht-7 empowers the virtue of center and nourishes the spirit within the heart. As the source point, Ht-7 provides a fresh reserve of *qi* to revitalize and calm the spirit. As a sedation point, Ht-7 can disperse relative excess within the heart to ease agitation and quell heart fire that disturbs the spirit. Ki-3 as the channel's earth point helps quiet anxiety and ease feeling of being overwhelmed by empowering the control of earth on water across the *ke* cycle. As the channel's source point, Ki-3 balances *yin* and *yang* at the root to help create a foundation of stability predicated on access to deep reserves of kidney *qi*.

Together, Ht-7 and Ki-3 help center and stabilize the heart kidney access to quiet the spirit and calm fear. CV-15 is the *mu* point of the heart protector channel. As such, CV-15 excels at calming the spirit and easing stagnation of both *qi* and blood in the heart. Ear *shenmen* is greatly calming to the spirit and enhances the hypnotic effect of *yintang*, GV-24.5. In the tradition of J. R. Worsley, *yintang* is called the "no name" point and considered to be a point on the governor vessel. *Yintang* has a deeply hypnotic effect and helps to quiet the spirit and sedate the mind's capacity to constantly think and make discernments of good and bad, right and wrong. This can help empower a distance from our problems so we may gain perspective on our current situation and wake up from treatment refreshed.

## JANINE

***Constitution:*** *Metal/Earth*
***Complaint:*** *Anxiety attacks*
***Diagnosis:*** *Possession*

Janine was a 38-year-old woman who came to treatment for what she termed high anxiety and panic attacks. I advised her that it would be a month before I could see her, and she implored me to allow her to come sooner. I decided to see her immediately with the provision that we would also schedule time in several weeks to conduct a full intake and pulse diagnosis. These attacks had been lifelong, and Janine reported that she had spent the "whole first grade throwing up from nervousness." During the intake she revealed she had just terminated an affair and was working on her marriage because of her three children. She said this, however, with absolutely no enthusiasm and seemed both nervous and distant. When I asked if she really wanted to save the marriage, she responded that, in fact, she had no love for her husband and really wanted to leave him but did not know how.

When asked to describe the essential problem in the marriage, Janine responded that she was lenient with the children and her husband was very authoritarian. She added, "With him, everything is either black or white. I tend to give the children more freedom to express themselves." She stated that her husband was both verbally and physically abusive but would not take legal action because, as a police officer, the repercussions for him would be severe. She had once asked him to leave the home and noted that ever since that request he had become the "perfect husband," trying in every way to please her.

Janine's pulse was tight in the *qi* depth with a fine vibration along its entire course. Deeper, in the blood and organ depths, Janine's pulse was both tense and slippery. Her tongue was peeled with a red tip and a deep line down the center to the tip.

### *Analysis*

It was clear from the moment Janine arrived at my office that she was living in a constant state of panic. Given her story regarding the level of her stress as a child, there appeared to be a high likelihood of severe dysfunction in her family environment and possibly abuse. Her distance and anxiety level lead me to conclude rapidly that, in fact, she was possessed by her fear. It seemed as though she was only breathing with the top three inches of her lungs for fear of opening herself to any feeling or outside influence.

Her statement that her husband saw everything as "black or white" was a projection of her own metal element's tendency to fail and draw clear distinctions between what is and is not of value in her life. This failure prevented her from letting go of her husband even though he was quite abusive. Her estimation that he had become the "perfect husband" reflected a tendency to look on the outside and avoid the depth of things. This reflects the inability of her metal to grasp essence and to concentrate on superficial appearances.

The tightness at the top of Janine's pulse indicated an agitated mind that was potentiating a condition of generalized *yin* deficiency. The tense and slippery qualities below suggested stagnation of *qi* and dampness in the earth element. This stagnation was congruent with her tendency to cater to others as reflected in her protection of her abusive husband. Her peeled tongue corroborated the finding of *yin* deficiency on her pulse, and the crack down the center suggested her heart weakness and agitation of her mind were constitutional issues.

### *Treatment*

Upon meeting Janine, it was clear she required treatment for possession. After spending five minutes ascertaining the information just presented, I had her lie down and I treated the internal dragon points as presented in Chapter 3. I also prescribed the formula Calm Spirit at a dosage of three pills to be taken three times daily.

I explained to Janine that her husband's saintlike behavior seemed suspect and probably was covering a lot of anger and resentment. Further it was likely that she resented him both for past abuse and because she had ended an affair with a man she cared about. She appeared to understand my points but felt wholly incapable of doing anything to change her situation.

***Result***

Janine returned after the first session and was amazed to report she had had absolutely no panic attacks for the previous two weeks.[24] She did, however, relate that her husband had blown up at her and actually strangled her in the presence of two of her children. I recommended that she consult with a local women's shelter and strongly consider taking legal action. However, she was still incapable of taking action. During this second treatment session, I tested for the presence of AE, which drained through the lung and heart protector *shu* points for one hour. Upon returning for her third session, Janine seemed changed. She was more in possession of herself and able to discuss realistically the serious nature of her situation. Still she reported no panic attacks and greatly decreased anxiety despite the events she was living through.

Just prior to receiving treatment, Janine looked directly at me and said, "I don't know what happened to the young girl I used to be. I truly believe she is dead." I found this to be an excellent sign, indicating an awareness of original nature and her distance from it. This indicates the conscious awareness both of true self and that work needs to be accomplished to return that spark into the world. This statement suggested to me that the amber in the formula was working to empower its virtues as discussed earlier. I therefore treated Lu-8, Lu-3, Ki-7, and Ki-24 in order to inspire her and awaken the memory of true self prior to her traumas in life. Lu-8 with Ki-7 helps strengthen the presence of essence (metal) in the depths (water) and empower the conception of true self. Lu-3 as the channel's "window" point can help empower the virtue of self-worth, which I deemed necessary if Janine was ever to extricate herself from her abusive relationship. Lastly, Ki-24 revives the *ling* spirit to allow us to experience ourselves as an effective force in the world and empower the potency to change the world around us.

---

## *Quell Anger, Quiet Heart*
## Chaihu Jia Longgu Muli Tang
## *(Bupleurum and Dragon Bones)*

### Bupleurum and Dragon Bones

| PINYIN | ENGLISH |
|---|---|
| Dahuang | Rhubarb root and rhizome |
| Muli | Oyster shell |
| Huangqin | Scutellaria root |
| Guizhi | Cinnamon twig |
| Dazao | Jujube |
| Banxia | Pinellia rhizome |
| Longgu | Dragon bone |
| Chaihu | Bupleurum root |
| Shengjiang | Fresh ginger rhizome |
| Fuling | Poria |
| Renshen | White ginseng root |

The *shaoyang* stage of illness indicates that an external insult in life is on the cusp of penetrating deeper to become an internal condition. In the *shaoyang* stage, an individual is engaged in a decisive conflict as if the opponent has her pinned down and, unless all strength is summoned, the battle will turn for the worse. Two formulas, Minor Bupleurum for weak constitutions and Major Bupleurum for strong constitutions, are archetypal for treating this stage of illness. Bupleurum and Dragon Bone formula (B&DB), a variation of Major Bupleurum, is useful for the person whose intensity of engagement in struggle is as, or more, damaging than the nature of any current conflict.

Bupleurum and Dragon Bone can act as a strong sedative to calm the spirit when excess heat in the liver causes belligerence and disturbs the heart to create anxiousness and an excessive need for control. As stagnant *qi* and excess heat build in the liver, people tend to explode in irrational violent outbursts of anger. Such a person is like a walking time bomb, always ready to go off at the slightest perceived injustice. Such spontaneous outbursts of anger can injure and unsettle the heart spirit. On the one hand, the patient may show an ongoing need for excessive control in many realms of life. On the other hand, the patient can show almost no self-control in regulating her temper.

Anger is a healthy and natural response to abuse in life. When suffering from abuse or when regaining memories of past transgressions, it is natural for a person to feel anger and rage. Anger is the emotion that accompanies our attempt to find creative ways around the obstacles in life that confront us. However, we may become so stuck in anger that the emotion takes on a life of its own and prevents healing rather than motivating growth. In such cases, B&DB can help calm us enough that we can gain sufficient perspective on our problems rather than continually reacting by knocking our heads against the wall.

***Pulse***

I expect the left proximal position to be relatively tense and pounding, indicating stagnant *qi* and excess heat. To the degree the liver is affecting other officials, this pulse may be found at other positions, on the entire left side, or bilaterally on both sides. The pulse may also be overflowing and rise above the *qi* depth, indicating a great amount of excess heat in the liver.

*Acupuncture*

POINTS

**Lv-3, LI-4**

**Lv-2, HP-8**

The archetypal acupuncture point combination I associate with this formula would be the combination of Lv-3 with LI-4. Known as "the four gates," sedating these points can greatly disperse excesses of *qi* and heat that result from a dysfunctional relationship between the metal and wood element.

Sedating Lv-2 and HP-8 helps drain excess fire from the liver and heart protector officials that creates heat and pressure and disrupts the spirit. Here belligerence in the liver is rising to disturb the heart. Both of these treatments can be appropriate when the pulses are generally tense and pounding. Sedating Bl-14 and Bl-18, the heart protector and liver *shu* points respectively, can also be helpful in this regard.

---

## *Stabilizing Sleep*

I consider the quality of a patient's sleep, water, food, and air to be foundational in supporting health. Of all the ways a patient can intervene in her own life to improve her health, these four areas are non-negotiable and must be intact if long-term healing is to be expected. I find seven to nine hours to be a healthy amount of sleep for the average adult. If a patient is getting less than seven hours of sleep regularly, it is unlikely she is functioning optimally in other realms of life. However, less sleep is needed if the patient has a regular practice of meditation. Nine hours of sleep should be enough for a healthy adult to feel well rested during the day. The finding that a patient needs more sleep, or does not feel rested after nine hours, indicates dysfunction.

The quality of a patient's sleep reflects the health of her heart spirit, and any disturbance in sleep suggests involvement of the *shen* as well as possibly the spirits of the other elements. When the *shen* is disturbed, it is unlikely it will be able to focus sufficiently into the depths of self for original nature to be restored and healing to take place. If a patient is exhausted from lack of sleep, she will be too easily overwhelmed by stress to focus sufficiently on the task of healing.

Therefore, I prioritize balancing patterns of sleep early in treatment. Initial clearing treatments such as draining AE or stabilizing the pulse often help improve sleep patterns by calming the *shen* and centering the heart. However, if sleep does not improve significantly after these measures it must be addressed directly as a therapeutic issue. As with every therapeutic issue, patterns of sleep dysfunction need to be differentiated in order to treat each patient individually.[25] To illustrate my approach, I discuss here a patent formula I have found to have good general applicability across a wide range of patients for improving sleep.

## Schizandra Dreams

| PINYIN | ENGLISH |
|---|---|
| Hupo | Amber |
| Kava Kava | Piper methysticum |
| Longgu | Dragon bone |
| Muli | Oyster shell |
| Wuweizi | Schizandra fruit |

### *Analysis*

Schizandra Dreams (SD) excels at treating insomnia in patients where the mind (*shen*) is agitated. By astringing the connection between the heart, lungs, and kidneys, the herb schizandra creates a clear strong connection between the upper and lower *jiao*. The connection between metal and water is vital to reinforce the renewal of self. In essence, this connection summons and strengthens the influences that empower conception.[26] Promoting communication between the heart and lungs helps stabilize the influence of heaven as it comes to us through the officials in the upper *jiao*. And stabilizing communication between the fire *(shen)* and water *(jing)* elements secures the very basis of insight into self. Dragon Bone and Oyster Shell are both heavy minerals and act to calm and root the heart spirit. Schizandra Dreams incorporates a Polynesian herb, Kava Kava, into the Chinese pharmacopoeia. Kava Kava is a warm, spicy herb that nourishes the heart and calms the spirit, in order to provide deep, restful sleep and peaceful dreams.[27] The herb amber was discussed earlier in the context of the formula Calm Spirit.

### *Application*

Schizandra Dreams can be helpful in cases of insomnia when patients waken at night with difficulty breathing or with night terrors associated with sleep apnea. Another benefit of SD is that it stimulates vivid dreaming, often allowing material to surface that has been suppressed due to a patient's lack of willingness to face it. Such material can be useful therapeutically in terms of its elemental associations and helping the patient regain memory of old traumas.[28]

Lastly, I find that in low dosages SD can work well to calm anxiety and quiet a restless heart even during the day. Hence I have found the formula useful for panic attacks, nervousness, and heart palpitations.

*Dosage*

I have found SD to work well at relatively low dosages to promote sleep. Generally, I prescribe from one to three tablets one half hour before bed. Occasionally I find a patient who needs as many as five pills before bed. If a patient wakes up at night I instruct them to have a pill by the bed with water and to take it immediately upon waking. When prescribing the formula for use during waking hours, I prescribe one pill in the morning and one in the afternoon.

*Acupuncture*

POINTS

| | | |
|---|---|---|
| **Lu-9** | *Taiyuan* | Great Abyss |
| **Lu-1** | *Zhongfu* | Central Treasury |
| **Ht-7** | *Shenmen* | Spirit Gate |
| **Ear *Shenmen*** | *Shenmen* | Spirit Gate |
| **CV-15** | *Jiuwei* | Dove Tail |
| **GV-24.5** | *(Yintang)* | No Name |

*Analysis of Point Selection*

Lu-9 paired with Ht-7 serve to stabilize the officials of the upper *jiao* and quiet the spirit. As their channel's source and earth points, Lu-9 and Ht-7 center and nourish the *shen* and the *po* and refresh these officials with deep reserves of *qi*. The inclusion of Lu-1 helps these points to stabilize the pulse by quieting the spirit and synchronizing the rhythm of the breath with the heart beat. Ear *shenmen* ("spirit gate") and CV-15, the *mu* point of the heart protector official, both help quiet the spirit. *Yintang* helps quiet the mind so it does not disturb the heart spirit.

The combination presented here is a core application aimed at quieting the heart spirit that is congruent with the intention of the herb formula Schizandra Dreams. Insomnia, like any symptom, must be differentiated in each patient. Points must be picked individually depending on the context of each treatment. For example, in an earth constitution, if excessive thought was disturbing sleep, I might add the point St-8, "head tied," with St-42, the source point on the stomach channel. I might also subtract the points Lu-9 and Lu-1. If liver fire was agitating the heart spirit, I might sedate Lv-2 and Hp-8 in conjunction with the last three points listed above.

---

### *Opening the Orifices: Niuhuang Qingxin Wan*[29]

I use the formula Niuhuang Qingxin Wan (NHQXW), translated as "ox gallstone clear the heart pill," for opening the heart orifice. I find this to be an excellent formula for opening E/E blocks in the chest when stagnation of heat and phlegm are presenting patterns. I prescribe this formula when the fire element, particularly the heart and pericardium, play a significant role in the patient's constitutional dynamics. Regardless of constitutional diagnosis, I expect that the patient who receives this formula will tend to evidence a slippery quality on the left distal position indicating phlegm obstructing the heart and pericardium. A long crack in the center of the tongue that may end at the tip (indicating heart involvement) and the presence of phlegm in this crack are other confirming signs for this formula.

## NHQXW

**Formula Ingredients**[30]

| PINYIN | ENGLISH |
|---|---|
| ***1. Huanglian*** | ***Coptis*** |
| Huangqin | Scute |
| Zhizi | Gardenia |
| Niuhuang | Calculus Bovis |
| Pianjianghuang | Curcuma |
| Zhusha | Cinnabar |
| | |
| ***2. Niuhuang*** | ***Calculus Bovis*** |
| Lingyangjiao | Cornu Antelopis |
| Renshen | Radix Ginseng Sileris |
| Danggui | Radix Angelicae Sinensis |
| Chuanxiong | Rhizoma Ligustici Wallichii |
| Gancao | Radix Glycyrrhizae |
| Baishao | Radix Paenoiae Lactiflorae |
| Renshen | Radix Ginseng |
| Rougui | Cortex Cinnamomi |
| Fangfeng | Radix Ledebouriellae Sesloidis |
| Ejiao | Asini Gelatinum |
| Shexiang | Secretio Moschus moschiferi |
| Zhusha | Cinnabar |
| Honey | |

This formula consists of four herbs that cool heat (coptis, scute, gardenia, ox gall stone), one herb that regulates *qi* and moves blood (curcuma), two herbs that extinguish liver wind (ox gall, antelope horn), two herbs that aromatically unblock the sensory orifices (curcuma and ox gall), and one herb that calms the *shen* (cinnabar).

*Intention of Formula*

This formula has both an inner and outer application. Externally, its main use is clearing excess heat resulting from febrile illness. Heat accumulating in the heart may produce wind, spasms, tremors, convulsions, and stroke. I have little experience using this formula in this way because most patients this sick are under the care of a physician and often are not well enough to come to my office. I do use NHQXW to clear heat from the heart and circulatory system to mitigate the risk of stroke. Here I focus on the inner uses of this formula. Internally, the main functions of NHQXW are to unblock the heart orifice, reestablish connection between the heart and kidney, clear heat from the heart and blood, move congealed blood and stagnant *qi*, and resolve phlegm. Later I examine each of these functions in terms of their inner meanings.

*The Nature of Consciousness*

With indications for symptoms such as coma, seizures, and mental illness, it is clear this formula has a strong effect on consciousness. Consciousness may be said to have both an internal and external aspect. Externally, the word *consciousness* may indicate an individual is able to perceive and respond to external stimuli. In this sense, the word may be taken to have a meaning opposite to that of the word *sleep*. However, in its internal meaning, consciousness may be taken to indicate an individual is aware of her motivation for acting in life. In Daoist alchemy and spirituality, health is evidenced by a natural spontaneity in life. One is able to respond freely to each new situation unfettered by the chains of past experience. The conscious individual perceives reality and then takes action in the world consistent with the intention she finds in her heart of hearts (the *yuanqi* and *jing*). The unconscious individual, in contrast, although perhaps wide awake, responds to life habitually reacting in a way determined by past experience. Unaware of the internal standard heaven has provided in her heart, she sows the seeds for her own destruction one step at a time. It is to these people that the alchemist Ge Hong refers to as "walking corpses," indicating that, although they move through the world, they are asleep relative to their true nature.[31]

### *Clearing of the Heart Orifice*

> The eye that is penetrating sees clearly, the ear that is penetrating hears clearly, the nose that is penetrating distinguishes odors, the mouth that is penetrating distinguishes flavor, the mind that is penetrating has understanding, and the understanding that is penetrating has virtue. In all things, the Way does not want to be obstructed, for if there is obstruction, there is choking; if the choking does not cease, there is disorder; and disorder harms the life of all creatures.
>
> All things that have consciousness depend on breath. But if they do not get their fill of breath, it is not the fault of Heaven. Heaven opens up the passages and supplies them day and night without stop. But man on the contrary blocks up the holes.[32]

A main function of this formula is that it unveils the sensory orifices. The proper functioning of *mingmen* preserves the integrity of the relationships that constitute health. A chief function of *mingmen* is to regulate the interpenetration of early (genetics) and later (life) heaven. In receiving life through the senses, reality (what is) must be channeled directly into *mingmen* uncolored by the mind's interpretation. The sensory orifices are windows into the world, and it is essential that they accurately convey reality to the inner fires of *mingmen*. To the degree that life is colored by the mind's interpretation, we are essentially feeding garbage into our internal furnace. Interpretations of experience that are not congruent with reality are of the same nutritional value spiritually as food additives.

Hence the phrase "unblocks the orifices" may be interpreted as indicating that a given herb empowers the accurate perception of reality. In the *Neijing Suwen,* the term *mingmen* is used to refer to the eyes, which suggests a reciprocal relationship between the function of Bl-1 *(jingming)* and the Gate of Destiny. When reality is accurately perceived via the senses, the fires of *mingmen* are fueled and burn brightly. In turn, the clarity of heaven's intent shines in the fires of *mingmen* and is evidenced in the brightness of one's eyes and the acuity of the senses in general.

When dysfunction has been embodied over the long term, the obfuscation of the sensory orifices may present as coma, epilepsy, and mental illness. However, these may be taken as extreme examples of loss of consciousness, which, according to my definition, may be present on quite subtle levels. I have found NHQXW to be an outstanding formula for aiding in the removal of the obstructions (phlegm, blood stasis, stagnant *qi*, and heat) that obscure the connection between the heart and mind.[33] Note that it is the aromatic properties of the ox gall and curcuma that allow this formula to cut through the damp and phlegm to unblock the sensory orifices.

### *Heart and Kidney Not Communicating*

It is said that coptis clears heart fire and relieves irritability and insomnia that results from "lack of communication between the kidneys and heart."[34] The heart is the seat of penetrating insight that empowers us to perceive accurately both our inner nature as well as the nature of reality as it occurs in the moment. The notion of the kidney and heart not communicating is important in terms of the alchemical physiology of *mingmen*. A function of heart *shen* is to illuminate the potential stored *jing*. Maintaining the interpenetration of the *shen* and *jing* is one of the key functions of *mingmen*. When the integrity of this relationship is broken, the will (*zhi*, the *shen* of the kidneys) tends to focus externally on material gain and exhaust our reserves of *jing* as we struggle to satisfy the habitual desires of the mind. It is the task of the traditional practitioner to help redirect the patient's intention (*shen* and *zhi*) back toward the source of her original nature as it is stored in the depths of self *(jing)*. In this way communication may be reestablished between the heart and kidney.

### *Drain Damp, Clear Phlegm*

A primary action of coptis, scute, and gardenia is that together they drain damp heat from the three burners. These three herbs occur in some versions of the formula. On an emotive/spirit level, I notice that damp heat often presents as fulminating resentment and bitterness, particularly as it affects the heart. All that we are exposed to in life must be transformed by the fires of *mingmen* so we abstract the highest that life has to offer us from every interaction. The abstraction of light depends in large part on the integrity of the functions that constitute the digestive system. All that is taken in must be broken down by the stomach. In turn, the small intestine must assimilate the essential into the blood (circulatory system and spleen function), which then proceeds to the heart. The large intestine must eliminate the refuse while absorbing the light that remains in the form of minerals.

The accumulation of dampness may be interpreted as a failure to eliminate the inessential from the past which is transformed into a burden (damp) that obscures the present. Under the appropriate guidance of the heart and small intestine, pain may be transformed into wisdom. Cut off from our heart, compassion may be lost for both self and others. Hence pain from the past may become stored as the toxic emotions of resentment and bitterness.[35] These emotions may be interpreted as unprocessed pain from the past poisoning the present. I find that the presence of these toxic emotions often presents on the pulse as a tight, biting, and slippery quality. These qualities tend to be found in the complementary positions for the *yang* organs, particularly in the large intestine, small intestine, and gallbladder positions.[36]

### *Cool and Move Blood*

Gardenia is a chief herb used to cool the blood, and curcuma has the property of moving the blood and breaking up congealedness. Blood is that part of ourselves that empowers both softness and vulnerability. The highest will of the heart protector in regulating the functioning of blood is to empower us to choose openness from a position of strength. It is in making the choice to be open that the beauty of life is revealed to us. Congealed blood may result from internal causes when intimacy and trust have been betrayed.[37] Heat in the heart protector may be interpreted as pain and/or unexpressed communications trapped in the heart by dampness or phlegm that obscures consciousness.[38] Feelings trapped in the heart may generate heat, which in turn may enter and, in time, damage the blood, thus contributing to a pattern of congealed blood. Congealed blood patterns in general may be due to a defensive mechanism that shuts down the heart and/or circulation when emotional pain is too threatening to assimilate.

### *Regulate* Qi

The herb curcuma circulates *qi* when constrained liver *qi* causes flank, chest, abdominal distension, or menstrual pain. When congealed blood cuts off the heart's communication and insight, the liver may fail to perform its function of regulating the smooth flow of *qi*. In this scenario the heart and heart protector sustain a blow that results in both separation (congealed blood) and the fixation of one's perspective in life (*qi* stagnation). For example, imagine a person whose blond girlfriend ends the relationship. The pain of perceived betrayal will tend to be embodied as blood stasis and the judgment that "blondes cannot be trusted" will tend to lead to *qi* stagnation. In this case, one's personalization of thought and feeling so fixes an experience that perspective is totally lost and the *hun* can no longer freely circulate to freshly assess life's changing circumstances. Liver *qi* stagnation, in turn, can impact the spleen in a way that creates dampness, which can manifest psychospiritually as stubborn adherence to one's view. Curcuma specifically addresses this dynamic by regulating *qi*, improving digestion, and moving blood.

This resignation is frequently congruent with stagnation of the *weiqi*, which evidences itself on the pulse as a cotton quality.[39] Generally, aromatic herbs are used to address this pulse quality and its corresponding type of *qi* stagnation. Think of cotton on the pulse as analogous to clouds that obscure the sun as grief in the lungs may obscure joy in the heart.[40] Similarly, phlegm in the heart and lungs may be considered a physiological correlate of sadness and grief.

### *Extinguish Liver Wind*

One property of ox gall is that it extinguishes the internal movement of liver wind and calms tremors. Wind is a chaotic influence that prevents the heart from exercising its mandate to rule our inner kingdom in an orderly fashion.[41] In the myth of the floods, Emperor Yu dispels the chaotic influence of wind as a necessary step in unifying the nation and ascending to fulfill his destiny as China's first ruler.[42]

### *Calm the* Shen

Cinnabar is a chief ingredient in this formula that specifically addresses the heart and has the property of sedating the heart and calming the *shen*. The transformative fire of life is found in humans in the cinnabar field or *dantian*, the internal alchemical furnace. In medicine, the "life gate fire" or "gate of destiny" *(mingmen)* overlaps the role of the cinnabar field in alchemy. As a metal, cinnabar can exist as a solid and liquid at room temperature. For this reason the Daoists considered it a symbol of flexible consciousness.[43] In the *Shennong Bencao Jing*, cinnabar is listed as the first herb in the group of 120 herbs that aid in the fulfillment of destiny. The *Shennong Bencao Jing* tells us, "Cinnabar tastes sweet and is slightly cold, it cures the hundred diseases of the body and the five *cang*. It nourishes the *jingshen*, makes the *hun* and *po* peaceful and benefits the *qi*. It brightens the eyes and kills demons and injurious ghosts. If you take it for a long time you can communicate with the spiritual brightness [*tong shenming*] and you will not grow old."

In this one paragraph we find many of the concepts discussed here in the context of the herb formula NHQXW. The function of nourishing the *jingshen* refers to empowering communication between the heart and the kidneys. Making the *hun* and *po* peaceful speaks to a deep level of spiritual balance predicated on a balance between the left and right halves of the *sheng* cycle.[44] Benefiting the *qi* is a general statement that may suggest a diverse range of actions from tonification to relieving constraint. We may take the concept of "brightening the eyes" to relate directly to the process whereby reality is directly perceived and channeled to fuel the fires of *mingmen*. Being in communication with the radiance of the *shen* *(tong shenming)* suggests our intention is in alignment with both the internal truth in our hearts and with the will of heaven as it exists externally to us. The idea of not growing old reflects the Daoist alchemical quest for immortality. I consider that gaining immortality indicates that one has fulfilled personal destiny and has made a universal contribution, the virtue of which never dies.

*Acupuncture*

POINTS

All the exit and entry points on the chest and head between the *yin* and *yang* channels
The *xi*-cleft points
The *luo* points
St-40
Sp-6
Lv-3
Lv-14
CV-15

## Clinical Case

Initially the patient, an adult Caucasian female, age 40, came to me in order to work with issues of commitment as they were pertinent to both career and intimate relationship. RB, as I call her, evidenced both a slippery quality on her left distal pulse as well as a wide deep crack that extended the length of her tongue. In this crack was a thick yellow mucus indicative of heart phlegm. RB's main imbalance was in the inability to accurately discern a path in life based on an internal sense of what gave her joy. At 40 she was unemployed and was not in touch with any direction to move in terms of pursuing a fulfilling career. Further, her relationships tended to be very entangled and complicated. She seemed to only pick partners who were unable to commit to her due to their own fears or limiting circumstances (being already married). RB kept a diary during treatment and has provided these notes regarding her reasons for coming:[45]

> At the time I was seeking much needed and greater clarity, insight that would illuminate my relationship with my world of work and partnership. I had gotten stuck in a vortex where I kept spinning into the same situations without any breakthrough insight emerging that would alter my paradigm, give me some lightness[46] in being, and allow me to see the interconnections between early events of my life and the present moment.

In relation to the effects of this formula, RB writes,

> I could feel its release throughout my heart center, lungs, bronchi, and then settle into my heart. Going from broad to specific location, loosening mucous congestion, almost immediately I would begin to cry. While the qualities of these insights were not completely new to me, the depth of these insights and intensity of emotion were astonishing.

RB's overwhelming sense is that this formula empowered a deep transformation relative to the emotion grief and around her own experience of insight and compassion. Currently, RB has enrolled in graduate school, put her house up for sale, which, to her, represents a clear break with her past, and has stayed out of relationship for a year so she may explore the workings of her own heart.

---

## *Opening the Orifices: Pathogens, Possession, and the Exit/Entry Blocks by Thea Elijah*[47]

Chinese medicine recognizes various pathogens of internal or external origin. When these pathogens occlude the sensory orifices, they can block our accurate perception of reality. If a patient presents with a significant degree of occlusion of the sensory orifices by internal or external pathogens, resolving these pathogens should be a first priority in treatment. Here I discuss two formulas, a modified version of Erchen Tang and Chuanxiong Chatiao San, that differentially resolve the occlusion of the sensory orifices due to either internal or external pathogens.[48] These formulas may be used to clear predisposition to chronic or recurring exit/entry (E/E) blocks in the head due to internal or external pathogens or, in more extreme cases of long-standing occlusion, they may be used to treat internal or external possession. Because the manifestations of internal and external possession in these cases are the further inward progression of the internal and external pathogen that initially caused the predisposition to E/E blocks in the head, the following discussion is presented primarily in terms of the E/E phenomenon itself.[49]

When patients present with a general tendency to E/E blocks in the head, we must assess the nature and cause of the pathogenic blockage, which is only possible if we have an understanding of what is being blocked. We must also understand what it means to enter and to exit and all that this implies about the concepts of "inside" and "outside."[50]

In English, we have only the single pair of antonyms: inside/outside. In Chinese, there are two distinct pairs of antonyms, both of which may be translated inside/outside, and yet they carry very important, very different meanings. One pair of terms for inside and outside are *nei* (內) and *wai* (外), used in the point names for HP-6 and TH-5, "inner" and "outer" "frontier gate," respectively. *Nei* is a character that depicts the concept of entry into an enclosure, such as a palace or, by implication, the body. The character *wai* depicts the time beyond which it is too late to perform a ritual of divination; the matter has passed outside of the boundary of time.[51] In both characters there is a clear sense of a boundary, and some things are inside this boundary and other things are excluded, outside the boundary. In usage, the inner is implied as more highly valued, more associated with the heavenly principle than the outer (e.g., *Neijing*, the inner classic).

The second pair of terms for inside and outside, *biao/li,* is quite different. *Biao* (表) and *li* (裏) imply the inner and outer face of the same thing. For example, a fur coat has an exterior aspect that is protective and suited to interfacing with the elements, and an inner aspect that is worn close to the body and likely to be finer than the coarse outer aspect of the garment. The outer aspect is associated with the character *biao*, which shows the cloak with fur on the outside. The inner aspect is associated with the character *li*, which shows the interior of a village, an established organization within which the intimate aspects of daily life take place. The important distinction compared to *nei/wai* is that with *biao/li* we have no sense of boundary; we have only the one thing, seen from the inside or the outside. This is the concept of inner and outer that applies to the officials: the gallbladder is the outer aspect of the liver; the kidney is the inner aspect of the bladder; none of the paired meridians are considered separate entities, but merely the inner and outer face of the same function.

Bearing these distinctions in mind, let us now consider the nature of the E/E pathways.

### *The Nature of E/E Blocks*

The concept of exit/entry is most commonly taught as the place where one meridian ends and the next begins. This description is incomplete because it does not take into account the deep pathways; for, in fact, when the meridian *qi* passes Lv-14, it continues internally along the deep pathway of the liver meridian to the top of the head (GV-20). And in making its way to the lung meridian, it travels internally to CV-12, where the lung meridian begins, before it finally surfaces to enter the lung channel at Lu-1. In the head as well, it cannot be said that the E/E exchange occurs where one meridian ends and the next begins because the E/E relationship in the head takes place along what in most traditions is considered a single meridian, that is, the *taiyang* (SI/Bl), *shaoyang* (TH/Gb), and *yangming* (St-LI) meridians.

In the head, E/E points are situated around those profound places of exiting and entering known as the sensory orifices. Thus the E/E points by their influence regulate the opening of the doorway between the outside world and the inside world. The sensory orifices are the openings whereby what is on the outside *(wai)* affects the inside *(nei)*. Although each of the senses is said to be ruled by a particular official (e.g., the kidney rule the ears, the liver rules the eyes), all of the sensory orifices also go to the heart. The primary official corresponding to a sensory orifice has responsibility for the mechanics of sight, smell, hearing, and so on, but it is the heart that allows us to be aware of what it is we are seeing and smelling. This is why the sensory orifices are also known as the orifices of the heart.

The inner/outer aspect of the orifices of the heart is a clear example of a *biao/li* relationship. The *yang* meridian E/E of the head are related to the sensory orifices, which are the outer *(biao)* aspect of the orifices of the heart. The *yin* meridian E/E of the chest are related to the inner *(li)* aspect of the orifices of the heart. The mind is associated with this outer *(biao)* center of awareness, and the heart is associated with the inner *(li)* center of awareness. Perception takes place when the orifices of the heart are clear and open, allowing external heaven to penetrate inside via the senses and internal heaven to pervade our hearts with consciousness. When the *yang* E/E points (or channels) of the head are blocked, it is hard for us to keep open the outward doorways of perception; when the *yin* E/E of the chest are blocked, it is hard for us to keep open the inward doorways of perception.

The inward always takes precedence over the outward, because it is internal heaven that gives us the capacity for insight and understanding. The sensory orifices in the head can only give us fragmentary perceptions, which our mind must bring into unity; we hear through two orifices, see through two other orifices, smell through two others, taste through another, and then we must bring together inside *(nei)* the perceptions from all these different sources to create in our mind a unified understanding of what is going on around us outside *(wai)*. By contrast, the orifices of the heart in the chest lead inward to the void of the heart where internal heaven dwells. This is a place of unified consciousness—not only unified within ourselves, but unified with all consciousness. Perception through the inward orifices of the heart brings us a direct knowing that can only come from a connection between the knower and the known that transcends the inside/outside *(nei/wai)* division between self and other, subject and object. This direct perception through the inner orifices of the heart rather than through the outer senses is known in the classics as *tong shenming* ("To be in communication with the spiritual radiance of heaven")(通神明).

In meditation, we are enjoined to "close the senses," but we do not close the orifices that lead to external heaven in the way they are closed by pathogens in the following discussion. Rather, we turn to face heaven inwardly *(nei)*, where there is no separation between our own consciousness and all consciousness, instead of outwardly *(wai)* through the holes in our head, where we can only perceive through the fragmentary awareness of our individual perspective.

Although primary importance is always accorded to our inner relationship with heaven, the outer is also absolutely vital to our health and development. At every moment, external heaven is attempting to awaken us, to guide us, to bring to fruition the destiny latent within us; thus it is very important to receive accurately the promptings of external heaven.

The first formula I discuss is Erchen Tang (Two Cured Soup) with Changpu, used when the head E/E points have clogged shut due to the accumulation of phlegm.[52] This phlegm is a result of pathology of the spleen leading to internal excess. The phlegm is an internal pathogen, which is now occluding the heart's perception of reality directly through the senses. The second formula is Chuaxiong Chatiao San (Ligusticum Powder Taken with Green Tea), used when the patient's inner vitality is not strong enough to suffuse the mind with the heart's awareness (via the blood), predisposing the patient to external invasion and a compensatory perceptual shutdown when life's movements are more sudden and changeable than the patient's mind can adapt to. These sudden changes in our environment that "invade" the mind effectively close our doorways of perception and are examples of external pathogens occluding the sensory orifices.

### Erchen Tang with Changpu

| PINYIN | ENGLISH |
|---|---|
| Banxia | Pinellia |
| Chenpi | Tangerine peel |
| Fuling | Poria |
| Gancao | Licorice |
| Shengjiang | Ginger |
| Dazao | Date |
| Changpu | Acorus |

Erchen Tang is generally considered a formula for transforming excess phlegm anywhere in the body. It is the spleen's job to transform our food, processing the incoming digestive material and fluids and transporting the resultant nourishment throughout the body. When the spleen fails to do this job adequately, half-processed food and fluids stagnate, and the accumulation thus produced is called phlegm. What might have been nourishment by default becomes a burden and a blockage.

The spleen rules not only physical digestion but also mental digestion, where concepts and ideas are our "food for thought." Phlegm on a mental level manifests as the accumulation of half-processed ideas and concepts that burden the mind with dull, thick conclusions. Old half-finished stories about "the way it is" are chewed on endlessly like chewing gum in the mind, without progressing to the next stage and without allowing space for the taking in and processing of anything new. In this way, phlegm creates blockage through accumulation on the mental level.

By itself, Erchen Tang may be used systemically for phlegm, although frequently one or two herbs are added to direct the phlegm-clearing function of the formula to a particular area of the body or a specific meridian. For the purpose of clearing phlegm from the E/E pathways in the head, Changpu (acorus), an herb from the open orifices category, is added.

Banxia (pinellia) is the primary herb for dissolving phlegm. It breaks up thick sticky digestive material that has coagulated into lumps, whether it is manifesting as thick white mucus in the digestive or respiratory tract or in the mind itself. Banxia dissolves thick blocklike concepts that are belaboring or even obstructing the progress of thought. Obsessions, fixations, or ideas that seem very definite and yet lack detail or a distinctly sluggish thought process may indicate this type of phlegm on a mental level.

Chenpi (tangerine peel) is used both to move digestive *qi* and to transform dampness. Its function is adjunctive to the primary herb, Banxia (pinellia). One of the primary ways that phlegm may develop is as a further consequence of dampness, especially in such situations where there is also stagnation of *qi*. Physically, in the digestion when food is incompletely transformed, this manifests as dampness. When there is also *qi* stagnation, this incompletely transformed substance (dampness) also stagnates, because it is not being moved by the *qi* along through the digestive system. By this means it eventually bogs down to the point of becoming a fixed obstruction, known as phlegm. On a physical level, Chenpi sees to it that the root of the phlegm accumulation is being addressed, by keeping the process of digestion from getting stuck in its movement from stage to stage along the digestive tract.

On the level of the mental digestive process, Chenpi is instrumental for thought that is going around and around in circles without moving on to the next stage of transformation. A person may have a sense that his or her mind is like a revolving door—not so completely stuck as to be utterly fixed on a topic, but more like a stomach that is churning, going around from possibility to possibility without actually transforming or transporting, like a delivery truck going around and around a traffic circle (CV-12, "middle duct") considering each possible exit in turn, but not actually going anywhere.

Fuling (poria) drains dampness systemically, thus benefiting the function of the spleen. It is said that the stomach likes dampness because its job is to receive food and liquids and homogenize them into a nutrient gruel *(guqi)*. On the contrary, the spleen likes dryness because it is the spleen's job to take this substance and begin to divide and shape it like clay, turning it into the muscles and flesh. On a mental level, it is the spleen that must come up with thoughts, ideas, and notions to present to the heart for consideration. When the spleen is waterlogged, on a physical level we feel heaviness in the flesh and muscles, making it hard to move. We may have edema, as opposed to the thicker, more lumpy accumulations of weight associated with phlegm. On a mental level, excess fluids lead to a lack of distinction in ideation; the mind is fuzzy, unable to come up with clear definitions and subtle distinctions. This is not the same as the thicker, more resiliently stubborn obtuseness or conceptual stuckness of phlegm; in the case of excess fluids, it is more that the mind is vague and muddy, unable to begin the thought process rather than obstructed by previous incompletely digested thoughts. Nevertheless, the presence of excess stagnant fluids does predispose a person to phlegm in that it significantly overburdens the transforming function of the spleen, and thus the Fuling helps give background support to the overall function of the formula.

Gancao (licorice), Shenjiang (ginger), and Dazao (dates) are three ingredients commonly added to formulas for their effect of harmonizing the earth element. They are known as "the three sweets" because their general effect is sweetly and gently tonifying the digestion and making it more receptive. Although the formula is primarily designed to clear excess, no situation is entirely one sided, and the three sweets address the hint of underlying weakness in the disharmony.

As previously mentioned, the formula is used for phlegm anywhere in the body, although it is frequently modified by the addition of one or two herbs to assure the formula's action is directed to a particular area of the body or a specific meridian. For the purpose of clearing phlegm from the E/E pathways in the head, Changpu (acorus) is added.

Changpu is said to open the orifices and vaporize phlegm. The orifices referred to are the orifices of the heart, and therefore in this context the sensory orifices in the head. When the sensory orifices are clogged by phlegm, we are unaware of what is going on around us; the perceptions simply cannot penetrate. At the extreme, when our orifices are completely occluded by phlegm and we have no awareness of external heaven penetrating our senses, this is a state of coma. When the orifices are intermittently occluded and the heart is fighting for awareness amid wind and phlegm, this is epilepsy.

When our thought patterns are so filled with sticky old stories and thick, dull conclusions that we would not even notice data to the contrary if it was right in front of our face, we are indeed living in a state of spiritual coma. The phlegm of our thoughts is blocking our heart's ability to receive the direct communication of the senses, and on some level we are no longer in contact with external reality; we live in a thought world of our own creation. This state can exist to a greater or lesser degree of obliviousness, and in some cases it is intermittent like epilepsy, causing a person to phase out and garble data only at certain times or on certain subjects. Changpu (acorus) vaporizes the phlegm and opens the orifices, allowing internal heaven and external heaven to make contact once again.

In summary, the formula Erchen Tang with Changpu addresses the spleen's function of thought (*si*: 思), which in this case is manifesting in its pathology of excess rumination, obsession, or worry. The action of the formula supports the power of the spleen to break down and integrate the elements of the thought process into a cohesive unity (integrity) that nourishes, rather than overwhelms, the emperor. In health, the power of the spleen is intention (*yi*: 意), the harmonious note or ambience offered to the heart—and indeed it is correct for our intentions to guide our perceptions somewhat. For example, if our intention is driving a car safely across town, our heart is focused by this intention to be more aware of traffic lights and pedestrians than of cloud formations in the sky. But when the dysfunction of the spleen produces the internal pathogen of phlegm, intention becomes obsession, and our heart cannot see beyond what we have been "keeping in mind" for far too long. In this case we may only attend to our own internally generated intention, which so fills the mind that there is no room to receive sensory cues from external heaven. For instance, when driving in traffic, it is our intention to attend first and foremost to traffic flow around us, but not to the point where we are unaware that our child in the backseat has been screaming for the last twelve minutes.

## Case Study

Dina was an earth constitution who originally came only for acupuncture because she insisted she could not bear the bad taste of any herbal formula. Her stated primary therapeutic issue was weight loss. Upon further conversation it became clear that she subsisted primarily on a diet of Twinkies and milk, soda, donuts, and sugary breakfast cereal, which she would eat dry as a snack. She was aware that her food choices were contributing to her inability to lose weight, but said she was so miserable in her marriage that the only way she could stand to remain with her husband and three small children was if she soothed herself by eating these foods. She would spend her days trying to care for three children in a messy house and think about what she could do to change all that was wrong with her husband, her children, her weight, and her home.

### *Interpretation of Findings*

Dina's CSOE are consistent with her being an earth constitutional type. The earth element is concerned with comfort, especially via taste, hence her rejection of herbs as a potential source of nourishment because the taste was unappealing and her choice of "comfort foods" rather than foods that would actually nourish her. Her excess weight can be viewed as an embodiment of all that she was unable to transform in her life. Her projection of all her problems as due to external sources is a sign of an excess condition. The slippery quality on her pulse and the thick coating on her tongue corroborated each other, indicating the presence of phlegm. All of these signs combined with the recurring presence of E/E blocks suggested phlegm occluding the sensory orifices.

### *Treatment and Outcome*

For the first few months of treatment, as well as sedating earth to clear the excess internal pathogen of phlegm, I found myself clearing various entry/exit points in the head practically every single time Dina came for a treatment. The results were seemingly miraculous, but unfortunately short lived, because the blocks would recur every few weeks. When I would clear SI-BL entry/exit, suddenly her husband became so much less sarcastic; now he understood what she was saying, did not twist her words into things she did not mean, and would respond with directness straight from the heart. Whenever I would clear a LI-St E/E block, suddenly her husband was so much more appreciative of her efforts around the house and found many small nonverbal ways of expressing his support and appreciation for her. She also found that her children were more polite and respectful, and thus she was much more tolerant of them in return. Whenever I would clear a TH-GB entry/exit, all of a sudden her husband would stop being so judgmental and the marriage would fall into an easy camaraderie with no more petty bickering. Over and over again as I cleared the E/E blocks, reopening Dina's ability to perceive reality outside of her own story, Dina would report fabulous changes in those around her. Finally, I managed to convince her to take a capsulized form of the formula just described, and within three weeks her husband was apparently a permanently changed man. Now that Dina was no longer blocking her sensory orifices with her own phlegm (causing her to believe she was "perceiving" what she was actually only thinking), the marriage was saved. Clearing these perceptual blocks was essential to Dina's being able to make some honest assessments about her own issues. After this point, treatment was able to progress far more rapidly into supporting lifestyle and dietary changes, as well as an inner exploration of what it means to nourish and be nourished.

## CHUANXIONG CHATIAO SAN

| PINYIN | ENGLISH |
|---|---|
| Chuanxiong | Ligusticum |
| Bohe | Mint |
| Xixin | Asarum |
| Baizhi | Angelica dahurica |
| Qianghuo | Notopterygium |
| Jingjie | Schizonepeta |
| Fangfeng | Ledebouriella |
| Gancao | Licorice |
| Cha | Green tea |

Chuanxiong Chatiao San (Ligusticum Powder Taken with Green Tea) is a formula primarily indicated for headaches that are triggered by weather changes or for a cold that is beginning with a tight headache. The formula is classified under "formulas that release exterior disorders with head and neck symptoms." For the purposes of this discussion, it is indicated when there is also an underlying pattern of deficiency of blood, rendering a person vulnerable to external wind.[53] As already discussed, Erchen Tang with Changpu treats an internal excess pattern of disharmony; the inner accumulation of stagnant thoughts, concepts, and ideas blocks the doorways of perception. This formula treats a primarily external excess pattern of disharmony: based on an internal deficiency, the person shuts down the doorways of perception because of an inability to adapt mentally to changing circumstances. In this case it is not that the mind is too strong, overwhelming the heart; it is the mind that is weak, unable to greet the constantly shifting perceptions of the outer world, because it is insufficiently nourished by the inner reality of the heart. It is under these conditions that the relatively excess exterior occludes the sensory orifices.

The release exterior category addresses primarily the lung meridian, in its function at the most superficial aspect of our being: the skin. The skin is the boundary of our selfhood, our personal demarcation of inside and outside *(nei/wai);* it is where we have contact and exchange with the exterior. Our degree of openness to the ambiance of the external environment is regulated by the opening and closing of our pores. In health, the *weiqi* regulates how open the pores should be under given circumstances, to allow free circulation but prevent invasion. In the event of an invasion, the pores shut in order to prevent further ingress; but this also by the same means can significantly impede the body's attempt to throw off the external pathogen. Herbs release the exterior function by reopening the pores to eject pathogens (via diaphoresis) that have entered from the outside and reestablish circulation at the surface.

On a physical level, the environmental pathogens breach our defenses by means of blowing in with the wind. The environmental factor associated with the wood element, wind is the volatile movement of life—which is not pathological until it invades us. It is lively, *yang* energy that keeps things moving all around us. In health, our *weiqi* allows our skin, via the opening and closing of our pores, to function as a self-adjusting windscreen.

This function of the *weiqi* exists not only on the level of the physical body, but of the mind as well—it is a mental as well as a physical windscreen which filters all that is blowing around us in our environment, a constantly adjusting structural compromise between stability, permeability of enlivening influences, and protection from harmful influences. Note that the aspect of stability actually derives from openness, not impermeability; it is the wider mesh that is less prone to being rattled by a strong gust of wind. Accordingly, it is the more open mind that is less disturbed by a highly unexpected turn of events.

What is it that makes it possible for a mind to keep its structural integrity and yet stay open to the wind? This is the central issue addressed by this formula. It is essentially a matter of balancing the *hun* and *po*. The *po* is the corporeal spirit, identified with the lung, the *weiqi*, the skin as windscreen, the boundaries of selfhood *(nei/wai)* by which we protect and maintain our structural integrity as individuals. The *hun* is the noncorporeal spirit, identified with the liver, the free flowing of blood and *qi*, and the spirit of the wind. The *hun* is also the emissary of the heart, the aspect of the *shen* that is able to travel.

We may liken the relationship between the *hun* and the *po* to a jack-in-the-box. Jack is the *hun*, the part of us always attempting to fly freely beyond ourselves. The *po* is the box, always attempting to contain and anchor the *hun* in the here and now of bodily existence.

On a mental level, *hun* is the imagination and *po* is the belief structure of the mind. To the degree that the *po* "opens the box" of the belief structure, the imaginative *hun* is able to fly freely and "think outside the box." To the degree the *po* constricts the boundaries of belief, that is, the limits of what is accepted as reality, the *hun*'s imaginative flight is curtailed.

If the *hun* is weak from *qi* or blood deficiency, resulting in a diminished ability to rise up to meet the new and changing winds with our own imaginative or inventive capacity, the tendency is for the pores of the mind to close, to "protect" ourselves from anything new enough or different enough to require our inventive response. Sudden or drastically changing conditions may trigger a complete defensive shutdown of the mind, and depending on the weakness of the *hun*, just having the local supermarket rearrange the location of its produce section may seem like too much change to adapt to. We may see this in people who because of depletion do not have the inner vitality with which to respond to life's continuous innovations and so protect themselves with a closed-minded conservatism by default. This compensation in turn leads to headaches because, after all, life is ceaseless change, and any mental structure that does not "breathe" with the winds of change is in opposition to life itself. Hence the tendency for this formula to address predisposition to entry/exit blocks with headache and pain; when we close our minds to the wind, the wind continues to beat at our doors. It is only when our own *hun* is well nourished from within and equal to meet the surrounding winds that our *po* is able to function protectively rather than defensively, that is, with a boundary structure that maintains its integrity through its selective openness, rather than by shutting down to external influences.

Chuanxiong (ligusticum) moves both *qi* and blood and releases the exterior. It does not perform this trio of functions as three separate acts; ligusticum empowers a systemic swirling of *qi* and blood all the way up to the head, all the way out to the skin, and beyond (release exterior). Chuanxiong is the quintessential spirit of the wood element; it is about keeping moving that which moves—*qi*, blood and wind, and, by extension, *hun*. Here the vitality of our own inner world flowing to our surface helps us meet outside influences such as wind as an equal partner in the dance of spontaneous creation. Chuanxiong nourishes the *hun* and encourages its freedom to rise and ride the winds, rooted in the experience of life's movement on the inside (blood) and our encounter with life's movement on the outside *(qi)*.

Chuanxiong began the action of the formula in the interior, bringing the spirit of the heart (via the *shen* in the blood) out to meet life at the exterior, where it may now fly freely as *hun*. The next six herbs in the formula are about opening the box, now that jack is strong enough to think outside of it.

Bohe (mint) is an herb that releases the exterior primarily from the neck upward and also alleviates constrained liver and gallbladder *qi* specifically by allowing it to flow in an upward and outward direction. The releasing of constraint takes place primarily at the level of "gate of hope" (Lv-14) so the flow of liver *qi* can continue up the internal course of the liver channel to ascend to the head. The release exterior function takes place at the sides of the head, at GB-1 and above it at GB-16 ("eye window"), gently opening the window for the *hun*'s free movement and return to flight beyond the confines of our own physical and mental boundary. This movement of the *hun* that allows us to see a situation from above and outside of ourselves is the essence of gaining perspective.

In considering the next two herbs, note the difference between the way the previous formula resolves cold phlegm by internal means, via the spleen's transformation of excess interior accumulation, compared to the following herbs that resolve cold phlegm by warming and releasing the exterior. In the latter case, cold phlegm has only accumulated in the lung because at the exterior wind/cold has entered and the pores are shut, inhibiting the flow of lung *qi* and its function of descending the fluids. This is how a person who is not normally prone to phlegm can suddenly be overflowing mucus when they catch a cold. When the *weiqi* shuts down the pores in the event of an external invasion of wind/cold, respiratory fluids immediately begin to stagnate, causing cold phlegm. Once the cold pathogen is released and the pores are opened via diaphoresis, the circulation of the lungs is no longer obstructed, which allows the cold phlegm to resolve.

Xixin (asarum) releases the exterior, tonifies the *yang* of the three heater, moves constrained gallbladder *qi*, and warms and dries the lung. Depending on the context of the formula in which it appears, Xixin may focus its action more in the region of the chest or in the face. When used in the context of the chest, it releases the exterior in the three heater and gallbladder *(shaoyang)* region of the shoulders (TH-16 and Gb-21) and moves and warms gallbladder *qi* through the chest in the region of Gb-22 to Gb-25. The unconstraining of the gallbladder *qi* allows the rib cage to expand, which allows the lung *qi* to circulate more freely. Combined with the resumption of the flow of warmth from the three heater, the lung is now able to resolve its accumulation of cold phlegm.

When directed by its placement in a formula such as the one currently under discussion, Xixin (asarum) also performs a similar function of releasing the *shaoyang* region of the head and assisting the lungs in warming and dispersing accumulated fluids in the respiratory system of the face. It is particularly helpful for addressing TH/Gb E/E block. It releases the exterior and relieves cold-constrained *qi* in the region of the three heater and gallbladder meridians at the temples and sides of the head (TH-22, TH-23, and GB-1 to Gb-4), allowing the lung *qi* to circulate more freely to warm and dry the cold phlegm in the face.

When the warmth and bold immediacy of spirit that is given by the *shaoyang* meridian is not flowing freely in the face, and moreover the face is clouded by a layer of cold phlegm, the face tends to feel like a heavy, lifeless mask that sits between us and the outside world. This is a common experience when we have a head cold; our face seems to hang like a thick veil over the skull, obscuring the radiance of our spirit. It can feel as though our face is immobile or frozen, that our animation somehow cannot penetrate our enclosing flesh. There may be a tendency toward a deadpan expression, as though dissociated from one's own face. Xixin (asarum) brings warmth and movement to melt through the mask of cold flesh, so our material face opens once again to bring its inner animation out to exchange with the winds of the outside world.

Baizhi (angelica dahurica) is an herb that releases the exterior and clears phlegm from the *yangming* (St and LI) channels of the face. It is particularly helpful for clearing LI/St blocks. Baizhi is often used to direct the effects of a formula to the front of the head and sinus area of the face, and it has particular influence in clearing phlegm from the "third eye" (the area of acupuncture point GV-24.5, *yintang*).

Phlegm in the respiratory system is a result of the failure of breath (spirit) and *jin/ye* (flesh) to interpenetrate, as demonstrated in the preceding paragraph. By contrast, phlegm in the digestive system (on a mental level) is the accumulated by-product of a thought process that has gotten burdened by its own results. As in the previous formula, this herb addresses a situation in which our ideas, theories, and stories about life now serve to block the momentary perception of truth. The difference is that in the previous formula, phlegm was generated internally; in this situation, as with the previous herb, the phlegm accumulation is a result, rather than the cause, of the LI/St block.

The moment we refuse to "welcome the fragrance" (LI-20) of the new breeze and close our eyes so they will not "receive tears" (St-1) when we look straight into the sun of the truth, we are closing our minds to what life is putting right in front of our face. Keeping our minds shut to the apparent requires developing an ever-thickening layer of phlegm obstruction. We generate conveniently opaque theories and conceptual structures in order to avoid seeing what is right in front of our eyes and smelling what is right under our nose. Baizhi reopens our mind's eye (and nose) and clears the mental constructs behind which we have been sheltering from truth, so we may receive the winds of reality anew with each breeze, each breath, each blink.

The next three herbs release the exterior and also treat *bi* (wind/cold/damp) syndrome. Herbs that release the exterior help reopen the boundary between the self and the environment while casting out pathogens. *Bi* syndrome herbs function as release exterior herbs, and they also help resolve dampness on the border between the self and the environment. This is not the same as internally produced dampness spilling over. It is a condition of the *weiqi* that allows environmental influences to penetrate and then linger on the surface between ourselves and the environment. This is why *bi* syndrome is primarily characterized by symptoms that come and go in response to environmental conditions.

Herbs that simply release the exterior address a defensive situation wherein the windscreen of the *weiqi* is no longer open to the breath of the moment. In the case of situations requiring the use of *bi* syndrome herbs, now there is also stickiness on the screen, allowing whatever was blowing in the wind yesterday (or a moment ago or years ago) to remain sticking on the windscreen today. In this case it is less that one is shut down to new environmental information than that one is actively clung to by old environmental information. These environmental sensory holding patterns both cause us to project on the environment the pathogen we ourselves are now carrying in our *wei* layer and also make us acutely vulnerable to these same pathogens when they do in fact appear in our environment. For instance, someone with cold/damp *bi* will both carry a sensation of coldness and dampness in the afflicted body part and also be the first person to sense (and to suffer) when the weather turns cool and rainy. Naturally, these environmental pathogens do not exist only on a physical level; pernicious influences may similarly penetrate and lodge in the outer layers of the psyche. The word *haunted* comes to mind to describe this state, and these herbs are among those used to treat possession.

The three release exterior herbs discussed here all focus their action in the area of the head and thus are capable of direct influence on the functioning of the sensory orifices. The *bi* syndrome herbs discussed later also affect the head but also have a greater affinity with the sensory experience of the body as a whole. This is because the primary sensory medium that *bi* syndrome herbs affect is the sense of touch. Eyes, ears, mouth, and nose all give us information about our environment from the vantage point of our head, but our kinesthetic experience of our surroundings is, in health, not a localized sensation. We feel our environment with our whole body, and in health, our whole body is in sensory agreement about the nature of our surroundings. The use of *bi* syndrome herbs is critical when one part of our body (such as our head) is trapped in an out-of-date sensory holding pattern that is different from the ambient kinesthetic experience of the rest of our body.

The first of the *bi* syndrome herbs, Qianghuo (notopterygium), is particularly indicated for wind/cold/damp *bi* that has settled in the *taiyang* (SI and Bl) meridian at the back of the head in a syndrome called "sleepy *bi*." It is a sensation of heaviness at the back of our head, leading us to want to let our heads fall backward into sleep. This may be contrasted with the frontal sensation of heavy-headedness that makes us want to fall asleep with our head fallen forward, which is associated with Baizhi (angelica dahurica), the herb with which Qianghuo is partnered in this formula. Here both the front and the back of the third eye have fallen asleep as the functions of the Baizhi and Qianghuo mirror each other in opening up the front and the back (unconscious) of the mind, respectively.

Although the experiences of sleepy *bi* just described are most common when we have a cold, they can also exist as a chronic state of having "fallen asleep" to our environment. In the case of sleepy *bi* at the back of the head, there is a strong relationship to the SI/Bl E/E block. All three of the E/E relationships on the head have their entry point situated directly beside the eye, and so all three of the E/E blocks relate to different aspects of compromised vision, based on the functions of the associated meridian. The *shaoyang* (TH/Gb) block has more to do with seeing movement and seeing what is new and changing in our environment. The *yangming* (St/LI) meridian has more to do with seeing light and the overt and obvious in our environment. The *taiyang* block, which Qianghuo (notopterygium) addresses, has more to do with peripheral and night vision, the ability to see what we cannot quite see clearly or directly. This extends to our sense of seeing the uncanny, things that confuse us, things on the edge of our awareness, and things we do not understand. If internal deficiencies leave us feeling unequal to responding to the subtle or ambiguous, we may choose to "close our eyes" to anything beyond our immediate ken. Sleepy *bi* indicates the loss of this natural awareness of invisible environmental phenomena such as predators, eyes in the darkness, and in spiritual terms the sense of being seen by the unseen. By releasing the exterior in the *taiyang* E/E region, Qianghuo restores the healthy function of the "eyes at the back of the head," the *taiyang* (SI/Bl) meridian's function of sensing with the outermost edges of sensitivity, symbolized by the hairs prickling up at the back of the neck in the *taiyang* region in response to something sensed behind one's back or beyond the realm of the knowable or the known.

Jingjie (schizonepeta) is a highly versatile herb for venting the exterior, particularly—like its partner in this formula, Bohe (mint)—in cases of unexpressed rashes. This is the case when something from the environment has penetrated inside that is irritating and needs to be discharged back out again. As a rule, release exterior herbs treat illnesses that are complicated by our shutting down to the environment only *after* the pathogen has entered. In some cases, this shutdown is more causative of illness than the original invasion.

Imagine a sudden gust of wind blowing straight into your eyes—naturally, your response would be to shut your eyes. But we must not leave them shut beyond the moment of wind. In the case of Jingjie, the problem extends one step further: imagine the wind has blown dust in your eyes and your eyes have tightly shut against the wind but only *after* the dust has gotten in. Now we have not only blindness as a result of our belated defense, but also the irritation of trapped dust. Jingjie helps us reopen to the environment and cast out the external irritant that is now lodged in our *weiqi*, so we no longer misperceive in our surroundings an irritant that we are actually carrying in our skin.

Fangfeng (ledebouriella) is a wind/cold/damp *bi* herb that is especially useful for wind-predominant *bi* that has penetrated so deeply it manifests as a pattern of internal wind as well. Physical manifestations of this combined wind *bi* and internal wind pattern might include trembling or painful spasms in the hands and feet, contracture of the limbs, and migraine headaches. On a mental level there is also trembling and contracture, a sense of being buffeted by the chaotic winds of circumstance from the outside world and a hurricane of conflict and indecision blowing around in the mind. The person who needs Fangfeng feels as though she is surrounded by a harsh swirling wind, when in fact the wind is now inside, in a feedback loop between the out-of-date sensory experience of the wind *bi* and the chaotic internal disorder of internal wind. For example, Fangfeng is the primary herb for sneezing, a response to external wind that resembles the convulsions of internal wind.

The *hun* travels because it continually seeks greater perspective, a vantage point that will give it a wider basis for assessing which way the winds are blowing. In order to make decisions about how to move forward into the future, the *hun* brings inner vision (blood) to match the outer vision of life's movement (wind). At times when circumstances are changing around us very swiftly, our *hun* is greatly challenged to ride the winds and make decisions based on continually shifting perspectives. Under these conditions, unable to find a stable perspective from which to view the future, we may feel paralyzed by inability to make decisions based on life's unpredictability. For instance, the chaos on the floor of the New York Stock Exchange is an example of a climate in which wind prevails. Here the decision-making abilities of the *hun* are challenged by the need to make swift decisions that reflect which way the wind is blowing, in a climate in which no particular wind may be counted on as prevailing. Some people, however, may stand in the middle of the supermarket feeling as though they are in the middle of the stock exchange, beset by an inner hurricane of indecision as though battling conflicting winds, just trying to figure out how to shop for the upcoming week. The resultant headache is typical of the kind of energetic that Fangfeng may address.

Just as there are many eddies and currents in a river, and yet ultimately the river is always flowing in one direction, so too we can get caught up in the superficial external whirlwinds of our worldly life and lose sight of the simple breath of *dao*, which is always blowing directly and steadily into our faces. This simple wind, this breath of *dao*, is always there and always constant, beneath the mask of moment-by-moment change. Fangfeng (ledebouriella) releases the phantom winds internally and externally, so the breath of *dao* is the only wind we feel.

Bohe (mint), Xixin (asarum), and Baizhi (angelica dahurica) work together to reopen the circulation of *weiqi* in the head to the exterior. They help reopen a closed mind to the enlivening influences that come from beyond the confines of our own perspective. Qianghuo (notopterygium), Jingjie (schizonepeta), and Fangfeng (ledebouriella) work together to free the body or an area of the body (in this case the head) from an experience of the surrounding environment that has in fact penetrated into our own skin and that we now carry with us.

These six herbs also work together in three pairs: Baizhu (angelica dahurica) and Qianghuo (notopterygium) work together to open the third eye in the front and the back of the head, the conscious and unconscious mind. Baizhu (angelica dahurica) is more focused in its action on the head; Qianghuo (notopterygium) brings awakening of "night vision" to the whole body, particularly the aspect of life that occurs both literally and figuratively "behind one's back."

Bohe (mint) and Jingjie (schizonepeta) both open up new vistas. Because they both vent rashes and Bohe (mint) also relieves stagnant liver *qi,* as a pair they help us free ourselves from irritation that was created by our previous perspective having been much too small.

Xixin (asarum) and Fangfeng (ledebouriella) both unmask; Xixin unmasks the radiance of our own face, when we are veiled by phlegm or accumulation of mundanity in our outward persona to the point where our own face feels like a thick dense veil between us and others (in health, to ourselves our own face is invisible, immaterial, nothing but consciousness and breath). Fangfeng unmasks the face of *dao* beneath the outside picture of worldly circumstance, so we can feel the breath of *dao* directly on our face.

These seven ingredients of the formula are harmonized by Gancao (licorice) and then are completed by being taken with green tea. Gancao is a sweet, moistening, spleen *qi* tonic herb that functions much like the great *luo* point Sp-21 ("great enveloping"): it is an ingredient added to many prescriptions in order to create a sweet harmonious spreading of the formula's action throughout the body, both in the meridians and in the flesh. Gancao also comforts the digestion. When we take an herbal formula, we are challenging the digestion to integrate the residue of sticks, rocks, roots, and sometimes even more difficult things. Many formulas therefore rely on the Gancao to be the proverbial "spoonful of sugar that makes the medicine go down." On a mental level, Gancao promotes the quality of tolerance. Tolerance lends to the mind a greater ability to digest and integrate comfortably whatever ideas and visions the *hun* may bring back from its journeys, which is particularly necessary if they are new and unusual.

Finally, we must consider why the formula is taken with green tea. To summarize the formula thus far: Gancao comforts the mind and increases tolerance; the six exterior releasing ingredients open the mind; and Chuanxiong (ligusticum), the main ingredient, fills the mind with blood so we will not be invaded by wind but instead can remain open to external forces without being overwhelmed by them. Chuanxiong brings blood to the skin and to the head and thus brings the spirit of the heart *(shen)* to the exterior and to the mind. When the mind is suffused by the inner life of the heart, it has no need to shut down to outside influence. When we live with our blood (heart's presence) circulating all the way to the outermost edges of our skin, we have no need to keep our pores shut to defend our boundary; we are able to remain open to the environment because we can exchange with it rather than be invaded by it. This is an optimal condition for the *hun*'s freedom of travel.

Nevertheless, to be practical and to keep from getting lost in the infinite, the *hun* must have, if not limits, then certainly a focus, so out of the vast expanse of all conceivable perceptions we choose a perspective that has bearing on our own life. Before the formula the openness of the mind's direct perception was too small; after the formula it is too vast, too big for the human mind. For this reason the formula is taken with green tea. Green tea is said to brighten the eyes. It does this by stimulating Gb-1, St-1, and Bl-1, all of the entry points in the head. It directs the *hun*'s vision by focusing the lens of perception for the human-eye view, to see on the level of what is here and relevant to our human life.

In summary, Chuanxiong Chatiao San treats predisposition to E/E blocks in the head when the causative disharmony is weakness of the *hun* (blood deficiency) leading to the need for overcompensatory actions of the *po* (shutting of the doorways to the exterior after the pathogen has gotten inside). In this state, the mind is caught in the limitations of its own defenses, unable to perceive beyond belief structures designed to create "closed mindedness." Chuanxiong Chatiao San nourishes and frees the *hun* by moving *qi* and blood to the exterior while simultaneously releasing the exterior in the area of the head, thereby allowing us to be protected by the *weiqi* rather than confined within our own skin with a pathogen.

Chuanxiong Chatiao San teaches us that it is only when our mind is not suffused with awareness from the inner life of our heart that it begins to shut down perception in defense against the unpredictable outer world (wind). Just as a fountain rising from a pool dances in the wind, responsive to every play of the breeze but remaining ruled by its continuous connection to its origin rather than shaped by external forces beyond the moment of their influence, so too does the mind rise from the heart and respond to the external play of circumstance without losing its primary connection to life from within.

## GIRA

***Diagnosis:*** *Water/earth within. Kidney/spleen.*

C: Blue/yellow
S: Groan/sing
O: Putrid
E: Fear/worry

***Complaint:*** *Migraine headaches, nausea, vomiting*

Gira was 32 when she first came to me for treatment. I had treated her mother for quite some time, and Gira, who lived far away, had come in for a visit. She had some lower back pain and called to ask if I would see her a few times while she was in town. I consented and treated her twice. Upon entering the office, I immediately took note of her blue color and the wide-eyed look of terror in her eyes as well as the dark circles that surrounded them. Having only two sessions to treat her, I addressed the external dragon points for possession right away.[54] She returned for the second treatment feeling substantially better. After this session as she stood in the hallway to leave, she looked straight at me and asked for my honest assessment of what was wrong with her. I said I thought existential terror had gripped her and whatever its source would be the fundamental issue to deal with. She was taken aback and asked how I could possibly know she lived in constant fear.

Two years later, Gira moved back to the East Coast with her new baby to live closer to her parents. At this time she approached me again for treatment. On conducting the intake I learned that, prior to her birth, her mother had had two cesarean sections. So when she was pregnant with Gira, her mother's physicians had scheduled her for a third C section. However the physicians miscalculated the date of delivery and delivered Gira at 34 weeks. This was discovered when her father went to look at Gira in the hospital's nursery only to find she had turned blue and was near death because her undeveloped lungs could not capture breath. All her life, Gira had been weak and vulnerable to illness. Although five feet eight inches tall, she weighed only 115 pounds. She found it nearly impossible to put on weight and her appetite suffered. Gira's eyebrows were quite thin, suggesting a weak nervous system, and she evidenced a blue/green color around her mouth that I associate with birth trauma.

Gira reported that she always felt weak and could tolerate no emotional stress at all. Conflict was too much for her and even the sound of music could easily overwhelm her. She was experiencing up to three migraine headaches a week with nausea and vomiting. She also reported feeling "deeply cold."

### *Pulse and Tongue*

Gira's entire pulse was thin and spreading at the blood depth. Her proximal positions, corresponding to the kidney, were both deep and wiry. Her tongue was pale and evidenced teeth marks around its perimeter. The veins under her tongue were engorged and purple.

### *Analysis*

Gira's constitution of water and earth reflected her deficiency of both innate and acquired *qi.* Her innate complement of *qi* had been compromised by her early delivery and associated birth trauma. Not having the benefit of full gestation, her lungs had not developed fully and her metal element was therefore unable to fully nourish her water element to forge the all-important link between metal and water responsible for renewing life around the *sheng* cycle. Her difficulty in acquiring and assimilating nourishment during life began with her first breath and had continued into the present. The thin and spreading qualities of her pulse suggested systemic *qi* and blood deficiency. The deep and wiry quality on her proximal positions indicated *jing* deficiency involving both *yin* and *yang.* The purple veins under her tongue suggested blood stasis, probably from an underlying deficiency of blood and *qi.*

### *Treatment*

I began working to harmonize the functional relationships of the water and earth elements by treating the kidney and spleen officials. Toward this end I prescribed Ginseng Nutritive Combination (Renshen Yangying Tong). From the first acupuncture treatments onward, Gira felt continually better. Her headaches continued at decreased intervals, but her nausea was greatly diminished and she no longer experienced vomiting. Although she was happy with her improvement, I was still concerned about the deep look of fear in her eyes. It was as though everything in her environment just overwhelmed her. I prescribed Chuanxiong Chatiao San at a dosage of three pills to be taken three times daily. This formula was taken for a period of one month. It has now been ten weeks and Gira has not reported having had even one migraine headache in that time. After taking the pills for two weeks Gira commented that she found herself able to listen to music again for the first time in years and felt far less overwhelmed by her environment in general.

# NOTES

1. Currently these products are available from the Kan Herb Company.
2. When choosing Bupleurum and Dragon Bones, I often use the version manufactured by Health Concerns named Ease Plus. The other two formulas mentioned here are also manufactured by this company.
3. Thea was also very helpful in helping me hone this chapter.
4. My orientation toward this material comes from my study of the five-element tradition of J. R. Worsley, my years of study with Leon Hammer, and from my own clinical experience. Both Worsley and Hammer emphasize the importance of stabilizing the heart and circulatory system in setting the groundwork for effective treatment.
5. I find it interesting that the Chinese characters *sanmai* (散脈) denote the *qi*-wild pulses and indicate the integrity of the pulse *(mai)* is dispersing like powder *(san)* in the wind. These characters are reversed in the name of the herb formula *Shengmai San* (生脈散), a central formula for restoring the integrity of the pulse.
6. This observation thanks to Thea Elijah.
7. I generally buy this formula premade in capsule form from one of a variety of manufacturers.
8. The analysis of each point selection presented in this chapter occurs within the context of the issue addressed by the associated herb formula. You can look up each point individually in Part IV for greater detail regarding the point's function.
9. There is some concern regarding the purity of Chinese patent formulas due to lack of stringency in the manufacturing process and possible adulteration with pharmaceutical substances. For this reason, some practitioners choose not to prescribe these formulas.
10. This according to Leon Hammer.
11. Note that in the five-element tradition the circulatory system may be seen as an extension of the heart protector official.
12. For a discussion of these two points, see *ND*, pp. 349–350.
13. Occasionally I am called on to use Chinese medicine as hospice work to aid the dying. I was once treating a patient who was dying of melanoma. I arrived that morning just as his physician was leaving and was advised my patient's lungs had collapsed and were working at 25 percent efficiency. I ascertained from the pulse that his lungs were filled with phlegm and *qi* could not circulate. I prescribed 9 grams of PM to be taken four times that day. Later that afternoon I received a call from the physician, who apprised me that the patient's lungs had been restored to 90 percent function. The physician was amazed, stating she knew of no drug that could have worked as well.
14. My orientation toward the use of this formula comes from my study with Ted Kaptchuk.
15. A Daoist term for the heart is *lingtai,* or "spiritual tower."
16. *ND,* pp. 351–354.
17. As with all conditions, blood stasis exists on a continuum that can be detected on the pulse. The process of "silting," whereby blood is slowly congealing, can be detected in qualities ranging from a smooth to a rough vibration on the pulse. Vibration on the pulse can indicate agitation of heart *qi* and *shen,* which can be congruent with the silting of blood and eventually blood stasis. By the time blood stagnation has become fully embodied as pathology (e.g., a tumor or clotted menstrual blood), the choppy quality is expected. Hence blood stagnation can be treated in psychospiritual realms preventively relative to an emotional trauma before significant congealing has occurred.

18. As discussed below, I have also found the "Women's Chamber" formula to be effective in treating women for issues of betrayal, particularly if they occur with gynecological complaints.
19. When treating Lv-2 and Hp-8 together, I would not include Hp-6 and TH-4 in the point selection. See my point selection in regard to the formula Bupleurum and Dragon Bones later.
20. Currently, this formula is available from the Kan Herb company.
21. For a discussion of blood and its relationship to vulnerability and betrayal, see *ND,* Chapter 11, and Jarrett, 1995a and 1995b.
22. The notion of amber reversing time and promoting law of cure reactions comes from practitioner Thea Elijah. I have also used Thea's interpretation of amber's dual functions of settling the spirit and moving blood stasis. For more on the law of cure, see *ND,* pp. 326–331.
23. Health Concerns lists the actions of the nutritional supplements as follows: "The enzymes Catalase and Peroxidase intercept free radicals produced during stress. Free radicals damage body tissues, especially those of the heart and brain, and interfere with normal energy production and with memory. Other enzymes derived from Aspergillus assist in the digestion of food, which is often a problem when stress levels are high. Magnesium is a natural tranquilizer and vasodilator and calms nervous activity; it also acts as a catalyst in the energy production that occurs in cell mitochondria. Taurine has been used to control heart arrhythmia and hypertension, particularly under conditions of stress." Health Concerns Product Literature.
24. Normally I would have seen her once a week, but her prior commitments prevented this.
25. I differentiate insomnia according to the five-element model in *ND,* pp. 375–376. The five shen are the *zhi, hun, shen, yi,* and *po* belonging to the water, wood, fire, earth, and metal elements, respectively.
26. For a description of the importance of this connection, see *ND,* Chapter 7.
27. This according to the manufacturer. I have witnessed heart palpitations in patients who take strongly concentrated dosages of Kava purchased from vitamin manufacturers. I have never seen such symptoms associated with the formula Schizandra Dreams.
28. The practitioner should never "interpret" the patient's dreams concretely. Lately, I have had patients recover memories of being abducted by aliens after visiting a psychotherapist who specializes in "alien abductions." To me, this illustrates a danger of some modern psychotherapy that seems to have specific agendas about the interpretation of the meaning of events in patient's lives and dreams. I often question the credibility of memories recovered under the direction of therapists who tend to lead their patients toward similar conclusions about the meaning of emotional material that arises during therapy. Often these conclusions seem to be sociopolitically motivated in some way. The natural imagery of Chinese medicine appeals to me for its timeless beauty, which seems to speak effortlessly to people without imposing on them. A patient's personal mythology should always be respected. Ultimately, however, I find it most useful to help people gain the perspective that their life story is, in fact, a personal mythology they have created with their unique interpretation of life events, which were, implicitly, meaningless. An important therapeutic goal is to help the patient comprehend the notion that if she is going to interpret life and create meaning, it is best done in a way that empowers virtue in herself and others.
29. There is some concern regarding the purity of Chinese patent formulas due to lack of stringency in the manufacturing process and possible adulteration with pharmaceutical substances. For this reason, some practitioners choose not to prescribe these formulas. Also note that this formula includes cinnabar, which contains mercury. Mercury can be lethal, and therefore I cannot personally recommend that practitioners prescribe it for

their patients. Note that, due to industrial pollution, many patients are probably exposed to mercury regularly and therefore it may not be judicious to expose them further by including cinnabar in their herb formula.

30. Here I list two forms of the formula. The second is a generally available patent I use often. The formulas have somewhat different applications, but the basic intent of cooling, nourishing, and clearing the heart is the same.
31. Ware, 1966.
32. Zhuangzi, in Watson, 1964a, p. 138.
33. I generally use the patent form of this medication, which comes sealed in a round wax egg in the form of gold-wrapped "gummy" balls.
34. Bensky and Gamble, 1986, p. 110.
35. These are discussed in *ND,* pp. 145–149, and here in Chapters 14 and 15.
36. These complementary positions on the pulse are elaborated in the Shen/Hammer system. See Hammer, 2001.
37. See Jarrett, 1995a and 1995b.
38. I consider phlegm to be congealed damp and to represent a more serious presentation of dampness. Dampness is relatively more wet, whereas phlegm is relatively more hard.
39. See Hammer, 2001, pp. 236–239.
40. I believe the function of Lu-2, translated as "cloud gate," addresses this functional dynamic. Hence by draining dampness from the lungs, Lu-2 can part the "clouds" that obscure the heart (sun).
41. See Jarrett, 1995b.
42. See *ND,* pp. 347–348.
43. For discussions of cinnabar and its use in internal alchemy, see the writings of Ge Hong in Ware, 1966.
44. See Chapter 4 for a review of these functions.
45. Note that the patient was only informed this formula was for clearing mucus and opening the heart.
46. The *Shennong Bencao Jing* states that herbs of the highest class will "make the body light."
47. Thea Elijah wrote this section and I contributed only the case study on "Gira" regarding my use of the formula *Chuanxiong Chatiao San.*
48. In powder form I prescribe these in doses of 1 to 3 grams up to three times daily.
49. For a discussion of possession and E/E blocks, see Chapters 3 and 5, respectively.
50. For an elaboration on the Chinese concepts of inside/outside, see Larre, Schatz, and Rochat de la Vallee, 1986.
51. For further elaboration of the character *wai,* see discussion of St-26 in Part IV of this text.
52. Note that this discussion refers to the E/E points being open or shut as a metaphor for the sensory orifices. The E/E phenomena is framed in relationship to acupuncture, which indeed addresses these blocks at the specific location of the individual E/E points. When such blocks are treated with herbs, it is my feeling that the individual orifice as well as the actual E/E channel is being addressed as a whole.
53. The formula focuses on resolving the acute treatment block; afterward we may effectively address the underlying pattern of disharmony. In the case of Erchen Tang with Changpu, the acute pattern is excess internal phlegm blocking the orifices; the underlying pattern might be spleen *qi* deficiency with dampness. In the case of Chuanxiong Chatiao San, the acute pattern is external wind obstructing the channels in the head; the underlying pattern is most likely to be blood deficiency.
54. These are discussed earlier in Chapter 3.

# 11

# OTHER BLOCKS

THE BLOCKS WE HAVE DISCUSSED THUS FAR ARE ASSOCIATED with specific therapeutic measures utilizing acupuncture and Chinese herbal medicine. However, other blocks of a more general nature can prevent treatment from progressing effectively. These blocks are not associated with a specific treatment protocol and may be addressed therapeutically in many different ways. I discuss these blocks here for the sake of completeness.

## *Qualities on the Pulse*

Specific qualities on the pulse are not elaborated to my satisfaction in the tradition of J. R. Worsley. Rather students are taught to assess the relative volume of the pulses corresponding to the *yin* and *yang* officials. This allows you to determine how to best maintain the functional balance of the twelve officials via transfers of *qi* using element points, *luo* points, or the application of E/E points. Students in the Worsley lineage are taught to intuit dysfunctional qualities on the pulse and clear them either by treating points on the constitutional channels or on the channel generating the quality. For example, if a patient is wood constitutionally and the liver pulse evidences a quality felt to be dysfunctional in some way, students are taught to prioritize clearing this quality with constitutional treatment. In this case, Lv-3 and Gb-37 might be treated to alleviate stress in the wood element. Students are also taught to use points for their classical functions when archetypal qualities such as slippery or wiry are felt. For example, if a slippery quality was found on the pulse, Sp-6 might be chosen for its function of resolving damp.

This notion of detecting and clearing dysfunctional qualities on the pulse is relatively unsophisticated compared to the huge vistas afforded by other traditions of pulse diagnosis into Chinese physiology. Hence I have found it quite beneficial to complement my clinical practice with a more sophisticated tradition of pulse diagnosis.[1] Every tradition has its relative strengths and weaknesses, and to be a well-rounded practitioner, I suggest you seek to supplement your skills by studying material that complements your own tradition of practice once you have discovered its limitations.

## *The Spirit Block*

Like the notion just discussed of clearing "qualities" on the pulse, the Worsley tradition alludes to, but does not explain to my satisfaction, the nature of the "spirit block." However, its very inclusion as a premise in treatment planning is a profound contribution to the modern practice of Chinese medicine in which knowledge of the importance of the spirit in illness and healing has atrophied. The fundamental concept of the spirit block is that a patient's progression in life is limited by some clouded aspect of spirit that can be cleared by treating the appropriate acupuncture points. *Nourishing Destiny* elaborates this notion in terms of medicine's role in assisting the fulfillment of spiritual purpose in life. It is a central role of the practitioner to identify how a patient's illness is an expression of the ego's personalization of thoughts and feelings. As self-image grows it increasingly obscures, and eventually smothers, the expression of spirit. The inappropriate identification with thoughts and feelings must be linked in the patient's mind with his or her false beliefs about the nature of self and life and the dysfunctional behaviors based on them. Identifying and rectifying these imbalances is the raison d'être of clinical practice. Health, as I have defined it in Chapter 12 of *Nourishing Destiny,* is a perspective that for each of us is based on choice. Recognition and treatment of a spirit block is a fundamental step that can be taken to mitigate the influence of conditioned mind and restore a patient's experience of authentic self. In this way the patient can be led to remember that what is expressed in this world as thought and deed is a matter of volitional choice. Renewal in the presence of spirit can provide an important motivation for only choosing actions that express the evolutionary movement of spirit. In this way the tendency toward stagnation can be broken as we generate a positive momentum in life and cease the creation of karma.

---

## *Structural Blocks*

Structural alignment in the skeletal system can be disordered to an extent that it slows or prevents progress in treatment. Various types of bodywork can complement effective treatment by bringing the spine and skeletal system into better alignment. I have also found exercise regimens such as Pilates or yoga to be effective in this regard. Of the bodywork paradigms, the Zero Balancing system formulated by Dr. Fritz Smith, an experienced acupuncturist and osteopath, is particularly effective.[2]

---

## *Scars*

Scars that cross a channel can compromise the flow of *qi* to the extent that blocks may not clear and ongoing treatment fails to hold. Therefore, if treatment is not progressing, helping *qi* bridge a scar to reinstitute its balanced flow within the affected channels is essential. I have found needling the exit and entry points before and after a scar can help restore the flow of *qi* in compromised meridians. Also needling the points just before and after the scar with the needles pointed in the direction of the flow of *qi* can be effective.

---

## *Lifestyle*

Addressing imbalances in lifestyle is a process that can take years as increasingly subtle layers of dysfunction are cleared. However, certain general realms of dysfunction must be addressed head on if treatment is not progressing as expected.

The four basic areas of life I consider to be non-negotiable are a patient's quality of food, water, air, and sleep. The first three can be thought of as falling under the auspices of diet. The importance of sleep is discussed in Chapter 10 in the context of the herb formula Schizandra Dreams. In general, people need a reasonable amount of cardiovascular exercise to circulate the *qi* and promote the health of the heart and lungs. Too much exercise, however, will deplete the vital resources of *jing*, *qi*, and *shen*.

I consider two of the greatest prognosticators of successful treatment to be the quality of a patient's relationship to work and family. People need right livelihood so their time at work offers them the opportunity to cultivate their potential virtues. Ideally, work should reflect the conscious choice to fulfill destiny. Too much work, or too little work, is detrimental and tends to indicate that a person is either driven or oppressed by unconscious motivations. The quality of a person's relationship to his or her family is also crucial. Dysfunctional separation from a loved one has the potential to compromise health until it is resolved.

Healthy sexuality is also an important contributing factor to overall balance in life. Too much or too little sex suggests a person is being either driven or suppressed by unconscious motivations.[3] I have previously discussed at length the importance of treating blocks associated with betrayal of intimacy.[4] Clearly if a patient is in an abusive relationship, helping him or her extricate himself or herself must be a primary goal of treatment.

Addictions are the surest indicator of habitual mind. Therefore, address any substance abuse, or addictions to sex, gambling, or food, from the outset. The entire process of treatment in a sense involves breaking addictions. At first these may be blatant such as addictions to smoking or drinking coffee. As these behaviors are let go, treatment may proceed to address increasingly subtle levels of healing the attachments of the ego and habitual mind. Prescription medications can also prevent treatment from progressing properly. For example, dependence on an antidepressant can effectively prevent patients from ever addressing the fundamental issue that weighs on them.

Exposure to chemical toxins and metals, or extreme environmental conditions, either at work or in the home, can prevent positive results in treatment. A patient who lives in a damp basement, for example, is not likely to see allergies readily improved. In one case, I had to suggest that a dental hygienist quit her job because of exposure to heavy metals and solvents. Only after doing so did her condition improve.

---

## *Dependence on Illness*

Finally, we must consider the possibility that a patient's illness serves the person to an extent that he or she is not willing to let go of it. The reasons for this can be many and varied. I have found almost uniformly that patients involved in lawsuits and workers' compensation cases progress more slowly in treatment than the average population. If the success of a quarter of a million dollar lawsuit is riding on the severity of patient's injury, how likely is it that he will get significantly better before the trial? I've frequently seen such patients improve dramatically after the trial was over, regardless of whether or not the decision was in the patient's favor.

Some patients hold on to their illness because it gets them sympathy from the practitioner or gives them control over significant others in their life. I am always immediately suspicious when a person complains about something and then fails to change his or her situation. I have to wonder precisely how the illness serves the patient. For example, recently a patient with untreated hypertension and prostate disease came to me for treatment. But he made it absolutely clear to me that he was not willing to stop smoking. In such an instance, you must assess the patient's real reasons for seeking treatment and what dysfunctional role the illness might play in the patient's life.

## *Questions*

1. What possible motivation could a patient diagnosed with hypertension have for not wanting to quit smoking?
2. Is the fact that the patient has come for treatment a sign she is willing to take positive action to help herself?
3. What is the practitioner's responsibility when he sees a patient engaging in behaviors that clearly defeat the goal of treatment?
4. At what point should a practitioner suggest the termination of treatment to a patient who refuses to alter such a behavior?
5. How much of their metabolic resources do most people expend resisting change?
6. If people truly want to change, why don't they do it immediately?
7. The nature of the authentic self is pure consciousness. From the perspective of the authentic self, there is no such thing as a subconscious that motivates behavior. In other words, everyone knows what they are doing, and why they are doing it, 100 percent of the time.[5]
    a. What are the implications of this principle for clinical practice?
    b. What would be the response of most of your patients if you informed them that their behavior was entirely a matter of choice?
    c. If all behavior truly is volitional, are we colluding with patients if we do not inform them of their culpability for all they choose to express?
    d. What part of a person would be invested in denying responsibility for, or making himself out to be a victim of, his own behavior?

# *NOTES*

1. My application of the pulse in this regard is elaborated in three case studies. See *ND*, Chapter 1, and Jarrett, 2002, pp. 152–166.
2. See Smith, 1986. See also http://www.zerobalancing.com.
3. Of course, a person can make a conscious decision to be celibate.
4. Jarrett, 1995a, 1995b, and 1995c.
5. Andrew Cohen calls this principle the "law of volitionality."

PART

# II

# POINT CATEGORIES

# INTRODUCTION

Now that we have studied specific protocols for clearing blocks and set the foundation for continued treatment, we examine different categories of points and their application. In Chapter 12, we begin with a discussion of the sixty element points as they form the heart of my clinical practice. These points may serve as icons to help you cultivate your own understanding of point function and life as seen through the window of the five-element model. This survey of point categories is essential to our discussion of the individual acupuncture points in Part IV. For the types of points covered in Part II, see the following list.

| CHAPTER NAME | POINT TYPES |
|---|---|
| 12 | Element |
| 13 | Source |
| 14 | *Luo* |
| 15 | *Xi*-cleft |
| 16 | *Mu* |
| 17 | *Shu* |
| 18 | Spirit |
| 19 | Windows to Heaven |
| 20 | Meeting |

# 12

# CULTIVATING THE FIVE ELEMENTS

THE SYNTHETIC AND HOLISTIC COGNITIVE STYLE INHERENT in the practice of the five-element tradition complements the linear and causal quality of thought that characterizes modern materialistic culture. The origins of synthetic thought are grounded in a deeper, more primal cognitive style that has been relatively obscured since the advent of Newtonian physics and the Industrial Revolution. As an environmentally based paradigm, the five-element system holds the potential for healing nature as it lies broken both within and around us. With the rise of materialism, the historical emphasis on discernment of qualities has been gradually eroded and replaced by quantitative analysis. Learning to distinguish increasingly fine shades of qualitative expression, as represented by the functions of the sixty element points, can strongly promote the dawning of integral and holistic forms of consciousness in the practitioner.[1]

Any of you can use the individual treatment paradigms discussed earlier, regardless of your tradition of Chinese medical practice, by merely adding them to your collection of techniques. You only need to understand the technical protocol involved in each and apply it correctly. But to truly grasp the five-element orientation toward healing, it is necessary to change your mind.

Here I present the five-element model as I use it in my clinical practice. This discussion occurs in the context of the five-element points on each channel and their various uses and relationships. We begin by reviewing the theoretical import of the five element points in both diagnosis, prognosis, and treatment (see Figure 12.1). In elaborating treatment I first present using "transfers" to harmonize relative excesses and deficiencies of *qi* along the *sheng* and *ke* cycles using the element points and *luo* points. I then present four-needle technique from the standpoint of tonifying and sedating *qi*. Next I discuss the notion of transmitting and receiving points in the context of Chinese medicine as a holographic science.

Finally, I take you through several exercises aimed at empowering the cultivation of the five elements as an embodied experience and worldview. This discussion centers around the idea of using the five-element points to differentiate clinical phenomena and to select element points appropriate to our assessment of clinical reality.

## *The Five-Element Model*[2]

The five-element points on each meridian are the basis of practice in the five-element tradition of Chinese medicine. These points provide a way to

| | Wood | Fire | Earth | Metal | Water |
|---|---|---|---|---|---|
| Ki | 1 | 2 | 3 | 7 | 10 |
| Lv | 1 | 2 | 3 | 4 | 8 |
| Ht | 9 | 8 | 7 | 4 | 3 |
| HP | 9 | 8 | 7 | 5 | 3 |
| Sp | 1 | 2 | 3 | 5 | 9 |
| Lu | 11 | 10 | 9 | 8 | 5 |
| | Metal | Water | Wood | Fire | Earth |
| Bl | 67 | 66 | 65 | 60 | 54 (40) |
| Gb | 44 | 43 | 41 | 38 | 34 |
| SI | 1 | 2 | 3 | 5 | 8 |
| TH | 1 | 2 | 3 | 6 | 11 |
| St | 45 | 44 | 43 | 41 | 36 |
| LI | 1 | 2 | 3 | 5 | 11 |

*Figure 12.1*
THE ELEMENT POINTS

access the functional influence of each element as it manifests within each of the twelve officials. The term *official* stems from Chapter 8 of the *Neijing Suwen* in which each organ is personified as an official in charge of specific functions. I use the term to refer to the sum total of a given organ's sphere of influence in all realms of a person's being. Each element is comprised of a *yin* and *yang* official, which in turn contains an implicit image of the *sheng* and *ke* cycles manifesting as the five-element points on each meridian. This relationship, portrayed in Figures 12.2 and 12.3 (p. 192), is the theoretical basis of the holistic and synthetic paradigm that lies at the heart of the five-element tradition.[3] In essence, the interpenetration of function offered by the five-element model represents a great elaboration of the synthetic thought inherent in *yin/yang* thinking. The five-element model provides you with increasingly fine shades of discernment relative to how constitutional predispositions are interacting with life to manifest physiological reality in each moment.[4]

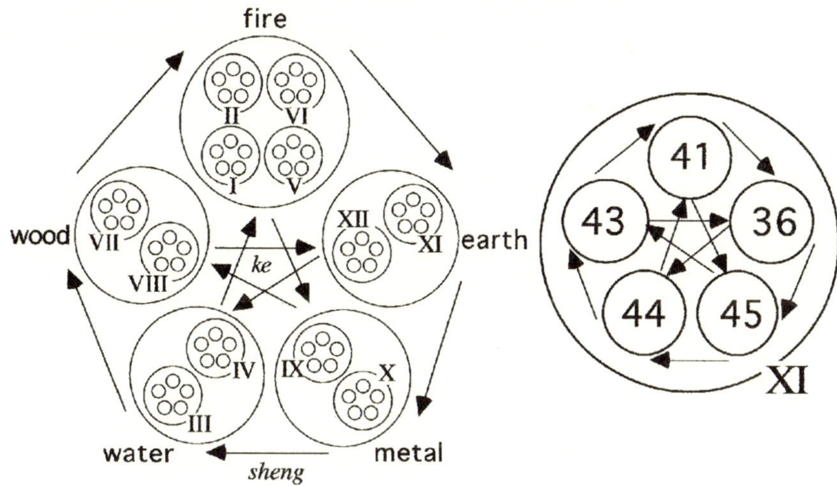


*Figure 12.2*
THE FIVE-ELEMENT POINTS

*a. The five elements are shown in their* sheng *and* ke *cycle relationships. Each organ is denoted in the order of flow of* qi *according to the Chinese clock, beginning with the heart (I). The elements create each other around the* sheng *cycle and control each other around the* ke *cycle. The elements are further divided into the twelve officials that comprise the* yin *and* yang *aspect of each element. Each official retains its own discrete function yet has within it the implicit representation of the whole five-element cycle. This representation exists as the five-element points associated with each meridian.*

*b. Here the five-element points associated with the stomach official are represented by their numerical position on the stomach meridian. Hence St-44 is the water point, St-43 is the wood point, and so forth. These points are depicted in Figure 12.3.*

The function of each of the officials is implicit in every official, indicated by the presence of the five-element points on each meridian. For example, if we consider the planning function of the liver, it is clear its integrity depends on the contribution of the functions of all the other officials. In order to formulate a harmonious plan, we must be able to make decisions (Gb), sort things out (SI), have access to resources (Bl and Ki), be receptive to the new and unencumbered by the past (Lu and LI), be able to nurture the plan as it unfolds (St and Sp), and be able to coordinate and integrate appropriately (Ht, TH) the contributions of each of these influences.

The functional relationships inherent in the *sheng* and *ke* cycles are balanced when each official manifests the dual states of autonomy and communion. These two states, autonomy and communion, become one when each official is single-mindedly devoted to fulfilling its function for the sake of the whole. In other words, each official is wholly itself and wholly in touch with each of the others "selves" (officials) that comprise the whole. In this state each official fulfills its role according to the natural hierarchical relationships inherent in the *sheng* and *ke*

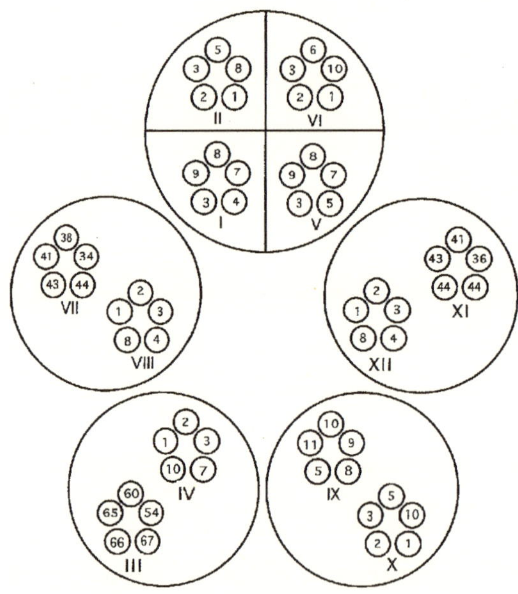


*Figure 12.3*

THE ELEMENT POINTS ON THE *SHENG* AND *KE* CYCLES

*The element points associated with each official are shown here with the designated number of the point as it occurs on each meridian. The meridians are numbered with roman numerals, beginning with the heart, from I to XII in the order of* qi *circulation according to the Chinese clock.*

cycles with the healthy and spontaneous *(ziran)* functioning of the organism as the result.

The five-element points on each channel form a central frame of reference in the five-element system. A knowledge of these points helps focus our intention in a way that allows us to craft a treatment that uniquely reflects the patient's functional dynamic in the clinical moment. For the functional relationships represented by these points exist, not just as discrete entities, but as the theoretical map that orients you toward the overall functional balance in every realm of the patient's being. Further, the element points help you match each treatment precisely to the overall quality and flow of *qi* both within the patient and within the external context of his life.

For the practitioner viewing the patient, the experience is like being in the center of a circle. During diagnosis, you feel pulled by the patient's color, sound, odor, and emotion (CSOE) toward one of the elements more than any of the others, and this direction is what allows you to determine the patient's constitutional type. In assessing the functional state of each official, evaluate the relative balance of each of the five elements within that official. The twelve officials, each containing five elemental influences, and five points to access these influences, yield a near infinite array of distinctions you can make in diagnosing and treating the functional dynamics unique to each person.

---

## *Uses of the Element Points*

### ***The Element Points and the Cultivation of Intuition***

As you become more familiar with the five-element system, the functional dynamics of every phenomenon in life becomes increasingly colored with nature's implicit expression of the elements. Eventually, there is nothing in life that cannot be experienced as an expression of this underlying movement of *qi*. Continually immersing ourselves in this phenomenological ocean, we may come to discern increasingly finer shades of the elements as momentary expressions of being. In time, this process may grant us the ability to acknowledge spontaneously the functional momentum underlying any phenomenon that occurs in our presence.

So tuned to the underlying dynamics that manifest physical reality, we approach the state of intuitively sensing the flow of life's river before any specific manifestation comes floating by. Hence the five-element system offers a superb model to empower the cultivation of intuition. In large part, the phenomenon of engendering intuition is what accounts for the five-element system's power in guiding patient rapport as well as its success as a preventive and holistic medicine. Cultivating intuition is synonymous with restoring original nature. Hence the practice of the five-element tradition is inherently a cultivational art that simultaneously treats both patient and practitioner.

### *The Element Points and the Power of Metaphor*

An evolved understanding of metaphor is essential in both diagnosis and treatment. Once you grasp the basic qualities of the five-element points and how the nature of each element is present within every official, you will develop the facility to observe any phenomenon and understand the relative balance of elements congruent with its manifestation. For all manifestations, from the interaction of subatomic particles to the movements of solar systems, are based on the flow of the elements as the *dao* winds its way through all things. Clinically, we must attend to the elemental dynamics contained in the metaphorical content of the patient's own language. For it is consciousness that chooses words and a human being's quality of expression is never arbitrary. Therapeutic resonance is achieved when the patient's own metaphorical expression is properly matched with the metaphors offered as medicine by the practitioner.

Metaphor is a most powerful medicine for engendering consciousness. Understanding the qualitative nature of the five-element points provides you with a theoretical base to tie every therapeutic suggestion into the deep context of a patient's life as it is based in nature. This allows for a consistency in the intention behind every needle you place, every herb you prescribe, and every word you speak.

I find it effective to talk to patients with a language that mirrors their constitutional dynamics using metaphors that flow from the names and elemental functions of the points and herbs I prescribe. Suggestions made in this way tend to bypass the mind's defensive mechanisms because they resonate with the patient's essential nature that is implicitly trying to express itself. Such suggestions are planted deeply to take root and eventually blossom in the world as virtue. In Chapter 22 I elaborate some general principles of how to make effective therapeutic suggestions.

### *The Element Points: Refining a Constitutional Diagnosis*

Although it is true that each person has a constitutional type related to one of the five elements, you may refine your diagnosis by evaluating the relative balance of each of the elements within the patient's constitutional type. The notion of "element in element" allows you to account for the compensatory influences of other organ systems as they contribute to a patient's complex functional dynamics. Refining a diagnosis to this degree can help you craft all aspects of treatment to suit the patient including herb and point selection as well as guide the suggestive process in therapy. For example, you may determine that a patient's constitutional type is governed by the kidney official. Yet within the sphere of function of the kidney official, you may assess that fire is the element most unbalanced. Hence the constitutional type of the patient may be designated as "water, fire within."

As we each gain clinical experience, our ability to discern fine shades of difference within each constitutional type evolves and deepens. Hence an advanced diagnosis may be stated as "water, fire, then earth within." This diagnosis indicates that water is the element of the constitutional type, and within water the elements of fire and earth are of secondary and tertiary importance, respectively.

The ability to formulate a highly refined diagnosis enables you to select a precise combination of points to ground a particular treatment. For example, a patient's constitutional type may be "fire, water within." Knowing that fire and water constitute the main functional issues for this patient, you may choose to use Ki-2 as a distal point in conjunction with a strong spirit point such as Ki-24. In this instance, you have chosen the element point corresponding to the patient's constitutional type (fire) as the distal point on the kidney official. This treatment is significantly different in quality than if you had chosen any other element point as a basis for the treatment. Consider also the example of a patient whose diagnosis is "wood, earth within." Choosing Lv-3, for its quality of being the earth point on the liver channel, is quite different from choosing Lv-3 as the channel's source point. Combining Lv-3 with Lv-13, the spleen *mu* point, could address elegantly the patient's constitutional dynamics in forming the core of a given treatment.

Lastly, knowledge of the five-element points can actually help you work backward to form a diagnosis. By noticing what points come to mind during the intake, and noting their elemental quality, you can gain valuable clues about the patient's constitutional type. For example, if while conducting an intake I feel very drawn toward treating Gb-34 on a particular patient, I would have to consider that wood and earth figure prominently in the underlying constitutional dynamics of the patient.

### *The Five-Element Points and Seasonal Treatment*

During every treatment session, I take into account a patient's constitutional diagnosis and presenting signs and symptoms, as well as the season, the weather, and the time of day. This view allows me to consider the patient's unique situation within the broader environmental context in which the treatment is occurring. The possibilities for using the element points in combination to balance a patient with the seasons are vast. Treatment in this way is one of the primary aims of the five-element system, which seeks to balance each patient with the natural transitions of life as expressed in the seasonal cycles of nature.

Patients generally display seasonal preferences and dislikes that mirror the nature of their elemental imbalances. People who are either excessively hot or cold tend to dislike summer or winter, respectively. Similarly, a patient who is damp internally tends to do worse during damp weather and to prefer drier climates. I expect that over the course of treatment patients will experience better harmony in each season and a more graceful flow of *qi* internally as the seasons change. When a patient who had reported feeling oppressed by summer heat comments it is no longer as troubling as it has been in the past, I know that treatment is helping instill a deep functional balance internally.

The element points provide a framework for treating patients in a seasonal context. Consideration of the patient's constitutional diagnosis and elemental balance may figure prominently in point selection for patients who are treated long term. Here I list several possible strategies for treating a patient with the five-element points in a seasonal context.

Let us assume a patient is wood constitutionally and governed by the liver official. Because wood corresponds to the spring season, several strategies using element points are possible to harmonize this patient with a given season throughout the year. The horary point Lv-1 (wood within wood) offers us the most explicit opportunity to harmonize the patient within the context of his or her elemental season. Treating Lv-1 at 1 to 3 A.M. on the vernal equinox offers a unique chance to draw on the quality of *qi* inherent in the spring season to empower the pure expression of wood within the patient.[5]

The water point on the liver channel, Lv-8, "crooked spring," can be used to good advantage in the spring for helping support the manifestation of the season within the patient if he is failing to draw on resources appropriately. Here the strength of winter, the previous season, is used to empower the elemental expression of the present season. During winter, Ki-1, the wood point on the kidney channel, may be treated to help set the stage for the expression of spring and the wood element when it arrives. In a similar fashion, Lv-2, the fire point on the liver channel, can be treated during spring in order to empower the expression of the fire element within the wood. In this way we can support the emergence of the flower that lies implicit within the wood so it blossoms during summer. Finally, during summer, H-9 or HP-9, the wood points on their respective fire meridians, may be treated to help bring the influence of the constitutional element to support the manifestation of the present season.

During the seasons of late summer and fall, element points can also be treated to harmonize the expression of the wood element at these times of year. For example, a patient who feels constrained by humidity during late summer may benefit from treatment with Lv-3, the earth point on the liver channel, or Sp-1, the wood point on the spleen meridian. During the fall, Lv-4 (metal) and Lv-1 (wood) are important points to consider for a wood element that is either over- or undercontrolled by the metal element during this season. Similarly, you may combine points in seasonal treatments. For example, you might combine Lu-8 with Lv-4 to strongly empower the virtues of metal within wood on the fall or spring equinox.

In another example, if a patient's constitutional type is "wood, water within" and the current season is summer, you may choose to treat Lv-8 (water) and HP-9 (wood) concurrently. Lv-8 is treated as the water point of the liver official, which can draw *qi* from the water into the wood element. Further, HP-9, as the wood point of a fire official, can then draw *qi* from the wood element to support the function of the heart protector official in its associated season of summer. The liver official has been joined to both its mother (water) and child (fire), thus integrating and empowering the entire left half of the *sheng* cycle.

The sixty element points provide a flexible enough foundation for treatment that a near limitless array of possibilities are available to address any patient's underlying functional dynamics as they occur within the daily rhythms of the Chinese clock and the yearly cycling of the seasons.

### *Element in Element: Guiding Prognosis*

The seasonal nature of the five-element model also offers you a way to hone your prognosis by helping guide your expectation of when a patient might improve during treatment. For example, I treated a woman for infertility who had tried in vain for four years to become pregnant. She was earth constitutionally and suffered from both spleen *qi* and blood deficiency. Having begun treatment in winter, I told her that I expected her to conceive by the end of August. This would allow seven months for the treatment to take hold, and I knew the late summer season would help empower the virtues of fullness and mothering associated with the earth element. In fact, by the third week of August she was pregnant as I had predicted.[6]

In another example, I was asked on two different occasions by patients with terminal illnesses when I thought they would die. Both were nearing death as fall approached, and their kidney pulses had grown progressively weaker during the summer months. In each case I predicted the first frost would break the final link between metal and water so crucial for sustaining life and death would soon follow.[7] Both patients in fact died the morning of the first frost.

In general, symptoms of excess worsen during a given season and symptoms of deficiency improve. For example, because my infertile patient was deficient in spleen *qi* and blood, it was reasonable to expect that if I worked to boost these prior to late summer, the onset of that season would support the influence of the earth element in creating these deficient resources. In contrast, if a patient's symptoms were based on the presence of dampness, these might worsen during the humid months of late summer but improve during fall or winter when dryness predominates. Hence a patient's constitution, the nature of his imbalances and symptoms, and the time of year treatment is initiated all inform my treatment plan.

---

## *The Five-Element Points and the Transfer of* Qi

Here we examine the practical application of the five-element points in treatment. I begin by reviewing basic tonification and sedation, proceed to relatively more complex transfers of *qi*, and end with a discussion of the four-needle technique.

### *Tonification and Sedation*

*What has surplus is reduced, what is deficient is supplemented.*
– *DAODEJING*[8]

The element points constitute an important method for tonifying or sedating the officials. Further, these points provide a way to transfer *qi* between the officials around the *sheng* and across the *ke* cycle. Here I examine some of the basic theory involved in using the element points to transfer *qi*.

#### *The Notions of Excess and Deficiency*

Before we discuss how to transfer *qi* using the five-element points, we must be clear about the concepts of excess and deficiency. At the outset we separate our discussion of signs and symptoms from the actual finding of excess and deficiency through pulse or tongue diagnosis. Understand that any specific manifestation can be based on a relative excess or deficiency of *qi*.

For example, a patient can display belligerence based on either a lack of self-esteem and/or arrogance. We may consider a display of anger and yelling as excessive in nature, whereas we think of a too quiet demeanor as reflecting deficiency. However, the only way to determine if either condition actually reflects a relative excess or deficiency of liver *qi* is to examine the pulse and tongue. Similarly, the headaches experienced by this patient can be predicated on either a condition of excess or deficiency as determined by pulse and tongue diagnosis.

Determining relative excess and deficiency of *qi* on the pulse yields a qualitative assessment of the functional state of each official. Here we are primarily concerned with the strength of the pulse in each of the twelve positions corresponding to the function of each official. The assessment of excess and deficiency of *qi* is based on considering the volume, amplitude, and intensity of the pulse in each position (see Figure 12.4).

The determination of relative excess and deficiency according to the criteria of pulse intensity alone can be a problem from the perspective of pulse systems that rely more explicitly on identifying pulse qualities. This is because a pulse that is thin, hard, and pounding (wiry) is actually just as deficient as a pulse that can barely be felt (feeble) or is actually missing (absent). The wiry pulse signifies a state of *jing* deficiency arrived at through the consumption of *yin,* and the feeble/absent (F/A) pulse represents a state of *jing* deficiency arrived at through the consumption of *yang.* Both the wiry pulse and the feeble/absent (F/A) pulse are equally deficient.

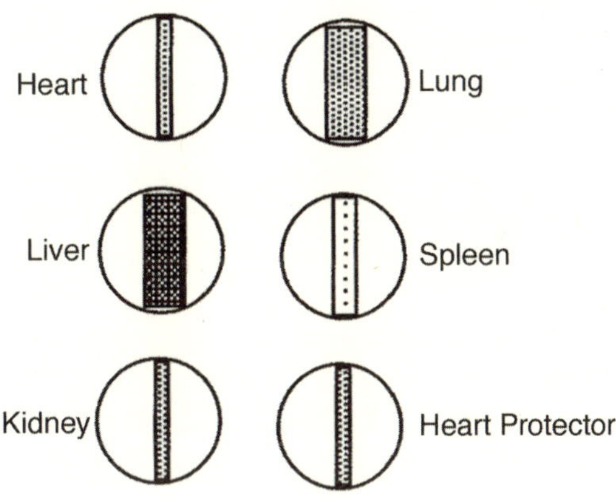


*Figure 12.4*

RELATIVE EXCESS AND DEFICIENCY ON THE PULSE[9]

*The circles each represent the primary pulse positions on the left and right wrists. Relative intensity in a given position is indicated by that position's depth of shading, and the volume of* qi *is denoted by width. Here the lung position is wider than that of the kidney, heart, and heart protector, indicating relatively more* qi *sustaining the function of the lung official. However, all four pulses are felt at the same relative intensity as indicated by their consistent shading, and, therefore, they are often mistakenly considered to be functioning equivalently. In fact, the kidney, heart, and heart protector pulses are tight (thin and hard), indicating a state of* yin *deficiency. The liver pulse is depicted as hitting the finger relatively more strongly and suggests a condition of stagnation and excess, whereas the position corresponding to the spleen is pictured as having the weakest intensity and the least* qi *supporting its function.*[10]

However, the wiry pulse is primarily deficient in *yin,* and the feeble/absent (F/A) pulse is primarily deficient in *yang*.

The problem occurs when you feel a pounding pulse that is *yin* deficient in one position and a soft, spreading, or F/A pulse, indicating *qi* and/or *yang* deficiency, in another position. Owing to the relative intensity of the *yin*-deficient pulse, as compared with the *qi*-deficient pulse, you might assume the *yin*-deficient position indicates a relative excess of *qi* in its corresponding official as compared to that of the *qi*-deficient position. Herein lies the fallacy because both positions are equally deficient, and sedating the *yin*-deficient position or trying to transfer *qi* from it is not likely to be fruitful because no sufficient reserve of *qi* is available to draw from in a *jing*-deficient organ. In Figure 12.4, the *qi* deficiency in the spleen could be tonified using Sp-1, the channel's secondary tonification point, to transfer the relative excess from the liver to support the function of the spleen official. However, I do not advise treating Sp-2, the channel's primary tonification point, because the heart and heart protector are *yin* deficient and do not have an excess of healthy *qi* to support the function of the spleen. Thus you must take into account more parameters of the pulse when designing transfers than merely the relative amount of force you detect on the pulse.

When treating a patient over time, never only treat the constitutional official. But remember everything is treated in relationship to this official. From a constitutional perspective, all transfers of *qi* are intended to support the function of the constitutional element and official. The therapeutic action taken in the scenario depicted in Figure 12.4 would depend entirely on your constitutional assessment of the patient as well as the context of the treatment as dictated by his or her presenting signs and symptoms and considerations such as the season, time of day, and climate.

### *Directing the Flow of* Qi

Each official is associated with tonification and sedation points that allow for a relative increase or decrease in the functional influence of that official systemically (see Figure 12.5, p. 202). The *qi* that supports the function of each official may be increased (tonified) or decreased (sedated) depending on the nature of the element points you select for treatment.

The primary tonification point is the point on each meridian that is of the same elemental quality of *qi* as the preceding element (its "mother") on the *sheng* cycle. For example, if we consider the liver meridian, Lv-8, the water point, it is the channel's primary tonification point because water is the element that precedes wood along the *sheng* cycle. When the function of the liver official is deficient relative to the function of the kidney official, Lv-8 may be used to draw from the relative excess of *qi* in the kidneys in order to support the function of the liver. Using a tonification point is a direct command to the *qi* to move down its concentration gradient from relative excess to relative deficiency. If the liver is deficient relative to the kidney, treating Lv-8 is a direct invocation to draw *qi* from the kidney to support the function of the liver official.

The secondary tonification point, available only on the *yin* channels, is the point of the same elemental nature of the element that is two elements before it on the *sheng* cycle (its "grandmother"). For example, the secondary tonification point associated with the liver official is Lv-4, the liver meridian's metal point. If the metal element is excessive relative to the function of the liver, Lv-4 can draw *qi* from the metal element to support the liver's function. The secondary tonification point works because *yin* officials can transfer *qi* across the *ke* cycle, whereas the *yang* officials cannot. Therefore, the *yin* officials each possess a primary and secondary tonification point. The *yang* officials, in contrast, each have only a primary tonification and sedation point (see Figure 12.5).

The primary sedation point is the point on each meridian that is of the same elemental nature of the element that follows it along the *sheng* cycle (its "child").[11] For example, the primary sedation point associated with the liver official is Lv-2. If the *qi* that supports the function of the liver official is excessive relative to the function of the heart protector, Lv-2 can send *qi* from liver (wood) to support the function of the relatively deficient fire official. Although tonification points direct the *qi* in an assertive and predictable fashion, the mode by which sedation points work is less predictable. That is, I would expect Lv-2 to disperse a relative excess in the liver official, but I would not necessarily expect this will be channeled to a relative deficiency in the fire element as predicted by theory. Certainly this may happen, but I find the excess will disperse and tend to find its way to whatever deficiency is most in need of tonification systemically. Hence when sedating Lv-2, I certainly expect the intensity of the liver pulse to diminish, but I must check the pulses to discern just how the *qi* has been distributed throughout all the officials and their related pulses.

The secondary sedation point, available only on the *yin* channels, is the point on each meridian of the same elemental nature of the element that is two elements after it on the *sheng* cycle (its "grandchild") and that it controls across the *ke* cycle. For example, the secondary sedation point associated with the liver official is Lv-3. If the *qi* that supports the function of the liver official is excess relative to the function of the spleen, Lv-3 may send *qi* from liver (wood) to support the function of the relatively deficient earth official. Again, this type of sedation is not as predictable in effect as tonification for the reasons already discussed.

| | Ht | SI | Bl | Ki | HP | TH | Gb | Lv | Lu | LI | St | Sp |
|---|---|---|---|---|---|---|---|---|---|---|---|---|
| 1° Tonification | 9 | 3 | 67 | 7 | 9 | 3 | 43 | 8 | 9 | 11 | 41 | 2 |
| 2° Tonification | 3 | X | X | 3 | 3 | X | X | 4 | 10 | X | X | 1 |
| 1° Sedation | 7 | 8 | 65 | 1 | 7 | 10 | 38 | 2 | 5 | 2 | 45 | 5 |
| 2° Sedation | 4 | X | X | 2 | 5 | X | X | 3 | 11 | X | X | 8 |
| Horary | 8 | 5 | 66 | 10 | 8 | 6 | 41 | 1 | 8 | 1 | 36 | 3 |

*Figure 12.5*

TONIFICATION AND SEDATION POINTS

*The numbers of the tonification and sedation points are given for each official as they correspond to the element points in Figure 12.1. An X indicates the* yang *officials, which do not possess secondary tonification or sedation points.*

### *The Use of* Luo *Points in Transfers*

*Luo* points have a wide range of functions that are sensitive to the contextual nature of each treatment. When employed in transfers, a *luo* point will always empower *qi* to flow down its concentration gradient from relative excess to relative deficiency. For example, if, according to pulse diagnosis, the liver official is relatively *qi* deficient as compared with the gallbladder official, then Lv-5, the *luo* point on the liver channel, will allow the relative excess in the gallbladder to tonify the relative deficiency in the liver.

### *The Transfer of Qi*

The tonification, sedation, and *luo* points may be used to transfer *qi* from an official that is relatively excess to one that is relatively deficient. In the five-element tradition, the use of the element points in this way constitutes one of the primary ways of establishing functional harmony among the twelve officials and five elements. Designing elegant transfers allows you a near infinite array of point combinations to ground each treatment in the patient's constitutional dynamics in a way that addresses concerns of excess and deficiency from a *yin/yang* perspective.

In Figure 12.6 (p. 205), I work through several different types of transfers. Notice in these examples that a relative excess is always being channeled to a relative deficiency. This allows you to emulate the virtue of Emperor Yu, who channeled through the mountains so the floodwaters inundating humanity could be directed safely to the sea.[12]

## GUIDELINES FOR TRANSFERS

1. A relative excess is always channeled toward a relative deficiency.
2. Points are always treated in order against the concentration gradient from deficiency to excess. For example, in Figure 12.6c, the points are needled in the following order: GB-37, Lv-4, Lu-7, and, finally, LI-11.
3. Needles are removed in the same order they were inserted.
4. Generally, the official we are transferring out of, or into, is the patient's constitutional organ. This is in keeping with the notion that the strongest or weakest pulse is most likely to correspond to the patient's constitutional official.
5. The pulse should change as predicted by theory in order for us to verify that the transfer has been effective. In other words, the relatively excess and relatively deficient pulses should have equilibrated after treatment.
6. *Qi* transfers from *yin* official to *yin* official and from *yang* official to *yang* official along the *sheng* cycle. In other words, if wood is excess relative to fire, and we tonify Ht-9, it is assumed the transfer is occurring primarily from the liver and not the gallbladder official.
7. *Qi* can be transferred between *yin* officials along the *sheng* or *ke* cycles. *Qi* can only be transferred between the *yang* officials around the *sheng* cycle. For example, if the liver is in excess relative to the spleen, Sp-1 can be treated to equilibrate the two officials. However, St-43, the wood point on the stomach channel, will not transfer a relative excess of *qi* from the gallbladder to the stomach official.
8. In designing a transfer, use the most direct route that requires the fewest needles when selecting transfer points.
9. You cannot transfer *qi* between the left and right half of the fire element. For example, if the heart has an excess of *qi* relative to the heart protector, there is no way to transfer directly between the two officials.
10. Avoid transferring through an official that is relatively more excess than the primary official you are transferring out of. For example, in Figure 12.6a (p. 205), imagine the lung pulse was rated at +2 (++) relative to the spleen at +1 (+). In this case, it is better to tonify the kidney using Ki-3 than to design a transfer using Ki-7 and Lu-9. This is because the lung official, already quite excess, is likely to hold on to the *qi* channeled through it so the kidney official will not see the functional benefits of the transfer.
11. Consider the patient's overall constitutional and physiological dynamics as well as the nature of the first point to be needled in designing the transfer. For example, if a patient is "fire within

earth"[13] constitutionally and earth is deficient relative to fire, it makes good sense to transfer from fire to earth using Sp-2. The nature of fire within earth is to empower us to be nourished through the internal cooking and assimilation of acquired essence. This transfer may therefore well address deep issues in a patient's life that transcend the mere mechanics of balancing *qi* according to theoretical concerns regarding relative excess and deficiency.

*Needle Technique*

When performing transfers, always treat points in reverse order along the concentration gradient from relative excess to relative deficiency. For example, in Figure 12.6c, points are needled in this order: GB-37, Lv-4, Lu-7, and, finally, LI-11. In this case, all needles after GB-37 are inserted perpendicularly to the meridian and no rotation is applied to the needles either in a clockwise or counterclockwise direction. These individual points are not being treated to affect the functions of their associated officials. Rather, these points are selected merely to establish a path for the *qi* to flow naturally down its gradient from relative excess to deficiency. The needles placed in this manner are called *carrier needles* in line with their passive function.

Needle Gb-37 first because it is the destination of the transfer and serves to establish the route for the transfer of *qi* when you place the carrier needles. Because the intent of the treatment is to tonify the function of the gallbladder official, insert the needle on the left side first and then on the right side. Then place each carrier needle in order on the left first and then the right side. After all the needles are in place, apply a strong tonification to GB-37 on the left and then on the right. Turn the needle clockwise until you feel *qi*, and then withdraw quickly as you seal the point with your finger. After taking the pulse to make sure the destination, in this case the gallbladder official, has been tonified, remove the carrier needles gently.

At the end of this chapter I provide several transfers for you to work through and solve to ensure you have grasped the method of transferring *qi*.

***Four-Needle Technique***

*In cases of deficiency, supplement the mother;*
*in cases of excess, reduce the child.*
– NANJING *(69th Difficult Issue)*[14]

In the five-element tradition, four-needle technique (4NT) provides a protocol for strongly tonifying or sedating the function of a specific official. Understanding the functional dynamics of this method will help you work with the fundamental principles of transferring *qi* around the *sheng* and the

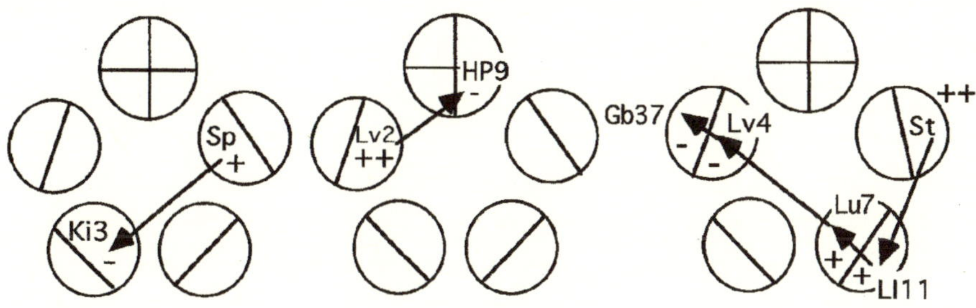


*Figure 12.6*
TRANSFERS OF *QI*

Qi *is channeled so it runs down its concentration gradient from excess to deficiency (symbolized by the plus and minus signs).*

*a. A simple transfer. A relative excess of* qi *is being channeled from the spleen official to tonify a relative deficiency of* qi *in the kidney official. In this transfer, Ki-3, the earth point on the kidney meridian, pulls* qi *across the* ke *cycle from the spleen official.*

*b. Transferring a relative excess to a deficiency around the* sheng *cycle. Here the liver official is found to be relatively excess to the heart protector official. In this scenario, two primary strategies can be employed that are not mutually exclusive. The first draws the relative excess from the liver to the heart protector by tonifying HP-9, the channel's tonification point. The second strategy sedates Lv-2, the fire and sedation point on the liver channel. Of course, both points could be treated together by sedating Lv-2 and subsequently tonifying HP-9. This strategy helps focus the dispersion of the relative excess in the liver so it supports the deficiency in the heart protector official.*

*c. A relatively more complex transfer.* Qi *is being channeled from the relatively excess stomach official to a relatively deficient gallbladder official. In such a scenario, the pulses associated with the earth element (the right middle position) may show qualities that typify stagnation of* qi *and* heat. *However, the wood pulses may show qualities such as "spreading," associated with* qi *deficiency. Acupuncture point LI-11 is the earth point and primary tonification point of the large intestine official and channels the relative excess from the stomach to the large intestine. The* luo *point of the lung, Lu-7, is then used to channel the* qi *into that official from the large intestine. The secondary tonification and metal point of the liver, Lv-4, is then used to channel the* qi *from the lung into the liver. Finally, the* luo *point on the gallbladder completes the circuit as the* qi *is drawn into the gallbladder from the liver. Such a complex transfer allows you to address the dynamics of dysfunction between any two officials with great specificity.*

*ke* cycles. Unlike the relatively simple transfers I discussed earlier, 4NT involves both tonification and sedation simultaneously in order to vigorously influence the function of an official that has not responded to simpler treatments. This technique is important because its provides access to a large array of point combinations that are useful for grounding treatments in a patient's constitutional dynamics. The point combinations that comprise the 4NT are listed in Figure 12.7. It also establishes the basis for the concept of transmitting and receiving points, covered later in this chapter.

*Tonification*

The essential strategy of tonification with 4NT is to disperse the element that controls the deficient meridian across the *ke* cycle while simultaneously tonifying the deficient meridian. For example, when tonifying the heart official, first disperse the controlling influence of the kidney. Sedate Ki-10 simultaneously with Ht-3, the water points on their respective meridians. Because Ki-10 as the channel's horary point is the transmitting point for the influence of water, sedating it simultaneously with Ht-3 diminishes the control by water of fire across the *ke* cycle.

By decreasing the controlling influence of water, the heart's fire is better able to thrive. After retaining the needles for up to forty minutes using a basic sedation technique, ascertain on the pulse that the left proximal position has

| | TONIFICATION | | SEDATION | |
|---|---|---|---|---|
| **Meridian** | **Tonify** | **Disperse** | **Disperse** | **Tonify** |
| Ht | Ht-9 Lv-1 | Ht-3 Ki-10 | Ht-7 Sp-3 | Ht-3 Ki-10 |
| SI | SI-3 Gb-41 | SI-2 Bl-66 | SI-8 St-36 | SI-2 Bl-66 |
| Bl | Bl-67 LI-1 | Bl-54 St-36 | Bl-65 Gb-41 | Bl-65 Gb-41 |
| Ki | Ki-7 Lu-8 | Ki-3 Sp-3 | Ki-1 Lv-1 | Ki-3 Sp-3 |
| HP | HP-9 Lv-1 | HP-3 Ki-10 | HP-7 Sp-3 | HP-3 Ki-10 |
| TH | TH-3 Gb-41 | TH-2 Bl-66 | TH-10 St-36 | TH-2 Bl-66 |
| Gb | Gb-43 Bl-66 | Gb-44 LI-1 | Gb-38 SI-5 | Gb-44 LI-1 |
| Lv | Lv-8 Ki-10 | Lv-4 Lu-8 | Lv-2 HP-8 | Lv-4 Lu-8 |
| Lu | Lu-9 Sp-3 | Lu-10 HP-8 | Lu-5 Ki-10 | Lu-10 HP-8 |
| LI | LI-11 St-36 | LI-5 SI-5 | LI-2 Bl-66 | LI-5 SI-5 |
| St | St-41 SI-5 | St-43 Gb-41 | St-45 LI-1 | St-43 Gb-41 |
| Sp | Sp-2 HP-8 | Sp-1 Lv-1 | Sp-5 Lu- 8 | Sp-1 Lv-1 |

*Figure 12.7*
FOUR-NEEDLE TECHNIQUE

decreased in intensity. We also expect a relative increase of intensity on the left distal position corresponding to the heart official. At this point we may then proceed by providing a strong tonification to the heart official by tonifying first Lv-1, the horary and wood point of the liver, and Ht-9, the wood point of the heart official. By decreasing the influence of water and increasing the influence of wood, the heart's fire may be strongly tonified. For the dynamics of this tonification, see Figure 12.8 (p. 208).

*Sedation*

The techniques of sedation and tonification are also applied simultaneously when using 4NT to strongly diminish the functional influence of an official. However, in this case, the points that sedate the official are dispersed and the points that empower control of the official across the *ke* cycle are tonified. Let's consider the example of using 4NT to sedate the heart official. In this case we would sedate both Sp-3 and Ht-7 together. Sedating Sp-3, the transmitting point of the earth element, in conjunction with Ht-7, the receiving point for earth on the heart channel, strongly sedates the heart official.

Monitor the pulse while retaining needles for up to forty minutes. When the heart pulse has decreased in intensity, tonify Ki-10 and Ht-3 to increase the control of the water element on the heart via the *ke* cycle. In this way, water's function of controlling fire is empowered while excess fire is dispersed. The functional dynamics of this application of 4NT are shown in Figure 12.8.

*Discussion*

Notice that the points Ki-10 and Ht-3 figure prominently when either tonifying or sedating the heart meridian using 4NT. In both cases, these points are used to either increase or decrease the influence of water in controlling the fire element across the *ke* cycle. By working through and grasping the fundamentals of 4NT for each official, you will gain the basic building blocks for treating each official in relationship to the three other officials using the element points. Hence you may use any portion of the 4NT technique to good advantage on its own in harmonizing the functional relationships among the officials.

For example, to tonify the heart official, treating Lv-1 and Ht-9 together can be quite effective. Similarly, choosing to sedate Ki-10 and H-3 on their own can help gently reduce the influence of the kidney in overcontrolling the heart without providing the stimulation of Lv-1 and Ht-9. This could be appropriate for a person whose heart's capacity for intimacy is overwhelmed by fear. In such a case a patient's anxiety and overly stressed nervous system might preclude a strongly tonifying treatment

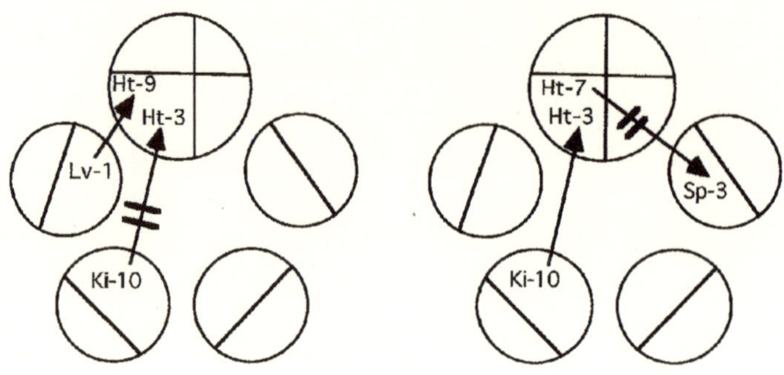


*Figure 12.8*
TREATING THE HEART OFFICIAL USING 4NT

*a. 4NT is applied to tonify the heart official. Ki-10 and Ht-3 are sedated, to mitigate the influence of the water element in controlling the fire element across the* ke *cycle. The double lines across the path of transmission from kidney to heart indicate the control of water over fire is being diminished. Then Lv-1 and Ht-9 are tonified to provide a strong boost of* qi *to support the functioning of the heart official.*

*b. 4NT is applied to sedate the functional influence of the heart. Ht-7 and Sp-3 are sedated, as indicated by double lines across the path of transmission from heart to spleen. Then Ki-10 and Ht-3 are tonified to enhance the kidney's ability to control the fire element across the* ke *cycle.*

such as Lv-1 and Ht-9. However, the gentle sedation provided by Ki-10 and Ht-3 might help revive the heart more gracefully.

Similarly, the components of 4NT that comprise sedation can be used independently. Thus Ht-7 combined with Sp-3 can offer a gentle sedation to the heart without having to add the stimulating qualities of tonifying Ki-10 and Ht-3. For a person experiencing manic-like symptoms, tonifying Ki-10 and Ht-3 can be effective to help reestablish communication between the kidney and the heart officials by empowering the functional influence of water within fire. Hence by understanding the dynamic of 4NT in relationship to the heart official, we may grasp a basic paradigm for treating the heart in relationship to the liver (Lv-1 with Ht-9), kidney (Ki-10 with Ht-3), and spleen (Ht-7 and Sp-3).

---

## *The Transmission of Virtue*

The four-needle technique forms the theoretical basis for the notion of transmitting and receiving points. It is in the paradigm of transmitting and receiving points that the holographic nature of the five-element system truly comes alive. The discussion of these points will form the basis for learning to differentiate any phenomenon and selecting two element points that resonate with its five-element dynamics. I begin with a discussion of horary points and their various functions.

### *Horary Points*

Each meridian possesses a horary point, the point with the same nature as the meridian's associated element. For example, the liver is associated with the wood element, and therefore Lv-1, the wood point on the liver meridian, is that channel's horary point. The name *horary* denotes the point's relationship to the high and low point of each channel according to the Chinese clock (see Figure 5.1). During this time, a horary point may be used in order to give an extra strong tonification or sedation to its official. In this regard, horary points are generally used when treating source points or tonification points has not served to tonify or sedate a given official sufficiently.

Horary points strongly empower the specific virtues associated with each official. Hence HP-8, a fire point on a fire meridian, is particularly effective for empowering the virtues of emotional warmth or passion as they are associated with the heart protector official. This is particularly true if treatment occurs at the time of day and seasonal peak associated with each official. For example, Lu-8, if needled between 3 and 5 A.M. on the fall equinox, would be particularly potent at empowering the virtues and functions associated with the lung official.

Horary points are also uniquely effective during the season associated with the point's elemental nature. Figure 12.9 (p. 210) lists the horary points in conjunction with their seasons. Although horary points can be used any time of year to enhance a treatment, they are particularly effective for harmonizing each person with the quality of *qi* present during his or her constitutional season. Hence treating Ki-10 on the winter solstice, at 5 P.M., on a water constitutional type, institutes an alignment between the patient's innate quality of being instilled at conception and the external movement of heaven and earth present in winter. In this way heaven within (constitution) and heaven without (the seasonal *qi*) are united.

We expect excess conditions will worsen during their associated season and deficient conditions will improve. For example, headaches associated with the gallbladder official predicated on excess are expected to worsen during the spring, and headaches based on deficiency should improve as the strength of the season tonifies the wood element within self and nature. You can use horary points during any season that contributes to functional instability. For example, if a patient becomes particularly agitated and develops insomnia every spring, Lv-1 can help harmonize his or her wood element most effectively during that season.

*Transmitting and Receiving Points*

The paradigm of transmitting and receiving points lies at the heart of the five-element system as a holographic model. Think of a horary point as a *transmitting point* capable of empowering a specific virtue associated with an official within any other official if it is needled simultaneously with an appropriate *receiving point* on another meridian. The receiving point is that point on a meridian which possesses the same elemental nature as the transmitting point. For example, a virtue associated with the liver official is self-esteem as empowered by the vision of what is fundamental in someone's life. As discussed in Chapter 31, an important point for empowering the virtue of self-esteem is Lv-1 ("great esteem"), the horary point on the liver channel. Imagine that we wished to empower the virtue of self-esteem and deep vision within the heart protector official. The appropriate points to choose according to this method would be Lv-1 as the transmitting point and HP-9, the wood point on the heart protector meridian, as the receiving point. If we wanted to empower the virtues of planning or vision within the lung official, we would choose Lv-1 and pair it with Lu-11, the wood point on the lung meridian. Generally, plan treatments so either the transmitting or receiving point is located on the patient's constitutional meridian.

***Horary Points***

| | HORARY POINTS | HIGH TIME | SEASONAL HIGH POINT |
|---|---|---|---|
| Water | Bl-66<br>Ki-10 | 3–5 P.M.<br>5–7 P.M. | Winter Solstice, December 21 |
| Wood | Gb-41<br>Lv-1 | 11 P.M.–1 A.M.<br>1–3 A.M. | Spring Equinox, March 21 |
| Fire | Ht-8<br>SI-5<br>HP-8<br>TH-6 | 11 A.M.–1 P.M.<br>1–3 P.M.<br>7–9 P.M.<br>9–11 P.M. | Summer Solstice, June 21 |
| Earth | St-36<br>Sp-3 | 7–9 A.M.<br>9–11 A.M. | Late Summer, August 21 |
| Metal | Lu-8<br>LI-1 | 3–5 A.M.<br>5–7 A.M. | Fall Equinox, September 21 |

*Figure 12.9*

HORARY POINTS, TIMES, AND SEASONS

Note that this method is not effective for transferring *qi* either by tonifying a deficiency or dispersing a relative excess. In the previous example, if liver is excess relative to the lung, treating Lv-1 in conjunction with Lu-11 will not disperse the liver or tonify the lung official. Rather this method allows you to address the functional relationship of two officials simultaneously regardless of either their *sheng* and *ke* cycle relationships or their relative state of excess or deficiency.

For example, a virtue associated with the lung official is receptivity. Patients who have suffered a traumatic loss in a relationship may have closed their heart protector in a way that leaves them no longer receptive (a characteristic of metal) to intimacy (a characteristic of fire). According to this method, you may choose to treat Lu-8 as the transmitting point and HP-5 as the receiving point, for the virtues of metal. Both Lu-8 and HP-5 are the metal points on their respective meridians. Your intention would be to empower the lung's virtue of receptivity and openness within the heart protector official. In this way the heart protector may again breathe more easily and let go of old pain to better receive joy. This point selection is depicted in Figure 12.10.

Because transmitting points are also horary points, their effect will be most powerful during the appropriate time of day and season associated with the point's element and channel. However, transmitting points can be used independently of their functions as horary points whenever we wish to integrate the functions of two different officials. Transmitting and receiving points only function between officials of the same *yin/yang* polarity. In other words, if the

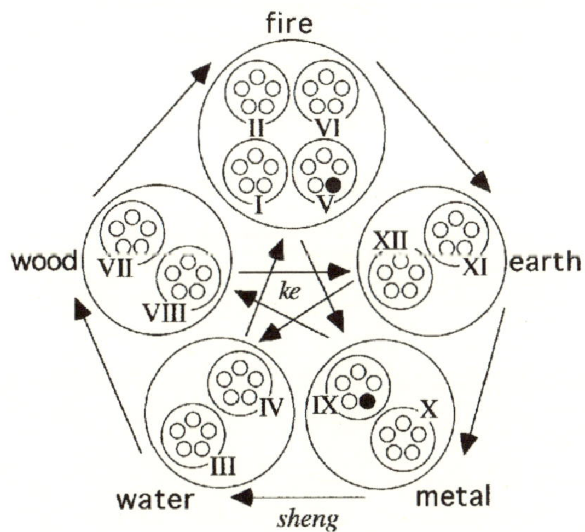


*Figure 12.10*

TRANSMITTING METAL TO FIRE

*Lu-8, metal within metal, transmits virtue to HP-5, a metal point within fire.*

transmitting point is on a *yin* channel, the receiving point must also be on a *yin* channel. This same principle holds true for the *yang* channels as well.

Note that the functionality of transmitting and receiving points figures prominently in the efficacy of 4NT. Each combination of points in 4NT uses two pairs of transmitting and receiving points. For example, consider using 4NT to sedate the liver. Here we would treat Lv-2 with HP-8 and Lu-8 with Lv-4. Sedating HP-8, the transmitting point of fire, with Lv-2, the receiving point for fire, serves to diminish greatly the presence of fire within wood. Therefore, wood will evidence less of a tendency to rapidly consume itself and cause the fire to flare up and burn out. Tonifying Lu-8, the transmitting point of metal, with Lv-4, the receiving point for metal, serves to increase greatly the presence of metal within wood and thereby extend the controlling influence of metal on wood across the *ke* cycle. By "disassembling" 4NT, we arrive at thirty-six pairs of points that can be used to increase or decrease the functional presence of one element within another utilizing the transmitting and receiving points.[15]

Each official is linked to five other officials by its element points. The possible combinations for the liver are listed in Figure 12.11. This analysis suggests that each official is capable of ten element point connections with other officials in the transmitting and receiving point paradigm. This yields a total of sixty unique two-point combinations for the twelve officials.

| Element | Transmitting | Receiving |
|---|---|---|
| Water | Ki-10 | Lv-8 |
| Wood | Lv-1 | Ht-9 |
| Wood | Lv-1 | HP-9 |
| Wood | Lv-1 | Sp-1 |
| Wood | Lv-1 | Lu-11 |
| Wood | Lv-1 | Ki-1 |
| Fire | Ht-8 | Lv-2 |
| Fire | HP-8 | Lv-2 |
| Earth | Sp-3 | Lv-3 |
| Metal | Lu-8 | Lv-4 |

*Figure 12.11*

TRANSMITTING AND RECEIVING POINT COMBINATIONS ASSOCIATED WITH THE LIVER CHANNEL

*Here are the ten possible combinations of transmitting and receiving points associated with the liver official. Extend this model to all the officials in order to attain a substantial grasp of five-element point combinations.*

I suggest you work through this model for each of the twelve officials so you understand all possible combinations of transmitting and receiving points. Of utmost importance is comprehending the quality of virtue empowered by each combination. For example, Figure 12.11 gives the combination of Ki-10 and Lv-8 for the liver official. Here the water element's virtue of grace is empowered as flexibility within the wood element. These virtues are alluded to by the name of Lv-8, "crooked spring."[16] This treatment can be appropriate any time the wood element is evidencing brittleness in any aspect of being. For example, dry skin, cracking nails, lack of physical or emotional flexibility, and being quick to anger can all be signs of the deficient presence of water within wood.

A good exercise is to imagine any aspect of being associated with a given official and how it is present implicitly within the function of every other official. Using the model of transmitting and receiving points discussed here, a point combination can be generated to address any such functional imbalance between two officials. Understanding the nature of the sixty transmitting and receiving point combinations can provide you with a potent metaphorical language and paradigm for both choosing points and discussing them with patients in a way that furthers the intention of the treatment itself.

### *Combining Element Points*

*He recovers the transgressions of many.*
*In assisting the self-becoming of all beings, he dares not act.*
– *DAODEJING, Chapter 64*[17]

*Wuwei* is a basic tenet of Daoism. It is based on the notion that in conducting affairs we should recognize the implicit direction that *qi* is flowing and impose nothing on the situation. Rather, we should try to assist the unfolding of life by aligning ourselves and others with the implicit flow of *dao* as it winds its way through life's events. Hence the role of the healer is to assist people in becoming themselves more effortlessly by helping remove the obstacles that impede their natural self-expression. The concept of *wuwei* is implicit within a basic tenet of treatment known as "the law of least action." This law tells us that the most efficacious healing is achieved with minimum invasiveness.

The theoretical pinnacle of this law applied to acupuncture would be the concept of the one-point treatment. Here a single point is utilized in a given treatment session. The point resonates so strongly with the dynamics of the patient's being that it produces a global functional change of lasting import. This theoretical ideal may not be practical in routine application, yet it can serve to help us focus our intention in treatment planning. Generally, my experience is that the more points a practitioner chooses to treat in a given session, the less firm is his or her grasp of the patient's situation. A focused treatment tends to direct *qi* clearly and concisely, whereas a treatment with many needles has a relatively low signal-to-noise ratio. That is to say, past some theoretical limit, each additional needle tends to diminish the import of the treatment's core intention.

Treating only points associated with the constitutional element can be helpful early in treatment to enable you in the beginning to discern the fidelity of your diagnosis. However, ongoing treatment often involves treating the constitutional element in relationship to the other elements and officials. I find most treatments involve treating two distal and one or two proximal points on two different meridians with possibly the addition of either a *mu* or *shu* point or a point on the conception or governing vessel. Distal points form the functional core of any treatment, and proximal points can be used to address specific issues and essentially fine-tune the treatment to capture nuances of your intention. The art of selecting element points allows you to match any treatment with a patient's five-element dynamics. Here I elaborate the possibilities of combining five-element points on any two channels to form the basis of treatment in the five-element system. Although I give specific examples of each treatment strategy here, you must work through as many combinations as possible until you grasp the essential nature of each method.

### *The* Sheng *Cycle: Mother/Child*

The mother/child relationship is of vital importance in helping harmonize the role of the constitutional elements in supporting the integrity of the *sheng* and *ke* cycles. The mother and child are conceived as any two elements in the order of *qi* flow around the *sheng* cycle. For example, the wood element is the child of water and the mother of fire. The "law of mother/child" states, "When the child is in distress, treat the mother." That is, if the mother is healthy, the child's needs will be well attended to. This law reminds us of the importance of always looking back toward the cause of an imbalance rather than merely attending to the symptoms that make the most noise.

When the constitutional element is conceived of as the mother, we often find that the next element along the *sheng* cycle, the child, tends to evidence more explicitly the signs and symptoms of imbalance. For example, if the wood element is constitutional, we often see explicit signs of imbalance in the fire element. Hence symptoms such as hypertension, heart arrhythmia, and insomnia, all manifesting in the fire element, might be secondary manifestations of an imbalance in the liver. After making a constitutional diagnosis, therefore, always consider the possibility that you have instead chosen the child, the element in most obvious distress, and look one element back on the *sheng* cycle, to the mother, as the possible constitutional source of the imbalance.

Treating the mother/child relationship in a given official with element points yields six possibilities for point selection. Figure 12.12 elaborates these in the context of treating the kidney official. To gain practice, work these relationships through for all the other officials.

*Mother/Child: Tonification*

Utilizing the first half of the tonifying protocol from 4NT, we can choose a horary point on a given meridian and combine it with the point of the same elemental quality on the meridian that follows it on the *sheng* cycle. For example, imagine the large intestine is the constitutional official. To tonify the large intestine by connecting it to earth, its "mother," we could

| | Transmitting | Receiving |
|---|---|---|
| 1 | Ki-10 | Lv-8 |
| 2 | Lu-8 | Ki-7 |
| 3 | Lv-1 | Ki-1 |
| 4 | Ki-10 | Lu-5 |
| | **Interpenetration of Function** | |
| 5 | Ki-1 | Lv-8 |
| 6 | Ki-7 | Lu-5 |

*Figure 12.12*
MOTHER/CHILD RELATIONSHIPS

*Six different point combinations are given for treating the kidney official in relationship to the lung and liver officials that precede and follow the kidney official along the* sheng *cycle. Combinations 1 and 2 derive from 4NT. Combination 1 can be used to tonify or sedate the liver, and combination 2 can be used to tonify or sedate the kidney, depending on the context of treatment. Combination 3 empowers the connection between the liver and kidney as the root and resource of life, respectively. Combination 4 can increase or decrease the functional presence of water within the lungs. Combination 5 pulls the root of wood down into water as resource (Ki-1) and stimulates the rising of resource out into the world (Lv-8). Combination 6 strengthens the functional connection between metal and water. On the one hand, the kidney is tonified to help the lungs grasp the* qi *(Ki-7), and on the other hand, the lungs are moistened (Lu-5). The notion of the interpenetration of point function is presented later.*

treat St-36, the earth point and horary point on the stomach channel, in conjunction with LI-11, the earth point on the large intestine channel.

Tonifying this combination will serve to strengthen the function of the large intestine, and sedating it will tend to decrease its function. These two points could be used as distal points in a treatment where we sought to balance the relationship between the earth and metal elements.

---

### ❖ Example: St-36, St-8, St-25, LI-11

**Analysis:** St-36 is one of the most important points for empowering us to harvest strength from the acquired constitution. The earth element provides substantial nurturance in the form of food. Harvesting the fruits of our labors effectively requires constant bending at the knee, the foundational joint where St-36 is located.

The large intestine derives nourishment for us by absorbing essence in the form of minerals while eliminating waste. In dysfunction, the metal constitutional type often compensates for lack of self-worth by seeking to fill the inner void with material possessions of increasing cost. However the material world is of transitory value, and only by reestablishing the virtue of self-worth internally can the destiny of the large intestine ever be fulfilled. Focusing obsessively on the external value of things, the large intestine may miss the intrinsic value to be gained in the process of living. In this case grief, longing, emptiness, and feelings of being alone may result as the large intestine fails to find the highest that life has to offer us.

Combining St-36 with LI-11 can help substantially to fill the emptiness we experience when the large intestine is dysfunctional. In this way we may be empowered to value the quality of nourishment available to us in life. Strengthened by the presence of its mother (earth to metal), the large intestine can empower us to value essence and to let go of stagnated pain over past loss that prevents the assimilation of what is truly of value in life. St-25, "heavenly pivot," is used here as a meeting point that unites the functions of the stomach and large intestine at the level of the umbilicus where the point is located. Earth as mother provides prenatal nourishment through the umbilicus, whereas the metal element provides inspiration from the heavenly father through connection to the essences. Hence St-25 can support the uniting of these two influences to help nourish a patient through the integration of heaven (metal) and earth.

St-8, "head tied," is used here as a point to calm the mind and quell the habitual worry to which the earth element is prone. Utilizing this point can help relax the mind enough so the stomach and large intestine can process nourishment in a way that is unconstrained by the mind's dysfunctional patterns of neediness. These points treat the exact same functional dynamics whether they are tonified or sedated, as dictated by pulse diagnosis.

*Mother/Child: Sedation*

To sedate an official, we utilize the first half of the sedation protocol from 4NT and choose the horary point on the child of the constitutional meridian. We then combine it with the point of the same elemental quality on the constitutional channel that precedes it on the *sheng* cycle. For example, let's imagine the heart protector is a patient's constitutional official. To sedate the heart protector we would sedate Sp-3, the horary and earth point of the spleen, in conjunction with HP-7, the earth point on the heart protector meridian.

By sedating the horary point of the same elemental quality as a meridian's sedation point, the overall reducing effect of the treatment is enhanced. Note that if the heart protector pulses are deficient, this combination can be tonified to increase the functional presence of earth within the fire using the paradigm of transmitting and receiving points. The presence of earth within fire can help provide a foundation for fire to burn on so it is more focused and less expansive. Hence this point combination can also be used to tonify the heart protector official.

Sp-3 and HP-7 could be used as distal points in any treatment where we seek to balance the relationship between the fire and earth elements.

---

### ❖ Example: Sp-3, Sp-16, HP-7, CV-15

**Analysis:** Like St-36, Sp-3 is a key point for helping us derive nourishment from acquired resources. A dysfunctional tendency of the heart protector is to fail to be nourished by intimate relationships. This failure can manifest as the habitual craving of intimacy that leads to endless superficial relationships or the shutting out of intimacy altogether because we never feel safe. By combining Sp-3 with HP-7, we can empower the presence of earth within the heart protector and allow it to be nourished by intimacy. This can ease the hunger of someone who habitually craves relationship, allowing the person to be more nourished by the sources of intimacy that are available to him or her. It can also help nourish a person who has shut out intimacy so he or she finds the strength to open up to it.

Sp-16, "abdomen sorrow," is an important point for healing the wound of not having been nourished in life. This is ideal for the person who, having failed to be nourished by love, has lost the appetite for life. CV-15, "spirit palace" (*shenfu*), is the *mu* point of the heart protector official.[18] As a residence of heart spirit (*shen*), CV-15 is an important point for revitalizing the spiritual essence of the heart protector. Our *shen* enables us to extend our spirit to touch others, and CV-15 may help ensure that such contact proceeds in a functional manner.

### *The* Ke *Cycle: Grandmother/Grandchild*

The grandmother/grandchild relationship always involves treating across the *ke* cycle. Hence we can choose either a transmitting or receiving point on the constitutional element and then the point of the same elemental quality on the official that either controls it, or is controlled by it, across the *ke* cycle. Treating the grandmother/grandchild relationship with element points yields six possibilities for point selection. These are listed in Figure 12.13.

#### *Tonification and Sedation Utilizing the Ke Cycle*

To either increase or decrease the functional influence of a given official, we can choose the second half of either the tonifying or sedating protocol from 4NT. In this case, the points used for tonification and sedation are

| | Transmitting | Receiving |
|---|---|---|
| 1 | Ki-10 | HP-3 |
| 2 | HP-8 | Ki-2 |
| 3 | Lu-8 | HP-5 |
| 4 | HP-8 | Lu-10 |
| | **Interpenetration of Function** | |
| 5 | HP-3 | Ki-2 |
| 6 | HP-5 | Lu-10 |

*Figure 12.13*
GRANDMOTHER/GRANDCHILD RELATIONSHIPS

*Six possibilities are listed for treating the heart protector to the elements of water and metal across the* ke *cycle. Combinations 1 and 4 are derivative of 4NT and can serve to increase or decrease the functional influence of water within fire or fire within metal, respectively. Combinations 2 and 3 can be used to increase or decrease the functional influence of fire within water or metal within fire, respectively. For example, combination 2 can draw the passion of fire into the depths to help dispel the presence of cold congruent with fear of intimacy. Combination 3 can empower the lungs' virtue of receptivity within the heart protector. Combination 5 can empower the penetration of fire into the depths (Ki-2) while allowing the wisdom of water to temper excessive passions (HP-3). And combination 6 can promote openness within the heart protector (HP-5) while simultaneously allowing fire to warm a cold and rigid metal element (Lu-10) that can keep us shut off and separate from others.*

the same. The choice of which action you take depends wholly on pulse diagnosis for an assessment of relative excess and deficiency. However, in this instance, the distinctions between excess and deficiency, and tonification and sedation, are not always so clear.

Any official can be tonified by sedating the horary point of its grandmother in conjunction with the point of the same elemental quality on its own meridian (see examples 1 and 4 in Figure 12.13). By utilizing element points in this way, we are able to inhibit the controlling influence of the grandmother element so the child may thrive. For example, if the liver is deficient relative to the lung, the lung may be overcontrolling the liver across the *ke* cycle. In this case, sedating the horary point of the lung (Lu-8) with Lv-4, the metal point on the liver meridian, will reduce the lung's overcontrol of the liver.

But if the liver is hyperfunctioning, tonifying Lu-8 and Lv-4 can increase the lung's control of the liver and thus help rein in the liver's dysfunctional tendency toward excessive growth. Note, however, that tonifying these two points can also tonify the liver in certain circumstances. For example, a plant may fail to thrive for lack of minerals that serve as nutrients. Similarly, plans may fail because of a lack of internal structure and value empowered by the metal element. By increasing the presence of metal within wood, it is thus possible to strengthen the liver.

If the presence of metal within wood is excessive, growth may not proceed in a healthy fashion because people always feel "cut down" whenever they branch out and choose a new direction in life. Hence sedating Lu-8 and Lv-4 can decrease the presence of metal within wood in a way that actually strengthens the liver's function in promoting healthy growth. The fact that the very same points can have either a tonifying or sedating effect given the same and differing needle techniques, and depending on the context of the treatment, emphasizes the importance of not resorting to formulaic prescriptions of points. Always select every point based on the unique merits of the situation at hand.

---

❖ **Example:** Lu-8, Lu-1, Lv-4, Lv-14

**Analysis:** Lu-8 is the metal and thus the horary point of the lung meridian. The point's name, "meridian gutter," alludes to the lung's function of maintaining purity by empowering receptivity to essence and exhalation of what is impure. It is this very function on which the virtue of self-worth is based. The liver governs planning by empowering a deep vision of our life's plan as contained in *jing*. Our ability to grow this plan into the world with fidelity is the foundation of self-esteem. Lv-4, "middle seal," addresses the relationship of metal within wood and the relationship between self-worth and self-esteem.

If the lungs become obsessed with purity, they may inhibit growth by leading us to find fault with every direction we take in life. Conversely, if we value our own ideals excessively, we may be willing to force our values and goals belligerently on others. By helping balance the relationship between our values (metal) and plans (wood), Lv-4 can help ensure that growth proceeds smoothly in a way governed by the virtues of benevolence (wood) and righteousness (metal).

The liver is responsible for helping detoxify the blood, and Lv-4 can support this function by empowering the lungs' virtue of purity within the liver official. Lv-14, "gate of hope," is the exit point on the liver meridian governing the virtue of aspiration. It is the *mu* point of the liver and supports unconstricted breathing by releasing anger and constraint stored in the diaphragm. Lv-14 and Lu-1 comprise the exit/entry combination between the liver and the lungs and further contribute to the healthy integration of the functions of these two organs.

Lu-1 is the *mu* point on the lung meridian and plays an important role in tonifying the *yin* and receptive qualities of the lungs while helping regulate the rhythm of breathing by strengthening the *zongqi.* This is a strong point for empowering the influence of heaven within us as it is received through breath.

With this point combination we have touched the virtue of metal inherent in Lu-8 and transmitted it to the wood element by treating Lv-4. We have then opened the connection between liver and lung with the exit/entry combination of Lv-14 and Lu-1. This combination of points can be either tonified or sedated to address the same issues, depending on the context of the individual treatment and patient.[19]

*The Grandchild/Grandmother Relationship*

Sometimes it is effective to treat the horary point on a given meridian with the point of the same elemental quality on its grandmother. For example, we could treat Sp-3, the channel's earth and horary point, in conjunction with Lv-3. In this case, either the spleen or the liver could be the constitutional official. Note that in this example, as contrasted with the one earlier, we are treating "backward" across the *ke* cycle from earth to wood. This treatment has the effect of either increasing or decreasing the presence of earth within the wood element. Earth both nurtures and stabilizes growth by both providing nutrients and grounding a plant's root structure. If the presence of earth within wood is deficient, growth may suffer due to lack of both nurturance and stability.

Sympathy, the emotion of earth, may be empowered within wood by treating Lv-3. In this way, wood's tendency toward belligerence can be tempered. This function is alluded to by the name of Lv-3, "happy calm."[20] The nurturance of earth is embodied within us as blood. The spleen creates blood and the liver must store and cleanse the blood. Treating Sp-3 and Lv-3 together is thus an effective way to promote both the quality and quantity of blood and empower it to support luxuriant growth.

A function of earth is to nourish wood so it may grow as it is directed from within by heaven's plan. On occasion this means sending out branches that will not yield fruit in order to test the possibility of growth in a new direction. If the presence of earth within wood is excessive, it may smother healthy growth in the same way that excessively coddling children can keep them from learning their own lessons in life. Hence if earth is counterattacking wood across the *ke* cycle, Lv-3 and Sp-3 can be sedated in order to diminish the influence of the spleen on the liver.

---

### ❖ Example: Sp-3, Sp-21, Lv-3, Lv-13

**Analysis:** Sp-3 and Lv-3 are treated together to help support the development of blood as it nurtures healthy growth. The liver is said to correspond to vision and to nourish the eyes. Hence the blood of the liver may be said to nourish our deep view of self that corresponds to self-esteem.[21] The presence of self-esteem indicates that the liver's virtue of benevolence is being manifested toward one's self.

Sp-3 and Lv-3 are source points on their respective meridians. Hence both points serve to ground and orient the overall functioning of their respective officials through connection to a primordial source of *qi*. Sp-21, "great enveloping," empowers the feeling of being embraced by life as though by the unconditional love of one's mother. The feeling of nurturance from within empowered by the selection of Sp-3 and Lv-3 is nicely complemented by the addition of Sp-21. In this way we may experience life around us as being unconditionally nourishing.

Lv-13, "chapter gate," is the *mu* point of the spleen and thus a meeting point of the liver and spleen officials. Helping ease constraint that inhibits growth, Lv-13 can balance the functions of these two officials so we are nourished during the process of our growth and not overly constrained by direction toward our goals. As we move through this gate we can open a new chapter in life.

### *The Interpenetration of Function*

The Chinese character *tong* (通) can denote the idea of two things being interpenetrated to the degree that only one thing is present. Complementary element points can be simultaneously needled within two officials to promote clear communication between them and effectively join their functions together.

### *The* Sheng *Cycle*

We can treat successive elements along the *sheng* cycle by needling in combination the element point of each within the other. For example, Ki-1, the channel's wood point, can be paired with Lv-8, the water point on the liver channel. This may be likened to helping a tree extend its roots into the depths to tap potential while at the same time helping it channel that potential into the world to promote growth. Similarly, we might join the function of Lv-2 with HP-9. In this way the influence of fire is increased within the wood (Lv-2), helping it burn while at the same time replenishing the presence of wood within fire (HP-9). Selecting such combinations as distal points can be particularly effective as one season changes into the next. The example just presented, therefore, can be most effective for strengthening the functional relationship between wood and fire elements as spring becomes summer.

### *The* Ke *Cycle*

The same strategy can be used in combining element points across the *ke* cycle. I consider this method similar to the herbal concept of astringing the relationship between two organs. Astringing suggests the creation of a clear, firm channel between two elements and officials that promotes open communication between them.[22] For example, we might choose to treat Ki-2, the fire point on water, and Ht-3, the water point on fire, simultaneously. In effect, we are strengthening the heart/kidney axis and allowing for the interpenetration of water and fire. This method is particularly effective on either the winter or summer solstice when treating a person who is either water or fire constitutionally.

Theoretically, a person has just one element that corresponds to his or her constitutional type. In clinical practice, however, some people have a second element that continually needs to be treated as well. For example, I have seen patients whose constitution seems to fluctuate back and forth between water and fire. Treating them on kidney will be effective for a period of time until I need to switch my emphasis to treating their fire element. The strategy discussed earlier of treating Ki-2 and Ht-3 together can help the two elements maintain functional contact with each other in a way that promotes greater stability to the constitutional dynamic defined by the two elements.

In the point combination of Ki-2 and Ht-3, Ki-2 treats the fire within water and helps fuel the flames of *mingmen* and draw consciousness (*shen*) into the depths. Ht-3, the water point within fire, can help keep the fire from burning out of control and depleting inner resources. I have used this treatment effectively with patients possessing a disharmony of the water and fire elements and who have a psychiatric diagnosis of bipolar disorder (formerly called manic depression). Such a treatment has also proven beneficial in some patients with seasonal affective disorder (SAD).

---

## *The Holographic Nature of the Five Elements*[23]

Each of the twelve officials possesses a unique function, yet the function of each official is implicit within all others. The interpenetration of function represented in the five-element chart (see Figure 12.2) is present and accessible in the relationship of the five-element points associated with each meridian. Here I elaborate how the function of the liver official is present within each of the other *yin* officials. For each relationship I specify a combination of transmitting and receiving points that addresses the functional dynamic of the two officials. These distinctions can serve as a template for you to work through every possible interrelationship of function according to the *sheng* and *ke* cycles.

**I.** The heart depends on the function of the liver for its penetrating insight and wisdom. In order to perform ritual effectively, the heart must be in constant touch with heaven's plan as it exists for us both externally and internally. This dynamic is contained in the transmitting and receiving point combination of Lv-1 and Ht-9.

**II.** The heart protector depends on the vision empowered by the liver so it may accurately discern which external events signify safety and which signify danger. The heart protector must be in touch with the inner plan so it may assess accurately the degree to which all relationships are congruent with true self. This dynamic is contained in the transmitting and receiving point combination of Lv-1 and HP-9.

**III.** The spleen depends on the function of the liver so it can embrace the vision of what constitutes nourishment, empowering us to embody the virtues of integrity and reciprocity. This is accomplished by comparing external sources of nourishment and opportunities for giving with our internal needs as present in the plan held by the liver. This dynamic is contained in the transmitting and receiving point combination of Lv-1 and Sp-1.

**IV.** The lungs' functions of receptivity and the ability to let go of what no longer serves are empowered by a healthy and fully functioning liver. By comparing the necessity of our real and desired possessions with the dictates of heaven's deep inner plan for us, we may be empowered to let go of what is inessential. In this way we may be open to receiving heaven's inspiration that may truly nourish our destiny. This dynamic is contained in the transmitting and receiving point combination of Lv-1 and Lu-11.

V. The kidney must empower the appropriate utilization of resources in accordance with our vision of the inner plan. The liver may be likened to a tree that sends down roots to tap the inner resources of the kidney official and bring them out into the world. This dynamic is contained in the transmitting and receiving point combination of Lv-1 and Ki-1.

### *Transmitting and Receiving Points on the* Sheng *and* Ke *Cycles*

The practice of five-element acupuncture is grounded in the understanding and application of the functional relationships contained in the *sheng* and *ke* cycles.[24] These basic relationships, as they are extended to the application of the five "element points" on each meridian, serve as the foundation of practice in the five-element system. Once grasped, the five-element model extends past the mere practice of healing to become embodied in every facet of our life experience. In essence, the five elements come to tint the window that we see life through and their dynamic expression is seen in all we experience.

Here I examine the fundamental relationships of the *sheng* and the *ke* cycles. The points that govern these relationships are listed as they are derived from 4NT. I discuss some general attributes for the quality of relationship between each elemental pair. Differentiate these general principles to understand how they might apply to each pair of transmitting and receiving points listed at the head of each section. For elaboration of these principles, look up the individual points in Part IV.

### *The* Sheng *Cycle*

The *sheng* cycle is the process by which the elements create each other. Proceeding in the order of the seasons, the *sheng* cycle is a qualitative standard against which the relative state of progression of all phenomena may be assessed. The functional integrity of the *sheng* cycle is imperative if the five elements within us are to manifest continually the evolutionary flow of life. If the flow of *qi* around the *sheng* cycle is disturbed, the entire integrity of the functional relationships among the officials will be compromised. Here I examine the five *sheng* cycle relationships as they pertain to the function of the elements and element points on their respective meridians.

*Water to Wood*

| Transmitting | Receiving |
|---|---|
| Ki-10 | Lv-8 |
| Bl-66 | Gb-43 |

*Careful, like crossing a river in winter,*
*Hesitating, like fearing neighbors on four sides,*
*Reverent, like being guests,*
*Dissolving, like ice beginning to melt,*
*Thick, like uncarved wood,*
*Open, like a valley,*
*Chaotic, like murky water.*
*What can stop the murkiness?*
*Quieting down, gradually it clarifies.*
*What can keep still for long?*
*Moving, gradually it stirs to life.*
*Those who keep this Dao,*
*Do not want to be filled to the full.*
*Because they are not full,*
*They can renew themselves before being worn out.*

– DAODEJING, *Chapter 15*[25]

During winter, growth exists only as the potential that incubates within the seed of the earth. Our potential for all possible manifestations during life is stored by the water element as our inherited endowment of *jing.* The function of the wood element as it exists within us is to send roots into our depths and tap our reserves, manifesting them in the flourishing growth of our outermost branches. Cut off from access to the depths of self, growth cannot proceed in a way that reflects our innate purpose. But if we push ourselves in order to grow more rapidly, we will tend to deplete our reserves prematurely and become worn out.

*Wood to Fire*

| Transmitting | Receiving |
|---|---|
| Lv-1 | Ht-9 |
| Lv-1 | HP-9 |
| Gb-41 | SI-3 |
| Gb-41 | TH-3 |

As water is the resource that sustains the healthy expression of wood, wood is the source of fuel that sustains fire. It is imperative for growth to occur in a balanced fashion if our efforts are gently to empower the opening of our hearts. Wood engenders the virtue of aspiration that drives us toward our goals as a plant strives toward the sun. The heart opening at the peak of life as a result of our efforts can be likened to the blossoming of flowers as summer approaches.

If wood is overly constrained and forces growth, we may never feel the joy that comes from attaining our goals. Never satisfied for long, we continually push toward new accomplishments and never take the time to rest. In this scenario, we may burn out as life becomes a joyless struggle. If the expression of wood is deficient within fire, we may not strive at all and appear hopeless. Resignation and depression often signify that wood and fire have lost functional contact as we fail to embrace the virtue of aspiration in all aspects of life.

*Fire to Earth*

| Transmitting | Receiving |
|---|---|
| Ht-8 | Sp-2 |
| HP-8 | Sp-2 |
| SI-5 | St-41 |
| TH-6 | St-41 |

We can liken the functional relationship between the fire and earth element to that of heat to cooking. The stomach and spleen officials essentially have to cook all potential sources of nurturance taken in during life so their essence can be assimilated as nourishment. If the fire within earth is deficient, the ability to be nourished by our life experiences can suffer. For lack of fire, what we ingest maybe turned into a burden in the form of dampness, instead of being transformed into blood, muscle, and a strong center predicated on integrity. If fire within the earth is excessive, our appetites will tend to be driven by habituated desire. In this case we may never be sated, regardless of how much we consume.

*Earth to Metal*

| Transmitting | Receiving |
|---|---|
| Sp-3 | Lu-9 |
| St-36 | LI-11 |

The earth element provides our connection to substantive nourishment and enables us to renew our body's resources. The metal element inspires our connection to heaven and to essential nourishment. These two influences must exist in balance so we humans can be nourished between heaven and earth. If earth is deficient within metal, we can lack a substantial center and too easily let go of what is of value in life. In this case we may be inspired by our ideals yet appear to others as though we do not have our feet on the ground. If the presence of earth within metal is excessive, we may feel uninspired and bogged down by worldly considerations. Hence the presence of dampness can obscure both the lungs' and large intestine's ability to abstract nourishment from life.

*Metal to Water*

| Transmitting | Receiving |
|---|---|
| Lu-8 | Ki-7 |
| LI-1 | Bl-67 |

In the *sheng* cycle, the transition from metal to water is the most crucial to perpetuating life. For it is at this juncture that our destiny hangs by a thread. The transition from metal to water is the turning point when we are given the opportunity to travel deep within to discover our original nature. If this opportunity is missed and the functional link between metal and water is broken, the dissolution of our life force begins as it returns "back into the mysterious workings of things." Hence the transition of metal to water plays an important role in the genesis of the husband/wife imbalance (see Chapter 4).

The points that strengthen the functional link between metal and water, Ki-7 and Bl-67, are crucial to perpetuating life by keeping *qi* flowing around the *sheng* cycle. Both these points figure prominently in breaking the husband/wife imbalance and resurrecting the will. If the presence of metal within water is excessive, unbalanced inspiration can drive us to deplete our resources. Always keeping busy can be a way of avoiding deep contact both with others and with ourselves.

### *The* Ke *Cycle*

Whereas the *sheng* cycle reflects the process by which the elements create each other, the *ke* cycle reflects the process by which the elements control each other. Harmony around the *ke* cycle is vital to promoting balanced function among all the elements and officials. In health, the elements control each other in a way that empowers each element's freedom of expression, yet prevents any element from becoming either excess or deficient relative to the others. For example, in health, if the presence of the fire element started to become relatively excess, the water element would spontaneously control the fire across the *ke* cycle and thus prevent its function from blazing out of control. Here I examine the five *ke* cycle relationships as they pertain to the function of the elements. Try and extrapolate these relationships to the functions of the element points on their respective meridians.

*Water to Fire*

| Transmitting | Receiving |
|---|---|
| Ki-10 | Ht-3 |
| Ki-10 | HP-3 |
| Bl-66 | SI-2 |
| Bl-66 | TH-2 |

Water represents the seed of potential for all of life's varied manifestations. It is the potential within this seed that ultimately limits its expression at the peak of its life, which is represented by fire. Hence the nature of innate constitution present in the acorn implicitly sets the limit on the quality of the oak tree that the seed may produce, given even the most favorable environment. The relative balance of wisdom and fear, the virtue and emotion associated with the water element, regulates the opening and closing of our heart and governs the degree of intimacy that we are capable of experiencing. If the presence of water within fire is excessive, it can be hard to experience joy because life always seems to "rain on our parade." If the presence of water is deficient, fire can blaze out of control, inevitably burning out.

*Wood to Earth*

| Transmitting | Receiving |
|---|---|
| Lv-1 | Sp-1 |
| Gb-41 | St-43 |

Wood controls the earth element in the same way the roots of plants can control the erosion of a hillside by holding it firmly in place. When wood and earth are in healthy relationship, they empower a functional balance between directional growth (wood) and the stability of our centers (earth). If the presence of wood within earth is excessive, our process of being nourished in life can be constrained just as a root-bound plant slowly strangles itself. If the presence of wood within is deficient, our centers can erode for lack of containment.

*Fire to Metal*

| Transmitting | Receiving |
|---|---|
| Ht-8 | Lu-10 |
| HP-8 | Lu-10 |
| SI-5 | LI-5 |
| TH-6 | LI-5 |

The relationship of fire to metal is illustrated in the alchemical transformation of lead, signifying mundane consciousness, into gold, signifying illuminated awareness. Compassion as governed by fire must be in perfect balance with the metal element's virtue of righteousness in order for justice to be served. The lungs and large intestine are mucous membranes that depend on moisture to regulate the interface they create between us and the external world. If the presence of fire within metal is excessive, these officials can become dry and fail to conduct essence inward. If the presence of fire within metal is deficient, water can accumulate because dampness can also obstruct the assimilation of essence.

*Earth to Water*

| Transmitting | Receiving |
|---|---|
| Sp-3 | Ki-3 |
| St-36 | Bl-54 (40) |

Forming the banks of a river, earth contains and channels water as a resource so its influence is nourishing and life supporting. Without the control of the earth, the water element can flood fields and destroy the crops in the same way our fears and ambitions can become overwhelming both to ourselves and others. If the presence of earth within water is excessive, the flow of water can be impeded as our potential is smothered and fails to manifest.

*Metal to Wood*

| Transmitting | Receiving |
|---|---|
| Lu-8 | Lv-4 |
| LI-1 | Gb-44 |

The relationship of metal to wood is one of both nourishment and limitation. On the one hand, minerals can support a plant from within and give it a strong internal structure necessary for healthy growth. On the other hand, metal can come to wood from without in the form of pruning shears. Pruning can limit growth, enabling it to proceed more fruitfully. If the presence of metal within wood is deficient, plants tend to be rather poor in quality. For lack of pruning, a plant tends to channel its limited resources into excessive growth and yield abundant fruit of diminished quality. If the presence of metal within wood is excessive, quality can also suffer as the plant is cut from within as if it were burned by the use of excessive fertilizer. Self-righteousness, a dysfunctional quality of being associated with metal, can limit our ability to plan by constraining growth in self and in others.

---

## *Differentiating Clinical Reality According to the Five Elements*

Here I guide you to an understanding of the holographic nature of the five-element model. When we finally grasp this model, we may comprehend experientially that everything that exists is present as an implicit representation within everything else that exists. The steps inherent in this exercise are elaborated in Figure 12.14.

First, think of some aspect of being that is essential to human nature as a virtue and, conversely, how it might be dysfunctionally expressed as a pathology. For example, a virtue of the heart is to acknowledge and communicate truth compassionately into the world. The dysfunctional expression of this capacity is lying. After identifying a given continuum of virtue and vice, differentiate its expression within each element and official. Once these relationships become clear, you can choose points that precisely touch this underlying dynamic as it is expressed uniquely within the patient. Here I differentiate the continuum of truth and lying according to the five-element model. I then differentiate several other aspects of being and how they are uniquely expressed through each of the five elements.

### *Virtue and Vice: The Acknowledgment and Denial of Truth*

A central function of the heart is to acknowledge the essential nature of self as it is stored in *jing* and to communicate this with fidelity into the world through speech and action that conveys truth. The heart's courage to be truthful with self and others is in large part based on feelings of safety in accordance with healthy boundaries established by the other fire officials. Safety is defined here as the context in which the heart may thrive. When boundaries function appropriately, we feel safe letting others

1. Discern the aspect of being you are differentiating.
2. How is it present as a strength and as a weakness?
3. Differentiate the aspect of being according to how it is present through the window of each of the five elements.
4. Choose a point combination that precisely reflects this dynamic in each patient.

*Figure 12.14*
DIFFERENTIATING BEING

know what is in our heart. This truth shines through the eyes as light reflecting the integrity of the fire burning in *mingmen.* Such light radiates as joy and compassion into the world and represents the spirit of the authentic self.

At the moment of losing original nature, the created self is conceived as a compensatory mechanism so the heart can survive in this world. The outer officials of the fire element help establish ego structures and defenses so the child's heart is less damaged by traumatic events in life. The created self is a lie, however, that does not reflect the original nature and potential virtues stored in *jing.*

As children grow into adults, they come only to know the self their mind has created as memory of true self slowly fades. Hence the fire element lies by wearing a mask in the world to protect the true self. The inner nature of this lie is not necessarily known consciously to the liar. This foundational lie serves to hide the memory of true self and the pain of its loss from conscious awareness. Externally, however, people learn how to hide their feelings with a smile and to feign joy, always telling themselves that others cannot see the pain in their heart. Hence the fire element can be said to govern the virtue of insight into true nature as well as the vice of lying and misrepresenting truth to both self and others. Now let's examine how these virtues and vices associated with the fire element express themselves through the other elements.

Here I elaborate point combinations using the concept of transmitting and receiving points that address how lying manifests through the dysfunctional expression of each element. You must understand that these are archetypal point selections for the issue at hand. Any group of points that serves to improve the function of an official would help empower the transformation of vice into virtue.

*Water*

The nature of water is that it contains true self in its depths in the form of *jing.* The virtue of water is wisdom, and it is the nature of *jing* to empower the development of wisdom as we learn to transcend our fears in life. If the influence of fire is dysfunctional within the water element, lying takes the form of secrecy as fear and ambition compel us to withhold information. The virtue of wisdom is distorted into the talent of cleverness as vital information is always held in reserve. When speaking to such a person, we sense an underlying current in each interaction suggestive of another agenda as the manipulative power seeker tries to assert ambition surreptitiously. The withholding of water expressed as lying is an expression of our failure to manifest destiny (bring truth into the world) in a way presided over by grace and empowered by *jing.*

Transmitting point: **Ht-8**
Receiving point: **Ki-2**

**Analysis:** Ht-8 is treated in conjunction with Ki-2 as the transmitting and receiving points for fire, respectively. This combination can empower the illumination of fire within the depths of water. Fire within water can help thaw the cold ambition that propagates secrecy.

*Wood*

The virtue of wood is to empower benevolence and justice in the world by allowing flexibility in applying standards based on the unique merits of each situation. Telling the truth for wood involves clear communication by the gallbladder of the liver's plan into the world through enlightened decision making. The virtue of flexibility is evidenced as the willingness to compromise while keeping our sights firmly on our goal. The habituated mind of wood lies by justifying the notion that the ends justifies the means. Dysfunctional wood fixates on a goal and is able to rationalize any means to attain its end to the point of perpetrating atrocities in the world in the name of justice.

Transmitting point: **Ht-8**
Receiving point: **Lv-2**

**Analysis:** When wood burns too intensely, it can become belligerent and overly determined in pursuit of justice. There are no measures too extreme to exact the toll that it deems necessary to rectify perceived inequities. Empowering the heart's compassion and insight within the wood element can help mitigate its burning passion for justice and help empower flexibility and compromise in reaching its goals.

*Earth*

The dysfunctional earth element leads us to lie through ingratiating behavior. The virtue of earth is integrity (*xin*), which implies a congruency between what a person thinks, says, and does. The sin of the earth element is ingratiation, which involves habitually hiding true feelings in an effort to win sympathy by dysfunctionally taking care of others. Lying in this way results in swallowing resentment, which often builds to eventually cause feelings of tightness and obstruction in the throat. Such plum pit *qi* is congruent with our lack of honest communication.

Transmitting point: **Ht-8**
Receiving point: **Sp-2**

**Analysis:** Often the main motivation behind ingratiation is pleasing people in order to be loved. Earth types smile and says "yes" when they should be saying "no." By taking care of others instead of self, sources of nourishment in life are eventually turned into burdens. This is most evident in a disease such as diabetes in which food is attained and eaten yet the nourishment cannot enter the cells. Such a person gives the impression of having gotten plenty of bread in life but little or no honey. By empowering the fire within the earth element, we may be better able to assimilate nourishment and to convey the heart's insight into the true nature of our needs into the world with integrity through speech and action.

*Metal*

Metal lies by misrepresenting the value of things. The virtue of metal is righteousness (*yi*), which may be distorted into the belief that we are closest to heaven and all nonbelievers are tainted. Hence a dysfunctional metal element tends to lead us toward fanaticism and to misrepresent spiritual teachings as justifying our own self-righteous behavior.

Transmitting point: **Ht-8**
Receiving point: **Lu-10**

**Analysis:** The tendency of metal is to become cold and piercing when inspiration untempered by compassion turns to zealotry. The truth without compassion is meaningless and can manifest as a coldhearted and self-righteous attitude. By empowering the presence of fire within metal, the metal may inspire the flow of open awareness and allow us to be receptive and appreciate the essence of heaven that lies at the center of all true spiritual teachings. In this way the specific form of the teachings that touch us can be let go of so we may better embody their essential truths.

***Differentiating the Concept of Boundary***

Each of the five elements empowers boundary from its own unique perspective. Here I elaborate each element's contribution to differentiating self from other. In this exercise I have not selected points to treat each element. Rather I have just given one example in my discussion of the wood element. I suggest you generate a unique point combination that addresses each element's contribution to the establishment of a healthy boundary.

*The Water Element as Boundary*

Water is unique in its ability to consume completely anything it comes into contact with. Water controls fire across the *ke* cycle, and it is often our fear (water) that limits the opening and closing of our heart and our capacity for intimacy (fire). Fear, the emotion paired with water, can be all consuming as we become literally frozen in life, unable to draw on our inner potential or move in any direction. As an iceberg separates from the water around it, fear may freeze and thus isolate any part of the body. For example, a woman who has experienced sexual abuse may embody subsequent fear of intimacy in her pelvis and thus become cold and infertile. Similarly, our digestion can suffer if we embody fear in a way that leads to stagnation of cold in the middle burner. In these examples, fear perpetuates separation.

At the other end of the spectrum, water represents the dissolution of all boundaries. For water is both the source and final resting place of all being. It is the water element within each person that empowers us to feel the dissolution of self as we merge with all of creation in the act of meditation and contemplation. The apparent separateness of the iceberg is actually an illusion, for there is a constant exchange between the ocean and iceberg at their interface. In essence, our human experience of being separate from some imagined "outside" world is an illusion. For we are an integral part of the very ocean of *qi* in which we are floating.

*The Wood Element as Boundary*

The wood element contributes to our defenses by empowering the vision of how external phenomena are aligned with our own internal plan. The liver detoxifies the blood and in this way helps protect us from pathogens. This detoxification of the blood assures a congruency between who we are in our template and what we incorporate into ourselves from the exterior.

A healthy, well-functioning liver empowers the natural expression of self-esteem. The virtue of self-esteem is present in a person's ability to stand up for whatever roots him or her into reality. Hence self-esteem regulates our boundary relative to how much we are willing to compromise in any given situation. If self-esteem is eroded, vigilance and anger can represent an attempt by the liver to keep others away and prevent them from influencing our agenda. Hence the wood element tends to establish boundary by drawing a "line in the dirt." "You can come this far but no further without transgressing the point at which I will act belligerently to defend my plans and decisions."

We may address the way the virtue of self-esteem contributes to the appropriate functioning of human boundary by treating the wood point on any meridian. For example, a patient might manifest poorly functioning boundaries related to lowered self-esteem. This, in turn, could compromise the ability to choose an appropriate partner with whom to have an intimate relationship. In this scenario, we might treat Lv-1 ("great esteem") in combination with HP-9 ("rushing into the middle"), the transmitting and receiving points of the wood element, respectively.

*The Fire Element as Boundary*

I have discussed the relationship of the fire officials to establishing human boundaries at length.[26] The functioning of the fire officials establishes four levels of defense from the outermost frontier in life to the inner world of the heart. We may liken the small intestine to the minister who stands outside the imperial chamber to convey essential communication into the emperor (the heart) and from the emperor to the outside world. Hence the small intestine serves to shield the emperor from mundanity so he can attend only to the affairs of heaven.

The heart protector official is like the keeper of the castle gate who must discern who is allowed to enter or leave the inner domain of the emperor. In this way the heart protector official governs human boundaries by regulating intimacy. Imagine the three heater as a fire that surrounds each individual and burns away pathogenic *qi* before it approaches the inner realms of function afforded by the other fire officials. Hence we can think of the three heater like the guard station at the great wall of China concerned with deciding who is allowed to enter or leave the country. In this regard, the three heater contributes to our defensive boundary known as *weiqi* that surrounds us as our first line of defense against exogenous attack.

*The Earth Element as Boundary*

For the first nine months of life, the fetus is tied to the mother by the umbilicus and completely dependent on her for nourishment through this connection. During this period the mother and fetus exist as one in what is ideally a symbiotic relationship. At birth when the umbilical cord is severed, the child's ability to gather nourishment shifts from belly to mouth. Still dependent on the mother, the infant suckles at her breast to receive all earthly nourishment. The quality of connection with the mother during gestation and breastfeeding can set the theme for the functional balance of the child's ability to nourish both self and others throughout life. Hence the earth element contributes to our boundary by establishing a healthy balance in our relationship to giving, receiving, and the fulfillment of others' needs as well as our own. This boundary is reflected in the nature of the virtues of integrity (*xin*) and reciprocity (*shu*) as they are associated with the earth element.[27]

*The Metal Element as Boundary*

It is said the lungs govern the defensive *qi* (*weiqi*) that serves as the shield which surrounds and protects us from external pathogens. A tendency of the metal constitutional type is to "cut off" in a way that establishes a "cold steel wall" around self so the person feels impenetrable by human contact. This hardness is often a defense mechanism secondary to the failure of the *weiqi* to protect us in a healthy, balanced fashion. Ideally, the lungs empower us to bring quality into our life while simultaneously filtering out all pernicious influences. In dysfunction the lungs may stop receiving altogether in a vain attempt to isolate us from the outside world.

The boundary established by the lungs and large intestine is mediated by moisture. When something is in these organs, it is, in effect, not within us until it is absorbed through their membranes into the blood. In this way the metal element creates a boundary concerned with maintaining our internal purity.

### *Differentiating the Cycles*

As *qi* flows around the *sheng* cycle and the seasons change within us, each element empowers some aspect of life's cycle. Here I differentiate the concept of cycles according to the five elements. Consider the implications of this material to the functioning of the five-element points.

#### *The Rhythm of Water*

> *The man of wisdom perceives calamity or good fortune*
> *when it is still remote, and understands what is beneficial*
> *or harmful when it is still early— . . . Seeing a beginning*
> *he knows what its end will be.*
> – *DONG ZHONGSHU*[28]

Each of the five elements has a rhythm to its expression that reflects a fundamental property of the endless cycling of *dao*. The rhythm of water possesses two beats that define the destiny of each human being. These moments of time reflect the conception and death of each thing that comes into existence. Life is turned on and off at its source like a stream that thaws and begins to flow in early spring and then ceases upon freezing again in winter. In between the points of conception and death, the flow of the water element must, through expenditure of the kidney's *jing,* lubricate all developmental processes in our being to assure they unfold gracefully.

Dong Zhongshu describes the vision of destiny empowered by the healthy presence of the water element, which represents the *dao* as the ultimate origin and destination of all things. The inherited constitution sets the limit on all that is capable of unfolding in our life from conception to death. The sage must be in contact with and acknowledge the quality and quantity of all available resources throughout life so these may be used wisely to empower the fulfillment of destiny.

*The Rhythm of Wood*

The rhythm of wood is qualitatively different from each of the other five elements in that it is continuous with no beat. The wood element ensures that life never proceeds in a circle but always in an upward evolutionary spiral. Hence the rhythm of wood is a continuous streaming that never falters, joining each moment to the next in the endless progression of all things toward heaven.

The circles found in a cross section of a tree are composed of channels known as phloem and xylem. These channels ensure that the tips of the outermost branches and the deepest root are joined in a way that promotes healthy growth. It is this connection that allows the growing branch to be always connected to the deepest root when discerning its direction. Similarly, the function of the wood element is to empower, through the virtue of benevolence, the interpenetration of the deepest aspects of self (*jing*) with the outermost radiation of our branches (*shen*).

*The Rhythm of Fire*

Fire governs the moment-to-moment presence in life reflected in the steady beating of the heart. Any deviation in the rhythm, rate, or intensity of the pulse speaks directly to the quality of our momentary presence governed by the fire element. Historically, a pulse that was either too rapid or too slow was thought to reflect the presence of either heat or cold, respectively. However, people in affluent cultures today are not subjected to such harsh environmental conditions as they were in the past. Unless there is compelling evidence to the contrary, any deviation of the pulse rate from normal must be considered a result of either a physical (e.g., car accident) or emotional (perceived betrayal such as rape, incest, or divorce) shock that impacted the integrated functioning of the fire officials.

*The Rhythm of Earth*

The cycle of the seasons around the earth creates a continuous rhythm that empowers humanity to find stability through all of life's changes. Hence Chen notes that the character *xin* (信), the virtue of earth, is connected in its meaning to the regularity and rhythm of life that inspires confidence in nature and the stability of humanity's place in the world.[29]

*The Rhythm of Metal*

The breath of *dao,* as described in Chapters 4 and 5 in the *Daodejing,* is a "whirling vortex," a great inhaling and exhaling that gives rise to all creation while receiving it back in the next moment. Upon exhaling (*yang*), the *dao* moves away from itself, imbuing the ten thousand things with their own natures. Inhaling (*yin*) in the next moment, it receives back all to which it has given birth. Chapter 4 of the *Daodejing,* which corresponds in number to the metal element as the fourth stage of *dao,*[30] describes the breath of *dao:*

> Dao *is a whirling emptiness (*chong*),*
> *Yet in use is inexhaustible.*
> *Fathomless (*yuan*),*
> *It seems to be the ancestor (*zong*) of ten thousand things.*
>
> – *DAODEJING*[31]

Chen interprets this chapter as describing the *dao* as "dynamic self-diffusive creativity," pouring out and receiving back all beings.[32] *Dao,* as the origin of all origins, is termed "the ancestor of ten thousand beings." The character *zong* (宗) for ancestor is the same character used for *zongqi* (宗氣), the ancestral *qi* of the lungs in the chest.[33] The *zongqi* is what empowers rhythmic movement in every aspect of our being. It is the breath of *dao* that powers our own breath as we mirror the basic functioning of the universe. The idea that breathing is a basic process of *dao* is supported in the *Daodejing,* Chapter 5:

> *Between heaven and earth, how like a bellows it is!*
> *Empty and yet inexhaustible,*
> *Moving and yet it pours out ever more.*[34]

The movement of *dao* is like a great whirlpool, rising and falling like a bellows, giving birth to all things at its periphery and receiving them back at its center.

### *Differentiating Sexuality*

In conclusion, I differentiate each element's contribution to sexuality. Transmitting and receiving point combinations are discussed for addressing the complex dynamics of sexuality when we wish to treat the functional relationship of any two *yin* officials. As an exercise, try extending this same quality of thought to the *yang* officials as well as to other phenomena.

## *The Nature of Sexuality*

Sexuality is generally the only context in which most people ever lower their boundaries enough to experience an ecstatic merging with another that transcends, for a moment, their separate sense of self. This moment of merging is also the closest that most people ever come to experiencing unity with the first cause (Big Bang) as the generative force of evolution. Hence the longing for unity that resides in each heart is often projected onto the sexual experience, which, because it is so highly conditioned by individual and cultural ego, is ultimately unfulfilling.

The heart's unfulfilled desires tend to be expressed as any number of displacement activities that are habitually driven by ego. These tend to include having affairs, overeating, overexercising, and overworking both physically and emotionally. Modern therapies often consider a disordered relationship to sexuality as constituting the basis of distortions in both our experience and expression of thoughts and feelings. This emphasis on sexuality represents a failure to embrace a fundamental truth of spirituality, that the basis of all suffering in life comes from failure to identify with and express the authentic self.

In harmonizing sexuality, or any imbalance for that matter, we must always bear in mind the functional dynamics that perpetuate a person's most fundamental division from self, which are always constitutional in nature. Hence, whenever a patient expresses the notion that either relationship or sexuality is a pressing issue, I always direct their attention deeper. And I always interpret the degree of urgency in his expression as being directly proportional to his denial of the true nature of his desire. For the authentic self is fully formed, always complete, and desires nothing except to be expressed.

*Water*

The water element governs potency and the transmission of essence *(jing)* and our ancestral lineage through sexual intercourse. Hence the kidneys provide both power and depth to sexuality. As our depth, the kidneys also represent the movement of our unconsciousness and the innate drives that motivate our sexual behavior. These drives, like the rising and falling of the tide, contribute a sense of surging and power to sexuality. Fear and anxiety associated with the kidneys can limit our capacity for intimacy and passion. Wisdom, the virtue of the kidney official, can help us maintain our potency by conserving resources and investing our energy in sexuality wisely. The bladder official, embodied as the nervous system, is the purveyor of mind and will and is responsible in part for the so-called electricity in the sexual connection.

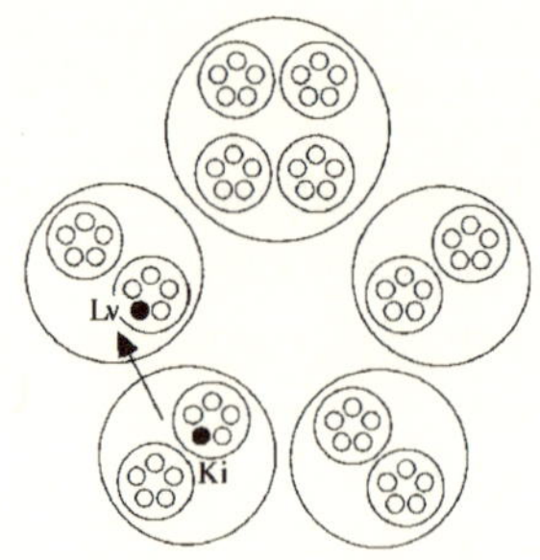


**Water to Wood**
Transmitting point: **Ki-10**
Receiving point: **Lv-8**

Here we tonify the kidney with its horary point to strongly empower the virtues of the water element. These are then transmitted to Lv-8, the receiving point on the liver channel for the influence of water. Hence the power of water is tapped and channeled up and out into the world via the liver, manifesting as strong directional growth. As the tonification point on the liver channel, Lv-8 empowers the upward rising tendency of wood to provide the sense of vigor and purpose inherent in the sexual experience. Conversely, if a person evidences heat congruent with an aggressive sexuality, this point combination can help cool and quiet the liver and help empower the virtue of benevolence in a way expressed as tenderness.

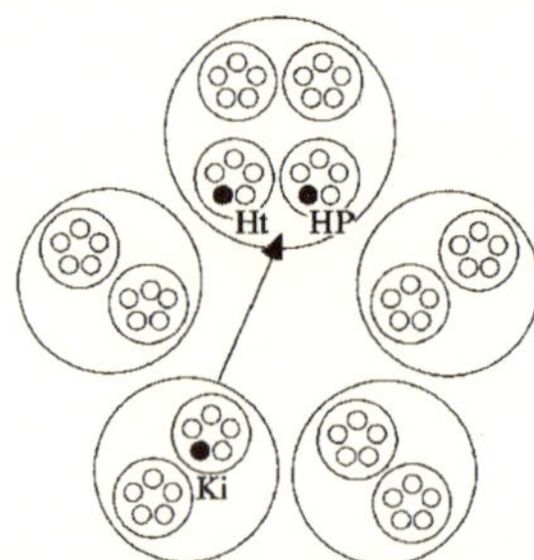


**Water to Fire**
Transmitting point: **Ki-10**
Receiving points: **Ht-3, HP-3**

When desires are unrealized or suppressed, a tightly held heart tends to generate heat that can unsettle the spirit. In contrast, heat in the heart tends to generate desires that are unending and, therefore, impossible to fulfill. This point combination can help cool the heart and empower the transcendence and wisdom of the kidney within the heart official. With the spirit settled we may better exercise wisdom in pursuit of our passions and thus derive joy from our relationships. If the presence of water within the heart is excessive, the heart's flame can be extinguished by fear. Diminishing the presence of water within can help fortify the heart's fire and increasing feelings of connectedness relative to the sexual experience.

If the presence of water within the heart protector is deficient, our passions can consume us. In this case, increasing the presence of water can empower a cooling influence so wisdom can temper our desires and quiet our spirit. If the presence of water within is excessive, fear can limit our capacity for intimacy. By dispersing the influence of water, the opening and closing of our heart's gate can better reflect our commitments and be less controlled by anxiety and fear.

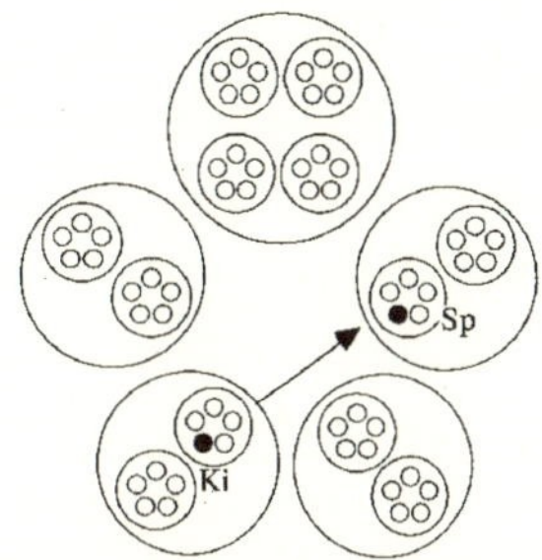


**Water to Earth**
Transmitting point: **Ki-10**
Receiving point: **Sp-9**

Water within earth empowers our ability to recognize the innate nature of our needs. In this way integrity (earth) is born of wisdom (water). By recognizing true self as it is inherent in water, the spleen can better process life so we are deeply nourished. Hence we can seek out relationships that resonate with our own inner natures. In this way we can cultivate our potential and become increasingly nourished by our relationship and physical contact. If the presence of water within is excessive, earth can turn to mud. This process is embodied as dampness that slows us down and leaves us feeling burdened by relationships and sexuality that could otherwise potentially nourish us. In this way integrity is undermined as fear overwhelms the potential stability afforded by earth.

If the presence of water within earth is deficient, we tend to fail to recognize the true nature of our needs. Hence appetite becomes excessive as fire within earth is uncontrolled and our desires and appetites proliferate. The habitual appetite of the mind can never be sated, however, and anything or anyone consumed leaves us feeling unfulfilled. By empowering the water within earth, we can cool excessive appetite and provide the memory inherent in water of what will deeply nourish original purpose. In this way sexuality can nourish, rather than undermine, our integrity.

The lungs govern the mucous membranes in the body, which must have the proper moisture content for sex to proceed comfortably. When the presence of water within is deficient, metal becomes dry and makes it difficult

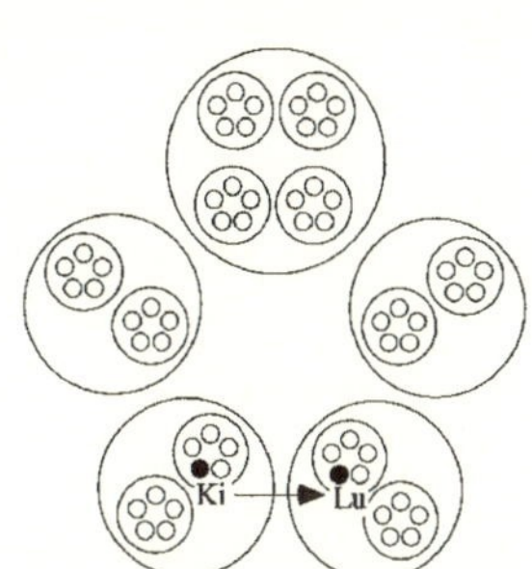


**Water to Metal**
Transmitting point: **Ki-10**
Receiving point: **Lu-5**

to receive. Heat in the lungs can make us fragile as metal becomes brittle and overly sensitive. Such heat is often congruent with perfectionism that leads us to be overly critical in relationship. The emotions of loss and longing can also generate heat in the lungs as we feel desperate to fill our internal void. In this situation we may be less than discriminating about the quality of our intimate connections as we grasp on to anyone who will temporarily allay our loneliness.

When metal becomes hard and brittle, we tend to insulate ourselves from relationship and cut off as if we are behind an iron door. This type of closing down is often in direct proportion to our degree of sensitivity. Hence such cutting off can be a self-protective mechanism in people who are "thin skinned." Empowering the water within the metal can cool heat in the lungs that gives rise to longing as well as ease our grief over past losses. In this way we may be fully present during the sexual experience without carrying the ghosts of lost loves along with us.

If the presence of water within metal is excessive, dampness in the lungs can also hinder our ability to receive. Hence inspiration can be smothered by fear as we fail to connect to the value in our relationship. Decreasing the presence of water within metal can empower lightness, joy, and inspiration with regard to sexuality.

*Wood*

The wood element governs the rising and directionality of sex. Wood engenders the strength and uprightness necessary to tap the potential in the kidneys to transmit it into the world. Being in a constant rush can lead to premature orgasm because the mind is always fixed on the goal rather than the process of the experience. Habituated frustration can lead us to work out our anger through our sexuality. The virtue of benevolence empowers the creative spontaneity of the sexual experience to occur in a way that is both exciting yet tender.

Wood is the fuel that feeds the expression of fire. If the presence of wood within is excessive, fire will burn too brightly and, eventually, burn out when its resources are consumed. Excess wood within fire can lead to

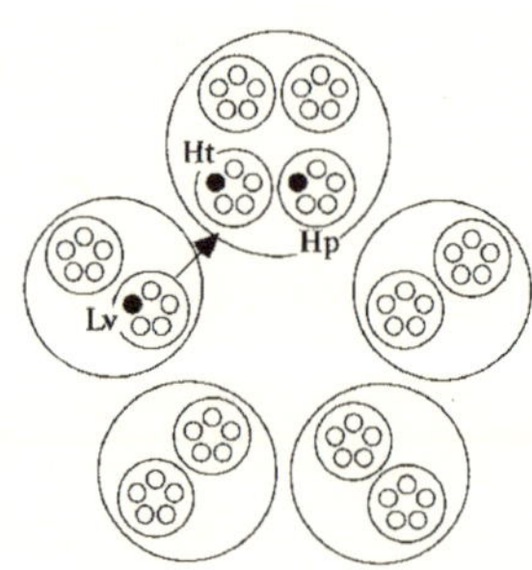


**Wood to Fire**
Transmitting point: **Lv-1**
Receiving points: **Ht-9, HP-9**

sexual aggressiveness based in part on the frustration that arises when our desires and fantasies are not realized. Of course, when wood excessively feeds fire, our desires can never be fulfilled as the mind continually generates new directions to grow in after each new experience or "conquest." Hence the spirit is continually agitated and never able to connect sexually from a place of tranquility.

If the presence of wood within is deficient, fire will fail to burn brightly enough as our hearts are left in the dark. For lack of the insight and understanding afforded by wood, the heart may be blown through life like a leaf in the wind. Then no clear direction is discerned in choosing intimate relationships and sexuality lacks purpose and resolve. With our fire so diminished, making contact with the heart of another can be an exercise in futility.

The presence of wood within the heart protector empowers our quality of discernment regarding who it is safe to let into the inner domain of our heart. If wood within fire is deficient we can engage in sex indiscriminately, allowing ourselves to be dominated and controlled by another's agenda, all in the vain hope of achieving intimacy. Such behavior is often based on a lack of self-esteem, which is a virtue empowered by the wood element. For lack of fuel, the heart protector may not be able to muster enough of an impulse to engage in relationship or to sustain intimate contact. Without the creativity empowered by wood, even sex can become dull as relationships tend to lose their glamour after the initial fire of attraction has faded.

If the presence of wood within the heart protector is excessive, we may be too analytical in selecting our mates because our heart's intuition is dominated by our mind's desires. Wood empowers vision, and if its influence is excessive then sexuality may be governed by ideas, concepts, and imagination in a way that keeps the heart from connecting to the reality of the person we are in relationship with. Hence sexuality can dominate the relationship as a way to avoid other deeper levels of contact that engender intimacy.

Wood controls earth as the roots of a plant keep soil from eroding on a hillside. Excessive judgment and anger can undermine the earth's tendency to create center and harmony. If the presence of wood within earth is excessive, we may be easily hurt by our lover's advances if we feel

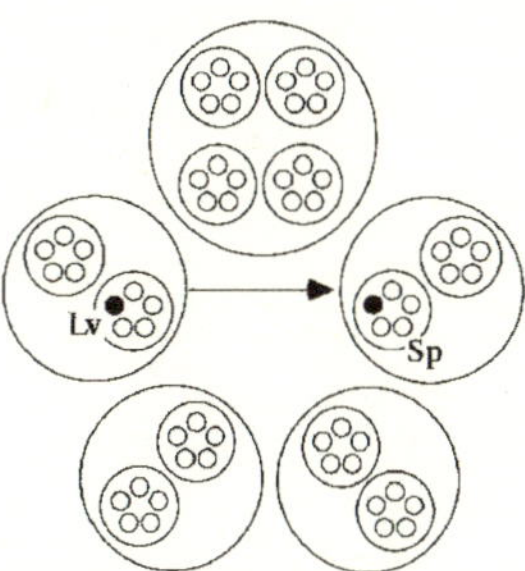


**Wood to Earth**
Transmitting point: **Lv-1**
Receiving point: **Sp-1**

they are too forceful or strong. We may also feel too easily judged by our lover for our own preferences regarding what nurtures us sexually.

If the presence of wood within is deficient, we may have no clear vision regarding the nature of our needs. The dysfunctional tendency of earth is to cater to the needs of others while ignoring what nourishes us. Sexually this can leave us both unfulfilled and resentful. Wood can help us gain clarity and help us initiate sexual behavior based on our own fulfillment rather than always waiting docilely for another to provide us an opportunity to serve.

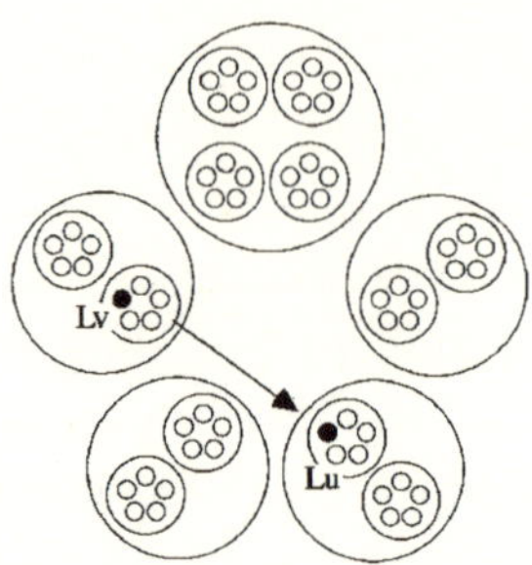


**Wood to Metal**
Transmitting point: **Lv-1**
Receiving point: **Lu-11**

The lungs govern breath and our synchronization to the primal rhythms of the universe. These rhythms are expressed within us as our primal urges, which are governed by the *po* spirit. These urges are a basis of sexual attraction both in the upper and lower *jiaos*. In the upper *jiao*, the lungs inspire attraction toward beauty and refinement. In the lower *jiao*, metal provides connection to water as essence is transmitted during procreation. This rhythm in the lower *jiao* is what accounts for our sexual response to the drums and bass in music as they align our urges to the primal rhythms of the universe.

The relationship of wood to metal is one of creativity and inspiration. Wood empowers the rising of our *yang*, and metal empowers the contraction of our *yin*. These complementary forces represent the directional movements of the *hun* and *po* spirits. If the presence of wood within metal is deficient, we may be excessively driven by our primal urges in life. In this case we may lack inspiration in the sexual experience as it becomes vulgar and unrefined. But if the wood within metal is excessive, our inspiration and freedom during sex may be constrained by the expectations and fantasies engendered by the wood element.

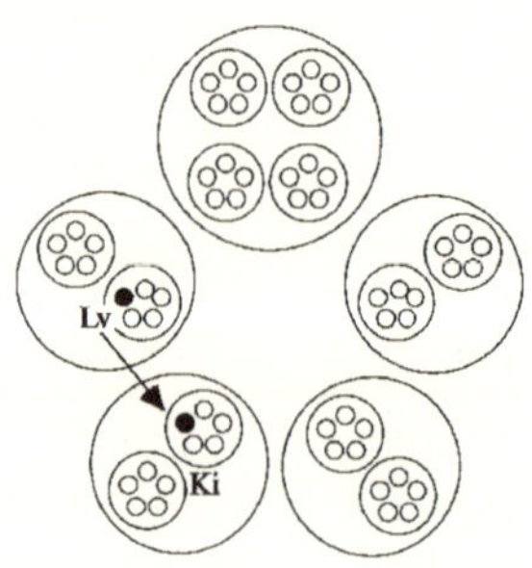


**Wood to Water**
Transmitting point: **Lv-1**
Receiving point: **Ki-1**

Wood within water empowers vision of the depths of self. These points effectively bring the roots of the tree that is the liver official down into the depths of the kidney to empower vision of our depths and tap innate resources. This treatment strongly opens the kidney at its source, "bubbling spring," to stimulate the rise of our resources into the world. If the presence of wood within water is deficient, our resources can lie dormant congruent with a state of impotency or indifference toward sexuality. If the presence of wood within is excessive, resources may be overutilized congruent with a sense of pressure and urgency regarding sexuality. Eventually overindulgence can also lead to a state of impotency as *jing* is consumed.

*Fire*

Fire is the passion that derives from and fuels the heart's desires for connection and intimacy.[35] The left half of fire (heart and small intestine) governs the quality of our connection to other human beings. The heart is both the source and goal of intimacy. The small intestine serves as an interface that must transmit reality both from, and to, the heart clearly. When the left half of fire is in alignment for both people in a sexual encounter, a clear channel is created so the two may merge as one. Here the heart of each provides connection to the depths of kidney *jing* so that, as the boundaries created by fire dissolve, both people merge in their depths at the level of water, ancestry, *jing*, and *dao*. In this way the heart provides the lightning bolt of attraction that occurs when two people come into alignment. This electricity is embodied as the functioning of the nervous system as the small intestine imparts our quality of mind to the essence of the heart as it is transmitted into the world.

The right half of fire (heart protector and three heater) governs passion, excitement, and the heat of sexual connection. The heart protector consumes passion as nurturance to empower the blood and circulatory system. The three heater and heart protector empower the initial attraction and the joy of sexuality, respectively. The heart protector governs the joy of sexuality that comes from lowering our boundaries to merge ecstatically with another human being. This is present in the feeling of melting and merging as our capillaries open and our blood quickens.[36]

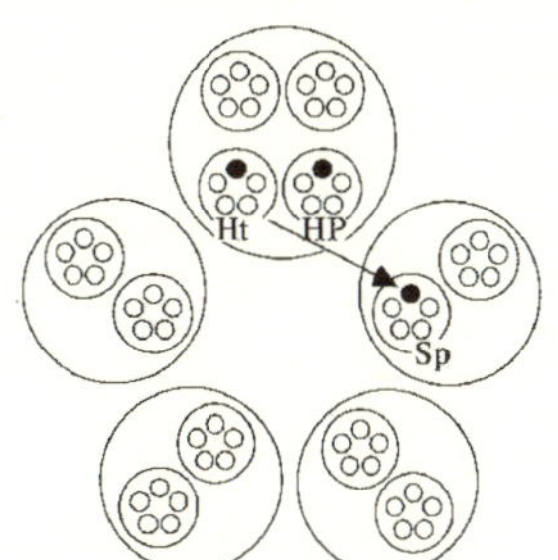


**Fire to Earth**
Transmitting points: **Ht-8, HP-8**
Receiving point: **Sp-2**

Fire within earth empowers the transformation of nutrients into muscle, blood, and flesh. The relationship between fire and earth must be balanced in the same way the fire within a stove nourishes the home with warmth and meals. If desires within the heart are repressed or if they are excessive, fire can rage in a way that overstimulates our appetites. Here the longings of the heart express themselves within the earth element as appetite fueled by excessive desire. Sexual longings that are unfulfilled can express themselves through the earth element as binge eating and strong cravings. Excessive fire from the heart or heart protector can express itself through the earth element as heat and inflammation in the muscles, which occurs in illnesses such as fibromyalgia or myofibrositis. In fact, this is one of the major point combinations I find useful in treating those disorders. I often find that women so affected have been sexually abused, and the chaos perpetuated in the fire element is expressing itself as fire within the muscles.

If fire within earth is deficient, food may fail to be properly "cooked," making it difficult for us to be adequately nourished. For lack of fire the spleen can fail to transform the fluids in a way congruent with the presence of damp. Failing to abstract nourishment from acquired sources in life, the heart in turn fails to be nourished by its efforts in the world and leads to a sense of resignation and joylessness. Increasing the presence of fire within can help nourish both the heart and spleen and therefore break this cycle and empower joy. In this way sexuality can once again nourish us rather than becoming a burden.

**Fire to Metal**
Transmitting points: **Ht-8, HP-8**
Receiving point: **Lu-10**

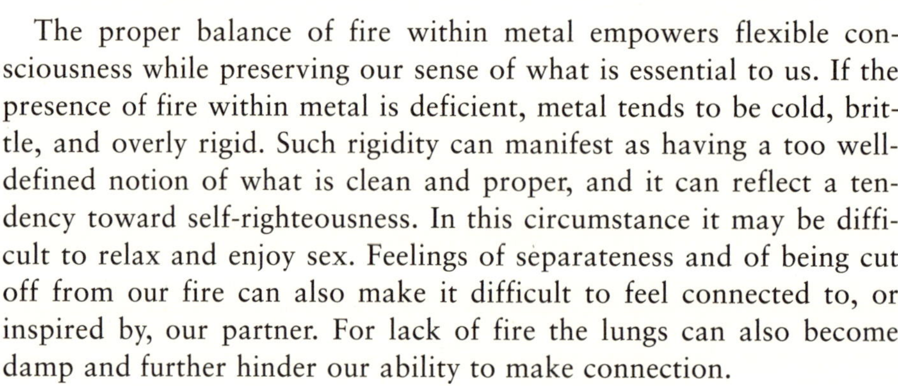

The proper balance of fire within metal empowers flexible consciousness while preserving our sense of what is essential to us. If the presence of fire within metal is deficient, metal tends to be cold, brittle, and overly rigid. Such rigidity can manifest as having a too well-defined notion of what is clean and proper, and it can reflect a tendency toward self-righteousness. In this circumstance it may be difficult to relax and enjoy sex. Feelings of separateness and of being cut off from our fire can also make it difficult to feel connected to, or inspired by, our partner. For lack of fire the lungs can also become damp and further hinder our ability to make connection.

If the presence of fire within metal is excessive, the lungs tend to become dry in a way congruent with longing. For lack of moisture in the lungs, it can become difficult to connect to essence in a comfortable way. Overcontrolled by our own fire we can become zealots straining to impose our sense of righteousness on others and converting them to our view of what is right, proper, and decent. Such behavior is most often a compensation for failure to connect to essence gracefully. By sedating the presence of fire within the lungs, connection can proceed more elegantly in a way that is less clinging and suffocating to our partner.

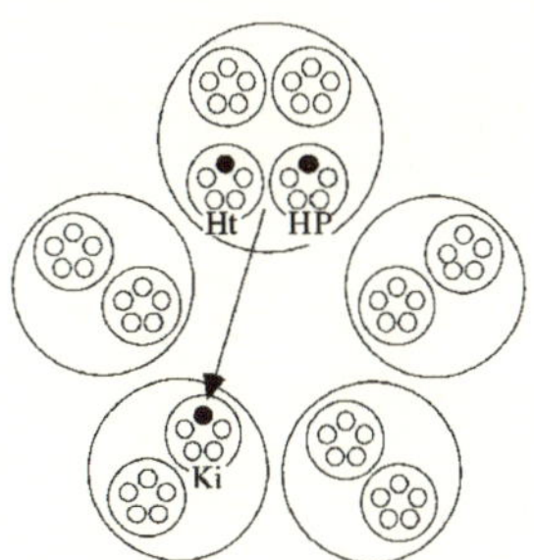


**Fire to Water**
Transmitting points: **Ht-8, HP-8**
Receiving point: **Ki-2**

Here fire is drawn down deep into the depths of the kidney. The presence of heart fire within the depths is congruent with the interpenetration of *shen* and *jing.* This is the very basis of self-knowledge and the cultivation of wisdom. The heart protector's fire can be conceived as located in both the upper and lower *jiao.* In the upper *jiao,* the heart protector governs the fire of intimacy, trust, and the joyous passion of merging with another human being. In the lower *jiao,* this fire is present as sexuality itself as we connect at the level of both ancestry and karma (water) and passion (fire). This mixing of water and fire is the essence of sexual alchemy and involves our merging with another human being. The presence of heart fire within the kidney is the basis of spiritual alchemy and depends only on our own recognition of original nature. When *shen* connects with *jing,* we merge with true self. When the heart protector's fire penetrates the depths, we are able to both attract and merge with another.

If the presence of fire is deficient within water, we can become cold, fearful, and closed to sexuality. For fear of knowing self (Ht) or other (HP), we tend to avoid connection and intimacy. Symptoms such as impotence and frigidity can often be associated with fear of intimate connection. If the presence of fire is excessive within water, we may be exhausted by our passions as our desires push us past our innate limits. In this way we can become *jing* deficient as our mind's desires habitually push us to expend inner resources in the pursuit of joy. Symptoms such as hot flashes, night sweats, and blushing can all be signs that fire within water is excessive.

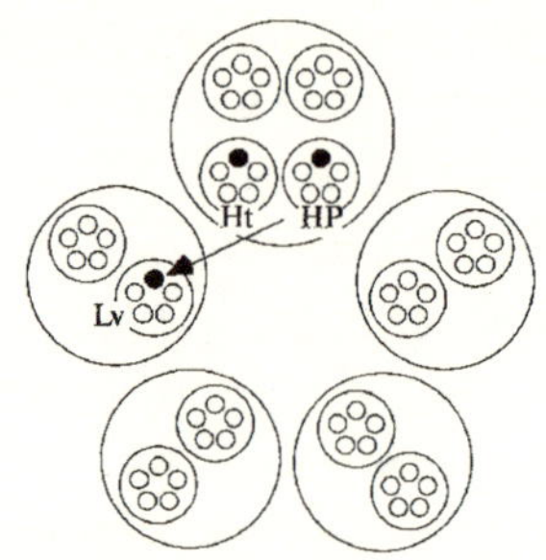


**Fire to Wood**
Transmitting points: **Ht-8, HP-8**
Receiving point: **Lv-2**

Fire within wood empowers the rising of our creative vision into the world. It is the nature of wood to aspire toward fire as spring becomes summer and our good works in the world lead to the flowering of the heart's joys and passions. Fire comes to wood from without as the sun whose light orients our growth and from within as that internal fire that rises through us from conception to death as our life's purpose. If the presence of fire within wood is deficient, resignation, despair, and hopelessness can predominate along with a lack of aspiration. It can be difficult to generate a sense of excitement about sexuality as it becomes divorced from any sense of purpose. "What's the use? Every time I love I never get anywhere." Sighing is often a sign that wood despairs of ever making fire or experiencing the joys inherent in directed growth. For lack of fire, wood tends toward dampness, and the flame in the heart itself may smolder and make connection a joyless experience. Impotence can be a sign that the passion of fire is unable to stimulate wood to rise forcefully.

If the presence of fire within wood is excessive, wood can be easily consumed as we feel increasingly driven toward our goals. As fire burns out of control, heat can enter the blood to fuel passions excessively in a way that further potentiates excessive fire. Here sexuality tends to be aggressive and passionate yet never sated as heat disturbs the spirit and agitates the heart protector. Such an insatiable appetite for sex can disturb the heart in a way congruent with heart attack or stroke as blind pursuit of our passions ultimately kills us.[37]

*Earth*

The earth element governs sensuality and our ability to feel nourished through physical contact. Earth is associated with our quality of appetite and our ability to identify and fulfill our needs sexually. The earth element influences our oral connection in sexuality. The tip of the tongue connects directly to the heart and is therefore related to the fire element. But the mouth itself, and its relationship to sexuality through the sense of taste, is related to the earth element. The earth element presides over the comfort, cuddling, and nesting aspect of sexuality. Earth governs the feeling that the sexual act is part of creating a home, a family, and a stable center. Dysfunctional eating can become a displacement activity for sex when the true nature of our desires is sublimated and transferred instead to food.

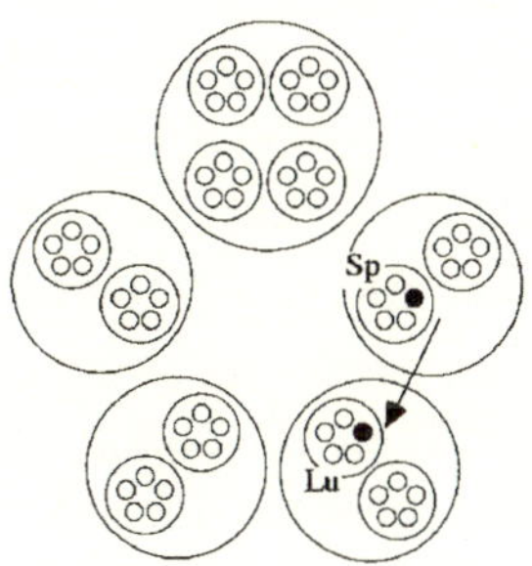


**Earth to Metal**
Transmitting point: **Sp-3**
Receiving point: **Lu-9**

Earth within metal empowers the presence of substantiality within essence. If the presence of earth within is deficient, we may fail to feel inspired or nourished by our relationships. Without a substantial center our relationships can tend to be based purely on our own inspiration without any real connection to our partner. Similarly, the sexual experience may be fast and inspired but never grounded enough to create comfort. In this case, we may look to sex to fill the emptiness we feel inside, although the void always returns if we have not connected to our partner with integrity in a way that nourishes our centers. Hence we may long for value in both relationship and sexuality that always seems to elude us.

If the presence of earth within metal is excessive, we can feel uninspired and burdened by physical contact. If we focus too much on the physical sensuality and connection inherent in sex, we may fail to connect to the transcendent aspects of spiritual essence exchanged during lovemaking. In this way our needs can smother our inspiration as we lose touch with the divine and more refined aspects of sexual connection.

Earth represents the acquired constitution, and its main function is to supplement the innate constitution. Hence a central function of earth is

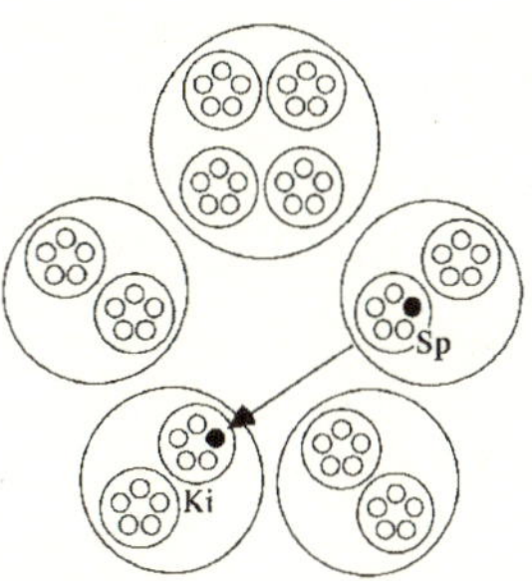


**Earth to Water**
Transmitting point: **Sp-1**
Receiving point: **Ki-3**

to contain water so resources can be channeled in a useful fashion. Earth represents our ability to recognize and meet our own needs in a way that nourishes us and helps us channel our innate resources efficiently into the world. Water represents our innate resources that nourish us from within as they flow out to manifest in life.

If the presence of earth is deficient within water, our fears can easily overwhelm us. Constant anxiety can make it difficult to settle down into our hearts and make contact with another in a way that nourishes us. For lack of earth, we can feel as though we are on a poor footing in a relationship and it is difficult to keep our heads above water. Hence we can feel easily overwhelmed and exhausted by sexual contact if anxiety leads us to indulge in constant sex without replenishment.

If the presence of earth within water is excessive, our sense of need may cause us to squander resources excessively. Such need may be congruent with dampness and heat in the lower *jiao*, representing the embodiment of burden that smothers our sense of potency and strength. Here earth essentially dams up our resources to prevent us from gracefully manifesting our potential. Hence our neediness can stop us from flowing gracefully in a sexual encounter.

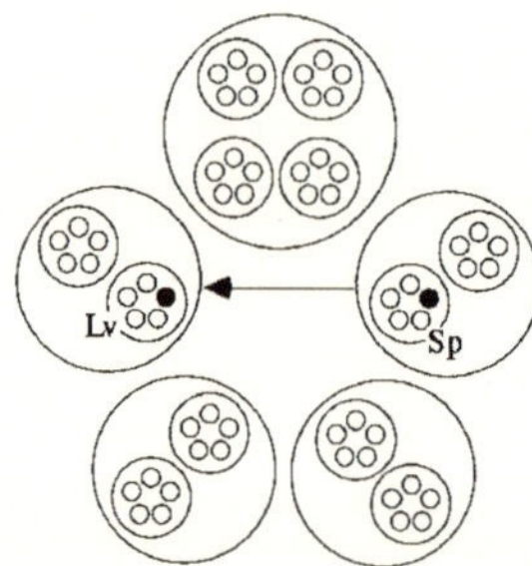


**Earth to Wood**
Transmitting point: **Sp-3**
Receiving point: **Lv-3**

Earth nourishes wood from within and provides stability and grounding from without. Earth empowers our centers so our creative impulses can be directed into growth in a balanced way that both flows from, and creates, integrity. The presence of earth as a circular process must exist in harmony with the linear goal-oriented striving of wood. If the presence of earth within wood is deficient, growth tends to constrain process so we are poorly nourished by our creative impulses. Healthy blood and *qi* depend on the earth element, and their deficiency can fail to nourish our creativity and motivations. Hence it can become difficult to stand up for ourselves in relationship, both figuratively and actually in terms of maintaining an erection or arousal.

For both sexes it can be intimidating to assert our needs or initiate sexual activity for lack of solid ground to stand on. Devoid of the sensuality and nesting instincts empowered by earth, sexuality can become impulsive, aggressive, and ultimately unsatisfying as we fail to be nourished in relationship and through physical contact. If wood predominates over earth in engendering sexuality, our minds can tend to push us habitually to seek new and exciting sexual experiences yet we may fail to build our centers to create the stability represented by family and home.

In implementing our plans in the world, the wood element must take its direction from kidney *jing* and use earth to nourish the manifestation of our inner resources out into the world. If the presence of earth within is excessive, our inner direction of growth as stored in the kidney can be smothered. The worldly needs and desires of the mind fuel our habitual motivations as the innate purpose stored in *jing* is obscured. Hence our appetite for sexuality can take on the hallmarks of sugar cravings as we aggressively, or passive aggressively, seek only comfort in sexuality as an immediate fix that never actually nourishes us. The manifestation of damp and heat in the liver can suggest that earth is burdening our creative impulses in this way. The presence of such pathogens often occurs along with conditions that impact sexuality such as prostatitis, sexually transmitted diseases, pelvic inflammatory disease, and various gynecological and bladder infections. Psychospiritually, such damp heat can present as resentment that poisons the heart and mind and taints the sexual encounter.

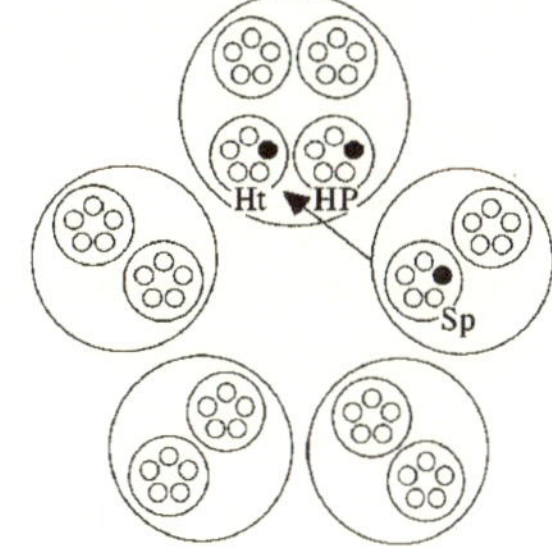


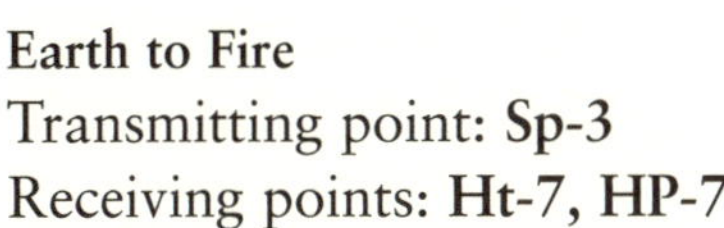
**Earth to Fire**
Transmitting point: **Sp-3**
Receiving points: **Ht-7, HP-7**

Earth provides a base for fire to burn on as well as a center to keep fire focused without dispersing. Fire serves earth by cooking our acquired sources of nourishment so we can abstract essence from it, and earth in turn nourishes fire with both *qi* and blood. If the presence of earth within fire is deficient, sexuality can be overly expansive for lack of a sufficient center. Here our fantasies and desires predominate in a blaze without ever being focused enough to nourish our hearts or create integrity in relationship. This dysfunction tends to perpetuate itself as insufficient earth fails to focus fire and overly dispersed fire fails to create earth. A heart not nourished is a joyless heart, and such people tend to give the impression that despite their best efforts they have never truly tasted and assimilated the sweet nectar of love or sensuality.

If earth within fire is excessive, our passions tend to be either smothered or fueled by our habitual needs and cravings. Hence we can tend to look to sexuality as a way of satisfying our cravings for comfort and stability. However, if these virtues do not arise from within, we may never feel contented and therefore always feel needy in relationship to others. In contrast, excessive earth can also extinguish fire entirely as our needs smother our passions. Here love, relationship, and sexuality can become just another responsibility to burden us. Dampness and heat within the heart can embody this dynamic as our neediness and cravings, embodied as cholesterol, for example, slowly choke our hearts and compromise our connection to the world.

*Metal*

The metal element empowers inspiration and receptivity during sex. Whereas fire governs connection with another through expansion, the metal element governs connection through the force of contraction and pulling the other in toward us. Metal provides our connection to quality and essence in relationship, helping assure us that we receive the best from our experience. Physiologically, this is present as the transmission of essence during the sexual act as the father's *jing* (semen) is transmitted from metal to the mother's blood (ovum). Outwardly, essence is conveyed through refinement, the honoring and respect paid to our partner, and the notions of honor and chastity. Because our love is precious, we keep what is of value pure until the ritual of courting is complete and the act of physical love is sanctified by heaven. Metal inspires the feeling that our love and our lover is special and the quality of our connection is uniquely ordained by heaven.

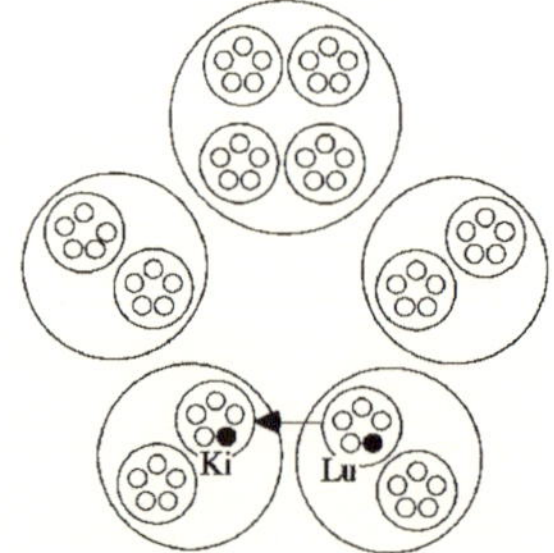


**Metal to Water**
Transmitting point: **Lu-8**
Receiving point: **Ki-7**

Metal within water is the diamond of original nature that is buried in our depths at conception. This essence is the light that attracts others to us when we are true to ourselves. The ability of water to grasp metal and pull it deeply within is vital if the *sheng* cycle is constantly to renew life.[38]

If the presence of metal within water is deficient, life itself can come to an end as *yin* and *yang* separate. For if the *qi* that supports the functioning of the kidneys is not renewed, the whole left side of the pulse collapses and gives rise to the H/W imbalance. With our will thus lying in ruins, the possibility of sexual connection is generally far from our thoughts as severely dysfunctional relationships are often associated with the H/W imbalance. The failure of water to attract metal mirrors our own lack of attractiveness to others as we feel wholly separated from the value that lies in our depths. Uninspired and uninspiring, it is unlikely we will make a sexual connection or muster a relationship at all.

If the presence of metal within water is excessive, dysfunctional inspiration can lead us to deplete our resources. Constantly keeping busy and generating excitement can be a way of avoiding deep contact with others and with ourselves. Always on the go we can run, but never hide, from the grief and longing that resides in our core. Of course, such nervous activity can eventually exhaust our reserves of kidney *yin*. In this case, sexuality is often exciting but tends to occur quickly as we never take time to luxuriate in the experience. Inspiration itself, however, is not enough to sustain a relationship and, if connection is not made to the depths, the relationship is not likely to last when inspiration is lost.

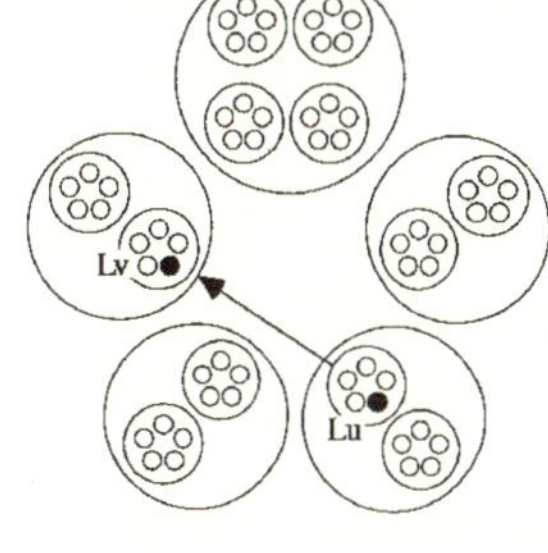


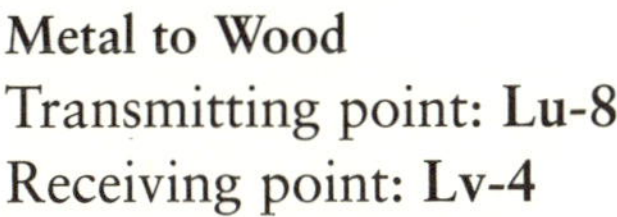

**Metal to Wood**
Transmitting point: **Lu-8**
Receiving point: **Lv-4**

Metal appears internally to wood as the minerals that nourish a plant and give it structure. Externally, metal appears to wood as the pruning shears help limit the possible directions of growth so inner resources are channeled efficiently. If the presence of metal within wood is deficient, growth tends to be excessive and of poor quality. For lack of control by metal, our minds tend to fantasize about every possibility of relationship and sexual contact and the process leaves us frustrated and eventually exhausted. However, the imagination of wood can suffer from a lack of inspiration or aspiration.[39] Then sexuality tends to be deficient as wood fails to strive toward anything. This lack of striving can present as a general lack of potency congruent with the inability to orient toward, and attract to us, what we value and desire in life.

If the presence of metal within wood is excessive, our best laid plans can be chopped down prematurely. Here growth can appear useless as every branch that we send out is immediately pruned either by the criticism of others or our own perfectionist tendencies. Hence we can feel constrained as our metal excessively limits the possibility of our wood's growth. Sexuality and relationship can be a frustrating experience if we feel like we are not able to satisfy either our partners or our own expectations. We can also feel frustrated if we are not free to branch out creatively in the directions we aspire to.

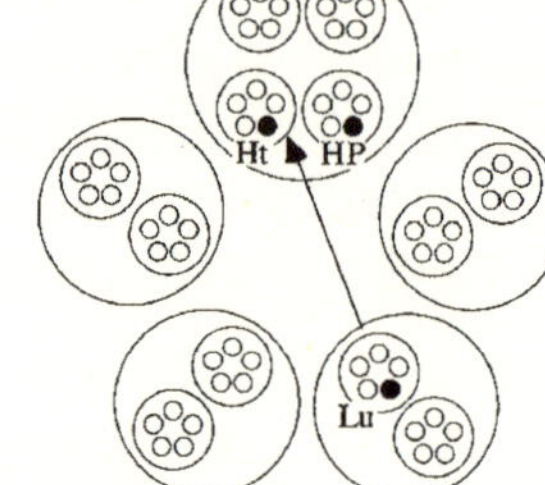


**Metal to Fire**
Transmitting point: **Lu-8**
Receiving points: **Ht-4, HP-5**

Metal within fire empowers the synchronization of the beating of our heart with our respiratory rhythm. The essence of metal within fire is the basis of alchemical transformation as impurities are burned away so only the highest inherent within our potential manifests in the world. Metal within fire represents the essences we transform as well as the essences that transform us. If the presence of metal within fire is deficient, relationships can stagnate as we fail to be transformed and inspired by them. Longing and grief can stagnate in the heart if we fail to abstract the highest that each loss has to offer us. Holding on to past relationships in this way can obscure our ability to be touched by new connections.

If the presence of metal within fire is excessive, we can be too attached to those we love. Afraid to let go and give them breathing space, we tend to suffocate them with our affection. We can also idealize our lovers as we fall in love with our own inspiration and fail to connect to our partner's inherent value. Sexuality can become an expression of desperation as we seek warmth not for the sake of connecting to another, but rather to avoid being alone.

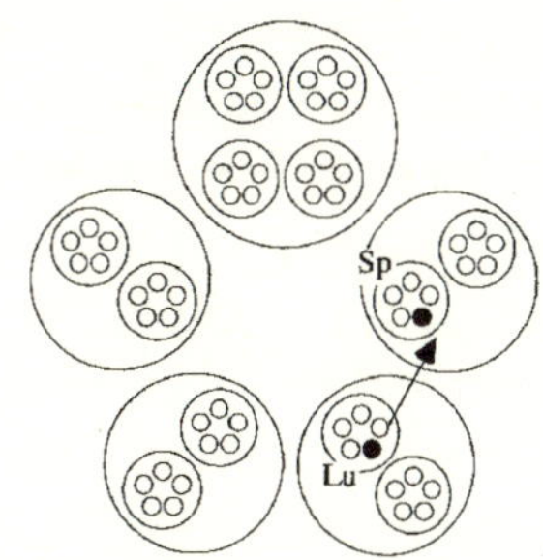


**Metal to Earth**
Transmitting point: **Lu-8**
Receiving point: **Sp-5**

The presence of metal within earth is represented by minerals in the soil that provide a structure that holds the earth in place and forms a significant part of the nutrient content of the food the earth produces. The balance of metal and earth is the balance between substantial (earth) and essential (metal) nourishment. It is the metal element that empowers the transcendence of both the suffering and comforts inherent in this world.

If the presence of metal is deficient within earth, we can easily become burdened by all sources of potential nourishment including sexuality. For lack of metal we may never transform our experiences into their essential value as they weigh us down like undigested food. Hence we can become buried under our habitual needs as we fail to transcend substance to grasp essence and let go of mundanity.

If the presence of metal within earth is excessive, we can fail to assimilate essence because we transcend form too quickly. Just as diarrhea prevents us from retaining what is of value in our food, we can let go of relationships prematurely before we are truly served by them. Here our inspiration may cause us to devour our partners without ever digesting the experience to create a solid foundation in relationship. In this way the center of earth slowly erodes and relationships lose their integrity.

---

## *Conclusion*

In this chapter I examined the interrelationships of the elements from the standpoint of the five-element points associated with each meridian. The study of Chinese medicine is the study of the quality of functional relationships among everything that exists. It is my hope that you will extend the quality of thought presented here to the point of transcending these theoretical constructs so as to arrive at fully possessing the five elements as an embodied experience in life.

## *Exercises*

1. Use this exercise to differentiate any aspect of being according to the five elements and to select a point combination to treat it. After presenting the steps of the exercise, I provide an example of how you might answer. Extending this protocol to other aspects of being can help you achieve a deep understanding of the five elements and their related transmitting and receiving points.
   a. Name an aspect of being you think is of clinical significance.
   b. What element governs the expression of this aspect of being?
   c. How is it expressed as a potential virtue or vice within each element and official?
   d. What is the transmitting point of the element that governs this aspect of being?
   e. What is the receiving point on each of the elements through which the virtue or vice can be uniquely expressed?
   f. How can you base a point selection on this combination for empowering the expression of the given virtue and mitigating the expression of the vice within each element?

   **Response**
   a. Appetite
   b. Earth
   c. (1) Within earth, appetite can help us nourish ourselves. If it is excessive we can become burdened, and if it is deficient we can be malnourished. (2) Within metal, appetite can engender inspiration and a hunger to transcend the material world through connection to essence. If appetite is excessive, we may either crave material possessions of increasing worth or adopt a fundamentalist view in our spiritual life. If appetite is deficient, we may feel empty for having failed to connect to quality in the essential aspects of life. (3) Within water, appetite can empower us to manifest our ambitions. If it is excessive, we may be overly ambitious and appetite can fuel us to exhaust ourselves. If it is deficient, we can become underachievers and never hunger for the fulfillment of individual purpose. (4) Within wood, appetite can empower growth and aspiration. If it is excessive, appetite can create stagnation engendering both frustration and belligerence. If appetite is deficient, we may be resigned and never hunger for growth. (5) Within fire, appetite can stimulate us to nourish our hearts. If it is excessive, the heart can be hungry and exhaust itself pursuing its passions. If appetite is deficient, the heart may starve, engendering sorrow as we never taste the fruit of our desires.

d. Transmitting points for appetite: Sp-3 and St-36

e. Receiving points: the earth point on each channel

f. For example, to treat the relationship of appetite to the gallbladder official, we could select St-36 and Gb-34 as the distal points to ground our treatment. Here the wood is nourished and the flow of *qi* is harmonized to quell frustration and calm appetites that drive us to excess. A strong center is empowered to root growth effectively, so less constraint is placed on the process of nourishment.

2. a. Work through all other two-point combinations using St-36 and Sp-3 as the transmitting points relative to the issue of appetite.

   b. What proximal points including *shu, mu,* CV, GV, and spirit points could you add to enhance these treatments?

3. In this chapter I differentiated sexuality according to the transmitting and receiving points on the *yin* officials. Do the same for the *yang* officials.

4. Here I have provided several cases of relative excess and deficiency along the *sheng* and *ke* cycle. Use these to practice designing transfers of *qi*. I have also left a blank diagram to help you design your own transfers.

   a. Lung excess, heart deficient.

   b. Stomach excess, spleen deficient.

   c. Small intestine excess, large intestine deficient.

   d. Practice makes perfect.

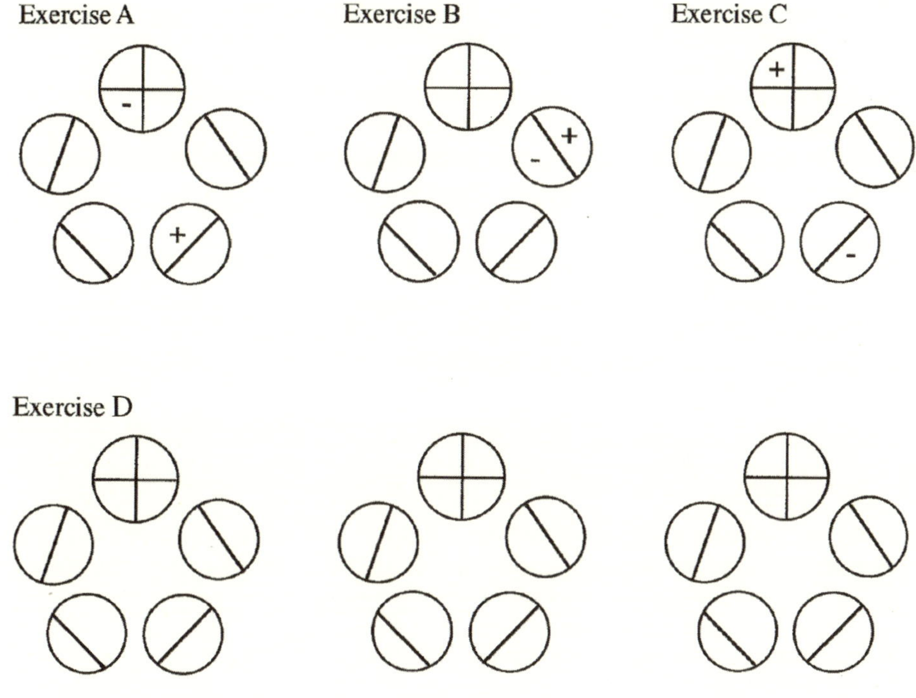

# NOTES

1. See my discussion of the spiral dynamics model at the end of Part V and Wilber, 2000. The origins of holistic thought in Chinese culture can be traced back to the *Yijing,* a time when the purple meme predominated the planet. The current wave of "yellow" and "turquoise" consciousness emerging now realizes for the first time the manifestation of a truly integral and holistic form of consciousness.
2. I suggest reviewing *ND,* Chapters 8 and 9, as preparation for this material.
3. See *ND,* Chapter 8, pp. 128–136.
4. The relationship between the five-element and eight-principle model is discussed in Chapter 37.
5. Note that some practitioners believe using the horary point is more efficacious in the middle of a season. Spring in the West begins on March 21 and ends on June 21. According to this way of thinking, the middle of May would correspond to the peak of the wood's functional influence in nature. Therefore this would be the most effective time to tap its potential in treatment. Note that Lv-1 may be either tonified or sedated at this juncture depending on the patient's pulses.
6. The effects of suggestion notwithstanding, I utilize this type of reasoning frequently and find my prognosis is confirmed whether I inform the patient of my prediction or not. Regardless of any effect my own expectation may have, I'm always gratified to see theory confirmed so precisely.
7. For a discussion of the vital link between metal and water, see *ND,* Chapter 7.
8. Chapter 77; in Chen, 1989, p. 223.
9. All pulse qualities referred to here are referenced to the Shen/Hammer system of pulse diagnosis. See Hammer, 2001.
10. In reality, the amount of *qi* supporting the function of an organ is generally indicated by several parameters of the pulse including amplitude, width, and intensity.
11. The term *child* refers to the next element in the *sheng* cycle whose function depends on the nourishment from the "mother" element that precedes it.
12. For a discussion of Emperor Yu and the floods, see *ND,* pp. 16–19.
13. In other words, he is an earth constitutional type and fire is the element of secondary concern.
14. Unschuld, 1986.
15. See Figure 12.7. If all redundancy in point selection is eliminated, we are left with thirty-six unique pairs of points that form the basis of 4NT.
16. For a further discussion of this point, look up Lv-8 in Chapter 31.
17. Chen, 1989, p. 203.
18. Here I have used one of the point's alternate names.
19. In the context discussed here, this point combination could overlap the therapeutic intention of the herb formula Linking Decoction (Yiguan Jian).
20. This name was ascribed by J. R. Worsley.
21. See *ND,* p. 309.
22. For example, the herb Schizandra astringes the connection between the heart and kidney.
23. See *ND,* pp. 127–135, for an elaboration of the holographic nature of the five-element system.
24. See *ND,* Chapter 8, pp. 128–136.
25. Chen, 1989, pp. 90–91.
26. See *ND,* pp. 203–224. See also Jarrett, 1995a, 1995b.
27. For more on these virtues, see *ND,* pp. 281–283.
28. Fung Yu-lan, 1983, vol. 2, p. 39; Dong Zhongshu (179–104? B.C.E.).
29. Chen, 1989, pp. 106–107.

30. The Chinese character for the number four, *si* (四), is a homophone with the character *si* (死), meaning death. Hence the fourth stage of *dao* may correspond to the death of primordial *dao* and the fall to the ten thousand things. Or it may correspond to the death of the body and the end of life or of ego, signifying the rebirth of the true self.
31. *Daodejing,* Chapter 4; Chen, 1989, p. 61.
32. Chen, 1989, p. 62.
33. The character *zong* refers to the building from which emanates the influence of the deceased ancestors over their posterity. Wieger, 1965, p. 101.
34. Chen, 1989, p. 64. Metallurgy was a highly developed art in ancient China. The use of the bellows as an image for the "whirling vortex" of *chongqi* between heaven and earth provides a tie between the lungs as the earthly manifestation of the breath of *dao,* the *zongqi,* and the metal element.
35. See *ND,* pp. 203–224. See also Jarrett, 1995a, 1995b.
36. Special thanks to Thea Elijah for this last insight.
37. Note that frequently impotence itself can be the body's way of protecting us from suffering a heart attack or stroke precipitated by overexertion.
38. The connection between metal and water is discussed more fully in Chapter 4.
39. Inspiration, a quality associated with the metal element, is congruent with the influence of the heaven that wood aspires to in its growth.

# 13

# SOURCE POINTS

THE CHARACTER *YUAN* (元), TRANSLATED AS "SOURCE," refers to the primordial center of *yuanqi* that lies in each person's depth. Source points empower the connection between this vital source of *qi* and the primal *dao* as the ultimate source of life. By virtue of this link, source points have a number of functions and thus broad application in treatment (see Figure 13.1).

After clearing all blocks and creating a stable foundation for further treatment, source points are often the first point to treat on the patient's constitutional meridian. By initiating treatment with the source point, you are accessing a deep source of pure *qi* that has the potential to reawaken the function of the constitutional official gently but effectively. In this way, the fundamental virtues inherent in *yuanqi* can be activated to serve as the guiding influence in the patient's life, thus providing a stream of fresh *qi* to erode the delusion of the created self from the inside out. By touching patients at their source, we have effectively reached back to the moment of conception prior to life's traumas to reinstitute the flow of purpose into the world. Such an invocation may serve notice to the deepest well of the patient's being that help is available and the time for healing is at hand (see Figure 13.2, p. 262).

Source points are unique because they can access every aspect of being addressed by every point on a given meridian but in a general way. Thus Lv-3, the source point on the liver channel, can access in a general way every function associated with the liver official. For example, Lv-1 is particularly associated with self-esteem as it is based on a vision of our roots, and Lv-14 is associated with the virtue of aspiration as it is based on a vision of our goals. Lv-3 can achieve both of these functions, although less specifically, by regulating the flow of *qi* to promote communication between our roots (Lv-1) and our outermost branches (Lv-14). Therefore, choose source points first when you want a distal point to ground treatment and influence an official in a general way.

Source points allow a person's deep inner nature to guide and moderate the effects of strong treatments. For example, if you select Ki-24, a very potent spirit point for treatment, you could moderate its effects by pairing it with Ki-3, the channel's source point. This pairing is much less directional than using Ki-2, the channel's fire point, as the distal point. The choice of a distal point such as Ki-2 is certainly not out of the question. In making that selection, however, you are making a very clear judgment about precisely how the *qi* is being manipulated. Selection of the source point affords the patient's own being a greater choice of how to utilize the treatment.

Let me illustrate this principle with the following example. If I make you a salad and know you very well, I may take the liberty of applying dressing before serving it to you. But by serving you the salad plain and offering you a selection of dressings, you are more likely to find one that best suits you in that moment. Source points, by virtue of their ability to touch any and all aspects of an official's function, permit patients to abstract what they most need from a given treatment in the moment.

Because source points are so balanced in their effect, you can always safely choose a meridian's source point to gauge the effects of "touching" an official with treatment if you are not sure what other distal point to use. If, for example, you wanted to treat the liver official but were not

| |
|---|
| 1. Revitalizes an official with primordial *qi*. |
| 2. Reestablishes connection to the virtues inherent in *yuanqi*. |
| 3. Activates every function of an official in a general way. |
| 4. Grounds strong proximal points so treatment is governed by nature. |
| 5. Effectively orients the officials toward center. |

*Figure 13.1*
FUNCTIONS OF A SOURCE POINT

sure whether or not to tonify the channel's fire point (Lv-2) or sedate the water point (Lv-8), you could always feel secure that choosing the channel's source point (Lv-3) will help ensure a balanced treatment.

The source points on the *yin* meridians are all earth points associated with their function of centering and nourishing their associated officials.

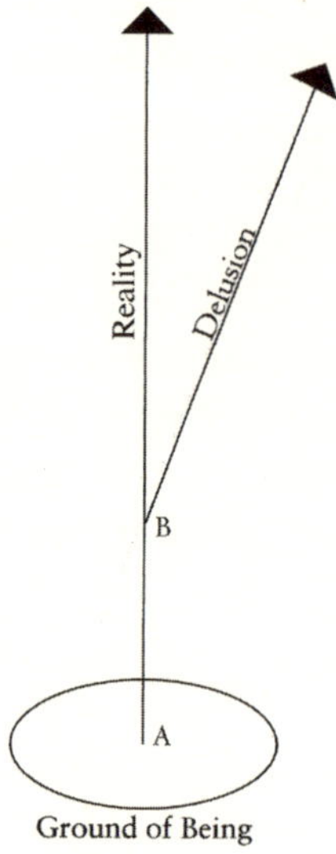


*Figure 13.2*
THE SOURCE OF AUTHENTIC SELF

*Fifteen billion years ago something came from nothing and, in a trillionth of a trillionth of a second, matter was formed and the universe began expanding. The outward momentum of this explosion is the motivating force of evolution itself and is denoted here by line (A). This line denotes the functional influence of* zhen-qi *in motivating the fulfillment of human destiny. The matter that constitutes a human being is moving at the same rate of change as the rest of the universe. Although reality always manifests faster than thought can process, it is possible for us to experience and respond to life at the speed that reality manifests. In effect, the authentic self surfs the outer edge of reality's continually unfolding wave. Living in this way can be thought of as being one with the first cause.*

*Constitutional type emerges at a point of original trauma in life, our own personal "big bang," and it is at this moment that ego is born and our life's motivation deviates from first cause (denoted by line [B]). This line denotes all that is crooked within us that is in need of rectification. In a moment of trauma we personalize a constitutional thought and feeling and the created self begins to gain its own momentum, eventually to obscure entirely the expression of the authentic self. It is the function of source points to reestablish our identification with the authentic self and the first cause as the guiding momentum in our lives. Source points reunite us with our ground of being and have the potential to begin healing the fundamental divisions within us.*

All *yin* source points are the third points proximal from the beginning or end of their meridian. Three is the number associated with the unity of heaven, human, and earth, which again alludes to the function of the source points in promoting harmony (see Figure 13.3).

Tonifying the *yin* source points tends to draw the mind inward toward the potential virtues stored in *jing*. For example, tonifying Lv-3 tends to focus the decision-making facility of the gallbladder inward so decision making is better informed by the plan stored in the liver and relatively less by the mind's desires. Sedating the *yin* source points helps relax the associated officials so the mind is less constrained in trying to assimilate and manifest inner purpose in the world. Hence sedating Lv-3 can help calm the urgency of planning so the gallbladder has time to focus on the details of implementation rather than being constantly pressured and overwhelmed by the big picture.

The source points associated with the *yang* officials clear the mind so it serves as an ideal window to unite the inner and outer worlds with fidelity and no coloration. The *yang* source points also activate the memory of original nature by drawing potential virtues from the depths out toward the mind. Upon recognizing original nature, the mind can better will actions that are congruent with manifesting virtue in the world. Hence tonifying Gb-40 can clear the mind and draw the plan inherent in the depths up into

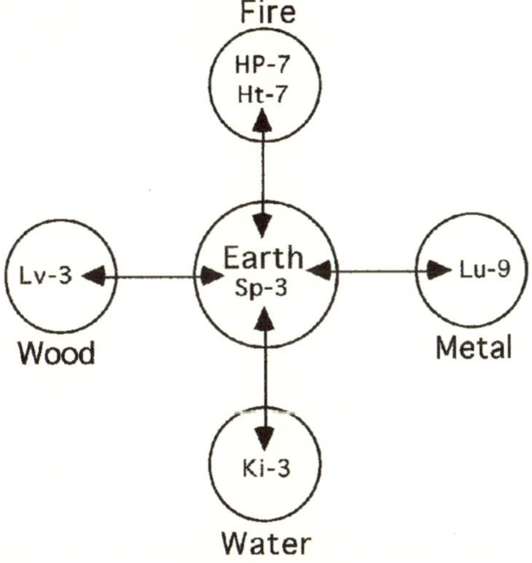


*Figure 13.3*
THE *YIN* SOURCE POINTS

*In the oldest charts of the five elements, the earth element occupies the central position around which the other elements are situated. This reflects the notion that earth is the transition point of change around which the four seasons revolve. The* yin *officials are all oriented toward the center by the functional connection between their source points and the earth element.*

conscious awareness. Dispersing or sedating the *yang* source points tends to relax the mind so that the influence of original nature can assert itself of its own accord. If the mind is overly constrained and habitually forcing growth, sedating Gb-40 can help ease constraint and thus allow the plan stored in the liver to emerge freely and spontaneously.

## QUESTIONS

1. Why are source points considered relatively safe to treat?
2. Could a patient have a negative reaction to the treatment of a source point? Explain a possible mechanism for such a reaction.

# 14

# *LUO* POINTS

LUO POINTS HAVE SEVERAL FUNCTIONS THAT CAN HELP maintain the integrity of the entire network of officials and their corresponding channels. These are summarized in Figure 14.1 (p. 266).

## *The Joining of* Yin *and* Yang *Officials*

The *luo* channels help form a functional yoke between the paired *yin* and *yang* officials associated with each element. In health, any local excesses or deficiencies generated within a given official are equilibrated by its paired official, which either tonifies its deficiency or accepts its excess via the action of the *luo* channels that join the two meridians. If this role of a *luo* channel is compromised, the communication between the *yin* and *yang* officials in an element becomes increasingly dysfunctional as the integrity of the element slowly erodes. The *luo* points on each meridian offer us a way to reestablish this communication. For example, Lv-5 is the *luo* point on the liver channel. If pulse diagnosis reveals a relative excess on the gallbladder meridian, treating Lv-5 will help equilibrate the two channels so the excess on the gallbladder is channeled to supplement the relative deficiency in the liver[1] (see Figure 14.2).

---

## *Balancing the Bilateral Channels*

The *luo* channels also balance the left and right courses of each pair of bilateral meridians. Hence if the right side of the liver meridian evidences a relative excess of *qi* as compared with the left side of the liver meridian, treating Lv-5 on the deficient left side can equilibrate the relative amount of *qi* in both meridians. The excess in the right half of the liver meridian is channeled to supplement the deficiency present in the left half of the meridian couple. The presence of one-sided symptomatology along a given meridian often suggests that treatment of the *luo* points in this way may be indicated. For example, sciatica traveling along the bladder channel on the left side of the body suggests that treating Bl-58 on either the left or right side as determined by palpatory diagnosis, or an akabane test, might be beneficial.[2]

---

## *Clearing Consciousness*

Think of *luo* points as windows that can be opened to vent the dysfunctional *qi* that supports thoughts, beliefs, and behaviors not congruent with true self to the exterior. *Luo* points can promote open awareness by clearing the mind and quieting the spirit. In essence, the *luo* points are like gates that provide access for each official into the depths of self and out into the world.[3] The *yangluo* points allow communication between the *yang* official and the outside world as well as into the interior as

| |
|---|
| 1. Form a functional yoke between the *yin* and *yang* officials in each element. |
| 2. Balance the left and right courses of each bilateral meridian pair. |
| 3. Clear consciousness. |
| 4. Direct consciousness relatively more internally or externally. |
| 5. Drain pathogens that are stagnant in a channel. |

*Figure 14.1*
THE FUNCTIONS OF LUO POINTS

represented by the function of the source point on the paired *yin* official. This dual function empowers the mind to integrate the external events of our lives with original nature as it arises spontaneously within. The *yinluo* points empower communication between the *yin* official and the *yang* official as well as into the interior depths of self as present in *jing*. The relationship of the *yin* and *yang luo* points is illustrated in Figure 14.3 (p. 268).

## Luo *Points as the Gates Between Human and Heavenly Will*

The human mind is juxtaposed between the ascending and descending influences of heaven's will. Internally, heaven's will rises through us as original nature and purpose assert themselves. Externally, heaven's will radiates to us as light descends to illuminate the events of our lives. The interaction of these two influences is mediated by the quality of the human mind as it regulates our will. In health, the mind empowers the alignment of heaven's will with human will to promote the interpenetration of heaven and earth, *shen* and *jing*. However, the tendency of the created self is to oppose the will of heaven by ignoring inner purpose and failing to accept the nature of external events on their own merits.

In response to shock, the *yang* officials tend to turn the mind outward and away from true nature.[4] As the mind attempts in vain to impose its will on the world, a natural conflict arises between the opposing forces of human and heavenly will. The friction that arises in this conflict causes heat that unsettles and agitates the mind and spirit. With the mind turned externally, the spirit fails to penetrate the depths and draw virtue out into the world. In this case the *yin* officials tend to overwork, trying to manifest

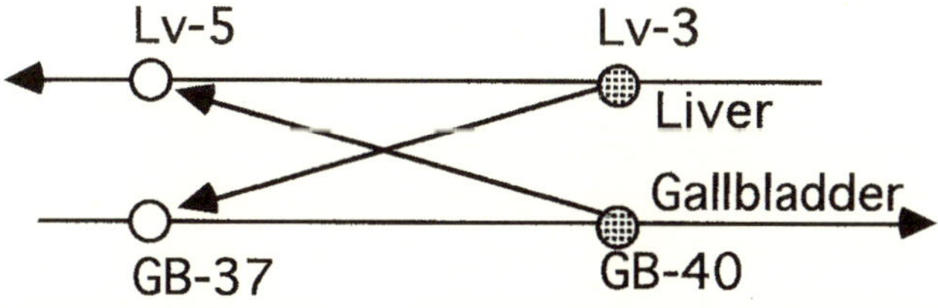


*Figure 14.2*

THE *LUO* POINTS AND ELEMENTAL INTEGRATION

*The* luo *point on each meridian is joined to the source point on the meridian of the complementary organ within each elemental pair. The source/*luo *pairings of Lv-3 with Gb-37 and Gb-40 with Lv-5 form a functional yoke that helps maintain the stability of the wood element by balancing relative excesses and deficiencies of* qi *that occur between its* yin *(liver) and* yang *(gallbladder) officials.*

destiny on their own and, in essence, push innate nature into the world. However, without the listening of the *yang* officials and the mind, all attempts to communicate virtue into the world are in vain.[5]

This process is best illustrated by realizing how frequently we hear that inner voice that never lies, only to ignore it. For example, have you ever had an argument with someone and heard your inner voice tell you not, under any circumstances, to say something hurtful, only to immediately say it anyway? The path of cultivating intuition and restoring original nature is one of heeding this inner voice at every opportunity. Every failure to do so represents a lost opportunity to cultivate virtue, the accretion of karma, and a distancing from true self.

The suppression of innate purpose by the mind results in friction between heaven's will as it arises from the depths of the *yin* officials and human will as it turns a deaf ear to innate purpose. Friction again causes heat and, over time, heat consumes fluid. Thus, as the *yin* officials overwork trying to channel purpose into the world, they tend to consume *jing*, the fluid that lubricates the smooth unfolding of human destiny. With *jing* consumed and purpose depleted, the mind and spirit become increasingly agitated.

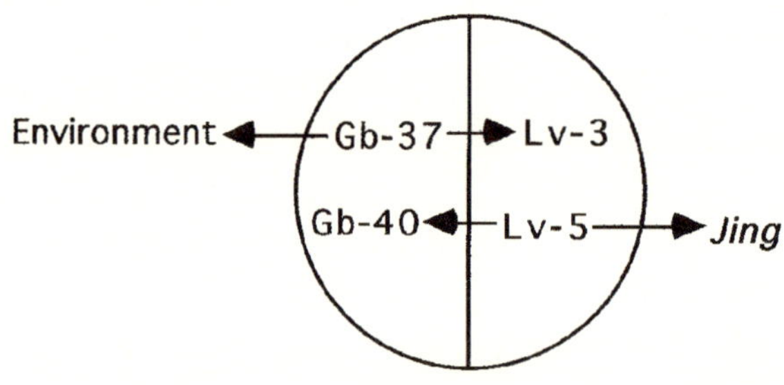


*Figure 14.3*

LUO POINTS AS INTERIOR AND EXTERIOR GATES

*The* yin *and* yang luo *points can help disperse the tension, heat, and stagnation that arises along with our struggle to accept heaven's will as our own as the guiding influence for our actions in life. Gb-37 serves to disperse excess to the exterior, thus clearing the mind and quieting the spirit. In this way the gallbladder official is afforded an elevated perspective regarding the nature of external events in life as they relate to the internal plan stored in the liver. Gb-37 can also help channel a relative excess of* qi *in the liver to supplement a relative depletion of* qi *in the gallbladder channel. Lv-5 can help clear stagnation in the liver so its internal plan as stored in* jing *can flow more effortlessly to inform the decision-making faculties of the gallbladder. Lv-5 can also channel a relative excess of* qi *in the gallbladder to supplement a relative deficiency in the liver official. As awareness follows the flow of* qi *into the interior, the inner nature of our life's plan as stored in* jing *is revealed.*

The *luo* points help settle the spirit and calm the mind by draining the heat and moving the stagnation that arises from conflicts between human and heavenly will. By simultaneously promoting communication between the *yin* and *yang* officials, *luo* points can empower a better alignment between humanity and the will of heaven.

---

## Luo *Points on the* Yin *and* Yang *Officials*

There is an intelligence built into *luo* points empowering the dual functions of dispersing relative excess or supplementing deficiency according to the prevailing functional dynamics of the patient at the moment of treatment. If stagnation is present, the *luo* points facilitate the dispersal of that stagnation to the exterior. But if deficiency is present, the *luo* points help supplement that deficiency by drawing on the relative excess from the source point on the paired official within a given element.

Stagnation causes heat, which in turn can contribute to increased pressure that agitates the mind and spirit. The *yangluo* points function to allow stagnation and heat that disturbs the spirit to vent to the exterior. Such stagnation can be of either external or internal origin. Clearing external excess involves draining the presence of pathogens, as discussed later. When stagnation is of internal origin, the *yangluo* points function to clear agitation from the mind and spirit that derives from habitual reactions to an element's emotion. This agitation generally stems from pathological emotional states that involve disordered belief systems predicated on a reactive mind and nervous system.[6]

For example, the bladder is the *yang* organ associated with the water element. Bl-58, "fly and scatter," is the *luo* point on the bladder channel. One function of Bl-58 is to clear anxiety based on fear that contributes to habitual overuse of willpower *(zhi)*. This function helps reduce the mind's reaction to both internal and external stress in life so fear is less likely to agitate the spirit. With the mind stilled, the will is more gently able to penetrate into the depths of self so *jing* is transformed into wisdom and fear is abated.

The *luo* points associated with the *yin* officials, in contrast, help clear stagnation and heat in the depths that cause emotions to become pathological so they agitate the mind and spirit. Pathological emotions arise congruent with the conflict between human and heavenly will. For example, the kidney works trying to assert potential in the world. However, the habituated mind of the bladder tends to ignore the kidney's innate wisdom and instead dominates and suppresses the kidney function as it tries to assert its own will in the world. This struggle tends to generate heat that can further unsettle the mind and obscure the spirit. Ki-4 ("great bell"), the *luo* point on the kidney channel, can call the mind of the bladder official back inward toward innate purpose by empowering the flow of *qi* from its source at Bl-64 toward Ki-4 in the interior. It can also disperse the heat that arises when the kidney official overworks trying to assert the will of heaven in the world. In this way the settled mind can better access faith and wisdom and once again will actions congruent with manifesting these virtues in the world. The relationships of the *luo* points to clearing consciousness is summarized in Figure 14.4.

## *Directing Awareness*

Conscious awareness mirrors the quality and flow of *qi*. The ability of *luo* points to channel a relative excess in one official to a relative deficiency in

| Elements | Points | Clears | Spirit | Virtue | Pathos |
|---|---|---|---|---|---|
| Water | Ki-4 | Fear | *Zhi* | Wisdom | Suspicion |
| | Bl-58 | Anxiety | | | |
| Wood | Lv-5 | Anger | *Hun* | Benevolence | Belligerence |
| | Gb-37 | Resentment | | | |
| Fire | Ht-5 | Sorrow | *Shen* | Propriety | Confusion |
| | SI-7 | Bitterness | | | |
| | HP-6 | Betrayal | | | |
| | TH-5 | Mania | | | |
| Earth | Sp-4 | Neediness | *Yi* | Integrity | Ingratiation |
| | St-40 | Obsession | | | |
| Metal | Lu-7 | Grief/Longing | *Po* | Righteousness | Self-Righteousness |
| | LI-6 | Disdain | | | |

*Figure 14.4*

LUO POINTS AND THEIR EFFECT ON CONSCIOUSNESS

*The* yangluo *points clear the outer pathological manifestations of internally generated emotions that stagnate like an infection. For example, SI-7 clears bitterness, the outer expression of the heart's sorrow. The stagnation of bitterness distorts the small intestine's ability to sort clearly the pure from impure in life. With the virtue of sorting eroded, the* shen *fails to cultivate the virtue of propriety, and confusion results. The* yinluo *points help settle the primary emotions associated with an element by clearing friction between an individual's will and the will of heaven. Friction produces heat, which agitates the spirit to eventually disturb the mind and distort the healthy emotions into their toxic counterparts as manifested through the* yang *officials.*

another is congruent with the ability of *luo* points to direct consciousness. A relative excess in the gallbladder as compared with the liver suggests the process of decision making is not adequately informed by the liver's function of planning. Treating Lv-5 to channel *qi* from the gallbladder into the liver official is synonymous with directing the decision-making facility of the gallbladder, as it represents the analytical facility of the mind, back inward toward the depths of the liver's plan. This shift of awareness is synonymous with the empowerment of introspection. Similarly, treating Gb-37 to direct a relative excess of *qi* from the liver to the gallbladder will help bring the liver's plan out into conscious awareness. This shift is synonymous with expanding the liver's awareness to include a greater perspective on our life's external circumstances. As *qi* is directed relatively more toward the interior or exterior, conscious awareness follows.

---

## *Coupling* Luo *Points with Source Points: Reintegrating Spirit and Virtue*

As illustrated in Figure 14.2, the *luo* point on each channel is coupled with the source point on its paired meridian. Treating the *luo* and source points together offers a simple protocol for reintegrating the axis of spirit and virtue within each element. *Luo* points can also be used in conjunction with source points to direct a patient's awareness in a relatively more internal or external direction.

There is a primary shock in life that is congruent with the loss of original nature. This shock initiates the separation of the *yin* and *yang* officials in a person's constitutional element. If a person is constitutionally strong in terms of quality and quantity of *jing,* shock tends to lead toward stagnation and excess in the constitutional official. If the person is constitutionally weak, shock tends to lead to deficiency of *qi*, *yang,* and other vital substances.[7]

Failure of communication between the *yin* and *yang* officials in the constitutional element is congruent with whatever disordered concept or belief is generated to help the mind cope with the trauma at hand. This story, in essence, sits between the two officials like a cloud that obscures the mind's ability to perceive reality. Treating the source point on the weaker official in conjunction with the *luo* point on the stronger official, as determined by pulse diagnosis, can help profoundly to reintegrate the functioning of the constitutional element.

Note that the function of a *luo* point used alone can be quite different than when it is used in conjunction with a source point. For example, if the stomach is excess relative to spleen, treating Sp-4 alone can work to transfer this relative excess internally. However, we can also address this same situation by treating the spleen's source point (Sp-3) in conjunction with the *luo* point on the stomach channel, St-40. My decision regarding which approach to take is based largely on pulse diagnosis. If the difference between the two officials is moderate and neither official evidences extreme imbalance, I am likely to just choose the *luo* point on the deficient channel. If, however, the *yang* official's pulse exhibits a true excess associated with stagnation of *qi* and heat, as evidenced by tense to tight, pounding, and biting qualities, I am more likely to treat the *yangluo* and *yin* source points together as elaborated here. Sometimes I retain needles in both points simultaneously and other times I treat them independently. In this case I retain the needle in the *luo* point until the pulse associated with the *yang* official softens, indicating to me that the stagnation has dispersed. I then tonify the source point on the *yin* channel to build healthy *qi* there in the relative absence of suppression from the mind of the *yang* official that has now been dissipated.

When the stomach official evidences a relative excess to the spleen, treating Sp-3 in conjunction with St-40 has several possible beneficial effects. As a *luo* point, St-40 ("abundant splendor") will disperse any relative excess in the stomach official that is agitating the spirit of the earth element and obscuring its communication with the virtue inherent in the *yin* official. Such agitation, heat, dampness, and pressure tends to support the functioning of the habitual mind and turn it outward away from the interior to support the existence of the created self. As a source point, Sp-3 will tonify the function of the spleen and revive its ability to assert the virtue of integrity with a fresh supply of primordial *qi*. It will also effectively draw *qi* from the *yang* official into the depths so the mind and spirit are reoriented toward the interior. Hence as stagnation is dispersed by the *luo* point, the awareness of the *yang* official is opened and redirected toward the *yin* official whose virtue is restored as the guiding influence in life.

However, let's imagine that the spleen evidences an excess relative to the stomach. Then treating Sp-4 in conjunction with St-42, the channel's *luo* and source points, can be equally beneficial in reintegrating the balanced functioning of the earth element. Sp-4 will disperse any excess and stagnation that obscures the nature of that official's virtue from asserting itself. Tonifying St-42 will strengthen the spirit (*yi,* thought) associated with the stomach official so it is better able to digest and integrate life experience in a way that allows the virtue of integrity to manifest in the world.

## Draining Pathogens

One function of *luo* points is to relieve the exterior by draining pathogens that have stagnated within a channel (see Figure 14.5). Pathogens are the embodiment of all we generate or incorporate into ourselves that is not congruent with original nature.[8] Pathogens obscure the communication of heart and mind, *jing* and *shen,* virtue and spirit. The presence of pathogens fuels the dysfunctional tendency of the *yang* officials to direct the mind outward into the world away and from the depths of self. Thus the mind tends to dominate the subtle influence of original nature in guiding awareness.

This process can be felt in pulse diagnosis when the complementary positions corresponding to the *yang* officials impinge on the principal positions corresponding to the *yin* officials.[9] By removing evil *qi* and moving stagnation, the patient is better able to introspect as true self is

| ***LUO* POINTS AND THEIR CORRESPONDING PATHOGENS** | | | |
|---|---|---|---|
| **Element** | ***Luo* Points** | **Point Names** | ***Luo* Function** |
| Water | Ki-4<br>Bl-58 | Great Bell<br>Fly and Scatter | Clears damp heat<br>Disperses wind & damp |
| Wood | Lv-5<br>Gb-37 | Insect Drain<br>Bright and Clear | Clears damp heat<br>Dispels wind, clears heat, transforms damp |
| Fire | Ht-5<br>SI-7<br>HP-6<br><br><br>TH-5 | Penetrating Inside<br>Support Uprightness<br>Inner Frontier Gate<br><br><br>Outer Frontier Gate | Clears heart fire & damp heat<br>Disperses wind, relieves exterior heat<br>Clears heat, transforms heart phlegm & fire, transforms summer heat & phlegm, expels wind phlegm<br>Relieves exterior heat, resolves toxins, dispels wind & wind heat |
| Earth | Sp-4<br>St-40 | Prince's Grandson<br>Abundant Splendor | Transforms damp & damp heat<br>Dispels wind & wind phlegm, clears stomach fire & heat, transforms damp, damp heat, & hot phlegm |
| Metal | Lu-7<br>LI-6 | Meridian Gutter<br>Side Passage | Disperses wind, relieves the exterior<br>Dispels heat, fire, & wind |

*Figure 14.5*
LUO POINTS AND PATHOGENS

*Here I have listed some traditional functions ascribed to* luo *points relative to their ability to drain pathogens.*

more clearly revealed. As evil *qi* is removed, it is expected the patient's pulse will relax and the complementary positions that correspond to the *yang* organs will impinge less on the principal positions. Clearing the presence of stagnation and its consequences is a necessary first step in restoring communication between the spirits and their potential virtues. *Luo* points can be used to drain the presence of internal or external pathogens that distort the function of either a *yin* or *yang* official. In this way we can remove a dysfunctional source of *qi* that fuels the distortions of the created self.

The *luo* points are often said to clear, invigorate, and regulate the channels (the main meridians and their collaterals). Their ability to clear stagnation and resolve latent pathogens relates directly to the function of the *luo* points in promoting and clearing awareness. When pathogens are contracted externally, symptoms tend to mimic the quality of the pathogen in nature. For example, the presence of wind/heat may produce a high fever and muscle aches that move around the body like the wind. If the presence of externally contracted pathogens is not resolved expediently, they can become chronic and stagnate in the channels.

Pathogens such as wind, heat, and damp can also be generated internally as the consequences of organ dysfunction. For example, incomplete digestion based on deficient spleen *qi* can lead to a condition of internal dampness. Excessive anger can generate heat and wind that stagnate and obscure the upright function of the liver official. The genesis of internal pathogens arises as a consequence of the conflict between human will and heavenly will as described earlier. The notion of internally and externally generated pathogens provides potent images that link the inner process of an individual to the greater context of his or her environment at large. The inner meanings of the pathogens addressed by the *luo* points are presented in Figure 14.6.

The acute phase of an illness is often typified by stagnation of wind, heat, cold, and dampness often in various combinations. In this scenario *luo* points are often chosen to drain the associated pathogen. The *luo* points also function to drain pathogens when they are generated internally due to morbid infatuation with one's emotions.

---

## *Summary*

*Luo* points have an array of functions that are context sensitive depending on the relative quantity of *qi* in the channels and the natures of the other points they are treated with. Generally, *luo* points work by dispersing

| Pathogen | Emotion | Attribute |
|---|---|---|
| Cold | Fear | Contractive: slows physiological processes. |
| Wind | Confusion | Chaos: things change rapidly. |
| Heat | Bitterness | Expansive: speeds up physiological processes, consumes *yin* over time. |
| Fire | Mania | Explosive: burns *yin* quickly. |
| Damp | Burden, Worry | Burdens physiological processes. |
| Dry | Grief, Longing | Causes friction and the generation of heat. |
| Trauma | Shock | Separates heart/kidney axis. |

*Figure 14.6*
INNER ATTRIBUTES OF PATHOGENS

true excess and channeling relative excess to relative deficiency. Consciousness follows the flow of *qi,* and *luo* points can be used to direct the mind in a relatively internal or external direction.

## NOTES

1. I use the N*anjing* pulse system to assess differences in the relative amount of *qi* between *yin* and *yang* officials of the same element. In this system the *yang* officials are considered superficial to the *yin* officials on the pulse.
2. Generally, the *luo* point on the side that is deficient is treated regardless of the side on which the symptom is present. The implications of such one-sided imbalances in the meridian system is discussed at length in Chapter 7 in the context of the akabane imbalance.
3. This function is predicated on that ultimate "gate of gates," the mysterious pass that serves as both entrance into the world as well as to the burial ground. See *ND,* pp. 20–21 and Chapter 7.
4. For a discussion of shock and its effect on the *yin* and *yang* officials, see Chapter 1.
5. For a discussion of the nature of listening, see the discussion of SI-19 in Chapter 25.
6. These pathological emotional states are discussed below and in Chapters 2 and 15.
7. Hence a person's constitutional type is likely to be felt on the pulse position that is either working the hardest or is the least functional.
8. For a discussion of the pathogens, see *ND,* pp. 176–177 (cold), 196–197 (fire), 235 (wind), 259 (dryness), and 280 (damp).
9. These are my own observations relative to the Shen/Hammer pulse system. See Hammer, 2001.

# 15

# *XI*-CLEFT POINTS

THE CHARACTER *XI* (郄) INDICATES A CLEFT OR FISSURE. At the *xi*-cleft points, *qi* and blood, which flow relatively superficially from the *jing*-well points, gather and penetrate more deeply into the interior (see Figure 15.1). In conditions of excess and stagnation, *qi* and blood tend to accumulate at a channel's *xi*-cleft point. *Xi*-cleft points excel at moving stagnation by regulating the circulation of *qi* and blood in the channels. The effects and causes of stagnation are unique for each official. If an official has a healthy reserve of *qi,* it will work to move whatever obstacle is suppressing its function. Excessive work generates heat, and, over time, fluid and *yin* will be consumed as well as the reserves of *qi* and *yang* which sustain that work. In this case *xi*-cleft points can help move stagnation and thereby alleviate the official from having to hyperfunction. If an official is weak and its reserve of *qi* is deficient, stagnation can result from failing to move and transform obstructions. Here stagnation tends to smother the expression of the official whose level of function will slow to a standstill.

In either the case of excess or deficiency, long-standing stagnation can lead to an accumulation of heat and toxicity. Generally the *xi*-cleft points are indicated in the treatment of acute conditions and pain; however, I have found these points on the *yang* channels to excel at helping move long-term stagnation in conjunction with pathological emotions and disorders of the spirit. I consider *xi*-cleft points unique in their ability to move the accretions of mundanity that inhibit the spontaneous expression of each official's true nature. The function of the *yang xi*-cleft points is related relatively more to issues involving *qi* and how we act in life, whereas the *yin xi*-cleft points tend to address issues involving the blood and our internal experience of ourselves. For example, SI-6, "nourishing the old," the *xi*-cleft point on the small intestine channel, drains bitterness, associated with heart's unfulfilled desires, that tends to manifest as sarcasm. In contrast, HP-4, "Cleft Gate," tends to help move sorrow accumulated from love lost that prevents us from trusting others.

---

## *Stagnant Emotional States and the* Yang Xi-*Cleft Points*

In Chapter 2 on aggressive energy, I discussed the implications of festering and toxic emotions and their similarity to chronic infection. This type of stagnation is often concurrent with the types of symptoms for which *xi*-cleft points are indicated. Swelling in the throat, carbuncles, furuncles, abcesses, gynecological masses, and vomiting can all be embodiments of such emotional toxicity.[1] Although the specific symptoms themselves may be acute, it is the long-term background of dysfunction represented by the

| **Element** | **Point** | **Name** |
|---|---|---|
| Water | Ki-5 | Water Spring |
| | Bl-63 | Golden Gate |
| Wood | Gb-36 | Outer Mound |
| | Lv-6 | Middle Capital |
| Fire | Ht-6 | *Yin* Cleft |
| | SI-6 | Nourishing the Old |
| | HP-4 | Cleft Gate |
| | TH-7 | Assembly of Officials |
| Earth | St-34 | Beam Mound |
| | Sp-8 | Earth Motivator |
| Metal | Lu-6 | Greatest Hole |
| | LI-7 | Warm Current |

*Figure 15.1*
*XI*-CLEFT POINTS

festering emotional states discussed that can make us vulnerable to expressing such symptoms physically. The *xi*-cleft points on the *yang* meridians may be used to help move the stagnation that supports the pathological expression of these emotional states. In conjunction with the *xi*-cleft points, I find the *luo* points (Figure 2.2) on the *yang* meridians particularly useful for draining the *qi* that perpetuates these negative emotional states. The *luo* points can vent the suppressed *qi* to the outside world and thereby deflate the internal pressure that feeds habitual nature. With this tension removed, the habit may be broken long enough for patients to gain perspective on their situation and to stop making it worse by perpetuating it with negative thoughts and behaviors.

## Yin Xi-*Cleft Points*

Whereas the *yang xi*-cleft points address issues that deal relatively more with *qi,* the *yin xi*-cleft points address issues relatively more related to blood stasis, deficiency, and bleeding. The relationship between the *yin xi*-cleft points and blood is summarized in Figure 15.2. The *yang xi*-cleft points address the consequences of mental/emotional orientations toward the external world. Hence bitterness, resentment, and secrecy constitute our responses to life and how we think about things. By addressing the blood, the *yin xi*-cleft points treat the internal consequences of how our attitudes and emotions come to be embodied and hurt us. Hence blood stasis in the heart or chest to the point of severe pain is often congruent with a distancing from self predicated on bitterness over past heartaches

| Point | Condition |
|---|---|
| Ki-5 | Menstrual difficulties associated with blood stasis or deficiency. |
| Lv-6 | Blood stasis in the uterus. |
| Ht-6 | Heart pain due to blood stasis; bleeding due to heat in the blood. |
| HP-4 | Pain associated with stasis of blood in the chest or heart.<br>Bleeding in the upper *jiao* associated with heat in the blood. |
| Sp-8 | Blood stasis in the uterus and abdomen. |
| Lu-6 | Coughing of blood. |

*Figure 15.2*

THE *YIN XI*-CLEFT POINTS AND BLOOD

*Here I have listed the functional relationship between the* yin xi-*cleft points and the blood. From the perspective of Chinese medicine, blood stasis can be a physiological correlate of suppression.*

and perceived betrayals. Similarly, the formation of abdominal or gynecological masses can be seen as based on a separation of our pain away from our consciousness and into the interior.[2]

### *Summary*

Acute symptomatology and pain for which *xi*-cleft points are used is often predicated on a background of stagnation. Such stagnation corresponds to the presence of false beliefs and thoughts that do not accurately convey true self as based in original nature. *Xi*-cleft points can address such stagnation during a crisis, and they can also serve during ongoing treatment to move stagnation preventively. I find these points to be particularly effective for relieving mental tension when emotional pain from past trauma has locked the mind into habitual patterns of functioning.

## *NOTES*

1. Deadman and Al-Khafaji, 2000.
2. For a discussion of blood stasis, see *ND*, pp. 307–310.

# 16

# *MU* POINTS

THE *MU* POINTS, LOCATED ON THE FRONT SURFACE OF THE body, provide deep access to the *yin* aspect of each official's realm of functioning (see Figure 16.1). The term *mu* (募) means "to collect" and implies that the *mu* points are places where the *qi* of the associated officials accumulates. Often *mu* points are referred to as "alarm points," which signifies that the points tend to become sensitive to pressure when *yinqi* (mundane *qi*) collects in a channel.

### *Treating the* Yin

We must distinguish between true *yin* and mundane *yin*. True *yin* represents the potential virtues inherent in essence, whereas mundane *yin* is synonymous with the accretions of all the influences we have assimilated during life that are not congruent with true self. *Mu* points have the facility of empowering true *yin* and removing mundanity.

| | | |
|---|---|---|
| Lu-1 | Central Palace | Lung |
| St-25 | Heavenly Pivot | Large Intestine |
| CV-12 | Middle Duct | Middle *Jiao,* Stomach |
| Lv-13 | Chapter Gate | Spleen |
| CV-14 | Great Deficiency | Heart |
| CV-4 | First Gate | Small Intestine |
| CV-3 | Utmost Middle | Bladder |
| GB-25 | Capital Gate | Kidney |
| CV-15 | Dove Tail | Heart Protector |
| CV-5 | Stone Gate | Three Heater |
| CV-7 | *Yin* Crossing | Lower *Jiao* |
| CV-17 | Primordial Child | Upper *Jiao* |
| GB-24 | Sun and Moon | Gallbladder |
| Lv-14 | Gate of Hope | Liver |

*Figure 16.1*
THE *MU* POINTS

---

## *Tonification*

*Mu* points are important conduits for the flow of essence into the world. Hence the *mu* point on each channel can effectively place that official in contact with a deep reserve of *jing*. This can empower the *yin* aspect of the virtues inherent in original nature. For example, the lung official can empower both *yin* and *yang* aspects of virtue. A *yang* virtue associated with the lung is the ability to acknowledge the quality in another's work. This is based in part on the *yin* virtue of feeling secure with our own worth and innate value. Hence Lu-1, the *mu* point on the lung channel, can invoke the lungs' *yin* virtues of openness and receptivity. Similarly, treating Lv-14, "gate of hope," can help soften the liver and the internalized wall of distension that is often congruent with frustration and belligerence.

The *mu* points are complementary in nature to the back *shu* points that provide access to a reserve of *yangqi* for each official. Treating both a channel's *mu* and *shu* points in the same session can effectively harmonize, tonify, or sedate the influence of *yin* and *yang* on an official.

## *Moving Stagnation*

Each *mu* point collects imbalances from the previous elements.[1] Hence Gb-24 and Lv-14, the *mu* points of the gallbladder and liver, respectively, are governed by the relationship of water to wood. Similarly, CV-14, the *mu* point of the heart official, is governed by the relationship of the wood to the fire element. Sensitivity found at a *mu* point on palpation can suggest either that stagnation is originating within the primary element or the previous element on the *sheng* cycle. For example, finding that Gb-24 is sensitive to pressure can suggest the stagnation is arising from either a primary dysfunction in the gallbladder official or that the gallbladder is accumulating stagnation from the water element. The later interpretation is furthered if we find that CV-3, the bladder *mu* point, is also tender. If we treat CV-3 and find the sensitivity in Gb-24 also improves, the tenderness at Gb-24 is likely to have reflected a bladder imbalance and did not occur due to primary dysfunction of the gallbladder official.

Divergent channels redirect external pathogens away from primary organs and into the joints. When a joint becomes saturated, the pathogen then continues its journey toward the target organ. Generally, the *yang* organs are affected first, and it is at the *mu* points that pathology will enter the *yin* organ as the presence of cold, wind, heat, dampness, or dryness. Such pathogens represent all we have embodied in life from the exterior that does not augment our true nature. Such pathogens congruent with mundanity are effectively drained at a channel's *mu* point.

# *NOTES*

1. From a lecture by Jeffrey Yuen.

# 17

# *SHU* POINTS

THE CHARACTER *SHU* (俞) CAN BE TRANSLATED AS "TRANSPORT," indicating the *qi* of the twelve officials is transported to the surface and is accessible through the *shu* points. The character *shu* is etymologically related to the character *yu* (愈), meaning to "heal." *Yu* depicts a boat (月) carrying a heart (心) from one shore to another. Located on the back, the *shu* points access particularly strong reserves of *qi* to provide strong tonification, or sedation, to the function of their corresponding official. Note that the *shu* points are located relatively over their respective organs and in the area of each organ's afferent and efferent innervation.[1]

## *Use of* Shu *Points*

Initially in treatment, *shu* points can play a role in clearing fundamental blocks that prevent constitutional treatment from progressing. In this regard, aggressive energy (AE) can be tapped at the *yinshu* points. Because of their ability to strongly tonify or sedate *qi, shu* points can also help correct an akabane or break a H/W imbalance that is resistant to treatment. Further, Bl-23 is included in the protocol for clearing internal states of possession. Its inclusion likely reflects its ability to drain cold and fear from the kidneys and to tonify *jing*, an innate source of original nature. Other than these instances, the use of *shu* points to strongly tonify or sedate a specific official is generally reserved for later in treatment after blocks have been cleared. *Shu* points are strong in effect and are useful in cases of serious disharmony when other more basic tonification or sedation techniques have failed to initiate substantive movement toward the restitution of functional balance. Once a basic balance has been achieved, *shu* points can be helpful in raising the overall level of *qi* available to support the officials, which should manifest as an overall increase of *qi* on the pulse.

The function of the *shu* points can embrace every discrete function associated with a given official. They may be used to reinforce other combinations of points in any treatment when we wish strongly to tonify or sedate the function of a given official. For example, if a patient's pulses indicate a moderate to severe amount of liver *qi* stagnation, a treatment of first choice might be to sedate Lv-3 and Gb-37, the source and *luo* points of the liver and gallbladder, respectively. If the expected change on the pulse is not significant, we might decide to utilize Bl-18 in this or another treatment to provide a stronger dispersion to the liver official.

*Shu* points are quite effective when treated with moxa for the presence of deficiency and cold in the *yin* officials. I have found that tonifying all the *yinshu* points in one treatment can be particularly effective to aid recovery when a patient has been left exhausted by a chronic illness. For example, a patient may report that a cold that had turned into bronchitis or pneumonia has left him debilitated. The *yinshu* points can literally rectify the *qi* to the degree that many people feel resurrected and back to their old selves immediately after the treatment.

---

## Shu *Point Relationships*

The relationship between the governor vessel points and the inner and outer *shu* points at a given anatomical level are of specific interest (see Figure 17.1). The governor vessel aligns us with the central axis of heaven. Hence the highest point on the governor vessel, GV-20, orients us to the North Star as the "heart of heaven." We can think of the governor vessel points as empowering the officials with a cosmological source of *yang*. Here the influence of *yang* can either be tonified or dispersed. In cases of deficiency, tonifying *yang* tends to have the effect of speeding up physiological processes, generating heat and expansiveness and causing things to ascend. For example, GV-8 ("sinew contraction"), located between the liver *shu* points, can empower us to stand up straight by tightening overly loose tendons. Such a process may empower liver *yang* to rise in a way congruent with self-esteem and the ability to stand up for one's self. In cases of excess, sedating or dispersing the governor vessel points tends to have the effect of slowing and relaxing physiological processes while easing constraint. Hence GV-8 can be used to sedate liver *yang* that rises to disturb the heart and is congruent with belligerence. In this way the sinews may relax as tension in the wood element eases.

The points on the "inner" line of the bladder meridian closest to the governor vessel are the *shu* points. These tap deep reserves of *qi* and *yang* to strengthen or sedate the functioning of each official. In cases of deficiency, *shu* points can be used to empower any virtue associated with a given official. For example, the ability of the earth element to nourish and hold the center is expressed as the virtue of integrity. Bl-20, the spleen *shu* point, can therefore empower integrity in any aspect of being where that virtue is lacking. Therefore, the point is equally effective in supporting the spleen to hold the blood within the vessels when there is bleeding or to empower the transformation of damp into blood and flesh. Similarly, the point can empower integrity by assisting us in learning to identify our

**GOVERNOR VESSEL AND *SHU* POINT RELATIONSHIPS**

| GV | Inner Line | Correspondence | Outer Line | Correspondence |
|---|---|---|---|---|
| GV-12 | Bl-13 | Lung | Bl-37 (42) | Gate of *Po* |
| X | Bl-14 | Heart Protector | Bl-38 (43) | *Gaohuangshu* |
| GV-11 | Bl-15 | Heart | Bl-39 (44) | Spirit Hall (*shen*) |
| GV-10 | Bl-16 | Governor Vessel | Bl-40 (45) | Wail of Grief |
| GV-9 | Bl-17 | Diaphragm | Bl-41 (46) | Diaphragm Border |
| GV-8 | Bl-18 | Liver | Bl-42 (47) | Gate of *Hun* |
| GV-7 | Bl-19 | Gallbladder | Bl-43 (48) | *Yang* Net |
| GV-6 | Bl-20 | Spleen | Bl-44 (49) | Thought Dwelling (*yi*) |
| X | Bl-21 | Stomach | Bl-45 (50) | Stomach Granary |
| GV-5 | Bl-22 | Three Heater | Bl-46 (51) | Vitals Door |
| GV-4 | Bl-23 | Kidney | Bl-47 (52) | Room of Will (*zhi*) |
| X | Bl-24 | Sea of *Qi* | X | X |
| GV-3 | Bl-25 | Large Intestine | X | X |
| X | Bl-26 | Origin Pass | X | X |
| X | Bl-27 | Small Intestine | X | X |
| X | Bl-28 | Bladder | Bl-48 (53) | Womb and Heart Diaphragm |
| X | Bl-29 | Sacrum | X | X |

*Figure 17.1*
THE *SHU* POINTS

*Here we can see the relative position of the points on the governor vessel to the points on the inner and outer lines of the bladder meridian.*

needs and speaking up for them. In cases of excess, the *shu* points can help ease constraint and moderate the function of an official. For example, the presence of damp can burden the spleen's function and cause it to overwork and generate heat congruent with insatiable appetite and neediness. Sedating Bl-20 can disperse excess and help slow a person's consumption of sweets and production of damp. In this way, the center can be strengthened, integrity restored, and neediness transformed into self-sufficiency.

The points on the "outer" bladder line access the emotional and spiritual realm of function for their corresponding official. This is particularly true for the *yinshu* points Bl-13, Bl-14, Bl-15, Bl-18, Bl-20, and Bl-23, although the principle can be applied elsewhere. Hence Bl-37 (42) ("*po* door"), the point on the outer bladder line congruent with Bl-13, the lung *shu* point, treats the *po*, the spirit associated with the lung official. The outer bladder points can be treated on their own if we wish to address specifically the spirit of a given official. They may also be treated in tandem with the inner *shu* points if you think the nature of a particular imbalance is driven by dysfunction at the spirit level or is creating dysfunction at the spirit level that is perpetuating illness. For example, if a patient evidences stagnation of *qi* and heat in his lungs, I might choose to treat Bl-13 for its ability to clear heat from the lungs and help them descend *qi*. In this case, I believe the stagnation is primary in the imbalance and not based on emotional or spirit-level dysfunction. However, if the stagnation appears to be predicated on, or significantly contributing to, grief, lack of inspiration, or loneliness, I might choose to treat Bl-37 in conjunction with Bl-13 or on its own in a separate treatment session.

Next I look at some of these specific relationships to illustrate the general principle of how these points are functionally connected. Look each of these points up later in the text for a more comprehensive comparison of individual point functions.[2]

---

### ❖ T3–T4: GV-12, Bl-13, Bl-37 (42)

Acupuncture point GV-12, "body pillar," is located behind CV-17, "primordial child." At CV-17 the breaths of heaven *(qi)* and earth *(jing)* meet to empower all rhythmic movements in our being and unite us with primordial *dao*. The spine is the structural pillar that holds up the body to unite heaven (the head) and earth (the torso). Hence GV-12 aligns the heavenly breaths with the central axis joining heaven and earth. Excess heat from the lungs is easily able to enter the heart to disturb the spirit. GV-12 can help drain lung heat that infiltrates the heart congruent with such manifestations of *shen* disturbance as mad walking, ranting, and raving, seeing ghosts, and murderous rage.[3] Such rage is typical of the self-righteousness that typifies the fanaticism that can accompany excess heat and dry lungs.[4]

Moving laterally, we find Bl-13, the lung *shu* point. Bl-13 has the potential to strongly tonify or to sedate the *qi* of the lung official. In cases of deficiency, Bl-13 can empower inspiration in all aspects of being. In cases of excess, Bl-13 can move stagnant *qi* and heat in the lungs and empower the virtues of openness and receptivity. Moving laterally again, we come to Bl-37 (42), "*po* door." The *po* is the spirit associated with the lung official.[5] Bl-37 can be particularly effective for addressing dysfunctional grieving or longing, as well as depression typified by feelings of emptiness, worthlessness, and loss.

---

## ❖ T4–T5: Bl-14, Bl-38 (43)

There is no governor vessel point at the T4–T5 level. Bl-14 is the *shu* point associated with the heart protector and can provide a strong tonification or sedation to that official. Habitually looking to love as the answer to our problems in life can leave a heart unfulfilled and tired. The reserve of *qi* accessed by Bl-14 can help revive such a weary heart. Sedating the heart protector can help calm the urgency that can drive us to exhaust ourselves in the pursuit of intimacy. The heart protector's *shu* point can also disperse heat that enters the blood through the heart protector. Such heat is often congruent with unconscious and unrealized desires that create internal pressure in the heart.

The function of the heart protector is to absorb blows that might otherwise harm the heart. If the heart protector becomes weak, due to chronic illness, or vulnerable, due to shock, illness may penetrate past the heart protector's defenses to reach the area between the heart and the diaphragm known as the Gaohuang. If this happens, Bl-38 (43), *gaohuangshu*, can be used to nourish the heart and heart protector and to unsettle illness from this vital region so close to the heart. In general, I find Bl-38(43) to nourish heart protector blood so it empowers the virtue of allowing us to choose to be open in life from a position of strength. Bl-38 (43) can help give us the "heart" and compassion toward ourselves that can help revive us and speed recovery from chronic illness.

---

## ❖ T5–T6: GV-11, Bl-15, Bl-39 (44)

Acupuncture points GV-10, *"lingtai,"* and GV-11, *"shendao,"* align the heart as the spiritual center of our beings to the North Star as the "heart of heaven." These two points address the *yin* and *yang* aspects of spirit, *ling* and *shen,* respectively. In cases of excess, these points are suitable for treating a psychospiritual presentation tending toward mania. In cases of deficiency, these points empower a perspective (GV-10) that initiates the positive movement of spirit (GV-11) into the world.[6]

Bl-15 as the heart *shu* point can provide a strong tonification or sedation to the heart official. I tend to use Bl-15 rarely because the emperor must always be approached only in the most serious of circumstances. However, Bl-15 can play an important role in commanding the heart as emperor to ascend the throne and retake the reins of the nation when other more gentle methods have failed to be persuasive. In cases of excess, sedating Bl-15 can disperse internal pressure in the heart resulting from stagnant heat and *qi*. Such pressure is often congruent with feelings of mania, rage, and being out of control. The name of Bl-39, "*shentang,*" alludes to the heart as a temple or hall where *shen* resides. "Spirit hall" allows us to nourish the heart *shen* so it is directed and focused in the pursuit of cultivating virtue. If the mind is too expansive, and continually wanders, "spirit hall" can call it home to the palace of the heart, thus helping us to focus. If the heart is exhausted and failing to serve as a guiding influence in orchestrating life, "spirit hall" can serve to renew the heart's commitment to its rule.

---

### ❖ T6–T7: GV-10, Bl-16, Bl-40 (45)

The name of GV-10, "spirit tower" *(lingtai),* is a Daoist name for the heart.[7] The name refers to a tower built for the emperor so he could gain an elevated perspective and thus see over the walls of his palace.[8] With his insight restored, feelings of seclusion and sorrow could be allayed. In cases of excess heat, GV-10 excels in treating mania. Bl-16 is the *shu* point associated with the governor vessel. The governor vessel itself serves as a type of tower aligning our entire being to the influence of *yang* and the axis of heaven. Although generally listed as a *shu* point for the governor vessel, I have never found Bl-16 useful in this regard. I have, however, used it to treat the heart, heart protector, and diaphragm and for draining heat and moving *qi* stagnation in these organs and in the area of the diaphragm. Bl-40 (45), "wail of grief," addresses sorrow and bitterness that affects the heart. I have found this point excellent for people whose emotional pain presents like a weeping wound. Such a condition is mirrored in symptoms like shingles when inflamed and weeping sores have appeared on the skin. Such grief and wailing suggests the emperor is indeed not comfortable on the throne and that sorrow is effectively preventing him from ruling the nation. Hence, if like King Xuan, a patient appears as if his heart is "like fire burning in the Heart-like fire burning in the hedges—My lonely Heart is as dried as the heat of summer; Sorrow in my burning Heart is like the clouds of steam rising from fire," I often consider treating Bl-40.[9]

---

### ❖ T7–T8, GV-9, Bl-17, Bl-41 (46)

Located at the level of the diaphragm, GV-9, "utmost *yang*," is credited with treating disharmonies in the upper and lower *jiao*. By strengthening the presence of *yang* to its "utmost," GV-9 can both tonify and warm the stomach and spleen in the middle *jiao*. By sedating excess *yang*, GV-9 can drain damp heat in the middle *jiao* often associated with jaundice. I have discussed elsewhere the stagnation of *qi* in the diaphragm from the perspective of separation and divorce.[10] Congruent with the inner conflict that gives rise to such stagnation, a patient often reports feeling as though he or she has been "stabbed in the back" in the area of GV-9. In this case, I often treat GV-9 to help release the diaphragm and relax the muscles of the middle back.

Bl-17 is the diaphragm *shu* point and can treat *qi* stagnation in the diaphragm. The diaphragm is an internal wall that separates the middle from the upper *jiao*. *Qi* tends to stagnate in the diaphragm as we internalize and come to embody the real or imagined walls that block our growth in life. Such stagnation can be congruent with limited mobility in the torso and compromised breathing due to *qi* stagnation in the diaphragm. Bl-41 (46), "diaphragm gate," can supplement the effects of Bl-17 in harmonizing the area of the diaphragm. As a gate between the middle and upper *jiao*, Bl-41 (46) can also promote communication between these two burners and move *qi* stagnation in the upper *jiao*.

---

### ❖ T9–T10: GV-8, Bl-18, Bl-42 (47)

The name of GV-8, "sinew contraction," alludes to the function of the liver official in presiding over the sinews. Hence GV-8 is indicated for conditions of wind congruent with either excessive movement as occurs in epilepsy or stiffness associated with tightness in the tendons. GV-8 is also indicated for symptoms of mania, suggesting that excess heat in the liver is rising to disturb the heart. This type of heat often manifests as belligerence that unsettles the spirit. Bl-18 is the liver *shu* point and can provide a strong tonification or sedation of *qi* to the liver official. In cases of deficiency, Bl-18 can address resignation, lack of aspiration, lack of motivation, and hopelessness. In cases of excess, Bl-18 can calm belligerence, mania, and aggressiveness. When used to treat either excess or deficiency, Bl-18 can empower vision either by elevating perspective and getting a person to stand up for himself (tonifying deficiency) or by empowering a belligerent person to step back from the obstacle that confronts him (sedation).

Bl-42, "*hun* gate," treats the *hun* spirit associated with the liver official. I find this point useful for treating conditions typified by a wandering, restless spirit. For example, disturbed dreaming and hallucinations can be examples of ungrounded creativity congruent with an unsettled *hun*. In contrast, depression, resignation, and hopelessness can signify spiritual stagnation and suggest the *hun* is failing to ascend. In either case the ability of the *hun* to empower evolution will be impaired.

---

### ❖ T10–T11: GV-7, Bl-19, Bl-43 (48)

The name of GV-7, "central pivot," alludes to this point's function of treating the middle *jiao* and benefiting the spine. Bl-19 is the *shu* point associated with the gallbladder and can strongly tonify or sedate that official. The name "central pivot" suggests the balanced role of decision making empowered by perspective in helping us find our way around the obstacles that confront us in life. The gallbladder tends toward stagnation and excess as we struggle against what obstructs us. In cases of excess, Bl-19 can support ease of decision making and discernment in the gallbladder official by empowering perspective. By relaxing constraint, Bl-19 can reduce the urgency in decision making so we have time to consider our options. In cases of deficiency, Bl-19 can empower decisiveness and commitment to action. The name of Bl-43, "*yang* net," refers to the mind and intellect as a net that empowers the cognizance of life. "*Yang* net" supports both purity and clarity of mind.

---

### ❖ T11–T12: GV-6, Bl-20, Bl-44 (49)

GV-6, "center of the spine," aligns the function of the spleen and middle *jiao* to the central axis of *yang*. By strengthening the ascending influence of *yang*, GV-6 can treat prolapses and hemorrhoids. Such failure to hold the center physically is often mirrored by a person's failure to identify and stand up for his or her own needs. This inability is often congruent with poor appetite and a general lack of pleasure in eating. Bl-20 is the spleen *shu* point and can strongly tonify or sedate that official. In cases of spleen *qi* deficiency, Bl-20 can help revive the spleen's function of integrating nurturance in life and thereby help foster the virtue of integrity in all aspects of being. In cases of excess, sedating Bl-20 can help disperse the burden of dampness that weighs us down and hinders our ability to assimilate nourishment. Sedating Bl-20 can also help disperse food stagnation and calm an insatiable appetite that drives us to consume nourishment too quickly. Bl-44, "thought dwelling," addresses the *yi* as the spirit associated with the spleen. The *yi* constitutes the digestive aspect of the mind that empowers us to seek out and effectively integrate life experiences that are congruent with nourishing original purpose.

---

### ❖ L2–L3: GV-4, Bl-23, Bl-47 (52)

GV-4, "gate of destiny," empowers the simultaneous infusion of early and later heaven, primordial *yin* and *yang*, and *shen* and *jing*.[11] Bl-23 is the *shu* point associated with the kidney and can strongly tonify or sedate the *qi* of that official. In cases of deficient *qi*, Bl-23 can strengthen the kidney's ability to draw on the potential of the inherited constitution. This infusion of *qi* can help us overcome our fears and empower any of the virtues associated with the kidney official including potency, ambition, willpower, or wisdom. In cases of excess, sedating Bl-23 can help diminish our habitual reaction to fear that causes us to squander our resources. Bl-47 (52) is named "ambition room" or "palace of essence," indicating its role in mediating the relationship between will, the spirit associated with the kidney, and *jing*, our innate resource.[12]

---

### ❖ L4–L5: GV-3, Bl-25

One of the key functions of GV-3 is to regulate the lower *jiao*. GV-3 also excels at treating pain and loss of mobility in the lumbar region, legs, and knees. Bl-25 is the *shu* point associated with the large intestine official and can provide a strong tonification or sedation of *qi* to that official. In cases of excess, Bl-25 can help us let go of all that has lost its essential value by moving stagnations of *qi,* blood, damp, or heat. Stagnation of *qi,* damp, and heat in the large intestine is often associated with feelings of pressure and bloating as well as self-righteous attitudes and behavior. Here we tend to feel compelled to point out and eradicate flaws and imperfections in others while failing to notice the error of our own ways. In cases of deficiency, Bl-25 can empower the function of the large intestine to sort pure from impure and better eliminate all that has lost value in life.

## *NOTES*

1. I suspect this is congruent with their powerful effect on the officials and their related organ systems. The first work I ever presented in the field of Chinese medicine was on the innervation of the *shu* points. See Jarrett, 1983.
2. You might also look these points up in other texts that present the points from a different perspective and try extrapolating the principles discussed here.
3. Deadman and Al-Khafaji, 2000, GV-12. Note that usually when a patient reports seeing, dreaming of, or fearing ghosts, I treat that patient for possession.
4. For more on fanaticism and the lungs, see *ND,* p. 262, and note 89, p. 298.
5. For a discussion of the *po,* see *ND,* pp. 259–260.
6. For a discussion of GV-10 and GV-11, see *ND,* pp. 348–351.
7. Zhuangzi uses the characters *lingtai* to refer to the heart. See Watson, 1968, p. 255.
8. Van Over, 1973, pp. 179–180.
9. For more of this poem, see my description of acupuncture point Ht-2 in *ND,* p. 357.
10. See my discussion of the herb formula Banxia Houpu Tang in Chapter 10.
11. For a detailed discussion of *mingmen,* see *ND,* Chapter 5, pp. 77–86.
12. The nature of this relationship is discussed in detail in *ND,* Chapter 4, pp. 62–76.

# 18

# SPIRIT POINTS

EVERY POINT HAS THE POTENTIAL TO BALANCE PHYSIOLOGICAL functioning simultaneously in physical, emotional, and spiritual realms of being. However, each point has its central core of efficacy at different places along the continuum of body, mind, and spirit. The function of some points is relatively more physical, and the function of others is relatively more emotional or spiritual. For example, SI-10, "shoulder blade *shu*," has a particularly broad-based effect on improving the range of motion (ROM) and reducing pain in the shoulder. It is possible that improved ROM and decreased pain will impact the functioning of the mind positively and therefore empower the expression of spirit. However, these results are congruent with a primary change in physical function.

The primary function of Ki-24, "spirit burial ground," however, is to resurrect the *ling* aspect of spirit. Certainly this point can be used in a mundane way to treat wheezing. But the depth of the point's efficacy lies in restoring the manifestation of spiritual potency. A knowledge of where each point's core of efficacy lies in the continuum of being is imperative to mastery of our medicine. Every point has some potential to touch an aspect of spirit, so I have not listed the spirit points here. Rather, I suggest you read the entire section on individual points and abstract for yourself the ability of each point to function as a spirit point.

---

## *The Nature of Spirit Points*

A point is referred to as a "spirit point" when its central core of efficacy lies in treating spirit-level imbalances. Spirit points work by harmonizing dysfunction at the spirit level that prevents a person from progressing in life. The spirit itself is always whole, shining, and ready to manifest whenever we chose to express it. The efficacy of spirit points is based on two simultaneous modes of action. One the one hand, spirit points can move stagnant thought or emotion to reveal a discrete aspect of spirit that has been obscured by conditioned mind. On the other hand, spirit points can actually touch that aspect of spirit directly, helping it cut through our conditioned senses like a fire burning from within. In both instances, what is restored is the memory of spirit as who we truly are, and as who were made at the moment of conception, prior to the arising of thought and the presence of feeling.

The aspect of spirit being touched by a specific point corresponds to a primary block that hinders destiny from expressing itself in the world. This block is congruent with some life trauma and concurrent coping mechanisms and beliefs that have kept a person stuck and unable to assimilate the lesson inherent in the trauma and move on. In essence, spirit points help us remember that, indeed, we do have a choice about what we express in this world. From this perspective, there is no such thing as a spiritual imbalance. In other words, the spirit is untouched by life, always perfect, and always ready to serve us if we choose to manifest its purpose. All of what falls under the auspices of spiritual illness in Chinese medicine can be viewed as being distortions in thought, feeling, and behavior perpetrated by ego.

The functions of window points, reviewed in the next chapter, are archetypal of how all spirit points work. Whereas the primary function of window points lies in revealing the spirit, other points often only serve as spirit points in particular contexts. For example, HP-8, "palace of weariness," is the fire point on the heart protector channel. It functions as a horary point and as a transmitting point for the virtues associated with the heart protector official. HP-8 can be used to provide a strong tonification or sedation to the heart protector in cases of extreme deficiency or excess. As the "palace of weariness," however, HP-8 has the spirit-level function of reviving a heart left weary from the pain of betrayal and loss in relationship. The ability to revive a heart weary from dysfunctional loving makes HP-8 a potent spirit point in the appropriate context.

But we can utilize HP-8 to sedate the official without invoking its ability to resurrect the heart. For example, HP-8 may be treated with the primary goal of removing heat from the blood with no concern for the issue of intimacy being a primary spiritual imbalance in the patient's life. Similarly, HP-8 can be treated to evoke the spirit of the point independent of primary concerns about relative excess or deficiency of *qi* or *yang* as they impact the functioning of the official.

---

## *Using Spirit Points*

When I choose to use a spirit point, that point serves as the thematic focus of the entire treatment. It constitutes the deepest level suggestion that I want the treatment to deliver to the patient. For example, consider the treatment Ki-7, Ki-24, Lu-8, and Lu-1. My intention is to use these points in the following ways. Ki-7 treated with Lu-8 strengthens the connection between metal and water and the kidneys' ability to grasp the breath.[1] These points empower the conception of self and return of original nature from the depths. Lu-1 strengthens the breath and the ancestral *qi (zhongqi)* that ties us to the rhythm of primordial *dao*. Ki-24 revives a person's sense of being a spiritually potent force in the world. Ki-7, Lu-8, and Lu-1 provide a physiological context for the deep spirit-level function of Ki-24 to emerge into.

In conjunction with this treatment I might also have chosen CV-17, "primordial child." CV-17 serves as a reunion point for the heart, heart protector, and lung officials. It also functions at the spirit level to empower the memory of how our hearts functioned as children prior to original shock and the onset of life's traumas. However, I generally only utilize one spirit point on one of the primary channels during each treatment session. Note that all points tend to be self-regulating in function. Always approach each treatment with focused intent, but remember that the patient's authentic self has its own wisdom. In general, treatment offered with the intention of promoting healing as I have defined it will orient itself toward the deepest level of dysfunction just as water tends to flow toward the depths.

When using a point to evoke its spirit, I almost always pair the point with a potent metaphor that is likely to be meaningful to the patient. This may involve merely mentioning the point's name to the patient upon needling or using a metaphor congruent with the point's spirit in conversation. For example, on needling Ki-24 I might mention to the patient that the point is named "spirit burial ground." Or, after needling the point, I might say, "It's finally time that you experienced yourself as a potent force in the world." Generally such metaphors are provided

after advising the patient to rest with the treatment and just prio
leaving the room.

Like the window points, I frequently, although not always, ut source point on the same channel as the spirit point to help moderate the treatment with nature's wisdom. This is a particularly good practice for those of you who are just beginning to use this material until you have become thoroughly familiar with the deeper functions of the points.

## *NOTES*

1. The implications of this connection are discussed in Chapter 4 on the husband/wife imbalance.

# 19

# WINDOWS TO HEAVEN

*If the mind does not have its heavenly wanderings,*
*then the six apertures of sensation*
*will defeat each other.*
– ZHUANGZI[1]

ANCIENT CHINESE MEDICINE IDENTIFIED THE HEART, RATHER than the brain, as the official that governs mental activity. In modern clinical practice, it is useful to distinguish between the mind as the faculty of data analysis, associated with brain function, and the heart's capacity to empower intuition by acknowledging the spontaneous nature of reality.[2] In health, the functions of the heart and mind are united as intuition and rational analysis balance each other. The role of the mind ideally is to will action consistent with the truth we find in our heart. The heart must be master to the mind as servant. Habitual behavior and ignorance, however, stem from loss of communication between the heart and mind. Actions are now dictated by the mind, which bases its decisions wholly on the faculty of data analysis and reasoning. Failing to compare its thoughts to the gold standard of truth that now lies dormant in the heart, the mind fails utterly to cultivate virtue and so only sows the seeds of habitual nature that obscure health.

I discuss the "heavenly window"(*tianchuang:* 天窗) points here as they pertain to harmonizing the relationship between the human heart and mind. With the exception of HP-1 and HP-2, these points are located on the neck and thus regulate contact between the body (earth/heart) and the head (heaven/mind). The window points are some of the strongest points for clearing blocks at the spirit level.[3]

In the moment of losing true self, we turn the focus of our minds away from ourselves and project our pain externally into the world. If we inquire deeply enough about the source of patients' suffering, it becomes clear that, in turning their back on their true nature, they have ultimately turned their back on heaven. People tend to believe their suffering constitutes proof that heaven is not virtuous and has forsaken them. The fire type questions, "If heaven is compassionate, how could I suffer so?" The water type groans, "If God supports me, how could I be so afraid?" The wood constitution asserts, "If heaven is just, how could such a thing have happened to me?" The earth type worries, "If heaven is nurturing, how could I feel so abandoned?" And the metal constitution cries, "If heaven values me, how could I be so alone?"

Several of the window points are associated with the divergent meridians[4] whose primary function is to keep external pathogens, or life events that are too threatening to assimilate consciously, from penetrating to a functional depth that could injure a primary organ. For example, wind/cold/damp that has entered the liver meridian could be diverted away from the liver and into the hip joint. Similarly, rage resulting from abuse could be diverted away from the liver by that official's divergent meridian. Part of the efficacy of window points in revealing the spirit is their ability to allow sublimated emotional material to resurface at a time in life when a person is no longer in proximity to a threatening event.

Children can only protect themselves by closing their hearts and suppressing their respiratory rhythm. Because they are so young and fragile, suppression is their only means of protection. The stories we create to protect ourselves from pain can help us survive when we are young. But these same stories only perpetuate dysfunction when they continue to motivate us unconsciously as adults. With the perspective afforded by time and distance from damaging events, and the influence of heaven empowered by the window point, the adult may be better able to contact the highest good in a previous difficulty. In this way he or she may let go of interpretations of traumatic events that have prolonged the pain and the dysfunctional state on which it is based. Hence window points possess the dual purpose of bringing up sublimated emotional material that has been repressed and simultaneously facilitating our ability to learn from past traumas in life (see Figure 19.1, p. 298).

### *The Wood Element as Window*

Interestingly, there are no window points on the wood meridians. However, the nature of the wood element itself suggests that every point on the liver and gallbladder meridians empowers some aspect of both inner and outer vision. By mediating the connection between *shen* and *jing* through the function of regulating the flow of *qi,* we can think of the entire wood element as a window.

I find that Gb-20 ("wind pond") can be treated as if it were a window point. This point is located at the top of the trapezius next to GV-16 and Bl-10, which are the window points of their respective meridians. I have found Gb-20 to be an ideal point in addressing the deepest levels of vision and discernment as they relate to mental and emotional functioning. Further, I consider this a potent point for "clearing the sensory orifices." Hence this point is said to "brighten the eyes," a phrase that suggests its action in empowering the reciprocal relationship between the accurate perception of reality as reflected in the brightness of the *shen* (reflected in the eyes) and the strength and clarity of the fires in the gate of destiny *(mingmen).*

| WINDOW POINTS | | |
|---|---|---|
| **Elements** | **Window** | **Divergent** |
| Water | Bl-10 | Bl, Ki |
| Wood | No Window Points | |
| Fire | SI-16<br>SI-17<br>HP-1 or HP-2 | TH, HP<br><br>Gb, HP |
| Earth | St-9 | St, Sp |
| Metal | Lu-3<br>LI-18 | <br>LI, Lu |
| CV | CV-22 | St, Sp |
| GV | GV-16 | |

*Figure 19.1*
WINDOWS TO HEAVEN

*The window points are listed by channel along with their association with the divergent meridians. In women, HP-2 can serve as a window point if propriety dictates not treating HP-1. The fact that the wood channels have no window points is discussed in the text.*

## *When to Consider Treating a Window Point*

You can use a source, or *luo* point, in a broad range of contexts and generally count on it to promote balance and stability. But because window points are so potentially powerful, it is particularly important to use them at precisely the right time and in the correct context. You must decide the patient is ready and able to assimilate the kind of information that can arise when treating a window point. If the patient is not ready, you may have a squandered a potentially therapeutic resource.

The primary consideration when using a window point is determining that the patient is able to assimilate truth, the foundation of restoring original nature. Telling a person the truth prematurely, however, can lack compassion and therefore contribute to further suffering. I remember a friend telling me only days after separating from my former wife that my marriage had not been a good one and I would meet someone else and be much happier. What my friend said was absolutely true, although at the time it just served to deepen my pain. It took another six months before I was ready to assimilate his spoken truth in a way that it could effectively offer perspective and hope and contribute to my healing.

In other words, if a person is stuck in a prison, providing a window to the outside world might empower hope or perpetuate despair. The determining factor often rests in how close the person is to actual liberation. Hence window points are most effective when the patient is nearing a turning point in treatment and the primordial *qi* is on the verge of reasserting its authority as the guiding influence in the patient's life.[5] This generally implies using the window points later in treatment after you have cleared blocks such as AE and restored a basic balance to the functioning of the *sheng* and *ke* cycles.

Utilizing a window at such a time can unblock the spirit at the deepest level of dysfunction that propagates the patient's suffering in life. A window can illuminate the moment of lost self and the fictitious nature of the story created to help the fragile young mind cope with its trauma. In this way a perspective is offered that can empower a person to see how his or her story has outgrown its usefulness. Hence by opening a window at the correct moment we have helped undermine a foundational pillar of the created self. A person who needs a window open often gives the impression of being "closed down" and of "operating in the dark." However, window points can also be too open and need treatment to help close them to create a better boundary between a person's spirit and the outside world. For example, hallucinogenic drugs often "blow open" the windows and leave a person dazed and disoriented. In such a person the analytic faculties of the mind are not integrated as determinants of correct action. A patient may seem idealistic to the point of dysfunction. Hence windows may serve effectively to "ground" an overly expansive person who walks around with his or her "head in the clouds."

Generally, I use window points on constitutional channels because the constitutional official ties patients to their unique expression of personal destiny. However, I often find it effective to utilize window points associated with any official when a patient evidences a deep mental, emotional, or spiritual block congruent with dysfunction in that official which is limiting his or her progress in treatment. Lastly, I almost always pair a window point with the source point on the same channel. In this way the potent functions of the window point are moderated by the control of nature. The source point can allow patients to take what they need from a treatment so they are less likely to be overwhelmed if the timing of the treatment is not precisely correct.

## *NOTES*

1. Watson, 1968, p. 301.
2. For a discussion of the heart and mind in relation to the *yin* and *yang* officials, see *ND*, pp. 169–172.
3. The three levels—body, mind, and spirit—are discussed in *ND*, pp. 323–325.
4. These are Bl-10, TH-16, LI-18, HP-1, St-9, and CV-22.
5. The significance of the turning point is discussed in *ND*, Chapter 7, and pp. 330–331.

# 20

# MEETING POINTS

MEETING POINTS ARE PLACES WHERE TWO OR MORE meridians intersect each other. Because of this meeting of channels, it is possible to influence the function of more than one official simultaneously. A knowledge of the meeting points enables you to design elegant and effective treatments utilizing a minimum of points. I often use meeting points locally to give a treatment focus by integrating the functions of all channels I have treated with distal points. For example, St-25 represents a crossing point of the stomach and the large intestine channels. It is therefore possible to utilize St-25 effectively for treating conditions of either or both the stomach and large intestine officials. Such a treatment might utilize St-36, the transmitting point of the earth element, in conjunction with LI-11 as the receiving point for the earth on the large intestine channel. Choosing St-25 as a local point could assist the treatment to empower the functional integration of the stomach and large intestine officials. Similarly, utilizing CV-17 as a reunion point of the heart, heart protector, and lung officials could help unify a treatment aimed at synchronizing the function of those three officials.[1]

Many of the meeting points are intuitively obvious once you arrive at a basic understanding of point functions. For example, all exit and entry points and *luo* points are meeting points. Hence Lu-1, the entry point of the lung channel, is a reunion point with the liver channel because *qi* flows from Lv-14 to Lu-1 in the exit/entry sequence. Lu-7, the *luo* point on the lung channel, is a meeting point with the large intestine channel because *qi* flows from LI-4, the source point, to Lu-7 via the *luo* channel. All the points of the eight extra meridians, other than the conception and governor vessels, are meeting points with their primary channels. For example, points Ki-9 through Ki-21 are all on *chongmai.* Hence these are meeting points between the *chongmai* and the kidney channel. Each channel has several meeting points (see list in Appendix C).

## *NOTES*

1. For an example of a point combination utilizing CV-17 in this way, see my point combination for stabilizing the pulse in Chapter 10.

# PART III

# ORIENTING TOWARD TREATMENT

# INTRODUCTION

In Part I, I discussed treatment paradigms for resolving shock and restoring authentic self, and in Part II, I examined various types of acupuncture points with an emphasis on their effects on consciousness. Here I discuss treatment planning, the suggestive process in treatment, and the nature of acupuncture point function itself.

From a certain perspective, patients must be considered freshly every time they arrive for treatment. Still, there are considerations in treatment planning that are generally applicable in clinical practice. Here we consider how to prioritize the information covered thus far in short-, medium-, and long-term treatment.

Metaphor is relevant in both diagnosis as well as in treatment. It is an essential diagnostic skill to be able to freely associate the symbolic nature of a patient's language and behavior with the relationships inherent in the five-element system. In order to treat effectively, we must then be able to offer metaphors that resonate with the patient. Such suggestions can be offered with the spoken word and reinforced with acupuncture points and herbal formulas, all of which possess their own rich metaphorical nature. In this way you can think of metaphor as a hinge between diagnosis and treatment. Hence I discuss the process of offering therapeutic suggestions before assessing the metaphors contained in the names and functions of the acupuncture points.

The nature of acupuncture point function is a continually unfolding mystery. Although the art has been practiced for nearly four thousand years, every generation of practitioner utilizes the same points to treat a being who is continually evolving. Hence as new aspects of being continuously arise, the function of the points themselves evolve always to include all previously ascribed functions. Here I discuss the dynamic nature of acupuncture points to create a context for consideration of their individual natures.

# 21

# TREATMENT PLANNING

## *Formulating a Diagnosis and Treatment Plan*

In general, my process of formulating a diagnosis involves first identifying the patient's constitutional type. This process is usually rapid and occurs within the first few minutes after meeting the patient. Unless compelling information to the contrary arises during the exam or later treatment, I generally stay with my constitutional diagnosis indefinitely. Constitution is the thread that joins together all observations regarding the relative balance of all functional relationships. The patient's constitutional type may, therefore, guide your intuition in interpreting diagnostic clues as the interview unfolds. Arriving at a constitutional diagnosis allows me to identify the virtues that are trying to emerge spontaneously. In part, these virtues define specific inner changes that will occur as healing proceeds, thus allowing for the close monitoring of progress in treatment.

Having established a five-element constitutional diagnosis, I then evaluate how the patient's physiology is expressing itself in relation to his or her constitutional type. This is done by comparing my observations of the pulse, tongue, and eyes with the dynamics of the constitutional diagnosis. I then proceed to formulate short-, intermediate-, and long-term therapeutic goals.

This phase may involve addressing obvious behaviors such as addictions (e.g., coffee, drugs, tobacco) or other self-destructive habits. In terms of the pulse, this means addressing the larger issues such as stability of rhythm, rate, and intensity. I often think of this stage of treatment as taking a person out of "shock," defined here as habituated behavior that keeps a person from self-discovery. The primary strategy involves clearing blocks that compromise the quality and flow of *qi* so constitutional treatment can proceed on a stable and strong foundation. Once a solid foundation has been set, I focus on integrating the functioning of the *yin* and *yang* officials associated with the patient's constitutional type. In terms of herbal treatment, this stage of therapy often entails administering formulas that are clarifying and stabilizing.[1]

As an intermediate and often secondary goal, I generally address the patient's main complaint. Of course, this may be done simultaneously with the short-term plan at the beginning of treatment. As habituated behavior decreases, there is often more authentic *qi (zhenqi)* available for healing. Thus this phase of treatment generally involves harmonizing the functional dynamics of the constitutional officials with the other officials involved in the pattern of dysfunction. For example, if lung (metal) is primary and heart protector (fire) is secondary, this stage of treatment might involve the harmonization of the balance between metal and fire across the *ke* cycle. During this stage of treatment I may introduce formulas that are constitutional in nature, in addition to formulas that are resolving or harmonizing.

My long-term strategy generally involves integrating the function of the constitutional organs with the functioning of the rest of the officials around the *sheng* and *ke* cycles. Hence, if a person is constitutionally metal, over time I would integrate the function of the associated organ systems (lung and large intestine) with the element's mother (earth), child (water), grandmother (fire), and grandchild (wood) in an order appropriate to the functional dynamics of the situation. This stage of therapy often involves administering one or two long-term herbal formulas that are constitutional in nature.

Of course, these are only general considerations, and you must assess the merits of each individual case. If there are signs of impending serious illness such as cancer or heart disease, you need to address them directly and aggressively in the initial stages of treatment. Furthermore, with occasional patients I sense that if they do not experience quick symptomatic relief, they may not return for further treatment. In such instances, constitutional points always serve as the basis for whatever local or symptomatic points I may treat.

## *Treatment Schedule*

Generally, I see patients once each week for six to eight weeks. I find this is enough time for people to have a sense they are receiving benefit from the treatments. After that, I see the patient every other week, once every three weeks, and then monthly. In serious cases involving aggressive and debilitating illnesses such as rheumatoid arthritis or multiple sclerosis, I may see a patient initially up to three times each week.

I find that an initial interval of one week between appointments affords me the opportunity to assess the effectiveness of a particular treatment as well as the patient's ability to sustain the effects of that treatment. After the first session, it is not unusual to have patients report having felt better for one or two days and then reverting to the state they were in before the session. As treatment progresses, the duration of benefit should increase in proportion to the patient's degree of awareness of the patterns of dysfunction that propagate his or her symptoms. As the benefits of treatment begin to last an entire week, the frequency of treatment is then moved to two weeks. In this way, the patient's inner resources are empowered to guide the process of healing as dependency on treatment diminishes.

My goal is that each patient should derive sufficient benefit from treatment so they consider it worthwhile to continue coming at a rate of about every six to eight weeks. For most people, I consider the first three to six months of treatment to be a time of "leveling the playing field." By the end of one year, most patients are receiving treatment at the longer intervals just mentioned. Once progress has been made with the initial complaints, and grosser levels of addictive behavior (tobacco, alcohol, etc.) have been removed, I find the opportunity arises to pursue directly the preventive and evolutionary aspects of therapy offered by Chinese medicine. These intervals must be considered in light of the fact that absolute healing does not necessarily take time. Ultimately, I find that three years constitutes sufficient time for most patients to restore a deep lasting balance.

My treatment regimen is in contrast to the practice of acupuncture therapy in modern China. There, patients typically receive acupuncture every day for an extended period (perhaps ten days in a row), with a short break of a day or two, followed by another course of ten days of treatment if needed. I believe this frequency of treatment is imposed by the state-run health care system whose main interest is the symptomatic relief of pain so people may return to work quickly. I also believe this approach represents a practice of acupuncture governed by principles more suited to herbal medicine. Here acupuncture point "prescriptions" are given daily in much the same way as a patient would be expected to take herbs.

Interestingly, in the ancient Chinese medical texts describing acupuncture therapy, virtually no mention is made of acupuncture frequency or overall duration of treatment. The role of the acupuncture points is discussed, and specific treatments (point selections, methods of inserting, stimulating, and withdrawing needles) are mentioned for particular ailments. However, overall treatment plans are never elaborated. In my view, this suggests that each acupuncture treatment stands alone as it is based on the unique merits of each clinical encounter.

---

## *Beginning to Apply the Material Clinically*

Practitioners who have graduated from a school in the Worsley lineage will likely find it easy to assimilate the material presented here into clinical practice. I have presented the foundational treatments utilized in this lineage according to the principles and values elaborated in *Nourishing Destiny.* Here I provide practitioners from other traditions with some guidelines for integrating this material clinically. Some practitioners will be inclined to abstract from this text a general knowledge along with a few techniques to complement whatever tradition they have already learned. I certainly think this is a valid approach. After all, although current traditions of practice may appear to represent unified bodies of knowledge, in truth they are based on the assimilation of diverse influences by their lineage holders over many generations. Learning to drain AE or treat possession holds great potential benefit to any practitioner wishing to reach his or her patients at a deeper level.

However, some practitioners may wish to venture deeply into this material and practice within the home ground of the tradition as it is presented here. Because I am relating this body of knowledge as it is unified within my own experience, I can only vouch for its effectiveness when practiced in the integrated way I have presented it. To practitioners interested in integrating this material substantially into their practice, I offer the following guidance on how to begin.

---

## *Prioritizing Initial Treatments*

During the initial stage of treatment, there is a specific order and priority for each protocol utilized in clearing blocks. Also, the choice of points is generally dictated by the specific protocol utilized. For example, when treating possession I choose only the seven points that address either internal or external possession. The priority assigned to these protocols also holds true should any of these blocks arise during ongoing treatment. For example, a patient who has been treated for several years may arrive for a regularly scheduled appointment and, upon taking the pulse, you may suspect an E/E block as well as the presence of AE. In this case, testing for the presence of AE always takes precedence over clearing the E/E block. Here I review the order in which I prioritize the clearing of specific blocks (see Table 21.1).

| ACUPUNCTURE | HERBS[2] |
|---|---|
| 1. Possession | 1. Stabilize pulse |
| 2. Umbilical pulse | 2. Calm spirit |
| 3. Aggressive energy | 3. Move stagnation |
| 4. Husband/wife imbalance or CV/GV | 4. Try constitutional formulas |
| 5. Akabanes | |
| 6. Exit/entry blocks | |

*Table 21.1*
***Priority of Treatment***

The umbilical pulse may be centered during the initial intake and prior to the application of either needles of herbs. This can help gently pull the patient to center and often will help balance the akabanes. In the presence of possession, none of the other protocols, or any treatment for that matter, is likely to be of lasting value. Therefore, if possession is present it takes priority over all the other treatments, including centering the umbilical pulse, and you should address it as soon as you diagnose it.

After clearing possession or performing any of the other treatments that transfer *qi,* test and drain AE if present. If AE is not drained, you run the risk of spreading evil *qi* throughout the other officials. Once AE is drained, recheck the akabanes and correct them if still unbalanced. In my experience this is unlikely, and I find that most often the akabanes do correct on their own after an AE drain. With *qi* flowing evenly in the twelve main channels, I then prioritize correcting any H/W or CV/GV block present. Finally, I clear any E/E blocks in the twelve main channels.

Concurrent with the strategies just outlined, you can prescribe herbs to stabilize the pulse, calm the spirit, and move any stagnations you find. In this way we have established a solid foundation for constitutional treatment and the return of original nature.

---

## *Initiating Constitutional Treatment*

Those of use who seek mastery through the practice of medicine must cultivate the skills to treat a patient literally from conception to the grave. In fact, it can be argued that the skill to treat prior to conception is needed when addressing infertility or optimizing a mother's health in preparation for pregnancy. The stage of treatment that ensues after the initial clearing of blocks can be lifelong and is open ended to the degree that no future session can be planned concretely. Every treatment is assessed in the context of the moment, and only the most general rules apply in point selection.

A useful analogy for treatment planning is the game of pool. We can liken the clearing of blocks to putting chalk on the cue and racking up the balls. Treating the constitutional official for the first time is like the break shot that sets the stage for the rest of the game. After the break shot, the goal of winning is held firmly in mind and specific rules apply to the game. However, every new shot must be addressed entirely on its own merits in order to further the eventual goal of winning. We cannot play with a fixed strategy from beginning to end because the game changes with every turn. Yet we can plan each shot intentionally in a way devised to best position the balls for our next turn with the cue.

The notion of constitution anchors treatment in the sense that the constitutional official is key. Knowing the patient's constitution gives us a vision of the general direction for each patient's progress. However, the specific steps taken in each session to arrive at that location are variable as we assess the patient in the context of his or her unique presentation every time the patient arrives for treatment. This same general notion holds true when addressing the fundamental balance of substances in Chinese physiology. For example, we may determine during the intake that a long-term goal of treatment is to diminish the presence of functional heat in a patient's blood. However, there is relatively great leeway in each session as to how this is best accomplished in the moment.

Thus you must always hold in mind a clear intention of the ultimate goal of all treatment rendered over the long term as well as the intention behind the point selection in the individual session. Never let the long-term goals constrain the momentary goals of treatment, and remember that short-term strategies must always further the overall goal. Keeping this in mind, I review some general guidelines for initiating constitutional treatment after having cleared the blocks discussed earlier.

## *The Break Shot*

A general rule of practice is that diagnosis is confirmed through treatment. In addressing the constitutional official for the first time, we are not only initiating treatment, we are afforded the opportunity of confirming our diagnosis as well. Frequently, my first constitutional treatment of a patient is to needle the source point on the constitutional official.

Choosing the source point as the first point has several advantages. The source point touches the official at its primal depth to renew its function with a clear reserve of *qi* untainted by life experience. Hence, after clearing blocks and diminishing the dysfunctional input of the patient's mind, we can reinstitute nature as a guiding influence in his or her life. The action of source points is gentle and not as directional in nature as selecting an element, *luo,* or spirit point. Hence treating Lv-3 is unlikely to destabilize the balance of the officials, whereas Lv-2, the channel's fire point, is very directional and could have undesired effects if our point choice is wrong. Lastly, source points are able to touch each specific aspect of an official's function in a general way so a global change can be initiated at the patient's core of dysfunction.

Upon treating the constitutional official's source point, a universal change in function throughout the patient's being confirms our constitutional diagnosis. We can ascertain this by noting changes in both CSOE and the pulse, as well as in our general sense of the patient's quality of being. The overall quality of the pulse is expected to improve, including parameters such as width and amplitude that suggest an overall increase in volume of *qi.*

Your facility to sense increasingly subtle shifts in function is paramount in clinical practice. When I treat a patient, I have a clear intention with every word said and every needle placed. It is my facility to monitor subtle changes in function in response to the therapeutic actions I take that allows me continually to refine my diagnosis and further contribute to the patient's healing. Consider the following analogy. Imagine sitting at a picnic in August with the sun shining and the fields full of summer's growth. Nature appears to be at its peak, yet, in one instant, the breeze shifts ever so slightly to rustle the leaves. This shift brings into awareness that the seed of autumn has been sown and the seasons will soon change. Sensing a universal qualitative shift after insertion of the first needle suggests that, indeed, the season of the patient's life is turning back toward balance and health.

---

## Luo *Points*

After receiving initial confirmation that our constitutional diagnosis is likely correct, we can integrate the function of the element's complementary *yin* or *yang* official by introducing that channel's *luo* point. For example, if we have received initial confirmation of our diagnosis by treating Lv-3 on a suspected wood constitutional type, we can then needle Gb-37. Restoring the integrity of the constitutional element with the source and *luo* points essentially reconnects the spirit *(yang)* with the potential virtue *(yin)* that resides in the depths. This alignment within the constitution will, through resonance, help restore the integrity of the heart/kidney axis at the patient's core as well as its expression within each element.

## *Continued Treatment*

In order to keep an open mind in the treatment process, I consider every session to have the potential of confirming my constitutional assessment. I always try and see each patient with new eyes and remain open to the possibility that after one or many sessions I may reassess the patient and modify my diagnosis. Continued treatment is an open-ended process based on simultaneously holding a vision of the overall therapeutic goal and the momentary goal of any given session. After initiating constitutional treatment, I then focus on restoring the integrity of the functional relationships inherent in the *sheng* and *ke* cycles. This involves integrating the function of the constitutional element with the other elements using transfers of *qi* and transmitting and receiving points as I see fit. Congruent with integrating the functional relationships of the *sheng* and *ke* cycle, I focus on spirit-level treatment by calling on the inner functions of acupuncture points that relate specifically to the patient's life destiny and the beliefs and behaviors that block its expression. At this point, for example, I may treat points in the windows to heaven category. The inner nature of acupuncture points is covered in Parts II and IV.

When beginning to integrate this material into clinical practice, it can be helpful to perform the first three to five treatments with points that are either on, or associated with, the constitutional element. For example, if we suspect the patient is metal constitutionally, we might limit treatment to points on the lung and large intestine channels as well as the *mu* and *shu* points associated with those officials. In this way we can best discern the precise effect of each treatment and the fidelity of our diagnosis to clinical reality.

## *Questions*

1. If, after treating a patient for several months, the practitioner modifies his or her diagnosis, does that mean the previous diagnosis was wrong?
2. Does modifying a constitutional diagnosis suggest the patient's constitution has changed in the course of treatment?

# *NOTES*

1. See Jarrett, 1995b (pp. 132–134), which covers herbal therapy utilizing Yunnan Baiyao, Meridian Passage, and Shengmai San in this regard.
2. The stages of prescription I give here can be overlapping. For example, the formula Shengmai San can be used to stabilize the pulse but can also be used as a constitutional formula. Similarly, a formula used to stabilize the pulse might calm the spirit or, in the case of Banxia Houpo Tang, move stagnation.

# 22

# THE SUGGESTIVE PROCESS IN TREATMENT

IN *NOURISHING DESTINY*, I DISCUSSED THE SUGGESTIVE process in treatment and the notion that, in fact, all therapeutic intervention is merely suggestion.[1] My ability to use metaphor is cultivated from twenty-three years of studying the language and cognitive style of Chinese medicine coupled with my eighteen years of clinical practice. The names of the points and herbs, as well as the language of Chinese physiology itself, offer potent metaphors that speak deeply to the human spirit. I believe, for engendering consciousness, that *metaphor is the most potent medicine on earth*. People make themselves sick with language by creating harmful myths. A well-placed metaphor can be a potent stimulus for wholeness and healing. This point is illustrated in the case study of Sorena in the section of Part IV that discusses acupuncture point St-30. My descriptions of the points in general, the case studies I have written, and much of my work in *Nourishing Destiny* will acquaint you with my orientation toward metaphor as medicine.

There are great subtleties, and an infinite number of variations, in offering therapeutic suggestions. Each must be tailored to the patient uniquely in the moment, and each must be offered at the precise time it is most likely to be effective. I consider the ability to offer clinically effective suggestions to be one of the highest skills of the master practitioner. Here I elaborate eight principles that empower the ability to make effective therapeutic suggestions. In essence, what I am describing here are the qualities of authentic speech applied to a therapeutic context.

## *1. Tell the Truth*

Efficacy is the goal of any therapeutic suggestion. The foundation of efficacy is truth. In the context of the tradition I am trying to convey, truth is operationally defined as that which supports the balanced expression of individual purpose in life. For this is the truth that flows from the innate influence of *jing, qi,* and *shen* to support the emergence of the authentic self. If a suggestion is congruent with the manifestation of innate purpose, it is likely to be well planted and cultivated. Suggestions made in this way empower an internal alignment in the patient that is immediately evident to the practitioner who listens and watches attentively. This alignment often occurs beneath the patient's own level of conscious awareness but can serve to reassure the practitioner that truth has indeed been spoken and the suggestion has been taken to heart.

## *2. Have No Personal Agenda*

You must have no agenda other than empowering the patient to take the next step on the path of fulfilling destiny. When offering a suggestion, we are only culpable for speaking the truth and can have no attachment to how soon that truth will manifest in the life of the patient. If truth is spoken, the *qi* will be rectified. But many other variables impact the patient's life that are beyond our control. Of course we want the best for our patients, yet, ultimately, the timing of healing is up to heaven as well as the patient's own conscious decision to initiate meaningful change in her life.

Patients often look to us for guidance when they are confronted by challenging situations in life. For example, a patient may be considering quitting her job or getting divorced. Our only concern in offering suggestions is that whatever course of action she chooses constitutes the next step in her path of healing and is not dictated by an unconscious reaction to avoid uncomfortable feelings. Hence we want only to ensure that a water constitutional type does not stay in his job because of fear or leave his job because of fear. The fire constitution must not choose divorce because she does not feel loved or stay in a loveless marriage because leaving makes her feel sad. Only when we choose actions on their own merits in a way unobscured by our thoughts or feelings can we ever be free in life.

If you hold personal agendas in making suggestions, the patient will never be well served. Such agendas may be politically, culturally, or economically based. For example, if you feel divorce is immoral and used this belief to guide therapeutic suggestions, the patient would not be well served. It is only our job to rectify the *qi* and help it flow effortlessly. We cannot be attached to specific outcomes, for those lie in the patient's hands and in the hands of heaven. The strength of Chinese medicine rests in its ability to generate a diagnosis and treatment plan unique to each individual. I feel strongly that it is unethical to integrate multilevel marketing schemes into our clinical practice. Food, air, water, and rest are good for every individual. Everything else is negotiable on an individual basis. Having a financial incentive for selling patients air purifiers, nutritional supplements, magnets, and so on, under the premise that they are "healthy for everyone" places the practitioner in an ethically compromised position that will undermine the efficacy of every other therapeutic suggestion.

---

## *3. Start at the Foundation*

When I was learning to teach martial arts, my master always emphasized identifying the single thing for my student to change that would improve the efficacy and beauty of her entire form. Teaching began from the ground up starting with foot position and proceeding to the ankle, knee, hip, waist, torso, shoulders, neck, and finally the alignment of the head. Only when the current lesson was mastered would I then proceed to identify the next issue to work on. Essentially, the goal is to empower each patient to see through her sense of possessing a self that is in any way separate from the whole. This means undermining the dysfunctional *qi* that supports the ego and helping the patient see through her mind.

In general, the foundation of all spiritual development is to first set the will on wanting freedom more than anything else. Once the will is set in this way, our choices in life are clarified. In this regard we should help the patient make a connection between what she complains about (her symptoms) and her dysfunctional beliefs, thoughts, and behaviors. In short, it is important to educate the patient regarding everything else she is choosing other than health.

The formation of a constitutional diagnosis yields a deep view into the lessons that patient is given during her lifetime. In formalizing a treatment plan we must prioritize what is the single most important lesson for the patient to grasp. We must identify the one concept, virtue, action, or communication that would most effectively improve the patient's life if she was able to embrace it. These will all be congruent with the patient's constitutional type and dynamics, for constitution is the foundation of life itself.

---

## *4. All Suggestions Must Be Congruent*

In every treatment session, all our therapeutic suggestions must be aimed at empowering the one foundational aspect of being until it is fully grasped. The process of ongoing treatment involves treating these issues internally while externally peeling away the outer layers of acquired self and ego like an onion until the ability of the heart and mind to communicate freely is restored. All therapeutic suggestions, whether they be acupuncture, herbs, nutritional advice, or counseling, must be guided by your coherence of intention. Like a laser, all suggestions must be coherent to illuminate the patient's authentic self in perfect form.

---

## *5. Don't Dilute the Message*

If treatment addresses too many issues simultaneously, we run the risk of not achieving any of them. Through many years of clinical practice and both training in and teaching the martial arts, I have come to believe in what I refer to as the "85 percent principle." This principle can be succinctly stated in this way: "Never assert will to attain a 100 percent result. Effort exerted past the point of 85 percent of the intended result tends to constrain and diminish the efficacy of the previous work accomplished." In any treatment session I am happy to attain 85 percent of the result I am looking for. If I perform a particular treatment and the pulses evidence an 85 percent shift, I consider that treatment to be complete. I find that if I continue to treat in an attempt to attain 100 percent of a theoretically achievable result, I may lose the first 85 percent of progress in the process. That is to say, a positive pulse shift can revert to its previous state if I keep inserting needles.

The same principle holds true for making therapeutic suggestions. Once the patient has grasped what you are trying to say, it is often best to stop talking and let the person assimilate the message. If I keep talking, trying to explain the point in different ways, or bring up other therapeutic issues, I run the risk of confusing and diluting the issue that has already been grasped. Silence is often the best response to a potent shift in a patient's flow of *qi*.

## 6. *Use the Patient's Own Language*

You must be attuned to the way patients express themselves and tailor your word choice and manner to match patients' own style of expression. The words and affect that I use are tailored to each patient individually. The variables that inform my manner are many and varied. For example, the language I would use to make a suggestion to a middle-aged attorney who appeared to be fairly conservative and intellectual might be very different than I would use to make the same suggestion to a young artist who appeared to be fairly open and emotional. Clinical experience may guide you to intuit how to make each patient comfortable to the degree she is increasingly receptive to suggestion.

The associations of each constitutional type offer a rich language to which each person of that elemental nature tends to be receptive. For example, if a person is wood constitutionally, words such as "justice," "fairness," "jealousy," "anger," and "growth" all tend to speak directly to the person in the way she orients toward life. We might choose to treat a wood constitutional type on the metal element to support the resolution of conflict by empowering metal's ability to help the wood "let go." In this case, words associated with the metal element like "essence," "quality," and "worth" can support the movement of *qi* in a patient before needles are even applied.

## 7. *Make the Suggestion an Extension of the Patient's Own Ideas*

To greatly increase the likelihood that a therapeutic suggestion will be effective, make that suggestion appear the logical consequence of everything the patient already believes to be true. In this way we can harness the momentum of the created self to help undermine its grasp on the patient. The entire force sustaining the created self is based on a belief generated at the moment that original nature is lost. Once we identify this belief, we can extend it via suggestion to embrace the possibility of positive change in the patient's life.

For example, a patient who is metal constitutionally may hold the belief she was not valued by her father and is therefore worthless.[2] Her smoking may be based on her lack of self-worth as she unconsciously attempts to fill her internal void. Our constitutional weakness tends to be compensated for by developing a compensatory "strength" in the world. Therefore her internal sense of feeling alone, empty, and worthless can be projected externally as pride and perfectionism. Making a connection for the patient between her smoking, her father, and the concept of value can be a potent tool for helping her beat her addiction. "You know, every time you smoke a cigarette you undervalue and hurt yourself more than your father ever did. You moved out of his house twenty-two years ago, yet you carry the dysfunction and pain inherent in that relationship in your shoulder bag [pointing to the pack of cigarettes] over your heart. You are so meticulous in your work, yet smoking is such a dirty habit. I think it's time to let go and move on."

A patient who is metal constitutionally cannot help but respond to a suggestion phrased in this way. Of course, the message must be delivered compassionately to assist it in penetrating to the heart.[3] Yet depending on the patient's five-element dynamics, the message may be delivered with either a soft or firm demeanor. The first half of the suggestion is rather confrontational and makes a connection between the patient's smoking and her pain. For she has shut herself off from her father yet ironically carries him around next to her heart. The trick is to get the patient to reject the cigarettes and open back up to healing her relationship with her father. We do this by pairing what she complains about, her father's lack of acknowledgment, with the act of smoking. We want every puff on her cigarette to become *consciously* paired with her father's look of disdain.

By acknowledging the patient as being "meticulous," I have supported the tendency of the habitual mind to compensate for an inner lack of self-worth by seeking external acknowledgment from others. In this way, I soften the initially confrontational part of the suggestion and gain the mind's trust. I then note the incongruity among the virtue the patient values, perfectionism, and the habit she is trying to let go of. Finally, I end the suggestion by gently reaffirming the metal element's ability to empower the virtue of letting go of all that no longer serves.

While making such a suggestion, watch attentively for the inner alignment created by the words. This alignment can be discerned at the patient's core, even when her mind reacts defensively. Finally, reinforce all suggestions with the proper acupuncture points and herbal prescriptions.

---

## *8. Acknowledge the Patient*

Dysfunction and illness that exists in the present is the result of coping mechanisms that form early in life. By the time many patients arrive for treatment, they have already begun to make positive changes in their lives of the precise nature that diagnosis suggests are necessary. For example, the life lesson of a patient who is earth constitutionally might be that of learning to identify and fulfill her own needs. Point out to the patient how the coping mechanism she evolved as a child that leads her to habitually care for others to the point of ingratiation no longer serves her. Certainly it worked as a child to help her survive, yet, as an adult, operating in the world based on the coping mechanisms formulated by a 6-year-old does little to foster the virtue of integrity. It is also important to acknowledge all the ways the patient has learned to establish boundaries with others as well as to recognize the ways she is taking appropriate care of herself.

### *Questions*

1. Is psychotherapy a valid part of Chinese medicine as a holistic medicine?
2. Why is it important to cultivate eloquence in the practice of healing?
3. What is the mechanism by which words injure or heal?
4. Think of a metaphor that has deeply changed your life for the better.
5. Discuss metaphor as medicine and its relationship to the principles of homeopathy.

## *NOTES*

1. *ND,* pp. 160–165, 183 (water), 203 (fire), 245 (wood), 267 (metal), 288 (earth).
2. A similar case was presented in *ND,* pp. 154–158.
3. The virtue of compassion is discussed in *ND,* p. 202.

# 23

# SOME THOUGHTS ON THE NATURE OF ACUPUNCTURE POINTS

To truly appreciate the function of acupuncture points, it is helpful to understand how the ancient Chinese thought about their world. Their conception of the universe is well explained in the Chinese mythology presented earlier in the text. When we understand this mythology (literally, spirit talk, *shenhua:*神話), the spirits of the points come alive and talk to us. Just as Emperor Yu traveled throughout China and became familiar with the spirits of the deep structures, so, too, must you know intimately the nature of the spirit present in each acupuncture point.

The meridians *(mai:*脈*)*running through the body are the internal rivers of the microcosm, each acupuncture point along a meridian representing and harmonizing a specific aspect of being in a person's inner kingdom. The acupuncture meridians and points reflect the way in which the Chinese saw the macrocosm of the universe as it is mapped onto the microcosm of the body. This map guides you in your efforts to balance the functional relationships that maintain the integrity of each human being.

Just as the *Yijing* is a tool to guide our understanding of the *dao*'s implicit movement in the world, so, too, a knowledge of the imagery of the points helps us access the ways in which the *dao* strives to express itself through each person and the ways in which that effort is blocked, resulting in imbalance and ill health. It is often your knowledge of the symbolism of each point that spells the difference between treating patients superficially and reaching them at their depth.

The unique property of acupuncture points is their ability, with stimulation, to restore our memory of original nature. Each point has the capacity to evoke some aspect of functioning that has been lost, buried under the accretions of life's habituating influence. The general characteristics of each of the five elements—water, wood, fire, earth, and metal—are elaborated in the discrete functions of the twelve *officials.* The function of each official is further elaborated in its associated acupuncture points. For example, the general qualities of the wood element are elaborated into their *yin* and *yang* aspects as the liver and gallbladder officials, respectively. A function associated with the liver official is planning. Thus the fourteen acupuncture points on the meridian of the liver official each address some discrete aspect of the function of planning.

Your developed knowledge of the individual points will guide you to identify and minister to subtle aspects of being that the patient is failing to access. For example, on the liver meridian, acupuncture point Lv-14, named "gate of hope," may allow you to empower that quality of being called hope within the patient. Hope can help ease internally generated constraints on our plans as we project them into the future. Lv-14, by empowering the balanced expression of "hope," may help harmonize unbalanced emotional extremes on a continuum ranging from despair to blind optimism. We could devote a lifetime to writing volumes on Lv-14 and the nature of hope as it presents in humanity. In fact, this job would be endless because our human understanding of the aspect of being that we call "hope" continually evolves. Hence the nature of any acupuncture point function evolves as our human experience of being evolves. The nature of acupuncture points is limitless and cannot be defined as narrowly as it has been in most modern texts.

The images contained in the point names do not define point functions, but they serve as foci for discussion about particular aspects of being harmonized by the point.[1] For example, discussing destiny *(ming)* in the context of the point GV-4, *mingmen,* does not mean GV-4 is "the point for destiny." Every point, used in the correct context and at precisely the right moment, may restore a lost aspect of self-expression that brings the patient closer to fulfilling his life's potential.

## *The Nature of Acupuncture Point Function*

Each acupuncture point is unique in its ability to touch some aspect of being that has been lost to the individual. By "touching" this aspect of being, the memory of original nature encoded within the point's function may be restored to the patient. Each point empowers an aspect of pure virtue that is untouched by any event that occurs in life. For example, HP-1, "heavenly pond," can provide the memory of safety within one's heart that is untouched by any abuse experienced in life. Having this experience of pure virtue and memory of true self, even for a moment, is often enough to initiate healing.

Acupuncture points work by harmonizing continuums of unbalanced and extreme expressions into the virtues from which they derive, precisely in the same way the *chongqi* is said to harmonize the dualities of heaven and earth into a state of primal unity. Another way of stating this is to say that acupuncture points work by dispelling ignorance based on duality through creating alignment with the absolute. An example on a physiological level is the function of Ht-7 ("spirit gate") in its ability to stabilize the pulse. Ht-7 can be used to equal advantage in an individual whose pulse is either excessively fast or excessively slow. In the former case, the function of the point contributes to calming the heart rate; in the latter case, the point helps raise the heart rate. Hence the function of Ht-7 represents the central point of balance between the extremes of heart function.

This same principle of harmonizing dualities operates in the realms of psychological, emotional, and spiritual functioning as well. For example, a person may be excessively belligerent in intimate relationships and at the same time timid in the workplace. These behaviors may be viewed as opposite ends on a continuum representing the unbalanced expression of the wood element. In this instance, the function of Lv-1, "great esteem," can serve to empower the virtue of self-esteem by harmonizing the unbalanced expression of both belligerence and timidity.

Another way to look at this is to consider that the function of Lv-1, in aligning a person with the absolute, allows him to let go of the need for self-esteem. So much of our stagnation in life, and failure to act with integrity, is due to our attachment to thoughts and feelings propagated by the ego in order to maintain its grip on us. Thoughts such as "I'm not enough," "I'm hopeless," or "I don't know enough" are just the mind's way of preventing us from embracing the absolute right now. So, on the one hand, we might consider that Lv-14, "gate of hope," empowers the presence of hope. On the other hand, it can empower a person to let go of the dysfunctional need for hope so he can take appropriate action now, having realized that nothing is in the way and there are no excuses. Whenever I state that an acupuncture point empowers a specific virtue, you must understand that it has done so by aligning a person with the absolute in a way colored by that point's function. An experience with the absolute can initiate healing, but it is solely our expression of the virtue discovered there, through word and deed, that makes a positive difference in this world. Experience itself, no matter how positive, does not necessarily lead to meaningful change. For this is always a matter of our willful alignment with the absolute as expressed through action.

The general principle of bringing balance by harmonizing dualities is central to understanding the opposing but complementary natures of Western and Chinese medicine. It is exemplified by the difference between "taking a position" in life and "making a stand." A position is always taken relative, and in opposition to, another view. Hence positions represent either/or alternatives to each other and often are taken in habitual and unconscious reaction to a contrary position adopted by another. For example, during the civil rights movement of the 1960s, some African Americans adopted a militant position regarding the bigotry prevalent among white people in America. The two opposing positions of the racist whites and militant blacks were fueled by habitual unconscious motivations on both sides. Rather than adopt a position in opposition to one view or another, Martin Luther King Jr. took a stand between these two unbalanced extremes. Instead of solely advocating for the rights of African Americans, King advocated for the rights and dignity of all human beings. In this way, he helped harmonize the two extremes of hatred and helped all Americans move closer to the promise and fulfillment of their national destiny. Hence, when we stand in the absolute, then the momentum of heaven and earth works through us to manifest destiny.

In a similar fashion, you must help to strengthen continually the center that harmonizes all forms of unbalanced expression in the patient's being. This center is defined by the patient's constitutional type, and the patterns of unbalanced expression he presents are based on his constitutional weaknesses and compensations. These imbalances may be addressed directly by your choice of treating acupuncture points and prescribing herbs that speak to the depth of the patient's being.

Access to the inner nature of acupuncture points is only available in the context of treatment whose overall aim is aiding patients to fulfill their destiny. That is to say, we cannot just throw a few of these points into a treatment plan and expect them to empower the virtues we have been discussing here. In the appropriate context, any point may be useful in harmonizing any imbalance in the patient's being. But in order to return the patient to his lost spontaneity and true nature, the sage as healer must be so united with variable circumstances that treatment is based on the functional dynamics of the patient at that moment.

For the practitioner, the patient is like a pointillist painting. During each treatment, you use your diagnostic skills to comprehend the functional portrait that emerges from the patient. In choosing a treatment, you are concerned with where in the portrait to place a dot (acupuncture point) and what color to make it (quality of *qi*) so the picture is complete in the moment. Between therapeutic sessions, the patient's functional dynamic will shift and, on each presentation, manifest a new picture that you will have to reassess each session. You must yourself respond spontaneously to each new presentation and not treat the same points repeatedly. Repeating points in an attempt to "cause" something to happen is analogous to forcing your will on the patient. Continually receiving the same points will cause the patient to stagnate as he becomes habituated to their effects. This is counterproductive because the goal of the highest medicine is to support the patient's evolution. Ideally, you are able to respond to each new presentation in a way that is unencumbered by your past experience with the patient. Even if a point is effective, avoid the inclination to use it repeatedly—hence Sunzi's warning not to repeat tactics that have worked successfully in the past but to let one's methods correspond to the unique merits of each new situation.[2]

Selecting the appropriate points from a constitutional perspective involves the following process: (1) identify the patient's constitutional type because all treatment is performed in relation to this element and official; (2) identify the functional dynamic of imbalance that exists between the patient's constitutional type and the other elements and officials; (3) identify the discrete aspects of the given functions that the patient is habitually failing to express; and (4) identify the individual points on the relevant meridians most likely to empower the expression of these virtues. Of course, the nature of a patient's signs and symptoms and consideration of point function from other perspectives such as the eight-principle model can also influence point selection.

The process of point selection is informed by input from many sources in your own life. You must be able to hold your long-term vision of the patient's path of healing while simultaneously responding to the unique circumstances of the therapeutic moment. This process often recedes into the realm of intuition when you are doing your best work. As in a brilliant musical improvisation, your selection of points expresses truth spontaneously as the rewards of practice mount and the constraints of theory fall away. Of course, we may always go back after the fact and analyze the performance or point selection. In truth, though, the note played or point selected emerges spontaneously out of the harmony of the moment. You literally have no other choice but to be a vessel for the creative flow of *dao* as expressed through the selection of points.

For the practitioner attuned to the functional relationships represented by the officials, the five-element system offers a method to discover the deep inner functions of the acupuncture points. Over many thousands of sessions, with proper intention, you may become increasingly aware of the way each point addresses discrete aspects of human function on all levels of being. Of course, this is a highly individual process. Clinical experience reveals to each of us truths about the points consistent with our own path, awareness, and belief system.

---

## *Aspects of Point Function*

Acupuncture points have many different levels of functioning, which range from a near cause-and-effect level of predictability to the possibility of evoking unforeseen miracles. I say "near cause and effect" because even when points are conceived as buttons we can push to yield specific results, they are never guaranteed to work exactly as theory dictates. Human beings are infinitely complex, and no matter how intellectually appealing it may be to think of ourselves as machines, the reality is we are not.

Any given point can have several levels of functioning that are expressed relatively more physically, emotionally, or spiritually. The more concrete the function being called on, the more predictable it will be. All point functions are context sensitive, and you must be clear on which aspect of point function you are evoking during the ritual of each treatment.

For example, Ht-7 can function on a purely physical level to diminish pain and improve range of motion in the wrist, as a source point, an earth point, a sedation point, or as a spirit point. Physically, Ht-7, because of its location on the wrist, can serve as a local point for symptomatic treatment for wrist problems. As a source point, Ht-7 can help bring other more stronger points on the channel, such as Ht-1, under the control of nature and help infuse the heart official with pure *qi*. As an earth point, Ht-7 can empower the virtues of earth within the heart, helping build a solid foundation and central integrity to empower heart function. As a sedation point, Ht-7 can disperse relative excess within the heart, manifesting physiologically as stagnation of *qi* and heat and emotionally as unexpressed desires. On a spiritual level, Ht-7 can be called on to regulate the appropriate opening and closing of the spirit gate so the *shen* can travel freely and come to rest within the heart safely.

## *The Effects of Acupuncture Points Are Not Predictable*

Each point has its own unique function, yet, because of the holographic nature of existence, is capable itself of evoking the function of any other point. In other words, each point tends toward certain functional effects yet is capable of effecting any change within the realm of human functioning.

The functions of Ht-7 just listed are only potential functions, and each is sensitive to the overall context of the patient at the moment as well as to the other points being treated at the same time. The functional system of the human being contains its own innate wisdom and inner regulatory mechanisms. The effects of each treatment are only in part determined by the known functions of the points and your intentions. Healing tends to go to that aspect of the being most in need.

The traditional functions ascribed to points only provide the qualitative direction of the point's function if a proper diagnosis has been made that is congruent with that specific application. The specific manifestation of any treatment is variable, however. For example, if we treat Ht-7 to improve wrist mobility, the results will vary within the narrow parameters of no improvement to a great improvement. But we cannot predict absolutely the other consequences of treating Ht-7. Because of the interrelationships of the entire functional system in a human being, any single point may yield any effect in a given patient at a given moment. Hence needling Ht-7 may improve the function of the lungs, bowels, or liver, or alleviate migraines or cure infertility, depending entirely on the functional dynamics of the patient involved.

Similarly, each point touches a unique aspect of spiritual and emotional being, yet the consequences of evoking these deeper aspects of point function are often far reaching in ways that are not entirely predictable. For example, the spirit of Ht-7 can be evoked to regulate the opening and closing of the heart via the spirit gate, but the extent of how this will manifest in the patient's awareness and behavior is not certain. Should the treatment be effective we can predict generally that the patient will be more relaxed, focused, and easily able to preside over his life according to the principle of *wuwei* (effortlessness). But the specific manifestation of this can vary. For example, if his spirit is called home to the heart, the memory of painful events in life can return and cause psychic distress as the patient processes whatever feelings might arrive in the face of his pain. Memory of true self can also help lay the foundation for deep continued healing. Balancing the relationship of the *shen* to its home in the heart can manifest as either peace or agitation as the psychic and spiritual facilities of the other officials come into alignment under the heart's influence.

## *Determinants of Point Function*

Acupuncture points have a multiplicity of functions determined in part by variables that lay implicitly within a given point and in part by external sources of input. These external sources range from the overall context of the treatment to your specific intention in treating the point. Next I discuss these different sources of input on the impact of acupuncture point function.

### *1. Functions Ascribed to Points*

If we read the major texts on acupuncture, each point has a seemingly endless array of functions ascribed to it. Further, each point can have a wide variety of symptoms for which it is said to be applicable, many of which seem to have nothing to do with each other. Every point has its own unique function, yet, because of the holographic nature of the human functional system, can initiate any possible result within the realm of human functioning depending on the patient and the overall context of the treatment. For this reason, traditional views of ascribing a limited range of functions to a point in a cause-and-effect fashion tends to limit our ability to truly grasp the essential nature of each point as well as the possibility of acupuncture treatment as a whole.

Physiological functions ascribed to points can only accurately be thought of as tendencies toward a specific direction or quality of functioning. Many of these functions can be deduced from the type of point (*luo*, source, *xi*-cleft, or spirit point) being treated and the nature of the official associated with the point.

These functions are often presented in a mechanistic and causal fashion such as, "St-40 drains damp" or "Lv-2 sedates fire." In fact, these point functions are context sensitive. Lv-2 has the potential to sedate fire if the liver official is in excess relative to a deficient fire element. However, Lv-2 can also tonify fire when the liver *yang* is deficient and not supporting the fire of the heart or heart protector. Hence the point's function is determined by variables relative to the entire functional system and not by variables that lie solely within the point itself.

### *2. Intention*

The role of the practitioner's intention in influencing point function is not emphasized enough in teaching or in the literature. From the standpoint of cultivating clinical awareness, you must know precisely why you are selecting a particular point for treatment. We can liken this focused intention to aiming an arrow toward the bull's-eye of a target. Only if our intention is focused on the object of treatment can we perceive the immediate feedback nature provides us about the efficacy of our point selection. Through knowledge of why we choose a point and the expected outcome of treatment according to parameters such as the pulse, CSOE, and other diagnostic signs, we can develop a rapport with nature that provides immediate feedback and allows us to practice in a way that is unconstrained by either theory or expectation. As important as knowing what we expect a point, treatment, or prescription to accomplish is the ability to assess accurately what actually occurred. We must try to ensure that our expectations of point function never constrain our ability to perceive the results of our treatments.

At an advanced stage of practice, you may develop a rapport with the points to such an extent that the direction of a point's function is influenced by your intention in needling the point. This aspect of practice involves embracing the authenticity that results from a deep alignment of your own *shen, jing,* and *ling* spirits, the physiological correlates of the absolute and divinity within us. Ideally, the spirit of each point is a metaphor that serves to unite the patient's internal physiological process with the practitioner's own exemplary virtue as it is expressed in every facet of his or her life.

## *3. Environment*

The greater context the treatment is occurring in also in part determines point function. Variables such as the season, weather, and time of day all can play an influential role in treatment. For example, Ki-10 is a horary point but only between the hours of 5 and 7 P.M. As a horary point it is particularly effective on the winter solstice.

## *4. Context*

The other points treated in combination with a given point influence its function. For example, if you treat a *luo* point on a *yang* meridian alone or in conjunction with a *xi*-cleft point, it tends to clear consciousness by channeling stagnation to the outside. If, in contrast, you treat it in conjunction with the source point on its paired *yin* channel, the *luo* point tends to promote communication between the *yin* and *yang* official in a way that focuses the mind internally.

## *Point Selection*

When acupuncture points or an herbal formula are prescribed, they are selected to complement the presenting functional dynamics of the patient in the moment. Practitioners seem to match herbs to a patient's pattern of dysfunction. For example, if a patient is determined to have deficient *qi* and *yang*, points and herbs are chosen for their ability to tonify these influences. If stagnant *qi* and excess heat predominate the clinical landscape, a treatment that moves *qi* and drains heat is chosen. Finally, if a patient appears to be belligerent in a way predicated on lack of self-esteem, treatment can be tailored toward increasing self-esteem and mitigating belligerence. This is certainly a valid way to approach treatment, although it does tend to emphasize a patient's pathology. We must keep in mind, however, that a basis of constitutional medicine is that a patient's greatest weakness is also his greatest potential strength.

An equally valid, although less utilized method of designing treatments, is to match the herbs and points you choose to a patient's strengths. This is possible with all acupuncture points and with herbs from the highest category of medicine that focus on the fulfillment of individual destiny.[3] For example, I might choose to treat Gb-40 ("wilderness mound") in a patient who lacks perspective and feels constrained by a perceived lack of options. However, I might also choose Gb-40 ("wilderness mound") in a patient who states, "I feel like I can see the entire span of my life for the first time. It's as though I've climbed a hill and can finally see the forest for the trees." In this case I am choosing the point because it resonates with the virtue of perspective and not with a pathology. This approach serves to reinforce the emergence of a strength and help empower a patient to truly come into his own.

## QUESTIONS

1. In a given patient, at a given moment, what is the single largest determinant of point function?
2. Does the practitioner's intention have a causal relationship to point function?
3. Is there a context too small or too large for the practice of Chinese medicine?
    a. Is using acupuncture to treat wrist pain too small a context?
    b. Is furthering the evolution of our species, and consciousness itself, too large a context?

# *NOTES*

1. Note the functional similarity between acupuncture points and the nature of Chinese characters as metaphors. Point function as well as the meaning of a given character both evolve in relation to the development of human awareness.
2. Sun Tzu, 1973, Chapter 6, line 28.
3. All acupuncture points harmonize specific issues along a continuum of imbalance by helping empower a center point of stability. For example, Ht-7 can lower or raise heart rate depending on the context of a particular treatment. In my experience, only the herbs most aligned with heaven can do this and usually only when they are prescribed in small amounts. For example, schizandra can help promote balanced sleep in a person who is too inspired at night to relax. However, the same herb can also figuratively wake a person up who is unmotivated and lacks inspiration.

PART

# IV

# THE ACUPUNCTURE POINTS

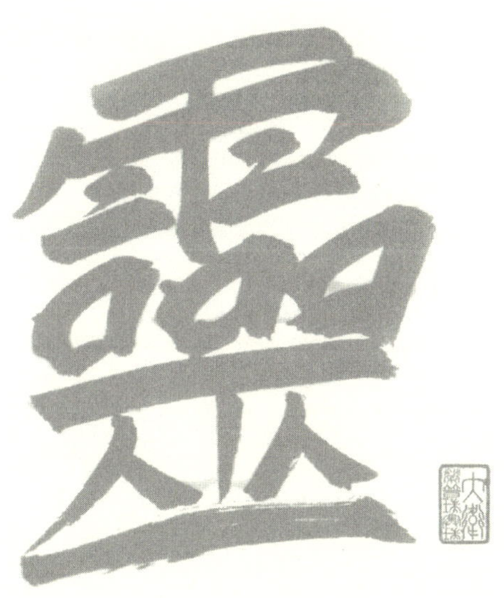

# INTRODUCTION

In Part IV, I discuss the functions of the acupuncture points on the twelve principal meridians. In *Nourishing Destiny*, I emphasized the relationship between Chinese mythology and the names and functions of twenty acupuncture points. Although I have included some similar material here, I emphasize my understanding of the points as it has emerged through my close to two decades of clinical practice.

The point numbering system and pathway descriptions are referenced to J. R. Worsley's book, *Traditional Chinese Acupuncture: Vol. I. Meridians and Points*. I have changed point names when I think the new rendering gives a better sense of the Chinese character. In any event, do not depend on English translations of point names to comprehend point function. Rather, take the time to familiarize yourself with the essence of the characters associated with the points. In this way you will grasp the metaphor of each point's function more deeply and broadly.

The point names presented here are referenced to Manfred Porkert's work in his book *The Theoretical Foundations of Chinese Medicine*. I have referenced each character in each point name to the appropriate etymological lesson in Wieger's text, *Chinese Characters*, as well as to the character number in *Mathews' Chinese-English Dictionary*.[1] This should facilitate your own research into acupuncture point names and functions so your knowledge of the topic is not restricted by my rendering of the Chinese or by the impossibility of arriving at a meaningful one-to-one translation into English for Chinese characters.

Following my discussion of the channel points, Chapter 36 presents several point combinations I have found helpful for empowering specific virtues. The material presented here represents my current thoughts in my ongoing inquiry into a topic of limitless nuance. The nature of acupuncture point function, like reality, evolves faster than the written word will ever grasp. The functions of the points I present here represent truths that are self-evident to me. I offer them only as insights into my own process of discovery and not as ultimate definitions of point function. At best, this work reflects only a momentary snapshot of my evolving inquiry into, and understanding of, acupuncture point function. A point may have entire realms of functioning that I do not discuss either because those functions are not congruent with my use of a point or simply because I am not aware of them. Hence the information provided here is not meant to contradict any understanding of point function presented in other texts. The practice of Chinese medicine as a path often entails cultivating the ability to embrace seemingly contradictory principles as reflecting complementary truths. To others who list the functions of points differently, I would just say, "and that, too."

## *NOTES*

1. See Character Index: Acupuncture Point Names.

# 24

# HEART

THE HEART CHANNEL BEGINS IN THE CENTER OF THE HEART'S complementary *yang* official, the small intestine. Another branch ascends through the esophagus to the eye. This branch allows for the radiation of our heart spirit into the world as the brilliance in our eyes and allows the heart to receive life directly through the eyes in a way that empowers intuition. A third branch ascends through the aorta, passes through the lungs, and travels to the axilla, where the heart channel emerges externally at Ht-1, the channel's entry point. From here the channel runs down the inner forearm to the inner nail point of the little finger.

## *Thoughts on the Channel*

The triumvirate of heaven, human, and earth correspond in number to the sides of a triangle (亼) that figures prominently in the character *ming* (命), meaning "destiny." The moon, stars, and sun invest destiny in our *jing*, *qi*, and *shen*, whose evolution is presided over by our three *hun* spirits. Three times three yields the number nine, which, in the Chinese enumeration of being, represents a state of completion and fullness. The nine points on the heart channel correspond to the destiny of the emperor fulfilled.

### MAIN FUNCTIONS

1. Empowers recognition of true self.
2. Initiates actions congruent with true self.
3. Coordinates the functions of all twelve other officials.
4. Empowers effortless control that flows from intuition.
5. Acknowledges reality.

### DISTAL POINT FUNCTIONS

***Wood:*** Empowers perspective, insight, and vision within the heart.
***Fire:*** Empowers the essential nature of the monarch's fire.
***Earth:*** Ensures that the heart is nourished in the process of governing.
***Metal:*** Connects the heart to its path, aligning it with breath.
***Water:*** Cools the heart and empowers connection to the depths of self.
***Xi-cleft:*** Moves stagnation of *qi,* heat, and dampness that obscures the heart, manifesting as pressure, repressed desire, and bitterness.
***Luo:*** Vents stagnation empowering clarity in communication with kidney *jing* and with the outside world via the small intestine.

---

## ❖ Ht-1 Utmost Spring

*Ji*[2]*quan*[2] Utmost Spring[1] 極泉

FUNCTION

Entry point virtues

1. Connects to the heavenly source of *yang.*
2. Aligns the human heart with the heart of heaven.
3. Empowers compassion, emotional warmth, and effortless control *(wuwei).*

Denoting the heart as being the first official in the order of *qi* circulation is consistent with an orientation toward the heart as emperor and an embodiment of heaven within us. In deference to its position of sovereign, the heart is the first official discussed in Chapter 8 of the *Neijing Suwen.*[2] The first brush stroke when writing the characters for the *yin* and *yang* of heart spirit, *ling* (靈) and *shen* (神), respectively, denotes the influence of heaven and primordial *qi* with the character *yi* (一), meaning "one." Hence Ht-1 as a source *(quan)* is given the designation of utmost *(ji)* respect. As the polestar is the center of the universe, the sun the center of the solar system, and the emperor the center of the nation, so too is the heart the center of our being. All of these centers play the same functional role, yet each has its own unique physical manifestation. The character *ji* denotes the ridgepole that at once separates and unites the dual poles of heaven and earth. Its use in the name of Ht-1 denotes this point's importance in aligning the heart with the universal centers just mentioned so we may be nourished from the primal source of *yang*.

Ultimately, all separation in life stems from and contributes to separation from heaven. If we are cut off from the "utmost source," we may appear cold and isolated, exhibiting a failure to exercise compassion both toward ourselves and others. Without the input of the heart and for lack of a spiritual center, life becomes a joyless struggle for control amid seemingly unending chaos. This deficiency tends to be reflected as a generalized spiritual emptiness apparent within all the officials and manifests as a dull and lifeless quality in the eyes and an ashen complexion. Absence or feebleness of the left distal pulse suggests severe depletion of both heart *qi* and *yang* and can require needling Ht-1 to reunite the heart with the universal sources of these influences.[3]

---

## ❖ Ht-2 — Cyan Spirit

| | | |
|---|---|---|
| *Qing*$^{1}$*ling*$^{2}$ | Cyan Spirit | 青靈 |
| *Qing*$^{1}$*ling*$^{2}$*quan*$^{2}$ | Cyan Spirit Source | 青靈泉 |

Prohibition: Forbidden to needle.

VIRTUES

1. Nourishes the *shen.*
2. Empowers effective performance of ritual.
3. Causes heart *qi* to rush.
4. Increases the potency of the heart as master.

### Qing

The character *qing* is composed of the character for plants growing (龶) over that of an alchemical furnace (丹) with cinnabar (丶) in it. The image contained in the character *qing* is that of the alchemical transformation and generative power of growth that takes place in plants during the spring. The character *qing* represents the blue-green (cyan) color of this growth, and the *Nanjing* assigns the liver the color *qing.*[4]

## *Alchemy, Ritual, and the King's Heart*

The transformative fire of life is found in humans in the cinnabar field, or *dantian* (丹田), the internal alchemical furnace. In medicine, the "life gate fire" seems to take over the role of the cinnabar field in alchemy. Cinnabar is listed in the *Shennong Bencao Jing* as the first herb in the upper class of those that nourish destiny. According to the *Shennong Bencao Jing*,

> Cinnabar tastes sweet and is slightly cold, it cures the hundred diseases of the body and the five *zang*. It nourishes the *jingshen*, makes the *hun* and *po* peaceful and benefits the *qi*. It brightens the eyes and kills demons and injurious ghosts. If you take it for a long time you can communicate with the spiritual brightness *(tong shenming)* and you will not grow old.

Cinnabar is considered the strongest herb to calm the heart, bringing stability to the emperor who presides over our inner kingdom of being. In fact, several emperors died of cinnabar toxicity, apparently poisoned by their court alchemists.[5]

The name of Ht-2, *qingling*, is the name of the terrace where the emperor went to receive spiritual influences[6]—hence the location of this point on the heart meridian. In reference to the character *ling*, Wieger points out that in ancient China, the shaman's most important role was to elicit rain from the heavens. The emperor's role was not so different because his duty was to be in charge of the performance of rites. In the *Yijing*, hexagram 51 corresponds to the "blue-green dragon," the arrival of spring. The hexagram tells us that even though the thunder may roll and spread terror for a hundred miles around, the ruler remains so "composed and reverent in spirit" that the sacrificial rite is not interrupted. Wilhelm continues, "This is the spirit that must animate leaders and the rulers of men—a profound inner seriousness from which all outer terrors glance off harmlessly."[7]

In this context, *qingling* may address the emperor's power to invoke rain from heaven, essential for new growth in spring, through the performing of rights. In general, *ling* may be thought of as the emperor's or heart's potency, as derived from fulfillment of his mandate *(ming)* to rule effectively.

A patient with a heart in which the *ling* spirit is unbalanced may appear out of synch in life. Symptomatically, this imbalance may appear as stuttering, heart palpitations, or insomnia. The person may also appear shaky and frightened.[8] When the *yin* and *yang* of heart spirit is balanced, things proceed "as if they were done by no one." Confucius refers to this balance of *ling* and *shen* spirits indirectly when he says that Shun, the great sage king, "merely placed himself gravely and reverently with his face due south; that was all,"[9] for "With correct comportment, no commands are necessary, yet affairs proceed."[10]

---

❖ **Ht-3** **Little Sea**
*Shao⁴hai³* Little Sea 少海
*Qu¹jie²* Crooked Joint 曲節

FUNCTIONS

1. Water point
2. Secondary tonification point

VIRTUES

1. Nourishes heart *yin.*
2. Calms the heart and mind.
3. Relaxes a tightly held heart and eases pressure generated by repressed or unfulfilled desires.
4. Empowers the kidney's virtues of wisdom, depth, coolness, and tranquility within the heart as the channel's receiving point for the influence of water.

As the water point on a fire meridian, Ht-3 is useful for harmonizing the relationship between the heart and kidney officials. A traditional function of this point is to calm heart spirit. If water fails to control the expression of fire, the desires of the conditioned mind can engulf us and obscure the pure intention of the heart, whose only desire is liberation from the tyranny of ego. The smaller the space an atom is confined to, the faster it vibrates and the more heat it generates. Similarly, if the heart is overtaxed or constrained through either the habitual pursuit or suppression of desires, its *qi* stagnates and heat accumulates. Such heat can agitate heart function, destabilizing the pulse and imparting a sense of urgency to all communications. Such a person will often seem out of control and feel victimized by his desire. Hence a tightly held and closed heart can be evidenced by stuttering, heat flushes, heart palpitations, and nervousness. This point may be "little" *(shao),* but as the sea *(hai)* point on the heart meridian it provides access to an ocean of *yin* that can cool and thus calm the heart's fire. If water overcontrols the expression of fire, then fear, the emotion associated with the kidneys, can extinguish the heart's flame altogether, manifesting physically as a heart attack or congestive heart failure and psychospiritually as lack of emotional warmth and connection to self and others. Such a person can feel out of control and victimized by his fears. In this case Ht-3 can be used to decrease the controlling influence of the water element over heart function.

The name "crooked joint" is an anatomical description of this point's location on the inner crease of the elbow.

---

### ❖ Ht-4 Spirit Path
*Ling²dao⁴* Spirit Path 靈道

FUNCTIONS

1. Metal point
2. Secondary sedation point
3. Cools heart fire

VIRTUES

1. Empowers the virtues of openness, receptivity, and righteousness associated with the metal element within fire.
2. Synchronizes the beating of the heart with the rhythm of the lungs.
3. Helps connect the heart to its spiritual path.

*Lingdao* is a name of the road that leads to the imperial mausoleum of the Chinese emperor. The *ling* spirit empowers us to perform ritual and thus allows us to be an effective force in the world around us. The metal within fire empowers connection of the heart to its spiritual path. If the presence of metal is deficient, the heart can wander aimlessly with no connection to transcendent values, vainly seeking satisfaction in the material world. If the influence of metal is excessive, we may lose touch with our hearts as the ego leads us to become self-righteous. In this case we may fail to value, and lose compassion for, nonbelievers. As the receiving point for the influence of metal on the heart channel, "spirit path" can empower the virtues of righteousness, openness, and receptivity within the heart so compassion is administered exactly.

Physiologically, Ht-4 can aid in synchronizing the rhythm of the heart and lungs. Treatment of "spirit path" can be indicated when we feel isolated from purpose, unable to overcome our identification with the pain, sadness, and loss we are experiencing that is, in fact, part of our spiritual journey. Hence balancing the metal within the fire can help us let go of pain and bitterness associated with the heart's losses and betrayals.

"Spirit path" is ideal for the patient who feels "burned by life." Here the affairs of the heart have been overcontrolling the metal element across the *ke* cycle. In such instances bitterness and excessive need for control can inhibit the rhythm of the breath and our ability to receive and let go spontaneously in life. As a secondary sedation point, Ht-4 can help cool and calm excessive heart fire. In this way we can let go of our attachment to manifesting all the mind's desires and in so doing reconnect to the transcendent values of the heart.

---

❖ **Ht-5** **Penetrating Inside**
*Tong*[1]*li*[3] Penetrating Inside 通里
*Tong*[1]*li*[3] Penetrating Principle 通理

FUNCTION

*Luo* point

VIRTUES

1. Directs the mind and spirit internally.
2. Vents heat and repressed desires from the heart.

The heart as emperor excels in insight and understanding.[11] In the *Shennong Bencao Jing,* the phrase "*tong shenming*" (通神明) indicates that medicines of the highest level (i.e., those that aid in the fulfillment of destiny) can empower communication between our hearts and the heart of heaven. Here the character *tong* conveys the notion of interpenetration or of being in communication with a principle or reason (*li:*理) in such a way that yields understanding. As a *luo* point, *tongli* brings *qi* into the heart, directing intention and awareness toward the interior. In this way the heart fire can penetrate the principles of true self that lie in the depths of being as contained in *jing*.

When the heart and mind separate, communication between the heart and small intestine is compromised. The habituated mind of the small intestine tends to turn externally in the world as it attempts to comprehend meaning in life through excessive sorting. Cut off from the heart's capacity to acknowledge truth, all sorting is in vain because the source of our suffering always lies within us. This is evident when a person uses "confusion" as an excuse for not taking appropriate action in the world. As the heart's *luo* point, Ht-5 can vent heat and phlegm, which agitates the *shen,* to the exterior. In this way the functions of the heart and small intestine can be reunited as the capacity for intuition is restored.

People who are fire constitutionally tend to hide pain by wearing a mask as a form of self-protection. Penetrating inside is ideal for the patient who habitually closes his heart to connection and intimacy and is therefore only able to experience superficial joy in life. Such a person might be smiling on the outside and wearing a brave face to cover his joylessness while inside he suffers in silence. This dynamic can be embodied as warmth, which is present superficially in a patient's body that is paired with the experience of being cold in the interior.

---

| ❖ **Ht-6** | ***Yin* Cleft** | |
|---|---|---|
| *Yin*[1]*xi*[1] | *Yin* Cleft | 陰郄 |
| *Shao*[4]*yin*[1]*xi*[1] | Lesser *Yin* Cleft | 少陰郄 |
| *Tong*[1]*guan*[1] | Communication Pass | 通關 |
| *Shi*[2]*gong*[1] | Stone Palace | 石宮 |

FUNCTION

*Xi*-cleft point

VIRTUE

Moves stagnation that obscures the heart and hampers the free movement of *shen.*

The character *xi* denotes a crack with light shining through it. As the *xi*-cleft point of the heart official, Ht-6 is able to move all manner of stagnation as it obscures the clarity and radiance of heart spirit. Hence this point is said to transform heart phlegm and to clear both heart fire and blood heat. Heart fire and blood heat correspond to feelings trapped in the heart that our minds cannot find a way to express comfortably. The more tightly our heart is held, the more the heart "vibrates" and generates heat that enters the blood through the heart. This vibration can evidence symptomatically as stuttering, heart palpitations, and flickering of the eyes corresponding to dissociation.[12] Such vibration can also present on the pulse and indicate a disturbance of the mind that prevents the spirit from resting peacefully in the heart. When agitated heart *qi* disturbs the blood, it can create heat that eventually leads to conditions of blood stasis.

Phlegm obstructing the heart is the embodiment of the ignorance and delusion that separates the heart and mind and impedes our ability to know true self. Often our desires can pose a threat to our minds because attempting to fulfill them would defy social conventions and our own ethical sensibilities. Even simple desires such as being in an intimate relationship can be threatening to the mind in the light of past pain and feelings of loss or betrayal. Threatening desires can be sublimated and transformed into unconscious urges that drive us to indulge ourselves in other less fulfilling ways. Unrealized desires for connection can be congruent with a hungry heart that can be expressed as overindulgence in sex, food, and drink as we search in vain for joy in life. Phlegm obscuring the heart often accrues from an overly rich diet driven by the mind's habitual attempt at satisfying worldly desires. By helping move stagnation, Ht-6 can restore communication between the heart and mind and help move old pain, bitterness, and unexpressed desire that has been trapped in the heart and has agitated the spirit.

---

| ❖ **Ht-7** | **Spirit Gate** | |
|---|---|---|
| *Shen*$^{2}$*men*$^{2}$ | Spirit Gate | 神門 |
| *Dui*$^{4}$*chong*$^{1}$ | Open Thoroughfare | 兑衝 |
| *Zhong*$^{1}$*du*$^{1}$ | Central Capital | 中都 |
| *Rui*$^{4}$*zhong*$^{1}$ | Valiant Center | 鋭中 |
| *Dui*$^{4}$*gu*$^{3}$ | Open Bone | 兑骨 |

FUNCTIONS

1. Source point
2. Earth point
3. Sedation point

VIRTUES

1. Oils the heart gate.
2. Allows the spirit to travel freely and rest within the heart.
3. Empowers the qualities of stability, center, and nourishment associated with the earth element within the heart official.

The name of Ht-7, "spirit gate," alludes to the facility of this point to regulate the mechanism that provides entry into, and out of, the imperial chamber of the heart. Ideally this function is mediated effortlessly beneath the level of our conscious awareness. Hence this gate must open and close according to the degree of safety inherent in any potential contact the heart as emperor might encounter. Safety is defined as the context in which the effortless governing of the heart can thrive according to the principles of *wuwei.*

The function of Ht-7 can be likened to oiling the heart's gate in order to facilitate the effortlessness of the emperor's rule. If the heart's gate "rusts" open, the mind can wander and be too expansive as it fails to focus the expression of spirit. Ht-7, as the earth point on the heart channel, can empower the virtue of center within the heart and help nourish the scattered *shen,* enabling it to rest within its home. It is important to discuss here the role of spirit in illness within the context of Chinese medicine. The notion of "scattered *shen*" implies a spiritual disorder. From my perspective, the spirit is always complete, untouched by life, and available as our deepest source of healing the moment we choose to identify with it. I have come to understand all spiritual disorders identified in Chinese medicine as being propagated by a disordered mind that is conditioned by ego. Hence a term like "scattered *shen*" actually identifies a dysfunction of mind that is not grounded in spirit.

If spirit gate is rusted closed, the mind can focus excessively on its unfulfilled desires, causing agitation and the accumulation of heat within the heart. In this scenario, oiling the spirit gate can help empower the spirit to feel less constrained and to enjoy a greater freedom of expression. The dynamic of the heart's gate rusting in either a shut or open position can present on a continuum ranging from depression to mania. When the virtue of Ht-7 is deficient, a patient can appear withdrawn and noncommunicative. When in excess, the patient tends to be overly excitable and talkative, evidence insomnia, and experience heart palpitations or, in extreme circumstances, hallucinations.

Drugs with hallucinogenic properties such as LSD erode the function of the spirit gate. The feelings of euphoria attained with these substances results from the dissolution of boundary established by the fire officials between the heart and the outside world. Hence one's sense of ego tends to be quelled as one feels merged with the universe. Used over extended periods of time, hallucinogens tend to make it difficult for the mind to convey the spirit with fidelity. In this case, the mind becomes scattered and thus the spirit may be said to not rest well within the heart. Certain dysfunctions diagnosed in the West as mental illness are also typified by feelings of being overly merged with the environment. Treating Ht-7 can help restore the boundary between self and the world to establish a basis on which a healthier sense of self, grounded in the absolute, can be built.

---

## ❖ Ht-8 Lesser Palace
*Shao⁴fu³* Lesser Palace 少府

FUNCTIONS

1. Fire point
2. Horary point; 11 A.M.–1 P.M., summer solstice

VIRTUES

1. Quells heart fire.
2. Calms the *shen.*
3. Reignites heart fire.
4. Diminishes the habituating force and urgency of repressed or unfulfilled desires.

The character *fu* (府) denotes Ht-8 as a storehouse where the heart spirit *(shen)* resides. The character *shao,* meaning "lesser," designates the heart as comprising part of the *shaoyin* complex along with the kidney channel. As the fire point on a fire meridian, Ht-8 is the horary point and uniquely able to tonify or sedate heart fire, particularly when treated between 11 A.M. and 1 P.M. on the summer solstice. This time of day and season represent the sun at its apex, indicating the influence of *yang* in nature is at its peak. "Lesser palace" can reignite the heart fire in cases where it appears to have "burned out." Evidence of this can include lack of brightness in the eyes and an ashen complexion. At the other extreme, this point is ideal for calming the fire of a heart that is straining and building up pressure from burning too brightly.

Excessive heat in the heart can evidence as a red tip to the tongue. Such heat often results from repressed desires that lie in the heart unexpressed. There is a delicate balance that must occur between commitment and suppression. We can stay in a dysfunctional relationship long after love has died out of a sense of commitment. Such an action often requires suppressing our desire for intimacy and our instinct to move on and take the next step in life. This scenario is joyless for the heart and its fire tends to either be smothered by such suppression or rage in excess as we hold our hearts too tightly. Sedating Ht-8 with SI-7 is an excellent combination for draining heat from the heart that results from excessive desires.

As a transmitting point for the influence of fire, Ht-8 can engender the virtues of insight, effortless control, and compassion within any other *yin* official when its fire point is treated simultaneously.

---

| | | |
|---|---|---|
| ❖ **Ht-9** | **Little Rushing In** | |
| *Shao⁴chong¹* | Little Rushing In | 少沖 |
| *Shao⁴chong¹* | Little Thoroughfare | 少衝 |
| *Jing¹shi³* | Meridian Beginning | 經始 |

FUNCTIONS

1. Wood point
2. Tonification point

VIRTUES

1. Empowers the virtues associated with wood including vision, benevolence, decision making, and planning within the heart.
2. Rekindles the heart's fire.

The term *shao* ("little") is present in Ht-9, Ht-3 (*shaohai,* "little sea"), and Ht-8 (*shaofu,* "lesser palace"). The concept conveyed here is not one meant to diminish the importance of the heart but rather to denote a concentration of power in a small space. Hence the emperor who is only one man and thus "small" is considered the emissary of heaven on earth and the spiritual center of his nation. The character *chong* denotes the motion of a whirlpool or geyser and qualifies the influence of the *qi* that unites heaven and earth. As the *chongqi* unites these two cosmic poles, so too do the emperor and the heart unite the nation and the functions of the twelve officials, respectively. Although "small" in the sense of being a *jing* well point, Ht-9 as the channel's tonification point can be quite powerful in strengthening the influence of the emperor in uniting the inner kingdom.

The natural relationship of wood to fire is that wood serves as fuel to sustain and nourish the fire's expression. If the influence of wood is deficient, the expression of fire is extinguished and coldness, lack of joy, and lack of compassion can predominate our internal landscape. If the influence of wood is excessive, fire can rage and ultimately burn out as it consumes all available resources like a wildfire in the mountains on a dry day. Within us, such excessive fire can be embodied as hypertension, heart attack, stroke, and an excessive need for control. As the channel's wood point, Ht-9 holds the potential for tonifying and nourishing the expression of fire when the heart's influence is waning. However, if a fire is nearly out, placing more wood on it can extinguish it completely. In this case it might be more appropriate to gently nourish the fire with Ht-7, the channel's earth point. After effectively creating a base for the fire's expression, we might then proceed to evoke the functions of Ht-9.

It is therefore important to discern why a patient's heart fire is deficient before choosing a method to revive it. The patient might have burned out from excessive need for control and overwork. In this case treating Ht-9 may only serve to enable the patient to continue to exhaust himself. If, however, the fire is deficient due to sadness and resignation, Ht-9 can engender the wood element's virtue of hope within the heart. In this way we can revive the heart's fire by offering it something to cling to as well as a goal to move toward.

As the receiving point for the influence of the wood element, Ht-9 can empower the heart's capacity for vision and clarity. The ability to trust in a grounded way involves integrating the vision of the liver with the insight of the heart. In trusting, we must utilize the heart's capacity to know truth as well as the mind's capacity to analyze data. Hence we must keep both our heart and eyes open as we favor people with our trust. By empowering the virtues of wood within the heart official, Ht-9 can unite the functions of the wood and fire elements to allow trust to occur in a balanced way.[13] Hence Ht-9 can encourage the patient to "look before he leaps" rather than to just "follow his heart."

The vision and planning facilities of the wood element can empower the virtue of insight within the heart as the rapid growth of spring empowers the blossoming of flowers in the summer. *Qi* rushes into the heart meridian at Ht-9, its *jing* well point. If the wood of the liver burns excessively bright, the heart tends to become agitated and a sense of uncontrolled "rushing" may be evident in all manner of personal expression. Conversely, if fire is cut off from the influence of wood, the heart as emperor tends to lack insight into both life and self and becomes joyless. Separated from the guiding light of the heart's fire and intuition, we may wander aimlessly like a leaf blown by the wind, neither discerning our direction from external cues or from inner knowing.

## *Exercise*

1. Discuss the significance of designating the heart official as first in the order of *qi* circulation as opposed to the lung official.
2. What is the functional relationship of Ht-4 *(lingdao)* to GV-11 *(shendao)* whose name can also be translated as "spirit path"?
3. How does the relationship of Ht-4 to GV-11 mirror that of the *ling* to the *shen* spirit?
4. Some traditions of practice, out of reverence for the emperor, do not treat points associated with the heart official. Is this traditional approach relevant in the context of the world situation and clinical practice today?

# *NOTES*

1. In the back of this text there is a glossary of all the characters used in the names of the acupuncture points. Every character is referenced to the appropriate lesson number in Wieger (1965) (W) and Mathews (1931) (M). To aid in your own research, just look up any character by its pinyin spelling. In this way you will not have to depend on any author's translation of the point names.
2. Larre and De La Vallee, 1985, p. 23.
3. This is particularly true if the right middle position evidences a relative excess as compared to the left distal position. This finding would indicate an E/E block between the spleen and heart officials as discussed in Chapter 5.
4. Unschuld, 1986, p. 170.
5. My translation.
6. Lecture with C. Larre (1986). *Ling* not only interacts with our own *shen* but may provide the facility for our communication with heaven. Thus it is our *ling* that attracts heaven's *shen*. In the performance of ritual it is an individual's potency *(ling)* that may summon a response from heaven.
7. Wilhelm, 1968, pp. 197–200.
8. These symptoms may indicate the use of cinnabar therapeutically with formulas such as Tianwang Buxin Wan that treat deficient heart *yin* (*yin* is associated with the *ling* aspect of spirit). Given the current levels of mercury in the environment due to pollution, prescribing cinnabar, because it contains mercury, may no longer be justified.
9. Fingarette, 1972, p. 4.
10. Ibid.
11. Veith, 1949, p. 133.
12. See Jarrett, 1995b, 1995c, and *ND*, p. 396.
13. In this regard, a particularly effective treatment may be combining Lv-1 with Ht-9.

# 25

# SMALL INTESTINE

THE SMALL INTESTINE CHANNEL BEGINS SUPERFICIALLY AT the ulnar nail point of the little finger at SI-1. It then ascends the posterior surface of the arm to transverse the rear of the scapula and arrive at the median line below the seventh cervical vertebra at GV-14. From GV-14 the pathway proceeds internally and runs anteriorly through the shoulder to St-12, where it divides into a superficial and a deep branch. The internal branch descends to the median line and meets the heart at CV-17. This branch passes through the stomach at CV-12 and CV-13, where it connects with its organ, the small intestine.

The superficial branch of the channel ascends the lateral aspect of the neck through SI-16 and then crosses the mandible to ascend the cheek and reach its termination point at SI-19 in front of the tragus of the ear. An internal pathway ascends from SI-18 to meet GB-1 at the lateral canthus of the eye and then proceeds to SI-19. Another deep branch leaves SI-18 to ascend to the medial canthus of the eye, where it joins the bladder channel at Bl-1.

---

## *Thoughts on the Channel*

For its first nine points, the posterior path of the small intestine channel mirrors the anterior path of the heart channel. The ascension of the channel past the axilla to the sensory orifice of the ear is congruent with the small intestine's role as a *yang* official to act as a conduit of mind.

### MAIN FUNCTIONS

1. Sorts pure from impure by burning away mundanity and empowering transformation in all aspects of being.
2. Abstracts essential *yang* from acquired *qi.*
3. Communicates heart essence into the world.
4. Empowers the virtues of listening and intuition.

### DISTAL POINT FUNCTIONS

*Metal:* Empowers the small intestine to discern and abstract essence.

*Water:* Regulates the expression of the small intestine's fire across the *ke* cycle.

*Wood:* Empowers vision and decision making within the sorting process.

*Fire:* Ignites or disperses the essential nature of the small intestine as a fire official.

*Earth:* Strengthens the assimilation of nourishment by the small intestine.

*Xi-cleft:* Moves stagnation within the small intestine manifesting as bitterness and resentment that obscures clear communication from and to the heart and hinders the assimilation of nourishment.

*Luo:* Vents stagnation within the small intestine to the outside world. Clears the mind and empowers communication with the heart.

---

| ❖ **SI-1** | **Little Marsh** | |
|---|---|---|
| *Shao⁴ze²* | Little Marsh | 少澤 |
| *Xiao³ji²* | Little Happiness | 小吉 |

FUNCTIONS

1. Entry point
2. Metal point
3. Secondary sedation point

VIRTUES

1. Cools heat in the small intestine.
2. Helps the small intestine filter the pure from impure.
3. Engenders the virtues of metal such as letting go and receiving, openness, and connection to essence within the small intestine.

Salt marshes and estuaries are areas where fresh water and salt water mix as rivers journey to the sea. Water from streams and rivers pass slowly through the marshes before arriving at the ocean. The marshes abstract nutrients carried downstream and are some of the most fertile areas on earth for supporting plant and animal life. Similarly, the small intestine helps abstract nourishment gleaned from digestion. Bringing metal into fire may be likened to burning leaves in the autumn to help eliminate the old growth of the past year that has lost its usefulness. In this way new growth in the spring can proceed unburdened by the past. The small intestine's fire burns away impurities as gold (essences) are retained and lead (mundanity) is passed on to the large intestine for elimination.

A virtue of metal is to empower the discernment of quality. As the metal point on the small intestine channel, SI-1 supports this official to filter the pure from the impure. If the presence of metal within the small intestine is deficient, the capacity of the small intestine to absorb only the finest essences into the blood may be compromised. If digestion is incomplete and the gut is overly permeable, virus-sized particles may be absorbed into the blood and trigger an immune response. This situation can result in allergies and decreased immunity over time because of overstimulation of the immune system. If metal within fire is excessive, the small intestine can be too selective, coinciding with conditions such as sprue in which the small intestine loses its cilia and is unable to absorb any nourishment whatsoever. Hence the proper balance of metal within fire empowers the small intestine's ability to absorb essence and pass the refuse on to the large intestine for elimination.

If the metal within fire is dysfunctional, our ability to sort is likely to be compromised and toxins are retained. Such toxicity can be embodied as boils, rashes, or lesions and inflammation in mucous membranes because the skin and membranes are governed by the metal element. Psychospiritually we may not connect to the good intentions in our hearts or the hearts of others as our failure to sort results in sarcasm and bitterness and our minds twist the meanings of all communications.

If the presence of metal within fire is deficient, it can fail to control the wood within the fire. In this scenario, lacking the proper internal balance of metal and wood, fire tends to rage out of control. Strengthening the influence of metal within fire brings a cooling and calming influence that mitigates wood's tendency toward constant striving. Hence the relationships of the *sheng* and *ke* cycle exist functionally within each official in precisely the same way as they exist among the elements overall.

---

❖ **SI-2** **Forward Valley**
*Qian²gu³* Forward Valley 前谷
*Shou³tai⁴yang²* Hand *Taiyang* 手太陽

FUNCTION

Water point

VIRTUES

1. Empowers the virtues associated with water within the small intestine.
2. Cools fire and tonifies *yin* within the small intestine.
3. Empowers "depth" of listening.

The name of SI-2 suggests its location just distal to the fifth metacarpal bone. The sequence of SI-3 ("back ravine"), SI-2, ("forward valley"), and SI-1 ("little marsh") are suggestive of the progression of a waterway to the sea as water flows from the forests (wood, SI-3), to the rivers (water, SI-2), to the estuaries and marshes where the rivers meet the abyss of the ocean (metal, SI-1).

If fire within the small intestine is excessive, SI-2 can empower the cooling and controlling influence of water across the *ke* cycle as well as increase the presence of *yin* within the small intestine. But if the presence of water is excessive, the transformative fires of the small intestine will be extinguished. As the water point on the small intestine channel, "forward valley" can help harmonize the relationship between the water and fire elements within the small intestine official. Desires accumulated within the heart can lead to heat building within the small intestine that over time consumes *yin*. As heat builds in the small intestine official it may be vented as sarcasm and bitterness because the essence of the heart is not accurately conveyed to the world.

Any shock that is significant enough in magnitude to create separation between the heart and mind compromises the heart/kidney axis and our ability to know true self through introspection.[1] The functional integrity of the relationship between the heart and small intestine is also likely to be affected as the mind turns externally and looks for the cause of its pain in the outside world.[2] Cut off from the heart's insight and intuition, the mind of the small intestine becomes confused because it lacks inner guidance in the process of sorting. In the midst of such confusion, the mind tends to struggle for control and generate stories about who we are and how life is. Physiologically, such excessive sorting can result in excess heat within the small intestine as it hyperfunctions.

"Forward valley" affects all secretions and can help regulate the balance between fire and water wherever tissue or joints are inflamed. Fire in the small intestine can be embodied as inflammation in the skin or joints or as lesions in mucous membranes as toxicity stagnates and is discharged. The influence of water is cleansing and can help wash away the accretion of impurities that results if the small intestine is not performing its function of sorting the pure from the impure. Fire can also manifest as burning urination or prostatitis as heat travels from the small intestine to the bladder as it is vented.[3]

This presentation often corresponds to the common pattern of heat traveling from the heart to the small intestine, to be vented by the bladder. I have seen this situation many times in women who experience bladder infections whenever they are sexually active. Here, desires in the heart are stirred by intimate contact yet are not able to be adequately expressed because of the fears and desires of the conditioned mind. The conflict between desire, commitment, and need generate heat within the heart that travels to the small intestine and manifests as confusion and excessive sorting regarding the nature of the relationship. This heat is ultimately vented through the bladder, receiving the biomedical diagnosis of "bladder infection" and a routine prescription of antibiotics. As the receiving point for the influence of water, "forward valley" can empower the water element's virtues of wisdom, coolness, and tranquility within the small intestine official. In this way the mind may slow to cease its habitual sorting based on fear and separation. The quiet mind may then be reunited with the guiding influence of the heart as the heart/kidney axis is rectified. I find this point particularly effective for stilling the mind when combined with Bl-66 (see Chapter 9).

---

### ❖ SI-3 Back Ravine

*Hou[4]xi[1]* Back Ravine 後谿

FUNCTIONS

1. Wood point
2. Tonification point
3. Master point of GV
4. Couple point of *yang* motility channel

VIRTUES

1. Empowers the virtues of the wood element within the small intestine.
2. Brings vision and clarity to the sorting process.

Located in a depression just proximal to the fifth metacarpal, SI-3 may be thought of as a "back ravine." The functions of the gallbladder and the small intestine are intimately linked through the interdependence of decision making and sorting. If the sorting function of the small intestine loses contact with the directionality of the wood element, growth tends to stagnate. We may become stuck on our journey in life as we sort endlessly but never make a decision about which path to take. As the wood point on the small intestine meridian, SI-3 helps empower the virtue of vision within the process of sorting.

If the influence of wood within the small intestine is excessive, our sorting capabilities may be overwhelmed by the gallbladder's habitual pressure to take immediate action. Here confusion results as the small intestine cannot sort fast enough to adequately inform the decision-making functions of the gallbladder. Now the gallbladder compensates by making impulsive decisions uninformed by the small intestine's capacity for listening to the heart.[4] In this case symptoms associated with excess heat in the small intestine may manifest due to an overabundance of wood fueling the small intestine's fire. Such a patient may appear flustered as the virtues of sorting and decision making are both compromised. Heat rising to the top of the small intestine channel can be experienced as tinnitus. Ringing in the ears can be evidence that the virtue of listening, as it guides the sorting process and development of intuition, has been obscured.

If the presence of wood within the fire is deficient, there may not be enough fuel to sustain the small intestine in performing its function of sorting. Cut off from the vision of the decision-making process, sorting comes to a standstill. In this scenario, digestion tends to stagnate as nutrients can no longer be effectively separated from waste for absorption. As the transformative fire of the small intestine slowly flickers and subsides, all of life can stagnate as the heart is unable to discern meaning and intuition slowly dies. All aspects of being may suffer as we fail to abstract the pure *yang* from life and our hearts fail to be nourished.

Balancing the influence of wood within the small intestine can empower clarity within the process of sorting. "Back ravine" can be an important point for "opening the sensory orifices" when they are obscured by the mind's delusions and desires. Hence SI-3 can help empower the accurate perception of reality especially when paired with points by the sensory orifices such as SI-19, "listening palace." Fire tends to be expansive, and the wood within fire can help give it structure so the perceptions and desires of the heart are rooted in reality.

As the channels' tonification point, SI-3 can be effective for moving stagnation in the small intestine and gallbladder by shaking up the way we listen to and see ourselves. Such stagnation can be predicated on our personalization of thoughts and feelings, which accumulate and obscure the upright sorting function of the small intestine. Strengthening the influence of wood within the fire can help us move on, by empowering the clarity of our vision and listening so that cognition of our life experience is authentic. In this way consciousness can cut through the complexity and confusion of the created self and focus once again on the simplicity and authenticity of essence.

---

### ❖ **SI-4** **Wrist Bone**
*Wan*[4]*gu*[3] Wrist Bone 腕骨

FUNCTION
Source point

VIRTUE
Purifies the *qi* of the small intestine.

"Wrist bone" is named for its location on the medial aspect of the wrist in the depression between the fifth metacarpal and the triquetral bone. We can view the wrist as the juncture between the core self and our extension into the outside world. The wrist is how we extend ourselves to make contact with others with a handshake, placing the world at large within our grasp. Similarly, the small intestine must convey the heart's essence into the world via speech and action as well as reach out into the world to bring nourishing essence into the inner realm of the heart. Hence the presence of wrist pain can be associated with failing to extend one's heart into the world with fidelity because of compromised functioning of the small intestine.

A function of this point is to clear dampness and heat that have stagnated in the small intestine. Psychospiritually, damp heat in the small intestine can manifest as the accretion of bitterness that festers internally. Ultimately, this toxic emotion can poison the heart and manifest as sarcasm, cynicism, and perversion if the essence of the heart is not transmitted accurately to the external world.[5] Hence, as the source point, SI-4 can empower the entire function of the small intestine to accurately convey and receive the essence of the heart in self and others.

As the channel's source point, SI-4 can renew the function of the small intestine, connecting it with a source of vital *yangqi* untouched by the vicissitudes of life. Unlike an element point, which is directional, SI-4 can best allow the context and functional dynamics of a given patient to determine the overall quality and direction of a given treatment. Hence stagnation can be moved, relative excess dispersed, and relative deficiency tonified, all under the auspices of the source point.

Sunlight is the essential source of postnatal nourishment that lies at the heart of all acquired forms of *qi*. This acquired *yang* is embodied within all we ingest whether it be food, air, or water. All that is not sunlight is *yin* and corresponds to mundanity that must be eliminated. We also acquire *yang* in the form of heaven's intent for us in all we experience. If we fail to grasp the highest in our experience, our stories, false interpretations, and the resulting suffering we generate in response to life correspond to acquired *yin*. By empowering the function of the small intestine with a source of pure *yangqi*, SI-4 can revitalize the official's ability to connect with and abstract *yang* in all realms of being.

The function of the small and large intestines are closely related, and treating SI-4 with LI-4 can help the function of each by empowering efficient assimilation of acquired *yang* and the elimination of mundane *yin*. The small intestine and large intestine both absorb *yang* in the form of amino acids and minerals, respectively. The large intestine then must eliminate all that has been acquired and lose its essential worth. For such waste is constituted only of mundanity and nothing celestial remains.

---

### ❖ SI-5 *Yang* Valley
*Yang*[2]*gu*[3] *Yang* Valley 陽谷

FUNCTIONS

1. Fire point
2. Horary point; 1–3 P.M., summer solstice

VIRTUES

1. Empowers the virtues of fire within the small intestine official.
2. Provides strong tonification or sedation to the small intestine.
3. Strengthens the transformative fire of the small intestine to burn away impurities.

As the fire point on the *taiyang* (great *yang*) fire meridian, SI-5 is *yang* in nature. Its location in the depression between the styloid process of the ulna and the triquetral bone is designated in the point name as a "valley." SI-5 ("*yang* valley") accumulates acquired *yang* as contrasted with Ki-10 ("*yin* valley"), where acquired *yin* tends to accumulate.[6] As the horary point associated with the small intestine official, SI-5 is particularly strong in shaking up the function of the small intestine official. The most effective time to treat SI-5 is between 1 and 3 P.M. on the summer solstice when the influence of *yang* is ascendant and the sun is highest in the sky.

Treating "*yang* valley" is like fanning the alchemist's flame and burning off the accretions of past experience that obscure the transformational aspects of the small intestine's fire.

Together, the bladder and small intestine constitute the *taiyang* channel and represent the outermost layer of functionality in the six-stage division of the meridians. We can think of the nervous system as composed of the *taiyang* channels. The bladder, as the water element, constitutes the form of the nervous system. Hence the bladder channel is the longest of the meridians running in proximity to the afferent and efferent innervation of the spinal cord.[7] In fact, the bladder meridian courses the entire length of the sciatic nerve, the longest nerve in the body. In contrast, the small intestine mediates the nature of the impulse communicated along the nerves and ensures the fidelity of all perceptions and actions to the needs of the heart as emperor.

As one of the two most *yang* points on a fire meridian (the other is TH-6), SI-5 empowers the fire of conscious awareness at its peak in life. This fire mediates our ability to perceive reality through the process of sorting and assimilation. All inessential sentiment must be burned away to ensure that only refined essence is communicated to the heart. Hence "*yang* valley" excels at rectifying the quality of our consciousness when it is obscured by excessive or deficient fire. If fire is excessive, delirium and mania can result, characterized by hallucinations, delusions, and excessive talking unfiltered by the healthy mind's ability to sort. More subtly, this can manifest as dissociated thought, or simply failing to discern the relevance of what is being communicated. Physically, excessive fire tends to manifest as heat and inflammation. Symptoms such as tinnitus, trigeminal neuralgia, gingivitis, and a bitter taste in the mouth can all be evidence of excessive fire compromising the function of the small intestine.

If the small intestine's fire is deficient, transformation slows to a standstill in all aspects of being. Symptoms similar to the those just described are based on deficiency and the presence of cold. In the absence of fire, the mind tends to grow slow and lethargic; communication is unclear because of laziness and disinterestedness rather than overengagement and mania. Clarity of hearing can be compromised if the process of assimilation proceeds too slowly. Here fluids can accumulate within the ear as the influence of fire wanes. As the fire point on its channel, "*yang* valley" excels at reigniting the fires of the small intestine to promote clarity of consciousness and transformation.

---

### ❖ SI-6 **Nourishing the Old**

*Yang*[3]*lao*[3] Nourishing the Old 養老

FUNCTION

*Xi*-cleft point

VIRTUES

1. Burns off impurities allowing for reconnection to nourishment.
2. Nourishes us in the face of old pain empowering the assimilation of life's lessons from past traumas.
3. Quells suffering.
4. Moves stagnation in the small intestine.

As the *xi*-cleft point, "nourishing the old" excels at clearing stagnation from the small intestine official by clearing the accretions of acquired mundanity that have smothered the fires of the heart and *mingmen.* Stagnation in the small intestine can lead to lethargy in all aspects of being and is ultimately embodied in weakness, pain, or paralysis of the arms and legs, rendering a person literally unable to sort things out.

Often the traumas that appear to be the source of our pain occurred in the distant past. Our present suffering is a product of our mind's twisted interpretation of the past feeding back on itself. Nourishing the old can assist the transformation of long-term chronic pains that have left us cynical and embittered. When the small intestine's flame is smothered, sarcasm, bitterness, and cynicism can manifest as we feel oppressed by the worst in everything. Further, confusion tends to present as our past noxiously colors the present, impeding us from interpreting the meaning of anything accurately. We can also have difficulty assimilating sincerity and feel uncomfortable in its presence because everything that comes to us appears tainted.

Such negative interpretations of life tend to reinforce the ongoing inhibition of the small intestine's virtue of transformation to the point that the fires of the heart and *mingmen* are eventually extinguished. After receiving this point in treatment, patients often report dreaming about people and places they had long ago forgotten. Such dreams suggest the processing of latent psychospiritual material. Further, patients can experience memories, feelings, or sensations such as smells that remind them of the past. By breaking the cycle of negativity, moving the psychospiritual basis of the stagnation, and assisting us to abstract the highest from our pain and move on, "nourishing the old" holds the potential to revitalize our entire being.

---

❖ **SI-7** **Support Uprightness**

*Zhi*[1]*zheng*[4] Support Uprightness 支正

FUNCTIONS

1. *Luo* point
2. Assembly point for the neck and head

VIRTUES

1. Vents stagnation to the exterior.
2. Clears the mind.
3. Reestablishes the fidelity of communication between the heart and the outside world.
4. Empowers the limbs to convey the heart's intention into the world accurately.

The name of SI-7, "support uprightness," alludes to the importance of the small intestine's function in rectifying *qi* by empowering clarity and intuition. The etymology of the Chinese character *de* (德), signifying both original nature and virtue, suggests we are able to know the world (十) directly (一) with our heart (心). To know the world in this way suggests the facility of intuition, which emerges when we stand upright (彳) between heaven and earth, perceiving life without coloring it with the mind's interpretation. The central function of the small intestine relates directly to the uprightness of connection between the heart (心) and mind (罒) denoted by the single brush stroke (一) in the character *de*. For this single stroke represents the number one, synonymous with the influence of heaven and the primordial *qi* in governing our lives. It is the essential nature of the small intestine to ensure that communication between our primordial *qi* and heaven occurs directly (一) in an upright way without distortion.

*Zhizheng* can also be translated as "upright branch," alluding to the function of SI-7 as the channel's *luo* point where it "branches" to meet with the heart official. The small intestine's function is to convey with absolute fidelity the heart's intentions into the world through both speech and action. Sarcasm, bitterness, and actions that perpetuate our own suffering and the suffering of others represent distortions of the heart's intention whose nature it is to always empower the highest in life. Often when such negative sentiments distort the heart's intention, we can feel we are not being understood or heard clearly as we fail to recognize the fault is our own. As the channel's *luo* point, SI-7 is useful for venting such stagnant emotions and thus removing the basis of their expression through speech and action. Hence the mind can be cleared as communication is reestablished with the guiding insight of the heart.

By uniting the function of the heart with the small intestine, SI-7 can empower the insight and intuition of the sovereign to guide the process of sorting so the wishes of the emperor are conveyed to the outside world with fidelity. We can think of the name "upright branch" as referring to the arms that are rooted in the shoulders and constitute the branches by which we extend our good works into the world. Symptoms such as pain and limited range of motion in the fingers, elbows, shoulders, and neck can be embodiments of the small intestine failing to grasp the intentions of our heart and thereby inhibiting its communication through virtuous deeds. The small intestine is specifically indicated when side-to-side motion of the head is limited.[8] Hence SI-7 is an excellent point for empowering free movement in the arms and shoulders in a way that reflects our commitments and is unhindered by confusion.

---

## ❖ **SI-8** **Small Sea**
*Xiao³hai³* Small Sea 小海

FUNCTIONS

1. Earth point
2. Sedation point
3. *He*-sea point

VIRTUES

1. Balances the relationship between sorting, as governed by the small intestine, and transformation, as governed by the spleen.
2. Serves as a foundation and center for containing the expression of fire.
3. Aids the small intestine in absorbing nourishment.

Here, at the channel's *he*-sea point, the river of nourishment born at SI-1 finally reaches the sea. As earth within fire, SI-8 addresses the role of the small intestine's fire in refining nutritional *qi* for absorption. The earth element's functions of transformation (spleen) and integration (stomach) are intimately related to the small intestine's function of sorting pure from impure. "Small sea" plays an important role in mediating these relationships. The spleen's central role is to transform all that we acquire in life into muscle, blood, and spiritual sustenance so we are nourished by, and come to embody, our life experience. The spleen helps accomplish this when the stomach fulfills the function of "rottening and ripening" all that we ingest. Hence all we take in is transformed into a nourishing soup (*guqi*:穀氣) that the small intestine can abstract essence from.

The spleen's function of building blood depends on the small intestine's function of absorbing essence. If the small intestine does not sort adequately, the spleen will not be able to build blood of sufficient quality. If the spleen fails to transform potential sources of nourishment beneficially, we may become bogged down with undigested material from the past that stagnates in us as dampness. Such dampness may present as confusion and a too slow thought process, making it more difficult for the small intestine to fulfill its function of sorting.

If the presence of earth within fire is deficient, the small intestine may fail to abstract nourishment adequately from life. When this is so, we may give the impression of having worked hard to earn our bread but of never having tasted honey or the fruits of our labors. Despite all available potential sources of nourishment, they somehow never seem to be assimilated to the point of touching our hearts, which can leave us sad and bitter. Earth serves as a foundation for fire and helps ground and contain it as a hearth warms a home. If deficient earth fails to hold the center, fire tends to be excessively expansive and blaze out of control, eventually burning out.

If the presence of earth within is excessive, the small intestine's fire may be smothered and extinguished as the presence of stagnation and damp slow the sorting process to a standstill. In either the case of earth excess or deficiency, confusion and sorrow can result as we fail to be nourished by life in all realms of being.

---

## ❖ SI-9 Upright Shoulder
*Jian*[1]*zhen*[1] Upright Shoulder 肩貞

As in the name of SI-7, the character *zhen* is used to convey the meaning of uprightness. An alternate translation of this points name is "shoulder divination," recalling that the ancient Chinese used scapulas as oracle bones in divination. Further, we may be able to divine the nature of shoulder problems by palpating this point.

SI-7, as a *luo* point, possesses the function of opening the channel along its entire route. In contrast, SI-9 helps empower the functions and virtues discussed in relationship to SI-7 locally within the shoulder. If the function of fire within the small intestine is deficient, our shoulder can become frozen as we are hindered from grasping life and conveying our virtue into the world through good deeds. Excessive fire can be associated with inflammation of the shoulder region.

---

## ❖ SI-10 Shoulder Blade Shu
*Nao*[4]*shu*[1] Shoulder Blade *Shu* 臑俞

FUNCTIONS

1. *Shu* point of the shoulder blade
2. Meeting point of small intestine channel and *yang* linking and *yang* motility vessels

SI-10 is a meeting point of the *yang* linking and *yang* heel channels. As such it links LI-15, LI-16, TH-15, and GB-21, all located on the shoulder with the small intestine channel. Because of its broad action in treating functional imbalances embodied within the shoulder, SI-10 is considered the *shu* point of the shoulder blade. I often utilize this as a local point for cases of frozen shoulder that involve functional imbalances of the small intestine. Despite the name of this condition, the shoulder may feel either cool or inflamed, suggesting an excess or deficiency of fire. I also may use this point when any of the channels it joins with are involved so as to broadly initiate movement of the *qi* through the shoulder region.

---

## ❖ SI-11 Heavenly Ancestor
*Tian*[1]*zong*[1] Heavenly Ancestor 天宗

VIRTUES

1. Connects us to our ancestry.
2. Empowers sorting on a spirit level.
3. Stimulates dreaming.
4. Addresses spirit-level imbalances that affect shoulder function.

In Zhuangzi, the ancestor of the human race is represented as Emperor *Huntun,* a phrase that can be translated as chaos.[9] In a world born of chaos, human life often becomes a struggle for meaning. Seemingly stuck in a whirlpool of fate, we may grasp on to stories and myths like a passing branch for the momentary stability they afford. However, the stability granted by belief is often fleeting as all human models and systems are eventually swept away by the flood of the *dao*'s rising waters. For someone who is troubled in the process of sorting, this point can empower the emergence of the heart's insight into original nature. True insight emerges when we have finally made peace with our mind's fundamental inability to know and comprehend life absolutely. *Tianzhong* brings the wisdom of the heavenly ancestor to the sorting process. For in the absolute purity of heaven, all is one and there is no "thing" to sort out.

The character *zong,* translated here as "ancestor," also denotes a gathering. SI-11 is a potent point for placing us in proper relationship to our own ancestry. Our own ancestors are the emissaries of the *dao* as our ultimate ancestor. The inner nature of SI-11 is to evoke the presence of the *dao* as ancestor so we may be guided by innate wisdom. I consider SI-11 to be in effect an "outer *shu* point" of SI-10 and to treat psychospiritual issues that are embodied as shoulder dysfunction.

I find "heavenly ancestor" to be a potent point for stimulating dreaming and the recovery of memories as unsorted psychospiritual material is processed during sleep. When insights are gained through treatment, a patient may become confused and overwhelmed as he tries to process recovered memories and new insights. In such circumstances, treatment of the small intestine official can help us assimilate the highest that past difficulties have held for us while we let go of our stories that perpetuate our suffering. "Heavenly ancestor" is a particularly helpful point in this regard.

---

### ❖ SI-12 Grasping the Wind

*Bing³feng¹* Grasping the Wind 秉風

FUNCTION

Meeting point of the small intestine, three heater, and gallbladder officials

VIRTUES

1. Releases wind that confuses the sorting process.
2. Promotes mental clarity by harmonizing the processes of decision making and sorting.

This point's name alludes to SI-12 as an entry point for wind. Wind is the environmental pernicious influence associated with the wood element. It is a disorienting influence that causes things to shift in a seemingly random fashion. Hence the interpenetration of decision making and sorting can be obscured as thoughts and feelings shift quickly and chaotically. Wind entering the shoulder may be embodied as stiffness and spasms or twitching in the musculature. SI-12 can help restore clarity by empowering the function of sorting and reorienting us to grasp the essential nature of life's shifting patterns. "Grasping the wind" can also help drain wind from the shoulder and reduce pain and inflammation, helping restore normal range of movement.

As a meeting point of the small intestine, three heater, and gallbladder officials, SI-12 helps harmonize the relationship between these wood and fire officials. The balance of our decision-making and sorting abilities is intimately related to three heater. The three heater helps regulate *weiqi* to protect us from external pathogens. The three heater must also integrate decision making and sorting with environmental cues in order for all three functions to help maintain homeostasis.

When wood and fire are out of balance in relation to each other, thoughts and speech may proceed too quickly as the wood agitates the fire. When fire is disturbed by wind, its tendency is to spread quickly and perpetuate the chaos. Hence wind can disrupt many diverse aspects of being as it compromises the three heater's ability to maintain balance between our inner selves and our environment. By draining wind, SI-12 can play an important role in eliminating its chaotic influence, helping restore clarity.

In designing a treatment to address effectively the dynamics just discussed, I might treat SI-3 and Gb-41, both wood points on their respective meridians, in conjunction with SI-12 and GB-21 as local points. Similarly, I might select Gb-41 with Gb-21 and TH-3 with TH-15, along with SI-12 as a meeting point, to integrate their functions.

---

### ❖ SI-13 **Crooked Wall**
*Qu*[1]*yuan*[2] Crooked Wall 曲垣

The small intestine official is part of the *taiyang* complex associated with our outermost defense to invasions by pathogens born on the wind. Points SI-9 through SI-13 crisscross the shoulder like the Great Wall of China that served to protect the country at its outermost boundary. Note that the concept of "crooked" stands in direct contrast to the small intestine's function of rectifying the *qi* inherent in the straight line (一) found in the character *de* (德), "virtue." When the flow of *qi* is impeded in the shoulder leading to pain and dysfunction, SI-13 can help sort out and straighten its flow.

---

### ❖ SI-14 **Outside the Shoulder *Shu***
*Jian*[1]*wai*[4]*shu*[1] Outside the Shoulder *Shu* 肩外俞

FUNCTION

Shoulder *shu* point

Like SI-10, this point is a *shu* point for the shoulder. I find its functions to be largely physical in nature, helping diminish pain and increase the shoulder's range of motion.

---

### ❖ SI-15 **Middle of the Shoulder *Shu***
*Jian*[1]*zhong*[1]*shu*[1] Middle of the Shoulder *Shu* 肩中俞

FUNCTION

Shoulder *shu* point

Like SI-10 and SI-14, this point is a *shu* point for the shoulder, helping largely in the physical domain to decrease pain and increase range of motion. It is particularly effective for softening the muscles and helping make them more pliable and therefore receptive to manipulation.[10]

---

❖ **SI-16** **Heavenly Window**

| | | |
|---|---|---|
| *Tian[1]chuang[1]* | Heavenly Window | 天窗 |
| *Chuang[1]long[2]* | Window Basket | 天蘢 |
| *Chuang[1]long[2]* | Window of Deafness | 窗聾 |
| *Chuang[1]long[2]* | Dragon Window | 窗龍 |

FUNCTION

Window to heaven

VIRTUES

1. Brings the perspective of heaven to the sorting process.
2. Empowers abstracting spiritual lessons and letting go of suffering.

As a window point, SI-16 provides clarity on a deep spiritual level to aid in the sorting process. When the function of this window is compromised, failure to sort appropriately can lead us to only find the negative in everything. Cynicism and bitterness can accumulate like toxins to obscure the small intestine's facility to assimilate the heart of self and life. This can evidence as an aversion to sincerity and suspicion over the motivations of those who act virtuously. The name "window of deafness" suggests this point's application in treating hearing loss, and the name "dragon window" suggests the point's usage in treating tinnitus congruent with rising *yang* or rebellious *qi*.

---

❖ **SI-17** **Heavenly Appearance**

| | | |
|---|---|---|
| *Tian[1]rong[2]* | Heavenly Appearance | 天容 |

FUNCTION

Window to heaven

VIRTUES

1. Brings the perspective of heaven to the sorting process.
2. Empowers the appearance of heaven's intent to cast light on our tribulations and burn away our suffering.

As window points both SI-16 and SI-17 are essential for the patient whose heart is separated from the heart of heaven. When in extreme pain we may ask ourselves, "If God is compassionate, how could I suffer so?" In asking this question we turn our backs on heaven and begin to suspect everyone's motivations, finding the worst in everything. For if heaven can't be trusted to be compassionate, then who can be?

As a window point, SI-17 is somewhat stronger than SI-16 in keeping with its relatively elevated status on the meridian. Rather than just providing a glimpse of truth through a window, this point can help make the decree of heaven manifest by placing us in direct contact with truth. Despite our imagined separation, heaven finds only the highest in us, and SI-17, in reuniting us with heaven, can empower us to rediscover the highest in ourselves and in life's challenges.

---

| ❖ **SI-18** | **Cheekbone** | |
|---|---|---|
| *Quan²liao²* | Cheekbone | 顴髎 |
| *Quan²jiao⁴* | Cheekbone Hole | 顴窌 |
| *Dui⁴gu³* | Exchange Bone | 兌骨 |

SI-18 is a local point that can be beneficial when the small intestine's failure to convey the heart's essence through speech is embodied as jaw pain and tension.

---

| ❖ **SI-19** | **Listening Palace** | |
|---|---|---|
| *Ting¹gong¹* | Listening Palace | 聽宮 |
| *Duo¹suo³wen²* | Place Where Much Is Heard | 多所聞 |

*Don't listen with your ears, listen with your mind. No, don't listen with your mind, but listen with your spirit. Listening stops with the ears, the mind stops with recognition, but spirit is empty and waits on all things. The way gathers in emptiness alone. Emptiness is the fasting of the mind.*

– *ZHUANGZI*[11]

FUNCTION

Exit point

VIRTUES

1. Empowers listening and the cultivation of intuition.
2. Empowers rectification of the heart.
3. Restores the ability to communicate clearly.

As an exit point, SI-19 governs the transition of *qi* from the small intestine to the bladder channel. With this transition the senses of hearing and seeing are integrated. The acuity of these senses depends on the integrity of the fires in *mingmen* and both engender, and are engendered by, conscious awareness.

The function of SI-19 is archetypal of the relationship between the heart and small intestine officials. The character *ting* (聽:listen) is etymologically related to the characters, both pronounced *de*, which refer to the rectitude of the heart (悳) and original nature (德).[12] The character *ting* (listen) is composed of the character that stands for the rectitude of the heart (悳) combined with that for the ear (耳) of the disciple (王) who is listening attentively. The overall sense imparted by this character is that, through attentive listening, our heart may be rectified. From the imagery of the character *ting*, we might define the ability to "listen" as the ability to hear our heart and the hearts of others without deviation. We who are "listening" in this way are able to know the nature of things immediately in our heart, directly bypassing the analytic faculties of our mind. Therefore, the capacity of listening may be said to empower intuition. The character *gong* (宮) designates the imperial private residence from the Qin dynasty.[13] This allusion to the emperor places further emphasis on the relationship between "listening" and the heart official as emperor in our inner kingdom.

The point's alternate name, *Duosuowen*, has three components. The character *duo* (多) suggests the idea of duplication and means "enough" or "many."[14] *Suo* (所) depicts an ax (斤) chopping at a door (戶) and denotes "a place."[15] The third character, *wen*(聞), depicts an ear (耳) next to a door (門) and means to listen attentively. Overall the name *Duosuowen* imparts the idea that the ear is a place where much can be heard if listening is attentive. The character *wen* can denote both the sense of hearing as well as smell, suggesting this point's ability to open the sensory orifices, which appear on the head like windows (*chuang*) or gates (*men*). As the exit point on the small intestine channel, SI-19 can benefit the eyes by empowering the flow of *qi* to Bl-1. The function of the small intestine and large intestine officials are closely related, and opening the exit point on the small intestine channel can promote the function of the large intestine channel that terminates at LI-20 on either side of the nose.

---

## *The Virtue of Listening*

The Chinese alchemical text "Secret of the Golden Flower" (*Taiyi Jinhua Zongzhi,* eighteenth century) describes the role of listening in aiding the heart's spirit to penetrate into the interior (depths of self). It paraphrases a legendary text, the *Danshu* (Book of the Elixir), and states,

> The hen can hatch her eggs because the heart is always listening. The hen can hatch her eggs because of the energy of heat. But the energy of the heat can only warm the shells; it cannot penetrate into the interior. Therefore she conducts this energy inward with her heart. This she does with her hearing. In this way she concentrates her whole heart. When the heart penetrates, the energy penetrates, and the chick receives the energy of the heat and begins to live. Therefore a hen, even at times when she leaves her eggs, always has the attitude of listening with bent ear. Thus the concentration of the spirit is not interrupted.[16]

This example serves as a metaphor for the way the function of the small intestine's capacity for attentive listening may empower the function of the heart. The elaborate ritual of the hen caring for her eggs is based on attentive listening. It is the concentration of our *shen* that brings intention into the world in a way that fulfills destiny. If habitual reaction to the emotions of sorrow or joy perpetuate a dysfunctional relationship between the heart and small intestine, the heart *shen* will not be focused in a way that promotes connection to life's purpose.

---

## *The Spirit of Listening*

Confucius alludes to the importance of "listening" when he describes for us the stages of his inner evolution. He tells us, "At sixty, my ear was an obedient organ for the reception of truth. At seventy, I could follow what my heart desired, without transgressing what was right."[17] Confucius, in saying that his "ear was an obedient organ for the reception of truth," precisely elaborates the quality of listening that was necessary for the ensuing rectification of his heart.

Hence "listening palace" provides a functional link between the small intestine and heart officials via the "aspect of being" termed "listening." The small intestine is like the emperor's (heart's) closest minister. Its functions are to relay to the emperor (heart official) the essence of what is going on in the nation (the other officials as well as the outside world) and to relate the essence of the emperor's intention to the nation.

Our sense of listening may be affected as we habitually reject momentary reality. Practitioners in the inner tradition should be aware that attentive listening on our part may contribute to the healing of another's heart.

## *Exercises*

1. In describing the stages of development, Confucius tells us,

*At fifteen I had my will* (zhi) *bent on learning,*
*At thirty I stood firm.*
*At forty I had my doubts.*
*At fifty I knew the decrees of heaven* (ming).
*At sixty my ear was an obedient organ for the reception of truth.*
*At seventy I could follow what my heart desired,*
*without transgressing what was right.*[18]

Will is associated with the bladder through the function of BL-47 (52), "room of will," and listening is associated with the small intestine official through SI-19, "listening palace." Together these form the *taiyang* meridian associated with the nervous system and therefore the mind.
   a. Discuss the role of the mind as it impacts both exertion of will and the ability to listen and its importance in rectifying the heart.
   b. In terms of the Chinese qualitative use of numbers, what is the significance of Confucius's heart being rectified at the age of seventy?
2. Why is the virtue of listening so vitally important to clinical practice?

# *NOTES*

1. See *ND,* pp. 207–210.
2. See *ND,* pp. 213–217.
3. The small intestine is the second channel in the order of *qi* flow, and bladder is the third. See Chapter 5 on E/E points.
4. For a review of the small intestine and its contribution to the virtue of listening, see *ND,* pp. 215–216, 358–359.
5. See *ND,* pp. 146–147.
6. Personal communication with Jeffrey Yuen, 1996.
7. Jarrett, 1983.
8. Difficulty turning the head while looking left to right implicates the gallbladder channel, difficulty moving the head side to side implicates the small intestine channel, and difficulty moving the head forward and backward implicates the bladder channel.
9. Girardot, 1983.
10. From lecture notes attributed to J. R. Worsley.
11. Watson, 1964a, p. 54.
12. Wieger, 1965, p. 37. See analysis of the character *de* in *ND,* p. 45.
13. Ibid., p. 228.
14. Ibid., p. 164, L64E.
15. Mathews, 1931, p. 754.
16. Wilhelm, 1962, pp. 41–42.
17. Legge, 1971, p. 146.
18. Ibid.

# 26

# BLADDER

THE BLADDER CHANNEL BEGINS SUPERFICIALLY AT THE medial canthus of the eye at Bl-1. It ascends through Bl-2 to the median line at GV-24 and then travels laterally to the midline to reach the vertex of the skull at Bl-7. From here an internal branch returns to the midline at GV-20 and then travels to connect with gallbladder points Gb-8 through Gb-12. A second branch of the superficial channel runs from Bl-7 to Bl-9 and then runs medially to GV-17. Moving laterally again, the channel arrives at Bl-10 to split into the inner and outer bladder lines that run parallel to each other as they descend the back.

The inner line descends to Bl-23, where a deep branch penetrates the kidney and then enters the organ of the bladder. The superficial channel continues to descend to the level of the fourth sacral foramen. It then rises medially to enter the first sacral foramen and then descends to Bl-35 just lateral to the coccyx. The pathway then moves laterally to Bl-50 and descends the rear surface of the thigh to meet the outer bladder line at Bl-54 (40) at the center of the popliteal fossa. The outer bladder line proceeds down the back in line with the medial border of the scapula to Bl-49 at the level of the fourth sacral foramen. From here it runs laterally to GB-30, where it descends to Bl-54 (40) to meet the inner bladder line.

Reunited, the single channel now descends the rear of the gastrocnemius. The channel moves laterally, passing posteriorly to the lateral malleolus, over the calcaneus and along the lateral edge of the fifth metatarsal bone. The channel terminates at Bl-67 at the lateral nail point of the little toe. From here it proceeds to the inner nail point of the little toe and on to meet the entry point of the kidney channel at Ki-1.

---

## *Thoughts on the Channel*

Like a mighty river, the bladder meridian runs from the inner canthus of the eye over the head and down the back extending to the outer nail point of the little toe. Like Ki-1, Bl-1 represents the opening and source of flow in its channel. Here the light that emanates from our inborn potential and rises through us meets with sunlight as it illuminates the events of our lives. These internal and external sources of light meet within *mingmen* to fuel the furnace of evolution, forming the very basis of health and vitality.

In keeping with their location on the head corresponding to heaven, Bl-1 through Bl-10 govern the illumination of the highest aspects of inborn potential as they combine with the heavenly *yang*. Hence these points all serve the function of "brightening the eyes," suggesting they empower the accurate perception of reality.

The points along the inner bladder line (Bl-11 through Bl-35) correspond to physiological reserves of *qi* that support the functioning of the officials and their most material manifestation in the organ systems. The outer bladder line, points 36 through 49, regulate the spiritual reserves corresponding to the highest aspect of each official as it governs the manifestation of virtue in life. The distal points, Bl-54 (40) through Bl-67, are the command points and provide access to each of the elements as they manifest within the function of the bladder official.

### MAIN FUNCTIONS

1. Regulates the storage and utilization of reserves.
2. Constitutes the mental aspect of will *(zhi)*.

### DISTAL POINT FUNCTIONS

*Water:* Addresses the essential nature of water within the bladder as a water official.

*Wood:* Taps the potential of water and empowers vision within the depths of self.

*Fire:* Empowers the interpenetration of water and fire, illuminating the depths of self to quell fear and anxiety. Thaws an overly cold will and cools heat congruent with nervous tension.

*Earth:* Controls water as the banks of a river contain the flow of a river.

*Metal:* Empowers the conception of self by bringing metal into water to renew the *sheng* cycle.

*Xi-cleft:* Moves stagnation within the bladder channel on which fear and anxiety are predicated. Reinstitutes flow born of faith and instinct.

*Luo:* Vents stagnation to the exterior, calming the mind and quelling anxiety.

*Source:* Revitalizes the bladder official with a pure source of *qi* drawn from the strength of the acquired constitution.

---

## *The Journey of* Qi *from Bl-1 Through Bl-7*

Bladder *qi* is the *yang* aspect of water and represents the manifestation of the mind as it emanates from, and guides, the interaction of *shen* and *jing*. The course of the kidney channel embodies the ascent of *jing* as it manifests internally as the cultivation of wisdom. The first seven points of the kidney channel represent a pooling and circling of *qi* as it concentrates strength for its ascent up the front of the body to Ki-27. The circle of points constituted by Ki-1 through Ki-7 empowers the conception of self. This same genesis is represented externally as the evolution of *qi* progresses from Bl-1 through Bl-7. Here the brilliance and illumination of our mind radiates the virtues inherent in our *jing* out into the world as cleverness and talent.

There are three sources of input by which the *yin* of water acquires *yang* as mind as it is constituted by the bladder official and the nervous system. At Bl-1, "eyes bright," the most refined *qi* acquired in life reaches the bladder from the small intestine. Light and *yang* also reach Bl-1 as heaven illuminates our lives with moon, star, and sunlight. These two sources of *yang* are congruent with heaven's intent as it is present in the highest that each life situation has to offer us. At Bl-1 *yin* is also infused with light emanating from *mingmen* via the heart. This light is constituted of the most refined innate *yang* as it arises from our primordial resources. Hence the influences of three outer luminaries, the moon, the stars, and the sun, and the three inner luminaries, *jing, yuanqi,* and *shen,* are confluent at Bl-1. Here *yang* as mind and spirit is infused into *yin* as represented by the function of the bladder official.

Bl-1 ("eyes bright") represents the source of bladder *qi* as the spirit (*shen*) and will (*zhi*) are conveyed by the *yang* aspect of water along the course of the bladder channel. Bl-2 ("collect bamboo") is a gathering of *qi* as the focus of spirit condenses and gains strength. "Eyebrows rushing" (Bl-3) represents the forceful ascent of bladder *qi (yin)* as it is guided by *shen (yang)* toward the top of the head. "Crooked servant" (Bl-4) serves as a reserve of *qi* to empower the flow of the bladder channel to reach the summit of the head. The ascent of *qi* to this point requires work, and "crooked servant" can help us go the distance when our minds are fatigued from overstrain.

"Five places" (Bl-5) represents another pooling and condensing of resources as *qi* approaches the summit of the head. "Receiving light" (Bl-6) illuminates the mind and depths with the guidance of heaven and ascended ancestry. At Bl-7 the ascendance of intellect and mind is complete as it literally "penetrates heaven" at the vertex of the head in proximity to GV-20, our embodiment of the polestar. Here, the bladder *qi* descends over the rear of the head and down the back like a mighty waterfall. This descent of *qi* represents the influence of our wisdom and insight as it informs the expenditure of reserve in all aspects of being. In this way the acuity of our mind and *shen* courses through and touches the functions of the various *shu* points on the bladder channel.

---

| ❖ **Bl-1** | **Eyes Bright** | |
|---|---|---|
| *Jing*$^{1}$*ming*$^{2}$ | Eyes Bright | 睛明 |
| *Jing*$^{1}$*ming*$^{2}$ | Illuminated Essence | 精明 |
| *Lei*$^{4}$*kong*$^{3}$ | Opening of Tears | 淚孔 |
| *Lei*$^{4}$*kong*$^{1}$ | Opening of Tears | 淚空 |
| *Mu*$^{4}$*nei*$^{4}$*zi*$^{4}$ | Inner Canthus of the Eye | 目內眦 |
| *Nei*$^{4}$*zi*$^{4}$*wai*$^{4}$ | Inner and Outer Canthus | 內眦外 |

FUNCTIONS

1. Entry point
2. Gate to *mingmen*
3. Brightens the eyes
4. Meeting point of the small intestine, bladder, and stomach channels with the *yin* and *yang* motility vessels and the governor vessel

VIRTUES

1. Unites inner and outer source of light.
2. Empowers accurate perception of reality.

An alternate name for Bl-1, based on a different character (精明) but also pronounced *jingming,* can be translated as "radiance of *jing.*" When the fires of *mingmen* burn brightly, the eyes shine with a radiance that reflects the purity of essential nature *(jing)*. Figure 5.3 depicts the physiology of *mingmen* as it relates to preserving the integrity of the key relationships between the *jing* and *shen,* primordial *yin* and *yang,* and early and later heaven. The integrity of these relationships assures the continued interpenetration of *yin* and *yang,* which serves as the deepest foundation for health and well-being. Early heaven, the influences received prior to the first breath, is represented by the foundational influences of *jing, yuanqi,* and *shen.* Later heaven, the influences received during and after the first breath, is reality as it occurs in life moment to moment.

All the intraelemental E/E points on the *yang* meridians are located on the head by the sensory orifices and play a crucial role in channeling later heaven into the fires of *mingmen* where they may interact with early heaven. Chief among these points are SI-19 and Bl-1. The two-way arrow in Figure 5.3 between Bl-1 and *mingmen* indicates the reciprocal relationship between these related functions. Momentary reality must be transmitted directly to *mingmen* without the deviation imposed by the mind's interpretation. When this occurs, the fires of *mingmen* are fueled, evidenced by the brightness of the eyes and acuity of hearing. Note that acupuncture points B-1 through Bl-9 are all said to "brighten the eyes," a metaphor that implies their efficacy at removing habituated influences to empower the accurate perception of truth. This function is associated with the point's ability to drain stagnations of wind, cold, and heat, the physiological correlates of delusion that obscure the connection between heart and mind.

I compare the functional effects of Bl-1 to how the quality of light changes after the winter solstice. The young light returns to fuel another round of evolution as *yang* begins to rise again through the summer solstice. As light diminishes during the fall and the year descends into the abyss of winter, our *qi* moves internally as potential condenses in a seed. In health, we recognize the importance of concentrating our *qi* during this time so we can lay a foundation of strength for our growth through spring and summer. This willingness to descend toward the depths suggests a transcendence of fear and a faith in heaven's promise of a new beginning each spring. If the water element is out of balance we can become depressed and tired as the light of the year is withdrawn and the influence of *yang* declines. This condition is known as seasonal affective disorder (SAD).[1] After the solstice, the quality of light changes, yielding hope and renewing faith in new beginnings. "Eyes bright" can empower this vision and help return our fire in the depths as well as our perception of heaven's light as it shines both within and without us as a guiding influence in our lives.

| ❖ **Bl-2** | **Collect Bamboo** | |
|---|---|---|
| *Cuan4zhu2* | Collect Bamboo | 攢竹 |
| *Shi3guang1* | Beginning Illumination | 始光 |
| *Ye4guang1* | Illuminated Darkness | 夜光 |
| *Ming2guang1* | Illuminated Brilliance | 明光 |
| *Yuan2zhu4* | Primordial Pillar | 元柱 |
| *Yuan2zhu4* | Official Pillar | 員柱 |
| *Yuan2zai4* | Official's Action | 員在 |
| *Mei2zhong1* | Eyebrow Center | 眉中 |
| *Guang1ming2* | Brilliant Illumination | 光明 |
| *Mei2ben3* | Root of the Eyebrow | 眉本 |
| *Xiao3zhu4* | Small Bamboo | 小竹 |
| *Mei2tou2* | Eyebrows | 眉頭 |

FUNCTIONS

1. Brightens the eyes
2. Alternate entry point

VIRTUES

1. Empowers balanced relationship to resources.
2. Stills the waters of anxiety.

Here the image of bamboo is used to symbolize the eyebrows as they emerge from Bl-2 as the plants might grow along a river. This image is further developed in the name of Bl-3, "eyebrows rushing." Behind the imperial throne was a piece of bamboo symbolizing the empty heart of the emperor as a vessel for receiving heaven. Bamboo was a great resource in China, used in writing, construction, the fabrication of tools, and weaponry. The image of gathering bamboo evokes the bladder's functions of storing and utilizing reserves.

I often use this point in place of Bl-1 if I want to retain needles during a treatment session. "Collect bamboo" excels at empowering the gathering of resources in a way that quiets anxiety. Psychospiritually this can help stem fear and empower the virtue of reserve. Physically it can benefit bladder function in a way that decreases urinary frequency predicated on anxiety. The first five names listed here suggest the evolution of awareness engendered by the higher functions of the bladder official as its *qi* ascends the forehead. These functions follow directly from that of Bl-1, "eyes bright."

| ❖ **Bl-3** | **Eyebrows Rushing** | |
|---|---|---|
| *Mei2chong1* | Eyebrows Rushing | 眉沖 |

FUNCTION
Brightens the eyes

The bladder meridian climbs directly up the temple from Bl-2 to reach the hairline at Bl-3. The character *chong* denotes a quick rising motion like a geyser erupting, a description applicable to the quickening of bladder *qi* as it ascends to Bl-3. *Meichong* can be useful for calming the mind when overactivity and exhaustion are predicated on pervasive anxiety and a sense of urgency.

---

❖ **Bl-4** **Crooked Servant**
*Qu[1]cha[1]* Crooked Servant 曲差
*Bi[2]chong[1]* Nose Thoroughfare 鼻衝

FUNCTION
Brightens the eyes
VIRTUES
1. Aids bladder *qi* in its ascent to the top of the head.
2. Helps strengthen resolve.

At Bl-4 the bladder meridian moves laterally on the head and gives the appearance of being crooked. The ascent of bladder *qi* from Bl-1 through Bl-7 represents the external evolution of the interpenetration of *shen* and *jing* as an accurate perception of reality empowers the sharpness of our minds. The journey between these points requires exertion as the *qi* ascends the forehead. This exertion parallels our effort in life to acquire knowledge and transform it into wisdom. A servant can aid us when we have overextended our reserves and are exhausted. "Crooked servant" can help us go the distance when our minds are fatigued from overuse of will.

The name "nose thoroughfare" denotes this point's ability to open the sinuses. Hence Bl-4 can be used simultaneously for sharpening the acuity of the senses of smell and vision.

---

❖ **Bl-5** **Five Places**
*Wu[3]chu[3]* Five Resting Places 五處
*Ju[4]chu[3]* Great Resting Place 巨處

FUNCTION
Brightens the eyes

The number five signifies a gathering together of resources as the bladder *qi* pools and condenses before continuing its ascent to reach the summit of the bladder channel at Bl-7. On a psychospiritual level this point can help a person rest when he is overwhelmed with the effort required to fulfill a task. Imagine climbing a mountain and, upon nearing the summit, being overwhelmed at the thought of continuing. Such a feeling of being overwhelmed can manifest as nervous exhaustion, anxiety, or headaches. "Five places" can help us gather resources and "pull it together" so we can attain our goal. The inner aspect of this journey is the illumination of our depths (Bl-6) and the penetration of heaven (Bl-7). On reaching the summit, fear is transformed into wisdom as conquering our fears grants a 360-degree perspective on our journey.

---

### ❖ Bl-6 Receive Light

*Cheng[2]guang[1]* Receive Light 承光

*And when their minds draw near to death,*
*nothing can restore them to the light.*
– *Zhuangzi*[2]

FUNCTION

Brightens the eyes

The character *cheng* means to receive in the sense of inheriting something. As the water element presides over the inherited constitution, the name "receive light" suggests the illumination of *jing* as a natural expression of our ancestry. The character *cheng* also means "to accept one's responsibility." Hence Bl-6 can empower us to relax and accept our destiny as mandated in a way that is not driven by anxiety or fear.

The ascent to Bl-6 is fueled by the internal fires of *mingmen* where inner and outer illumination meet. The initiation of the movement of this *qi* began in the depths of the kidney at conception with the light gleaned from karma and ancestry as *yuanqi*. Here at Bl-6, one step from the channel's summit at Bl-7, we are empowered to receive light once again from ancestry. In this process heaven illuminates the quality of our minds by empowering brilliance, itself the outer shining and *yang* aspect of wisdom as it has ascended from *jing*.

I find "receiving light" useful when a patient's mind has grown dark and he has lost his way and sense of purpose. On the one hand, the patient may be completely in the dark regarding the nature of his destiny. On the other hand, he may be aware of what is required but his ego may be struggling against accepting what heaven is asking of him.

In the face of destiny it is human nature to struggle against the unavoidable tide of reality. For how frequently do we perceive the correct course of action to be taken, yet resist it, even though we know our fate is assured? Bl-6 can help illuminate the nature of purpose in our depths and inspire the mind by aligning it with heaven's purpose as it comes to us from above.

---

| ❖ **Bl-7** | **Penetrate Heaven** | |
|---|---|---|
| *Tong[1]tian[1]* | Penetrate Heaven | 通天 |
| *Tian[1]bai[2]* | Heaven White | 天白 |
| *Tian[1]jiu[4]* | Heaven's Mortar | 天臼 |
| *Tian[1]bo[2]* | Heaven's Respect | 天佰 |

FUNCTION

Brightens the eyes

The character *tong* in the name of Bl-7 imparts the notion that we are inexorably linked to heaven, *tian*. For heaven penetrates our foundation as its will is imprinted on our *jing* at conception, and it extends itself to us every moment of life as the moon, stars, and sun shine on us. Here at the vertex of the bladder channel, these internal and external sources of light meet. Therefore, "penetrate heaven" is found directly adjacent to GV-20, our embodiment of the North Star and life-giving center of the universe.

Water constitutes the depths of self, and its arrival at Bl-7 represents the greatest height it can attain. Here, the spark planted within our depth at conception has carried the *yin* as close to the center of heaven as possible. In proximity to the North Star, the water element is once again infused with light before the channel begins its long descent down the rear of the body at Bl-8. The infusion of heavenly light gleaned at Bl-7 merges with the external shining of mind as it transmits the essential wisdom of the heart and kidney into the world.

The central function of Bl-7 is to empower resonance between the light of heaven and that of our minds. The virtues inherent in our *jing* can shine into the world as talent and intellectual brilliance. Upon "penetrating heaven," our minds are illuminated by the very source of light itself, to burn away mundanity, quell lingering doubts and fears, and renew faith. In this way we are best prepared for the long journey back into our depths as the *qi* reaches Bl-8 to descend the mighty river that is the bladder channel. At Bl-6 our minds have received light and influence from heaven above; at Bl-7 the light from our minds is evoked to penetrate heaven. For all mundanity *(yin)* must be shed as the highest within us ultimately reaches the North Star as purified virtue. This is because only virtue can travel to the heart of heaven as the wisdom and spark of our ancestry returns to itself upon death having been elevated in its journey through us.

The points Ki-1 through Ki-7 lay the foundation for conception of the spiritual embryo, and the points Bl-1 through Bl-7 address the pinnacle and outer manifestation of this journey as it expresses itself through the brilliant radiance of mind. The illumination gleaned by the ascent of bladder *qi* through these first seven points helps ensure that the expenditure of reserves in every level of being, as accessed by the *shu* points, will be presided over by the virtue of wisdom and not by the reaction to fear.

---

❖ **Bl-8** **Connecting Decline**

| | | |
|---|---|---|
| *Luo⁴que⁴* | Connecting Decline | 絡卻 |
| *Luo⁴xi¹* | Connecting Cleft | 絡郄 |
| *Qiang²yang²* | Strong *Yang* | 強陽 |
| *Nao³gai⁴* | Brain Cover | 腦蓋 |

FUNCTION

Brightens the eyes

Having reached its apex at Bl-7, the bladder meridian now begins its descent down the rear of the head and body. Bl-8 is the point that connects the channel to this descent, hence its name. Having "penetrated heaven" at Bl-7 to be illuminated by the North Star, the bladder *qi* must now travel the length of the channel communicating the message of destiny as light to every aspect of being. This spiritual light is carried by the bladder *qi,* via the *zhi,* to every other official. Hence *yang* is at its full force here as it begins its descent as denoted by the name "strong *yang.*" The term *naogai,* given as the fifth name, refers anatomically to the top of the skull.

---

❖ **Bl-9** **Jade Pillow**

| | | |
|---|---|---|
| *Yu⁴zhen³* | Jade Pillow | 玉枕 |

FUNCTION

Brightens the eyes

This point is named for its location on the occiput where the head comes into contact with a pillow during sleep. An allusion is made in the point's name to resting, a process vital to renewing reserves as presided over by the bladder official. I use this point to address mental exhaustion and the inability to rest due to anxiety.

## ❖ Bl-10 Heavenly Pillar
*Tian*[1]*zhu*[4] Heavenly Pillar 天柱

FUNCTIONS

1. Window to heaven
2. Meeting point of the bladder, small intestine, gallbladder, and three heater channels

VIRTUES

1. Connects us to an inner pillar of strength.
2. Empowers the transcendence of fear.

In Chinese mythology, the body of our heavenly ancestor Pan Gu was the pillar that unified heaven and earth before the human race lost its original nature.[3] "Heavenly pillar" is situated at the top of the trapezius muscle directly under the occipital bone. The trapezius is the pillar that literally holds up the head, which is our embodiment of heaven. As the spine is the pillar of the body (addressed by GV-12, "body pillar"), Bl-10 is the pillar of the spirit empowering us to hold our heads up and stand tall. The ascendancy of *yang* that produces marrow to strengthen the bones manifests psychospiritually as self-confidence. Healthy confidence springs from the accurate assessment of our capabilities in relationship to any given task. If our minds react habitually to fear, our relationship to our abilities and reserves will be distorted in a way that undermines or artificially boosts our confidence.

In essence, Bl-10 engenders a stabilizing influence on the neck and shoulders so the head (heaven) and the body (earth) can communicate clearly. In this way will can descend and marrow can ascend unimpeded by our reaction to fear. As a window point, Bl-10 can empower a healthy relationship to our fears by placing us in contact with a sense of strength at the very core of our beings. Hence, faith in ourselves, and in heaven as the ultimate support of our lives, can be restored. I have often used this point in combination with Bl-54 (40), GV-3, and St-36 in order to empower an individual to "stand up for himself."

### PAUL

***Age:** 32*
***Complaint:** Sciatica*
***Diagnosis:** Water/Earth within*

Paul was my first patient after I graduated from school and opened my clinical practice. He complained of pain radiating from his right buttock, down the rear of his leg, progressing all the way to his ankle. Paul's color was dark blue and his voice evidenced a deep groaning quality. A carpenter, he was continually fearful he was not getting enough work and would not be able to make his expenses. Paul also complained continually about his girlfriend and how she was dragging him down and driving him crazy.

*Interpretation*

Paul's color, sound, and emotion (blue, groaning, and fear) confirmed his nature as a water constitutional type. His constant fear regarding financial resources had compelled Paul to overwork, resulting in continued strain on his back that eventually manifested as sciatica. Complaining about a situation without changing it can be a dysfunctional quality associated with the earth element. Complaining can also impart a singing tone to the voice, substantiating the earth element as constituting Paul's secondary constitutional element "within."

*Treatment*

For the first six sessions I addressed basic blocks such as AE, akabane imbalances, and exit/entry points. I also worked on the constitutional officials of bladder and stomach. In this time Paul experienced a moderate amount of relief in his legs as his pain concentrated in his lower back and buttocks in the area of Bl-50 (36). During his seventh session Paul groaned bitterly about what a burden his girlfriend had become and how she weighed him down. He was afraid to break up with her because she helped manage his carpentry business. On this session I treated Bl-10 and Bl-64 in combination with GV-3. I explained to Paul that these points empowered a fortitude born of inner strength. I suggested he picture a pillar of black marble at his center while he lay on the table during the treatment.

*Result*

For his next session Paul returned smiling with a sparkle in his eyes I had not seen before. His walk was confident and no longer seemed to falter due to pain. On entering the treatment room Paul announced his sciatica had disappeared entirely. With a laugh he related that the day after his last treatment he had broken up with his girlfriend and the pain had left completely within twelve hours. He exclaimed, "I realized I am perfectly capable of supporting myself and that she was the pain in my rear!"

---

### ❖ Bl-11 Great Shuttle

| | | |
|---|---|---|
| *Da⁴zhu⁴* | Great Shuttle | 大杼 |
| *Bei⁴shu¹* | Back *Shu* | 背俞 |
| *Bai³lao²* | One Hundred Labors | 百劳 |

FUNCTIONS

1. Sea of blood
2. External dragon point
3. Meeting of the bladder channel and governor vessel
4. Meeting point of the bones

The characters *jingluo* (經絡) refer to the meridian system and are etymologically related to a depiction of the warp and woof of a loom. The function of Bl-11 can be compared to the shuttle of a loom that weaves back together the fabric of life when it unravels. Often *jing* deficiency is the basis of dysfunction when life begins to unravel at the seams. The name "one hundred labors" alludes to the toll that life can take in depleting us. "Great shuttle" addresses the relationship between *jing*, marrow, and the production of blood to weave these vital resources back into a functional fabric that supports life. As a sea of blood, Bl-11 can be used for general tonification when the pulse evidences qualities associated with blood deficiency. I find this point helpful both in aiding recovery from chronic illness or after blood loss.

---

❖ **Bl-12** **Wind Gate**

| | | |
|---|---|---|
| *Feng*[1]*men*[2] | Wind Gate | 風門 |
| *Re*[4]*fu*[3] | Heat Storehouse | 熱府 |

FUNCTIONS

1. Resolves wind
2. Meeting of the bladder channel and governor vessel

The name refers to the point's function of clearing externally contracted wind/cold or wind/heat. The next point, Bl-13, is the lung *shu* point, an organ particularly susceptible to invasion by wind.

---

## *The* Shu *Points*

Each *shu* point constitutes a physiological reserve of *qi* for its associated official. The points of the inner bladder line from Bl-13 through Bl-35 address physiological issues relative to the generation and distribution of *jing, yuanqi, qi,* and blood. The points on the outer bladder line from Bl-36 (41) through Bl-49 (54) tend to address relatively more psychospiritual issues associated with the officials and their spirits *(zhi, hun, shen, yi, and po).*

Two different systems are in current usage for numbering the points of the bladder channel. In the tradition I practice, the bladder channel is conceived of as traveling from Bl-35 (*huiyang,* "meeting of *yang*") on the sacrum to Bl-36 (*fufen,* "attached branch") at the top of the scapula. From there the channel descends down the outer bladder line and the rear of the leg through each point in turn until arriving at Bl-67. Other traditions consider that the bladder channel travels from Bl-35 down the rear of the leg to *weizhong* (designated as Bl-40) located in the rear of the knee crease. From here the channel rises to the point *fufen,* numbered Bl-41, to begin its descent down the outer bladder line. In this text the outer bladder points are numbered as they occur in my own tradition. For those of you who use the latter system, I have provided the alternate point number in parentheses.

---

| ❖ **Bl-13** | **Lung Shu** | |
|---|---|---|
| *Fei⁴shu¹* | Lung *Shu* | 肺俞 |
| *San¹jiao¹zhi¹ jian¹* | Third Burning Space | 三焦之間 |

FUNCTION

Lung *shu* point

*Feishu* provides access to a strong reserve of *qi* for the lung official. The lungs govern the *weiqi* and are particularly vulnerable to invasion by pathogenic wind. The rear of the neck is most vulnerable to such invasions, and, in the spirit of prevention, it is best to advise patients to keep this area covered from fall through early spring because these are the months during which exposure to wind is most likely. The lung *shu* point can be used to tonify deficiency of *qi* and *yang,* disperse and sedate excess, and move stagnation.

When the distal pulses that correspond to the upper *jiao* exhibit deep, feeble, and/or absent qualities associated with *qi* or *yang* deficiency, Bl-13, Bl-14, and Bl-15 can play a vital role in restoring the functional influence of the heart and lungs. Such emptiness often corresponds to deep sadness and resignation as the heart fails to be touched in life and the lungs fail to inspire. These upper *shu* points are often well paired with the upper kidney points (Ki-23, Ki-24, and Ki-25) that lie directly in front of them on the chest.

The name "third burning space" denotes Bl-13 as one of six points—*feishu* (BL-13), *xinshu* (BL-15), *geshu* (Bl-17), *ganshu* (BL-18), *pishu* (BL-20), and *shenshu* (Bl-23)—that drain heat from the five zang (see Figure 26.1). The "burning space" *shu* points are numbered according to their association with the dorsal vertebrae. *Lingshu* 51 uses *jiao* (焦), as in *"sanjiao,"* to designate the vertebrae, possibly as a mnemonic reminding us of the efficacy of moxa in treating these points.[4]

| Point | Name | Vertebrae | Correspondence |
|---|---|---|---|
| Bl-13 | Third burning space | Third dorsal | Lung |
| Bl-15 | Fifth burning space | Fifth dorsal | Heart |
| Bl-17 | Seventh burning space | Seventh dorsal | Diaphragm |
| Bl-18 | Ninth burning space | Ninth dorsal | Liver |
| Bl-20 | Eleventh burning space | Eleventh dorsal | Spleen |
| Bl-23 | Fourteenth burning space | Fourteenth dorsal | Kidney |

*Figure 26.1*

THE SIX BURNING SPACE *SHU* POINTS

*These six points can drain heat from the* zang *officials.*

---

❖ **Bl-14** **Tower Gate Shu**[5]

*Que⁴shu¹* — Tower Gate *Shu* — 闕俞

*Jue²yin¹shu¹* — *Jueyinshu* — 厥陰俞

*Jue²shu¹* — *Jueshu* — 厥俞

FUNCTION

Heart protector *shu* point

The heart protector empowers balanced boundaries like the wall that surrounds the imperial palace. The character *que* signifies a lookout tower, which might be found at the imperial gate. Hence this point's name speaks directly to the heart protector's function of regulating boundaries and empowering feelings of safety. "Tower gate *shu*" empowers a deep reserve of strength, rectifying the *qi* of the heart protector official so it can stand tall like a fortified sentinel tower. The names *Jueyinshu* and *Jueshu* denote the heart protector as a *jueyin* official. The *jueyin* channel is composed of the liver and heart protector meridians. For further discussion of the etymology of the character *jue,* see acupuncture point Bl-58.

---

❖ **Bl-15** **Heart *Shu***

*Xin¹shu¹* — Heart *Shu* — 心俞

*Bei⁴shu¹* — Back *Shu* — 背俞

*Wu³jiao¹zhi¹ jian¹* — Fifth Burning Space — 五焦之間

FUNCTION

Heart *shu* point

*Xinshu* provides a strong reserve of *qi* for the heart official. In my clinical practice I tend to use this point with far less frequency than the other *shu* points. The heart as emperor must be approached with reverence, and a private audience is rare. The *shu* points are powerful and I only approach the heart *shu* if other more gentle methods of influencing the heart's *qi* and *yang* are unsuccessful.

---

### ❖ Bl-16 Governor *Shu*

| | | |
|---|---|---|
| *Du*$^{1}$*shu*$^{1}$ | Governor *Shu* | 督俞 |
| *Gao*$^{1}$*yi*$^{4}$ | Tower Benefit | 高益 |
| *Gao*$^{1}$*gai*$^{4}$ | Tower Cover | 高蓋 |

FUNCTION

Governor vessel *shu* point

Bl-16 provides a strong reserve of *qi* for the governor vessel channel. I use Bl-16 when there is a general deficiency of *yang* on the pulse in several or in all positions. Hence the governor vessel can be reinvigorated with *yangqi* in cases of severe depletion resulting from trauma, chronic illness, or inborn constitutional weakness.

An alternate name for Bl-16 is *gaoyi* (高益), meaning "eminent benefit." The character *gao* depicts a pavilion (亠口) raised upon a substructure (口) covering a hall (冂). The character *gao* imparts the meanings of high, lofty, and eminent in the way such an important building might impress us. This image can be applied as a metaphor to our physical structure: the building represents the head, the substructure our body, and the covered hall the spinal cord.

Rising *yang* carries marrow up the spine toward the brain as we transform fear into wisdom. This *yang* serves to help us stand up in all aspects of being and assert our purpose and intention in the world. Hence the *qi* and *yang* presided over by the governor vessel is of "eminent benefit" in helping support our "building" by ensuring integrity from our foundation in *jing* to the top of our heads, which serves as a roof for our wisdom. Hence another name for Bl-16 is *gaogai* (高蓋) meaning "tower cover."

---

### ❖ Bl-17 Diaphragm *Shu*

| | | |
|---|---|---|
| *Ge*$^{2}$*shu*$^{1}$ | Diaphragm *Shu* | 膈俞 |
| *Qi*$^{1}$*jiao*$^{1}$*zhi*$^{1}$*jian*$^{1}$ | Seventh Burning Space *Shu* | 七焦之間 |

FUNCTIONS

1. Meeting point of blood
2. Diaphragm *shu* point

Bl-17 is effective in moving *qi* stagnation in the diaphragm. Mechanical sources of such stagnation include lifting excessive weight, working in a hunched-over position, or walking with a cane. Internally such stagnation results from the dynamic of conflict present during the painful separation of an intimate relationship. Here anger rising from the middle *jiao* meets with suppressed feelings of tenderness for the person being left that emanate from the upper *jiao*.[6] As these two opposing forces collide, *qi* stagnation results in the diaphragm. "Diaphragm *shu*" is an important point for promoting communication between the upper and middle *jiao* and moving stagnation even years after the separation has been completed. Bl-17 is also useful in cases of *qi* deficiency when weakness in the diaphragm contributes to difficulty in breathing.

As a meeting point of blood, Bl-17 is able to address every type of dysfunction involving blood including stasis, deficiency, and heat in the blood. The aorta and vena cava pass through the diaphragm, and any constriction here can impede their function of supplying blood to the body effectively. Hence *qi* stagnation in the diaphragm can increase pressure on the heart and lungs as well as restrict their blood supply. In this case the spiritual functions presided over by the upper *jiao* can languish due to lack of nourishment.

---

❖ **Bl-18** **Liver *Shu***
*Gan¹shu¹* Liver *Shu* 肝俞
*Jiu³jiao¹zhi¹jian¹* Ninth Burning Space 九焦之間

FUNCTION
Liver *shu* point

Like Bl-17, "liver *shu*" plays an important role in treating *qi* stagnation in the diaphragm by diminishing the source of rising *yang*. I often sedate this point when the entire pulse evidences qualities of liver excess. Such an approach can be helpful in helping aggressive and belligerent people relax and feel more equanimity. In contrast, by tonifying the *qi* and *yang* of the liver, Bl-18 can help a person with poor self-esteem stand up for himself. Similarly, this point can help harmonize a continuum of expression ranging from depression, resignation, and lack of striving to excessive goal-oriented behavior to the point of anger, judgment, and frustration.

---

❖ **Bl-19** **Gallbladder *Shu***
*Dan³shu¹* Gallbladder *Shu* 膽俞

FUNCTION
Gallbladder *shu* point

The gallbladder tends toward stagnation and excess. Bile congealed in the gallbladder forms sludge and stones that are the embodiment of the obstacles we encounter in life and cannot discern a way around gracefully. Heat is generated as we confront such emotional and physical walls in life. Stagnant *qi* and heat can present as a distended feeling under the rib cage, particularly in the area of Gb-24, the channel's *mu* point. This tends to coincide with a burning sensation starting from CV-12 and rising as a bitter taste in the mouth as bile ascends. Often, patients feel pain in the back around the location of Bl-19 and directly behind GB-24. *Danshu* is useful for dispersing such stagnations of *qi* and heat by helping relax the functioning of the gallbladder official. This can be likened to empowering a person to rest and stand back from an obstacle that is confronting him in order to receive a broader perspective.

The symptoms listed here may also occur in cases of *qi deficiency* because the gallbladder is unable to move obstacles due to its weakened function. In such cases *danshu* can empower us to rise to the occasion and find a way around obstacles to which we have resigned ourselves. In cases of liver *yang* deficiency, *Danshu* can help revive the liver by empowering the gallbladder to provide direction and decisiveness in overcoming obstruction.

The character *dan* can also be translated as "bravery," referring to the *yang* aspect of the wood element in empowering decisive action in the world. In harmony, the gallbladder assists the liver as general in manifesting plans in the world based on insight into the root of self. In excess, gallbladder imbalance can manifest as belligerence and frustration as we become willing to force our plans on self and others. In its deficient presentation, the gallbladder can be associated with timidity as we fail to stand up for what we know is just.

---

| ❖ **Bl-20** | **Spleen *Shu*** | |
|---|---|---|
| *Pi²shu¹* | Spleen *Shu* | 脾俞 |
| *Shi²yi¹jiao¹zhi¹jian¹* | Eleventh Burning Space | 十一焦之間 |

FUNCTION

Spleen *shu* point

*Pishu* provides a strong reserve of *qi* for the spleen official and helps assist its functions of transportation and transformation. Spleen *qi* deficiency often coincides with a general failure to identify appropriate sources of nourishment in life. And, even when these are acquired, the spleen tends to fail to transform them into nourishment, engendering instead the burden of dampness. *Pishu* can help reinvigorate the spleen so we are better nourished by our work in the world and better able to receive and process the abundance that life has to offer.

---

### ❖ Bl-21 **Stomach *Shu***
*Wei[4]shu[1]* Stomach *Shu* 胃俞

FUNCTION

Stomach *shu* point

*Weishu* provides a strong reserve of *qi* for the stomach official to empower the integration of nourishment in all aspects of being. Integrity is the virtue of the earth element, and the stomach helps us embody this virtue physically by strengthening our *hara* and psychospiritually by helping us integrate our life experience into a meaningful whole. If stomach *qi* is weak, the alignment between our intentions, speech, and actions is likely to be compromised in diverse aspects of being. *Weishu* can help rectify these relationships by strengthening the *qi* that creates and holds us to our center.

---

### ❖ Bl-22 **Three Heater *Shu***
*San[1]jiao[1]shu[1]* Three Heater *Shu* 三焦俞

FUNCTION

Three heater *shu* point

*Sanjiaoshu* provides a strong reserve of *qi* for the three heater official. This helps us access that aspect of three heater function associated with kidney *yang*. This relationship is addressed by the presence of this point in proximity to the kidney *shu* point (Bl-23) and *mingmen* (GV-4). The quality of the *qi* distributed by the three heater is both warm and wet like lava, reflecting the nature of the *yuanqi*. Differentiated into its *yin* and *yang* components, the kidneys govern the relatively *yin* watery aspect of *yuanqi*, and the three heater governs the warm *yang* aspect.

I use *sanjiaoshu* any time I find imbalances of warmth or cold in any aspect of being. When treating this point I combine it with other points to direct its effect to the area where I wish its function to be evoked. For example, I might treat Bl-22 with TH-4 and TH-17 in order to direct warmth to the head and empower the *weiqi* as a protective mechanism against invasions of wind/cold or to strengthen a person's boundary in social situations. Often points on the conception and governing vessel can be used to direct the effects of BL-22 in this way. Therefore, I might treat Bl-22 with TH-4 and CV-4 to empower warmth in the lower burner, aiding conception (with TH-11) or connection through sexuality (with TH-12).

I also find it helpful to combine Bl-22 with other *shu* points. For example, I might treat Bl-22 in conjunction with Bl-13 if I want to bring warmth to the lungs or upper *jiao*.

---

❖ **Bl-23** **Kidney *Shu***

| | | |
|---|---|---|
| *Shen⁴shu¹* | Kidney *Shu* | 腎俞 |
| *Jing¹gong¹* | Essence Palace | 精宮 |
| *Gao¹gai⁴* | Tower Cover | 高蓋 |

FUNCTION

1. Kidney *shu* point
2. External dragon point

Located on either side of *mingmen, shenshu* provides a strong reserve of *qi* for the kidney official. I use this point in every manner of kidney imbalance including stagnation and *yin* and *yang* deficiency. In cases of excess heat and stagnation I have found Bl-23 to excel in helping move kidney stones.

*Shenshu* is a powerful point to reinvigorate the connection between will *(zhi)* and the resources of *jing* and *yuanqi*. In this regard, notice it shares the alternate name "essence palace" with Bl-47 (52), "room of will." It is human nature to force our will and overtax our reserves in a way that leads us to become deficient in kidney *yin* and *yang*. The patient must be educated about how best to conserve and strengthen the particular reserve of *qi* accessed through any *shu* point being treated. This is most important when treating the kidney *shu* point because it helps us access our deepest reserves of will and *qi*. Repeated tonification without instruction will enable the patient dysfunctionally to continue the very behaviors and beliefs that have exhausted him in the first place. Such treatment will not further the patient and, in the long run, will result in even greater deficiency.

The name *gaogai*, "tower cover," is shared with Bl-16, the *shu* point of the governor vessel. The tower referred to in the point names is the spinal cord that conveys *yang* from the base of the spine up to the pinnacle of the head at GV-20.

---

❖ **Bl-24** **Sea of *Qi Shu***

| | | |
|---|---|---|
| *Qi⁴hai³shu¹* | Sea of *Qi Shu* | 氣海俞 |

FUNCTION

Sea of *qi shu* point

Located directly behind CV-6, "sea of *qi*," this *shu* point helps both tonify and regulate the sea of *qi*. The function of the sea of *qi* is congruent with the function of *mingmen* and the golden gate in internal alchemy.[7] Bl-22 and Bl-23 touch the *yang* and *yin* aspects of kidney function, respectively. In the "sea of *qi*" (Bl-24), these are united as our resource of *yuanqi*. CV-6, located just below the umbilicus (a prenatal source of *yuanqi*), comprises a *yin* aspect of the sea of *qi*, and Bl-24, located just beneath *mingmen*, comprises a *yang* aspect. If either kidney *yin* or *yang* are deficient, I treat Bl-23 or Bl-22, respectively. If, however, both kidney *yin* and *yang* are equally deficient, I often treat Bl-24 first to strengthen their source. Note that, in this regard, Bl-26, "primordial gate *shu*," is also useful.

---

### ❖ Bl-25 **Large Intestine *Shu***
*Da⁴chang²shu¹* Large Intestine *Shu* 大腸俞

FUNCTION

Large intestine *shu* point

*Dachangshu* provides a strong reserve of *qi* for the large intestine official and helps move stagnation, sedate excess, and tonify *qi* and *yang* deficiency. I find this point often allows tense muscles in the lower back to let go, making it particularly effective for many types of lower back pain. Stagnation of *qi* and heat in the large intestine manifests as pressure internally and compromises the ability to let go across diverse aspects of being. Emotionally such pressure tends to manifest as self-righteousness and perfectionism as we become dysfunctionally engaged in the pursuit of quality in life. Physically we can tend toward constipation as heat consumes fluids and dries the large intestine. Bowel movements when they occur can be explosive and mirror an attempt to hold on with excessive force even to that which has lost its value to us.

If the *qi* of the large intestine is deficient, we can tend to let go of the people and things we value too easily. Feelings of emptiness and loneliness can predominate as what we value slips through our fingers. Here the lower back tends to be weakened as the muscles do not have enough strength to support and grasp the spine adequately. Similarly, bowel movements tend toward being loose as we let go of the stool before having adequately absorbed its mineral content.

---

### ❖ Bl-26 **Primordial Gate *Shu***
*Guan¹yuan²shu¹* Primordial Gate *Shu* 關元俞

FUNCTION

Primordial gate *shu* point

The characters *yuanguan* denote the mysterious pass referred to throughout Daoist writings as the gateway between being and nonbeing.[8] This reference ties the function of Bl-26 to that of both CV-1 and Bl-63, *jingmen* ("golden gate": 金門), which is another name for the mysterious pass. The character *yuan* can also be translated into English as the word "first," again referencing CV-1 and suggesting the importance of Bl-26 as the "first gate *shu*" point.

"Primordial gate *shu*" is an important point for evoking the strength of *yuanqi* (primordial *qi*) in all aspects of being. Bl-26 is located directly behind CV-4, which governs the *yin* aspect of *mingmen*. Note that alternative names for CV-4 include "destiny gate" (*mingmen:* 命門), "sea of *qi*" (*qihai:* 氣海), and "essential dew" (*jinglu:* 精露) indicating the relationship between *jing,* the gate of destiny, and the sea of *qi.* The primary names of CV-4, "source pass" (*guanyuan:* 關原) and "primordial pass" (*guanyuan:* 關元), use the characters *yuan* (原) and *yuan* (元) to denote the source *qi* and the primordial *qi* that it regulates. The name of BL-26 includes the character *yuan* (元), referring to primordial *qi.* Although both characters are prononced *yuan,* and are therefore homophones, there is a slight shade of difference in their meanings. Source *qi* (原氣) comprises the aspect of inborn constitutional *qi* (*xiantianqi:* 先天氣) that is activated and employed in physiological processes.[9] Primordial *qi* (元氣) comprises the aspect of inborn constitutional *qi* as it exists as undifferentiated potential *(jing),* mirroring the fundamental qualities of *dao.*[10]

"Primordial gate *shu*" regulates the opening and closing of all the other gate points such as Ht-7, HP-6, and TH-5. If a particular gate repeatedly becomes stuck, the "primordial gate" can empower its balanced functioning from the very source of the patient's being, for this is the gate of incarnation. For example, HP-6 helps regulate the opening and closing of the inner frontier gate relative to establishing the balanced functioning of human intimacy. If a patient is continually unable to sustain openness from a position of strength, Bl-26 can provide a reserve of *qi* to support the ongoing function of HP-6. I also find treating Bl-26 to be essential if I am not getting the results I expect from treating the other *shu* points.

---

❖ **Bl-27** **Small Intestine *Shu***
*Xiao³chang²shu¹* Small Intestine *Shu* 小腸俞

FUNCTION

Small intestine *shu* point

*Xiaochangshu* provides a strong reserve of *qi* for the small intestine official and helps move stagnation, sedate excess, and tonify deficiency. Stagnation in the small intestine manifests as pressure internally, compromising the ability to sort pure from impure in diverse aspects of being. Emotionally such pressure tends to manifest as urgency in communication as we feel misunderstood and not heard by others. Physically such excess tends to manifest as excess heat and damp affecting assimilation and contributing to signs and symptoms such as burning urination, lesions on mucous membranes, and a bitter taste in the mouth. If heat is too excessive, it can burn the cilia in the small intestine, compromising its ability to assimilate nourishment. Dampness tends to obscure the process of assimilation by clogging the small intestine and forcing it to work harder, which in turn generates more heat, or extinguishing the fire of the small intestine to compromise assimilation.

If the *qi* of the small intestine is deficient, the gut can become overly permeable and assimilate unselectively. Entry of toxins into the blood can lead to boils and other lesions as they are transmitted to the exterior through the skin. By-products of incomplete digestion can also trigger an immune response after they enter the blood. In time, the immune system itself can become compromised from being overstimulated, leading to increased vulnerability to illness.

---

### ❖ Bl-28 — Bladder *Shu*

*Pang²guang¹shu¹* — Bladder *Shu* — 膀胱俞

FUNCTION

Bladder *shu* point

*Panguangshu* provides a strong reserve of *qi* for the bladder official and helps move stagnation, sedate excess, and tonify deficiency. Stagnation in the bladder manifests as pressure internally, compromising the ability to regulate reserves adequately in all aspects of being. Emotionally such pressure tends to manifest as a general sense of urgency and anxiety that is projected onto any situation at hand. The patient feels compelled to use his will to push ahead and squander resources at any cost. Physically such stagnation can manifest in diverse ways including prostate inflammation, urinary dysfunction, and pain in the lower back that is sensitive to touch.

If the *qi* of the bladder is deficient, reserves tend to be retained poorly and contribute to urinary problems such as stress incontinence.[11] Pain in the lower back may be relieved by touch as increased sensation tonifies the internal deficiency. In the case of deficiency, the emotions of anxiety and urgency proceed with diminished force. In cases of excess, there is a sense the patient is overwhelmed and struggling to "keep his head above water." In cases of deficiency, the *qi* is already depleted and anxiety comes from exhaustion and having given up the struggle.

---

| ❖ **Bl-29** | **Middle of the Backbone *Shu*** | |
|---|---|---|
| *Zhong[1]lu[2]shu[1]* | Middle of the Backbone *Shu* | 中膂俞 |
| *Zhong[1]lu[2]* | Middle of the Backbone | 中膂 |
| *Zhong[1]lu[2]nei[4]shu[1]* | Middle of the Backbone Inner *Shu* | 中膂內俞 |
| *Ji[2]nei[4]shu[1]* | Inner Spine *Shu* | 脊內俞 |
| *Xuan[2]shu[1]* | Revolving *Shu* | 旋俞 |

FUNCTION

Middle of the back *shu* point

"Middle of the backbone *shu*" on the inner bladder channel is congruent in name with Bl-33, "middle bone" *(zhongliao)*. I use both points only on the physical level for treating low back pain. Points such as Bl-24, Bl-26, and GV-4 address the transmission of primordial *qi* that is channeled up the spine for distribution by all the other *shu* points. Points Bl-29 and Bl-31 to Bl-34 address an outer manifestation of this process as it empowers the strength of the lower back muscles and spine. In deference to its designation as a *shu* point, I usually treat Bl-29 when I treat any of the other points from Bl-31 to Bl-34 for pain in the lower back. The name "revolving *shu*" denotes the importance of the lower spine in empowering rotational movement in the torso and this point's efficacy in restoring such movement when it is compromised.

---

| ❖ **Bl-30** | **White Ring *Shu*** | |
|---|---|---|
| *Bai[2]huan[2]shu[1]* | White Ring *Shu* | 白環俞 |
| *Yu[4]huan[2]shu[1]* | Jade Ring *Shu* | 玉環俞 |
| *Yu[4]fang[2]shu[1]* | Jade Chariot *Shu* | 玉房俞 |

FUNCTION

White ring *shu* point

White is the color of the metal element, and the ring referred to in this point's name is the anal sphincter. Bl-30 is effective in treating problems there such as prolapse, hemorrhoids, or spasm. On deeper levels the point can be used when the large intestine dysfunctionally compels us to hold on to things, making us uptight and retentive. The anal sphincter is also addressed in the name of Bl-37, *pohu* ("*po* door"), which differentially addresses the spiritual issues of the metal element relative to our process of letting go in life. In Daoist alchemy the "white ring" is referred to as storing the *jing*, hence a function ascribed to Bl-30 is one of stabilizing the essence.

Functionally, the large intestine helps us retain essence by empowering us to hold on to what is of value in life. In this regard, note that the act of conception involves the transmission of metal essence *(jing)* into water.[12] The phrase *yuhuan*, present in the third name given here, means "jade bracelet" and refers to the moon.[13]

---

❖ **Bl-31** **Upper Foramen**
*Shang⁴liao²* Upper Bone Hole 上髎
*Shang⁴jiao¹* Upper Hole 上窌

FUNCTION

Meeting of the bladder, kidney, and gallbladder channel[14]

The character *liao* (髎) consists of the character *gu* (骨), meaning "bone," paired with the character *liao* (翏), denoting "the sound of the wind," suggesting an empty place or hole. Here I have translated the character as "foramen," consistent with the location of these points over the sacral foramen. Bl-31 through Bl-34 are the four bilateral foramen ("bone hole") points on the sacrum. These are used locally to treat pain, atrophy, and loss of range of motion (ROM) in the lower back. Generally, I treat the functional basis of any symptom before I start using such local points to address the relatively more physical expressions of imbalance. After I see improvement emanating from the patient's depth as expressed through the pulse, disposition, tongue, and CSOE, I begin to utilize local points to address the symptom directly. But there are times when quick symptomatic relief is the most significant contribution that can be made to a patient. For example, if a patient is in so much pain he cannot sit still for an intake, I often proceed directly to treatment. When such cases involve lower back pain, these eight sacral points are often my first choice.

---

❖ **Bl-32** **Second Sacral Foramen**
*Ci⁴liao²* Second Sacral Foramen 次窌
*Ci⁴jiao⁴* Second Hole 沈髎

I use Bl-31 through Bl-34 as local points to treat pain, atrophy, and loss of ROM in the lower back.

---

❖ **Bl-33** **Central Foramen**

| | | |
|---|---|---|
| *Zhong*[1]*liao*[2] | Central Foramen | 中髎 |
| *Zhong*[1]*jiao*[4] | Central Hole | 中窌 |
| *Zhong*[1]*kong*[1] | Central Hole | 中空 |

FUNCTION

Meeting point of the bladder, liver, and gallbladder channels[15]

I use Bl-31 through Bl-34 as local points to treat pain, atrophy, and loss of ROM in the lower back.

---

❖ **Bl-34** **Lower Sacral Bone**

| | | |
|---|---|---|
| *Xia*[4]*liao*[2] | Lower Sacral Bone | 下髎 |
| *Xia*[4]*jiao*[4] | Lower Hole | 下窌 |

I use Bl-31 through Bl-34 as local points to treat pain, atrophy, and loss of ROM in the lower back.

---

❖ **Bl-35** **Meeting of *Yang***

| | | |
|---|---|---|
| *Hui*[4]*yang*[2] | Meeting of *Yang* | 會陽 |
| *Li*[4]*ji*[1] | Gain Motion | 利機 |

FUNCTION

Meeting point of the bladder and governor vessel channels

The lowest point on the inner bladder line, Bl-35 represents a convergence of the *yang* channels, bladder, and governor vessel, in the depths. Note that these channels meet again at GV-20, "hundred meetings," on the vertex of the head. "Meeting of *yang*" is effective to help raise *yangqi* in any realm of being whether it manifests as physical debility, prolapses, or a weakness of will and motivation associated with depression. When pain and dysfunction in the lower back and legs is based on a functional state of *yang* deficiency, "uniting *yang*" can help strengthen these areas. The character *ji* refers to motion as the primary motivating force of the universe and has secondary meanings of "seizing an opportunity" and of secrecy and the occult.[16]

## The Outer Bladder Line

### ❖ Bl-36 (41) Attached Branch
*Fu⁴fen¹* Attached Branch 附分

FUNCTION

Meeting point of the bladder and small intestine channels

*Fufen* is the first point on the top of the outer bladder line, having branched off from the inner bladder line at Bl-35 *(huiyang)*. I generally use this as a local point for pain in the neck, shoulder, and scapula region. It can also be good when a patient's neck pain is the embodiment of his projection that other people are a "pain in the neck."[17] Located just above the lung inner (Bl-13) and outer (Bl-37) *shu* points, *fufen* is also useful for supplementing the lungs and dispersing wind cold.

### ❖ Bl-37 (42) *Po* Door
*Po⁴hu⁴* *Po* Door 魄戶

Adjacent to Bl-13, the lung *shu* point, Bl-37 addresses the *po* spirit. The *hun,* associated with the liver, is a manifestation of the evolutionary instinct that drives the ascension of the virtue we cultivate during life. Upon death, the *hun* exits through GV-20 to ascend to heaven as light and report on the merit we have cultivated during our incarnation. Upon death, the *po,* representing all within us that is still mundane, exits through the anus (the *po* door) and returns to earth, providing the fertilizer for future rounds of incarnations.

Just as the body must let go of the spirit upon death, so too must the individual let go of what no longer serves and has lost its essential value during life. Grief occurs when our attachment to the physical form of someone or something we have lost prevents us from contacting its immortal essence. The *po* is that urge in us governing peristalsis and allowing us to attract value into our lives. The desires of the habituated mind can become overly attached to the form of things in this world and distort the *po*'s search for quality. Regardless of the earthly value of material goods, we are left feeling spiritually empty and alone if we fail to be inspired by spirit. Bl-37 helps ease the *po*'s longing and helps us reorient toward valuing essence in life. I find Bl-37 to play a vital role in helping reinspire patient's spiritually when they are depressed, resigned, or worn down by chronic illness.

My experience suggests that dreams of flying during sleep are often associated with the wandering of the *po* spirit. I find such dreams frequently begin with feelings of inspiration but end dysphorically with difficulties in breathing associated with conditions such as sleep apnea or asthma. It is my feeling that the *po* is actually exhaled from the body through the "*po* door" as it travels in search of some spiritual essence that is missed during waking. In this regard, note that after death, the disincarnate *po* were thought to become wandering souls searching for the respect of their families.[18] I find that "*po* door" is most effective in treating the spiritual basis of longing as well as the outer manifestation of symptoms such as sleep disturbed by breathing difficulties.

---

| ❖ **Bl-38 (43)** | **Rich for the Vitals** | |
|---|---|---|
| *Gao¹huang¹shu¹* | Rich for the Vitals | 膏肓俞 |
| *Gao¹huang¹* | *Gao Huang* | 膏肓 |

The character *gao* in ordinary speech refers to oil or fat and has the connotation of "rich" both in terms of nutritional content and as a metaphor for the wealthy who can afford to eat "rich" food. In a medical context, *gao* refers to the region beneath the heart.[19] The character *huang* refers to the area between the heart and diaphragm, translated here as "the vitals."[20] I think of this area as somewhat larger in the form of a circle whose diameter touches CV-14 on its bottom and CV-17 on its top (see Figure 26.2).

Ki-16 is the root of the *gaohuang* and has the function of tonifying heart essence. CV-14 and CV-15 are the heart and heart protector *mu* points, respectively, and CV-15 is the source point of the *gaohuang*. I think of the *gaohuang* as representing a deep level of the heart whose pathology often relates to profound karmic issues regarding a conflict between one's individual purpose in life and ancestral issues. Pain regarding unresolved issues regarding ancestors can play a role in illness here. Dark secrets around family members who may have committed suicide, committed a crime, or perpetrated incest can also be involved. Also shame regarding our own past actions can lodge here to poison heart function.

Such issues represent a type of karmic stagnation that must be addressed to empower the possibility of transcending the limitations of a tainted past. This region is the area where we often feel the pain of betrayal and separation from loved ones. It is the area affected when we feel "heartsick," like someone has placed a knife in the center of this circle and is slowly turning it.

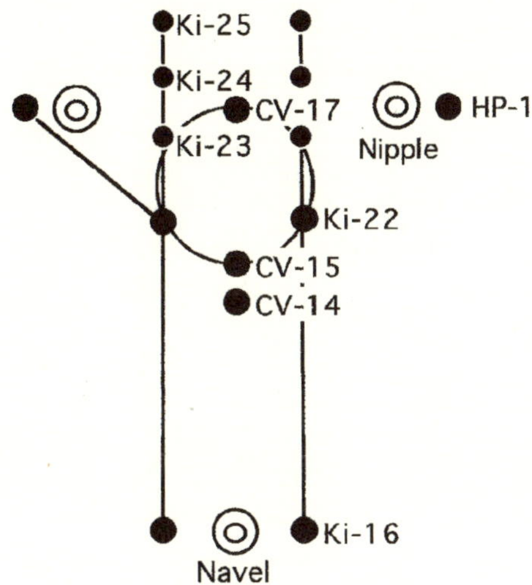


*Figure 26.2*
SOME THOUGHTS ON THE *GAOHUANG* REGION

*Here are depicted several important functional relationships relative to the* gaohuang *region. At Ki-22 the kidney meridian steps up onto the "verandah" of the rib cage. The channel splits into two as the main course of* qi *flows toward the light as represented by HP-1. The subsequent points on the kidney channel, from Ki-23 upward, direct essence into the inner domain and burial ground of the heart as emperor. It is in the final transformations, as represented by the functions of the upper kidney points, that* jing *is refined into the spiritual potency of the emperor that is* ling. *The points from CV-15 and Ki-22 upward represent the "inner frontier" that is accessed by HP-6. "Inner frontier gate," HP-6, is the couple point of the penetrating vessel whose highest point is Ki-21, located at the level of CV-15, the heart protector's* mu *point. Here* qi *and blood, the refined essence of heaven and earth, rises to nourish the heart. If the functions of empowering* (jing/ling) *and nourishing the heart with blood and* qi *are disturbed, purpose atrophies, self is lost, and eventual illness is the result. In such cases, treating the* gaohuang *region can help tonify deep levels of deficiency and promote healing through resurrection of the heart/kidney axis. Note that one homophone, also pronounced* huang *(巟), depicts the devastation caused by the overflowing rivers; another (荒) means "wild," "barren," and "draught"; and a third (慌) denotes that one is scared because the heart (忄) is running wild (荒).*[21]

CV-15, the source point of the *gaohuang*, lies exactly halfway between Ki-21 ("dark gate") and Ki-22 ("walking on the terrace").[22] As *qi* transitions through these two points it makes a journey into the inner frontier as alluded to in the name of HP-6 ("inner frontier gate"). *Qi* passes through "dark gate" and it moves off the abdomen and onto the rib cage to enter the inner domain of the heart. Ki-22 is the exit point where the main flow of *qi* leaves to enter the heart protector channel at HP-1. The following five points on the kidney channel represent the road leading to the imperial mausoleum and the burial ground of the heart as emperor. In health, *qi* makes a graceful transition between Ki-22 and HP-1 as darkness turns to light. This transition signifies the transcendence of our fears as we make intimate connection with our own hearts, the hearts of others, and the heart of life itself. As fear is transcended, the finest essence rises from *jing* to travel the spirit road toward Ki-27. In this journey, essence reaches its final state of refinement as it is transformed into *ling* to become spiritual potency. For this essence represents that aspect of our *jing* that has been fully realized and is therefore suitable to nourish the heart and complement the *shen.*[23] Hence a homophone also pronounced *huang* (恍) depicts the heart (忄) seeing the light (光) and suggests the phenomenon of sudden insight.

Ki-21 is also the highest point on the extra meridian *chongmai,* the Sea of Blood or penetrating vessel. In *chongmai, yin* and *yang,* and the inherited and acquired constitutions (via the contributions of the kidney and stomach officials), are combined in a way that fills our center with the highest nutritional essence. This essence fills us up to Ki-21 where it then travels upward to nourish the heart and lungs. Blockage in the area of the *gaohuang* prevents the upper *jiao* from receiving this essential nourishment, and the organs there slowly starve. This pattern is often typified by a pulse picture in which the distal positions corresponding to the upper *jiao* are either feeble or absent bilaterally.

In illness typified by heart break, *qi* fails to make the healthy transition between Ki-22 and HP-1 and leaves the heart and heart protector isolated from connection to the kidney.[24] Cut off from the heart protector's warmth, the cold northern influences of the kidney are diverted toward the upper kidney points and the burial ground.[25] Now potency is drowned by sorrow, fear, and darkness as the heart's fire is slowly extinguished by mundanity *(yin).* I find this dynamic typifies AIDS, an illness frequently characterized by shame and isolation from family and loved ones.[26] I also find this pattern in many chronic illnesses typified by shame, heart sickness, and isolation. *Gaohuangshu* is an important point for treating such illness when a patient has "lost heart" and fails to manifest the strength that always resides in spirit. As a point that empowers the warmth and spiritual qualities of the heart protector, *Gaohuangshu* is particularly responsive to moxa, which I often apply over many treatments to slowly nourish the spirit back to health.

*Gaohuangshu* is quite effective in treating psychospiritual issues related to the heart and heart protector officials. I find this point excels at stimulating the production of blood in a way that nourishes the vital center of the heart as well as the heart protector. Bl-38 (43) empowers the heart protector's contribution to blood, specifically the ability to be open from a position of strength. This blood nourishes the heart protector in a way that allows us to feel safe and comfortable within our own hearts, offering hope that darkness may once again flow to light.

---

### ❖ **Bl-39 (44)** **Spirit Hall**
*Shen²tang²* Spirit Hall 神堂

The name of Bl-39 has two shades of meaning, both alluding to the heart as a storehouse of *shen.* The character *tang* refers to the hall that provides access to the imperial chamber of the emperor and inner chamber of the heart. The upper kidney points (Ki-23, Ki-24, and Ki-25) constitute the *lingdao,* or "spirit path," that leads to the tomb of the emperor where his virtue is preserved in death. This path is the *yin,* internal aspect of the emperor's spiritual journey made by the spirit metaphorically during life and in actuality after death. "Spirit hall," in contrast, leads to the inner chamber within the emperor's palace and represents the *yang* aspect of the emperor's path as he cultivates and exercises virtue during life. The upper kidney points allow the possibility of reviving the heart spirits, *shen* and *ling,* when they are buried in darkness and sorrow. By comparison, "spirit hall" allows us to nourish the *shen* so it is directed and focused in the pursuit of virtue during life.

Another ancient meaning of the character *tang* is "temple," alluding to the heart as the holy place where *shen* resides. The image of the heart as a temple containing *shen* is the embodiment of the historic structure known as the *mingtang* (明堂), or "illuminated palace." The *mingtang,* referred to first in the *Zuozhuan (Tsochuan)* and the writings of Mencius, constituted both a spiritual retreat for the emperor as well as his ancestral temple.[27] Successively destroyed and rebuilt over the centuries, the concept of the *mingtang* served as a focal point for the development of Chinese cosmology. Thinkers of different generations sought to design the *mingtang* to embrace architecturally all the constructs of Chinese enumerative thought. Although Han dynasty models were cited by modern historian Luo Guang as the "most concrete expression of five element thought," later designs were architectural monstrosities that were inclined toward the architecturally impossible.[28]

The characters *mingtang* are also the name of the acupuncture point GV-24. An alternative name of GV-24 is *shentang,* or "spirit hall," showing further connection with the function of Bl-39. In Chinese alchemy the *mingtang* constitutes the upper cinnabar field or sea of *qi.* It resides one inch directly behind the center of the eyebrows and is the temple of the *shen* in the head. The *Baiwen Bian* refers to the *mingtang* as the first of the nine rooms within the brain, denoting it as the *chongyuan,* ( 中元 ) or "primordial center."[29] The term *chongyuan* is also synonymous with the heart as the middle of the three cinnabar fields. Interestingly, *Han* commentators on the *mingtang* traced its origin to the *lingtai,* or "spiritual tower," referred to in the writings of Mencius. *Lingtai* is both a Daoist term for the heart as well as the name of GV-10, located directly behind the heart on the center line just below Bl-39.

From the above we may conclude that Bl-39, *shentang,* addresses the spiritual nature of the *shen* as it radiates to direct affairs within both the heart and the mind. With this one point, heart and mind can be united in purpose as the *shen* is brought back to center in all realms of being.

---

### ❖ Bl-40 (45) Wail of Grief, Exclamation of Joy

| | | |
|---|---|---|
| *Yi⁴xi¹* | Wail of Grief, Exclamation of Joy | 譩譆 |
| *Wu³qu¹shu¹* | Five Openings *Shu* | 五胠俞 |

*So it is said, grief and happiness are perversions of virtue; joy and anger are transgressions of the way; love and hate are offenses against virtue. When the mind is without care or joy, this is the height of virtue.*

– *Zhuangzi* [30]

The characters *yi* and *xi* denote sounds of exclamation that can convey either joy when we are delightfully surprised or our shock upon receiving bad news.[31] Many texts state that *"yixi!"* is the sound a patient makes when this point is pressed on.

The diaphragm plays an important role in empowering both breath and speech. Often when we receive painful news unexpectedly it can feel as though we "have had the wind knocked out" of us. The gasp emitted upon hearing such news signals that shock has reached past our heart to the level of the diaphragm. This is particularly true when confronted with painful separation from someone we love, for example in divorce.[32] Located between the outer *shu* points for the heart (Bl-39) and the diaphragm (Bl-41), Bl-40 addresses the wail of anguish that accompanies the ties of the heart being torn asunder. Although eventually the wailing will stop, the pain, shock, and sorrow may become embodied as stagnation in the region of the diaphragm. When a person is drowning in the sorrow of a traumatic loss, Bl-40 can assuage his pain and help him avoid having his suffering stagnate in the diaphragm where it can reside unresolved indefinitely.

I have found this point to excel at treating shingles, an illness I often find is the embodiment of deep pain trapped in the heart and diaphragm region expressing itself on the skin as a weeping wound or "wail of grief." I always treat shingles by first draining AE and most frequently include a needle to treat Bl-40 as well.

---

### ❖ Bl-41 (46) **Diaphragm Border**
*Ge²guan¹* Diaphragm Border 膈關

Like Bl-40 and Bl-17, "diaphragm border" tonifies *qi* and moves stagnation in the diaphragm. I use this point to supplement the effects of Bl-40 or on its own to provide variation in treatment.

---

### ❖ Bl-42 (47) ***Hun* Gate**
*Hun²men²* *Hun* Gate 魂門

Adjacent to Bl-18, the liver *shu* point, Bl-42, addresses the *hun* spirit. In *Nourishing Destiny,* I stated that the *hun* spirit of the liver is comprised of the *jing,* the *qi,* and the *shen.* I was introduced to this notion in the writing of C. A. S. Williams.[33] Although unable to find such a reference in the primary literature, I am intrigued by Williams's assertion and it has influenced my understanding of the *hun.* In early texts, the *hun* is discussed as a single spirit, and it is only later in history that the concept of three *hun* emerged.[34] The *hun* is the evolutionary soul that travels through GV-20 upon death to ascend to the heart of heaven as symbolized by the North Star, where it reports on the degree of virtue we have cultivated in life. The relationship of the *hun* to heaven is symbolized by the inclusion of the cloud radical *yun* (云) in the character for *hun.*

Destiny is conferred by the three luminaries: the moon, the stars, and the sun. These three invest us with light at the moment of conception, granting us the three treasures of *jing, qi,* and *shen.* The evolution of our spirit *(hun)* is synonymous with our willful manifestation of the potential virtues present in these three primordial influences. The *hun* resides in the liver, halfway along the *sheng* cycle between the water and fire elements. My conception of the *hun* as three is that the *jing* resides in the kidney, the *qi* is presided over by the liver, and the *shen* is governed by the heart. We can conceive the movement of the *hun* as the unified action of these three treasures in motivating the fulfillment of our destiny as presided over by the wood element. The wood element governs evolution by regulating *qi* and spanning the distance between heaven and earth as exemplified by the character *ren* (仁). Hence, through the marshaling of *qi,* the wood element sends roots into the depths of water to tap potential *(jing)* and raise it up toward heaven *(shen)*. Further through the regulation of *qi* the wood element frees the center to empower the open communication of *shen* in the upper burner and *jing* in the lower burner. Hence the evolution of our *hun* spirit is synonomous with our cultivation of virtue and is fueled by the will of heaven invested within our *jing, qi,* and *shen.*

This point can be effective in treating a continuum of imbalance ranging from depression to chronic frustration. Depression is often typified by a diminished quality of aspiration, indicating the ascension of the *hun* is being suppressed by resignation. Frustration, in contrast, results from a habitual drive toward growth that diminishes perspective. "*Hun* gate" is an important point for resurrecting the evolutionary thrust that propels spiritual evolution as presided over by the functional relationships inherent in the left half of the *sheng* cycle.

A function of the liver is to purify the blood, and Bl-42 excels at helping cleanse and detoxify the mind and spirit. Addictions tend to obscure perspective in life as habitual need for a given drug overshadows reason. Drugs compound the problem by causing physical damage and generating chaos in the liver official. Procuring and using the drug of choice eventually becomes the addict's only concern with no care for the long-term consequences of his actions to self or others. "*Hun* gate" excels at treating addictions whether they are to coffee, prescription medications, or illegal drugs. By going to the very root of the person's spiritual reason for having been incarnated, "*Hun* gate" can help reorient the liver's spirit toward purpose and heaven.

Out-of-body experiences during sleep are often associated with the wandering of the *hun* spirit. Such experiences are typified by full consciousness within the "dream" as the spirit explores expressions not allowed by the ego during wakefulness. "*Hun* gate" can help bring an awakened perspective to our "unconscious" desires and help us be better aware of our motivations in life. This point can also help quiet the egoic mind so the spirit can rest better within the body. In this regard, Bl-42 (47) can improve restless sleep or conditions of insomnia.

---

### ❖ Bl-43 (48) *Yang* Net

*Yang[2]gang[1]* *Yang* Net 陽綱

The character *yang* denotes that the gallbladder is the *yang* official associated with the wood element. The character *gang* depicts the head rope of a fishing net and means by extension a link, principle, or the essence of a thing. As the outer *shu* point of the gallbladder official, Bl-43 presides over the psychospiritual aspects of judgment and decision making. The mind can be conceived as a net of *yang* that we cast over life as we fish with our thoughts and perceptions that link us to the essential principles in all we perceive. "*Yang* net" can help clarify our thought processes and expand the horizons of the mind, yielding a wider perspective in life.

---

### ❖ Bl-44 (49) **Thought Dwelling**
*Yi⁴she⁴* Thought Dwelling 意舍

The *yi* is the spirit *(shen)* associated with the spleen official that governs the processes of thought and ideation. The character *she* depicts a home and can mean "to reside." Thought is the digestive aspect of the mind that enables us to process and be nourished by our life experience and to take productive action in the world that is congruent with our intentions.

Bl-44 can help harmonize thought on a continuum from overly slow thought processes to obsessiveness. Dysfunctionally, the spleen tends toward expressions of lethargy and boredom as the *yi* becomes bogged down and turns all potential sources of nourishment into burden. In time, lack of psychospiritual nourishment leads to exhaustion and apathy. Even the thought of moving may seem too much as we become obstinately set in our ways. Or failure to be nourished emotionally and spiritually can lead us to become self-centered as we seek obsessively to be taken care of in life. Here the mind races from one thing to another as a person drowns in his thoughts. Whether thought is excess or deficient, the end result is the same, as little productive work is accomplished in the world and what is accomplished fails to nourish us.

"Thought dwelling" can help support the spleen's function so obsessive thought is transformed into productive action rather than continued deliberation. By nourishing the center *(hara)* of the mind and spirit, we can be empowered to digest our life experience in a way that nourishes us so we can continue to contribute to life productively.

---

### ❖ Bl-45 (50) **Stomach Granary**
*Wei⁴cang¹* Stomach Granary 胃倉

As the outer *shu* of the stomach official, Bl-45 provides access to deep reserves of spiritual nourishment. A finding that the entire right side of the pulse is thin and feeble in relation to the left side suggests a person has been malnourished in life. This can be due either to neglect by others or poverty during childhood, neglect of self as an adult, eating disorders, a nutritionally poor diet, or weak digestion that fails to assimilate nourishment effectively. Whatever the cause, such a pulse finding suggests that no matter how hard a person works he will not be able to reap effectively the harvest of his efforts.

In reaction to having starved in life we may lose the ability to feel sympathy appropriately for self and others. Hence we may become needy or callous as our imbalance relative to nourishment deepens. "Stomach granary" can be effective in helping us open to receive nourishment in the most subtle aspects of being. In this way we may better identify and meet our own needs and become more sympathetic to the needs of others.

A central function of the earth element is to empower the virtue of integrity by processing life in a way that creates a firm center in all aspects of being. Emotionally threatening material that is too difficult to assimilate can sit like a lump of undigested food as a burden we have to carry through life. The character *zang* translated as "granary" can also be translated as "storehouse." We can conceive of Bl-45 as providing access to the storehouse of such undigested psychospiritual material in life. By strengthening the "stomach's storehouse" the mind can be empowered to digest stagnant material so we can move on, less burdened in life, and cultivate integrity.

---

**❖ Bl-46 (51)** **_Huang_ Gate**
*Huang*[1]*men*[2] *Huang* Gate 肓門

The *huang* is the area just above the diaphragm discussed earlier in the context of Bl-43. The diaphragm defines the border between the middle and upper *jiao*. As the outer *shu* of the three heater official, Bl-46 can help eliminate stagnation and promote communication between the middle and upper *jiao*. I find this point particularly effective when the conditioned mind suffers from resignation and the spirit fails to ascend into the upper *jiao*, the domain of the heart.

---

**❖ Bl-47 (52)** **Room of Will**
*Zhi*[4]*shi*[4] Room of Will 志室
*Jing*[1]*gong*[1] Palace of Essence 精宮

*Short well ropes won't dip up deep water.*
– ZHUANGZI[35]

Acupuncture point Bl-52 is intimately associated with the relationship between the human heart *(xin)* and the fulfillment of destiny *(ming)* through the recognition and cultivation of inborn potential as stored in *jing* (essence). According to Zhu Xi, "The will *(zhi)* lies in the deepest recesses of the mind *(xin)* and therefore the doctors say the will *(zhi)* belongs to the kidneys."[36] The 34th Difficult Issue of the *Nanjing* tells us that "the kidneys store the *jing* and the *zhi*,"[37] and the *zhi* is the spirit *(shen)* of the kidneys. The character *zhi* is present in the name of Bl-52 *(zhishi)*, which has been translated as "ambition room"[38] and "room of will."[39] Bl-52 also has the alternative name *jinggong*, or "palace of essence."[40] That the same acupuncture point can be used to treat both the *jing* and the *zhi* simultaneously illustrates the intimate relationship between them.

The "authentic" *(zhen)* heart is lost in the individual's inevitable fall from original nature *(de)*. The "memory" *(zhi)* of this true nature is stored in *jing* as a mandate from heaven. It is in directing the mind "down into" the *jing*, the depths of self, via the *zhi* (fixing the will), that the "lost" individual may rediscover heaven's commands and return to bringing his heart back into the world fully expressed. Hence the function of Bl-52 is to harmonize the relationship between kidney *jing*, heart *shen*, and human will *(zhi)*. With the careful direction of the practitioner, this point may serve to "soften" an overly "hard" will and protect a depleted *jing* or strengthen the will to focus the *shen* on unused potential.

In a sense, the function of Bl-47 is archetypal for all points on the entire bladder meridian inasmuch as they contribute to empowering the appropriate storage and utilization of reserves. Harmonizing the will can have a beneficial effect in every realm of being as we more efficiently utilize, conserve, and cultivate resources.

---

## ❖ BL-48 (53) Womb and Heart Diaphragm
*Bao[1]huang[1]* Womb and Heart Diaphragm 胞肓

The heart protector and three heater comprise the "right" half of the fire element along the *sheng* cycle (Figure 12.2). This manifestation of fire is unique because it expresses itself in both the upper and the lower *jiao* as compared with the heart, which resides in the upper *jiao*, and the small intestine, which resides in the middle *jiao*. In the upper *jiao*, these two officials regulate the opening and closing of the gates that allow us to make heart contact and experience emotional intimacy with another. In the lower *jiao*, these two officials preside over sexual intimacy as a physical manifestation of our connection to another's heart. Bl-48 addresses sexual intimacy as governed by the heart protector and expressed in the lower *jiao*.

Often this crucial link can be compromised due to abortions and miscarriages or physical trauma and sexual abuse. When a person feels betrayed in an intimate relationship, he often responds by suppressing the expression of his fire. Over time, this can have the effect of producing coldness in the lower *jiao* associated with poor sexual functioning, inability to achieve orgasm, urinary dysfunction, lumbar back pain, menstrual problems, blood stasis, or infertility. Bl-48 is an effective point to treat when rekindling the heart's fire if its balanced expression has been compromised, resulting in any of these manifestations. I consider the contribution of this point to treating such issues to be unified in intention with prescribing variations of the formula Guizhi Tang (Cinnamon Twig Soup).

---

❖ **Bl-49 (54) Sequential Limit**
*Zhi⁴bian¹* Sequential Limit 秩邊

Bl-49 is the last point on the outer bladder line before the meridian leaves the lower back to run down the rear of the leg. Hence this point defines the limit of the bladder channel on the back. I use this as a local point for lower back, hip, and sciatic pain. It can also be effective in cases of difficult elimination for its local effects on the anus and large intestine.

---

❖ **Bl-50 (36) Receive Support**

| | | |
|---|---|---|
| *Cheng²fu²* | Receive Support | 承扶 |
| *Pi²bu⁴* | Skin Region | 皮部 |
| *Cheng²fu²pi²bu⁴* | Skin Region Support | 承扶皮部 |
| *Yin¹pi²bu⁴guan¹* | *Yin* Skin Division Pass | 陰皮部關 |
| *Pi²xi¹* | Skin Cleft | 皮郄 |
| *Rou⁴xi¹* | Flesh Cleft | 肉郄 |

Located at the base of the buttocks where they join with the legs, Bl-50 helps strengthen the lower back and regulate the flow of *qi* when stagnation is contributing to weakness and pain along the channel. I have also used this point effectively when such pain is associated with a person's feelings that he is not supported in life or feels overwhelmed by the task of supporting others.

---

❖ **Bl-51 (37) Prosperous Gate**
*Yin¹men²* Prosperous Gate 殷門

The water element governs our innate and acquired reserves in life. The degree to which we are prosperous in life is proportional to how appropriately we invest our resources. Overwork may lead us to accumulate worldly gain, but as our internal reserves of *yin* and *yang* are expended we can experience weakness in the lower back and legs. "Prosperous gate" can strengthen and provide flexibility to the lower back, hip, and knee muscles when their dysfunction is associated with inner weakness. Active largely on the physical level, this point can be combined with others such as Bl-23 and Bl-47 to help harmonize the will.

---

❖ **Bl-52 (38)** **Superficial Cleft**
*Fu²xi¹* Superficial Cleft 浮郄

This point is found superficially in a cleft between two tendons, hence its name. I have used this only as a local point for pain and inflammation in the rear of the knee where the two tendons insert.

---

❖ **Bl-53 (39)** **Servant *Yang***
*Wei³yang²* Servant *Yang* 委陽

FUNCTION

Meeting point of the bladder and three heater channels

Both the three heater and the bladder constitute the *yang* aspect of kidney function. Here at Bl-53 the functions of both these officials are united in promoting the balance of water and fire in all realms of being. Maintaining the equilibrium of water and fire is a central function of the three heater official because it regulates the body's thermostatic mechanisms. The bladder contributes to this process by helping regulate reserves across the entire spectrum of human function.

If either the three heater or bladder are a person's constitutional official, both officials will often need to be treated in relation to each other. For example, if a person is bladder constitutionally, the three heater will also need to be treated. The expansive nature of the three heater's fire tends to overheat water, which can result in stagnation of damp and heat. Hence a traditional function of Bl-53 is to disperse damp heat in the lower *jiao,* expressing itself symptomatically as nephritis, pain in the lower back, stiffness and swelling in the leg and foot, urinary infection, and fever.

---

❖ **Bl-54 (40)** **Central Servant**

| | | |
|---|---|---|
| *Wei³zhong¹* | Central Servant | 委中 |
| *Wei³zhong¹yang¹* | Central Servant *Yang* | 委中陽 |
| *Zhong¹xi¹* | Central *Xi* | 中郄 |
| *Xi¹zhong¹* | Central *Xi* | 郄中 |
| *Xue⁴xi¹* | Blood *Xi* | 血郄 |
| *Tui³wa¹* | Leg Hollow | 腿凹 |
| *Qu¹qiu¹nei⁴* | Inner Crook Harvest | 曲秋內 |

FUNCTIONS

1. Earth point
2. Command point of the back

VIRTUES

1. Empowers the virtues of earth within the bladder official.
2. Contains overwhelm.
3. Empowers stability.

The earth element strengthens and holds the center within us by promoting the virtue of integrity. Hence Bl-54 serves the center by empowering earth to control water across the *ke* cycle. Note that the character *wei,* meaning "center" or "central," is a homophone of the character *wei* (胃), meaning "stomach." The function of "central servant" is similar to that of utilizing earth to shore up and contain the banks of a river that is overflowing. Just as Emperor Yu dug deep channels to carry the excess floodwaters out to the sea, Bl-54 can help provide the inner stability needed to control anxiety and fear associated with the water element.[41] This function is underscored by the presence of Bl-40 at the rear of the knee, a foundational joint that empowers the virtues of balance, strength, and stability. Note that, in English, calling someone "weak kneed" is another way of saying he is a coward. By harmonizing the balance of the earth element within water, we may feel the strength that comes from having adequately focused and contained reserves in the face of our fears.

If the influence of earth on water is deficient, water may overflow its banks. In this case we may experience pervasive anxiety and evidence a tendency to be easily overwhelmed for lack of adequate reserve. Physically this may manifest as frequent urination or loss of bladder control. This is in concordance with the observation that animals overwhelmed by fear often lose control of their bladders. If the presence of earth within water is excessive, dampness can inhibit the free flowing of reserves. Physically this can manifest as edema and difficult or incomplete urination. In either case, the excess or deficient presence of earth within water tends to be typified by the compounding of worry with fear, the emotions associated with the earth and water elements, respectively.

The names "central *xi*" and "blood *xi*" denote this point's function of clearing the blood, moving blood stasis, and draining heat from the blood. The name "leg hollow" is a reference to the point's anatomical location in the rear of the knee, and "inner crook harvest" suggests the association of Bl-54 with the earth element. It is interesting to note that "harvesting" blood, the earth element's bounty, at this point with a needle is particularly effective for draining, cooling the blood, and moving blood stasis.

❖ **Bl-55** **Uniting *Yang***
*He²yang²* Uniting *Yang* 委中

"Uniting *yang*" strengthens the influence of *yang* to empower the legs and lower back as foundational pillars of support for the body. Located between the two heads of the gastrocnemius muscle, Bl-55 unites these muscles to strengthen us as we work to manifest our potential in the world.

❖ **Bl-56** **Supporting Muscles**

| | | |
|---|---|---|
| *Cheng²jin¹* | Supporting Muscles | 承筋 |
| *Chuai⁴chang²* | Heel Intestine | 踹腸 |
| *Chuan⁴chang²* | Calf Intestine | 腨腸 |
| *Zhi²chang²* | Rectum | 直腸 |

*Discipline the mind; the body will follow.*
– MASTER JOHN HOLLOWAY

Bl-56 helps support the muscles of the legs as they in turn support us in carrying our works into the world. The strength in our legs and muscles is an embodiment of both our inherited and acquired constitutions. The inner strength and will to move our muscles in productive work is based in the kidney official and the water element. The muscles must also be nourished by the earth element and the productive work they do in life. Hence the strength of our muscles and the resolve of our minds are intimately related. By strengthening the muscles, the resolve of the mind can in turn be strengthened, and by strengthening the mind the muscles can be directed through will and intention to work in a way that aids us in manifesting our life's purpose. The name "calf intestine" has been used in the classical literature to refer to the area at the back of the lower leg.[42] The characters *Chuaichang* can also be translated as "trampled intestine." This meaning, along with the fourth name above that, designates the rectum and suggests this point's efficacy in treating hemorrhoids, incontinence of stool, and other disorders of the intestines.

❖ **Bl-57** **Supporting Mountain**

| | | |
|---|---|---|
| *Cheng²shan¹* | Supporting Mountain | 承山 |
| *Chang²shan¹* | Intestine Mountain | 腸山 |
| *Shang¹shan¹* | Injured Mountain | 傷山 |
| *Rou⁴zhu⁴* | Flesh Pillar | 肉柱 |
| *Yu²yao¹* | Fish Loins | 魚腰 |
| *Yu²fu⁴* | Fish Belly | 魚腹 |

Similar in function to BL-56, this point strengthens the legs and lower back. *Chengshan* is located in the lower tip in the belly of the gastrocnemius muscle that can be thought of as resembling a mountain. Ellis et al. note that as the two halves of this muscle split at this point they create an indentation that recalls the character *ren* ( 人 ), meaning man.[43] The image of a man supporting a mountain evokes the spirit of this point in strengthening our resolve to bear up under the burden of our responsibilities and life's challenges. I tend to use Bl-56 relatively more when treating the physical level of muscular weakness and Bl-57 when addressing psychospiritual issues relative to helping patients find the fortitude to shoulder their burdens in life. The reference to the intestines in the second name listed here denotes that several points in this area benefit the intestines. The name "injured mountain" may refer not just to the gastrocnemius muscle or the body as a whole but also to the anus. This point, like several that precede, can therefore benefit disorders of rectal prolapse or hemorrhoids where the "mountain" of the body is injured and falling.

---

| ❖ **Bl-58** | **Fly and Scatter** | |
|---|---|---|
| *Fei*[1]*yang*[2] | Fly and Scatter | 飛揚 |
| *Fei*[1]*yang*[2] | Flying *Yang* | 飛陽 |
| *Jue*[2]*yang*[2] | *Jue Yang* | 厥陽 |
| *Jue*[2]*yang*[2] | *Jue* Scatter | 厥楊 |

FUNCTION

*Luo* point

VIRTUES

1. Quells anxiety and calms the mind.
2. Protects reserves from being dissipated by nervous tension.

The function of "fly and scatter" can be compared to regulating a reservoir's sluice to empower the appropriate retention and utilization of reserves. The point's name serves as an ideal image for the exhaustion of *yin* and rising of *yang* engendered when we are driven by ambition to overwork emotionally. I have found this to be a most useful point in helping still the mind and nervous system by draining tension manifesting as anxiety and associated constant vigilance.[44]

The name "flying *yang*" suggests this point's function of dispersing rebellious *yang* and redirecting it downward. The natural tendency of *yang* is to ascend and of *yin* to descend. The power of *yin* is to root the *yang* by evoking it to descend and overcome its natural inclination to rise. The tendency of the mind *(yang, shen)* as presided over by the bladder channel and *yang* officials, generally, is to compel us to expend our reserves as we strive for success in the world. The innate power of *jing* (*yin* as compared with mind/*shen*) is to attract *shen* (mind) into our depths so we are able to introspect and cultivate reserves rather than exhaust them.

Our unconscious response to fear and anxiety can lead to a state of chronic vigilance that, over time, depletes the kidney and leads to *yin* deficiency. Our reaction to fear can push us to work excessively hard emotionally or physically and result in depletion of both *yin* and *yang*, respectively. As *yin* becomes depleted it eventually fails to anchor the *yang* and causes the mind to take flight as evidenced by constant fantasy and anxiety. Hence the first name listed here literally means "to soar, as a bird."[45] "Fly and scatter" can help quiet the mind by dissipating fear and redirecting it back down into the depths of self. Bl-58 is indicated for symptoms characterized by excess, heat, and *yang* in the upper part of the body accompanied by deficiency and cold below.[46] This pattern may further explain the names that make reference to flying and the ascension of *yang*.

The notion of working excessively to the point of exhaustion and the separation of *yin* and *yang* is also contained in the *jue* (厥).[47] This character has two main components of interest in discerning its meaning in the name of Bl-58. The first element depicts a cliff (厂), which when climbing it puts us out of breath.[48] The second, also pronounced *jue* (欮), denotes breathing problems such as hiccup, cough, asthma, or suffocation and depicts an obstacle (屰) that impedes breathing (欠).[49] Hence the character *jue* (欮) imparts the meaning of having expended our resources to the point that our breath is exhausted. Therefore, Bl-58 is indicated for several breathing disorders including rhinitis and nasal congestion. The character *jue* (欮) is also present in the designation of the liver and heart protector channels as constituting the *jueyin* (欮陰) channel. *Jueyin* illnesses are characterized by irregularities in the distribution of heat and cold, *yin* and *yang*, and by symptoms of collapsing or counterflow of *qi*.[50] Hence the character *jue* may be present in the name of Bl-58 to denote the symptoms of counterflow such as cough, hiccup, and asthma that can be addressed by the point.

---

❖ **Bl-59** **Instep *Yang***

| | | |
|---|---|---|
| *Fu¹yang²* | Instep *Yang* | 趺陽 |
| *Fu⁴yang²* | Instep Flourish | 跗揚 |
| *Fu⁴yang²* | Dependent on *Yang* | 附陽 |
| *Fu⁴yang⁴* | Transfer *Yang* | 付陽 |

FUNCTION

*Xi*-cleft point of the *yang* motility vessel

The point's location above the instep on the bladder, a *yang* channel, may account for its name. "Footbone *yang*" is useful for helping the bladder eliminate toxins by moving stagnant and polluted water. Physically, these can result from food poisoning, allergic reactions, invasion by pathogenic factors, or the accumulation of toxicity in the body over time. Foul-smelling sweat or urine is often evidence of the presence of such toxicity. It often produces a caustic smell similar to ammonia, indicating that the water of the body is polluted. Cleansing toxic accretions in psychospiritual realms can help clear the mind and quell anxiety.

---

| ❖ **Bl-60** | Kunlun **Mountain** | |
|---|---|---|
| *Kun[1]lun[2]* | Kunlun Mountain | 崑崙 |
| *Xia[4]kun[1]lun[2]* | Lower *Kunlun* | 下崑崙 |

FUNCTION

Fire point

VIRTUES

1. Balances the expression of fire within the bladder official.
2. Promotes insight in the depths.
3. Helps balance *yin* and *yang*.

Bl-60 is located at the base of the lateral malleolus (ankle bone), which is likened to the mythical Kunlun Mountain in the point's name. In early Chinese mythology, the brother and sister, who represent the primordial *yin* and *yang (yuanqi),* land on Kunlun Mountain and copulate, rekindling the life of the human race after the great flood.[51] Kunlun Mountain was conceived as the pillar that joined heaven and earth, representing the axis of all creation.[52] As the root of heaven and earth, Kunlun was thought to balance the primordial *yin* and *yang* and to radiate this power through the expression of the five elements on earth—water, wood, fire, earth, and metal.[53] As a fire point on a water meridian, Bl-60 embodies the function of helping balance *yin* and *yang*.

Note that Bl-60 and Ki-3 are located exactly opposite each other on the lateral and medial aspect of the ankle, respectively.[54] Ki-3 is the channel's source point capable of tonifying *yin* and *yang* in equal proportion. Needling Bl-60 through to Ki-3 can be a strong way of tonifying *jing*. This treatment captures the metaphor of the primordial brother and sister uniting on top of Kunlun Mountain to rekindle the flame of the human race after it is extinguished by the floods.

Bl-60 represents fire on the mountain as contrasted with Ki-2 ("blazing valley"), which represents fire in the valley. This designation is consistent with the functions of the bladder and kidney as *yang* and *yin* officials, respectively. Girardot states, "The 'place' of creation as the gap or fissure in Heaven (the *Lieh-ch'ueh*) that spits out the fire of transmutation . . . can also be transposed into the mythically equivalent terms of cosmic mountain (*Kunlun*)."[55] Here at Kunlun Mountain the mythological fire of creation meets with the waters of the flood and reunites heaven and earth and resurrects life itself.

We can consider the image of the "fire of transmutation" from both an internal and external perspective. Internally the fire that burns in our depths is the *yuanqi* sustaining the transmutation of inborn potential into manifestation as the promise of our constitution is realized in the world. As a fire point within the water element, Bl-60 addresses the functional basis for the alchemical interpenetration of *yin* and *yang,* water and fire, the very foundation of life. In balance, fire within the *yang* of water (bladder) helps direct *yin* upward toward the brain as *jing* is transformed into marrow and fear into wisdom. Hence in Daoist alchemical maps of the human body, the upper regions of the spine or top of the head often depict Kunlun Mountain whose presence there stands as a metaphor for the ascension and transformation of *jing* into marrow manifesting as wisdom.

Externally, the image of fire on the mountain represents the transcendent wisdom that may come to us in a flash like a bolt from heaven above. This flash of transformation can also be thought of as the fire and spark of mind because the Daoists identify Kunlun Mountain with the head. The imagery of Emperor Yu convening the hundred spirits to unify China on Mount Mao, or of Moses receiving the ten commandments on top of Mount Sinai, imparts a sense of the functional significance of "Kunlun Mountain."[56]

The image of water boiling can be applied metaphorically to the agitation of the nervous system and mind when the influence of fire within water is excessive. Such heat disturbs the spirit *(shen)*, and I have found Bl-60 to be particularly effective as a point for easing a mind unsettled by pain anywhere along the bladder channel. If the presence of fire is excessive, the patient can give a general impression of urgency and anxiety as the mind is agitated by petty fears. Physically, this can be embodied as burning urination.

If the presence of fire within the bladder official is deficient, coldness can slow the transformation of *jing* into marrow and inhibits its ascension to engender wisdom. In this case we can be coldhearted and lack compassion as fear drives our ambitions to overwhelm others. Or self-expression can slow to a standstill as the flow of our wills freezes for lack of fire.

---

❖ **Bl-61** **Servant's Aid**
*Pu²can¹* Servant's Aid 僕參
*An¹xie²* Quieting of Evil 安邪

FUNCTIONS

1. Meeting point of bladder and *yang* motility vessel
2. External dragon point

Here, seven points from its end, we have nearly reached the extremity of the river that we embody as the bladder channel. Seven is the number of return and renewal and, as we approach completion of our journey, reserves may need replenishing. When fear dictates the expenditure of our resources, reserves of will and strength are diminished. Hence undertakings frequently fail in their final steps before completion. "Servant's aid" can provide the necessary help needed to supplement our strength so we can continue on our way. The concept of having a point that works as a reserve near the end of a channel is also present in the function of St-36 and Ki-25 and Ki-27. As a meeting point with the *yang* heel channel, Bl-61 can help tap the depths of this extra channel in a way that serves us to continue onward toward our destination.

The alternate name, "quieting of evil" *(anxie)*, may refer to the efficacy of Bl-61 as a dragon point in helping clear possession.

---

❖ **Bl-62** **Extended Meridian**
*Shen¹mai⁴* Extended Meridian 申脈
*Yang²qiao¹* *Yang* Motility 陽蹻
*Gui³lu⁴* Ghost Road 鬼路

FUNCTIONS

1. Master point of the *yang* motility vessel
2. Ghost point

The character *shen* refers to the ninth of the twelve earthly branches that is correlated with the time of the bladder channel (3–5 P.M.) on the Chinese clock. The *yang* motility vessel begins at this point and extends upward, yielding the name of the point. This extra meridian also governs the attachments of the limbs to the body, which is how we extend ourselves into the world. Hence the function of Bl-62 can address the relationship between our utilization of resources, the strength of our limbs, and the quality of our wills. I frequently use this point for pain and limited range of motion in the ankles or shoulders when they arise from pushing too hard in either exercise or work.

---

❖ **Bl-63** **Golden Gate**
*Jin¹men²* Golden Gate 金門
*Liang²guan¹* Bridge Pass 梁關

*Though floodwaters pile up high to the sky,*
*he [the sage] will not drown.*
– *ZHUANGZI*[57]

FUNCTIONS
1. *Xi*-cleft point
2. Meeting point of the bladder and *yang* linking vessel

VIRTUES
1. Promotes balanced flow in all domain of life.
2. Moves stagnation.
3. Opens the sensory orifices.

In Daoist mythology, the entrance to the kingdom of the mysterious *Xiwangmu,* queen mother of the West, is pictured as a golden gate (*jinmen:* 金門) and a place of "ultimate safety."[58] At this gate, she receives both the souls of the dead and the survivors after the deluge. From the womb of the queen mother the life-giving waters flow, and to her tomb, all return in the flood's wake. CV-1 is also named *jinmen,* and its function addresses the deep cosmological relationships related to Chinese creation mythology. Bl-63 embraces these same issues on the relatively more embodied level of regulating the flow of water in the body and helping empower the appropriate utilization of reserves.

The "golden gate" is located functionally between metal and water along the *sheng* cycle.[59] The connection between metal and water is referenced in this point's name and function. Metal is the element associated with the terrestrial branch *shen* (申).[60] This branch presides over the period 3 to 5 P.M., which is the high time of the bladder and the low time of the lung according to the Chinese clock. During this time the *qi* and blood of the bladder official flow through the golden (metal) gate. If this flow is blocked, the all-important connection between water and metal may be compromised.

As the channel's *xi*-cleft point, Bl-63 helps move the stagnations of wind, cold, or damp that compromise the smooth flow of water in all aspects of being. Such stagnation can be congruent with habitual fear that tends to compel either stillness in life, to the point of being frozen, or excessive movement associated with agitation of the mind and nervous system. Such fear tends to either inhibit or disinhibit the flow of water in the body. Resolving stagnation and fear can help us when we are overwhelmed and feel as if we are drowning in responsibilities and life circumstances. The point's function of "opening the sensory orifices" can help dispel fear and empower the clear perception of reality. By helping move stagnation when we are frozen with fear, Bl-63 may better align ourselves with *dao* and "going with the flow." In this way the life-giving virtues of the *sheng* cycle are reaffirmed.

---

❖ **Bl-64** **Capital Bone**
*Jing[1]gu[3]* Capital Bone 京骨

FUNCTION
Source point

VIRTUE
Empowers in a general way all functions associated with the bladder official.

The character *jing* (京), referring to a capital, was used historically for the character *yuan* (原), meaning "source."[61] As the source point associated with the bladder official, Bl-64 can ground the entire course of the meridian and its associated functions. This is particularly important because the bladder official empowers access to our inner reserves. These reserves are represented by the function of the *shu* points that provide access to the deepest level of each organ's functional reserve of *qi*. This reserve of *qi* is mediated by the mind and nervous system because each *shu* point lies directly over its organ's afferent and efferent nerves.[62] Hence Bl-64 is said to "clear the channels," "invigorate the collaterals," "benefit the backside of the body," and "calm the spirit and clear the brain."[63] The strength of "capital bone" lies in its ability to affect the functioning of all the officials by harmonizing the bladder official in relationship to fear and empowering its ability to regulate reserves appropriately in all domains of being.

---

❖ **Bl-65** **Bone Binder**
*Shu[4]gu[3]* Bone Binder 束骨
*Ci[4]gu[3]* Thorn Bone 刺骨

FUNCTIONS

1. Wood point
2. Sedation point

VIRTUES

1. Empowers the virtues of the wood element within the bladder official.
2. Empowers vision regarding reserves.

A function associated with Bl-65 is that of strengthening bones, hence the point's name. The presence of wood within water can be likened to the roots of a tree that reach down deep to tap reserves. Hence "bone binder" can tap the potential of *jing* to build marrow in a way that strengthens the bones.

If the presence of wood within water is deficient, water will tend to accumulate as potential lies untapped in the depths. Hence the decision-making faculty of the gallbladder may not be adequately informed by a clear vision of our reserves. In this case the mind chooses our direction based only on its goals and desires that are untempered by an adequate assessment of capability. Thus our actions can become compulsive and no longer reflect our inner virtues. When wood fails to mobilize water, multiplicative bone growth can appear, presenting as calcium deposits, stenosis of the spine, and heel spurs. Such conditions can feel sharply painful as though we are being stuck by a thorn, which may explain the point's alternate name, "thorn bone." Hence Bl-65 is effective for both strengthening the bones and dispersing stagnation if bone growth is excessive.

If the presence of wood within the bladder is in excess, then water tends to be depleted as we overutilize our reserves. Here the mind compulsively pursues growth leading to constant anxiety as the bladder is never afforded the opportunity of replenishing reserves. This can manifest as frequent urination accompanied by the presence of fear. The excessive presence of wood within the bladder can be embodied as a condition known as *lin* (淋) illness. The character *lin* contains the water (氵) radical and also depicts two trees (林). The condition is typified by a woody feeling in the urethra and by urination that is difficult and incomplete. Bl-65 can help disperse the influence of wood within water so urine as well as our reserves of *qi* flow into the world with less constraint. I have also found Bl-65 to be helpful as a sedation point in helping kidney stones exit the body.

By empowering vision in our depths, Bl-65 can help quell fear that both results from, and potentiates, either under- or overutilization of resources. Such vision can lead to the type of insight and flowering of mind empowered by Bl-60 as the wood within the water engenders fire and the cultivation of an intelligence that may best serve wisdom. As a point that clears vision, Bl-65 can be powerfully combined with Bl-1 to help "brighten the eyes" and empower the accurate perception of reality.

---

### ❖ Bl-66 Penetrating Valley

*Tong*[1]*gu*[3] Penetrating Valley 通谷

FUNCTIONS

1. Water point
2. Horary point; 3–5 P.M., winter solstice

VIRTUES

1. Transmits the virtues associated with the bladder to all other water points on *yang* channels.
2. Quiets and cools the nervous system.

Totaling sixty-seven points, the bladder meridian is the longest of the channels, and its course may be likened to that of a great river. The name "penetrating valley" suggests the image of this river winding its way through a valley as it journeys to the sea. As noted, the *shu* points lie over the efferent and afferent nerves as they enter and leave the spine.[64] I have found Bl-66 useful in calming the nervous systems of people who evidence generalized fear and anxiety, in effect helping them "cool out."[65] The use of Bl-66 as a transmitting point to quiet the mind is discussed in Chapter 9.

This point shares its name with Ki-20 ("through the valley"), also named *tonggu.* Ki-20 addresses our spiritual journey and helps guide us through dark passages that can cause fear and hinder evolution. Bl-66, in contrast, helps empower our wills to flow effectively into the world in a way that is not driven by anxiety. If the *yang* aspect of the water element guides us in a balanced way, our actions proceed with grace and quiet reserve. Having contained and cultivated our reserves, the appropriate exertion of power is effortless as we meet each challenge with the resources required of us yet never feel overextended.

If the influence of Bl-66 is deficient, we may have difficulty focusing our wills in a resourceful way. In this case it is as though we are stuck in a continual flight or fight response to life because all actions we take are based on fear. If the water within bladder is excessive, our wills and ambition may coldly overwhelm all that lies in our path as we assert power inappropriately over everything and everyone in an attempt to run from our own fears.

---

### ❖ Bl-67 Extremity of *Yin*

*Zhi*[4]*yin*[1] Extremity of *Yin* 至陰

FUNCTIONS

1. Metal point
2. Tonification point
3. Point for breaking the H/W imbalance

VIRTUE

Draws *qi* through the golden gate from metal to water.

The name "extremity of *yin*" alludes to Bl-67 as the final point on the bladder channel. As the meridian's exit point, *qi* flows from Bl-67 to the entry point of the kidney channel at Ki-1. Here the river that is bladder extends our will to meet the ocean of our potential presided over by the kidneys. This transition represents the attainment of our life's purpose as the ultimate goal for expending our resources. In our life's journey, this place where the river meets the ocean is the final destination of our will. It is precisely at this point that potential can be renewed or tapped at a deeper level to empower us to finish our life's work and fulfill destiny.

As the metal point within water, Bl-67 is a key point for breaking the husband/wife imbalance by helping draw *qi* through the golden gate from metal to water that mediates both birth and death.[66] Ki-7, the metal point on water's *yin* channel, empowers conception of self and other. As the metal on water's *yang* channel, Bl-67 can be effective to stimulate contractions during labor and help orient a fetus's head toward the vaginal opening. In this way the fetus may become an infant as it moves through the "door of the mysterious female" and out into life.

## *Exercises*

1. Several points on the bladder meridian address the issue of shouldering responsibility without being burdened or exhausted by it. These include Bl-6 ("receiving light"), Bl-10 ("heavenly pillar"), Bl-50 ("receive support"), Bl-56 ("supporting muscles"), and Bl-57 ("supporting mountain"). Compare the functions of these points as they address this issue across different levels of being.
2. What is the difference in the quality of light received at conception and the quality of light that comes to us during life through our senses?
3. Compare the functions of Ki-2 ("blazing valley"), Ki-6 ("illuminated sea"), Ki-12 ("great brightness"), Ki-21 ("dark gate"), Ki-24 ("spirit burial ground"), Ki-26 ("amid elegance"), and Bl-6 ("receiving light"). How do each of these points differentially address the issue of illumination as it impacts the transformation of fear into wisdom?
4. Compare the function of Bl-11 with that of Ki-26 as they both address revitalization through evoking the expression of *jing*.

5. Compare the function of B-14 ("tower gate *shu*") with the function of HP-6 ("inner frontier gate") and GV-10 ("spirit tower").
   a. Why is the symbolism of a gate or tower associated with the function of the heart and heart protector?
   b. What are the virtues of a good gate or tower, and how are these inherent in the functions of the three points in question?
6. Work through the rationale for the point combinations provided in the discussion of Bl-22.
7. Devise a treatment for utilizing Bl-22 to empower digestion in the middle burner. Explain the relative contribution of each point you have selected in this combination.
8. In my discussion of Bl-23 I have emphasized the importance of teaching patients to conserve resources when providing supplementing treatments.
   a. For each of the *shu* points, what instruction might you give to empower patients to most beneficially direct their new reserve of *qi* toward healing?
   b. Discuss the physiology of how tonification in the absence of education can be harmful to patients over the long term.
9. What are the functional relationships among CV-1, Bl-26, Bl-24, Bl-23, and Bl-22 in terms of the differentiation of *yin* and *yang*?

# *NOTES*

1. A central thrust of the five-element system is to harmonize humans with the seasons. Therefore, to a degree, all imbalances can be thought of as being seasonal in nature.
2. Watson, 1964a, p. 32.
3. See *ND,* p. 15.
4. In the *Leijing, Zhang Jiebin* tells us that, "The meaning of *jiao* is vertebrae." Henry Lu suggests that the use of the term *jiao* was a transcription error for "vertebrae." B1-17, the meeting point for blood, can be used to drain heat from the blood. I will elaborate my interpretation of these points in a future article.
5. The translation of *que* as "tower gate" is from Mathews, 1931, p. 241.
6. For a discussion of this dynamic, see my discussion of the liver/lung E/E block in Chapter 5.
7. *ND,* p. 279. For a discussion of the golden gate, see *ND,* pp. 20–21.
8. *ND,* pp. 20–21.
9. Porkert, 1982, p. 172.
10. Ibid., p. 173.
11. If bladder *qi* and *yang* is deficient, the physical signs and symptoms can be the same as those listed for excess. A general principle is that any given manifestation can have an underlying basis of either excess or deficiency. It is the pulse, tongue, and overall context that determine the physiological basis of a functional condition. Any given symptom in isolation only tells us the outermost expression of the dysfunction. Signs and symptoms must be differentiated to determine their physiological basis in terms of excess or deficiency.

12. *ND,* pp. 103–117, 88, 363.
13. Mathews, 1931, p. 1148.
14. Ellis, Wiseman, and Boss, 1989, p. 166.
15. Ibid., p. 168.
16. Mathews, 1931, p. 54.
17. From lecture notes attributed to J. R. Worsley.
18. After death the *hun* ascends to heaven as *shen* and the *po* stays in between heaven and earth as *gui.* The spirits of those not meritorious enough to be honored by their families would wander aimlessly stealing offerings of others' graves.
19. Mathews, 1931, p. 495.
20. Ibid., p. 338.
21. See Wieger, lesson 12J, p. 41.
22. The first chapter of the *Lingshu* ("The Spiritual Pivot") denotes CV-15 as the source point of the *gao.*
23. For a discussion of *shen* and *ling,* see *ND,* pp. 49–57.
24. This is addressed by treating the exit/entry block between the two points Ki-21 and HP-1. See Chapter 5 for a complete description.
25. See the description of Ki-23 in Chapter 27 for an explanation of this imagery.
26. I find HP-6, CV-15, and Bl-43 to play an important role in treating shame generally. It is interesting to note that Deadman and Al-Khafaji cite CV-15 as useful for "excessive sexual activity leading to exhaustion in youths." Deadman and Al-Khafaji, 2000, CD-ROM, CV-15.
27. Henderson, 1984, pp. 75–76.
28. Ibid., pp. 77–78.
29. Homann, 1976, pp. 12, 59, 80.
30. Watson, 1968, p. 169.
31. Mathews, 1931, pp. 361, 443.
32. See the description of BL-17 earlier.
33. Williams, 1974, p. 462.
34. Three *hun* was apparently discussed first in a ninth-century Daoist scripture titled *The Chu Sanshi Jiuchong Baosheng Jing (Scripture of How to Preserve Life by Expelling the Three Deathbringers and Nine Worms) (Daozang, 871).* Texts in the Daoist canon (*Daozang*) are organized according to Schipper, 1975. This scripture states, "The three spirit (*yang*) souls are located beneath the liver. They look like human beings and all wear green robes with yellow inner garments. Every month on the third, thirteenth, and twenty-third, they leave the body in the evening to go wandering about." See Kohn, 2002, p. 17.
35. Watson, 1964a, p. 115.
36. Munro, 1985, p. 312.
37. Unschuld, 1986, p. 367.
38. Worsley, 1979.
39. Ming, 1982, p. 295.
40. Ellis, Wiseman, and Boss, 1989, p. 180.
41. *ND,* pp. 16–19.
42. This reference appears in the *Systematized Canon of Acupuncture and Moxibustion* (cited by Ellis, Wiseman, and Boss, 1989, p. 184).
43. Ellis, Wiseman, and Boss, 1989, p. 184.
44. Note that a function of Bl-58 in this regard is to "disperse *taiyang* evil *qi.*" As previously mentioned, the bladder and small intestine constitute the "*taiyang*" nervous system.
45. Mathews, 1931, p. 1086.
46. Deadman and Al-Khafaji, 2000, CD-ROM, Bl-58.
47. Porkert discusses *jue* ("flexus") as the "yielding and collapse of an energy circuit." Porkert, 1983, p. 109.

48. See Weiger, 1965, L59A, p. 154, and 102D, p. 248.
49. See ibid., L99A, p. 242, and 102D, p. 248.
50. Porkert, 1983, p. 109.
51. Girardot, 1983, pp. 173–174.
52. Acupuncture point Bl-60 is named "Kunlun Mountain" and Bl-10 is named "heavenly pillar," referring again to Kunlun. Both points are located on the bladder meridian, which is consistent with the bladder's role in regulating water flow within the body and the cosmological function of Kunlun in regulating the balance of the primordial *yin* and *yang*.
53. Kohn, 1992, p. 110.
54. Practitioner Jonathan Alexander Daniel pointed out this relationship to me after he read *Nourishing Destiny.*
55. Girardot, 1983, p. 93.
56. For a discussion of Emperor Yu and the floods, see *ND,* pp. 16–19.
57. Watson, 1964a, p. 27.
58. Lagerwey, 1987, pp. 39–41.
59. *ND,* Chapter 7, pp. 103–117.
60. The heavenly stems and terrestrial branches are an important part of Chinese phase energetics. See Porkert, 1982, pp. 55–106.
61. Mathews, 1931, p. 158.
62. This was the first professional work I presented on Chinese medicine. See Jarrett, 1983.
63. DeLaney, Leonard, and Kisch, 1989, Bl-64. Remember the spirit never needs calming. In fact, it is spirit that the mind must rest in.
64. See Jarrett, 1983.
65. Note that Dr. Leon Hammer states that the first two points on each meridian, as one moves proximally from the toes and fingers, treat imbalances in the nervous system. See Hammer, 1990, p. 312.
66. See *ND,* pp. 106–114.

# 27

# KIDNEY

TRAVELING DEEP FROM THE VENTRAL SURFACE OF THE LITTLE toe, the kidney meridian begins at Ki-1 between the second and third metatarsal bones. The channel follows the points in order to Ki-8, where a deep branch splits to join with Sp-6 and then rejoins the main channel at Ki-9. Ascending to Ki-10 at the medial border of the popliteal fossa, the channel runs from the knee over the medial surface of the thigh and into the groin. From here it runs internally to the tip of the coccyx at GV-1 and continues up the spine to the level of GV-4, the "gate of destiny," where it then enters the kidneys.

An internal branch leaves the kidney to enter its paired *yang* organ, the bladder. From the bladder, this internal branch travels to the midline at CV-4, descends to CV-3, and then travels laterally to Ki-11 on the superior edge of the pubic symphysis. From here the channel travels superficially up the abdomen to the fifth intercostal space, where it joins Ki-22, the channel's exit point. From here the channel ascends to terminate at Ki-27 just below the clavicle.

Another internal branch of the channel leaves the kidney and ascends to enter the liver and then continues onward to enter the lungs. From here it proceeds up the trachea to the root of the tongue. A branch of this pathway leaves the lungs to enter the heart and connect with CV-17 in the center of the chest, where it unites with the heart protector meridian.

---

## *Thoughts on the Channel*

As *qi* rises from Ki-1 up to Ki-27, it becomes refined in a way that mirrors the life transformation of the kidney constitutional type whose destiny it is to transform fear into wisdom.[1] The first points on the meridian (Ki-1 through Ki-10) govern conception and the renewal of life. The middle points on the meridian (Ki-11 through Ki-15) govern conception through early childhood. Points Ki-16 through Ki-27 govern the transformation of *jing* (potential) into *ling,* spiritual power attained through the cultivation of wisdom. The function of the kidney official is to empower conception, gestation, birth, and subsequent development of one's being. In life this process governs the cultivation of the spiritual embryo as it incubates within the adept. This represents the continual refinement of kidney *qi* until it reaches the level of the heart to become *ling* and mingle with the heart *shen.* It is through the interaction of *shen* and *ling* that spiritual potency is cultivated as destiny is fulfilled.

The path of the kidney meridian begins in the depths by providing contact with the earth as the cosmological pole of *yin* at Ki-1, "bubbling spring." Here the primordial depths of water and its potential are tapped at their source. This represents the genetic and karmic depths of the individual as it is invested by heaven as *jing* at conception. The *yin* of the conception vessel is genetic, forming the basis of our structural manifestation in life, whereas the *yin* of the kidney is karmic in nature and imparts structure to our spiritual path during each incarnation.

At Ki-2, "blazing valley," water is heated, causing it to rise and initiate the manifestation of our potential in its evolutionary path. At Ki-3, "great mountain stream," the *qi* of water becomes substantial and gains force as embodied by the earth element and the source point of the kidney meridian. The *qi* then descends down toward the ankle and Ki-5 as if spilling over a waterfall. This force carries the *qi* to Ki-6, "illuminated sea," the master point of the *yin* motility vessel and the coupled point of the conception vessel. Here our genetic and karmic potential are fused directly over Ki-2, the receiving point for fire within water, where they are again heated and begin to rise under the influence of fire and the heart spirit, *shen.*

The next three points preside functionally over conception and the interpenetration of *yin* and *yang* as it fuels the dynamic movement of the *sheng* cycle. Ki-7, "returning current," signifies the *qi* is now ascending again directly toward its destination in the upper *jiao*. "Returning current" presides over the moment of conception and the interpenetration of the sperm and egg, *jing* and blood, and metal with water along the *sheng* cycle. At conception, heaven imparts a destiny to the newly created being, reflected in the name of Ki-8, "exchanging pledges." The spiritual or physical embryo now resides within the womb as presided over by Ki-9, "building guest."

At Ki-10, the meridian's sea point, the *qi* travels deeply within to begin its ascent toward the spiritual frontier. At Ki-12, "great brightness," the spark of ancestry is kindled within the ovaries and within the being. This further illumination fuels the continual rise of the kidney *qi* and essence. Next the *qi* passes through the "door of infants" at Ki-13. At Ki-14, "four full," the embryo is near completion, and at Ki-15, "middle flowing out," the pregnancy has come full term and birth approaches.

At the level of Ki-16, the root of the *gaohuang*, kidney *qi* blends with heart essence. From Ki-18 through Ki-21, this essence travels through a series of points as it transitions to the upper burner. Named in succession "stone border," "*yin* capital," "through the valley," and "dark gate," the *qi* now journeys into the inner realm of the heart spirit. The Forbidden City of the heart as emperor is embodied as the rib cage. At Ki-22 the channel ascends onto the rib cage and the path of the kidney *qi* diverges. The general circulation of *qi* flows from Ki-22, the channel's exit point, to enter the heart protector channel at HP-1. However, the most refined essential *qi* travels past Ki-22 to continue its journey up toward Ki-27. Here, it enters the inner sanctum of heart spirit as alluded to in the name of Ki-24, "spirit burial ground."

Points Ki-23, 24, and 25 preside over the interpenetration of the *shen* and *ling* spirits. *Ling* is the highest expression of *jing* manifesting as the spiritual power and potency that we have cultivated in performing the ritual of our life's journey.

## MAIN FUNCTIONS

1. Empowers the flow of life's purpose into the world.
2. Empowers potency.
3. Constitutes our depths.
4. Lubricates the graceful unfolding of human destiny.

## DISTAL POINT FUNCTIONS

***Wood:*** Enters water as the roots of a tree travel deeply to tap potential and channel it upward toward heaven.

*Fire:* Impulse that stirs water from within and summons it from without.

*Earth:* Like the banks of a river, earth contains and directs the innate tendencies of water to support life.

*Metal:* Imparts essence to water and gives it value.

*Water:* Imparts the essential qualities of the water element to the kidney official.

*Xi-cleft:* Moves stagnation within the kidney official, reinstituting a natural flow born of faith and instinct.

*Luo:* Directs the mind inward toward potential and purpose.

---

❖ **Ki-1** **Bubbling Spring**

| | | |
|---|---|---|
| *Yong³quan²* | Bubbling Spring | 湧泉 |
| *Di⁴chong¹* | Earth Thoroughfare | 地衝 |
| *Di⁴qu²* | Earth Thoroughfare | 地衢 |

FUNCTIONS

1. Wood point
2. Entry point
3. Sedation point

VIRTUES

1. Empowers our connection to the cosmological pole of earth, allowing us to receive water at its source.
2. Initiates the rising of essence through us toward heaven, thus propelling evolution.
3. Pulls the influence of heaven down through our roots ensuring that all growth is grounded in a vision of our depths.

CV-1 connects us to the cosmological pole of earth *(yin)* as it is contrasted with heaven *(yang)*. In contrast, Ki-1, located on the bottom of the foot, connects us to *yin* as it is expressed on earth as the elemental phase water. The *Daodejing* elaborates the virtues of water as embodying the essential nature of *dao* as it is manifest on earth. The name "bubbling spring," the channel's entry point, images the very source of water as it percolates up from the ground. Here, at the spring's source, the purist water can be tapped to refresh and cleanse our entire being. The name "earth thoroughfare" denotes this point of great activity where our feet touch the earth and water flows from its source.

The function of Ki-1 can be likened to drawing the roots of a tree into the depths of the earth to tap potential as a resource for growth. As the channel's wood point, Ki-1 extends the reach of the liver into our depths so it can extract our life plan from our *jing* to use as a template for evolution.

In this way our aspirations and motivations are linked to innate purpose as our potential is channeled from our roots to our outermost branches. As wood within water, "bubbling spring" empowers vision within our depths, ensuring that potential will be mobilized with clarity of purpose.

"Bubbling spring" also provides a strong stimulation to the entire kidney meridian to motivate the rising of *qi* and *jing* in its evolutionary path toward heaven. This movement is represented by the left half of the *sheng* cycle as the potential in *jing* is tapped by wood and channeled upward to support the fire element and the opening of the heart. The nature of this movement is conveyed in an alternate name for Ki-1—*dichong* (地沖), or "earth surge."[2] Here the character *chong* alludes to the *chongqi* that rises from earth toward heaven like a geyser as the two cosmological poles interpenetrate each other. Hence Ki-1 simultaneously accesses water at our source, draws mind (heaven and *yang)* down through us to our very roots, and initiates the rising of our inborn potential toward heaven.

If the presence of wood within water is deficient, potential may lay fallow and untapped in our depths. The creative impulse of the *sheng* cycle will be compromised as growth is choked off in any and all domains of being. Symptoms such as exhaustion, depression, lack of motivation, and purposelessness can all be evidence that our momentum in life has been severed at its root. Divorced of reason, and an adequate assessment of capability and purpose, our motivations will tend to be governed by a habituated mind. Planning and decisions making will no longer be free-flowing natural expressions of *jing*. Instead, the mind will exhaust us further as it exercises our potential without vision.

In modern TCM, the kidney is never considered to function in an excess state. All internal syndrome patterns are thought to be rooted in either kidney *yin* or *yang* deficiency. However, I find my patients do in fact exhibit patterns of kidney excess relative to the use of their willpowers *(zhi)* as it manifests their ambitions. This pattern can present on the pulse as qualities that indicate stagnation of *qi* (tense) and heat (pounding) in the left proximal position. In such cases, Ki-1 can be used as a sedation point to disperse the relative excess in the kidney official. The actual instances of kidney excess that I have described here are less frequent than cases of kidney *qi, yin, yang,* and *jing* deficiency. In these cases Ki-1 can be tonified utilizing its function as either the entry point, or the wood point, of the kidney meridian.

I often use Ki-1 in conjunction with GV-20 to help establish a patient's connection to heaven and earth. Ki-1 can be thought of as activating a connection to earth while at the same time pulling the influence of heaven down toward the patient's roots. GV-20 helps establish our connection to the influence of heaven while simultaneously pulling *qi* toward the top of the head. In this way the influences of heaven and earth may be initiated at their source while both poles are stimulated to interpenetrate each other through us. This is an ideal treatment when patients are stuck inside themselves and feel either unconnected, or overconnected, to outside influences.[3]

---

| ❖ **Ki-2** | **Blazing Valley** | |
|---|---|---|
| *Ran²gu³* | Blazing Valley | 然谷 |
| *Long²yuan¹* | Dragon Abyss | 龍淵 |
| *Long²quan²* | Dragon Spring | 龍泉 |
| *Ran²gu³* | Blazing Bones | 然骨 |

FUNCTIONS

1. Fire point
2. Secondary sedation point
3. Point of the *yin* motility vessel

VIRTUES

1. Helps establish and secure the heart/kidney axis.
2. Increases the functional influence of kidney *yang*.
3. Regulates the presence of fire within the kidney.

"Bubbling spring" evokes the image of water percolating up from its source deep within the earth. The source of a spring is freezing cold and therefore Ki-1 is often followed in a later treatment by Ki-2, "blazing valley." Here at Ki-2 water is heated to aid its ascent toward heaven as represented by the upper *jiao* and heart. The transformation of fear into wisdom is the destiny of the water element. This is a dual process having both a *yin* and *yang* aspect. In its *yang* aspect, *jing* ascends the governor vessel and bladder channel to nourish the brain with marrow and thereby engender wisdom. In its *yin* aspect, *jing* ascends the kidney channel and conception vessel as it is transformed into *ling*, spiritual potency, at the level of the heart. The image of *yang* rising from the depths is also provided by the point names "dragon abyss" and "dragon spring." Dragons are the embodied image of rising *yang*, and the character *yuan* (淵) denotes a primal deep whirlpool, imaging the *dao* as the spring from which all of life's manifestations flow.

The name of Ki-2 evokes the image of fire in the valley as compared with Bl-60 that images fire on the mountain. The presence of fire within water is established from two sources. The first source is gleaned at conception, as heaven imprints a flame within our *jing* and manifests as *yuanqi*. While in the womb, the *yuanqi* guides the entire differentiation of the embryo and fetus. During life, the *yuanqi* is the inner fire that fuels all developmental processes such as making blood, the growth of bones, emotional and psychic development, and the ascent of the spirit. The second source of fire within water arrives from our *shen,* which has ascended during gestation from our *jing* to rest in the palace of the heart. Think of the *yuanqi* as the core of fire burning at the center of the earth as opposed to the *shen* that can be likened in function to light emanating from the sun. *Yuanqi* guides physiological processes that occur beneath the level of conscious awareness. *Shen* allows us to inquire willfully into our own natures and therefore direct the development of our purpose in life.

In keeping with the two sources of fire within water, the function of "blazing valley" also has a dual purpose. On the one hand, it can help tonify kidney *yang,* empowering us with that innate spark that drives our ascension in life. On the other hand, Ki-2 can draw fire from the heart into the depths of self to strengthen or resurrect the heart/kidney axis. The stability of this axis is the very foundation of health, immunity, and self-knowledge.[4] The physiological basis of introspection involves the radiance of *shen* as it illuminates the depths of self stored in kidney *jing.* When we suffer a shock in life, our mind turns our intention away from our depths as we search futilely for the cause of our pain externally. By empowering the fire within water, "blazing valley" can redirect consciousness back into our depths in a way that illuminates personal destiny and allows us to comprehend the highest lesson our pain holds for us. By strengthening the *yuanqi* in our depths, innate purpose and drive are revitalized, helping fuel the ascension of *jing* up the heart/kidney axis. Hence in the function of Ki-2, heart spirit *(shen)* as the fire in the upper *jiao* is reunited with its source as *jing* and *yuanqi* in the lower *jiao* and kidney.

If the presence of fire within water is deficient, coldness tends to predominate our physiological processes as evident in patterns of kidney *yang* deficiency. Here our evolution slows as the presence of cold impacts physiological function in any and all domains of functioning. "Blazing valley" can help thaw us when we are frozen in life and our potential is failing to manifest in any realm of being. If the presence of fire within water is excessive, *yin* will tend to be consumed, resulting in any of the myriad patterns associated with *yin* deficiency. In this case we may fail to introspect as our minds are diverted away from innate purpose by worldly desires. This tends to result in depletion of inner resources as we use our wills to drive ourselves to the point of exhaustion.

The name "blazing bone" may refer to this point's efficacy in treating conditions of *yin* deficiency such as steaming bone syndrome,[5] night sweats, and hot flushes. On a physical level, Ki-2 along with Bl-60 are important points for regulating the temperature of the feet when they are either too warm or too cold.

---

❖ **Ki-3** **Great Mountain Stream**
*Tai[4]xi[1]* Great Mountain Stream 太谿
*Lu[3]xi[4]* Thin Tube 呂細

FUNCTIONS

1. Earth point
2. Secondary tonification point
3. Source point
4. Point for breaking the H/W imbalance

VIRTUES

1. Tonifies the *yin* and *yang* aspects of kidney function.
2. Harmonizes the innate (water) and acquired (earth) constitutions.
3. Balances all spirit-level kidney treatments by grounding them at their source.

The image evoked by the name of Ki-3 is one of a spring gushing out of its source high in the mountains and flowing downward into a valley. Hence the flow of *qi* descends from Ki-3 through Ki-4 and down to Ki-5 as a stream descends a mountainside. The location of Ki-3 next to the medial malleolus (the mountain), and an alternate translation for this point's name of "great ravine," speaks to this image as does the name "thin tube."

If the presence of earth within water is deficient, the flow of water may not be adequately controlled as fear overwhelms us like a river breaching its banks. In this case our innate stores of potential can be wasted. *Yijing* hexagram 52, "mountain," represents the earth element and is comprised of the trigram for mountain and earth doubled. In the trigram for mountain (☶), one *yang* line sits on top of two *yin* lines. Because *yang* has fulfilled its natural tendency to ascend and *yin* has fulfilled its tendency to descend, the image evoked by this hexagram is one of stillness and meditation. As an earth point on a water meridian, Ki-3 may empower the stability and stillness of the earth element within water to help contain fear and effectively channel the resources associated with water. Here we call on the controlling influence of earth on water inherent in the *ke* cycle relationship of these two elements.

Whenever water is deficient in any aspect of being, the kidney's source point can be called on to stimulate its flow. In fact, a character translated as spring (*quan*:泉) is a component of the character translated as "source" (*yuan*:原). The character *quan* depicts a spring gushing up from the ground, and the character *yuan* depicts a spring flowing out of a cliff to denote the origin or source of a thing.[6] The kidney is the source of our inherited constitution as contained in *jing*. Earth, in contrast, represents our acquired constitution as it is gleaned from the stomach and spleen officials. Hence Ki-3, the earth point on the kidney meridian, can promote the interpenetration and strength of our inherited and acquired constitutions.

If the presence of earth within water is excessive, it can deplete potential like a sponge as the habituated needs of the earth element soak up and deplete innate resources. In this case the kidney struggles to support the self-centeredness of the spleen. Negative attributes associated with the earth element like neediness and worry tend to promote fear in the water element in a way that paralyzes the expression of innate potential. Earth can also congest the expression of inborn potential in the same way a landslide may dam the flow of a river. Stagnation of damp in the lower *jiao* tends to indicate that water is congealing in the kidneys and bladder due to overcontrol by the earth element. Hence sedating the earth point within water can help move stagnation in the kidneys and liberate the expression of the inborn constitution from the excessive control of the earth element.

---

### ❖ Ki-4 Great Bell, Great Cup

*Da[4]zhong[1]* Great Bell, Great Cup 大鍾

FUNCTION

*Luo* point

VIRTUES

1. Directs mind toward innate purpose.
2. Quiets the mind and stills ambition.
3. Vents ignorance embodied as dampness and heat that stagnates to obscure original nature and block the expression of inborn potential.

The character *zhong* can be translated as either the English words "bell" or "cup." The image of a great cup suggests the capability of this point to help us "dip into" our reserves. As a "great bell" this point can be likened to the bell at the center of a town that calls all the inhabitants and alerts them to their purpose through its resonance and tone. As the channel's *luo* point, Ki-4 can be conceived of as a gate into our depths that, when opened, can clear away influences that obscure insight into original nature. Hence the point is said to "benefit the *jing,*" "calm the spirit," and "clear the brain."[7]

A natural tendency in response to fear is to turn our minds outward, away from original nature, as we struggle for survival. This fight or flight response to life may become habituated to far outlast the source of any specific threat. In time, kidney *yin* and *yang* are depleted as our habituated response to fear compels us to overwork emotionally and physically just to keep our heads above water. Such depletion can in turn lead to stagnation as our potential fails to follow its nature and flow into life spontaneously. "Great bell" can help quiet the mind by moving stagnation and dispersing fear. In this way we may be reconnected to our deeper purpose that was lost to us in a moment of shock and panic. As the "great cup," Ki-4 can help reinvigorate us through connection to a deep reserve of *yuanqi* and *jing*. In this way original purpose can serve as the source of our motivation instead of fear, and a newfound reserve of strength can once again place us on the path of fulfilling destiny.

---

### ❖ Ki-5 Water Spring
*Shui³quan²* Water Spring 水泉

FUNCTION

*Xi*-cleft point

VIRTUES

1. Reinstitutes flow in all aspects of being.
2. Removes the tarnish of mundane *yin* from obscuring the influence of the inherited constitution.

Here the theme of water flowing is continued as the kidney meridian winds its way toward the heart of the upper burner.[8] As the *xi*-cleft point associated with the kidney official, Ki-5 is able to move stagnation and clear the kidney *qi* so it flows with the fresh purity of a clear spring.

I often use this point when I have the impression that a patient's inherited constitution is "tarnished." This image is present in the archetype of an old professor who, although wise, comes across as muddled and whose clothes are threadbare and worn by the passage of time. As the channel's *xi*-cleft point, Ki-5 can serve to clear the quality of the water element by moving stagnation. In this way it can help put us back in touch with constitutional strengths, similar to refurbishing an old tarnished antique to restore its shine. We can think of Ki-5 as a secondary source point on the kidney channel. As noted in the description of Ki-3, the character *quan* (泉), meaning "spring," is a central component of the character *yuan* (原), meaning "source."

Cold is the environmental condition that affects the kidney, and habitual reaction to fear tends to cause us to freeze in life as we fail to progress and manifest in all aspects of expression. Physically, fear and cold can manifest as rigidity or atrophy in the spine as marrow fuses or fails to nourish the bones. Psychospiritually, we can build a prison around ourselves as we fear contact with the outside world. This condition can be congruent with a wide range of disorders from agoraphobia and anxiety attacks to paranoia. The point "water spring" can initiate flow in all aspects of being and help revitalize physical structure as well as support the flow of our potential into the world around us.

---

| ❖ **Ki-6** | **Illuminated Sea, Reflecting Sea** | |
|---|---|---|
| *Zhao⁴hai³* | Illuminated Sea | 照海 |
| *Yin¹qiao³* | *Yin* Motility | 陰蹻 |

*In cleansing your mirror of the dark,*
*can you make it spotless?*
– *DAODEJING*[9]

*Men do not look into running water as a mirror, but into still water; it is only the still water that can arrest them all and keep them in the contemplation of their real selves.*
– *ZHUANGZI*[10]

*I am calm like the sea.*
– *DAODEJING*[11]

FUNCTIONS

1. Master point of the *yin* motility vessel
2. Coupled point of the conception vessel

VIRTUE

Empowers the virtue of reflection.

An habituated reaction to fear can be inborn or spring from a specific life experience. If the source of our fear is karmic, meaning it emanates from issues gleaned prior to first breath, it tends to act in a way that disturbs the solid formation of the foundation of our being. Such fear is brought into our lives through *jing* and can therefore erode the foundation of our integrated functioning. Fear emanating from life experience tends to obscure the expression of potential as governed by the kidney official. Shocks of significant magnitude can also penetrate to disturb the functioning of the eight extra meridians through the kidney. Whatever its specific etiology, chronic fear clouds the mind and suppresses the generation of wisdom as a virtue in life.

In Daoism, the mind of the sage is likened to a still sea that, like a mirror, accurately reflects inner nature and the nature of life around him. The chronic presence of anxiety and fear can cloud the mind in much the same way as ripples on the surface of water prevent it from revealing its depths or accurately reflecting the nature of anything reflected in it. Thick mucus in the chest, or concentrated urine, both symptoms for which Ki-6 is indicated, are the embodiment of murkiness in the water element. Psychospiritually, such obfuscation can manifest as free-floating anxiety and a sense of urgency and feeling of being overwhelmed that attaches itself to whatever circumstances are at hand.

"Illuminated sea," as a meeting point of the kidney official and the eight extra meridians, can help clear these channels of fear and still the waters of the mind by illuminating the unknown nature of the fears that lurk in our depths. In this way the reflective and contemplative aspects of kidney function can be empowered to promote the virtue of inner reflection. The character *qiao,* translated here as "motility," is composed of the character *zu,* meaning foot (足), with the character *gao* (高), meaning "tall," and the character *yao* (夭) for "incline." *Qiao* gives the sense of something rising from the foot, which is what the *yin* motility vessel does.

---

| ❖ **Ki-7** | **Returning Current** | |
|---|---|---|
| *Fu⁴liu¹* | Returning Current | 復溜 |
| *Fu⁴liu²* | Hidden Restraint | 伏留 |
| *Fu²liu²* | Hidden | 復留 |
| *Fu²bai⁴* | Hidden White | 復白 |
| *Chang¹yang³* | Glorious *Yang* | 昌陽 |
| *Wai⁴ming⁴* | Beyond Destiny | 外命 |

*On the seventh day comes return.*
– YIJING[12]

FUNCTIONS

1. Metal point
2. Tonification point
3. Archetypal point to break the husband/wife imbalance

VIRTUES

1. Empowers conception.
2. Draws *qi* through the metal gate (*jinmen*).

In the Daoist enumeration of being, the number seven corresponds to both the loss and return of original nature. The importance of Ki-7 in breaking the husband/wife imbalance is such that it merits particular attention. Named "returning current," Ki-7 is the metal point and the tonification point on the kidney meridian.[13] The functional dynamics of the transition from hexagram 23 to 24 precisely correspond to the function of Ki-7. Hexagram 24, "the return," is representative of the reappearance of *yang* within the primordial *yin* and the continual renewal of water that occurs on the winter solstice. This function is also pointed to in the name "glorious *yang*." The second, third, and fourth names given here all allude to the presence of metal as it lies hidden within water.

*The Book of Balance and Harmony* states, "The inner medicine is the primordial point of true *yang*, the celestial. It is likened to the center line in the *Yijing* trigram heaven. When it mates with earth, that forms water. The center line of the trigram for water represents true inner sense, which is firm and hence symbolized by metal, so it is called metal in water. These are all names for ultimate vitality. When the ultimate vitality is stable, it reverts to generative energy."[14] It is this generative "energy" that fuels another round of evolution as the seasons of life move along the *sheng* cycle. In this same manner, Ki-7, as the metal point within the water element, tonifies kidney *yin* and *yang* so the integrity of the primordial *qi* remains strong, the fires of *mingmen* are kindled, and the influence of heaven is not exhausted by mundane *yin* influences.

An alternate name for Ki-7, the key point for helping a patient return, is *waiming* (外命), meaning "beyond destiny."[15] This name indicates that, if one has "failed to return at the correct time," physical illness may have proceeded further than treatment is able to restore. For the illness now has its own life and has gone further than even the fulfillment of destiny can resolve. In this usage, Ki-7 may still help the patient in his transition from life to death as he returns to the primal *dao*.

---

## ❖ Ki-8 Exchanging Pledges, Communicate Faith
*Jiao*[1]*xin*[4] Exchanging Pledges, Communicate Faith 交信

FUNCTION

*Xi*-cleft point of *yin* motility vessel

VIRTUES

1. Renews and empowers our commitment to manifesting purpose in life.
2. Empowers faith.

The first seven points on the kidney meridian preside over the loss and return of original nature. Ki-7, "returning current," presides over the moment of conception of the original and reborn self. Destiny is a bipartite treasure existing both within ourselves and within heaven. Ki-8, "exchanging pledges," represents the binding contract given by heaven to humanity as it instills destiny within us.

It is at conception that heaven communicates our natures to us and instills faith as a virtue of the water element. Hence the character *xin* combined with the character *de* (original nature, virtue) means "faith" 德信. Faith as a virtue can be equated with self-confidence predicated on our innate trust (*xin:* 信) in heaven to support us. It is faith that empowers us to steer through life's challenging waters in the absence of external guidance by turning our attention toward the truth *(xin)* that rests in our depths. Hence "exchanging pledges" can strengthen both *yuanqi* and *jing* as guiding influences in our lives while reaffirming our pact with heaven to manifest destiny.

---

❖ **Ki-9** **Building Guest**
*Zhu²bin¹* Building Guest 築賓
*Zhu²bin¹* Building Embankment 築濱

FUNCTION

*Xi*-cleft point of the *yin* motility vessel

VIRTUE

Nourishes the womb and fetus.

With conception completed successfully (Ki-7) and destiny imparted (Ki-8), a guest in the form of a embryo now lives within the building of the womb. This "guest" must also be built within the womb as the commands within *jing* are implemented by the *yuanqi* during the incubation and development of the fetus. Points Ki-7, 8, and 9 are important for empowering the continued flow of life as it manifests in conception and the development of the fetus. The term *fetus* can also serve as a metaphor for the spiritual embryo that incubates within each of us as we awaken in life and pursue our path of personal cultivation. In this case, these three points can be used to empower the conception of a new self based on awakening to original nature.

---

❖ **Ki-10** ***Yin* Valley**
*Yin¹gu³* *Yin* Valley 陰谷

*Nothing under heaven is softer or weaker than water,*
*Yet nothing can compare with it in attacking the hard and strong.*
– *DAODEJING*[16]

FUNCTIONS

1. Water point
2. Horary point; 5–7 P.M., winter solstice
3. Transmitting point for all virtues of the kidney official

VIRTUE

Empowers fluidity in all aspects of being

At Ki-10, the meridian's *he*-sea point, the kidney *qi* runs deep into the interior of our being. The point's location in the crook of the knee provides the image of a mighty river *(yin)* running through a valley toward the sea. By treating the water point associated with the kidney official, we can address the overall function and quality of the water element as it lubricates, cleanses, and cools all aspects of our being.

Envision the crevice of the knee where the point is located as a great bend in a river. It is the nature of water to flow around all obstacles as it follows the path of least resistance flowing effortlessly toward the ocean. Fear and anxiety can obstruct the flow of kidney *qi,* causing us to exert excessive effort and overutilize our wills *(zhi)* as we struggle to manifest the goals of the habituated mind. Excessive effort can contribute to knee problems as this foundational joint fails to be lubricated and the resources of the kidney dwindle. Hence, on a mundane level, this point is often indicated for knee problems. Inwardly, "*yin* valley" can empower the kidney official so we do not exercise our wills habitually in reaction to fear. In this way fluidity of movement can return as we more gracefully manifest our purpose in life.

Ki-10, "*yin* valley" is in part complementary in function to SI-5, "*yang* valley." At "*yin* valley," *yin* accumulates from postnatal *qi,* whereas at "*yang* valley," *yang* accumulates from postnatal *qi.*[17] Hence Ki-10 can help us cleanse all aspects of our being by washing away the accretions of mundane *yin.* In contrast, SI-5 can burn away the stagnation of acquired influences and thereby help us more effectively extract essential *yang* (sunlight) from life.

---

| ❖ **Ki-11** | **Transverse Bone** | |
|---|---|---|
| *Heng²gu³* | Transverse Bone | 橫骨 |
| *Heng²gu³* | Horizontal Valley | 橫谷 |
| *Qu¹gu³* | Crooked Bone | 曲骨 |
| *Qu¹gu³* | Bent Bone | 屈骨 |
| *Xia⁴ji²* | Lower Extreme | 下極 |
| *Sui³gong¹* | Marrow Hollow | 髓公 |

FUNCTION

Point of the penetrating vessel

VIRTUES

1. Helps kidney *qi* bridge the pubic bone.
2. Integrates sexual functioning with conception and incubation.

The name of Ki-11 refers to the pubic bone that separates the genital region from the womb. In effect, this bone divides the lower *jiao* into upper and lower halves. The region below the pubic bone relates relatively more to issues of sexuality and the genitalia; the region above this bone relates relatively more to conception and nourishing the fetus within the womb. "Transverse bone" can help integrate these levels of function and empower conception as *qi* is brought across the pubic bone to Ki-12.

As a meeting between the kidney channel and the penetrating vessel, this point is particularly effective for treating symptomatology of the genital region including low sperm count and sexually transmitted diseases (STDs). The character *chong* (虫) figures prominently in the character *gu*, depicting insects and their toxins (蟲) proliferating in a basin (皿). This is a compelling image for the notion of bacteria or cells proliferating within the womb. *Gu* illness (蠱) was a deeply psychospiritually based disease having its basis in superstition and the occult (see the description of Lv-6). The superstitious belief in *gu* possibly overlapped with the shame and fear associated with sexually transmitted disease and gynecological illnesses. Such shame sullies the honor of one's family lineage whose desecration can be embodied as patterns of disharmony in the lower *jiao* and associated infertility. "Transverse bone" can help heal the lower *jiao*, mitigate the symptoms of STDs, and tonify *jing* in a way that can promote fertility. For it is through the act of procreation that the family lineage is resurrected. This point's ability to tonify *jing* is suggested in the name "marrow hollow." The character *gong*, translated as "hollow," can also mean "impoverished." Hence the name *suigong* might be translated as "marrow impoverishment," imparting a sense of *jing* deficiency.

---

## ❖ Ki-12 **Great Brightness**

| | | |
|---|---|---|
| *Da⁴he⁴* | Great Brightness | 大赫 |
| *Yin¹guan¹* | *Yin* Pass | 陰關 |
| *Yin¹wei²* | *Yin* Link | 陰維 |

FUNCTION

Point of the penetrating vessel

VIRTUES

1. Empowers conception.
2. Illuminates the depths, promoting our transcendence of fear and shame.

> Before one's father and mother give birth to one's body, when the male and female *qi* of *yin* and *yang* interact, a point arises that comes forth from emptiness. This is called the true, unified, ancestral *qi* of early heaven. This *qi* enters the *jing* and the blood and fuses *(daoyong)* them back into a chaotic unity. Having no form, yet it gives birth to form. Having no substance, yet it gives birth to substance. Internally, the five *zang*, six *fu*, five palaces, and hundred bones change and transform, becoming complete, according to the principle of natural spontaneity.[18]

Located directly over the womb, "great brightness" is an important point for empowering fertility and conception. For this purpose, Ki-12 is most effectively utilized when the patient has responded well to ongoing treatment and everything else is in place for conception to occur. Then "great brightness" can be utilized in direct proximity to the time she is likely to be most fertile. The character *he* suggests an awe-inspiring, bright, and glorious manifestation. Such is the light of the moon, stars, and sun, which impart destiny by shining on the act of procreation to bind conception. Hence Ki-12 can engender the heat and light from heaven to illuminate conception in the lower *jiao*.

Transcending our fear of the unknown is a crucial step in the transformation of fear into wisdom. Hence "great brightness" can also empower the conception of our spiritual embryo when fear prevents us from journeying into our depths and introspecting. Symptoms in the lower *jiao* such as vaginitis, low sperm count, vaginal discharge, and genital pain can all indicate that the water in the lower *jiao* is toxic and murky. So too can the unconscious be full of frightening murky thoughts like shadows that slither in the depths just beyond our recognition. "Great brightness" can illuminate the unfaced nature of our fears while clarifying the quality of water governed by the kidneys.

The historical meaning of the character *he* suggests an intense emotional state characterized by blushing, shame, and fear.[19] These conditions tend to occur when *yin* is deficient and unrooted *yang* ascends. Hence the names "*yin* pass" and "*yin* link" may refer to this point's ability to both tonify kidney *yin* and channel the *yang* back down into the *yin*. "Great brightness" can be useful for illuminating the unconscious nature of our shame and fears as they impact sexuality and conception. Ki-12 is an important point for helping us overcome both fear and coldness with compassion and warmth.

---

| | | |
|---|---|---|
| ❖ **Ki-13** | **Door of Infants** | |
| *Zi³hu⁴* | Door of Infants | 子戶 |
| *Qi⁴xue⁴* | *Qi* Cave | 氣穴 |
| *Bao¹men³* | Uterus Gate | 胞門 |

FUNCTION

Point of the penetrating vessel

VIRTUES

1. Empowers conception and birth.
2. Addresses therapeutic issues associated with infancy.

Ki-13 helps open the door to the womb and empowers both conception of the fetus and birth of the infant. "Door of infants" is ideal when therapeutic issues in a patient relate to variables of consciousness dating from birth to early childhood. Often traumas experienced during this time are not available as concrete memories to the adult. I have found "door of infants" to be helpful in recovering direct memories or in stimulating the emergence of somatic memories or dream imagery. Even when memory does not emerge, Ki-13 can help *qi* flow "past" a specific life trauma and continue to rise and support the higher manifestations of destiny governed by the points on the rest of the kidney channel. In this way the patient can move forward in life less hampered by fears predicated on childhood traumas. Similarly, this point can be effective for helping patients move past fears and doubts that arrive early, in the "childhood" of their spiritual path.

---

| | | |
|---|---|---|
| ❖ **Ki-14** | **Four Full** | |
| *Si⁴man³* | Four Full | 四滿 |
| *Sui²fu³* | Marrow Palace | 髓府 |
| *Sui²fu³* | *Sui* Palace | 隋府 |
| *Sui²zhong¹* | Marrow Center | 髓中 |

FUNCTION

Point of the penetrating vessel

VIRTUE

Relieves distension in the lower *jiao*.

For fullness and distension in the lower abdomen, this point treats stagnation of food, *qi*, blood, and dampness. This function is similar to the application of the herbal formula Danggui and Magnolia (*Wujisan*), also called the five accumulations. I have also used this point to good advantage for helping women with irregular menstrual cycles get their periods when they are late. Often the patient feels bloating in the lower *jiao,* suggesting her period is ready to arrive but is unable to start for dysfunctional reasons.

I also utilize "four full" for uterine and ovarian fibroids that impart a sense of fullness to the area of the point. Sometimes the generation of fibroids is a dysfunctional embodiment of a woman's unfulfilled desire to have children. Hence I often see such fibroids in women age 32 to 45 who are either without children or who desire more children but whose life situation will not permit it. In this case, resources such as *qi,* blood, and *jing* are channeled into the dysfunctional growth of a fibroid where a fetus might have been. As a point of the penetrating vessel, "four full" can help nurture the patient with *qi* and blood and help relieve the emotional and physical issues underlying this stagnation.

The name "marrow mansion" makes reference to the kidney as the Sea of Marrow. Ki-14 can stimulate the production of marrow from *jing* to nourish fertility, thereby leading to a fullness in the four directions as the embryo is conceived and thrives.

---

### ❖ Ki-15 **Middle Flowing Out**
*Zhong¹zhu⁴* Middle Flowing Out 中注

FUNCTION

Point of the penetrating vessel

VIRTUE

Tonifies the center and regulates water metabolism.

Ki-15 is located just laterally to CV-7, the *mu* point of the lower heater and the place that the three heater's internal channel enters into the *dantian* (丹田). Hence the ministerial fire flows from this point into the cinnabar field to fuel the alchemical transformations engendered by *mingmen.* As the pure and impure are separated, the impure *qi* travels to the bladder for elimination and the pure *qi* nourishes *mingmen* and flows to the viscera.

When the center is not strong enough to contain water it can flow out in all directions like a flood. This can manifest as swelling in the periphery, particularly in the hands. If water is contained excessively, urination can be difficult. "Middle flowing out" can regulate fluid metabolism by promoting the balanced flow of water. The point's name can also be translated as "central flow," denoting that kidney *qi* flows here into the penetrating vessel that constitutes the central core of our functional network.

❖ **Ki-16** **Heart Pit *Shu***
*Huang*[1]*shu*[1] Heart Pit *Shu* 肓俞

FUNCTIONS

1. Point of the penetrating vessel
2. Root of the *huang* region

VIRTUE

Tonifies heart essence.

The character *huang* refers to the area beneath the heart as well as to the bladder. The import of the *huang* region is discussed at length in the context of acupuncture point Bl-38 (43). *Huangshu* is located between CV-8, "spirit deficiency," and St-25, "heavenly pivot." "Spirit deficiency," located in the center of the umbilicus, addresses the transmission of *yuanqi* from mother to child during gestation. This primordial influence is innate as it is gleaned before the first breath. "Heavenly pivot," a meeting point of the stomach and large intestine officials, allows us to effectively abstract nourishment from food to nourish our centers with acquired *qi.* Ki-16 addresses the innate and acquired constitutions as it promotes the formation of *qi* and blood from primordial *yin, yang* and *jing. Huangshu* is able to utilize these resources to nourish the heart essence. These three points—CV-8, Ki-16, and St-25—all serve to strengthen our centers and thus empower the virtue of integrity.

Before the functions of the upper *jiao* have been activated in the fetus, it receives blood and breath through the umbilicus rather than through its heart and lungs. The place defined as the *gaohuang,* the area between the diaphragm and lower aspect of the heart, is, I believe, a meeting ground of innate and acquired influences as they nourish the heart and help establish an important foundation of the heart/kidney axis. This is a place where ancestry and purpose, attributes associated with the kidney, meet with the higher aspects of heart function. At Ki-16 the channel makes functional contact with the heart as it ascends toward the upper *jiao.* The series of transitions presided over by the upper kidney points empower the transcendence of fear in life and the evolution of wisdom. This process culminates at points Ki-23, 24, and 25 where *jing* is transformed into *ling,* the *yin* aspect of spirit.

As a point on a water channel at the level of St-25, the *mu* point of the large intestine official, Ki-16 can be effective in regulating the balance of water in the intestines. Hence Ki-16 can be useful for treating both constipation and diarrhea when excess or deficient fluids or accumulation of cold, a pathogen associated with the water element, is an issue.

❖ **Ki-17** **Crooked Merchant**

| | | |
|---|---|---|
| *Shang*[1]*qu*[1] | Crooked Merchant | 商曲 |
| *Shang*[1]*she*[2] | Merchant Abode | 商舍 |
| *Gao*[1]*qu*[1] | High Bend | 高曲 |

FUNCTION

Point of the penetrating vessel

I envision the "crooked merchant" as a traveler who metaphorically embodies the spiritual journey signified by the evolution of *qi* along the kidney channel. When the traveler becomes tired of living, resigned, and sad, "crooked merchant" can help revitalize him by renewing his sense of purpose. The notion of "crooked" can be juxtaposed with that of straight (一) as it figures in the character *de* (德), meaning virtue. All kidney points on the torso can be thought of as rectifying the path of kidney *qi* as it ascends toward the heart in the upper *jiao*.

In the process of building blood and *qi*, the penetrating vessel must integrate the contributions of both the innate and acquired constitutions. The character *shang*, translated as "merchant," implies the type of exchange that occurs between innate and acquired resources as they are integrated to form *qi* and blood.

❖ **Ki-18** **Stone Border**

| | | |
|---|---|---|
| *Shi*[2]*guan*[1] | Stone Border | 石關 |
| *You*[4]*guan*[1] | Western Pass | 右關 |
| *Shi*[2]*que*[4] | Stone Tower Gate | 石闕 |

FUNCTION

Point of the penetrating vessel

VIRTUES

1. Softens hardness resulting from fear.
2. Helps transcend fear and promote the flow of kidney *qi* toward the upper *jiao*.

In ascending to the heights of the kidney meridian, *qi* must pass through several portals ("door of infants," "stone border," "dark gate") that symbolize stages of our spiritual journey in transcending fear. "Stone border" signals our approach to a center of the kidney's influence as signified by the name of the next point, Ki-19, "*yin* capital." Such a border calls to mind the function of the great wall protecting the heart of the nation as symbolized by the Forbidden City. Similarly, "stone border" can be conceived as an outer barrier in the approach of kidney *qi* to the upper *jiao*.

There is often a congruence of function between points on the conception vessel and points on the stomach and kidney channels at the same anatomical level. Hence CV-11 is a central point for addressing *qi* stagnation in the middle *jiao*. Just lateral to CV-11 is Ki-18 ("stone border") and lateral to that is St-22 ("border gate"). The names of both Ki-18 and St-22 contain the character *guan*, denoting a border pass. Hence at this level we can address the ascent of kidney *qi* and the descent of stomach *qi* in a way that promotes harmony in the middle *jiao* by integrating the inherited and acquired constitutions.

Both the names of Ki-18, "western pass," and Ki-21, "dark gate," allude to the mysterious pass *(yuanguan)* as entryway into the kingdom of the immortal Xi Wang Mu, the Queen Mother of the West. West is the direction of the metal element, and as kidney *qi* transitions into the domain of the upper burner it enters the province of the lungs. The character *shi,* meaning "stone," can relate to any condition of hardness or coldness that this point is known to treat such as infertility, constipation, or blood stasis. The character *que,* translated as "tower gate," is composed of the character *men*(門), meaning "gate," and the character *jue* (闕) depicting an obstacle (屰) that impedes breathing (欠).[20] The image of a stone gate as an impediment to breath is congruent with this point's application in treating hiccuping, which is a literal meaning of the character *jue.*

The water element's virtue of flow can be compromised as our reaction to fear causes us to freeze and harden ourselves to the cold realities of life. Such a response can manifest as abdominal pain and hardness, stomach spasms, constipation, and infertility. "Stone border" can soften our hardness and help us continue our journey in a way that is relatively more guided by breath and relatively less encumbered by fear.

---

| ❖ **Ki-19** | ***Yin* Capital** | |
|---|---|---|
| *Yin[1]du[1]* | *Yin* Capital | 陰都 |
| *Tong[1]guan[1]* | Communication Pass | 通關 |
| *Shi[2]gong[1]* | Food Palace | 食宮 |
| *Shi[2]gong[1]* | Stone Palace | 石宮 |
| *Shi[2]lu[3]* | Food Tube | 食呂 |

FUNCTION

Point of the penetrating vessel

VIRTUE

Stills fear that undermines the functions of the middle *jiao.*

The kidney is a *yin* official, and the designation of this point as a "capital" suggests it is a center that influences the function of the kidneys. Ki-19 lies between CV-12, "middle duct," and St-19, "not at ease." CV-12 helps equilibrate the middle *jiao* by addressing issues of tension and stagnation. "Not at ease" addresses these issues by helping calm the earth element's tendency toward obsession and worry. "*Yin* capital" helps still the waters in the middle *jiao* by quieting the underlying fears that can unsettle and erode the earth element's virtue of building integrity.

The names "food palace" and "food tube" refer to the descent of acquired *qi* in the stomach channel in the process of alimentation. Lubrication is required for digestion and assimilation to proceed gracefully, and if *yin* is deficient, conditions typified by hardness can occur. The name "stone palace" may refer to the conditions of fullness beneath the heart, as well as distension and pain in the abdomen, difficult defecation, infertility, and blood stasis in the uterus for which this point is indicated.[21]

---

## ❖ Ki-20 **Through the Valley**
*Tong*[1]*gu*[3] Through the Valley 通谷

FUNCTION

Point of the penetrating vessel

VIRTUE

Strengthens faith to support the transcendence of fear.

Having left "*yin* capital," the kidney *qi* now journeys "through the valley" on its way to "dark gate." Just as water runs through the valley on its way to the sea, so too must we pass through the valley of our own fears as we manifest destiny. Our *jing,* in its ascent toward the upper *jiao,* must lubricate our transitions through the valley of our life experience if wisdom is to be engendered. If communication between the heart and kidney is compromised, this valley can be a dark and foreboding place as we are cut off from the illumination and guidance of the heart. With no light at the end of the tunnel we can lose faith in the purpose of our journey and the nature of our destination. If fear prevents *jing* from flowing toward its destination, progress in life can come to a standstill in any and all aspects of being.

"Through the valley" empowers us to embrace faith in our inner purpose so we can continue our journey and ultimately transcend our fears. I use this point to support a patient who feels lost and in the dark during his process of healing. In another scenario, fear can compel a person to take risks continually as ambition drives him to manifest his mind's purpose at any cost to self and others. In this case "through the valley" can help connect the patient to the unconscious fears that compel him and empower him with a more realistic sense of his capabilities and limits.

A valley is a sheltered and flourishing place nourished by the river passing through it as it carries resources from its origin out to the sea. The river also helps carry away waste to the sea, thus lubricating and revitalizing all aspects of being that it touches. If the flow of the river is impeded, conditions typified by bloating and accumulation of fluids tend to result. "Through the valley" can help stimulate the movement of fluids and accumulation of phlegm and damp in the middle and upper *jiao*.

---

| ❖ **Ki-21** | **Dark Gate** | |
|---|---|---|
| *You¹men²* | Dark Gate | 幽門 |
| *Shang⁴men²* | Upper Gate | 上門 |

FUNCTION

Point of the penetrating vessel

VIRTUE

Empowers transcendence of fear to promote flow.

After making the journey "through the valley" we arrive at the "dark gate." Ki-21 is the last point on the abdomen after which the *qi* flows to the exit point at Ki-22 and onward to meet the heart protector channel at HP-1. The name "dark gate" symbolizes the entry into the domain of the upper kidney points and the burial ground of the emperor. Upon entering the dark gate, we approach the imperial mausoleums, a place of reverence for the soul of the dead emperor. Here the *qi* also makes a transition to the inner domain of the heart where *ling* and *shen,* the *yin* and *yang* aspects of spirit, intermingle. Here they empower a potency and efficacy in the world that is presided over by the virtue of *wuwei.* On a physical level, the phrase *youmen* refers to the pyloric valve; on a metaphysical level, it refers to the underworld.[22]

Communication between the kidneys and the heart is essential if the potential in our depths is to be illuminated by *shen.* If our reaction to fear shuts the "dark gate," the effects are twofold. On the one hand, *shen* will not be able to penetrate into the depths of the kidney. Here the unfaced nature of our fears results in us turning our mind's outward looking for external sources of reassurance as we fail to introspect. On the other hand, kidney *jing* will fail to evolve and become *ling,* resulting in feelings of impotency as we lose the ability to effect change in the world and perform ritual effectively. In both cases fear compels us as we fail to face and transmute our depths of self symbolized by kidney *jing* and its evolution to the imperial burial grounds in the upper *jiao*.

*Youmen* is the traditional name for the bottom of the stomach and in modern Chinese medicine is equivalent to the pyloric valve. An alternate name for Ki-21 is *shangmen* (上門), translated as "upper gate." This name is more in line with the location of Ki-21 near the top of the stomach. When these gates become stuck physically, we may experience feelings of bloating and heaviness in the stomach as well as distension and tightness rising up the center of the chest along the midline. Such stagnation can be congruent with feelings of pressure around the heart as stagnation of the earth element hampers the effortless expression of our heart's fire.

The names of points Ki-18 through Ki-21 have a dual meaning. On the one hand, these names allude to the ascension of kidney *qi* as it transitions onto the rib cage and into the inner realm of the heart. On the other hand, these point names refer to the descent of stomach *qi* as it ascends into the abyss of the middle *jiao*. For example, the name "dark gate" may be taken to refer both to the entry of kidney *qi* into the imperial burial ground as represented by the functions of the upper kidney points as well as to the function of the pyloric valve, which helps regulate the descent of stomach *qi*.

---

❖ **Ki-22** **Walking on the Verandah**

| | | |
|---|---|---|
| *Bu⁴lang²* | Walking on the Verandah | 步廊 |
| *Bu⁴lang²* | Walking Gentleman | 步郎 |

FUNCTION

Exit point

At Ki-22 the kidney meridian rises off the abdomen and steps (*bu:*步) up onto the rib cage, denoted in the point name as a "verandah." The character *lang* gives the sense of a corridor, veranda, or "upward path." The names of Ki-18 through Ki-21, "stone border," *yin* capital," "through the valley," and "dark gate," respectively, tell a story of a journey through darkness as *jing* ascends to the upper *jiao*. This ascension is congruent with the arrival of our purpose into the world and the generation of virtue as we discover who we are and take appropriate action. As the kidney meridian reaches the highlands of the rib cage, the flow of *qi* shifts to HP-1.

We must make an interesting distinction in comprehending the transition in the quality of *qi* as it flows from Ki-21 to Ki-22. On the one hand, the kidney *qi* is entering the upper *jiao*, which corresponds to the functional influence of heaven. This is a *yang* influence empowered by light and illumination emanating from the heart spirit *(shen)*. Hence as the *qi* makes its transition to HP-1, darkness dissipates and joy is renewed. On the other hand, the most refined essence continues its upward journey into the inner realm of spirit concordant with the burial ground of the emperor.

The points that follow the channel's exit point (Ki-23 to Ki-27) represent the deepest reserves of spiritual *qi* accessible on the kidney meridian. These points form a corridor along the rib cage similar to the figures found lining the spirit road *(shendao)* leading to the ancient imperial mausoleums (see Photo 29.1).[23] In fact, the name of Ki-24 *(lingxu),* "spirit burial ground," evokes the imagery of these imperial burial places. This realm represents the highest evolution of *jing* as spiritual potency that is embodied in the function of Ki-24. This burial ground can appear as a dark and foreboding place to those who have not cultivated the virtues of faith, wisdom, or reverence for the will of heaven.

The E/E combination of Ki-22 to HP-1 can empower us to make the transition from the spiritual depth of our journey to transcend its attendant fears so we may fully embrace the joys and pleasures governed by the heart protector official. For one who avoids the depths by diverting his *qi* excessively toward the pursuit of pleasure, Ki-22 can help channel essence toward the upper kidney points and the inner realm of the heart.

## *The Upper Kidney Points*

❖ **Ki-23** **Spirit Seal**
*Shen[2]feng[1]* Spirit Seal 神封

VIRTUES

1. Unblocks the expression of heart *shen.*
2. Affirms actions that arise spontaneously from the heart without needing external confirmation.

*Shen* is the character for heart spirit and, in a larger sense, the active impulses that emanate from heaven. *Feng* (封) is composed of the character for earth doubled (圭), alongside the character for a hand affixing a seal of authority (寸). Wieger explains the character: "The ancient character represented a tree upon a tumulus. . . . This knoll, surmounted with a tree, represented the imperial possession of the land. A similar knoll, but smaller, was erected in the fief granted by the emperor to a feudatory."[24] In ancient China, when the emperor invested a noble, a mound of earth would be taken from the imperial altar and placed on the noble's altar as a symbol of the emperor's authority.

*Photo 29.1*

*Here statues of various officials line the spirit road on the way to the imperial mausoleum. These evoke the image of the upper kidney points, Ki-22 through Ki-27, as they denote entrance into the spiritual (*shen *and* ling*) domain of the heart.*

The left half of the character is an image of a mound of earth erected for religious purposes. This mound represents the gods of the earth (*she:* (社) who were worshipped in ancient China. The *she* (earth altar) stood in sacred groves, which themselves may have earlier been the object of the cult. In ancient times, mounds were marked by a sacred tree and a pole. Thus the *she* were quite open to the air. As telluric deities, it was paramount that they remain exposed to atmospheric influences in order to imbibe constantly from the heavenly *qi* and *shen.* To deprive them of power, as in the conquest of a state, it was necessary only to enclose them with a roof and walls, thereby shutting off their access to sunlight and air.[25]

When the Shang empire was overthrown, their *she* was enclosed with an opening that faced north so only debilitating influences could reach it. Here the potential power of earth *(yin)* had been cut off from the sunlight *(shen)*, the activating influences from heaven. Thus the power of the dynasty dwindled as it lost its mandate from both heaven and emperor. This scenario is similar to what happens in the individual when he receives only influences from the north (water element) and no activating impulses from the south (*shen,* or heart). Cut off from the warmth of his "sealed" heart, the power that stems from his mandate (*ming,* or destiny) diminishes.

In the following passage, Zhuangzi virtually describes the genesis and progress of kidney depletion to which this point speaks:

> Men's little fears are mean and trembly; their great fears are stunned and overwhelming. . . . They fade like Fall and Winter—such is the way they dwindle day by day. They drown in what they do—you cannot make them turn back. They grow dark as though sealed with seals—such are the excesses of their old age. And when their minds draw near to death, nothing can restore them to the light.[26]

This is a person whose heart spirit has been sealed so the *shen*, the brightness of life, cannot manifest and activate his inborn potential. The patient for whom this point is indicated may show a lack of authority on all levels. Often he may exhibit a sense of being out of touch with his purpose in life and his spiritual identity. "Spirit seal" can help establish the realization that no external confirmation in life is needed to choose a course of action. We need only follow the inner knowing that this direction is present in our heart, placed there by heaven, the highest authority. Ultimately, "spirit seal" may help restore the interaction between the potential present in the kidney official and the mandate from one's own heart and the heart of heaven *(shen)*.

---

| | | |
|---|---|---|
| ❖ **Ki-24** | **Spirit Burial Ground** | |
| *Ling²xu¹* | Spirit Burial Ground | 靈墟 |
| *Ling²qiang²* | Spirit Wall | 靈墻 |

VIRTUES

1. Resurrects the *ling* spirit.
2. Empowers potency that attains from the fulfillment of destiny.
3. Empowers us to be an effective force in the world.

The etymology of the character *ling,* as discussed earlier, relates to the power and potential of the heart spirit to effect change. *Xu* (虛) means emptiness or that which contains nothing,[27] and in Daoism refers to the void. Used as a medical term, *xu* means deficiency or exhaustion. The character *xu* pictures two men on a hill looking in all directions, yet nothing can be seen, for they are in a high upland that is wild and barren. The imperial burial grounds in ancient China were located in exactly such places.[28] Hence adding the earth radical (土) to produce the homophone *xu* (墟) yields the meaning of "burial ground."

*Ling* appears in the title of the *Lingshu,* the "spiritual axis." Both characters *xu* and *ling* are associated with the potentiality of the empty vortex whirling between heaven and earth. According to the *Daodejing,* the *dao*'s axis is "empty *(xu)* yet inexhaustible,"[29] and it is precisely this emptiness that gives the *dao* its use.[30]

When the aspect being addressed by Ki-24 is in balance, a person may feel connected to the wellspring of *dao,* life's greatest resource, and experience himself as a potent and effective force in the world. Ki-24 is indicated therapeutically when the potential *(ling)* to manifest in life is exhausted *(xu),* giving the sense that the *ling* spirit has died. The patient's life may appear like a barren wasteland, scorched by the impulses of the heart's *shen,* with little manifestation of potential. With the *ling* spirit dried up and depleted, the individual may grow sad as he becomes increasingly cut off from his spiritual source and power in life. This exhaustion on a basic level may be predicated on a weakened *jing* and deficient *yin.* The patient evidences an internal spiritual crumbling, which parallels the physical disintegration taking place as his life's resources dry up.

Ki-24 speaks to the spiritual aspect of the imbalance by treating the relationship between the heart and the kidneys in the upper burner. "Spirit burial ground" can help restore the patient's experience of himself as a potent force in the universe by returning him to his spiritual source. The functional quality present in this point may be likened to bringing water to the desert so life may flourish.

---

## ❖ Ki-25 **Spirit Storehouse**
*Shen²cang²* Spirit Storehouse 神藏

VIRTUE

Provides access to a reserve of *shen.*

The first character, *shen,* as in Ki-23, indicates the heart spirit. The character *cang* means to hide or conceal and also has the meaning "storehouse."[31] Here we are given the image of a reserve of spirit *(shen)*, which is stored in the heart. Thus, when a patient's *shen* is deficient or hidden, Ki-25 can act as a storehouse of *qi* to support the spirit.

*Cang* is a homophone of the character *cang* (臧), meaning compliancy. This character is an image of an official kneeling prostrate before his master whose authority may be symbolized by the halberd.[32] "Spirit storehouse" may not only access a reserve of *shen,* but also help the heart-mind (emperor) enforce its commands with authority and garner the respect it deserves from its officials (the other functions in one's inner kingdom of being).

Three points, Ki-23, Ki-24, and Ki-25, are of paramount importance in maintaining balance between the *yin (ling)* and *yang (shen)* of heart spirit. Figure 27.1 (p. 456) depicts the relationship among these three points.

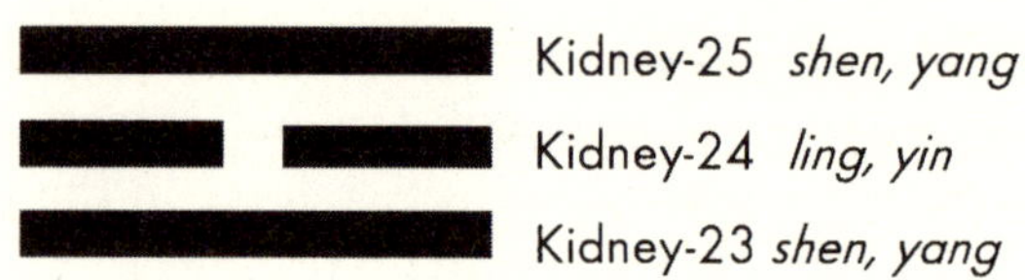


*Figure 27.1*

ANALYSIS OF RELATIONSHIP AMONG KI-23, KI-24, AND KI-25

*Ki-23, Ki-24, and Ki-25 address the* shen, ling, *and* shen *spirits, respectively. Assigning a solid* yang *line to each of the* shen *points (Ki-23 and Ki-25) and a broken* yin *line to the* ling *point (Ki-24) produces the* Yijing *trigram for fire* (li).[33] *These points lie on the kidney meridian, a meridian associated with water, over the heart, an organ associated with fire in the upper burner, which corresponds to heaven. Hence these points relate intimately to the spiritual alchemy of water and* fire, ling *and* shen. *They address the intrinsic harmony of* yin *and* yang *as it manifests the balanced expression of the human spirit. The functional balance of* ling *and* shen *is essential if life is to proceed effectively and with spontaneity.*

---

❖ **Ki-26** **Amid Elegance**

| | | |
|---|---|---|
| *Yu⁴zhong¹* | Amid Elegance | 彧中 |
| *Yu⁴zhong¹* | Within the Frontier | 域中 |
| *Huo⁴zhong¹* | Possible Center | 或中 |

*But I've heard that if the mirror is bright, no dust settles on it; if dust settles, it isn't really bright.*
– *ZHUANGZI*[34]

VIRTUE

Removes tarnish from original nature.

The essential nature of the inherited constitution is like a diamond buried in our depths. This diamond is the primordial influences of *jing* and *shen* invested within us by heaven at the moment of conception. When the *ling* and *shen* spirits interpenetrate in the way presided over by the functions of Ki-23, Ki-24, and Ki-25, elegance is one of the emerging virtues. Hence we can rule our lives with grace and ease as *jing* lubricates all transitions in life and our virtues shine forth effortlessly.

Shock tends to erode the stability of the heart/kidney axis, and in time the brilliance of our innate endowment may become tarnished due to the accretion of negativity dysfunctionally assimilated during life.[35] Ki-26, "amid elegance," can help remove the tarnish of acquired experience that obscures both perception and manifestation of our innate beauty. I have often used this point to good effect when I assess that a patient is worn down and his or her appearance seems tattered like an old sweater that could use mending. "Spirit burial ground" (Ki-24) can reawaken our identification with our deepest spirit as it flows from its source in the kidneys. "Amid elegance," in contrast, addresses the outer luster of our spiritual constitution as it radiates as virtue into the world.

The upper *jiao* as presided over by the heart is the "inner frontier" alluded to in the name of HP-6, "inner frontier gate." The name "within the frontier" denotes the location and function of Ki-26 as being within the inner domain governed by the heart.

---

❖ **Ki-27** **Storehouse**
*Shu*[1]*fu*[3] Storehouse 俞府
*Shu*[1]*fu*[3] Tribute Mansion 輸府

Storehouse is the highest point on the kidney channel and therefore closest to heaven. This relationship is symbolized by its location at the same anatomical level as Lu-1. As a reserve of kidney *qi,* "storehouse" empowers the kidneys to grasp *qi* and promote balanced respiration. In the depths, the interpenetration of metal and water presides over conception as governed by "returning current" (Ki-7). Here the water element grasps the metal, as the mother's blood (ovum) attracts the father's *jing* (sperm), to initiate conception. Ki-27, however, empowers water to grasp metal at the height of the kidney channel. In this way we can receive the heavenly essence that continually inspires our conception of true self. For this is the lightest and most refined *qi,* similar in quality to the air we might encounter on a mountain peak as symbolized by the presence of Ki-27 and Lu-1 at the top of the lungs.

The habitual reaction to fear can lead us to exhaustion from overexpending our reserves. "Storehouse" provides a reserve of kidney *qi* to help quiet the spirit from above so it does not undermine the reserves stored in the lower *jiao* below. In this way we may be encouraged to just "breathe" rather than react to anxiety and fear.

## Exercises

1. The names of "blazing valley" (Ki-2), "illuminated sea" (Ki-6), and "great brightness" (Ki-12) all allude to a quality of light and illumination. Compare the functions of these points.
2. Compare the function of Ki-4 and Gb-39 relative to the imagery of the

word "cup" in each point name and these points' relationship to accessing reserves.

3. Compare the function of Ki-5 in revitalizing the inherited constitution to the related functions of Ki-26 and Bl-11.
4. In my discussion of Ki-16, Ki-18, and Ki-19, I analyzed the functional relationships between various points on the conception vessel, kidney, and stomach channels that are found at the same anatomical level.
   a. Discuss the functional relationships between CV-12 ("middle duct"), Ki-19 ("*yin* capital"), and St-21 ("bridge gate").
   b. As acquired *qi* descends, inherited *qi* ascends. Discuss the functional relationships among all conception vessel, kidney, and stomach points that are found at the same anatomical level.

## *NOTES*

1. It is interesting to note that the heart official is discussed first in the *Neijing Suwen* and has a total of nine points. The kidney official is presented ninth and has a total of twenty-seven points. The number nine signifies a position of completion and power in the Chinese enumeration of being. The heart channel in having nine points (3 x 3) has its own concentrated power of impulse. The kidney channel in having twenty-seven points (3 x 9) has a great power to manifest potential. In balance, our potential to manifest is always in greater abundance than the impulse to manifest. That is to say, one little spark is enough to ignite the manifestation of a tremendous amount of potential. Therefore perhaps the heart is in need of only nine points to govern the manifestation of the potential inherent in the twenty-seven kidney points.
2. This name is listed in Ellis, Wiseman, and Boss, 1989, p. 196.
3. See the case study of Jill in Chapter 3.
4. For a discussion of the heart kidney axis, see *ND*, pp. 204–210.
5. Steaming bone syndrome, which can occur in cases of severe *yin* deficiency, is characterized by heat felt in the bones.
6. Weiger, 1965, p. 289.
7. DeLaney, Leonard, and Kisch, 1989.
8. The "depths" are reflected in the point names and functions of the upper kidney points.
9. Chen, 1989, p. 78.
10. Watson, 1964a, p. 65.
11. Chen, 1989, p. 20.
12. Wilhelm, 1968, p. 97. The number seven corresponds to the return or loss of original nature. The seven holes in the human head correspond to the senses and self-awareness. It is in retracing our steps and closing these apertures that we are able to experience the true reality that lies within.
13. Note that the *Baiwen Bian* (The Hundred Questions), a late-eighth-century alchemical text, calls the kidney the "metal radiance" *(jinguang)* and "metal essence" *(jinjing)*. Homann, 1976, p. 48. Homann fixes the time of this text to the school of Lu Dongbin, who was born in 755 C.E.
14. Cleary, 1989, p. 22.
15. Hicks, 1985, p. 16.
16. Chapter 78, Chen, 1989, p. 18.

17. From lecture with Jeffrey Yuen.
18. The character *hun* refers to the "chaotic" nature of the *dao* and may also mean "to blend." Throughout my translation, I have interpreted the character *hun* as the blending of two seemingly opposite factors back into a unity beyond human comprehension that is patterned on the *dao* of early heaven. For further discussion of this topic, see Girardot, 1983. Quotation from Liu I-ming, *Symbolic Language: Breaking Open Doubt.*
19. Weiger, 1965, p. 291.
20. See Wieger, 1965, L102D, p. 248, as well as my discussion of the character *jue* in the context of Bl-58.
21. Deadman and Al-Khafaji, 2000, CD-ROM, Ki-19.
22. Mathews, 1931, p. 1124.
23. This photograph originally apeared in Paludan, 1991, p. 160. My thanks to Ann Paludan for her permission to use this photograph.
24. Weiger, 1965, p. 205.
25. Bishop, 1933, pp. 24–43.
26. Watson, 1964a, p. 32. The reference to receiving light brings to mind the point Bl-6 ("receiving light").
27. Weiger, 1965, pp. 80–81.
28. Fischer, 1930. The burial grounds and mausoleums of many of the emperors contained the character *ling* in their name.
29. *Daodejing,* Chapter 5; in Chen, 1989, p. 5.
30. *Daodejing,* Chapter 11; in ibid., p. 82.
31. Mathews, 1931, p. 985.
32. Weiger, 1965, p. 214. Although the characters are homophones and very similar in appearance, they do not necessarily share the same etymology. Nevertheless, the information yielded from their comparison is still interesting.
33. For an explanation of the symbolism of the *Yijing,* see Wilhelm, 1968.
34. Watson, 1964a, p. 66.
35. *ND,* pp. 207–210.

# 28

# HEART PROTECTOR

THE HEART PROTECTOR MERIDIAN BEGINS IN THE pericardium and travels superficially to emerge at CV-17, between the nipples, in the center of the upper *jiao*. One branch descends the midline to pass through CV-12 and terminate at CV-7 just below the umbilicus in the lower *jiao*. A second branch runs laterally to emerge at HP-1, the channel's entry point, just lateral to the nipple in the fourth intercostal space. From here it arches over the axilla and runs down the anterior aspect of the arm, through the middle of the wrist and hand, to end at HP-9, the radial nail point of the middle finger. An internal branch splits off at HP-8, the channel's exit point, and travels to the ulna nail point of the ring finger, where it connects with the three heater channel at its entry point, TH-1.

## *Thoughts on the Channel*

The nine points on the heart protector channel correspond in number to the nine points on the heart channel. The course of the heart protector's meridian parallels that of the heart channel, a relationship appropriate to its function of protecting the heart. Located on the medial surface of the forearm, the heart protector channel opens as we receive another into our hearts and into our arms through a loving embrace.

### MAIN FUNCTIONS

1. Empowers the virtue of openness from a position of strength.
2. Protects the heart.
3. Discerns what internal and external cues signify a condition of safety. Safety is defined as the context in which the heart thrives.
4. Governs circulation, intimacy, and the influence of fire in sexuality.

### DISTAL POINT FUNCTIONS

*Water:* Quiets fear that limits the heart protector's capacity for intimacy by empowering a sense of purpose in relationship.

*Wood:* Empowers clarity of vision within the heart protector, serving as fuel for joy and intimacy.

*Fire:* Empowers the essential qualities of fire within the heart protector official.

*Earth:* Empowers the heart to be nourished by intimacy.

*Metal:* Cools grief stemming from lost love. Empowers the heart protector's discernment of quality.

*Xi-cleft:* Helps the heart protector let go of past pain from heartbreak and perceived betrayal.

*Luo:* Empowers appropriate function of the gate leading into the inner domain of the heart.

---

## ❖ HP-1 Heavenly Pond

*Tian¹chi²* Heavenly Pond 天池
*Tian¹hui²* Heavenly Meeting 天會

FUNCTIONS

1. Window point
2. Entry point
3. Intersection point of the heart protector, liver, and gallbladder channels

VIRTUE

Empowers a memory of safety that is untouched by life experience.

Each acupuncture point empowers a virtue as it exists perfectly within us, untouched by negative interpretations associated with our life experience.

As a window point, "heavenly pond" helps restore the memory of our heart as a place of ultimate safety before it became burdened by life's sorrows. The experience of a pure virtue, even for an instant, can be enough to sweep away a lifetime of accumulated ignorance and pain. In clearing the effects of past betrayal, we can once again come to experience the world and our hearts as a safe place for our spirit to rest.

If we are unable to feel compassion toward ourselves, it often becomes difficult to experience connection to our own heart. We then tend to project our need for intimacy eternally by seeking someone else to embody love and intimacy for us in a way that we cannot manage for ourselves. Relationships entered into out of dysfunction become unfulfilling because the same mechanism that prevents us from communicating with our own hearts will eventually prevent us from connecting to the hearts of others after the initial fire at the beginning of the relationship begins to wane. "Heavenly pond" transports us to a place where we may safely nourish and connect to our own hearts. Upon experiencing compassion and love for ourselves, our old wounds may heal and allow for the possibility that we may connect to another in a more functional way.

As an entry point, HP-1 receives *qi* as it flows from the kidney channel at Ki-22. The specific nature of this exit/entry block is that it addresses the relationship between fear (kidney) and intimacy (heart protector). Note that the names of the first three points on the heart protector meridian allude to water. Hence 3 x 3 is equivalent in number to the nine points on the heart protector channel and 3 x 9 yields the number twenty-seven, equal in number to the points on the kidney channel. This is congruent with the heart protector official being related to kidney *yang* as it occupies the proximal position pulse on the right wrist. Hence the heart protector and three heater officials can be thought of as constituting the presence of fire within water. This designation evokes for me the image of lava flowing out of a volcano as well as the quality of heart protector blood as it empowers the virtue of choosing intimacy from a position of strength.[1] Lava, like blood, embodies the virtues of both warmth and flow. Just as the fire element creates earth as *qi* transitions along the *sheng* cycle, so too does lava extend the land's mass into the ocean.

HP-1 is forbidden to needle on women (see my discussion of HP-2). However, in my opinion it is quite feasible for experienced practitioners to needle this point in women with small-sized breasts. Because of its position, male practitioners must be sensitive to issues regarding propriety if they choose to needle this point on a woman. I have found this to be a most potent point in empowering the overall spiritual well-being and function of the heart protector official.

### ❖ HP-2 Heavenly Spring

| | | |
|---|---|---|
| *Tian¹quan²* | Heavenly Spring | 天泉 |
| *Tian¹shi¹* | Heavenly Damp | 天濕 |
| *Tian¹wen¹* | Heavenly Warmth, Heaven's Revival | 天溫 |

FUNCTIONS

1. Alternate entry point
2. Alternate window point

VIRTUE

Empowers feelings of safety untouched by life experience.

HP-1 is forbidden to needle on women and HP-2 is recommended instead.[2] Although it is feasible to treat HP-1 on many women, HP-2 can serve as an alternate entry point and window in cases where a woman's breasts are simply too large to locate the point or when propriety dictates the practitioner not treating a point located on the breast. Used in this context, HP-2 can empower the virtues listed earlier associated with HP-1.

A spring is more active than a pond and implies more vigorous movement. "Heavenly pond" (HP-1) denotes a quiet place of safety, and the name "heavenly spring" suggests the initiation of movement and action. Upon bringing someone to heaven's pond we are providing the person the opportunity to bask safely in the rays of his own heart. This experience is rejuvenative, and not much is to be expected of the patient while he enjoys a recuperative rest on the shores of heaven. However once rested, it is important to move back into the world and use what he has learned in an active way. "Heavenly spring" helps initiate action in the world to flow from the heart with a strength and compassion born of healing. The name "heavenly revival" may be taken to refer to this point's action in reviving the heart as an emissary of heaven within us.

The names "heavenly warmth" and "heavenly damp" refer to the nature of the heart protector's fire as belonging to the provenance of the water element as kidney *yang* and to its nature as a fire official. The heart protector official "warms" the blood (damp, moisture) so the heart's radiance flourishes to flow into the world as joy.

### ❖ HP-3 Crooked Marsh

| | | |
|---|---|---|
| *Qu¹ze²* | Crooked Marsh | 曲澤 |

FUNCTIONS

1. Water point
2. Secondary tonification point

VIRTUES

1. Quiets fear that limits intimacy.
2. Empowers the virtues of water such as fortitude and contemplation within the heart protector.

"Crooked marsh" is a key point for establishing the balanced relationship of the water element as it expresses itself through the heart protector official. The functioning of the heart protector and the heart are intimately related. Therefore, shock to the heart protector tends to undermine the balanced functioning of the heart/kidney axis in a way that disorders the healthy control of water over fire across the *ke* cycle. This often manifests as disharmony between the water and fire elements as they contribute to the balanced relationship between fear, intimacy, and the appropriate setting of boundaries. Lack of functional connection between the heart protector and kidney official can be diagnosed if the left proximal pulse associated with the kidney is excessive as compared with the right proximal pulse associated with the heart protector. This condition corresponds to the presence of an exit/entry block between the two officials that can be treated according to E/E protocol with Ki-22 and HP-1.[3] However, this same dynamic can also be treated using HP-3 as a secondary tonification point to draw the relative excess from water to the heart protector across the *ke* cycle.

If the presence of water within the heart protector is deficient, the heart protector's fire tends to rage out of control. As a reaction to perceived betrayal, our hearts may be too open and expansive as we try to ease our pain and heartache by habitually loving. Conversely, our heart protector can close in reaction to pain. In this scenario, repressed feelings in the heart can generate heat and lead to excessive fire. Such excessive fire tends over time to consume fluids, leading to a *yin*-deficient condition in the heart protector. Such deficient fire is often expressed as nervousness, anxiety, and impulsiveness relative to intimacy. "Crooked marsh" can help reestablish the healthy control of water over fire across the *ke* cycle. In this way fire's tendency toward expansiveness can be mitigated as heat and pressure within the heart is cooled and dissipated.

If the presence of water within fire is excessive, our capacity to experience the joy of intimate connection may be limited by our fears. Hence fear can habitually rain on the heart's parade and result in a chronic lack of connection and joylessness. People often project past pain onto their present relationship. They interpret feelings of fear regarding intimacy as a sign that they are not safe in the moment. In reality, fear can occur whenever a person is reaching a new stage of intimacy and signal the opportunity for pursuing a deeper connection with the loved one. Hence sedating HP-3 can limit the excessive control of water, thus allowing the fire of the heart protector to express itself in a way that is not limited dysfunctionally by fear.

---

## ❖ HP-4 Cleft Gate

*Xi*[1]*men*[2] Cleft Gate 郄門

FUNCTION

*Xi*-cleft point

VIRTUE

Moves old pain and bitterness trapped in the heart.

As a *xi*-cleft point, HP-4 clears stagnation resulting from past heartbreaks and betrayals. Reaction to such experiences tends to obstruct the spontaneous opening and closing of the heart protector's gate in regulating human boundary and intimacy. Hence relationships are entered into in our vain attempt to satisfy the habitual desires of our minds rather than nourishing the instincts and intentions of the heart. This point can help resolve the belief that relationships are either the cause of, or answer to, our suffering.

"Cleft gate" is also an important point for harmonizing the function of the diaphragm and moving the stagnation that results during painful separations such as divorce. In the process of individuating from a mate, a person is forced to repress the tender feelings felt for the other. These tender feelings emanate from the heart in the upper burner and sit on top of the feelings of anger generated by the liver in the middle burner. It is the opposing forces of the tender feelings being shoved down and the anger rising that cause the stagnation of *qi* and heat halfway between the middle and upper burner in the diaphragm.[4,5] After experiencing such a separation, the heart protector can hold on dysfunctionally to the pain of the heartbreak by generating the belief that intimacy is not safe. HP-4 can help move this stagnation and empower us to let go of our attachment to past betrayals so we may once again experience intimacy with ourselves and with others.

---

## ❖ HP-5 The Intermediary

*Jian*[1]*shi*[2] The Intermediary 間使
*Gui*[3]*lu*[4] Ghost Road 鬼路

FUNCTIONS

1. Metal point
2. Secondary sedation point
3. Meeting point of the heart, heart protector, and lung officials
4. Ghost point

VIRTUES

1. Cools grief stemming from lost love and betrayal.
2. Empowers the heart protector to let go.
3. Empowers the virtues of metal within the heart protector official.

The heart protector official is the intermediary between the inner sanctum of the heart and the outside world. Like CV-17, HP-5 is a meeting point acting as an intermediary between the lung, heart protector, and heart officials. Hence HP-5 joins the functions of the lungs and the heart protector both as a meeting point and as the metal point on the heart protector channel. As the channel's metal point, HP-5 balances the expression of the metal element within the functioning of the heart protector official. The image of metal within fire represents the alchemical transformation whereby lead, mundane consciousness and attachment to the world, is turned into gold, or open, nonattached awareness. In health, metal empowers us to receive and let go with our hearts in life as effortlessly as we breathe. If the presence of metal within fire is unbalanced, grief and longing can color the quality of our relationships as we habitually hold on to, or shut ourselves off from, intimate connection.

If the presence of metal within fire is deficient, we may have a hard time attracting quality relationships or holding on to those precious relationships that our hearts value. Grief stemming from metal may combine with the sadness of the fire element to manifest as longing for love lost or unattained. Without the openness and receptivity engendered by metal, the heart protector can have a difficult time connecting to essence in both self and in others. In this case relationships tend to be chosen for their emotional appeal rather than for their essential value to us.

If metal within fire is excessive, grief and longing can oppress the fire of the heart protector as clouds obscure the sun. The dysfunctional tendency of metal to hold on to what has lost its value can compel the heart protector to cling to intimate relationships that have lost their value to us. Or the dysfunctional influence of metal within fire can cause the heart protector to shut the iron door on all new relationships because of past pain. Perfectionism born of self-righteousness engendered within the heart by a dysfunctional metal element can lead to our finding flaws in any new relationship and result in separation and lack of intimate connection.

The heart protector, via the effortless opening and closing of its inner frontier gate, must "breathe." It is this breath that empowers the heart's need for connection in the world to be fulfilled. If dysfunctional metal does not allow the heart protector to let go of attachments and desires associated with past loves, the capacity for intimate connection can be constrained. In this case excessive heat and pressure stagnate within the heart protector as the mind attempts to control the opening and closing of boundaries in intimate relationships. As the channel's secondary sedation point, HP-5 can cool the heart's fire by sedating the heart protector. Grief over love lost or longed for is often congruent with resignation and the manifestation of the cotton ("sad") quality on the pulse. "The intermediary" is useful for moving such resignation and can play an important role in resolving the cotton pulse and its attendant *weiqi* stagnation.[6]

Metal is associated with the *po* spirit that presides over peristalsis and our ability to attract quality into our lives. If metal is dysfunctional, we tend to hold on to or let go of what we value inappropriately. An alternate name of HP-5 is *guilu* (鬼路), or "ghost path," suggesting its efficacy for treating possession. The metal point on the heart channel is *lingdao,* or "spirit path." This name refers to the road leading to the imperial mausoleums where emperors are buried. As opposed to the virtuous spirit of the emperor, the ghost alluded to in the name of HP-5 is a malevolent spirit, or *gui.*[7] The character *po* (魄) consists of the character *gui* (鬼) plus the character *bai* (白) for white, the color associated with the metal element. If the expression of the *po* is unbalanced, we may be possessed by our urges, longings, and desires. Such unconscious urges tend to be expressed through the heart protector as lust. The heart protector can also be possessed by the ghosts of lost loves as we never seem to be able to leave the past behind and be fully present in our current relationship. As the metal point within heart protector, HP-5 can empower us to let go of past loves that haunt us and resolve the heart's longing.

## Lea

***Age:*** *32*
***Diagnosis:*** *Earth, fire within.*
***Complaint:*** *Fibromyalgia*

Lea was a vivacious, extremely funny, and neurotic woman whose main complaint was fatigue and burning in her muscles. One hundred and thirty pounds overweight, Lea had long since let herself go. Despite her pain and exhaustion, Lea always found the time to make a joke or laugh at one and evidenced a wonderful humor about herself and her condition despite its difficulty. She felt trapped in a loveless marriage and each week reported, either furiously or laughing, or both, the horrific fights she was having daily with her husband. Lea exhibited obsessive and compulsive tendencies to the degree that, when food shopping, it could take her half an hour just to determine which container of milk to buy.

Lea's intake was punctuated with one fantastic story after another. These ranged from partial memories of seeing dead bodies buried behind her uncle's house when she was a girl to stories of how her neighbor constantly spied on her. All such stories were quite vague and never left me convinced of their actual occurrence.

Lea's tongue evidenced a red color, yellow coating, teeth marks, and a red tip. Her pulse was tense, pounding, slippery, and hesitant in all positions. Her color was yellow, and the sound in her voice clearly had a singing quality. The laughing sound and red color were prominent whenever her humor manifested, which was frequently.

*Interpretation*

Lea's CSOE were all congruent with the earth constitutional type, and her constant laughter suggested the presence of fire as the element within. Lea seemed to me to be a woman with a tremendous appetite for life that burned unexpressed within her heart. Unable to manifest her desires in an intimate relationship, these were projected onto food as her size increased as a protective mechanism to keep her husband at bay. No amount of displaced consumption can satisfy the heart's desire for love. Hence her heart fire raged dysfunctionally within her muscles as her earthly appetites fueled her fire, and her fire in turn burned her earth in a self-perpetuating cycle of imbalance.

Integration is a virtue of the earth element, and Lea's stories all represented unintegrated aspects of her life experience. Like undigested and stagnant food that weighed her down, each story burdened Lea and made it difficult for her to move on in life and attend to the present. Lea's tongue and pulse both suggested the presence of stagnant *qi,* damp, and heat systemically. The red tip to her tongue suggested heat trapped in her heart and the presence of unfulfilled desires. The hesitant quality on her pulse suggested the dominance of worry and obsession, both dysfunctional emotions associated with the earth element.

*Treatment*

I treated Lea weekly for two years during which time her symptoms of fatigue and muscle pain disappeared completely. Treatment focused on establishing functional harmony between the fire and earth elements. On one particular session Lea asserted that, although she felt much better physically, she could not bring herself to let go of her dysfunctional relationship with her husband. In their most recent fight he had ripped all the phones off the walls and thrown one of them through the living room window. She also complained of tightness in her chest while relating this story and pointed to CV-17. For her treatment I selected Lu-8 in combination with HP-5 as the transmitting and receiving points for metal. I also treated CV-17, "primordial child," as a meeting point and for its spirit of healing the child's heart within us.

***Result***

Lea returned for her next treatment one week later smiling and laughing as usual. When queried about how she was doing, she exclaimed, "I don't know what points you treated last week, but after leaving your office, I went food shopping. I ran into Jim, the man I dated in ninth grade, for the first time since high school. I've filed for divorce and Jim and I are getting married." Lea and Jim are still happily married and very much in love fifteen years later. Her symptoms of fatigue and muscle pain never returned.

---

### ❖ HP-6 Inner Frontier Gate
*Nei⁴guan¹* Inner Frontier Gate 內關

FUNCTIONS

1. *Luo* point
2. Master point of the *yin* linking vessel
3. Coupled point of the penetrating vessel

VIRTUE

Empowers the heart protector to regulate boundaries to the inner frontier of the heart according to the principle of *wuwei.*

The function of the heart protector official can be likened to that of a drawbridge providing access both into, and out of, the forbidden city of the heart. In reaction to past pain, the heart protector may close to protect the heart. Although this may protect the acquired self from the pain of intimacy, it also tends to trap old pain within the heart that may accrue physiologically as stagnation and heat. As the channel's *luo* point, HP-6 may help vent such stagnation to the outside and, in effect, oil the "inner frontier gate" so it may open and close in a way not constrained by our habitual reaction to past pain. In this way we may cease projecting old pain onto our present relationships.

As the gate to our inner frontier, HP-6 helps direct conscious awareness into the depths of the heart. "Inner frontier gate" excels at calming a restless heart and quieting a mind confused by issues of intimacy and its betrayal as occurs in rape, incest, or divorce. This is a particularly effective point for opening up the area around the xiphoid process that contains CV-14 and CV-15, the *mu* points of the heart and heart protector, respectively. This is the region where we tend to feel as though we have been shot or stabbed when experiencing perceived betrayal or a painful separation. "Inner frontier gate" is appropriate for someone who is "eating his heart out" over a relationship or when affairs of the heart are constraining his ability to receive nourishment. In this regard, note that the Chinese character *ai* (愛), meaning "love," literally means "to swallow one's heart."[8]

Note also that the area around the xiphoid is congruent with the kidney meridian entering the upper *jiao* and the domain of the spirit burial ground. Hence the "inner frontier gate" referred to in the point name has a direct relationship with Ki-20, Ki-21, and Ki-22, the points that embody our journey into our own hearts. When our inner journey is constrained by fear, the emotion of the water element, the compassion, connection, warmth, and light empowered by the heart protector's fire can empower us to proceed onward.

---

| ❖ **HP-7** | **Great Mound** | |
|---|---|---|
| *Da⁴ling²* | Great Mound | 大陵 |
| *Zhu³xin¹* | Heart Master | 主心 |
| *Gui³xin¹* | Ghost Heart | 鬼心 |

FUNCTIONS

1. Earth point
2. Sedation point
3. Ghost point

VIRTUES

1. Empowers the heart protector to be nourished through intimate connection.
2. Helps quiet a hungry heart.

As the earth point on the heart protector meridian, the name "great mound" evokes the imagery of the imperial mausoleums as giant mounds of earth. The character *ling* (陵), meaning "mound," is a homophone for the character *ling* (靈), referring to the spiritual potency of the emperor that empowers him to perform ritual effectively. As a source point, "great mound" can help nourish and revive a heart buried under life's sorrows. As the channel's earth point, HP-7 can help empower the virtues of integrity, center, and groundedness within the heart protector official.

Earth serves as the foundation on which we can build a fire. If the presence of earth within the heart protector is deficient, our pursuit of relationship may be both ungrounded and unfulfilling. Without a center that defines integrity within relationship, the heart protector tends to be driven only by vain desire. Relationships that only feed the ego can never fulfill or nurture the heart. In time, the starved heart tends to become weak and weary as it lies buried under a mound of acquired sorrow and pain.

As an earth point, HP-7 can address the functional relationship between the spleen and heart protector's relationship to healthy blood. Hence HP-7 can allow us to choose intimacy from a position of strength by fostering the virtues of earth within fire to create healthy blood and nourish the heart protector. "Great mound" is ideal for a person who has been left exhausted and unnourished by intimate relationships.

If the presence of earth within fire is excessive, our hearts may always be hungry for intimacy. The habituated mind can become addicted to the pursuit of earthly pleasures and desires. To the degree the heart protector functions habitually, we will never be nourished regardless of the amount of stimulation received or sexual intimacy experienced. As the channel's sedation point, HP-7 can still the appetites of the heart protector that are driven solely by the mind and allow us to connect to deeper sources of nourishment with our heart spirit.

An alternative name for HP-7 is *guixin,* "ghost heart," identifying it as one of Sun Simiao's points for treating possession. HP-7 as the "ghost heart" can be indicated for one who is possessed and exhausted by lust. As we are less driven by desire and more nourished, our heart is restored to its rightful place as master, a function alluded to in the name *xinzhu,* or "heart master."

---

## ❖ HP-8 Palace of Weariness

| | | |
|---|---|---|
| *Lao²gong¹* | Palace of Weariness | 勞宮 |
| *Gui³lu⁴* | Ghost Road | 鬼路 |
| *Wu³li³* | Five Miles | 五里 |
| *Zhang³zhong¹* | Palm Center | 掌中 |

FUNCTIONS

1. Fire point
2. Horary point; 7 P.M.–9 P.M., summer solstice
3. Ghost point

VIRTUES

1. Serves as transmitting point for all virtues of the heart protector official.
2. Resurrects a heart unfulfilled and weary from loving.
3. Quiets mania and addiction to joy.

The character *lao* (勞) depicts lamps (火火) in a room (冖) where one continues to work (力) at night. This signifies the extraordinary vigilance exercised by the heart protector in protecting the heart whose presence is indicated by the character *gong* (宮), meaning "palace." As the channel's horary point, HP-8 can provide strong tonification or sedation to the heart protector, particularly when treated between 7 and 9 P.M. on the summer solstice. As the channel's transmitting point, HP-8 can empower the heart protector's virtues of openness, warmth, and safety within any other *yin* official when its fire point is needled simultaneously.

Deficiency of the heart protector's fire can impact the functioning of all the officials as a lack of joy and warmth becomes pervasive. The heart can become so weary from the pain of past heartbreaks that no strength or conviction can be gathered to engage in intimate relationships. As the channel's horary point, "palace of weariness" can rekindle the fires of the heart protector and empower the experience of joy and safety within the context of intimacy. HP-8 can induce a state of bliss within the heart that helps us transcend past pain, empowering us to regain the courage to love again.

If the heart protector's fire is excessive, we can be compelled to look to intimacy, sex, and love as the resolution of our pain in life. However, relationships entered dysfunctionally in this way are rarely fulfilling, especially if we cannot transcend the fire of initial attraction to connect at a deeper more spiritual level in a relationship. If the desire of the heart protector pours too much heat into the blood, we may be run by lust and exhibit behaviors that tend toward mania and an addiction to bliss. In this case, "palace of weariness" can be used to sedate the heart protector's fire to quiet and cool the heart.

---

| ❖ **HP-9** | **Rushing into the Middle** | |
|---|---|---|
| *Zhong*[1]*chong*[1] | Rushing into the Middle | 中沖 |
| *Zhong*[1]*chong*[1] | Central Thoroughfare | 中衝 |

FUNCTIONS

1. Wood point
2. Tonification point

VIRTUES

1. Empowers vision and self-esteem within the context of relationships.
2. Directs the mind toward the heart.

The name of HP-9 suggests the image of *qi* rushing into the center of the heart. The heart protector must have full access to the vision and discernment of the wood element if intimacy is to be regulated adequately. By harmonizing the influence of wood within fire, HP-9 can direct the mind inward toward the heart and help quiet the mind so it ceases to agitate the heart.

If the influence of wood within the heart protector is deficient, we can feel lost in relationship to intimacy. Rational data from the mind tends to be neglected as we attempt to "intuitively" follow the heart's desires. Without looking to see who is actually coming across the heart protector's drawbridge, relationships are dictated only by our vain desires. In this case we tend dysfunctionally to allows others into the inner realm of our hearts who should not be there. Failing to draw on the perspective of the wood element, we may become entangled in dysfunctional relationships that do not create a context of healthy intimacy in which the heart can function safely. Hence relationships that should nourish the heart tend to become sources of sorrow because of lack of intimacy.

If the presence of wood is not strong enough to sustain the heart protector's fire, the heart protector may not have enough *qi* to engage in relationship at all. In this case the patient's sorrow results from a lack of any intimate contact with self and others. As the channel's wood point, "rushing into the middle" can help integrate the virtues of discernment and self-esteem as associated with the wood element, with the heart's capacity for intuition. As the channel's tonification point, HP-9 can help feed the heart protector's fire and enable it to sustain an intimate relationship or reinvigorate a heart protector that is burned out from heartbreak.

If the presence of wood within fire is excessive, we can tend to engage in relationships from a mental level without any desire for intimacy. Such contact can be aggressive in nature as the mind attempts to express its unresolved anger through sexuality. In this case we can habitually crave the initial excitement of sexuality in a new relationship to the exclusion of ever journeying to a depth of spiritual intimacy. This dynamic can present as sexual addiction as the drive of the liver overwhelms the heart protector's capacity for trust, tenderness, and intimacy. In this case the name "rushing into the middle" can suggest a preoccupation with sexuality to the exclusion of intimacy. Efforts to "follow our hearts" may just be based on the attainment of momentary excitement. The wood element's tendency toward creativity and branching out can lead us into a series of successive relationships that overstimulate the heart as we become exhausted pursuing our passions. Sedation of HP-9 can reduce the influence of wood within fire, helping quell the mind's desires so the heart and heart protector can love more openly and with less of a sense of urgency and constraint. In this way we may connect more deeply with the hearts of our loved ones rather than just with the idea of relationship itself.

### *Exercise*

The theme of one point initiating a virtue and the following point empowering its manifestation occurs regularly.

a. In this regard, compare the functions of HP-1 with HP-2, Ki-1 with Ki-2, and GV-10 with GV-11.

b. Identify at least two other sequential points on any meridian that evidence this quality of relationship.

c. What are the therapeutic implications of this type of relationship between two points relative to treatment planning?

d. Discuss the difference between having a spiritual experience and choosing to live that experience as expressed through words and deeds.

e. Are spiritual experiences, regardless of how profound they might be, enough to guarantee meaningful change in a person's life?

## *NOTES*

1. *ND,* pp. 309–331.
2. Worsley, 1982, p. 113.
3. See Chapter 5 for a discussion of exit/entry blocks.
4. See Jarrett, 1995a, 1995b, and 1995c.
5. See a further description of this dynamic in terms of the E/E block between liver and lung in Chapter 5.
6. For more on the cotton quality, see Hammer, 2001.
7. See Chapter 3 on possession.
8. Weiger, 1965, p. 243.

# 29

# THREE HEATER

The three heater channel begins superficially at the ulna nail point of the fourth finger. It runs along the posterior surface of the hand, wrist, and forearm to the elbow at TH-10. It continues up the posterior surface of the arm to TH-14, located in the depression that is inferior to the acromion. From here the channel turns medially over the dorsal part of the shoulder to TH-15. An internal branch leaves from TH-14 and travels to SI-12 to reunite with the main channel again at TH-15. The entire channel then moves internally to cross Gb-21 on its way to meet St-12 in the supraclavicular fossa. From here it moves medially and descends to CV-17, where it connects with the heart protector. It then continues down the median line, through the diaphragm to the area of the middle *jiao* at CV-12 and continues on to the lower *jiao* at CV-7.

From CV-17, another internal branch ascends back to St-12 and travels posteriorly to join GV-14. The pathway then returns to the shoulder where it reemerges superficially just inferior to TH-16. From here the channel travels to TH-17 at the mastoid process and outlines the rear of the ear until it reaches its apex at TH-20. Once again the channel travels internally to pass through Gb-5, Gb-4, and Gb-14, to descend to Bl-1 at the inner canthus of the eye. It then travels down the side of the nose to turn onto the cheek and end at SI-18.

An internal branch leaves TH-17 to enter the auditory canal and becomes superficial again at SI-19. From here the channel travels through TH-21 to TH-22, the channel's exit point, and then onward to its final point, TH-23, at the lateral edge of the eyebrow. From here the channel travels internally again to descend and connect with the entry point of the gallbladder meridian at Gb-1.

---

## *Thoughts on the Channel*

Whereas the heart protector channel travels along the inner surface of the arms to empower the warmth of an embrace, the three heater channel runs along the outer surface of the arms and is exposed when we are closed or take on a defensive posture. These anatomical relationships embody the relative functions of these officials in empowering intimate and social connections, respectively.

### MAIN FUNCTIONS

1. Maintains homeostasis by promoting communication among all aspects of being.
2. Promotes communication with our environment.
3. Empowers the protective functions of defensive *qi (weiqi).*
4. Regulates social relationships.

### DISTAL POINT FUNCTIONS

*Water:* Controls the expression of fire to help maintain homeostasis.

*Wood:* Serves as fuel for fire, empowering vision to the outer limit of our boundary.

*Fire:* Empowers the essential qualities of fire within the three heater official.

*Earth:* Empowers the earth's virtues of center, stability, integrity, and nurturance within fire.

*Metal:* Helps maintain the balance of metal and fire as they delimit our boundary in life.

*Xi-cleft:* Moves stagnant heat that obscures appropriate relationship to the environment.

*Luo:* Vents heat and stagnation to the exterior that hamper the three heater's ability to read external cues and maintain homeostasis.

## ❖ TH-1 Rushing the Frontier Gate

| | | |
|---|---|---|
| *Guan[1]chong[1]* | Rushing the Frontier Gate | 關沖 |
| *Guan[1]chong[1]* | Rushing the Frontier Gate | 關衝 |

FUNCTIONS

1. Metal point
2. Entry point

VIRTUES

1. Harmonizes the relationship between metal and fire as they constitute *weiqi.*
2. Addresses the balance of inspiration and joy as they govern social contact.

"Rushing the frontier gate" addresses the functional relationship between the metal and fire elements as they empower the balanced functioning of *weiqi. Weiqi* defines an external boundary that constitutes the most subtle edge at which we contact the world around us and thus plays an important role as the first line of our defense and immunity. The fire element expands to define a perimeter around us that constitutes our outermost border. This perimeter defines the farthest extent to which our spirit, light, and warmth can extend itself into the world. On the one hand, this fire can be extended to subtly touch, and receive touch, from others. On the other hand, this fire can be thought of as a boundary that incinerates any noxious influence before it has the opportunity to touch us in a harmful way.

With each inhalation, the lungs assimilate that aspect of *qi* trapped by air as sunlight (heavenly *yang*) and reject all that has no value in sustaining life. The lungs thus construct a barrier between our inner and outer world in a way that defines what is self and not-self. The protective boundary established by fire is an expansive force, and its outer limit, as conveyed by the triple heater official, represents the outermost level that our consciousness can extend. The boundary established by the lungs is a contractive force that represents the outermost limit of where we are able to draw quality into our lives. I think of this limit as the edge of our force of "gravitational pull," that, along with the boundary created by fire, defines where we end and the outer world begins.

If the presence of metal within the three heater is deficient, the unbalanced expression of our outermost fire can lead us to touch and be touched in ways that are not selective. Social contact can occur in a way not grounded in the virtue of self-worth as inspired by the metal element. On the one hand, we may let others in to touch us whose essence is not congruent with our own inner purpose. On the other hand, we can fail to receive inspiration from our connections in the world as all joy from social contact is filtered out before it reaches the heart. In this case we can feel uninspired, never to be drawn out of our shells to venture into the outer frontier of relationship. Eventually sorrow and loneliness, emotions associated with the fire and metal elements, respectively, will tend to predominate our inner landscape. If our *qi* is not sufficient to establish an external boundary, we can fall prey to pathogenic factors whether they be viruses, bacteria, or the desires of others that are not congruent with our own needs or purpose. In these circumstances, "rushing the frontier gate" can empower us to extend ourselves past the boundary of our flesh and out into the world in an expansive, inspired, and protected way.

If the presence of metal within the three heater is excessive, we can tend to feel overly exposed as our inspiration compels us too quickly into the outer frontier of connection and relationship. The spirit of the lungs has been likened to that of a spirited horse and, if the influence of metal is excessive, we can feel compelled to rush the frontier gate like a wild horse that has escaped the corral. This dynamic is present in an individual who feels exposed after inappropriately revealing too much of himself early in a relationship. The effect of metal as a *yin* element is to quiet and cool excessive fire. By diminishing the influence of metal within fire, TH-1 can allow relationship to proceed according to the inherent quality of any given connection rather than merely being fueled by inspiration born of the love of relationship itself.

Rushing unprotected into the outer frontier, we can easily fall prey to external pathogenic factors. A function of TH-1 as the channel's *jing*-well point is to dispel wind and heat and help stimulate the release of latent pathogens. As the channel's metal point, this function can be thought of as empowering the metal element's virtue of letting go of what no longer serves within the fire element.

*Qi* flows from HP-9, the channel's exit point, to TH-1, the entry point of the three heater meridian. Note that as the last point on the heart protector channel HP-9, "rushing into the middle," directs *qi* toward the inner frontier of the heart. In contrast, TH-1, as the first point on a *yang* official, directs *qi* toward the exterior and the outer frontier. It is also interesting to compare the function of TH-1 with TH-23, the channel's last point. "Silk bamboo hollow" (TH-23) functions to return the three heater's fire from the outermost frontier back to its origin in the depth of the heart.

---

❖ **TH-2** **Fluid Secretion Gate**

| | | |
|---|---|---|
| *Ye⁴men²* | Fluid Secretion Gate | 液門 |
| *Ye⁴men²* | Armpit Gate | 腋門 |
| *Ye⁴men²* | Armpit Gate | 掖門 |

FUNCTION

Water point

VIRTUES

1. Moistens mucous membranes. Lubricates and cools the surface where we make intimate contact with others.
2. Mediates balance of water in the three burning spaces.

Maintaining the equilibrium of water and fire is an important role of the three heater official as it regulates the body's thermostatic mechanisms. As the channel's water point, "fluid secretion gate" regulates the presence of water within fire as it contributes to the balanced function of the three heater. As the name of the point implies, TH-2 controls fluid secretions and may be indicated when there is an excess or deficiency of fluid in any aspect of being. The name "armpit gate" evokes the image of the armpits as gates from which sweat (a fluid secretion) flows.

This is an important point to consider when there is an uneven distribution of warmth such as when the hands and feet are either too warm or too cold. Similarly, TH-2 can be indicated when a person runs either too hot or too cold emotionally or fluctuates between these extremes. The three heater as the body's thermostat is located in every aspect of being and does not have a centralized location. However, inasmuch as the official is thought to correspond to kidney *yang*, it can be considered to address issues involving the balance of water and fire stemming from the lower *jiao*. As the channel's water point, TH-2 can balance the expression of warmth (fire) and cold (water) in the lower *jiao* as they impact sexual function and intimacy. Yet, because the three heater also contributes to the function of *weiqi* and the establishment of boundaries at our periphery, TH-2 can also harmonize imbalances of external fire as they govern social contact. Hence this one point can address the balance of water and fire across a broad continuum of human contact and connection.

If the presence of water within the three heater is deficient, fire tends to expand out of control. Water within fire may be deficient for one of two reasons. In the case of *yin* deficiency, water is deficient of its own accord and fails to temper the fire of the three heater across the *ke* cycle. For lack of control by water, the three heater's fire in turn tends to consume more *yin* and exacerbate the initial condition of *yin* deficiency. However, the three heater itself can exhibit a pattern of stagnation and excess that consumes *yin*. Here the *yin* deficiency is secondary to the primary instability that led to the original excess in the three heater official. In either case, TH-2 can temper fire in any aspect of being by helping increase the functional presence and flow of cool, clear water.

Fire not effectively mediated by the presence of water will tend to consume fluid, with dryness and inflammation as the result. Often such inflammation occurs in mucous membranes as typifies such conditions as chronic hoarseness, vaginal dryness, dry eyes, or interstitial cystitis. These conditions are often characterized by anxiety and dryness. Here social contact is driven dysfunctionally by an overactive mind and nervous system that consumes *yin* gradually. As *yin* is consumed, the mind grows increasingly agitated and leads to conditions such as insomnia, anxiety, tinnitus, and hot flushes. Concentration may be difficult as the mind wanders expansively away from present situations toward the outer frontiers of fantasy. When deficient, water fails to still the mind so relationship can proceed from the depths of self. With fire raging, connection is often made for connection's sake alone. By increasing the presence of water within the three heater, "fluid secretion gate" can resolve dryness and temper the excessive expression of the three heater's fire.

Sexual contact and intimacy depends on the proper balance of water and fire. Fire provides the passion and warmth of the connection, and moisture allows for actual physical intimacy to occur as the essence of two lovers commingle. During intercourse, physical connection at the surface of the flesh is a relatively outer level of contact that is presided over by the three heater. Dryness of the vaginal mucosa can limit sexual contact and intimacy as the physical connection fails to penetrate to the interior to reach the heart/kidney axis. Further, if the sexual encounter is presided over by the three heater's external projection of expectations born of fantasy, and not the heart/kidney connection, the three heater's fire may lead to a state of internal dryness that mirrors the quality of lack of intimacy inherent in the encounter.

"Fluid secretion gate" can help address the fear as well as the mind's expectations and fantasies that limits sexual intimacy and help lubricate mucous membranes, allowing for a deeper level of sexual and intimate connection. When the presence of fire is excessive, social contact can tend to burn those we encounter as we cross their boundaries without their consent. In this case, "fluid secretion gate" can help moderate and soothe the contact we make with others at our periphery so it proceeds in a more graceful way as presided over by the water element. This dynamic can also be addressed by TH-6, "flying tiger," the fire point on the three heater channel.

The expansive nature of the three heater's fire can also overheat water in a way that results in stagnation of damp and heat in any of the three burning spaces. This is congruent with symptoms of stagnation and excess that typify conditions such as chronic bladder infections, conjunctivitis, or malaria. Malarial diseases of a *shaoyang* nature are characterized by excessive sweating and shivering and indicate instability of the three heater in regulating thermostatic mechanisms.[1] In time, excess heat will consume fluid in a way that will lead to a concurrent state of *yin* deficiency. By generating healthy *yin,* "fluid secretion gate" can help the three heater promote the movement of stagnant fluids and diminish the presence of excessive heat throughout our being.

If the presence of water in the three heater is excessive, it can inhibit the expression of the official's fire. Such stagnation of water can present as edema, dampness, and cold in any of the three burning spaces. When excessive fluid in the ears leads to tinnitus, the sound heard by the patient is often characterized by a whooshing sound similar to the flowing of water or the sea. Difficulty in concentrating is characterized by feelings of being "swept away" by one's thoughts as though the tides of the mind are not under centralized control. When our skin is physically burned, fluid is generated at the site of the trauma that serves to moisten and cool the damaged tissue. Similarly, when we are burned in relationship fear, the emotion of the water element can arise to limit future contact and protect us from further pain. If fear stagnates to become habitual, we may have no fire available for social connection. "Fluid secretion gate" can promote the movement of stagnant water so it does not overwhelm the healthy presence of the three heater's fire.

---

### ❖ TH-3 **Middle Islet**
*Zhong[1]zhu[3]* Middle Islet 中渚

FUNCTIONS
1. Wood point
2. Tonification point

VIRTUE
Empowers vision toward the horizon.

As our thermostat, the three heater plays a unique role in maintaining homeostasis throughout diverse aspects of being. Therefore imbalances involving this official tend to manifest globally. Conversely, when many officials are evidencing distress and chaos seems to be pervasive, the three heater official is often indicated for treatment. As wood empowers the virtues of birth, growth, and hope, "middle islet" can help engender the birth of getting well by strengthening the connection of wood to fire. The three heater meridian terminates by the ears (TH-22) and the eyes (TH-23), both important sensory orifices for empowering accurate perception of reality. As the channel's wood point, TH-3 has a particularly strong effect in stimulating mental function and opening the sensory orifices to sharpen their acuity. "Middle islet" can empower the virtues of vision and clarity regarding our horizons in life. These virtues help us to recruit data from our periphery to inform all internal processes so homeostasis is maintained and we are able to live in relative harmony with our environment.

If the presence of wood within fire is deficient, fire itself tends to be deficient throughout our being. Conditions such as glaucoma, cataracts, or tinnitus can suggest a dulling of the senses associated with this condition. A patient can give the overall impression of being nearsighted and disconnected from his surroundings, having no clear picture of the overall context of his life. Poor coordination, balance, or frequently injuring ourselves can also indicate we are "out of touch" with the world around us. Socially, a person may tend to misread cues relative to the nature of his relationships and regularly mistake the degree of openness appropriate to any given interaction. "Middle islet" may empower vision within the three heater in a way that helps us better make the momentary discernments necessary to exist functionally in the world.

If the presence of wood is excessive, the three heater's fire will tend to generate too much heat and speed up metabolic processes. As heat rises, such excess can lead to inflammatory conditions affecting the eyes and ears. This may also present as glaucoma or tinnitus as increased heat generates internal pressure. In this scenario, the mind is constantly vigilant regarding external details in the periphery and often fails to notice important details closer at hand. Such an imbalance can lead people to be excessively social but miss the nuances of personal expression that transcend superficial chatter. "Middle islet" can diminish the presence of wood within fire to decrease the fuel supply and thus temper the function of the three heater.

---

## ❖ TH-4 ***Yang* Pond**

*Yang²chi²* *Yang* Pond 陽池
*Bie²yang²* Separate *Yang* 別陽

FUNCTION

Source point

VIRTUES

1. Refreshes the three heater with a clear source of *yangqi*.
2. Plays a vital role in regulating thermostatic mechanisms in all aspects of being.

The point's name alludes to the depression between the ulna and carpal bones in which the point is located as a pond. The three heater is the body's thermostat and it performs its function of maintaining homeostasis by regulating the relative balance of fire and water, hot and cold, and *yin* and *yang* in all aspects of being. Hence a "pond" (water) of *yang* (fire) is a fitting image for the source point associated with this fire official. The *yang* "pooling" at this source point is derived and, in a sense, "separated" from *mingmen,* possibly explaining the point's alternate name.

Traditional functions ascribed to this point are relieving heat and moistening dryness, suggesting the three heater's ability to balance the relationship between water and fire. As the source point on the three heater, "*yang* pond" plays an important role in helping this official maintain appropriate temperatures and rate of metabolic function in all aspects of being.

The three heater and fire element govern not only our outermost border as defined by *weiqi* but also the extension of our physical touch into the world. The wrist, as the demarcation between the arm and hand, mediates the extent of both our reach and grasp. Of the six points encircling the wrist (Ht-7, HP-7, Lu-9, LI-5, TH-4, SI-5), all but Lu-9 are either fire points or points located on a fire meridian. Pain and limited range of motion in the wrist can indicate dysfunction of boundaries and our ability to make contact in a healthy fashion. This dysfunction can also be embodied as a differential in warmth between the arm, wrist, and hands, all of which may be noted during pulse diagnosis. Hands that are too hot or too cold can indicate either an excessive need for contact or that emotional warmth has been withdrawn. In cases of excessive warmth, "*yang* pond" can help diminish the urgency of our need for physical connection with others so our fire can manifest in a way that is less clinging.[2] In cases of deficiency and cold, "*yang* pond" can supply a clear stream of *yangqi* to warm our hands and help us extend our hearts into the world in a more balanced way.

---

## ❖ TH-5 **Outer Frontier Gate**
*Wai[4]guan[1]* Outer Frontier Gate 外關

FUNCTIONS

1. *Luo* point
2. Master point of the *yang* linking channel
3. Coupled point of the governor vessel

VIRTUES

1. Vents heat to the exterior.
2. Harmonizes the interior and exterior.
3. Allows the mind to focus by harmonizing the exterior.
4. Helps regulate appropriate boundaries in social relationships.

The name "outer frontier gate" alludes to the three heater as similar in function to the Great Wall of China that protects the periphery of the nation by defining its outermost border. The function of a border pass is to allow for the active discernment of who may enter and leave the nation. Similarly, TH-5 regulates our external boundary and helps us make contact with beneficial influences in life while defending us from pathogenic influences, whether they be people or viruses. TH-5 addresses dysfunction in our boundaries along a continuum of imbalance ranging from an inability to journey up to or past our borders, to moderating our behavior when we are habitually driven toward inappropriately exposing ourselves in the outer frontier.

The "outer frontier gate" tends toward one of three dysfunctional states being either stuck open, stuck closed, or opening and closing in a seemingly random fashion that is not congruent with the nature of the specific connection at hand. If the three heater's gate is stuck closed, we tend to have trouble extending ourselves into the world, journeying to our horizons, or allowing others to enter our "country," so contact is only made in the most superficial of ways. For failing to have extended ourselves into the world to make meaningful connections, our emotional landscape can become bitter and frozen. In this case, "outer frontier gate" can empower us to come out of our shells and initiate social contact from our depths so the external warmth and *yang* received can be channeled to nourish our interiors.

If the three heater's gate is stuck open, however, we tend to be constantly exposed without selectivity to influences that can be harmful to us. This can manifest as embarrassment, feelings of shame, and generally compromised immunity. Here fire tends to be focused externally as a means of avoiding intimacy. Hence we may tend toward excessive chatter that never touches the heart of the matter or toward making too many social commitments as a means of avoiding intimacy with our mates. In this scenario TH-5 can help close our "outer frontier gate," allowing us to choose, rather than be compelled toward, connection.

Lastly, the "outer frontier gate" may swing open and shut in a seemingly random fashion. In this scenario a person tends to run hot and cold both physically and emotionally as the three heater's gate constantly opens and closes in reaction to the mind's habitual fears and desires. This can manifest as feelings of being exposed coupled with a lack of ability to make sustained connection, mood swings shifting between sorrow and joy, and extreme fluctuations in temperature as found in hot flashes or Raynaud's syndrome. In this circumstance, TH-5 can help mediate the function of the three heater's gate so it is less controlled by the mind's reactions and desires and relatively more congruent with promoting the balanced communication between interior and exterior necessary for the maintenance of homeostasis.

One virtue of the *luo* points on the *yang* meridians is that they are able to drain external pathogens. Hence TH-5, an outer official of the fire element, relives exterior and hot conditions. In this respect, TH-5 is like a valve that can vent internal pressure and relieve the entire continuum of function represented by the fire officials. Superficial heat that agitates the mind and compels us toward excessive need for contact with others can be dispersed through the regulatory mechanisms afforded by TH-5. By draining this heat TH-5 can allow us to focus more clearly on our horizons without being compelled by our minds to be ever vigilant at our borders. Thus we may see more clearly at our periphery in a way uncolored by the habitual desire for contact with others. In this way we may better rest in our hearts, and our minds may be better informed by our depths.

---

❖ **TH-6** **Flying Tiger**
*Fei[1]hu[3]* Flying Tiger 飛虎
*Zhi[1]gou[1]* Branch Ditch 支溝

FUNCTIONS

1. Fire point
2. Horary point; 9 P.M.–11 P.M., summer solstice

VIRTUES

1. Quells inappropriate contact.
2. Grounds rising *yang*.

The notion of a flying tiger conjures images of abundant strength and energy. We can only imagine how much inappropriate contact tigers could make if they could fly. The tiger is a *yin* animal, and its place is on the earth rather than in the heavens flying. The tendency of fire in excess is to expand and rise, and TH-6 can harmonize the balance of *yin* and *yang* and help bring excessive *yang* back down to earth. As the horary point, TH-6 can provide a strong stimulus or sedation to the three heater official, particularly on or near the summer solstice between the hours of 9 and 11 P.M. The alternate name for TH-6, "branch ditch," alludes to the three heater's function of regulating the flow of water in a way similar to the function of irrigation channels. Hence this point is implicated in helping regulate fluid metabolism when excess or deficient fire either consumes or fails to mobilize water.

Because the three heater controls our thermostat, any excess or deficient condition in the official can manifest globally or in any aspect of being. When the fire of the three heater fire is excessive, the body tends to be hot and metabolism proceeds at a too fast rate. Hence traditional functions ascribed to this point include quelling fevers and reducing excess heat. Typically such excess fire can be embodied in symptoms as diverse as constipation, cystitis, fibromyalgia, bronchitis, or fevers. I find "flying tiger" to be of great help in treating conditions such as poison ivy when the toxin is spreading through a patient's system like wildfire.

I also find TH-6 particularly useful in quelling fire in conditions such as malaria and dengue fever, which often present with excess heat in the *shaoyang* channels (gallbladder and three heater). Such conditions are typified by fevers followed by cold sweats. In psychospiritual realms, such fluctuations of the three heater often present in people who run hot and cold emotionally. In such cases people tend to exude a great deal of social fire that burns out quickly as relationships begin to require a deeper heartfelt connection. Such excess fire can be fun to be around socially, but it becomes overwhelming if contact is sustained. Over time such expansiveness can lead to hypertension, heart attack, and stroke as excessive fire causes damage to the circulatory system.

If the three heater's fire is deficient, we may be cold in any and all aspects of being as metabolic processes proceed too slowly. In such cases people tend to appear joyless as they are unable to sustain the fire of connection long enough to be warmed by it. Deficient fire can slow metabolism in any of the three heaters and produce symptoms as diverse as asthma (upper *jiao*), poor digestion and assimilation (middle *jiao*), and loose stools or frequent urination (lower *jiao*). Deficient fire is often accompanied by a corresponding excess of water embodied as swelling, edema, and cold arthritic conditions. As the channel's horary point, TH-6 can give a strong boost to the *yangqi* of the three heater official, helping provide warmth, mobilize stagnant water, and increase metabolism.

---

### ❖ **TH-7** **Assembly of Ancestors**
*Hui⁴zong¹* Assembly of Ancestors 會宗

FUNCTION

*Xi*-cleft point

VIRTUES

1. Moves stagnation in all three *jiao*.

2. Mediates the influence of ancestral wisdom as imprinted within *jing* and radiated by heaven's *shen.*

The three heater is an official of the fire element and thus is associated with the summer season. The meeting *(hui)* of the feudal princes (officials) at the summer court in ancient China was denoted by the character *zong,* which can be translated here as "official" or "ancestor."[3] The function of the three heater official is to unite and integrate the functions of all the other officials in the same way that a well-functioning thermostat maintains the internal environment so all processes function together harmoniously.

As the *xi*-cleft point associated with the three heater official, TH-7 helps move stagnation in all three burners and therefore can impact all the officials and their related functions. Stagnation of wind, cold, heat, and damp can be considered the physiological embodiment of the encrustation of the fires of *mingmen* by acquired experience. Hence TH-7 is an ideal point in helping burn off the accretions of mundane consciousness that obscure the influence of original nature. In this way the entire functional network of the officials and the meridian system is revitalized.

The three heater functions to maintain homeostasis by mediating the connection between everything that exists externally to us with everything that exists within us. Internally, the foundation of our life is laid through our genetic and karmic connection to ancestry. In part the three heater's function is to channel *jing,* the basis of our connection to ancestry, to inform every aspect of being. "Assembly of ancestors" can help clear away stagnation to realign us with the wisdom and virtue of our ancestors as it exists in our template and serves as our foundation for fulfilling destiny. Rooted internally to ancestral wisdom we may be better aligned with external circumstances in life as they convey the will of heaven. Hence TH-7 functions as a point of connection between heaven's will and radiance *(shen)* as it exists internally in our *jing* and as it arrives to us externally as sunlight *(shen).*

Our individual destiny is always an expression of the lineage supporting it both in terms of our own previous incarnations as well as our familial and ethnic heritage. In keeping with the three heater's function of governing social relationship, "assembly of ancestors" can be effective in treating issues regarding identification with one's genetic or ethnic lineage. In this way we may be placed in contact with the strengths associated with our heritage and experience a greater context of support and understanding to address our individual struggles in life. The point can also be useful when concepts of who we are based on the past limit our possibility in the present.

---

❖ **TH-8** **Three *Yang* Junction**

| | | |
|---|---|---|
| *San[1]yang[2]luo[4]* | Three *Yang* Junction | 三陽絡 |
| *Tong[1]jian[1]* | Connecting Interval | 通間 |
| *Tong[1]guan[1]* | Communication Pass | 通關 |
| *Tong[1]men[2]* | Communication Gate | 通門 |

FUNCTION

Meeting point of the small intestine, large intestine, three heater
*Note:* Forbidden to needle

VIRTUE

Helps mediate the functional relationship between assimilation and letting go as governed by the small and large intestine, respectively.

Uniting the three *yang* meridians of the arm, TH-8 helps regulate warmth and movement of *qi* to promote activity in these officials. The functions of the small intestine and large intestine are intimately tied together. Both officials sort pure from impure to aid in the assimilation of essence and the elimination of waste. Dysfunction in either official is likely to undermine the efficacy of the other. "Three *yang* junction" offers an opportunity to call on the three heater to help mediate the relationship between these two officials and to promote homeostasis.

Attaining harmony between the small intestine and large intestine can have wide-ranging effects in decreasing pain and increasing function of the arms and shoulders, which are traversed by the meridians of these officials. This point can be particularly effective when pain and dysfunction in the arms and shoulders is accompanied by either the presence of cold or heat and inflammation. The senses of smell, taste, vision, and hearing can benefit from this one point as the three channels it mediates terminate at the ears (TH-22, SI-19), nose (LI-20), and eyes (TH-23). As essence is more effectively assimilated and negativity is eliminated, a patient's interpretation of life tends to be relatively more congruent with reality. It is expected he will increasingly evidence the virtues of clarity and sincerity as his communications become less tainted by bitterness and disdain, pathological emotions associated with the small and large intestine, respectively.[4]

---

❖ **TH-9** **Four Rivers**

| | | |
|---|---|---|
| *Si[4]du[2]* | Four Rivers | 四瀆 |

VIRTUES

1. Helps regulate the flow of water in all aspects of being.
2. Moves stagnation that obscures hearing.

The point's name refers to its efficacy of regulating the flow of water and helping harmonize excesses and deficiencies of water wherever they occur. The three heater can be conceived of as embodying the network of channels dug by Emperor Yu when he harmonized the waters of the great flood. By channeling the flooding waters to the sea, Yu restored balance and united ancient China.[5] Hence the three heater governs all the connections in our being that permit homeostasis to be maintained by allowing all aspects of being to be in communication with each other.

The "four rivers" empower water to cleanse us by carrying away impurities. As the three heater channel terminates by the ears at TH-22, "four rivers" is particularly effective in helping reduce the stagnation of water and impurities that accumulate within the ears. Moving such stagnation can restore hearing and thus promote a more balanced communication with others. In this way we may live in better harmony in the context of our social environment.

---

## ❖ TH-10 **Heavenly Well**
*Tian[1]jing[3]* Heavenly Well 天井

FUNCTIONS

1. Earth point
2. Sedation point

VIRTUE

Mediates the interpenetration of innate and acquired *jing* as our deepest resources.

Part of the three heater's function in maintaining homeostasis is to assure congruency between our internal needs as contained in inherited *jing* and the sources of nourishment we acquire *jing* from externally during life. The image of TH-10 as the "heavenly well" alludes to the three heater's function of mediating the distribution of innate and acquired *jing*, our deepest resources, throughout our entire being. As the channel's earth point, "heavenly well" provides access to a deep source of nourishment for any aspect of being that is undernourished. Whereas the function of Ki-24 can be likened to bringing water to someone who has been lost in the desert, the function of TH-10 may be likened to bringing that person a nourishing meal. "Heavenly well" excels at treating adults who were not adequately nourished as children and who feel separated from heaven's universal love and support.

If the presence of earth within fire is excessive, fire tends to be excessively fueled by appetite. Such a person can be said to have a "hungry heart" that never feels sated. This type of neediness is often congruent with the presence of damp/heat that hampers the digestive process as sources of potential nourishment are burned to become unpalatable. Neediness associated with the earth element can eventually smother the expression of fire so no source of acquired *qi* is effectively digested or assimilated. The habituated drive toward sensuality, bliss, and connection can lead us to burn out emotionally or be embodied as a heart attack or stroke as we try in vain to fulfill ourselves. As the channel's sedation point, TH-10 can quell excessive fire in the three heater official and help engender moderation in our lust for life.

Fire must be grounded in order to serve humanity in a balanced way, and the earth element serves to stabilize fire and give it a foundation to rest on. If the presence of earth within fire is deficient, fire can lack stability and focus and be unable to sustain itself. Lack of desire tends to leave the internal landscape barren as we fail to connect to sources of nourishment in life. I find this a particularly good point for addressing fire or earth constitutional types who feel sorrow in midsummer and have difficulty assimilating the joyfulness and fullness of the season. "Heavenly well" can be an important point when the heart, and our fire element in general, is not nourished by the fruits of our labors. Like SI-8, this is an important point for people who have had bread but never really tasted the honey that life has to offer.

---

| ❖ **TH-11** | **Pure Cold Abyss** | |
|---|---|---|
| *Qing[1]leng[3]yuan[1]* | Pure Cold Abyss | 清冷淵 |
| *Qing[1]leng[3]quan[2]* | Pure Cold Source | 清冷泉 |
| *Qing[1]ling[2]* | Cyan Spirit | 青靈 |

VIRTUES

1. Channels warmth to thaw coldness.
2. Empowers compassion toward self and others.

"Pure cold abyss" has the dual function of (1) clearing heat and draining fire, and (2) rekindling fire in aspects of being from which it has been withdrawn. The three heater tends to dysfunction by creating excess heat or withdrawing warmth from areas associated with trauma in life. Because the three heater is a fire official, the heart and sexual organs are often affected when the three heater dysfunctions. Hyperfunctions of the three heater tend to engender excess. Physically this heat can be embodied as vaginitis, prostate inflammation, hot flashes, or heart palpitations and a too fast pulse. Emotionally we can tend to "burn" others in relationship as we overstep their boundaries. Excessive sexuality can serve as a protective mechanism to keep us away from the heart of a relationship. "Pure cold abyss" can help cool such fire so our connections are made from our hearts and are less driven by habitual desires.

A person who has been "burned" in relationship can tend to retreat from intimate contact. This retreat can manifest as physical coldness embodied in the area of the sexual organs, in a handshake, or as a lack of emotional warmth. "Pure cold abyss" can be effective in the restoration of warmth to the uterus and sexual organs when it has been withdrawn as a reaction to perceived betrayal. Further this point can help warm the interior and the heart in a way that empowers the virtue of compassion. *Qingling* ("cyan spirit"), an alternate name of this point, is also the name of Ht-2, and both points are found in proximity to each other.

---

## ❖ TH-12 Thawing the River

| | | |
|---|---|---|
| *Xiao[1]luo[4]* | Thawing the River | 消濼 |
| *Xiao[1]shuo[4]* | Melting Shining | 消鑠 |
| *Xiao[1]shuo[4]* | Melting Brilliance | 消爍 |
| *Xiao[1]li[4]* | Thawing Trickle | 消瀝 |

VIRTUES

1. Thaws inner cold that obscures compassion.
2. Empowers the flow of warmth to engender compassion and sensuality.
3. Quells excess fire.

The names of TH-12 allude to the point's function of harmonizing the expression of fire on a continuum from tonifying deficiency to dispersing excess. The names all suggest the alchemical aspect of the three heater's function in empowering transformation through the interpenetration of fire with the other elements to eliminate mundanity and support the heart's fire. All four names begin with the character *xiao,* which can be translated as either to "thaw," "melt," or "disperse," and suggest the promotion of flow and transformation in what has stagnated. The second character of each name contains the character *lo* (樂), denoting both music in the sense of ritual and ceremony as well as the emotion of joy as it is associated with the fire element.[6] The character *lo* appears in conjunction with the radical for water (氵), metal (金), and fire (火), respectively.

Following on the function of "pure cold abyss," the name "thawing the river" alludes to a hypofunctioning of the three heater official as a frozen river that is failing to warm and nourish us. In the face of pain and heartbreak that we perceive as betrayal in life, warmth can be withdrawn from any aspect of self. This can be expressed as the inability to sustain contact with others who may find us emotionally cold. Such coldness can lead to a lack of sexual desire or potency as well as difficulty in "letting go" to achieve orgasm. The spirit of "thawing the river" can be called on to empower warmth and flow in any aspect of being that we have frozen and separated out from ourselves because it is too painful to embrace.

The name "dispersing brilliance" suggests this point's function in quelling the excessive expression of the three heater's fire. The expansive nature of fire often leads the three heater to foster excessive contact with those around us. When fire is excessive, a person can be habitually driven by lust, leading to symptoms as diverse as premature ejaculation, frequent sexual encounters with no sustained intimacy, and poor boundaries leading to a failure to discriminate social from intimate relationships. In this case a patient can project his lack of internal connection to self externally by overattending to the business of others.

By utilizing TH-12 to disperse the excess heat born of desire, we may be better able to relax our need for control socially and therefore enjoy ourselves inwardly. The name "relax and joy" does not represent a direct translation of the Chinese characters *(xiaoluo)* for the name of this point. However, this name given by J. R. Worsley to TH-12 uniquely expresses the spirit of this point in empowering the virtues of the three heater official. This is an important point for empowering "being" rather than "doing" in relationship to others. Excessive need for control can manifest as an inability to let go during sex, making it difficult to climax. A physiological function associated with this "letting go of control" is the ability of TH-12 to restore deficient vaginal secretions that hinder enjoyment of sex.

Note that a given symptom, in this case difficulty achieving orgasm, can exist on either end of a continuum addressed by a point's function. When the presence of fire is deficient, cold and fear can prevent us from connecting with our hearts to achieve union with another. When fire is excessive, our own desires and fantasies can engender a need for control that also diminishes our capacity for connection and fulfillment with another. In either case the spirit of TH-12 can be evoked to harmonize the continuum of fire's unbalanced expression and promote connection with self and other in a way that engenders the bliss of union. The sexual impulse itself is a relatively lower expression of the impulse toward communion with the divine. All points on the heart protector and three heater channels have the potential to harmonize the sexual urge when it limits one's experience of connection to the evolutionary impulse itself.

❖ **TH-13** **Shoulder Meeting**
*Nao⁴hui⁴* Shoulder 臑會
*Nao⁴jiao²* Shoulder Crossing 臑交
*Nao⁴liao²* Shoulder Foramen 臑髎

FUNCTION

Meeting point with the *yang* linking vessel

Named for its location, "shoulder meeting" is an excellent point any time warmth is needed to promote healing and movement in a shoulder frozen from internal cold or from exposure to external cold.

❖ **TH-14** **Shoulder Bone**
*Jian¹liao²* Shoulder Foramen 肩髎
*Jian¹jiao⁴* Shoulder Hole 肩窌

FUNCTION

Meeting point with the *yang* linking vessel

"Shoulder bone" is similar in function to TH-13 but addresses issues of both coldness and excessive warmth. This can be an effective point when fluctuations or extremes in temperature affect, or are evident in, the shoulder region.

❖ **TH-15** **Heavenly Foramen**
*Tian¹liao²* Heavenly Foramen 天窌
*Tian¹jiao⁴* Heavenly Bone 天髎

FUNCTION

Meeting point with the *yang* linking vessel

VIRTUE

Empowers warmth in the shoulder to assist us in extending our hearts into the world.

The upper edge of the shoulder can be conceived of as a plateau that serves as the interface between heaven (the head) and earth (the body). Hence the designation of heaven in the point name can refer to the role of TH-15 in mediating this relationship. Whereas TH-13 and TH-14 address the issue of heat and cold in the shoulder on a relatively more physical and thermodynamic level, TH-15 addresses relatively more the psychospiritual issues regarding the underlying reasons warmth has been withdrawn from this area. "Heavenly bone" can also address how our emotional state is being impacted by exposure to external cold that has invaded the three heater channel to cause pain and limit movement in the shoulder.

The function of this point is similar to that of SI-11 in addressing the spirit as it impacts the arms and shoulders. Limited range of motion in the arms can be congruent with physical and emotional coldness that prevents us from reaching out to make social and intimate contact with others. Hence TH-15 can improve circulation and allow a warmth that arises from blood and spirit *(shen)* to flow back into a frozen arm or shoulder. In this way we may be empowered to better touch and be touched by the world.

---

### ❖ TH-16 **Heavenly Window**
*Tian[1]you[3]* Heavenly Window 天牖

FUNCTION

Window to heaven

VIRTUE

Empowers a glimpse of our spiritual connection to heaven
as it comes to us through love and light.

As a window point, TH-16 can empower insight into our communications, connections, and the overall context of our lives because these issues are mediated by the function of the three heater. The three heater governs the connection of every aspect within us to all aspects of the world externally that impact us. When we have lost touch with a part of ourselves, TH-16 can help empower connections that restore effective communication internally so we are less driven by unconscious motivations.

Often, psychospiritual material is prevented from entering consciousness because the mind has severed ties to an internal aspect of being in an attempt to avoid pain. "Heavenly window" can shine a light into our depths so the warmth and compassion of the fire element can illuminate these unintegrated parts of ourselves. This can benefit people who run hot and cold emotionally and are not facing their motivations in connecting or disconnecting in relationship. This dysfunction can be embodied as disparate temperatures in different regions of the body, with some being too warm and others too cold.

---

### ❖ TH-17 **Wind Screen**
*Yi[4]feng[1]* Wind Screen 翳風

FUNCTION

Intersection point of the bladder and three heater channels

VIRTUES

1. Tonifies *weiqi.*
2. Empowers us to be less susceptible to other people's opinions about us.

The name "wind screen" refers to this point's function of stimulating the three heater to strengthen our *weiqi* to form a protective screen around us. This "screen" guards the shoulders and neck from wind by strengthening the outer defensive functions of the fire element.[7] In nature, wind creates movement so our surroundings are not stable. Such a chaotic influence can hinder the three heater's function of assuring congruency between our internal and external environments. Hence a well-functioning three heater official must be able to maintain internal stability even when the world around us is changing. If the *qi* of the three heater is insufficient to establish a protective boundary, we can be susceptible to external pathogenic factors that are born on the wind such as wind/heat, wind/cold, or wind/damp. The presence of internal pathogenic wind can be evidenced by symptoms and signs that change rapidly and in an unpredictable fashion such as muscle twitches that move around the body or an erratic emotional state.

Rumors can be considered a form of wind as people's opinions and gossip circulate around us and we feel exposed. Hence we use the saying "my ears are burning" when we accidentally overhear others talking about us. This expression evokes the spirit of TH-17 as it is located on a fire meridian by the ear. Inflammation in the ear, a feeling of pounding in the vessels behind the ear, or tinnitus can all be embodiments of feeling overexposed to the influence and opinions of others. This dysfunction can also be evidenced in one who is overly concerned about social appearances and glosses over deeper conflicts that appear unseemly. I have used this point to good effect with a 15-year-old girl who did not report she had been raped for fear of what others might think of her. In this sense, "wind screen" can help protect us from feelings of shame associated with being exposed as the *weiqi* is strengthened to better insulate us on both emotional and spiritual levels.

I have also found this point to excel at treating psychospiritual disorders when patients feel overly merged with their environment. Such imbalances tend to have the biomedical diagnosis of schizophrenia. For example, this point was helpful in treating Jill whose case study is reported in Chapter 3. Lastly I have found the point to be effective in treating apprehension about public speaking, stage appearances, and crowds, all conditions characterized by a fear of public exposure.

---

❖ **TH-18** **Spasm Vessel**

| | | |
|---|---|---|
| *Ji$^4$mai$^4$* | Spasm Vessel | 瘈脈 |
| *Zi$^3$ti$^4$* | Assisting the Body | 資體 |
| *Ti$^4$mai$^4$* | Body Vessel | 體脈 |

VIRTUES

1. Nourishes the mind and nervous system.
2. Relaxes muscle spasms in the neck.

The name "spasm vessel" suggests this point's efficacy for muscle spasms in the neck and shoulder region as they are impacted by our nervous reaction to stress in life as well as by exposure to wind/cold or wind/heat. I often associate such spasms with issues regarding the struggle for excessive control in life. Convulsions, for which TH-18 is also indicated, can be thought of as severe dysfunction in the three heater's ability to maintain internal control through regulating homeostasis via the central nervous system. The nervous system can be thought of as an embodiment of the three heater official as it forms a network that maintains connection among all realms of functioning.

The name "assisting the body" refers to the three heater as a distribution network for nourishment, a function also alluded to in the name of TH-11, "heavenly well." Evoking the spirit of this point is like bringing a warm nourishing meal to every aspect of being that is shut off and cold, starving for love, attention, and warmth.

---

❖ **TH-19** **Skull Breathing**

| | | |
|---|---|---|
| *Lu$^2$xi$^2$* | Skull Breathing | 顱息 |
| *Lu$^2$xin$^4$* | Skull | 顱囟 |

VIRTUE

Allows the skull to breathe, easing constraint of the mind and spirit.

As recognized by modalities such as craniosacral therapy, the skull does indeed breathe. "Skull breathing" can be effective when a person appears to be stuck in the head or "bottled up." I have used this point often to good advantage in treating head injuries, particularly when these have occurred early in life and malformation of the skull is evident. In such cases I have the sense that the patient is effectively either trapped inside or outside his own head as mental processes appear to be constrained or overly expansive.

Trapped inside his head, the patient can evidence an intellect that is overly strong and a deficiency of compassion toward himself as well as others. Trapped "outside" his head, a patient's *shen* is scattered, and he has a hard time focusing to learn new things or implementing what he has learned so he can apply it effectively. Here the three heater is dysfunctional in a way that the individual is unable to connect what he has learned to everything else he knows or to its practical application. "Skull breathing" can help ease constraint in the head and mind, thus enabling the spirit to communicate more freely with self and the outside world.

---

### ❖ TH-20 **Angle Grandson**
*Jiao³sun¹* Angle Grandson 角孫

FUNCTION

Intersection point of the small intestine, gallbladder, and three heater channels

A grandson (孫) is the connecting (系) line of the offspring (子) that bridges future generations with the past. So too does the three heater function to integrate innate and acquired sources of *qi.* This point is located at the apex of the three heater channel as it makes an angle around the ear. Similarly, the grandson is the end of the family line before it turns the corner to future generations.

As a meeting point for the small intestine, gallbladder, and three heater officials where they converge at the ear, TH-20 can be particularly effective for treating any disorder of this orifice or of hearing in general. The gallbladder channel terminates at the eyes, and TH-20 is said to "brighten" the eyes, suggesting its ability to empower the accurate perception of reality. By harmonizing the relationship between seeing and hearing as governed by the gallbladder and small intestine, respectively, TH-20 can empower the virtues of clarity, sorting, and intuition associated with these officials.

---

### ❖ TH-21 **Ear Gate**
*Er³men²* Ear Gate 耳門

One of the strongest points for treating diseases of the ear, I find this point to be relatively more effective physically for improving auditory perception as compared with SI-19, "listening palace," which empowers the spiritual basis of listening in a way that allows one to abstract the essence of meaning from what is heard in life.

---

❖ **TH-22** **Harmony Foramen**

| | | |
|---|---|---|
| *He[2]liao[2]* | Harmony Foramen | 和髎 |
| *He[2]jiao[4]* | Harmony Hole | 和窌 |

FUNCTION

Exit point

VIRTUE

Levels and quiets the mind to stop it from agitating the spirit.

A line drawn between the bilateral TH-22 points defines the horizontal axis of the head. By extension a function of TH-22 is to level the mind so thought and spirit are harmonious. *Qi* exits TH-22 to enter the gallbladder channel at Gb-1. Both TH-22 and Gb-1 are meeting points of the gallbladder, small intestine, and three heater channels. These three *yang* meridians are prone to stagnant *qi* and excess heat that can agitate the mind and cause dysfunction in our senses of hearing and vision that preclude accurate perception of reality. In my experience, TH-22 is an important point for quieting the mind and harmonizing all manner of imbalances as they undermine clarity of mental function.

---

❖ **TH-23** **Silk Bamboo Hollow**

| | | |
|---|---|---|
| *Si[1]zhu[2]kong[1]* | Silk Bamboo Hollow | 絲竹空 |
| *Ju[4]liao[2]* | Great Foramen | 巨髎 |
| *Mu[4]liao[2]* | Eye Foramen | 目髎 |
| *Yue[4]liao[2]* | Moon Foramen | 月髎 |

*So openness is the great root of the world.*
*This may be symbolized by bamboo.*
*Dealing with events directly,*
*Dealing with the world with adaptability,*
*Managing the mind with flexibility,*
*Managing the body with calmness—*
*This is like the resilient strength of bamboo.*
*Forgetting emotions in action,*
*Forgetting thoughts in stillness,*
*Forgetting self in dealing with events,*
*Forgetting things in adopting to change—*
*This is like the inner emptiness of bamboo.*
– *The Book of Balance and Harmony*[8]

FUNCTION

Intersection point of the small intestine, gallbladder, and three heater channels

TH-23 is the terminal point on its channel and therefore represents the outermost aspect of the fire element's sphere of influence. The function of "silk bamboo hollow" is to return our outer extension of fire back in toward our depths. This function is alluded to metaphorically in the point's name with the metaphor of the bamboo plant channeling the external manifestation of its flower (silk) back in toward its empty core. Both silk and bamboo were important resources in ancient China, and the fire we extend into the world, as well as its internal origin in the heart, are important personal resources. Ayscough affirms that the presence of bamboo in the imperial palace "symbolizes the 'empty heart,' which is ready to receive all goods and virtuous suggestions. So should the emperor be ready to listen to the advice of his ministers."[9]

"Silk bamboo hollow" helps empower connection to our own core when we have failed to be nourished internally as we overextend ourselves trying to make external connections with others. This dysfunction can manifest as using social connection as a means for avoiding intimacy. Such a person can have many acquaintances but few friends. Physically, this pattern can be embodied in a patient who evidences sensations of heat externally while reporting feeling cold in the interior.

## *Exercises*

1. Compare the names and functions of TH-1 with TH-23 as the first and last points on the three heater meridian.
2. Compare the names and functions of HP-1 with HP-9 as the first and last points on the heart protector meridian.
3. Compare the functions of Ht-1, the "deepest" point on a fire channel, with those of TH-23, the "outermost" point on a fire channel.
4. Compare the name and function of each channel's first and last point relative to the function of the given official.
5. Compare the name and function of the exit and entry points of each successive official.
6. Compare the functions of TH-2 with Ki-2 as they address temperature regulation and fluid metabolism in the hands and feet.
7. Compare the functions of these same two points as they address emotional warmth and human contact.

8. The character *zhi* (支) in one name of TH-6 may be translated as "descendant." The character *zong* in the name of TH-7 makes reference to our ancestors.
   a. What functional relationship does the three heater have to the transmission of inherited influences?
   b. How are the functions of TH-6 and TH-7 connected relative to the notions of descendants and ancestry?
9. Compare the function of TH-15, LI-15, and Gb-21 as they treat the neck and shoulder and mediate the relationship between heart (body) and mind (head).
10. I have discussed TH-19, "skull breathing," in relationship to its function of easing mental constraint. In this regard compare the function of TH-19 to that of St-8, "head tied," and Gb-4, "loathsome jaws."

## *NOTES*

1. The term *shaoyang* refers variously to the gallbladder and three heater channels as they form a functional pair and to the "half inside half outside" stage in the progression of wind/cold as it penetrates into the interior.
2. Note that the *Yijing* hexagram for fire is named *Li,* "the clinging." See *ND,* p. 199.
3. Mathews, 1931, p. 1016.
4. See my discussion of pathological emotional states in Chapters 2 and 14.
5. *ND,* pp. 17–19, 347–348.
6. The character *le* has the meaning of both music and joy, which are often discussed together in the Confucian analects. According to Confucius, the purpose of ritual (*li*) and music is to permit human desire and emotion to be expressed in a healthy fashion without excess. Often, in medical literature, the character *xi* (喜) is used to denote pathological joy, whereas the character *le* denotes the healthy expression of joy. See *ND,* pp. 198–199.
7. The function of this point reminds me of the Jade Screen formula containing astragalus, which is said to "seal in the *weiqi.*"
8. A thirteenth-century Daoist text. Cleary, 1989, p. 181.
9. Ayscough, 1930, p. 74.

# 30

# GALLBLADDER

THE GALLBLADDER CHANNEL BEGINS AT THE OUTER CANTHUS of the eye at Gb-1, the channel's entry point. From here the channel descends as it runs laterally to Gb-2 located just anterior to the base of the earlobe. It then ascends to Gb-4 and descends again to Gb-7 at the apex of the pinna just anterior to the ear. The channel outlines the ear as it descends to the base of the occiput at Gb-12. It then arches back over the head to reach Gb-14, one ACI[1] superior to the supraorbital notch. Again the channel travels posteriorly and arches back over the head to reach Gb-20 at the base of the occiput. From here it proceeds laterally to Gb-21 on the anterior border of the trapezius muscle. An internal branch of the pathway splits off from Gb-21 to travel to GV-14 inferior to the seventh cervical vertebra. This branch runs laterally through Bl-11 and SI-12 to turn anteriorly, becoming superficial at St-12.

Four deep branches of the gallbladder channel are located on the head. The first internal branch leaves Gb-1 and descends the cheek to St-5, ascends again to SI-18, and then descends through St-6 to reach St-12. The second internal branch leaves Gb-7 and joins TH-20. The third branch exits Gb-14 and descends to Bl-1 at the inner canthus. The fourth internal branch exits Gb-20, proceeds anteriorly to TH-17, and then enters the ear to emerge at SI-19.

Both a superficial and deep pathway descend the body from St-12. The superficial path descends to the fourth intercostal space at Gb-22 and then travels through Gb-23 to Gb-24 in the seventh intercostal space. It then descends laterally to the hip, where it joins Gb-29. Here the pathway moves internally and travels posteriorly to descend the sacrum via Bl-31 and Bl-33 to reach GV-1 at the tip of the coccyx. It then returns to join the superficial pathway in the center of the hip at Gb-30.

The internal pathway descends from St-12 through the thorax, where it passes the superficial pathway at Gb-24. From here it travels to Lv-13, where it enters the organs of the liver and gallbladder. It then descends to St-30 at the superior edge of the pubic bone and turns laterally to join the superficial pathway at Gb-30. Reunited, the single meridian now travels superficially to travel down the lateral surface of the thigh, through the lateral surface of the knee and calf, and runs anteriorly to the lateral malleolus at Gb-40. It then moves over the dorsal surface of the foot between the fourth and fifth metatarsal bones to terminate at Gb-44, the lateral nail point of the fourth toe. From Gb-41, the channel's exit point, an internal branch travels to join the liver channel at its entry point, Lv-1, located at the medial nail point of the big toe.

---

## *Thoughts on the Channel*

The lateral course of the gallbladder channel is consistent with its function of empowering discernment and perspective. As the channel descends the body, it passes through many major joints at Gb-20 (neck), Gb-30 (hip), Gb-33 and Gb-34 (knee), and Gb-40 (ankle). The gallbladder official tends toward one-sided symptomatology, frequently the embodiment of a limited perspective that allows us to see only one side of a given issue. The joints are the articulations where we literally branch out in life. Dysfunction of the joints is often the embodiment of an underlying dysfunction in the way our gallbladder official regulates our growth around perceived obstacles. Like giant knots in a tree, our joints can become disfigured and dysfunctional congruent with the gallbladder's failure to smoothly implement our plans in the world.

### MAIN FUNCTIONS

1. Directs growth of the liver's plan into the world.
2. Empowers decisiveness and perspective.
3. Empowers external vision.

DISTAL POINT FUNCTIONS

*Water:* Empowers fluidity of growth within the wood that manifests as flexibility. Controls the fire within wood to moderate wood's tendency toward directional growth.

*Wood:* Empowers the virtues of wood and transmits them to the other officials.

*Fire:* Empowers the growth of wood from within and constitutes the goal of all growth from without.

*Earth:* Nourishes wood internally and creates outer stability by supporting the root.

*Metal:* Empowers the letting go of all aspects of self not conducive to healthy growth.

*Xi-cleft:* Moves stagnation within the gallbladder channel on which resentment and jealousy are based.

*Luo:* Drains heat and wind from the gallbladder channel that obscure clarity of vision and quality of discernment.

---

| ❖ **Gb-1** | **Pupil Foramen** | |
|---|---|---|
| *Tong²zi³jiao⁴* | Pupil Foramen | 瞳子窌 |
| *Tong²zi³liao²* | Pupil Foramen | 瞳子髎 |
| *Tai⁴yang²* | Great *Yang*, The Sun | 太陽 |
| *Qian²guan¹* | Before the Pass | 前關 |
| *Hou⁴qu²* | After the Curve | 後曲 |

*After the death of Pan Gu, his breath became the wind and clouds, his voice the thunder, his left and right eyes the sun and moon . . .*
– SHUYIJI *(Sixth Century)*[2]

FUNCTIONS

1. Entry point
2. Meeting point of the small intestine, three heater, and gallbladder channels.

VIRTUE

Empowers clarity of vision.

Gb-1 is named for its location in the depression of the orbital bone at the outer canthus of the eye. The character *zi* is an honorary suffix, which occurs in the names of many of the great philosophers such as

Laozi or Zhuangzi. Here the term denotes Gb-1 as particularly efficacious in treating imbalances that affect vision. Of special note is that the character *zi* is also the name of the terrestrial branch, according to Chinese phase energetics, that corresponds to the hours of 11 P.M. to 1 A.M., the hourly high point of the gallbladder official according to the Chinese clock. As the channel's entry point, *qi* arrives at Gb-1 at 11 P.M. The name *Taiyang* refers to the eyes' function of receiving light, the only true source of nourishment available to us from our first breath onward. The last two names, "before the pass" and "after the curve," make reference to the physical location of this point next to the orbital bone.

This point's function helps mediate the quality of our discernments regarding the inner nature of self and our relationship to the world around us. Even though life can at times appear to us as chaos, we will always be able to navigate if we can maintain connection to a stable reference point. Both our internal and external reference points are accessed by the liver, the *yin* official associated with the wood element. Internally, the liver connects to the plan stored in *jing*, and externally, through GV-20, the liver connects us to the North Star as the immovable heart of heaven that has invested destiny within us.[3] The gallbladder's function is to create alignment between our inner plan and our life events as mediated by accurate vision.

Traditional functions ascribed to this point include draining heat and wind. The gallbladder, as the *yang* official associated with the wood element, empowers the creative growth of our inner plans into the world. The generation of excess heat by the gallbladder is the physiological byproduct of an underlying psychospiritual process based on frustration. In essence, some issue has blocked our progress in life, and as we work and try to move the obstacle, friction generates heat. Heat tends to rise and, in so doing, can generate wind, the environmental pathogen associated with the wood element. Wind and heat that rise to the top of the gallbladder channel can disturb vision and be congruent with conditions such as heart attack and stroke.

Symptoms such as dizziness, cataracts, or glaucoma can suggest that wind and heat have obscured our connection to stable reference points internally and externally. What we see in the world can no longer be aligned with the picture emerging from our depths in a way we can reconcile with our minds. Heat engenders internal pressure, and symptoms engendered by wind tend to move quickly and unpredictably. When wind and heat obscure our vision we are unable to discern a clear picture of our lives, which can appear to us like an unrelated string of seemingly random events. Frustration ensues as we are unable to discern our way through the chaos around us.

We tend to compensate for lack of proper orientation in one of two ways. For lack of an internal reference point we may depend excessively on external signs to lead us in life. In this case we may rely dysfunctionally on the opinions of others to guide our decision-making process. Such a process can be based on a lack of the inner vision on which self-esteem is based. Or we may compensate for lack of an appropriate external reference point by overrelying on our own internal view of what is right and what is wrong. Hence we may become rigidly inflexible and belligerent, unable to consider anyone else's point of view. "Pupil foramen" can harmonize the expression of our vision by clearing wind and heat, thereby empowering the realignment of our internal and external reference points in life. In this way belligerence is transformed into benevolence as the virtues of the wood element, so dependent on harmonious vision, are restored.

---

| ❖ **Gb-2** | **Hearing Assembly** | |
|---|---|---|
| *Ting¹hui⁴* | Hearing Assembly | 聽會 |
| *Ji¹guan¹* | Hinge | 機關 |
| *Ting¹he¹* | Hearing Laughter | 聽呵 |
| *Hou⁴guan¹* | After the Pass | 後關 |

VIRTUES

1. Harmonizes anger that tightens the jaw and obscures hearing.
2. Empowers the virtues of benevolence, listening, and intuition.

Located in front of the ear, Gb-2 is named for its function of addressing a broad continuum of hearing disorders ranging from tinnitus or pain in the ear to failure to discern correctly the informational content inherent in what we are listening to. The character *ting* (聽) contains the characters *de* (德), meaning both "virtue" and "original nature," as well as the character *de* (悳), meaning "rectification of the heart."[4] Hence the inner nature of listening implies listening to life in a way that original nature is restored and the heart is rectified. Listening in this way, intuition is restored as we come to know life directly with our hearts bypassing the analytical facilities of the mind. All aspects of hearing converge (*hui:*會) functionally at Gb-2, hence the name "hearing assembly."

In reaction to perceived injustice in the world, the gallbladder official tends to keep us overengaged in work and unable to relax. Hyperfunction of the gallbladder tends to manifest as either excess or deficient heat whose rising is congruent with symptoms such as headaches that are typified by pounding along the gallbladder channel, ringing in the ears, pain under the occiput in the area of Gb-20, and hypertension. Accompanying such symptoms is often a feeling of rushing and pulsing along this channel from Gb-20 to Gb-1. Commonly used for tinnitus, Gb-2 is specific for ringing in the ears characterized by a rushing quality. Hence "hearing assembly" is located just anterior to the ear in a depression directly over a pulsing blood vessel. When this point is indicated, patients tend to report feeling they can feel a pounding in their ears or they can hear their blood flowing. Rising heat generated by the gallbladder can be congruent with frustration, anger, and resentment that manifests when we fail to flow smoothly around life's obstacles.

When these emotions occur habitually, they obscure the virtue of intuition as it is empowered by listening. As the virtues of wood erode, belligerence tends to fuel our habitual need to be right. Anger and frustration tend to lock the jaw and contribute to symptoms such as trigeminal neuralgia, grinding of the teeth, and temporomandibular joint syndrome (TMJ). Hence an alternate name of Gb-2 is *jiguan* (機關), meaning "hinge," and referring to this point's location over the mandibular bone. Note that a name of Gb-1, *qianguan,* meaning "before the pass," is juxtaposed with that of Gb-2, *houguan,* meaning "after the pass." Both names make reference to the positions of these points before and after the mandibular bone, respectively.

Another name of Gb-2, *tinghe* (聽呵), "hearing laughter," suggests the efficacy of this point in empowering joy by reducing ringing and pain in the ears. When we are habitually driven by anger, we can lose contact with our own hearts as well as the hearts of others. The need to be right tends to obscure any other consideration in relationship. Hence "hearing laughter" can ease habitual anger related to ringing in the ears and tension and pain in the jaw. In this way we may once again listen to our hearts so intuition is restored.

---

| ❖ **Gb-3** | **Above the Pass** | |
|---|---|---|
| *Shang⁴guan¹* | Above the Pass | 上關 |
| *Ke⁴zhu³ren²* | Guest Host Man | 客主人 |
| *Ke⁴zhu²* | Guest Host | 客主 |
| *Rong²zhu³* | Easy Host | 容主 |
| *Tai⁴yang²* | Great *Yang*, The Sun | 太陽 |

FUNCTION

Meeting point of the three heater, stomach, large intestine, and gallbladder channels

This point is located on the upper edge of the mandibular bone, often referred to in Chinese as a gate *(guan)*. As a convergence of four *yang* channels anterior to the ear, "upper pass" can be effective in treating conditions of the jaw and ear in a way similar to Gb-2. I find Gb-3 to be relatively more effective physically, whereas Gb-2 addresses relatively deeper psychospiritual aspects of functioning. The names of the first three points on the gallbladder channel, "in front of the pass," "after the pass," and "above the pass," may make reference to the trilogy of heaven, human, and earth and be present in the name of Gb-3 as "guest, host, man." Heaven is guest, earth is host, and humanity mediates the interaction of both.

---

❖ **Gb-4** **Loathsome Jaws**
*Han⁴yan⁴* Loathsome Jaws 頷厭

*The man of benevolence is tranquil.*
– CONFUCIUS[5]

FUNCTION

Meeting point of the three heater, stomach, large intestine, and gallbladder channels

The character *yan* can be rendered as to "detest," "hate," and "reject" or to be "tranquil" or "serene." Anger not expressed as clarity during waking hours can manifest as clenching of the jaw and grinding of the teeth at night during sleep. Over time this stress can contribute to symptoms such as trigeminal neuralgia, TMJ, and worn-down teeth. "Loathsome jaws" helps provide perspective on life's conflicts by quieting the mind and easing tension in the musculature of the jaw and head that is associated with repressed anger and seething. Whereas Gb-3 and Gb-5 address relatively more physical manifestations of pain and dysfunction, "loathsome jaws" addresses the underlying dynamic of suppression that contributes to such tension in this area.

---

❖ **Gb-5** **Suspended Skull**
*Xuan²lu²* Suspended Skull 懸顱
*Sui²zhong¹* Center of Marrow 髓中
*Sui²kong³* Marrow Opening 髓孔
*Mi³nie⁴* Grain Chewing 米嚙

FUNCTION

Meeting point of the three heater, stomach, large intestine, and gallbladder channel

If we trace the gallbladder meridian from Gb-2 through Gb-7, we can imagine the channel as a hook and rope suspending the skull. "Suspended skull" can be useful for local symptomatology such as one-sided headache, facial pain, and pain in the lateral canthus of the eye. Like the preceding points on the channel, Gb-5 can help resolve imbalances of wind and heat congruent with gallbladder dysfunction. In so doing the mind may be cleared, vision improved, and the virtue of patience empowered. The function of decision making may be better guided by the virtue of discernment and relatively less by habituated anger.

Gb-39 is the meeting point of marrow, and the names "center of marrow" and "marrow opening" allude to the gallbladder as a "curious" organ that receives its nourishment from kidney *jing* via the production of marrow.[6] The gallbladder strengthens the *yang* aspect of the nervous system by focusing and directing spirit. The kidneys, in contrast, empower the *yin* structural aspect of nervous system functioning. A function of Gb-5 is to channel marrow up toward the head to strengthen both the brain and the skull. This function is based on the relationship of wood to water as wood sends down roots to tap and raise innate potential into the world.

---

### ❖ Gb-6 **Suspended Tuft**

*Xuan²li²* Suspended Tuft 懸釐

FUNCTION

Meeting point of the three heater, stomach, large intestine, and gallbladder channels

This point's name reflects the fact that a tuft of hair must be lifted in order to access the point.[7] Like Gb-3, Gb-4, and Gb-5, "suspended tuft" is a meeting point for the *shaoyang* and *yangming* channels comprised of the gallbladder and three heater and the stomach and large intestine officials, respectively.[8] The *shaoyang* channel is congruent with the transition of wood to fire and the ascendancy of the *sheng* cycle toward the outermost manifestation of fire at the peak of life. This transition is expressed as the most exterior flowering of our creativity as fueled by wood and expressed through the fire element. The *yangming* channel governs the transition of earth to metal as the influence of *yang* wanes and the *sheng* cycle descends into the abyss of winter.

These two transitions constitute complementary movements of *qi* along the *sheng* cycle. The *shaoyang* officials govern the rising momentum of our creativity, whereas the *yangming* officials empower us to be nourished in the process of growth and to let go of the specific outcome of our actions. In this way we may be nourished by channeling heaven's will into the world for the sake of its expression alone without excessively imposing the constraints of our own egos on our actions. If these relationships fall out of balance, our attachments to specific outcomes can fuel a habitual drive that prevents us from ever being nourished in the creative process.

The *shaoyang* officials can lead us to overengage in the world in an expansive way. Driven by anger and impatience, the habitual planning and decision making of the wood element can cause us to be constantly vigilant of external details. Overly attached to the outcomes of our efforts, we tend to exert the force of our wills to effect change in the world too quickly. However, there is a limit to how much work can be accomplished effectively in the world, and, when this limit is reached, frustration and anger can push us to work past these limits. As we overwork, wood excessively fuels fire, which can rise in a way associated with symptomatology along the three heater and gallbladder channels in the shoulders, neck, and head. In this case pressure may be experienced along the gallbladder channel as we become habitually addicted to creating and overly attached to the injustice we perceive when we do not achieve the results we seek from our works. Excessive striving can leave us unnourished in the process of our growth as frustration keeps us always focused on our goals and takes us away from our momentary experience.

In dysfunction, the *yangming* officials can keep us overengaged in our internal process and obsessively concerned with our own needs. We become overly attached to our immediate comfort and seek to quell our habitual appetites through consumption. Trying in vain to fill our internal void creates a vacuum of consumption that can possess us to have a life of its own. However, there is a limit to how much we can efficiently process, and, once this threshold is passed, acquired forms of *qi* become burdens that no longer nourish us. Overwork of the digestive system can lead to stagnation and the accumulation of heat. Such heat can rise congruent with symptomatology along the stomach and large intestine channels in the neck and face. Excessive concern with our own comfort can lead us to always focus on our momentary needs and ignore the outcomes of our actions.

When these relationships become dysfunctional, stagnation and heat are generated that can rise to the head and disturb mental and emotional processes. Over time, excess heat tends to consume *yin*, and deficient heat can also rise to disturb the heart and mind. Symptoms such as pounding in the head, tightness in the jaw, headache, hypertension, heart attack, stroke, insomnia, and an inability to disengage with the world internally or externally can be evidence of these processes. The points Gb-3 through Gb-6 can disperse this internal pressure and help calm the rushing of *qi* along the gallbladder channel as well as quell the anger and impatience that limits our perspective in life. As meeting points of the *shaoyang* and *yangming* channels, Gb-3 through Gb-6 can help harmonize the relationship between these officials so expansion and contraction are harmonized as equal and opposite movements and functional integrity of the *sheng* cycle is restored. In this way the relationship between the expansiveness of creativity and the inwardness of being nourished in process can enhance rather than compete with each other.

The imbalances discussed here involve the *hun* and *po* spirits associated with the wood and metal elements, respectively. The *hun* governs the evolution and expansion of our destiny into the world, and the *po* governs the contraction of peristalsis and our assimilation of nourishment as expressed through the left and right sides of the *sheng* cycle. When imbalances of the *hun* and *po* are congruent with a *yin*-deficient condition, I often prescribe Yiguan Jian (Linking Decoction), which links the ascension and descending actions of these spiritual influences. When either excess of deficient heat rises to cause symptomatology along the gallbladder channel on the head, I often select from Gb-3 through Gb-6. In this way constraint of the mind and pressure can be relieved and allow us to disengage long enough from our goals and the obstacles that confront us to gain a healthier perspective on our situation.

---

### ❖ Gb-7 Crooked Hair on the Temples

| | | |
|---|---|---|
| *Qu¹bin⁴* | Crooked Hair on the Temples | 曲鬢 |
| *Qu¹fa³* | Crooked Hair | 曲髮 |

FUNCTION

Meeting point of the bladder and gallbladder channels

From Gb-4 through Gb-7, the gallbladder channel descends toward the ear. Upon reaching Gb-7 the channel turns to ascend to the top of the ear at Gb-9. Often such changes in a channel's direction are denoted with the character *qu,* meaning "crooked" or "curved."[9] Gb-7 is located just in front of the temporal hairline. Like the preceding points, Gb-7 can be useful for pain and dysfunction in the jaw, ear, and head that has an underlying etiology of gallbladder imbalance.

❖ **Gb-8** **Cricket Valley**

| | | |
|---|---|---|
| *Shuai⁴gu³* | Cricket Valley | 蟀谷 |
| *Shuai⁴gu³* | Leading Bone | 率骨 |
| *Shuai⁴jue³* | Net Angle | 率角 |
| *Er³jian¹* | Ear Tip | 耳尖 |

FUNCTION

Meeting point of the bladder and gallbladder channels

VIRTUE

Empowers the practical application of perspective.

This is the highest of all the valley points in the body, in keeping with the gallbladder's function of empowering perspective. "Wilderness mound" (Gb-40), the channel's source point, is located in a relatively low position on the ankle and has the function of helping elevate our perspective in a way similar to taking us up a hill to see over the forest that is obstructing our vision. In contrast, "leading valley," located on the head, can empower us to implement our elevated perspective by bringing us down off the mountain and back into the valley to continue our journey. Traditional indications such as clearing wind and treating vertigo speak to this point's function of empowering clarity and perspective.

Gb-8 is a meeting point with the bladder channel and, as such, can address the relationship between vision (wood) and the unknown depths of our journey that can be inhibited by fear associated with the water element. Note that Bl-66, a transmitting point for the influence of water, is named "penetrating valley" *(tonggu)*. Bl-66 empowers fortitude born of faith, enabling us to continue on our way unhindered by fear and lack of self-confidence. Hence the tendency of fear to limit perspective can be addressed at Gb-8, where the bladder and gallbladder channels intersect.

---

❖ **Gb-9** **Heaven Rushing**

| | | |
|---|---|---|
| *Tian¹chong⁴* | Heaven Rushing | 天冲 |
| *Tian¹qu²* | Heaven's Meeting | 天衢 |

FUNCTION

Meeting point of the bladder and gallbladder channels

VIRTUE

Quiets a rushing mind.

The designation of heaven, that which is highest, corresponds to this point's location on the head at the apex of the ear. The character *chong* means to "rush" or "surge" and denotes the *chongqi* (沖氣), that whirling abyss which mediates the interaction of heaven and earth.[10] The name "heavenly meeting" refers to the meeting of the bladder and gallbladder channels that occurs at this point.

Aspiration, creativity, and growth are virtues of the wood element. Such attributes are empowered by, and in turn engender, our engagement with the world. The gallbladder's dysfunctional tendency is to engage excessively with life as the mind strives to attain its goals through excessive decision making and action. Overwork of the mind and nervous system depletes *yin*, which can lead to a state of rising *yang*. Without the proper balance of *yin* (water), the wood element tends to burn excessively and create an overabundance of fire. Such fire can enter the blood as heat and consume the *yin* of the arteries, decreasing their elasticity and constricting them as blood pressure rises.

The tendency of fire is to rise, and, in so doing, it can often create symptomatology along the gallbladder channel congruent with dysfunction of the gallbladder official. Fire rising along the gallbladder channel enters the head (congruent with the designation of heaven in this point name) at Gb-20, "wind pond," and can collect there to manifest as a surging *(chong)* sensation as well as pain in the occiput. Rising heat tends to accumulate at Gb-20 to engender wind that can disturb the mind.[11] Internal wind and heat can be associated with biomedical diagnoses such as hypertension, pounding in or around the ears, migraine headaches, dizziness, vertigo, or seizures.

"Heaven rushing" addresses both the manifestation of rising *yang* as well as the underlying issue of being overly engaged and "rushing heaven" to manifest our goals rather than letting things unfold effortlessly of their own accord. As a meeting point of the bladder and gallbladder channels, "heaven rushing" can help empower the influence of water within wood at the level of the mind to help dispel wind and quell heat, thus promoting clarity, benevolence, and perspective—all virtues of the gallbladder official.

---

### ❖ Gb-10 **Rising White**
*Fu²bai²* Rising White 浮白

FUNCTION

Meeting point of the bladder and gallbladder channels

The character *fu* (浮白) can mean to "rise" or to "exceed" and refers here to the tendency of excess *yang* to rise and disturb the functioning of the gallbladder official. The character *bai* refers to the color white associated with the metal element. Metal can dysfunctionally constrain wood by overcontrolling it across the *ke* cycle. Metal's tendency toward perfectionism can constrain the decision-making and planning functions of the wood element. When wood is constrained in this way, the *qi* of the gallbladder as a *yang* official can become stagnant and lead to excess heat that tends to rise. "Rising white" helps disperse rising *yang* and wind that disturb the tranquil functioning of this official.

---

### ❖ Gb-11 — Head Hole *Yin*

| | | |
|---|---|---|
| *Tou²qiao⁴yin¹* | Head Hole *Yin* | 頭竅陰 |
| *Zhen³gu³* | Pillow Bone | 枕骨 |

> The emperor of the South Sea was called Shu [Brief], the emperor of the North Sea was called Hu [Sudden], and the emperor of the central region was called Huntun [Chaos]. Shu and Hu from time to time came together for a meeting in the territory of Huntun, and Huntun treated them very generously. Shu and Hu discussed how they could repay his kindness. "All men," they said, "have seven openings so they can see, hear, eat, and breathe. But Huntun alone doesn't have any. Let's try boring him some!" Every day they bored another hole, and on the seventh day, Huntun died.[12]

FUNCTION

Meeting point of the bladder and gallbladder channels

VIRTUES

1. Clears the sensory orifices.
2. Empowers accurate perception of reality.

The character *tou* (head) helps distinguish Gb-11 from Gb-44 ("foot hole *yin*"). The holes in the head referred to in the point name are the sensory orifices. Hence Gb-11 is said to treat the eyes, nose, mouth, and ears. "Head hole *yin*" empowers the clarity and perspective of the wood element within each of the senses. Our sensory orifices are windows that mediate the fidelity of our connection to the world. If these windows are clean and function properly, we are able to recognize the nature of reality without making artificial interpretations. In this way the influence of heaven internally and externally unites to nourish our purpose as it flows effortlessly through us. The function ascribed to Gb-11 of "clearing the sensory orifices" is a metaphor that suggests the point's efficacy in empowering the accurate perception of reality by harmonizing disorders of the wood element that obscure balanced judgment and perspective.

Ego obscures the virtue of spontaneity in a way that distorts our vision of both inner nature and the nature of events that occur in the world around us. When we are guided by our minds rather than our hearts, the window of our senses becomes colored by thoughts, beliefs, and desires that are not congruent with true self. Conditions affecting the sensory orifices such as tinnitus, glaucoma, nasal congestion, or a bitter or sour taste in the mouth are the embodiments of such separation. Psychospiritually, anger, belligerence, and lack of perspective suggest the deeper aspects of vision empowered by the wood element have been compromised. By helping clear the senses of disorienting influences such as wind and heat, Gb-11 can help harmonize the functional basis of this pathology and thus restore the virtues of perspective and connection to reality.

---

### ❖ Gb-12 **Final Bone**
*Wan²gu³* Final Bone 完骨

FUNCTION

Meeting point of the bladder and gallbladder channels

*Wangu* is the traditional Chinese name for the mastoid process. Gb-12 is located in the angle formed by the posterior border of the mastoid process and the inferior edge of the occipital bone. Here the gallbladder channel descends to this "final bone" at the base of the skull before it begins its ascent back over the head to Gb-13. I use this point when wind and heat rise in the gallbladder channel congruent with pounding and pain at the base of the skull in the region of this point.

---

### ❖ Gb-13 **Root Spirit**
*Ben³shen²* Root Spirit 本神

*For every needling, the method is above all,*
*not to miss the rooting in the Spirits.*
– LINGSHU[13]

FUNCTION

Meeting point with the *yang* linking vessel

Chapter 8 of the *Lingshu* is titled *Benshen* ("Rooting in the Spirits") and discusses the importance of restoring the spirit as the root of treating all illness. The *ling* and *shen* spirits comprise the *yin* and *yang* of spirit associated with the kidneys and the heart, respectively. *Ling* is the highest emanation of *jing* as it rises to the upper *jiao* and interacts with *shen* in a way that cultivates spiritual potency.[14] The interaction of *shen* and *jing* depends on the smooth flow of *qi* empowered by the wood element. These three—*jing (ling), qi,* and *shen*—fuel the rising of the *hun* spirit, associated with the wood element, that mediates evolution and presides over the left half of the *sheng* cycle and pulse. Hence the kidney, gallbladder, and heart channels, as well as the governor vessel that mediates the ascension of *yang*, have points that access both the *shen* and *ling* spirits. For a list of these points, see Figure 30.1.

Located between water and fire along the *sheng* cycle, the wood element must empower a vision that extends from our deepest roots in *jing* to the flowering of our spirit *(shen)* into the world. Hence wood effectively "roots" the *shen* into our *jing* so our actions and thoughts reflect our potential in a virtuous way. Further, wood, as the source of fuel for fire, can also be said to be its root. The wood element mediates the communication of the kidney and heart by regulating the flow of *qi* along the *sheng* cycle and by allowing free communication through the middle *jiao*. The relationship of the gallbladder official to *shen* and *ling* is similar to that of a tree to the water *(jing)* tapped by its roots and the sunlight *(shen)* it captures with its highest branches. Sunlight provides the warmth and metabolic fuel empowering the tree to raise potential from its depth to manifest as new growth at its height. Similarly, as *shen* flows down through us, the potential of *jing* is tapped and elevated to become *ling* in the upper *jiao*.

If the wood element is likened to a tree, the highest aspects of the gallbladder channel on the head are its outermost branches. The location of Gb-13 on the head corresponds to the highest perspective afforded by the tree's top branches as they touch, and receive, the influence of heaven's *shen*. *Shen* is the aspect of spirit that heaven extends to touch us from on high. "Root spirit" helps us receive this influence so it may extend from our heads, down through our hearts, and ultimately to our roots. When wood agitates the spirit and engenders excessive fire and constraint, Gb-13

| | Kidney | Gallbladder | Heart | GV |
|---|---|---|---|---|
| *Shen* | Ki-23, Ki-25 | Gb-13 | Ht-7 | GV-11 |
| *Ling* | Ki-24 | Gb-18 | Ht-4 | GV-10 |

*Figure 30.1*
SHEN AND LING

*Here I have listed the acupuncture points whose primary name makes reference to either the* shen *or* ling *spirit.*

can help ease the mind and spirit to empower perspective. In this way the virtues of benevolence (wood) and propriety (fire) can be cultivated.

---

### ❖ Gb-14 *Yang* White
*Yang²bai²* *Yang* White 陽白

FUNCTION

Meeting point of the gallbladder, three heater, stomach, and large intestine channels, and the *yang* linking vessels

VIRTUE

Brightens the eyes.

The character *yang* refers to the position of Gb-14 on the head as well as the fact that it is a meeting point of five *yang* channels. The character *bai* refers to the whites of the eyes and is also a metaphor for clarity, suggesting the efficacy of Gb-14 in treating vision. The entire flow of *qi* in the gallbladder channel converges at Gb-14 and is focused toward the eyes before the channel turns to flow back over the head and descend the body. Located directly over the pupils, "*yang* white" can be conceived as a higher pair of eyes treating both the physical and functional aspects of vision.

The wood element governs vision directed both inwardly into ourselves and externally into life. Whereas the liver as a *yin* official presides over inner vision and self-esteem, the gallbladder, in accordance with its status as a *yang* official, governs external vision.[15] External vision itself has two components. The outer aspect of vision consists of the physical mechanics of actually seeing with our eyes. Thus "*yang* white" has the traditional functions of eliminating wind and clearing heat that can contribute to diverse symptomatology associated with visual problems.

The point's function of "brightening the eyes" suggests its efficacy in treating deeper aspects of vision. These inner aspects include our projection of ourselves into the external world through the capacity of sight. Hence emotions such as jealousy and envy represent dysfunction of our vision as it relates to our concept of our relative position to the external world. Anger and judgment that result from habitually seeing others in a relatively higher or lower position than ourselves represents a loss of the wood element's virtue of benevolence. Benevolence is the capacity to have a broader perspective than others without becoming arrogant.[16] It also constitutes our capacity to remain humble with the realization that no matter how broad or elevated our personal perspective, it is always relative and limited as compared with the absolute.

Although the physical sense of vision is embodied in our eyes, we can think of each set of bilateral points on the gallbladder meridian as representing different subtle aspects of vision as it exists psychospiritually. For example, we may think of Gb-24, "the sun and the moon," as a pair of eyes on the rib cage. Each pair of points from Gb-14 through Gb-20, all in line with the pupil, can also represent a pair of eyes and address a discrete aspect of inner and outer vision.

---

## ❖ Gb-15 **Head Before Crying**

*Tou²lin²qi⁴* Head Before Crying 頭臨泣

FUNCTION

Meeting point of the gallbladder and bladder channels and the *yang* linking vessel

VIRTUES

1. Brightens the eyes.
2. Opens the nasal orifice.
3. Empowers perspective to relieve frustration.

The character *tou* ("head") helps distinguish Gb-15 from Gb-41 (*zulinqi,* "foot before crying"). Like Gb-41, this point addresses frustration to the point of tears. In keeping with its location on the head, Gb-15 empowers an elevated perspective on life's challenges. Hence we may better discern heaven's intention in our life circumstance and abstract the appropriate lesson from each problem that confronts us. Physically, Gb-15 can address tearing in the eyes that results from allergies or conjunctivitis as well as helping open and clear the nose. Both functions are based on clearing wind and heat that obscure these sensory orifices. Extreme wind and heat can be congruent with vertigo or seizures, whose presence suggests great disorientation toward both self and the external world.

External wind suggests the world is shifting around us in a chaotic way that prevents us from orienting to it. This puts stress on the decision-making and planning facilities of the wood element and results in headaches, dizziness, and visual disturbances that are the embodiment of our frustration and lack of focus. Internal wind arising from liver blood deficiency is often associated with a lack of self-esteem that keeps us from adequately assessing our place in the world relative to others. Frustration and anger can further lead to heat through a path of excess and eventual *yin* deficiency.

With any of these internal etiologies, the presence of dizziness suggests a lack of congruence between our internal and external vision. In other words, dizziness tends to manifest when we cannot reconcile what we see in the world with what we believe to be true inside ourselves. "Head before crying" can relieve frustration and anger, empowering a greater alignment between internal and external reality as gleaned through vision. In this way we may feel more properly oriented toward the context of our lives and discover creative solutions around the obstacles that confront us.

---

❖ **Gb-16** **Eye Window**
*Mu⁴chuang¹* Eye Window 目窗
*Zhi⁴rong²* Greatest Glory 室榮

*Those who discriminate fail to see.*
– ZHUANGZI[17]

FUNCTION

Meeting point with the *yang* linking vessel

VIRTUES

1. Brightens the eyes.
2. Clears stagnation between the mind and spirit that obscures vision.

"Eye window" is one of the highest points on the gallbladder channel and thus can empower the most elevated perspective the official has to offer. The character *zhi* in the name *zhirong,* "greatest glory," can be rendered as "solstice," in this case signifying the greatest height to which *yang,* empowering perspective and vision, can ascend. Our spirit *(shen)* is informed by the vision of heaven's intent as it exists within our *jing* and in the events of our lives. When the path of our spirit into the world is clear, compassion and virtue manifest effortlessly through both speech and deed. Undue focus on past events can prevent the gallbladder from adequately making the momentary discernments necessary for healthy growth in the present. In dysfunction every new situation is interpreted according to our past regrets or future expectations, rather than being assessed on its own unique merits.

The created self is based on our habitual need to be right about who we are, how life is, and the nature of the meanings we attach to our traumas in life. Our attachments to such judgments can often prevent us from healing because our illness is in part a justification for a given point of view. "Eye window" can empower us to release judgments against self and others by bringing both current and past events into perspective.[18] The wind and heat cleared by this point are often congruent with such stagnant judgments that limit our perspective. I think of this point as a window that can enlighten any aspect of vision which does not reflect reality.

When vision of self is obscured, a patient may not realize the progress and subtle changes occurring during the course of treatment. Frequently this is because the patient's vision is fixated externally as he seeks the source of his troubles outside of himself. Even when a patient thinks treatment is not helping at all, his friends and family will often be able to discern vast improvements in both his attitude and spirit. "Eye window" can be useful for empowering a patient to perceive the subtle changes within himself as healing occurs.

## GEORGE

***Diagnosis:** Fire constitution, small intestine*
***Complaint:** Tinnitus*

George was one of my first patients. He was 32 years old, married, and taught languages at a local college. For several months he had experienced a high-pitched ringing in his ears that was greatly distracting to him. George's pulses were tense and pounding, and his small intestine and gallbladder pulses were quite tight and biting. His tongue was generally red with a yellow coat and a bright red tip.

### *Analysis*

The theme of George's life was communication, evidenced in his career teaching languages. His CSOE were all consistent with the fire constitutional type. His pulse and tongue indicated that stagnation and heat originating in the gallbladder and small intestine channels were rising to the head and the likely basis of the ringing in his ears. The fiery red tip to his tongue suggested that heat was trapped in his heart. I often connect such heat with unexpressed desires.

### *Treatment*

I treated George weekly, sedating the gallbladder and small intestine officials and working to vent heat from the heart and heart protector channels. On the eighth treatment George informed me he was receiving no relief and felt absolutely no benefit from the treatment. I requested that he please give me two more sessions to make a difference because I could clearly discern his pulse, tongue, and demeanor were improving and I felt confident that eventually this would manifest as improvement in his tinnitus.

However, to my disappointment, by ten treatments George still felt no relief and, because he was moving away to accept a professorship at a new university, he terminated treatment.

***Result***

I took my failure to help George as a defeat. I had confidence in my diagnosis and treatment plan and was dismayed that his tinnitus had not improved. Several weeks after his last appointment I received a phone call from George's wife, who was in tears. She stated, "I don't know what you've done, but since George has been seeing you I feel like I have my old husband back for the first time in years. He's loving and physically affectionate like he used to be and has started making time to listen to me again. I just don't know how to thank you."

This was a great lesson for me early in my practice to trust my instincts and never measure my success solely according to improvement in a patient's primary complaint. By working on the gallbladder and small intestine officials, and the fire element in general, George's hearing had greatly improved. His heart had opened and, as I had suspected, he was surely healing. In all likelihood, with such healing occurring in his depths, eventually had he continued treatments, his tinnitus would have improved as well. I also learned to trust my diagnostic capabilities and to have faith in the medicine. Patients are more likely to know what they want than what they need. Healing will always proceed at the functional depth of an imbalance before specific symptoms improve. Perhaps administering Gb-16, "eye window," could have yielded George some insight into just how far he had come.

---

## ❖ Gb-17 **Upright Living**

*Zheng[4]ying[2]* Upright Living 正營

*When virtue* (de) *embraces all things, we have benevolence.*
– ZHUANGZI[19]

FUNCTION

Meeting point with the *yang* linking vessel

VIRTUES

1. Empowers living in a way aligned with original nature.
2. Nourishes vision of true self.

The character *zheng,* translated here as "upright," is related in meaning to the character *zhen* (真), meaning "true" or "genuine." In medicine the character *zhen* refers to our true, unified, and authentic *qi* as granted at conception. *Zhenqi* is the *qi* of manifest destiny flowing through us in an unbroken stream as we stand "upright" between heaven and earth. According to Porkert, *zhenqi* sustains the integrity of an individual and protects and defends him against exogenous and endogenous attacks and disturbances.[20]

The character *zhen* is related to the right component of the character *de* (德), meaning original nature, virtue, and intuition.[21] *De*, often translated as "virtue," is composed of three key components. The first is a picture of a man walking (彳) and implies movement or action. The second means "perfectly right" (悳) and suggests a thing scrutinized by the eye (罒) from all directions (十) has shown no deviation (一). The last component denotes the heart/mind (*xin:*心).[22]

The straight line (一) between the mind, as represented by the eyes (罒) and the heart (心), reflects the notion of "uprightness" *(zheng)* between heaven above and earth below reflected in this point's name. In this context the character *zheng* refers to living life virtuously in an "upright" manner that preserves original nature, generates virtue, and empowers intuition. The character *de* can be interpreted to mean the virtuous person's behavior perfectly reflects his or her heart, which, under scrutiny, shows no deviation. The power of *de* may be said to grant the ability to be straight, keeping true to one's essence, and maintaining an invariable direction such as the downward flowing tendency of water.[23]

Another character containing the notion of "perfectly straight" and "uprightness" is *ren* (仁), the virtue associated with the wood element. The character *ren* consists of the radical for "man" on the left (亻) and the character for the number two (*er:*二) on the right. Its etymology is generally interpreted to indicate the benevolence and reciprocity that exists between each person and his or her neighbor.[24] However, the number two itself represents the reciprocal relationship between heaven and earth, and the character *ren* could be taken to depict a person standing upright between these two poles of the cosmos. In this context, *ren* would indicate the upright *(zhen)* posture of the sage who fulfills destiny by unifying heaven and earth.

Although there are differences in the interpretive nuances between the two characters *de* and *jen,* they both convey the notion of "uprightness" *(zheng)* alluded to in the name of Gb-17.[25] In nature, trees are a prime example of these virtues when they grow straight toward the sky to mediate the interaction between heaven and earth. Within us these virtues are empowered by the wood element.[26] Hence Gb-17, the highest point on the gallbladder channel, helps empower our ability to grow straight toward heaven and carry ourselves through life in an upright manner congruent with the virtues just discussed.

The second character in the name of Gb-17, *ying,* has several relevant meanings in the context of the point's function. The character *ying* may be defined as "to regulate," "manage," "plan," or "build." In this context of the point's name, these meanings all converge to yield the sense of "to live" one's life in an upright manner. *Ying* also refers to the nutritive aspect of blood. Blood is the embodied basis of self-esteem as an inner vision that penetrates to our roots. Here, the character *ying* implies this point's efficacy in empowering blood to nourish vision. Hence at Gb-17 the influence of blood and *qi* converge to empower a broad perspective on our lives and strengthen us to live in an upright manner congruent with the flow of *qi* between heaven and earth, root and branch, heart and mind.

---

### ❖ Gb-18 Receiving Spirit
*Cheng²ling²* Receiving Spirit 承靈

> *Spirits* [shen] *attain the One thus are efficacious* [ling]. . . .
> *Spirits* (shen), *without that which makes them efficacious* (ling), *would, I'm afraid, be powerless.*
> – *DAODEJING, Chapter* 39

FUNCTION

Meeting point with the *yang* linking vessel

VIRTUES

1. Empowers the ascent of *ling* to the heart and mind.
2. Empowers the *ling* to attract *shen.*
3. Eases constraint of the rational mind, allowing for connection to the power that arises from the unconscious.

The character *cheng* has several meanings in English including (1) to receive, to accept, to inherit, (2) to hold, contain, support, (3) to hear, listen, be informed, (4) to contract for, to undertake, (5) to continue, to carry on (a theme, etc.), and (6) to confess or to acknowledge. The character *ling* refers to the spiritual potency cultivated as the highest expression of our *jing*. Taken as a whole, *chengling* yields the sense of our receiving the spirit inherited at conception and thus continuing the theme of our ancestry. Hence during life we are vessels containing spirit whose evolution is the "backbone" and essential support of our lives. In accepting spirit, we enter into a contract with heaven. And by listening to spirit, we acknowledge original nature and are informed of the purpose to be undertaken in this life as we fulfill destiny.

*Chengling* is located at the region of the head that the ancient Chinese termed the "cover of the heavenly spirit."[27] *Ling* is the highest spiritual emanation of our *jing* as it ascends to the upper burner to mix with *shen.* By living in an upright manner (see Gb-17) congruent with original nature, *jing* is transformed into *ling* and we attain the spiritual potency to evoke changes in the world around us through the effective performance of ritual.[28] Ritual is the most passive action that can be taken, for it entails the evocation of change rather than the taking of a direct action to "make" something happen.

The act of evocation implies creating an opening to receive *(cheng)* heaven as it extends *(shen)* its influence to us. Hence our *ling,* the *yin* aspect of spirit, attracts *shen,* the *yang* aspect of spirit, so we can "receive" the influence of heaven in our lives. The function of Gb-18 mediates the interface between our personal power arrived at through the cultivation of destiny and the *shen* of heaven as it extends itself toward us. Entering the top of the gallbladder meridian on the head allows heaven's influence *(shen)* to penetrate through us down to our roots.[29]

The character *cheng* can mean to receive something in the sense of inheriting it from ancestry, and *ling* refers to that aspect of ancestral spirit which guards us during life. *Jing* is the greatest asset inherited from our ancestors, and *ling* is its highest expression. It is the function of the wood element to draw the inherited potential out of the kidney and channel it upward toward the head and heart to engender wisdom and compassion. Wood supports the expression of spirit by empowering us to receive the spiritual potency of *ling* with our hearts and minds. Hence *cheng* can also mean to "support," yielding the translation of *chengling* as "supporting spirit." In this regard, Gb-18 can mediate the extension of our potency into the world as we effect changes around us.

As the kidney is a vessel containing *jing,* we are vessels containing spirit. *Shen,* associated with the fire element, illuminates our lives so we gain conscious awareness of the nature of self and life. *Shen* empowers the mind to know truth by illuminating the distinctions between the world's myriad forms. *Ling,* in contrast, corresponds to our spiritual depths in the water element and is relatively more associated with our instincts and the mystery of the unknown. The wood element spans the distance between the lower and upper *jiao* by sending roots to our depths and branches to our heights. Wood blends and regulates the flow of *qi* between heaven and earth, integrating the facilities of unconscious and conscious knowing, intuition, and rationality.

When the wood element is dysfunctional, the gallbladder and liver officials lose communication with one another. Having lost the capacity for inner vision, the gallbladder official can become obsessed with being right as a way of making sense of the world. The three-dimensional mind loses touch with the intuitive, spiritual, and mystical nature of *ling.* "Receiving spirit" helps relax the constraints of the rational mind and awaken personal connection to the *yin* aspect of spirit. Hence *chengling* can be thought of as a potent point for strengthening the influence of *yin* within the wood element at the level of mind and spirit.

---

❖ **Gb-19** **Brain Hollow**

| | | |
|---|---|---|
| *Nao*[3]*kong*[1] | Brain Hollow | 腦空 |
| *Nie*[4]*ru*[2] | Temporal Bone | 顳顬 |

FUNCTION

Meeting point with the *yang* linking vessel

VIRTUES

1. Stimulates the brain and clears the mind.
2. Opens the sensory orifices.

The progression in point function from Gb-18 to Gb-19 typifies a functional relationship found on many meridians. Often points are grouped together that address similar issues from a relatively more physical, emotional, or spiritual perspective. Hence Gb-18 empowers *ling* as the highest spiritual expression of *jing*. Gb-19 addresses the nervous system and brain as the highest, most complex physical structures to arise out of *jing* through the production of marrow. The nervous system, mind, and spirit are related phenomena in different levels of being. Hence Gb-18, "receiving spirit," is followed by Gb-19, "brain hollow," reflecting the notion that the spirit is the basis of both mind as well as neurological functioning.

The nervous system is the physical substrate supporting the transmission of *shen* as it is congruent with neurological impulse. Hence the Chinese for nervous system is *shenjing* (神經) or, literally, "spirit wires." The authentic mind itself is an emanation of spirit as it manifests through the workings of the nervous system. Gb-18 is applicable when the conditioned mind fails to manifest the *yin* nature of *ling* spirit. Gb-19 is used relatively more when disturbance of the mind is congruent with neurological dysfunction. Hence Gb-18 might be relatively more applicable for delusion, belligerence, or emotional inflexibility, whereas Gb-19 is more appropriate for tinnitus, tremors, or epilepsy.

"Brain hollow" is also useful for addressing the brain as the most material form of mind when treating mental illness. Hence Gb-19 is said to "clear the sensory orifices," which is another way of saying the point empowers the accurate perception of reality. "Brain hollow" is also useful for clearing gallbladder fire when heat rises to cause pounding in the rear of the skull and pressure along the channel to Gb-1. Such a manifestation can be congruent with hypertension, emotional constraint, belligerence, and anger.

### ❖ Gb-20 Wind Pond
*Feng[1]chi[2]* Wind Pond 風池

FUNCTION

Meeting point with the *yang* linking vessel.

VIRTUES

1. Disperses wind.
2. Restores orientation, perspective, and mental clarity.

The environmental condition associated with the wood element is wind, and Gb-20 is a key point for eliminating this pathogenic influence. When external events are rapidly changing, the facility of the liver and gallbladder to make decisions and implement plans is critical. Pathogenic wind can be congruent with an external or internal etiology. The nature of external wind is that it moves unpredictably, making it difficult for us to navigate and orient ourselves to our surroundings. Hence externally contracted wind tends to obscure the orifices and cloud the mind, yielding such symptoms as sinus congestion, plugged ears, and runny eyes. Internal wind tends to obscure our vision of self as evidenced by constantly changing plans and decisions or the belligerent adherence to plans for lack of being able to accommodate to life's changing circumstances.

Habitual reaction to anger tends to obscure communication between the liver and gallbladder officials. As the function of these officials separate, an internal state of wind can be engendered. Hence such wind is often dispersed with Gb-37, the *luo* point that empowers communication between the liver and gallbladder. The physical presence of internal wind can be indicated by any symptom that exhibits chaotic and unpredictable movements. For instance, convulsions, muscle twitches and spasms, headaches, or pains that change location rapidly may signal the presence of wind. Emotionally, wind can manifest as anger that blows up like a storm whenever we must alter our plans in order to accommodate present circumstances. With vision so obscured by anger, we may be unable to contact the fixed reference point provided by the liver's plan. Indecisiveness and poor planning may make it difficult for us to chart a course as we appear to be blown through life like a leaf in the wind.

In such a scenario, symptoms of dizziness can present, indicating our inability to navigate when life changes so rapidly and unpredictably. The presence of dizziness suggests a lack of congruence between the internal and external aspects of vision. In other words, dizziness can result when we are unable to reconcile what we see in the world with our sense of self. Patients often become dizzy when points such as Gb-20 are needled to treat wind disorders. Such dizziness indicates the treatment is successful in eliminating the wind pathogen. By draining wind, Gb-20 can restore communication between the wood officials and thus align the facilities of decision making and planning. In this way the clarity that arises from the congruence of inner and outer vision may be restored.

Note how point function progresses from Gb-18 through Gb-20. Gb-18 governs the reception of heaven's *shen* as it is summoned by our own personal potency. Gb-19 addresses the nervous system as it transmits and receives *shen,* and Gb-20 clears wind that creates chaos in the nervous system and mind. Note that Gb-20 is at the same level as GV-16, "wind palace," an important point for draining wind from the governor vessel. As a pair of points, Gb-20 can be thought of as the eyes on the back of the head. "Wind pond" can help clear the stagnation of past regrets and thus enlighten vision about present circumstance.

---

### ❖ Gb-21 **Shoulder Well**

| | | |
|---|---|---|
| *Jian*[1]*jing*[3] | Shoulder Well | 肩井 |
| *Bo*[2]*jing*[3] | Shoulder Well | 膊井 |

FUNCTION

Meeting point of the three heater, stomach, and *yang* linking vessels

*Jianjing* is named for its location in a well-like depression in the center of the trapezius muscle. The plateau defined by the top of the shoulders represents the highest aspect of the torso. From here the neck rises to join the head and body as they represent heaven and earth, respectively. Every bilateral pair of points along the gallbladder channel addresses a specific form of constraint that can disempower the smooth flow of *qi* and disrupt communication between various aspects of being.

The wood element empowers the virtue of benevolence that manifests as a broad perspective in life not limited by judgmentalness or belligerence. When separation occurs between head and heart due to anger and constraint, the shoulders often become tight in a way that limits perspective because the head is unable to turn fully. Such tension can obscure a patient's vision of the highest aspects of himself and others, resulting in harsh judgments and inappropriate anger.

Gb-21 helps regulate the smooth flow of *qi* between heart and mind by empowering perspective and emotional flexibility and keeping the neck and shoulders relaxed so they can turn freely. In this way the heart's insight is freely accessible to the mind, and the virtue of benevolence can be restored.

❖ **Gb-22** **Armpit Abyss**

| | | |
|---|---|---|
| *Yuan*[1]*ye*[3] | Armpit Abyss | 淵腋 |
| *Quan*[2]*ye*[3] | Armpit Spring | 泉腋 |
| *Ye*[4]*men*[2] | Armpit Gate | 腋門 |
| *Ye*[4]*men*[2] | Fluid Secretion Gate | 液門 |
| *Yuan*[2]*ye*[4] | Abyss of Secretions | 淵液 |

Gb-20 ("wind pond"), Gb-21 ("shoulder well"), and Gb-22 ("armpit abyss") all allude to water in their names. The progression of imagery from a pond to a well, and ultimately to a deep whirlpool (*yuan:* "abyss," depicts water [氵] flowing into the depths [㶞]) is associated with the location of these points in successively larger holes in their respective muscles. The *qi* has transitioned over the course of these three points from the head (Gb-20) to the interface between the body and head on the shoulders (Gb-21) and finally to the body itself (Gb-22). At each stage the gallbladder official helps regulate the smooth flow of *qi* so it can journey from the head (heaven) to the torso (earth) in a way unconstrained by anger or judgment.

Gb-22 is useful for pain that radiates up the side of the rib cage from Gb-25 up to Gb-22. I also find this point useful when belligerence constrains and agitates the heart.

❖ **Gb-23** **Attached Tendon**

| | | |
|---|---|---|
| *Zhe*[2]*jin*[1] | Attached Tendon | 輒筋 |
| *Shen*[2]*guang*[1] | Spirit Radiance | 神光 |

FUNCTIONS

1. Meeting point of the gallbladder and bladder channels
2. Gallbladder *mu* point

VIRTUES

1. Strengthens muscles and tendons.
2. Motivates flexibility in action.

The character *zhe* indicates the side of a chariot where weapons were hung. *Zhejin* is located in just such a place where the muscles of the rib cage (weapons) are attached to the torso (chariot). The character *jin* denotes the tendons and ligaments, which are governed by the wood element. Here the radical for bamboo (⺮) denotes the relationship of the tendons to the wood element by evoking bamboo as the archetype of healthy growth.[30] Underneath are the radicals for flesh (月) and strength (力).

Taken together, the point name yields the sense of the strength and flexibility empowered by healthy tendons as they reflect the underlying qualities of the wood element.

The gallbladder official presides over the tendons and ligaments that anchor our muscles and empower flexibility in action. Tendons and muscles implement our motivations in the world and help us stand upright. Whereas Gb-17, "upright living," addresses our spiritual disposition toward proper motivation in life, Gb-23 addresses the physical component of proper disposition and conduct as it manifests in the strength and flexibility of the tendons and ligaments. Hence J. R. Worsley has named Gb-23 "neglected muscles," indicating the point's efficacy in treating illnesses typified by atrophy.[31]

One alternate name of Gb-23 is *shenguang,* or "spirit radiance." Located just below the armpit at the level of the heart, Gb-23 helps maintain the proper balance between the emperor (heart) and the general (gallbladder) by ensuring that the wood element (mind, facility of data analysis) does not constrain and dominate the intuitive capacity of the heart. In this way the radiance of the spirit can manifest to reflect the balance between reason and intuition.

As a meeting point, Gb-23 facilitates the functional union of the bladder and gallbladder officials. The bladder empowers upright behavior by strengthening the spine and allowing us to stand firmly with our back straight and our head held high. The gallbladder, by governing the tendons and ligaments, empowers flexibility in our posture and perspective as well as the virtues of strength and decisiveness in our movement.

---

| ❖ **Gb-24** | **Sun and Moon**[32] | |
|---|---|---|
| *Ri$^4$yue$^4$* | Sun and Moon | 明 |
| *Dan$^3$mu$^4$* | Gallbladder *Mu* | 膽募 |
| *Shen$^2$guang$^1$* | Spirit Brightness | 神光 |

FUNCTIONS

1. Gallbladder *mu* point
2. Meeting point of the gallbladder and spleen channel, and the *yang* linking vessel

The name of this point comprises the character for sun (*ri:*日) placed next to the character for moon (*yue:* 月). Together these characters compose the character *ming* (明), meaning "illumination." The left half is the sun (日) and represents outer illumination: the vision that brings "things" into the world. It is the vision of creation that proceeds from the opening of the senses, which allows us to perceive the phenomenal world. The right half of the character represents the moon (月): the quality of light at night that "blends all things into one." This inner illumination is the vision that results from shutting off the senses, allowing a look into the depth of things. For Zhuangzi, it is the man of "far-reaching vision" who is able to roll the ten thousand things back into one, "illuminating all in the light of heaven."[33]

It is our vision of "things" that creates the phenomenal universe. The two eyes are emblematic of the fall from the unity of the one, where all things are implicit within each other, to the two, where distinctions arise between the good and the bad and, ultimately, between the self and the *dao*. The balanced functioning of discrimination and judgment are presided over by the gallbladder official. The sage is able to use these faculties without being deluded that personal discriminations and judgments constitute ultimate reality. We must be able to use the faculties of the mind, such as discernment, to know the world as it manifests in the bright light of day. However, we should not be deluded by our judgments and forget it is the unity which all things return to at night that is ultimately real. When the *Daodejing* tells us in Chapter 41 that the "[i]lluminating *dao* appears dark," it is referring to the inward gaze of the sage, who always returns to the vision afforded by the dim light represented by the moon in the character *ming*.

The character *ming* may serve as an icon for the functional relationship between the liver and gallbladder, which are the *yin* and *yang* officials that comprise the wood element. In a state of functional balance, these officials empower the integrated vision of our inner and outer world. Internally, the liver (moon/*yin*) empowers the vision of *dao* contained in our primordial endowment. The gallbladder (sun/*yang*) must bring the internal vision of the liver into the world as well as convey clearly the reality outside our self back into our depths. It is in this balanced alignment of inner and outer vision that the sage finds clarity.

The dysfunctional tendency of the gallbladder official is to become split, perceiving alternatives as being either good or bad, black or white, or right and wrong. This can result in an internal tearing apart congruent with the one-sided symptomatology associated with the gallbladder official. Personal judgments of good and bad, beautiful and ugly, split the world apart in a way that does not reflect the spontaneous nature of *dao*. Hence Gb-24 is useful for empowering us to perceive the fundamental unity behind what we imagine are diametrically opposed alternatives in life.[34] In this way we may gain a broad perspective that harmonizes both judgment and constraint. I have also found this point to be useful for treating people who are overly optimistic or pessimistic—able to see only the good or bad in life. Lastly, Gb-24 can be effective for the person who refuses to judge anything or anyone because everything is perceived as being relative and therefore equal.

An alternate name of Gb-24, *danmu,* indicates this is the *mu* point of the gallbladder official. Hence *danmu* may be used in palpatory diagnosis to assess stagnation in the gallbladder official as well as treat such stagnation.

---

❖ **Gb-25** **Capital Gate**

| | | |
|---|---|---|
| *Jing¹men²* | Capital Gate | 京門 |
| *Qi⁴fu³* | *Qi* Storehouse | 氣府 |
| *Qi⁴shu¹* | *Qi Shu* | 氣俞 |
| *Shen⁴mu⁴* | Kidney *Mu* | 腎募 |

FUNCTION

*Mu* point of the kidneys

The designation as a capital implies the importance of this point in marshaling the activity of the kidney official. A capital is a central location where officials gather to conduct the affairs of the country. Hence Gb-25 is the *mu* point of the kidneys where kidney *qi* gathers. In this point's name, the character *jing* (京) for capital is related to that of *yuan* (原), meaning source.[35] Note that the character *jing* (京), meaning "capital," is a homophone with the character *jing* (精), denoting kidney essence. As the *mu* point of the kidney, Gb-25 provides access to a strong reserve of *qi* for the kidney official that presides over *jing* and *yuanqi,* as resources of the inherited constitution.

"Capital gate" is located over the gallbladder and can be useful for treating symptoms of that organ as well as helping reinstitute the smooth flow of *qi* in the official and its channel after the gallbladder has been removed.

---

❖ **Gb-26** **Girdle Vessel**

| | | |
|---|---|---|
| *Dai⁴mai⁴* | Girdle Vessel | 帶脈 |

FUNCTION

Meeting point with the girdle vessel

Named after the fourth of the eight extra meridians, this is an important point for activating the functions of *daimai.* The genesis of the eight extra meridians recapitulate the ontogeny of being as discussed in Chapter 1 of *Nourishing Destiny.* The conception vessel is the first to emerge as an expression of *dao* as undifferentiated potential. The governor vessel is next to emerge as an expression of heaven's influence. These two form the dual poles of heaven and earth within the emerging form of the fetus. Between them arises *chongmo* to blend the polarities of heaven and earth, *yin* and *yang,* within us. Here the development of the universe has been recapitulated as heaven arises from the eternal *dao* and the two cosmic poles of heaven and earth are in turn blended by *chongqi.*

The fourth vessel to emerge is *daimai,* which encircles the other three vessels and defines the central perimeter around which the rest of the body will develop. The function of *daimai* is to unify and bind together all the vessels with just enough force to create integrity and with enough ease to prevent constraint. *Daimai* conducts the *qi* of the entire organism in the correct direction and to its final destination.[36] The conception vessel, governor vessel, and *chongmai* define the front, back, and middle of being in two-dimensional space, but it is *daimai* that creates the expansion of being to give it volume. At this stage in embryological development, the two (*yin* and *yang*) have been doubled to yield four meridians (CV, GV, CM, and DM) that complete the torso of the fetus's body.

Note that the function of all bilateral point pairs along the gallbladder meridian has been to unconstrain *qi* in some aspect of being. Here, at Gb-25, that function is emphasized as *daimai* regulates the relationship between the upper and lower halves of the body. If judgment constrains the mind, our centers will tighten and the heart and kidneys will not be able to communicate freely. Shut off from the kidneys' wisdom as contained in *jing,* the heart will not be able to govern compassionately according to the principle of *wuwei.*

The point *daimai* promotes communication between the upper and lower *jiao* by easing constraint in the center. In this way the perspective of the heart may be restored and the potential destiny stored in kidney *jing* can again flow effortlessly into the world.

---

## ❖ Gb-27 Fifth Pivot

*Wu³shu¹* Fifth Pivot 五俞

FUNCTION

Meeting point with the girdle vessel

Located at the center of the torso, this point is one of the five that allude to a pivot in their name. The others are St-25 ("heavenly pivot"), Gb-28 ("outer pivot"), GV-5 ("suspended pivot"), and GV-7 ("central pivot"). Note that the other four pivot points are also located on the center of the torso. The character *wu,* meaning "five," denotes all four directions plus the center as an immovable reference point. Gb-27 helps the body rotate flexibly around its central axis to embody the gallbladder's function of promoting decisiveness and flexibility in both movement and thought. As a point of *daimai,* Gb-27 helps regulate the central axis of the body in the ways discussed relative to Gb-25.

---

### ❖ Gb-28 **Binding Path**

| | | |
|---|---|---|
| *Wei²dao⁴* | Binding Path | 維道 |
| *Wai⁴shu¹* | Outside Pivot | 外俞 |

FUNCTION

Meeting point with the girdle vessel

*Daimai* wraps around the conception and governing vessels and *chongmo*, "binding" them together with a dynamic tension that creates form yet allows *qi* to flow smoothly between the upper and lower *jiao.* The hips are a pivotal joint embodying the gallbladder's function of choosing direction decisively in life. Indecision may find us habitually trying different paths as we continually branch out but never get far in any particular direction. "Binding path" can empower the virtue of decisiveness in staying without deviation on one's chosen course of action while also maintaining the virtue of flexibility empowered by the gallbladder official.

---

### ❖ Gb-29 **Dwelling in the Bone**

| | | |
|---|---|---|
| *Ju¹liao²* | Dwelling in the Bone | 居髎 |
| *Ju¹jiao⁴* | Dwelling Hole | 居窌 |

FUNCTION

Meeting point with the *yang* motility and *yang* linking vessels

Gb-29 is located in a small depression above the ilium and thus can be said to "dwell" in the hipbone. The divergent meridians channel pathogens into the joints in an attempt to divert them away from the organs. The liver official tends to be damaged by pathogens characterized by wind, cold, and damp. Pathogens can be directed away from the liver and into the hip joint at Gb-30, which is the upper confluent point of the gallbladder and liver divergent channels. When such pathogens are "dwelling in the bone," they can cause pain and limit movement. Use of moxa on Gb-29 can be effective for warming the gallbladder channel and helping remove such pathogens.

## ❖ Gb-30 Jumping Circle

They forget liver and gall, cast aside ears and eyes, turning and revolving, ending and beginning again, unaware of where they start or finish. Idly they roam beyond the dust and dirt; they wander free and easy in the service of inaction. Why should they fret and fuss about the ceremonies of the vulgar world and make a display for the ears and eyes of the common herd?[37]

| | | |
|---|---|---|
| *Huan²tiao⁴* | Jumping Circle | 環跳 |
| *Huan²tiao²* | Circle Spear | 環銚 |
| *Huan²gu³* | Circle Valley | 環谷 |
| *Kuan¹gu³* | Hipbone | 髖骨 |
| *Bi⁴shu¹* | Hip Socket | 髀樞 |
| *Bi⁴yan⁴* | Weary Hip | 髀厭 |
| *Bin⁴ku³* | Kneecap | 臏骨 |
| *Shu¹he²zhong¹* | Harmonious Central Pivot | 樞合中 |
| *Shu¹zhong¹* | Central Pivot | 樞中 |

FUNCTION

Meeting point with the bladder channel

Located in the center of the hip joint, "jumping circle" empowers the ability to move flexibly and decisively in a manner unconstrained by thought. Flowing movement of the hip joint reflects a spirit that is able to wander freely and spontaneously. The sage is able to follow the direction of his own nature spontaneously, unhampered by conditioned thoughts of "should" or "shouldn't." Gb-28 helps bind the indecisive person to his path, and Gb-30 helps empower flexibility in our movement through life.

## ❖ Gb-31 Wind Market

*Feng¹shi⁴* Wind Market 風市

Wind is the environmental influence associated with the wood element. Because a market is a gathering place, wind tends to collect at this point where it may be treated with acupuncture and moxibustion. Symptoms associated with wind accumulating may include pain or numbness and decreased range of motion in the lower back or legs, muscle spasms or tremors, or itching.

---

| ❖ **Gb-32** | **Middle Ditch** | |
|---|---|---|
| *Zhong*$^{1}$*du*$^{2}$ | Middle Ditch, Middle River | 中瀆 |
| *Zhong*$^{1}$*du*$^{2}$ | Middle Calf | 中犢 |

Gb-32 is named for its location in the center of the lateral thigh in a depression between the two muscles that resembles a ditch or river. I use this point for pain, numbness, and decreased range of motion (ROM) along the gallbladder channel on the leg. Such symptoms are often associated with the presence of wind and cold in the gallbladder channel.

---

| ❖ **Gb-33** | ***Yang* Pass** | |
|---|---|---|
| *Yang*$^{2}$*guan*$^{1}$ | *Yang* Pass | 陽關 |
| *Guan*$^{1}$*yang*$^{2}$ | Pass *Yang* | 關陽 |
| *Guan*$^{1}$*ling*$^{2}$ | Pass Mound | 關陵 |
| *Han*$^{2}$*fu*$^{3}$ | Cold Storehouse | 寒府 |

Gb-33 is named for its location along the lateral edge of the knee on a *yang* meridian. The character *xi,* meaning "knee," is sometimes included in the point's name *(xiyangguan)* to distinguish it from GV-3, *yaoyangguan,* or "lumbar *yang* pass." Both the lower back and knee are foundational joints in governing movement. The flow of *qi* and *yang* that empowers vigorous movement must "pass" through these joints unobstructed, or damage to the tissue can result. Hence it is vitally important when practicing any discipline such as yoga or the martial arts to attain correct form before exerting strong effort.

Both GV-3 and Gb-33 help move stagnation, alleviate pain, increase ROM, and reinstitute the flow of *qi* and *yang* in their respective joints. The name *hanfu,* "cold storehouse," refers to the knee joint as a storehouse of cold in *bi* (i.e., arthritis-type) syndromes and alludes to the usefulness of this point in treating painful obstruction and dispersing cold.

---

| ❖ **Gb-34** | ***Yang* Mound Spring** | |
|---|---|---|
| *Yang*$^{2}$*ling*$^{2}$*quan*$^{2}$ | *Yang* Mound Spring | 陽陵泉 |
| *Yang*$^{2}$*ling*$^{2}$ | *Yang* Mound | 陽陵 |
| *Yang*$^{2}$*zhi*$^{1}$*ling*$^{2}$*quan*$^{2}$ | *Yang*'s Mound Spring | 陽之陵泉 |

FUNCTIONS

1. Earth point
2. Meeting point of the sinews

VIRTUE

Provides stability and nourishment to the wood element.

The character *yang* denotes that Gb-34 is located on a *yang* channel and differentiates this point from Sp-9, *yinlingquan,* or "*yin* mound spring." The character *ling* suggests the point's location in the depression just anterior and inferior to the head of the fibula, which is likened to a mound of earth. As the meeting point of the sinews, Gb-34 nourishes and moistens the tendons and ligaments as a spring nourishes the earth.

Blood itself is actually a type of connective tissue possessing an extracellular matrix in the form of plasma. The nutritive content of the plasma is created by the spleen. Healthy muscles, associated with a thriving earth element, nourish the tendons with a robust supply of blood. As the earth point on a wood channel, Gb-34 tonifies liver blood and nourishes the sinews. Hence "*yang* mound spring" is potentially useful for a wide variety of conditions that involve the tendons. These include conditions of atrophy and paralysis congruent with blood deficiency or loss. The sinews facilitate the movement of the muscle so intention *(yi)*, the spirit of earth, is brought decisively and flexibly into the world in a way presided over by the virtues of the wood element. The balanced tension of the sinews is the embodiment of the upright posture and healthy growth empowered by wood. Sinews that are overly tight or loose tend to reflect a person's constrained or aloof relationship to growth, respectively.

In order to grow tall, a tree must possess a firm root structure anchoring it into the earth. Similarly, the decisions initiated by the gallbladder must be firmly rooted in the liver's plan. Earth provides the stability needed to prevent a tree from falling due to overextension of its height and reach. Whereas Lv-3 governs earth as it nourishes wood from within, Gb-34 governs the relationship of earth to wood externally. Hence the muscles, an emanation of the earth element, surround the sinews as earth surrounds the roots of a tree.

If the presence of earth is not sufficient to support wood, growth tends to be impulsive and not grounded as our plans and decisions fail to take effective root in the world. Without sufficient rooting we may become timid and hesitant to initiate actions, and our capacity for vigorous decisive movement is compromised. Hence Gb-34 can dispel timidity and promote decisiveness by nourishing and rooting the gallbladder official so we may stand tall as we pursue our goals. Tonifying the influence of the earth within the wood can ease constraint and allow us to branch out as our *qi* can once again flow creatively and freely. "*Yang* mound spring" is a key point for helping stabilize and nourish the mind when it feels constrained and frustrated that growth is not occurring quickly enough.

If the presence of earth within wood is excessive, the seed of our plans may be smothered and never be able to manifest. Excessive wood can swallow up and overwhelm the earth, leading to a type of constraint that can be likened to that imposing on a root-bound plant. Whereas the gallbladder is committed to decisiveness in movement, the earth element empowers process. Excessive process and deliberation can frustrate the impulse toward growth empowered by wood. Here dampness associated with the earth element can cause stagnation in the gallbladder congruent with the congealing of bile. Eventually stones can form as dampness obstructs the flow of *qi* through the gallbladder official. Similarly, the knees can manifest inflammation and swelling as earth congeals water and congests wood at this pivotal joint. In this regard, note that all the command points by the knee are either earth or water points. A knee so affected can be likened to a knot that disfigures the upright growth of a tree. "*Yang* mound spring" excels at reducing inflammation and swelling in the knees when congested earth is at the root of the dysfunction. Thus a traditional function of Gb-34 is to clear and cool damp heat. By reducing the presence of earth, the wood element can once again be free to assert the direction of its growth clearly and forcefully.

---

❖ **Gb-35** **_Yang_ Crossing**

| | | |
|---|---|---|
| *Yang²jiao¹* | *Yang* Crossing | 陽交 |
| *Bie²yang²* | Divergent *Yang* | 別陽 |
| *Zu²jiao⁴* | Leg Bone Hole | 足窌 |
| *Zu²liao²* | Leg Bone Hole | 足髎 |

FUNCTIONS

1. Meeting point with the *yang* linking vessel
2. *Xi*-cleft point of the *yang* linking vessel

Here the gallbladder meridian crosses with the *yang* linking vessel, one of the eight extra meridians. The name of the point alludes to this meeting of channels.

---

❖ **Gb-36** **Outer Mound**

| | | |
|---|---|---|
| *Wai⁴qiu¹* | Outer Mound | 外丘 |

FUNCTION

*Xi*-cleft point

The character *qiu,* translated here as "mound," is also present in the name of Gb-40: *qiuxu,* or "wilderness mound." Here the designation of "outer" refers to the point's location on the lateral aspect of the calf. Gb-36 is said to disperse heat and inflammation and resolve toxins.[38] Such stagnation tends to present as a hot and sour taste in the mouth, a burning and sour feeling in the area of CV-12 to CV-15, esophageal reflux, and boils. Heat and inflammation can express itself through the gallbladder official as resentment that festers like an infection. Heat can also express itself as excessive judgments about self and others and overattachment to the outcome of one's plans and decisions. "Outer mound" can also be used to address intense dislike or fear of wind, the environmental pathogen associated with the wood element.[39] As a *xi*-cleft point, "outer mound" can help move and thus resolve these "toxic" emotions, and their physiological correlates, that often accompany gallbladder stagnation.

---

## ❖ Gb-37 **Bright and Clear**
*Guang[1]ming[2]* Bright and Clear 光明

*To see the small is called illumination* (ming).
*To abide by the soft is called strength.*
*Use the bright light* (guang),
*But return to the dim light* (ming).
– *DAODEJING, Chapter 52*

FUNCTION

*Luo* point

VIRTUES

1. Harmonizes the relationship between inner and outer vision.
2. Rids pathogens and concepts that obscure communication between the gallbladder and liver officials.

Chapter 52 of the *Daodejing* juxtaposes the characters *ming* and *guang* as signifying the relationship between transcendental vision *(ming)* and the vision of the material, causal world *(guang).* The character *ming*, meaning "illumination," was discussed at length in the context of Gb-24. Laozi advises that we must know how to make our way through the material world using the "bright light" to aid our distinctions and discernments, a facility governed by the gallbladder official. However, the vision of all things being separate and possessing unique properties must be recognized as merely a tool for navigation. We must always hold to the deeper vision *(ming)* of *dao* empowering the knowledge that, in reality, all things are one.

The name of Gb-37, *guangming*, evokes the balanced vision of the sage who can use the intellect to steer through the world yet always possesses a deeper view of the forces that support its manifestation. In fact, this is the very function empowered by Gb-37, the *luo* point on the gallbladder channel. Hence "bright and clear" empowers a balanced vision of the external context of one's life as well as the inner plan accessed by the liver and stored in the *jing*. By "transforming damp heat," this point can clear resentment harbored against others that festers in the gallbladder official like an infection. As the channel's *luo* point, Gb-37 helps clear heat, wind, and damp, pathogens that can obscure clear communication between the liver and gallbladder officials. In this way ignorance can be dispelled and the ability to discriminate between what is real and what is illusion can be empowered.

Symptoms addressed by Gb-37, such as muscle spasms, rigidity, paralysis, or nerve pain or numbness, can all be embodiments of our inability to flow smoothly through life. "Bright and clear" is an important point for treating one-sided symptomatology along the lateral aspects of the body corresponding to the path of the gallbladder channel. One-sided signs and symptoms can reflect the tendency to see only one side of an issue, suggesting a dysfunctional gallbladder official is limiting our perspective. Such symptomatology also suggests the possibility of an akabane imbalance. Often akabane imbalances, regardless of the channel they occur on, can be corrected using Gb-37 unilaterally on the side of the gallbladder channel determined to be relatively deficient (see discussion of the akabane test in Chapter 7).

---

### ❖ Gb-38 — *Yang* Support

| | | |
|---|---|---|
| *Yang[2]fu[3]* | *Yang* Support | 陽府 |
| *Fen[1]rou[4]* | Divided Flesh | 分肉 |

FUNCTIONS

1. Fire point
2. Sedation point

VIRTUES

1. Quells fire.
2. Harmonizes both resignation and excessive striving.

The name "*yang* support" evokes the functional role of wood in supporting the expression of the fire element. Wood serves as the fuel for fire and there must be just the right proportion of each if healthy growth is to occur. To the liver, fire is the motivating source that fuels growth from within. To the gallbladder, fire represents the external goal that all growth is directed toward.

If the presence of fire within wood is deficient, wood will not be able to engender fire effectively. In this case we tend to feel resigned to our life's circumstances and lack the strength and inclination to find our way creatively around the obstacles that block our growth. Such resignation and despair is characterized by frequent sighing as our breath *(qi)* stagnates in the diaphragm, a physical embodiment of all walls we encounter in life. The sun as the ultimate source of fire is the goal toward which all growth is directed. Hence by strengthening the influence of fire within wood, resignation can be resolved as hopefulness and striving toward our goals is revived.

If the influence of fire within wood is excessive, growth can overwhelm our facilities of decision making and planning. As internal pressure mounts, decision making tends to proceed hastily in a way not congruent with our life's plan. Impulsive growth is never directed toward a healthy goal, and eventual burnout is inevitable. Symptoms such as headaches, high blood pressure, and ringing in the ears can all be signs of heat rising when wood burns too strongly. Heart attack and stroke are both embodiments of burnout as the excessive drive of the gallbladder overstrains the heart and circulatory system.

If wood is in excess relative to fire as determined by pulse diagnosis, Gb-38 as the channel's sedation point can sedate wood and build fire. This is particularly effective when Gb-38 is paired with either SI-3 or TH-3. In this scenario, as excess is being sedated on the gallbladder channel it can be directed specifically to either the small intestine or three heater using that channel's tonification (wood) point.

## ETTA

***Diagnosis:*** *Wood, fire within. Gallbladder constitution.*
***Complaint:*** *Shoulder pain*

Etta was my second patient after opening my clinical practice. Eighty-nine years old, she had a good sense of humor and a tremendous spirit. Etta experienced arthritic pain in all her joints, which was most severe in her right shoulder. Her pulses were ropy and pounding in all positions and missed beats irregularly. Her tongue was peeled and bright red in color.

### *Assessment*

Etta's CSOE were all characteristic of the wood constitutional type. My diagnosis was that fire from her gallbladder official was rising to disturb her heart and cause inflammation at the joints all along the course of the gallbladder channel. I explained to Etta that my main concern was the instability in her heart, secondary to a gallbladder imbalance, and I was addressing it as I attended to her shoulder pain. However, Etta insisted nothing was wrong with her heart and I should only focus on her shoulder.

*Treatment*

Sedating the gallbladder's fire included treating Gb-38 and SI-5 in tandem with Gb-21 and SI-10. These points helped calm Etta's gallbladder, and, over several treatments, she experienced good relief from the arthritic pain throughout her body. However, after experiencing such relief she decided not to pursue continued treatment because "nothing else was wrong" with her.

*Outcome*

I didn't hear from Etta again for nearly two and a half years. Then one day I received a phone call from her daughter telling me that Etta needed to talk to me and had requested I come to her home for a visit. I was informed that Etta had recently been diagnosed with gallbladder problems and had sustained a heart attack. Entering Etta's room I found her lying in bed breathing oxygen through a tube and panting very hard.

Seeing I had entered her room Etta summoned me to her bedside. As her voice was quite weak I leaned close to her mouth. Etta squeezed my hand and smiled, saying, "You were right. It was my gallbladder hurting my heart." Her pulses were quite strong on the top but completely insubstantial upon pressure. This "empty" quality suggested her feeble *yin* was failing to root her *yang,* and her life force, synonymous with *yang,* was floating away.

Etta died later that evening. I have always been impressed that the presence of fire within her wood was so strong, she felt compelled to acknowledge to me I had been correct in my diagnosis of her only hours before her death at the age of 93. A sense of justice burned within her, and she could not rest until "settling" this score.

At her funeral, her daughter showed me a picture of Etta when she was 17. Etta sat upright on the side of a boat with a gleam in her eye and a smile, looking into the camera and out toward the horizon of her life. What a contrast in form yet similarity in spirit to the old woman I had known!

---

| ❖ **Gb-39** | **Hanging Cup** | |
|---|---|---|
| *Xuan²zhong¹* | Hanging Cup | 懸鐘 |
| *Jue²gu³* | Broken Bone | 絕骨 |
| *Sui²hui⁴* | Marrow Meeting | 隨會 |

FUNCTIONS

1. Sea of marrow
2. Meeting point of the gallbladder, stomach, and bladder channels

The lateral malleolus resembles a cup that can be thought of as hanging from this point. The image of a hanging cup suggests potential support held in reserve. Only if this cup is grasped can it fulfill its function of providing nourishment. As a sea of marrow, Gb-39 is an important point for nourishing the *yang* aspect of the nervous system and for strengthening the bones. This function is alluded to in the alternate names, *suihui* (隨會), "marrow meeting,"[40] and *juegu,* "broken bone."

---

### ❖ Gb-40 Wilderness Mound
*Qiu[1]xu[1]* Wilderness Mound[41] 丘虛

FUNCTION

Source point

VIRTUE

Empowers perspective.

The character *qiu* depicts men (丘) standing on a hilltop who can see in all four directions without obstruction.[42] The character *xu* depicts these same men standing on a plateau in the wilderness, and, although they look in all directions, nothing can be seen, indicating the region is deserted and barren. *Xu* can be translated as a hill, ruins, or burial ground.

Gb-40 is located at the base of the lateral malleolus whose shape is similar to a hill. We can liken its function of Gb-40 to climbing a peak when lost in the wilderness. At the summit we may gain a perspective on where we have been, where we are, and where we are going. Hence "wilderness mound" can be an ideal point for someone who is lost in his life journey and "can't see the forest for the trees." As the source point on the *yang* meridian associated with the wood element, Gb-40 empowers clarity of vision relative to our interpretations and judgments regarding the external world and our relationship to it. Such a perspective can empower the realization that our personal opinions are always contextual, relative, and never absolute. With this realization the virtue of benevolence may become manifest as our vision becomes aligned with the absolute itself.

---

### ❖ Gb-41 Foot Near to Tears
*Zu[2]lin[2]qi[1]* Foot Near to Tears 足臨泣

FUNCTIONS

1. Wood point
2. Horary point; 11 P.M.–1 A.M., spring equinox
3. Transmitting point for the virtues of the wood element

VIRTUE

Empowers the acknowledgment and expression of frustration and anger so tears can be released and stagnant emotions resolved.

The character *zu* distinguishes the name of Gb-41 from that of Gb-15, whose name is *toulinqi,* or "head near to tears." The character *qi* (泣) means "to weep silent tears."[43] The character *lin* (臨), meaning "to be near to," is a homophone of the character *lin* (林), which means "forest." The gallbladder, as an official of the wood element, is associated with the emotion anger, a feeling that accompanies directed growth. Such motivation can present as either a pathological excess or deficiency. In excess, we may constantly knock our heads against all walls we encounter in life. As we overwork trying to move the stagnation symbolized by the real and imagined walls that confront us, internal heat is generated. When motivation is deficient we stop pushing onward in our journey and become resigned to life's apparent obstacles. Both scenarios are characterized by diminished perspective and the inability to find creative solutions to our problems. By empowering the essence of vision, "near to tears" can help us find our way creatively around obstacles and thus dispel the source of our identification with feelings of frustration or resignation.

As the channel's horary point, Gb-41 is capable of transmitting the virtues of the wood element to any other *yang* official on which the wood, or receiving point, is simultaneously treated. For example, to empower decisiveness within the stomach official, Gb-41 and St-43 could be treated in combination. In this case increasing the virtue of perspective associated with wood could dispel the tendency of earth toward excess deliberation and worry.

---

### ❖ Gb-42 Earth Five Meetings

| | | |
|---|---|---|
| *Di⁴wu³hui⁴* | Earth Five Meetings | 地五會 |
| *Di⁴wu³* | Earth Five | 地五 |

All three characters in the name of Gb-42 denote a convergence, or meeting, of influences. The earth is the gathering point and provides the stability of a solid center through all of life's transitions. *Wu,* the character for five, symbolizes the four directions and a center located between the poles of heaven and earth. Hence earth is the fifth element to arise in the order of elemental generation. The character *hui* denotes the collection of things into a whole. The foot is the location where the five toes meet the earth, and Gb-42 is the place where the fifth toe meets with the other four. The toes, like the roots of a tree, bind us into the earth and provide a strong foundation that can empower flexible growth. Hence the name of Gb-42 evokes the convergence of the wood and earth element at the foundational level where our feet (roots) contact the earth. Traditionally, Gb-42 is said to treat symptoms such as mastitis, breast distension, and insufficient lactation, all of which can be based on the dysfunctional dynamic of wood constraining earth at the level of the chest.

---

❖ **Gb-43** **Valiant Stream**

| | | |
|---|---|---|
| *Xia²xi¹* | Valiant Stream | 俠谿 |
| *Jia¹xi¹* | Pressed Stream | 夾谿 |

FUNCTIONS

1. Water point
2. Primary tonification point

VIRTUE

Empowers the ability to flow with grace around life's obstacles.

The character *xia,* meaning "bravery" or "chivalry," contains the man radical (亻) and the phonetic *jia* (夾), depicting a man with outspread arms (大) holding two people (人 人) he is rescuing. The character *xi* refers to a ravine that a mountain stream would flow through. The name of Gb-43 evokes the image of a stream flowing valiantly toward its goal of reaching the sea regardless of what obstacles it might encounter on its journey. Whereas Lv-8 empowers flexibility as an internal virtue, Gb-43 empowers a flexible perspective on obstacles that confront us on our journey. When a stream encounters an obstacle, it flows around it gracefully until eventually the barrier is eroded and washed away. As the water point within the wood element, Gb-43 helps us embody the virtue of graceful flow in the process of growth.

If the presence of water within is deficient, wood tends to become brittle and dry, losing its ability to grow flexibly. Without water to control the fire within wood, excess heat tends to consume fluids, leading to a state of *yin* deficiency and constraint along the gallbladder channel. Such constraint is suggested by the point's name: the character *xia* can mean "to pinch," and the character *xi* can refer to a gully that narrows the flow of a mountain stream. In this case the name of Gb-43 can be translated as "pinched ravine," suggesting constraint in the flow of the gallbladder's *qi*. As fire rages out of control, rising heat can generate wind congruent with such symptoms as hypertension, heart attack, and stroke. Belligerence tends to explode in spontaneous outbursts that appear as unexpectedly as sudden thunderstorms in spring. Strengthening the presence of water within wood can help calm fire, dispel arrogance and anger, and promote tranquility as the graceful flow of *qi* is restored.

If the presence of water within is excessive, wood tends to become damp as the presence of fire within wood is extinguished. Wet wood loses its strength and tends toward mold and rot. As fire is extinguished, our quality of aspiration and self-assertion suffers as we cease to strive toward our goals. Excessive fear associated with the water element can keep us from ever manifesting our plans as we bend too easily in the face of life's adversity. In this case we may compensate for our fear by overrelying on our intellect in a struggle to "keep our heads above water." By diminishing the excessive influence of water within, wood may once again stand up straight and assert its spontaneous direction of growth toward heaven.

---

**❖ Gb-44** **Foot Hole *Yin***
*Zu²qiao⁴yin¹* Foot Hole *Yin* 足竅陰

FUNCTIONS

1. Metal point
2. Exit point

VIRTUES

1. Opens the sensory orifices.
2. Helps us let go of what is inessential to empower balanced growth.

The character *zu,* meaning "foot," distinguishes this point from Gb-11, *tou qiaoyin*, translated as "head hole *yin.*" The character *qiao* means "portal," and, like Gb-11, the point's name makes reference to its use in treating conditions that obscure the sensory orifices. At Gb-44 *qi* exits the channel to enter the liver meridian at Lv-1. The character *qiao* can be translated as "aperture," suggesting Gb-44 is a "hole" in the "foot" and allows *qi* to flow to the liver channel, which is *yin* in nature.

As the metal point on the gallbladder meridian, Gb-44 regulates the metal element's control of wood across the *ke* cycle. Gallbladder is a *yang* official, and, as such, the qualities of metal come to it externally. Hence the influence of metal on the gallbladder can be likened to that of pruning shears to a plant. The quality of good pruning is that it eliminates the unessential so growth can proceed in a focused manner. Although it may hurt us to let go of a potential direction of growth, in the long run we are empowered to channel our limited resources more fruitfully. For example, if a tomato plant is not pruned it will produce a lot of fruit that will tend to be relatively small in size. Pruning helps the plant channel its mineral resources to produce fewer tomatoes although of larger size.

Both wood and metal empower different aspects of structure within our lives. Wood empowers that aspect which flows flexibly from within as we creatively manifest destiny. This can be likened to the rings of a tree that in cross section represent the tree's growth yet constitute the channels within the tree that connect the deepest roots to the outermost branches. Metal, however, constitutes the internal crystalline lattice of our lives that springs from essence and is not negotiable. This aspect of self flows from heaven through our *jing* within and from life without. It is the function of metal to ultimately limit the creativity of our growth so all our life's expressions are in line with heaven's plan. When wood and metal, the *hun* and the *po,* are in balance, there is an alignment between the creative thrust of the human mind (wood) and heaven's intention (metal) for each of our lives. If these influences are not aligned, the quality of our growth can suffer.

If the presence of metal within wood is deficient, our quality of growth can emulate a tree that sends out branches in many directions yet never grows very far toward any specific goal. We may fear letting go for lack of a clear vision about what to let go of or what direction to move in once we do let go of our attachments. Empowering metal within wood may help us prune away only those aspects of self that are unnecessary for balanced growth. In this way our intention and direction can be better focused as inspiration, a virtue associated with metal, meets aspiration, a virtue born of wood.

The resolution of anger is often found in our ability to let go of our attachment to our interpretations of past experience. The mind's futile search for justice on earth often constrains the wood element because no legal remedy is sufficient to empower us to let go of our anger and pain. Such constraint is often associated with a sour or metallic taste in the mouth associated with the wood and metal elements, respectively. Harmonizing the presence of metal within wood can help soften the quest for earthly justice with the knowledge that all is just and in accord with heaven's plan. In this way the metal element's virtue of righteousness can be empowered within the wood to help us truly let go and heal from past trauma and perceived injustices. True healing is always characterized by such reconciliation with heaven's will.

If the presence of metal within is excessive, wood tends to be constrained as it is overcontrolled. In this case we can feel we have been "cut down in our tracks" every time we have initiated an action in life. This can lead to anger and resentment against self, others, and ultimately heaven for unjustly stopping us from pursuing our chosen path. Constantly being "cut down" can lead to despair, resignation, and timidity as we cease to believe there is any use even trying to assert our own wills in the world. Timidity can reflect our fear of heaven's ax coming to constantly chop down our best laid plans. Often this dynamic is characterized by sighing as we weakly let off steam, thinking, "what is the use?" By sedating Gb-44 we can inhibit the excessive control of metal over wood, thus allowing wood to better direct growth according to our inner plan.

I have found this point to be good for nightmares and fear of ghosts. This fear keeps people up at night when they are unable to let go of the past. Here a person's regrets over past decisions, injustices, and paths not taken returns to haunt him, making sleep difficult. Such insomnia typically occurs during the peak hours of the wood (11 A.M.–3 A.M.) and metal (3 A.M.–7 A.M.) elements according to the Chinese clock.[44] Thoughts of "I should have done this," "I should be doing that," "I should never have . . ." keep the patient awake and unable to let go into sleep. Harmonizing the metal within the wood can be helpful for this type of insomnia and empower us to let go into sleep.

## *Exercises*

1. Compare the functions of all the points that surround the eye (Gb-1, St-1, Bl-1, and TH-23) as they differentially empower vision.
2. The *shaoyang* channel is comprised of the gallbladder and three heater officials. Gb-1 and TH-23 and Gb-2 and TH-22 are located by the eyes and ears, respectively. How do these four points differentially integrate hearing and vision?
3. Both SI-19 and Gb-2 are located next to the ear and contain the character *ting,* meaning "to hear." Compare the functions of these two points as they address the inner and outer aspects of hearing.
4. Compare the functional relationships between Gb-8 and Gb-10 with that of GV-10 and GV-11 relative to the empowerment of perspective and its practical application.
5. Analyze the point combination Bl-66, Gb-43, Gb-8 from the standpoint of quieting fear, empowering perspective, and promoting movement through life.
6. Discuss the nature of the *shen* and *ling* spirits as they influence the functions of the points listed in Figure 30.1.
7. Each of the bilateral pair of points from Gb-1 through Gb-20 may

be conceived of as a pair of eyes.

a. Pick any pair of points and elaborate the aspect of vision addressed by the point's function.

b. Differentiate the aspects of vision addressed by the functions of Gb-1 through Gb-20.

c. How does each set of points address the internal and external aspects of vision?

8. How do wind and heat obscure vision spiritually, emotionally, and physically?
9. The points Gb-17, Bl-7, and GV-20 are all located in a line at the top of the head on their respective channels. Discuss the functional relationship among the three points as they relate to the connection among the related concepts of center, heaven, mind, spirit, evolution, original nature, uprightness, and destiny.
10. Compare the function of Gb-13, "root spirit," with Gb-18, "receiving spirit," relative to how each point addresses *shen* and *ling*, respectively.
11. The following are key points on the gallbladder channel that address constraint in different aspects of being: Gb-4, Gb-15, Gb-21, Gb-24, Gb-34, and Gb-40.
    a. Differentiate the aspect of constraint addressed by each point.
    b. How is the point's location on the body associated with the aspect of constraint it addresses?
12. Compare the functions of Ht-4, GV-11, and Gb-30 relative to the idea of adhering to a path in life.
13. Gb-40 empowers our clarity of vision regarding our place in the world, whereas Lv-3 empowers the vision of our own inner plan. Compare the relative inner and outer orientation of functions for the source points on each of the *yin* and *yang* paired officials, respectively.

## NOTES

1. ACI = anatomical Chinese inch.
2. As quoted by Girardot, 1983, p. 194.
3. For more on the relationship of the North Star to Chinese physiology and cosmology, see *ND,* Chapters 1 and 2.
4. See *ND,* pp. 44–46.
5. Legge, 1971, p. 192.
6. The curious organs are the bones, the gallbladder, the brain, the womb, the blood vessels, and the marrow.
7. Ellis, Wiseman, and Boss, 1989, p. 256.
8. Here I am referring to these channels only as paired meridians and not as relative depths of illness as is done in the six-division model.
9. For example, SI-13, Lv-8, LI-11, and Bl-4.

10. For a discussion of the *chongqi,* see *ND,* Chapters 1 and 11.
11. I often utilize the herbal formula Gastrodia and Uncaria (Tianma Gouteng Yin) to harmonize such a dynamic.
12. Zhuangzi, in Watson, 1964a, p. 95.
13. Larre and de la Vallee, 1993, p. 2.
14. For a discussion of *shen* and *ling,* see *ND*, pp. 49–57.
15. For a discussion of the differences between *yin* and *yang* officials, see *ND,* pp. 169–172.
16. For a discussion of the virtue of benevolence, see *ND,* pp. 239–241.
17. Watson, 1964a, p. 39.
18. For a discussion of the clinical use of this point, see *ND,* pp. 254–255, for a case study.
19. Watson, 1968, p. 171.
20. Porkert, 1982, p. 171.
21. See Wieger, 1965, lesson 10 K, L, and O. The imagery of the character *de* also has an overtone suggesting the empowerment of intuition. According to the etymology of the character, intuition may be defined as the ability to bypass one's mind directly and know spontaneously with one's heart the heart of all things.
22. Weiger, 1965, pp. 36–37.
23. Ibid.
24. Ibid., p. 28.
25. For a discussion of these differences, see *ND,* pp. 238–239.
26. For a discussion of bamboo as the archetype of healthy growth, see *ND,* pp. 234–235.
27. Ellis et al., 1989, p. 267.
28. Note that the character *de* (得), meaning "to attain," is a homophone of the character *de* (德), meaning both "original nature" and "virtue."
29. See discussion of Gb-13, "root spirit."
30. For a discussion of bamboo, see *ND,* pp. 234–235.
31. Worsley, 1982, p. 155.
32. See the quotation from Chapter 52 of the *Daodejing* in my description of Gb-37, as it has relevance to the function of Gb-24 as well.
33. Watson, 1964a, p. 36.
34. Chen, 1989, p. 123. Another acupuncture point that may address this aspect of vision is GV-24.5 [Ex-HN3, or *yintang*], which is not named in some traditions. Naming creates duality and a "two-eyed" vision of self that is separate from the *dao.* GV-24.5 addresses the function of the "third eye," which grants one the insight that comes from the vision of unity. Hence Worsley denotes this the "No Name" point. See Worsley, 1982, p. 281.
35. According to the selected explanations of point names as cited by Ellis et al., 1989, p. 274.
36. See Larre and de la Vallee, 1997, pp. 136–157.
37. Watson, 1964a, p. 83.
38. DeLaney, Leonard, and Kisch, 1989.
39. From lecture notes attributed to J. R. Worsley.
40. This name is listed in Ellis et al., 1989, p. 285.
41. The character *xu* (虛) depicts a barren place such as where burial grounds (*xu:*墟) are located. Hence to arrive at the character *xu* in this point's name we add the earth radical (土) to the character *xu* discussed in Wieger, 1965, in lesson 27H.
42. Wieger, 1965, pp. 80–81.
43. Mathews, 1931, p. 75.
44. For a discussion of the Chinese clock, see *ND*, pp. 129–130.

# 31

# LIVER

THE LIVER CHANNEL BEGINS AT THE LATERAL NAIL POINT OF the big toe and travels over the top of the foot between the first and second metatarsal bones, passing in front of the medial malleolus. It rises up the medial surface of leg, posterior to the tibia, and continues up the medial aspect of the thigh through Lv-10, Lv-11, and Lv-12 in the inguinal region. A deep branch rises from Lv-11 through Sp-12 and Sp-13. Another internal branch runs medially from Lv-12 and arcs around the genitals to rise up the median line of the abdomen through CV-2, CV-3, and CV-4. This branch then rises laterally to Lv-13 at the tip of the eleventh rib. The channel emerges from Lv-13 to run superficially again to its exit point at Lv-14 on the inferior edge of the rib cage in line with the nipple.

An internal branch leaves from Lv-13 to enter the liver, connect with the gallbladder, and then return to Lv-14. It then rises through the diaphragm and ascends posterior to the trachea to pass through the nasal cavity and connect with the eye. From here it rises up the forehead and along the top of the head to end at GV-20. A branch of the internal pathway leaves the eye to move down the mandible and circle the mouth around the inside surface of the lips. Another deep branch leaves the liver to ascend through the diaphragm and enter the lungs, where it connects with the entry point, Lu-1.

---

### *Thoughts on the Channel*

The liver meridian can be conceived of as a tree with its roots anchored in Lv-1 and its outermost branches embodying the function of Lv-14. Each point on the liver channel empowers the free flow of *qi* in some aspect of being, helping promote unconstrained growth at a rate that is healthy for the individual. If growth is driven by habituated desires, frustration with accompanying stagnation of *qi* and heat will be the result. If *qi* and *yang* are deficient and fail to empower striving, resignation will manifest as growth comes to a standstill.

The liver channel terminates at Lv-14, "gate of hope," located on the rib cage under the diaphragm. Think of the diaphragm as the embodiment of all the walls we encounter in life. So when the smooth flow of *qi* is disrupted because we fail to find creative ways around the obstacles that confront us, pain and distension are often embodied in the region of Lv-14.

#### MAIN FUNCTIONS

1. Empowers planning and striving.
2. Empowers a vision of our depths congruent with self-esteem.
3. Empowers the virtue of benevolence.
4. Generates creativity to direct growth according to the principle of flexibility.

#### DISTAL POINT FUNCTIONS

***Water:*** Empowers fluidity, gracefulness, and flexibility in growth.

***Wood:*** Empowers the essential nature of wood within the liver as an official of the wood element.

***Earth:*** Nourishes wood internally.

***Metal:*** Provides the inner structure that guides growth and purpose.

***Xi-cleft:*** Empowers the smooth flow of *qi* around obstacles that we have carried along with us.

***Luo:*** Clears stagnation of wind, cold, damp, and heat. Resolves judgments and resentments over perceived injustices.

---

❖ **Lv-1** **Great Esteem**

| | | |
|---|---|---|
| *Da²dun¹* | Great Esteem | 大敦 |
| *Da⁴shun⁴* | Great Compliance | 大順 |
| *Shui³quan²* | Water Spring | 水泉 |

*A promise that never fails is the heart of heaven and earth.*[1]

FUNCTIONS

1. Wood point
2. Horary point; 11 P.M.–1 A.M., spring equinox

VIRTUE

Empowers vision of those aspects of self that root us into our ground of being and cannot be compromised.

As the channel's horary point, Lv-1 addresses the essence of the wood element. "Great esteem," the first point on the liver meridian, is located on the big toe, which provides our physical root and grounding to the earth. This point empowers the specific virtue of self-esteem that emerges from the vision of those principles that spring from our deepest nature. In essence, these principles root us into the ground of our being. In pruning a plant, we can remove unessential branches so growth may be channeled more fruitfully. However, the roots that anchor and feed the plant must not be compromised or the plant itself will wither and die.

Physiologically, our roots consist of our genetics and our life's purpose. One gene codes for many potential traits just as the strength of one root supports the manifestation of many branches. Our destinies constitute the very root of the purpose for our incarnation. The presence of any given genetic defect suggests it is likely to have manifested in other ways. For example, a cleft palate suggests the likelihood of other anomalies, which are perhaps not as obvious. Similarly, when a fundamental principle of our life's purpose is compromised, the implications for healthy functioning are broad reaching. To follow our inner nature as it grows from within is to comply (*shun:*順) with the *dao*. Thus the character *shun* depicts a person aligning his head (頁) with the current of a river (川). The name *dashun,* "great compliance," alludes to the importance of vision in empowering us to align ourselves internally with the flow of *dao* in and around us.[2] For this is the main way to avoid constraint in life.

Self-esteem can be defined as the ability to stand up for the vision that emerges from the depths of self. The wood element supports self-esteem by empowering a vision of our depths (liver) and building our life's plan into the world in an upright manner (gallbladder). When we compromise basic principles in life, self-esteem erodes as we gradually lose vision of our depths. Compromise becomes gradually easier until we entirely lose insight into our true nature. As the root of our vision erodes, all the officials are deprived of the liver's virtues of perspective and discernment. Losing touch with what is fundamental, we tend to act as though any compromise we are asked to make is a personal affront. Hence belligerence over relatively simple points of compromise often indicates a failure to stand up for what is fundamental in other areas of our life. Lv-1 along with Lv-14 can help empower the discernment of the difference between our life's roots (fundamental principles) and branches (those aspects of self that can be compromised), respectively.

"Great esteem" can be an important point for treating impotence. The ability to initiate and sustain an erection depends partly on the force of rising *yang*. The imagery of *yang* rising forcefully from the root to empower growth easily conveys this dynamic. Men with high-powered jobs tend to overwork both physically and intellectually. Lawyers and politicians, for example, have careers that require constantly being in their heads as they overuse their intellect to survive based on cunning and aggressiveness. Acquiring external power, such men often become *jing* deficient through a lifetime of overwork. As *yin* is consumed, *qi* and *yang* rises to their heads, often associated with migraines, neck pain along the gallbladder channel, and hypertension. As *yang* accumulates to congest the head and mind, it is unavailable below to raise and maintain an erection.

In this case sexual potency is inversely proportional to the amount of intellectual strength and aggressiveness cultivated. Self-esteem tends to erode in direct proportion to loss of potency, and belligerence increases as an external compensation for internal feelings of inadequacy. Lv-1 can help draw the *yang* out of the head and back down toward the root. It is therefore potentially helpful in both reducing migraines and increasing potency while increasing self-esteem and harmonizing belligerence. Note that I have found the formula Gastrodia and Uncaria (Tianma Gouteng Yin) similarly helpful in this situation.[3]

---

❖ **Lv-2** **Walk Between**

| | | |
|---|---|---|
| *Xing[2]jian[1]* | Walk Between | 行間 |
| *Da[4]shun[4]* | Great Compliance, Following the Great | 大順 |

*When fire arises in wood, the evil, having once begun, is sure to go on to the destruction of wood.*

– ZHUANGZI[4]

FUNCTIONS

1. Fire point
2. Sedation point

VIRTUES

1. Quells fire manifesting as belligerence.
2. Empowers compassion and benevolence allowing for moderation in all things.
3. Dispels excess fire that supports the justification "the ends justify the means."

The name of Lv-2 denotes the point's location between the first and second metatarsals. Fire within wood fuels the transformative process of aspiration and growth. If the presence of fire within is deficient, growth will slow correspondingly, and if fire is excessive then growth can proceed out of control to the point of burnout. The tendency of wood is to see the world in terms of dualities such as good and bad, and right and wrong. Benevolence *(ren),* the virtue of the wood element, helps harmonize dualistic thinking and empower moderation and compromise in the pursuit of justice. "Walk between" can empower us to choose the middle path between perceived opposites, suspending judgments of good and bad, or right and wrong. Such is the virtue of benevolence depicting a human (亻) standing upright between the two poles of heaven and earth (二).

If the presence of fire within is deficient, wood will tend to be overly damp and bend too easily in the face of adversity. Weak sighing can be a sign of yielding too quickly to life's challenges. Such resignation indicates the failure of wood to burn and empower the virtue of aspiration and upright growth. The despair associated with chronic illnesses is often congruent with the liver failing to engender a vision of "the light at the end of the tunnel." Tonifying the presence of fire within wood can offer a glimmer of hope that healing is possible and help strengthen our resolve toward that goal.

If the presence of fire within is excessive, internal pressure tends to mount as we become incapable of sustaining such rapid growth. Excessive fire tends to generate wind that can be embodied as muscle tremors, heart attack, headache, or stroke. Excess liver fire can rise to disturb the heart. This typifies the dynamic of a person who has a cause that "burns" within.[5] Excessive fire within wood tends to fuel the obsessive need to be right and allows us to justify any action deemed necessary to our chosen purpose. Occasionally in life we learn all too painfully that something is more important than being right. For without compassion, the possession of truth is meaningless.

As the channel's fire point, Lv-2 addresses the relationship between compassion, a virtue associated with the fire element, and benevolence, a virtue associated with wood. Compassion toward self and others can empower benevolence when one's mind is obsessed with judgment and perceived injustice. Sedating fire within wood can disperse the internal pressure underlying the habitual need to be right. In this way we can choose a path of moderation and "walk between" the extremes that typify this seemingly dualistic world. Hence belligerence can be dispelled as the heart is free to rule of its own accord and is less bullied by the dictates of the habituated mind.

---

### ❖ Lv-3 Supreme Rushing

*Tai*[2]*chong*[1] Supreme Rushing 太冲
*Happy Calm*[6]

FUNCTIONS

1. Earth point
2. Secondary sedation point
3. Source point

VIRTUES

1. Eases constraint to empower benevolence.
2. Nourishes wood from within.

In Daoism the character *tai,* meaning "great," refers to the ultimate unified principle of life, the *dao* as the great source for all of life's varied manifestations. The character *chong* refers to the *chongqi,* that vast whirling abyss that blends heaven and earth back into a unified whole. The liver is situated in the middle burner between heaven (the upper burner) and earth (the lower burner). A key function of the liver is to help smooth the flow of *qi* between these two poles within us. In this way *jing,* our life's potential stored in the lower *jiao,* can ascend as we learn from life and cultivate wisdom. And our spirit *(shen),* stored in the heart, can descend as we inquire into our true natures. Like the *chongqi,* the central function of the liver is to allow for the free interpenetration of *shen* and *jing* as the influences of heaven and earth commingle within us. As a source and earth point, "supreme rushing" is able to maintain a balanced center between these two poles, allowing *qi* to flow freely between them. In keeping with this spirit, J. R. Worsley has named this point "happy calm."[7]

The liver's function is to ensure that growth occurs smoothly. In dysfunction, the liver tends to either accelerate growth and overwork or to collapse as we push against perceived obstacles in life. If the presence of earth within is deficient, growth tends to be undernourished. Too fast a rate of growth strains the earth's capacity to nourish and sustain us. Here belligerence tends to overwhelm sympathy as resentment for being stuck in life is externalized and we project on others our inability to find creative solutions to our problems. This dynamic is often present in diabetes and hypoglycemia when outbursts of anger are associated with blood sugar. Earth represents the fruits of our labor. Wood tends to become consumed with attaining goals and fails to allow the leisure time for us to be nourished during the process of creation. Even when a goal is reached, the liver can tend to initiate new plans, never allowing enough time for us to relax, recoup, and taste the fruits of our labors.

Diabetes can embody the dynamic of wood invading earth as glucose is trapped outside our cells, effectively denying us the benefit of our hard work. This generates severe anger, which is frequently blood sugar dependent, as the person with diabetes or hypoglycemia (sometimes a prediabetic condition) grows frustrated as he constantly pushes himself to work yet never seems able to be nourished by his harvest.

If the presence of earth within is excessive, growth can be smothered just as too much earth can smother a seed. A dysfunctional tendency of the earth element is to mitigate our own needs in order to avoid conflict. However, every time we say "yes" when we should be saying "no," a little bit of resentment is swallowed. As resentment predicated on undelivered communication builds, stagnation grows in the digestive system and slows the functioning of the earth element as pressure mounts up toward St-9. Eventually we can feel like vomiting as we are unable to "take it anymore." Such stagnant emotions tend to produce what is known as "plum pit" *qi,* experienced as feeling a lump of something is stuck in the throat. This lump, however, is insubstantial and results from the conflicted relationship of the earth and wood elements. Lv-3, as the channel's earth point, can help ease such conflict and disperse the swellings, distensions, and unexpressed communications associated with liver *qi* stagnation.

Liver *qi* stagnation can occur at any level from Lv-1 up to the top of the internal branch of the liver channel at GV-20. Such stagnation is often typified by constraint of the middle in a way that inhibits the smooth flow of *qi* from ascending or descending properly. Weakness, pain, and congestion in the ankles, knees, hips, reproductive organs, digestive system, the center of the chest, the throat, jaw, temples, or vertex of the head can all be associated with liver *qi* stagnation. Such stagnation is often associated with congestion of *qi* and damp within the earth element. A pathological tendency of earth is to become bogged down in processing. When this occurs, what should have nourished us in life is instead transformed into burden. Burdens, whether they manifest as unprocessed emotions or as excess weight, tend to slow the liver from realizing its goals, for, as weight increases, our journey becomes more difficult. In helping regulate the smooth flow of *qi,* "happy calm" can help support growth to occur more freely in a way less burdened by unprocessed anger and resentment.

When liver *qi* is unbalanced it can ascend congruent with such physical presentations as nausea, vomiting, and esophageal reflux. The character *chong* also has the meaning of "shooting up," in the sense of a geyser erupting. Hence a key function of "happy calm" is to sedate rebellious *qi*. The earth element supports wood by nourishing it from within. A tendency of wood is to grow impatient and to feel constraint in the process of realizing its goals. The creative mind can see endless possibility in life and grows frustrated with the process of implementing plans and decisions in the world. Whereas the work of the mind is instantaneous in conceiving a project, the spleen must slowly nourish the process of realizing the liver's goals. Wood can see the beginning and know the end in a moment, but the earth must grow, harvest, prepare, ingest, digest, and build our blood, muscle, and tissue as we work to bring our plans to fruition. Many of the symptoms of stagnant or rebellious liver *qi* just listed can be the embodiment of wood "yelling" at the earth and digestive system to "hurry up!"

As a secondary sedation point, Lv-3 can disperse the excessive influence of earth within wood. In this way wood can be less constrained by process and assert itself more freely without being burdened by dampness or having to carry along undigested past experience. As a source point, "supreme rushing" can help renew the liver official by connecting it to a pure source of primordial *qi*, helping to once again ground the liver's vision in heaven's plan.

---

### ❖ Lv-4 Middle Seal

*Zhong¹feng¹* Middle Seal 中封
*Xuan²quan²* Suspended Spring 懸泉

FUNCTIONS

1. Metal point
2. Secondary tonification point
3. Point for breaking the H/W imbalance

VIRTUES

1. Addresses the relationship between self-esteem as governed by wood and self-worth as associated with the metal element.
2. Harmonizes the control of metal on wood.
3. Cools inflammation within wood.
4. Quells judgment by empowering the appreciation of intrinsic value.

The character *zhong,* meaning "center," denotes both that the liver is an official of the middle *jiao* located between water and fire along the *sheng* cycle as well as the fact that Lv-4 is located in the middle of the ankle between two large tendons. The character *feng* represents a seal like the emperor might affix on a written decree.[8] Taken as a whole, the point's name suggests the imparting, recognition, valuation of, and proper perspective on personal identity as invested by heaven (metal) within our roots (wood).

The tendency of the *hun*, as governed by wood, is to expand and rise as it empowers evolutionary growth. The *po,* in contrast, associated with the metal element, represents a contractive force calling us to center. Metal controls wood across the *ke* cycle, and "middle seal" plays an important role in mediating the relationship between these two elements.

The wood element, by governing the tendons and sinews, empowers the virtues of both flexibility and aspiration in growth. As a *yin* official, metal comes to the liver internally in the way minerals confer inner structure to a plant. Plants (wood) digest minerals (metal) within the earth and bring this essence into the world in a form we humans can assimilate. Plants grown in soil that is poor in mineral content are generally inferior in quality, having too soft a center due to a weakened internal structure. But soil too rich in minerals can "cut" or burn a plant internally and constrain growth.

The metal element's contribution to *jing* constitutes the latticework that is the inner structure of our being. This latticework must be at once solid yet fluid so our inner matrix supports growth without confining it. The solidity of our matrix reflects heaven's will as an influence in our life, constituting the highest within us and inspiring us toward the highest without. The fluidity of this matrix is congruent with heaven's grace in forgiving us when we fail to live up to our highest standards. Wood sends down roots to contact heaven in the form of minerals and, at its highest branches, receives the most refined *qi* abstracted from heaven above in the form of sunlight. Heaven above joins with heaven below to form this essential latticework permeating our entire being.

Think of the relationship of this metal lattice to the wood element as similar to that of a framework placed in a garden so tomato plants can grow off the ground, preventing them from rotting into the earth. Such a framework must elevate the plant without overly constraining it, thus providing the opportunity for maximum growth. Internally, this latticework is conferred by minerals that supply the inner structural strength of the plant.

Writing is worth only the paper it is printed on until the emperor affixes his seal *(feng)* on it. At that precise moment, equivalent to conception, a law becomes a decree conferred through the emperor by the authority of heaven. Similarly, at conception, heaven invests us with the authority to manifest its highest purpose for us during life. This authority represents the most essential value within us and constitutes the very foundation of self-worth during life. As the metal within, "middle seal" addresses the relationship between self-worth and self-esteem as governed by the wood element. Self-esteem as empowered by the liver (Lv-1) derives from the vision of who we are in our depths, whereas self-worth, as empowered by the metal element, is the valuation of what we find there.

If the presence of metal within is deficient, growth may occur for the sake of growth alone. Divorced from self-worth, our growth may be forceful but will be devoid of the inner structure and inspiration of heaven's guidance. In this case our motivations for exerting effort tend to be driven by anger and vengeance with no connection to transcendent values. Without metal's moderation, self-assertion tends to occur belligerently with little respect for self or others. Jealousy, envy, and resentment, often based on lack of self-worth, lead us to perceive injustices everywhere we turn. Such emotions constrain the wood element as our growth in life is controlled by the habituated mind and no longer reflects the inner structure of heaven's plan. Or, for lack of metal's inspiration, growth may cease entirely as we fail to see any value whatsoever in exerting effort in life.

The liver's function of detoxifying the blood depends in part on the metal within to empower the discernment of what is of value and what needs to be filtered out of the blood. Hence the liver must leave helpful minerals in the blood while eliminating what is not essential for growth. If metal within is deficient, the liver and blood tend to lack the nutrients required for healthy growth. In this case our lives may seem meaningless because we lack both inspiration and aspiration. If the quality of metal within wood is lacking, we may tend to see only the negative in ourselves and others.

If the presence of metal within is excessive, our quality of growth tends to be constrained and overly rigid. If metal overcontrols wood, we may become inflexible and constantly judge ourselves as we fail to meet our highest standards. In this way the metal element's tendency toward perfectionism can constrain wood across the *ke* cycle. We may be cut down by the internalized voice of people we respected when we were young, such as parents, teachers, or religious figures who harshly criticized us. Although we may no longer be in relationship with these people, we may still carry their voices of self-righteousness and judgment along with us. The internalized voices of our detractors becomes our mind's weapon to limit the upright assertion of our own vision in the world. In the extreme, constraint may be so severe that it becomes hard for us to find room to breathe. As wood is constrained, *qi* has a difficult time flowing freely across the diaphragm from Lv-14 and enter Lu-1, resulting in an exit/entry block between the liver and lung channel.

The dynamic of metal constraining wood often is often associated with a metallic or bitter taste in the mouth. As metal limits the expression of wood, anger tends to be repressed. Here anger may vent only as a weak sigh as its full force is always cut off in mid-expression. Often such anger is cold and piercing as the person cuts off, unable or unwilling to engage the expression of his wood element. Moxa can be quite effective to warm and soften the metal within wood at Lv-4, allowing *qi* to flow so we can stay engaged. In this way metal may less constrain wood and growth may proceed guided by an equal balance of both human and heaven's will. Illnesses characterized by inflammation such as hepatitis can be treated by needling Lv-4 to provide the cooling, *yin,* influence of metal as it controls and quells the liver's fire.

---

| ❖ **Lv-5** | **Insect Drain** | |
|---|---|---|
| *Li³gou¹* | Insect Drain | 蠡溝 |
| *Jiao¹yi²* | Intersection Apparatus | 交儀 |

FUNCTIONS

1. *Luo* point
2. Drains stagnations of *qi,* heat, damp, and wind that obscure the relationship of the liver and gallbladder officials

VIRTUES

1. Dispels annoyance over details by empowering a vision of the big picture.
2. Helps the liver detoxify the blood.

The character *li* denotes a wood-boring insect, and the character *gou* literally means "canal." As the channel's *luo* point, Lv-5 has the dual function of focusing the mind inwardly toward our depths and of opening the liver channel so stagnation can vent to the exterior. Stagnation of *qi,* damp, heat, and wind can be the physiological correlates of delusion that obscure the relationship between the mind of the gallbladder and the innate purpose of the liver official. As these stagnations are vented, the relationship between the gallbladder and liver officials is rectified and the true nature of our plan as stored in the liver is revealed to the mind. The name "intersection apparatus" alludes to the function of Lv-5 as a *luo* point empowering the intersection of the bilateral halves of the liver channel as well as that of the liver and gallbladder meridians.

A traditional function ascribed to Lv-5 is the potential to tonify both liver *yin* and blood.[9] A central physiological function of the liver official is to clear and detoxify the blood. Stagnation of *qi* or damp can lead to a buildup of heat that presents as a range of dysfunctional qualities in the blood depth of the pulse. Viral infection of the liver, as occurs in mononucleosis or hepatitis, can appear as a slippery quality in the organ depth of the liver pulse, suggesting toxicity and possible liver inflammation. Stagnation of damp and heat in the liver can manifest as any number of types of aggravating skin conditions such as eczema or psoriasis that appear like bugs on the flesh. Wind affecting the liver can also result in skin conditions resulting in annoyances that patients often describe as feeling like "bugs crawling" on their skin. On a psychospiritual level, heat in the blood can present as frustration and aggravation and cause us to feel an internal pressure congruent with belligerence.

Livers so compromised can lose the ability to clean the blood effectively. Autoimmune illnesses, as well as food and chemical sensitivities, tend to develop as the immune system hyperfunctions and responds to every perceived threat no matter how minute. This dynamic can present psychospiritually as we focus excessively on annoying details to the exclusion of the big picture. In this sense Lv-5 is indicated for the person whose picnic is always ruined by ants, helping, in effect, to "get the bugs out of the system."

Excessive attachment to our vision of how things "ought to be" in life can constrain our heart's ability to connect with self and others. For instance, a mother may judge her daughter's husband harshly because he does not meet her expectation that the daughter would marry a physician. This detail regarding the specific form of the son-in-law's career may annoy, frustrate, and lead to judgment and resentment on the part of the mother. However, the son-in-law may, in fact, be the best mate for her daughter, which is really what the mother wants for her daughter in her heart of hearts. "Insect drain" can empower a deeper vision of heaven's plan, helping us let go of our attachment to specific outcomes in life that constrain us.

The liver is the only channel that passes directly through the genitals. The character *li* (蠡) contains the character *chong* (虫) for insect doubled. A homophone for *chong,* meaning "insect," is the character *chong* (衝), denoting the penetrating vessel *(chongmai)* that figures prominently in the treatment of many gynecological disorders. The proliferation of bacteria or cell growth in the reproductive organs that occurs in disorders such as Candida albicans or dysplasia may be conceived of as insects and their toxins (蟲) proliferating in a basin (皿) (the womb). This point's metaphorical function of draining insects alludes to its ability to treat such gynecological disorders and to drain dampness and heat stagnating in the lower burner.

The character *gu* (蠱) depicts insects proliferating in a basin. Note that the three worms depicted in this character correspond in number to the *jing, qi,* and *shen,* the three treasures that fuel our evolution and the emergence of all virtue during life. Daoism posits the existence of three worms that must be guarded against with disciplined practice to prevent them from eroding our virtue and causing illness and an untimely death. The character *gu* refers to illnesses that were attributed to evil spells cast by witches. Witches were believed to place many poisonous insects, worms, and snakes in a container and to leave them there until only two were left. These final two were thought to reproduce and yield a toxin that could be transmitted to a person in order to afflict them. Such illnesses might be typified by fear and shame in the same way as sexually transmitted diseases are, and they also might be considered to result from either suppression of, or indulgence in, the sexual impulse.

Lv-5, in "draining insects," can both address gynecological disorders and quiet the urge toward immediate sexual gratification, and gratification in general, that is compelled by a dysfunctional liver official. By clearing stagnation, the virtue of benevolence and virtue in general may be rectified.[10]

---

| ❖ **Lv-6** | **Middle Capital** | |
|---|---|---|
| *Zhong¹du¹* | Middle Capital | 中都 |
| *Zhong¹xi¹* | Middle Cleft | 中郄 |
| *Tai⁴yin¹* | Supreme *Yin* | 太陰 |

FUNCTION

*Xi*-cleft point

VIRTUE

Moves liver *qi* stagnation.

The name "middle capital" refers to the point's location in the middle of the leg as well as to the liver as an official that resides in the middle *jiao*. Liver *qi* stagnation often manifests as a band across the part of the body it is affecting. For example, liver stagnation can manifest as knee pain (the middle of the leg), groin pain (middle of the lower burner), pain across the middle burner in the area of CV-11 and CV-12 (middle of the torso), tightness in the upper burner in the middle of the sternum, or constriction in the center of the throat.

As the *xi*-cleft point of the liver, this point excels at moving stagnation along the entire course of the liver channel and throughout the body. Such stagnation can present psychospiritually as frustration, judgment, despair, and hopelessness—all emotions that tend to be associated with lack of healthy growth in life. Constant sighing can be a sign of stagnant liver *qi* failing to ascend past the diaphragm, the embodiment of all walls we confront in life.

---

### ❖ Lv-7 **Knee Border**
*Xi¹guan¹* Knee Border 膝關

Located on the border of the knee, Lv-7 is used as a local point for conditions affecting the function of the knee. "Knee border" is especially good for arthritic conditions exacerbated by wind, the environmental pathogen associated with the wood element.

---

### ❖ Lv-8 **Crooked Spring**
*Qu¹quan²* Crooked Spring 曲泉

*Bent, thus preserved whole.*
– *DAODEJING*[11]

FUNCTIONS
1. Water point
2. Tonification point

VIRTUES
1. Empowers the virtue of flexibility.
2. Empowers the ability to flow around obstacles while staying focused on a goal when the external context of our life conflicts with our plans.

Empowering the qualities of water within wood, "crooked spring" nourishes the virtue of flexible movement in the face of life's challenges. Like a spring that winds its way around all obstacles to always find its way home to the ocean, so too does healthy wood, by virtue of the water within, bend around any impediment that obstructs its reach toward heaven.

Bamboo embodies the archetypal virtues of the wood element as it empowers healthy growth. Bamboo derives its strengths from its emptiness, rootedness, and flexibility. The flexibility of bamboo is in large part provided by its ability to tap deep reserves of water through its extensive root structure. When a wind blows, bamboo bends in exact proportion to the strength of the wind blowing against it. Its rootedness allows it to yield without falling over, and its emptiness represents nonattachment in the moment to its goal of rapid directional growth. Hence bamboo is "empty" in the sense of not trying to fight the direction it is being taken momentarily. As the wind subsides, bamboo springs up immediately to reassert its purpose and pursue its path. Exhibiting the virtue of benevolence, bamboo carries no grudge toward the wind that has temporarily waylaid its progress. Rather, it grows continuously, unencumbered in its journey toward heaven. The water within wood empowers these virtues within us as spiritual benevolence and the capacity for flexibility. Physically, water as *yin* nourishes the tendons, allowing us to embody the virtues of bamboo.

If the water within is deficient, wood grows brittle and loses its flexibility. This tends to manifest psychospiritually as belligerent attachment to the outcome of our plans and decisions. The water within wood is a functional basis of liver blood. If liver *yin* and blood are deficient, our sinews can dry out as we grow increasingly tight and dry physically. "Crooked spring" can tonify liver *yin* and blood to nourish the tendons and allow us to more gracefully embody the virtues of bamboo as we follow our path through life.

Because the deficiency of water is unable to control the fire within wood, excess heat tends to create internal pressure that manifests as an habitual drive toward growth. Such a person lives at the point of snapping and cannot take even minor stresses without becoming unduly angry. The overwhelming feeling accompanying this dynamic is of being on a short fuse ready to explode at any moment. Over time, excess heat tends to consume fluid and lead to a state of liver *yin* deficiency. Excess heat tends to consume the *yin* of the arteries, which lose their elasticity in conditions such hypertension, stroke, and atherosclerosis. "Crooked spring" can harmonize the presence of water within wood to help cool and moderate the drive toward excessive growth. This can mitigate the tendency toward liver *yin* deficiency, helping make growth more supple and effortless in all aspects of being.

If the presence of water within is excessive, wood becomes waterlogged and bends too easily, unable to assert itself. As the fire within is slowly extinguished, our quality of aspiration tends to suffer and we become too willing to compromise in the face of life's challenges. This dynamic can present as despair, hopelessness, and depression, all based on our inability to stand up for ourselves. This state is often typified by the struggle to keep our "heads above water" as all effort exerted is based on our flight from being overwhelmed and from fear. If we are losing this struggle to keep afloat we can appear fearful and desperate as though we are drowning. Talk of suicide can accompany such hopelessness if fear finally overtakes us. Physically, excess water within wood manifests as damp and heat collecting in the lower burner. This dynamic can be embodied in conditions such as discharges from the genitals, dysentery, or urinary infections. Dispersing the influence of water within wood can help diminish the habitual fear that fuels panicked growth. As fire within wood reasserts its influence, the virtue of aspiration is once again ignited, and hope for a brighter future is restored.

❖ **Lv-9** **_Yin_ Wrapping**
*Yin[1]bao[1]* *Yin* Wrapping 陰包

VIRTUES

1. Harmonizes liver *qi* stagnation affecting the genital region and reproductive organs.
2. Harmonizes anger embodied as stagnation in the genitals and womb.

The character *bao* depicts a fetus within the womb, and the designation of *yin* refers to the location of the point on the liver as a *yin* channel. The liver meridian is the only channel that passes directly through the genitals, providing both vigor and impulse in initiating and maintaining sexual activity. In a man this empowers the ability to sustain erection, and the imagery of bamboo growing is compelling here. In a woman, liver blood nourishes the menstrual cycle and reproductive process, and the virtue of aspiration fueled by the liver empowers fetal development within the womb.

"*Yin* wrapping" can address liver *qi* stagnation as it affects the lower *jiao* and reproductive organs. Stagnation of heat and dampness in the lower *jiao* manifesting in gynecological or prostate problems can benefit from this point. These conditions often represent the embodiment of resentment (stagnant heat) and unfulfilled need (dampness) stored in the lower *jiao* when sexual frustration and appetite form the basis of stagnation in the liver official. Anger born of abuse can be embodied as stagnation of *qi*, damp, and heat that accumulates in the genitals or womb. Such stagnation can be associated with a wide variety of gynecological disorders including fibroids, endometriosis, or eventually cancer. In men this same dynamic tends to manifest as conditions involving inflammation of the prostate.

❖ **Lv-10** **Foot Five Miles**
*Zu[2]wu[3]li[3]* Foot Five Miles 足五里

Lv-10 is five points away from Lv-14, the exit point of the liver channel. The character *wu,* meaning "five," designates the five directions: north, east, south, west, and the center. The number five itself suggests the notion of center because five is the number associated with the earth element. The character *li* (a measure of distance) and the character *li* (理), meaning "to rectify," were not always distinguished in classical Chinese.[12] Therefore, in the context of this point's name, these two characters can be taken as having similar meanings. Hence a function of Lv-10 is to rectify the center and harmonize the *qi*. *Zuwuli* complements the functions of Lv-9 but on a relatively more physical level, addressing issues of liver *qi*, damp, and heat stagnation in the lower *jiao*.

---

**❖ Lv-11 *Yin* Angle**

*Yin[1]lian[2]* *Yin* Angle 陰廉

Located on a *yin* channel, this point is found on the angle of the groin crease at the top of the thigh. "*Yin* angle" helps diminish tension in the muscles and tendons of the groin and is efficacious in easing childbirth, allowing *qi* to flow smoothly through the groin. I have also found the point useful for soothing menstrual cramps associated with stagnant liver blood and *qi*.

---

**❖ Lv-12 Urgent Pulse**

*Ji[2]mai[4]* Urgent Pulse 急脈

VIRTUE

Harmonizes the relationship between anger, self-esteem, and sexuality.

Liver *qi* and *yang* provide the thrust and force necessary for engaging in sexual activity. The throbbing felt in the genitals when aroused gives a good sense of the quality of functioning addressed by this point. I've found "urgent pulse" useful for treating sexual frustration and for people who express their anger through sexual aggressiveness. On the one hand, this point can help calm feelings of internal pressure around sexuality that manifest as tension and "pulsing" in the genital area. On the other hand, Lv-12 can be useful for impotence as well as lack of sexual desire when liver *yang* fails to rise vigorously enough to support an erection. In this case Lv-12 can disperse cold stagnation in the liver channel that is inhibiting the expression of liver *yang*.

---

**❖ Lv-13 Chapter Gate, Gate of Law**

| | | |
|---|---|---|
| *Zhang[1]men[2]* | Chapter Gate, Gate of Law[13] | 章門 |
| *Chang[2]ping[2]* | Long Tranquility | 長平 |
| *Zhou[3]jian[1]* | Elbow Tip | 肘尖 |
| *Pi[2]mu[4]* | Spleen *Mu* | 脾募 |
| *Lei[4]liao[2]* | Rib Foramen | 肋髎 |
| *Ji[4]lei[4]* | Last Rib | 季肋 |
| *Xie[2]jiao[4]* | Rib Hole | 脅窌 |

*In reconciling a great injury,*
*There is sure to have some injury left.*
*How can this be good?*
*Therefore the sage holds the left tally,*
*He does not blame others.*
– *DAODEJING*[14]

FUNCTIONS

1. *Mu* point of spleen
2. Meeting point of the liver, gallbladder, and spleen channels
3. Meeting point of the five *yin* officials
4. Point of the girdle vessel
5. Assembling point of the *yang* officials

VIRTUES

1. Treats existential writer's block.
2. Dissolves walls that block vision and frustrate growth.
3. Empowers letting go of old injuries so we can move forward in life.

The character *zhang* is the numerical classifier for both trees and documents, affirming a relationship to the wood element. *Zhang* depicts a strain of music or writing (音) that is complete as represented by the character *shi* (十). *Shi,* meaning "ten," suggests the finishing of something to perfection.[15] The name "chapter gate" invokes the image of empowering us to turn the page and move on to a new chapter in life. This function of Lv-13 is embodied by its location on the tip of the eleventh rib, the final juncture to be crossed before the liver *qi* reaches Lv-14, and from there aspires to heaven as represented by the function of Lu-1. The name "elbow tip" alludes to the fact that, with our arms hanging at our sides and our palms turned outward, this point can be found on the torso next to the tip of our elbow.

The liver, gallbladder, and spleen officials all converge at Lv-13. The functional dynamics of disharmony between the wood and earth element were discussed in the context of Lv-3 and Gb-6.[16] In this scenario our creative drive as mediated by the wood element comes into conflict with the very process needed for creation to occur as nurtured by the earth element. This conflict can lead to a variety of symptoms including bitter taste in the mouth, constriction anywhere from CV-12 up to the throat, plum pit *qi,* heart palpitations, ulcers, diabetes, and a wide range of digestive dysfunctions. As a meeting point for the involved officials, Lv-13 is ideally suited to harmonizing this disharmony and helping restore balance between the officials of the middle *jiao*.

Holding on to the past can prevent us from ever moving on to open a new chapter in life. Resentments may so color our vision of the present that we are unable to respond to any new situation based on its own merits. Hence creativity becomes impossible as we are constantly limited by ingrained thought patterns. "Chapter gate" is ideal for harmonizing frustration that arises in the creative process, and I have used it to good advantage with people suffering from "writer's block." Often artists become bogged down in the process of their work and lose sight of their goals as well as the purpose of their creation. This dysfunction is typified by earth obscuring the process of creation by smothering the wood element. As the *mu* point of the spleen and as a meeting point of wood and earth elements, Lv-13 holds the potential to help resolve this disharmony and unburden the creative process.

The character *zhang* can also refer to laws, regulations, and rules. An alternate translation of this point's name as "gate of law" makes reference to the wood element's association with the notion of human justice. Lv-13 as the "gate of law" can be ideal for people who hold a grudge to the point of harming themselves. This type of behavior is found in those who engage in lengthy lawsuits to prove a point even though the ultimate expense of money, time, and energy far exceeds what they could have settled for in the first place. As acrimony builds so does frustration and lack of perspective.

When we suffer an injury there will never be a satisfactory resolution in terms of human justice. As long as we persist in distinguishing between right and wrong, scars and lingering damage will result. No human resolution can entirely make up the loss created by injury. The only real healing comes from rolling the two of right and wrong back into the one of primordial *dao* in which all opposites are harmonized. Along these lines, the *Daodejing* advises us not to seek justice but rather to "repay injury with *de* (virtue)."[17] We can only be considered healed when the damaging events of life no longer limit self-expression and the manifestation of our individual destiny. I consider healing complete when a patient can look himself right in the eye and say clearly, "I would change nothing in my life if it meant not being here now." "Chapter gate" can help us to turn the page and begin looking from the present moment onward toward the future. As we turn the page, and *qi* once again flows freely through "chapter gate," it arrives to empower the functions of Lv-14, "gate of hope." The name "long tranquility" alludes to this function of easing constraint, empowering benevolence, and regulating the smooth flow of *qi* through transitions in life.

---

| | | |
|---|---|---|
| ❖ **Lv-14** | **Gate of Hope** | |
| *Qi²men²* | Gate of Hope | 期門 |
| *Gan¹mu⁴* | Liver *Mu* | 肝募 |

*They forget the liver and gall, cast aside ears and eyes, turning and revolving, ending and beginning again, unaware of where they start or finish. Idly they roam beyond the dust and dirt; they wander free and easy in the service of inaction.*
– *ZHUANGZI*[18]

FUNCTIONS

1. Exit point
2. Liver *mu* point
3. Meeting point with the spleen channel and *yin* linking vessel

VIRTUES

1. Resolves resignation.
2. Empowers hope.

Lv-14 is the anatomically highest point on the liver meridian and empowers the quality of aspiration. Here, at the top of the tree that is the liver channel, the highest branches reach up to touch heaven, which is represented by its connection to the lung meridian at Lu-1. The E/E block between Lv-14 and Lu-1 is perhaps the most frequently encountered of all the E/E blocks. This is because of the circuitous route the *qi* must make to breach the diaphragm and find its way to Lu-1. Think of the diaphragm, separating the middle from the upper *jiao,* as the embodiment of all the walls that confront our growth in life. Hence liver *qi* tends to stagnate here, resulting in distension in the ribs and pressure in the chest.

This block is often congruent with a loss of aspiration as empowered by the liver and inspiration as empowered by the lungs. The virtue of aspiration is engendered as we feel the *qi* of the wood element rising through us. Acknowledging the nature and direction of the plan implicit in our growth, we aspire to fulfill our purpose. Inspiration fills us from without and draws us ever onward toward the highest in life. Stagnation resulting from lack of communication between Lv-14 and Lu-1 is often congruent with feelings of anger, frustration, despair, hopelessness, resignation, and depression. "Gate of hope" can help dissolve perceived obstacles to our growth and empower the finding of creative solutions to our problems. By harmonizing emotions on a continuum from resignation to rage, Lv-14 can promote clarity of vision regarding the congruence of our own purpose with the purpose of heaven. In this way we may be empowered to stop "knocking our heads against the wall" and turn our eyes toward the future with optimism. Hence "gate of hope" is often useful for treating the person who "can't see the light at the end of the tunnel."

Lv-14 can also treat us when we are overly optimistic. Sometimes we may stagnate because we put off making changes until the future, in the vain hope that things will improve of their own accord. Hence we can cling to hope dysfunctionally rather than taking action based on our commitments and goals. Always hoping our situation will eventually improve, we stay stuck in front of the walls that confront us in life. The notion of having time in some imaginary future is the ego's way of ensuring its survival and preventing us from initiating meaningful change in our lives. "Gate of hope" can empower an accurate perspective of the moment, for, in reality, there is only now, and the future is an illusion.

## *Exercises*

1. Compare the functions of Lv-4 to those of the herbal formula Yiguan Jian, or "Linking Decoction."
2. Elaborate the function of Lv-4 in relationship to the *hun* and the *po*.
3. Discuss how Lv-3, Lv-8, Lv-9, and Lv-14 harmonize the flow of *qi* at the level of the feet, knees, groin, and diaphragm, respectively.
4. Discuss sexual constraint from the perspective of the five-element points on the liver channel.
   a. What is the unique aspect of constraint harmonized by each point?
   b. How can such constraint be uniquely predicated on a relative excess or deficient presence of each element within the liver official?
5. The wood element presides over our vision of time by governing growth from conception to death. Discuss how attachment to the past and future can limit perspective and cause stagnation.

## *NOTES*

1. Chen, 1989, p. 152.
2. For a discussion of the characters *shun*, "compliance," and *ni*, "to go against," see *ND*, pp. 316–317.
3. Thea Elijah introduced the use of the formula to me in this way.
4. Legge, 1962, p. 259.
5. See the case study on Etta associated with Gb-38.
6. Name attributed to J. R. Worsley.
7. From class notes, Traditional Acupuncture Institute, 1984.
8. The character *feng* has been discussed at length in the context of Ki-23.

9. Deadman, Mazin, and Baker, 1989.
10. For a discussion of the relationship of the liver's virtue of benevolence to virtue in general, see *ND,* pp. 238–240.
11. Chen, 1989, verse 22, p. 110.
12. Ellis, Wiseman, and Boss, 1989, pp. 298–299.
13. This translation according to Omura. See Omura, 1982, p. 110.
14. *Daodejing*, Chapter 79; in Chen, 1989, p. 226.
15. Weiger, 1965, Lesson 73, p. 187. Note that the meaning of *shi* in this sense is contained in the name of the herb formula Shiquan Dabu Wan, or "Ten Complete Repair Pill." Like Lv-13, this formula treats both the wood and earth element, nourishing liver blood and spleen *qi.*
16. Also see *ND*, pp. 319–320.
17. Chen, 1989, p. 63.
18. Watson, 1964, p. 83.

# 32

# LUNG

THE LUNG CHANNEL BEGINS AT CV-12, DEEP WITHIN THE area of the stomach, and descends to loop around the transverse colon at CV-9. From here it ascends the midline to penetrate the diaphragm and bifurcates into each lobe of the lung. The meridian continues to ascend bilaterally on either side of the trachea to the level of the larynx. Each branch then descends to become superficial at Lu-1, the channel's entry point. From here the channel arches over the shoulder and descends the lateral aspect of the biceps to Lu-5 at the flexure of the elbow. It then runs down the anterolateral surface of the forearm over the wrist and up onto the thenar eminence. From here it travels over the anterolateral edge of the thumb to its nail point and exit point, Lu-11. A deep branch leaves from Lu-7, the *luo* point, to travel between the first and second metacarpal bones and connect with the large intestine channel at LI-4.

## *Thoughts on the Channel*

The lungs can be pictured as two mountains on either side of a valley with the lung meridian representing a path from the top of the mountain to the bottom. Stone steps wind their way down the mountainsides, and altars for rest and meditation appear in the form of each acupuncture point along the lung channel. A stream flows at the mountain's peak, picking up momentum as it descends to form a river flowing through the valley below. At the mountain's top is a temple of serenity high above the clouds and mist (Lu-1). Ascending to the very peak we reach a gate (Lu-2) where we begin our descent to another temple in the clouds (Lu-3). Thus inspired (Lu-4) we descend lower to pass a marsh (Lu-5) as the stream narrows (Lu-7 and Lu-8) to fall over an abyss (Lu-9). At the bottom of the waterfall is a pool where a local villager catches fish (Lu-10) to carry them off to market (Lu-11).

### MAIN FUNCTIONS

1. Receives purity.
2. Empowers the transcendence of material form to allow connection to essence.
3. Empowers self-worth born of inspiration.

### DISTAL POINT FUNCTIONS

***Wood:*** Empowers benevolence within righteousness, equilibrating the relationship between human (wood) and heavenly (metal) justice.

***Fire:*** Tempers the metal with compassion to burn away impurities.

***Earth:*** Empowers substantiality within the empty abyss that is the lung official. Harmonizes the relationship between substantial (earth) and essential (metal) nourishment.

***Metal:*** Empowers the essential nature of the lung as an official of the metal element.

***Water:*** Regulates the balance of moisture in the lungs, empowering the virtues of boundary and receptivity.

***Xi-cleft:*** Moves *qi*, heat, and dampness that have stagnated within the lung as grief and longing.

***Luo:*** Vents stagnation to the exterior and creates an internal state of open receptivity and connection to essence.

---

| ❖ **Lu-1** | **Central Treasury** | |
|---|---|---|
| *Zhong[1]fu[3]* | Central Treasury | 中府 |
| *Fu[3]zhong[1]shu[2]* | Central Treasury *Shu* | 中府俞 |
| *Fei[4]mu[4]* | Lung *Mu* | 肺募 |
| *Ying[1]zhong[1]shu[2]* | Center of the Breast *Shu* | 膺中俞 |
| *Ying[1]shu[2]* | Breast *Shu* | 膺俞 |

*Man's life is a coming together of breath. If it comes together, there is life; if it scatters, there is death.*
– *ZHUANGZI*

FUNCTIONS

1. Entry point
2. *Mu* point
3. Intersection point with the spleen channel

VIRTUE

Empowers inspiration and connection to essence.

The flow of *qi* from the exit point Lv-14 to the entry point of the lungs at Lu-1 provides a connection between the inner virtue of aspiration that propels us toward our goals and the inspiration afforded by the ultimate goal of all virtuous endeavor, which is heaven. Inspiration has both an internal and external aspect. Internally, inspiration arises from our connection to heaven as it is present as the potential virtue that lies within our *jing*. Externally, inspiration is empowered by our ability to connect with and abstract the nourishing *yang* inherent in all that comes to us in life.

The virtue of metal, *yi*, righteousness, implies an exactness in the way the lungs conducts its affairs. Our breath joins heaven within and heaven without as the highest potential inherent in our *jing* meets with the most essential essences abstracted from life to form *zhongqi* (宗氣). This refined *qi* collects in the center of the chest at CV-17 just as the treasury must collect and store taxes. It is the lungs' connection to quality and essence that enable them to empower the virtue of inspiration. As quality is drawn into our lives with each inhalation, the lungs must surrender with each exhalation what is of no value. This dynamic is contained in the close functional relationship between the lungs and the heart and the circulatory and respiratory rhythms, all of which are empowered by *zhongqi*, our central treasure.

The *zhongqi* as "ancestral" *qi* empowers the synchronicity of all rhythmic movements within us and joins us in breath to both our personal lineage of ancestry as well as to the creative breath of eternal *dao* as the momentary cause of our being. Our personal ancestry includes what we bring to each moment from our past, whereas our connection to *dao* is a momentary phenomenon that spontaneously gives birth to us newly with each breath and heartbeat. Our source of inspiration then comes from joining the highest we possess from our past (our ancestry) with the highest available to us in each instant. Hence it is through breath that our past inspires our present.

A child often responds to early trauma and disappointments in life by shutting off his heart and suppressing his respiratory rhythm. This dynamic is also addressed by CV-17, "primordial child," the meeting point of the lung, heart, and heart protector officials and storehouse of *zhongqi*. Depletion here is suggested by the presence of a caved-in chest, shallow or obstructed breathing, and shoulders that are hunched forward. Characteristic of this imbalance is frustration giving way to despair as liver *qi* stagnates and we lose touch with our inner drive of aspiration and fail to be inspired toward our goals. This dynamic is evidenced by an internal emptiness and loneliness because the lungs have failed to bring quality into our inner landscape or to make contact with our inner worth (the central treasure).

As the *mu* point of the lungs, Lu-1 empowers the receptive aspects of lung function associated with lung *yin*. This function is emphasized in the point's alternate names of *yingzhongshu* and *yingshu*, which can be translated as "receiving center *shu*" and "receiving *shu*," respectively.[1] In fact, the phrase *ying tianming* (膺天命) means to receive *(ying)* the destiny *(ming)* appointed by heaven *(tian)*. Later heaven radiates as sunlight toward humanity in an attempt to nourish the seed placed within by early heaven at conception. The sunlight that lies at the heart of all things is the source of nourishing *yang* the lungs must extract from air from our first breath onward in life. Treating Lu-1 may be likened to taking someone up to the top of a mountain where the air is clear and the finest most refined *qi* is available to inspire him. For here we are closest to the sun, embodied in the upper *jiao* as the human heart.

---

## ❖ Lu-2 Cloud Gate

*Yun²men²* Cloud Gate 雲門

VIRTUE

Clears grief that obscures the heart.

Grief in the lungs can obscure the heart's fire in the way that clouds obscure the sun. The chronic presence of grief can make us feel like heaven has forsaken and forgotten about us. Reacting to the presence of grief, the lungs can eventually fail to contact essence due to anticipation of its inevitable loss. Hence we can feel empty inside as we reject what is of greatest value both internally and externally in life. With connection to the sun and heaven so obscured we may become both uninspired and uninspiring. This cloud of grief can be embodied as phlegm in the lungs, a chronic cough representing the lungs' rejection of heavenly *qi*, and constant clear sinus dripping, symbolizing the embodiment of grief as internal tears.

For a person who is chronically negative as if "followed by a cloud," "cloud gate" can renew the virtue of inspiration by allowing a glimpse of heaven. "Cloud gate" can resolve grief and allow the heart's intention to shine as the sun burns through the clouds on an overcast day. To imagine the quality "cloud gate" can impart to consciousness, just think of how it feels to glimpse the sun through the clouds after weeks of rain. Such a vision provides hope and joy born of inspiration when heaven's light meets the light of our own hearts.

I use this point, as well as Lu-1 and Lu-3, for treating the quality of *qi* stagnation that produces the cotton quality on the pulse.[2] The cotton quality is felt as an obfuscation of the pulse that mirrors the metaphor of clouds (stagnant *weiqi*) obscuring the sun (the impulse felt in the artery). It is as though the impulse itself is hidden by sheets of cotton. The cotton quality arises when we take a blow in life that is too strong to bear. Such a blow can be associated with the inhibition of the circulatory and respiratory rhythm discussed earlier in the context of Lu-1. Failing in its protective function, the *weiqi* effectively collapses and smothers the functional dynamics of *qi* circulation in the same way resignation smothers the expression of spirit. Over time, our innate influences (*jing, qi,* and *shen*) will stop trying to express themselves as the left side of the pulse becomes deep and possibly feeble in a way that is congruent with a H/W imbalance. Hence it is therapeutically important to root out resignation and keep our expression of spirit flowing freely into the world. "Cloud gate" can play an important role in this by clearing grief and thus calling the heavens to part and reinspire us.

Located at the level of Lu-1 and Ki-27, Lu-2 plays an important role in helping the lungs fulfill their function of descending water and of helping the kidney to grasp the *qi*. If the lungs fail to descend water, phlegm can form that in turn will hinder the kidney from grasping *qi*. Or if the kidney fails to power the breath, *qi* circulation will be compromised and phlegm may form. "Cloud gate" can function to both clear and tonify the lungs and is therefore useful in either of these two situations.

---

### ❖ Lu-3 Heavenly Palace
*Tian[1]fu[3]* Heavenly Palace 天府

FUNCTION

Window to heaven

VIRTUE

Empowers us to find the highest within ourselves as inspired by heaven.

The character *fu* indicates a building where records are kept; hence Mathews translates *tianfu* as "the storehouse of god-eternity."[3] The pathology of the metal element is that once inspiration and self-worth are compromised, we tend to find the worst in ourselves and others. The lungs' virtue of connecting to essence is thus distorted into perfectionism and disdain for anyone or anything we consider soiled. The sensitivity of the lungs to insult is such that people with weak lungs often feel tainted in life or like they are "damaged goods." However, virtue lives purely within each of us untouched by any event in life. In fact, heaven can only ever see the highest in us. For only the virtue we have cultivated during life ascends to heaven upon death to join the light of the moon, stars, and sun. "Heavenly palace" can empower us to acknowledge that heaven always finds the best in us. Hence our slate is clean so we may find the best in ourselves and move forward in a way that is untainted by the past.

The virtue associated with the lungs is justice *(yi)*.[4] Whereas the liver is associated with human justice, the lungs are associated with heavenly justice. The wood element's connection to justice is embodied in the role of the attorney who must argue persuasively for his position. The metal element's role is embodied by the judge who must listen to both sides of a story and abstract the relative truth from each. Human justice is always a matter of judgment and compromise. Hence the *Daodejing* states, "in reconciling a great injury, there is always sure to be some injury remaining. How can this be good?"[5] Heavenly justice always repays injury with original nature *(de),* the very basis of self-worth. "Heavenly palace" can be conceived as providing access to inspiration as it is grounded in the spiritual depths of self-worth. This point may truly enable us to forgive, let go of the past, and be receptive to the guidance of divine inspiration so we can move ahead in life less burdened.

It is interesting to compare the virtue of self-worth in contradistinction to self-esteem as empowered by Lv-1. Self-esteem can be said to be predicated on a balanced vision of those aspects of self that root us into our ground of being and cannot be compromised. This vision must discern these foundational principles as compared with the peripheral aspects of self, which may be likened to branches that can be pruned and relinquished as we channel resources to direct new growth. Self-worth, in contrast, is predicated on our respect for, and value of, the treasures we find in our depths. If we heed only the desires of our minds and fail to value heaven's will, the basis of self-worth will eventually be eroded at its root. "Heavenly palace" can restore our ability to acknowledge the best in ourselves and in others.

People tend to externalize their relationship with their own spirit by projecting their connection to heaven on external figures such as spiritual teachers and institutions. Eventually many such relationships sour when the disciple finds hypocrisy within the person or group he projects as embodying his connection to heaven. Often, in severing a connection with a spiritual teacher or institution, the disillusioned turn their backs on heaven. In this way they are shut off from the essence of their connection to value both internally and externally as respect for self and others is compromised. "Heavenly palace" can help reestablish our connection with heaven as it inspires us within as breath and without as sunlight. Hence we may once again become receptive to the influence of spirit. In this way we may retain the lessons learned from past spiritual encounters without clinging to the person or organization that was a vehicle for them.

---

❖ **Lu-4** **Valiant White**
*Xia[1]bai[2]* Valiant White 俠白
*Jia[1]bai[2]* Pinched White 夾白

VIRTUE

Harmonizes the dysfunctional expressions of resignation on the one hand and self-righteousness on the other.

White is the color associated with the metal element, inspiring us with its brilliance and purity. The character *xia* also means "hero" and refers here to the purity of intentions of one who is truly inspired by heaven. Think of the brilliance of heaven and how it inspires service in the warrior whose intentions are singular and pure in serving the emperor. This brilliance is embodied in the warrior's perfectly honed sword when heaven guides his hand to act with righteousness, the virtue of the metal element. I have found this point useful for helping someone find the inner strength to act on his inspiration. But the virtue of righteousness can be distorted into self-righteousness when the function of the lung official is compromised. In this case "valiant white" can be used to temper the lungs' tendency toward fanaticism.

---

❖ **Lu-5** **Foot Marsh**
*Chi[3]ze[2]* Foot Marsh 尺澤
*Gui[3]shou[4]* Ghost Reception 鬼受
*Gui[3]tang[2]* Ghost Hall 鬼堂

FUNCTIONS

1. Water point
2. Sedation point
3. Ghost point

VIRTUES

1. Cools and clears the lungs.
2. Helps the lungs empower a boundary that defines what is self and what is not.

During the Zhao dynasty (1122–255 B.C.E.), the character *chi,* translated here as "foot," was a standard unit of measurement that corresponded to the span of a man's hand from the thumb to the pinky. This is approximately the distance on each person from Lu-9 to Lu-5. In fact, the phrase *chize* denotes a small pond but also refers to the pulse in the arm.[6] The two alternate names of Lu-5 reference its use to treat possession. The character *shou* means to receive in the sense of confining something into a recipient.[7] It also yields the sense of suffering through a tribulation. Hence the name *guishou* speaks directly to the notion of possession.

A function of the lungs is to allow water that rises in the body to condense and to then descend in the same way that clouds form in the dome of heaven to create rain. Healthy moisture in the lungs and large intestine forms the interface between our internal and external world. Moisture helps these organs draw quality into our being and discharge what has been metabolized and no longer serves. In this way the lungs and large intestine are responsible for defining the boundary between self and not self.

If the presence of water within the lungs is excessive, phlegm can obscure breathing and hamper the process of assimilation from outside to inside. In this case phlegm can be seen as the embodiment of negativity and grief that keeps us clinging to the past and unable to receive. In this scenario the lung pulses are expected to exhibit tense and slippery qualities associated with stagnation of *qi* and damp. Here we may evoke the function of Lu-5 as a sedation point to disperse the excess in the lungs, allowing it to flow onward toward the water element just as Emperor Yu channeled the excess floodwaters to the sea.

If the presence of water within is deficient, dryness can impinge the lungs' function. When we lose what we have valued in life, we can feel burned and resent heaven for our losses. Here the upper *jiao* can become like a desert as the flower of the heart and lungs fails to bloom for lack of moisture and inspiration. In this scenario the lung pulses are expected to exhibit qualities associated with *yin* deficiency. The patient can experience rapid and shallow breathing and anxiety to the point of panic attacks. Such anxiety comes from failure of the lungs to grasp life and be inspired, paired with a feeling of urgency that what is valued in life is slipping away and cannot be held on to.

By regulating the moisture content of the lung official, Lu-5 can help both establish a healthy boundary between self and the outside world and inspire the assimilation of heavenly *qi.* Hence "foot marsh" can help resolve dampness in the lungs as well as ensure an adequate moisture content when the lungs are dry.

---

### ❖ Lu-6 Greatest Hole
*Kong*[3]*zui*[4] Greatest Hole 空最

FUNCTION

*Xi*-cleft point

VIRTUE

Helps move the oppression of grief.

As the channel's *xi*-cleft point, Lu-6 can help move stagnation in any aspect of being presided over by the lung official. This stagnation can correspond to phlegm embodied in the lungs as well as to old grief or longing that impedes the lungs' function of keeping us rhythmically linked to the movement of *dao* via breath. The name "greatest hole" is similar to that of Lu-9, "very great abyss," in alluding to the nature of *dao* as the source and resting place of all things. By channeling old grief into the abyss, Lu-6 empowers the virtue of emptiness so we may better appreciate and receive the value that is present to us in each moment of life.

Resignation associated with loss can manifest as stagnation of the *weiqi* evident in the pulse as a cotton, or "sad," quality. The *weiqi* protects the surface of the body and also helps constitute our emotional protection so we are not overly sensitive or "thin skinned." Long-term stagnation of *weiqi* can contribute to the presence of slow-growing tumors that represent the accretions of resignation and sorrow. Such "heavy" emotions tend to suppress the healthy expression of joy and inspiration. By helping break up stagnant emotional states and promote movement of the *weiqi,* Lu-6 can help inspire the virtue of lightness in being.

Psychospiritually, stagnation in the lungs can present as grief over value that has been lost in life. Holding on to memories and longing for old loves, friends, and objects that have been lost can prevent us from extracting the spiritual value that is an essential part of our life experience. Grief arises as an emotion because the pain felt over having lost the form of something valued keeps us from connecting to its spiritual essence, which is eternal. In moving the stagnation of grief, Lu-6 can empower the momentary experience of transcendence of loss and connection to essence and allow us to move forward in a lighter way, less burdened by our attachment to the past.

| | | |
|---|---|---|
| ❖ **Lu-7** | **Broken Sequence** | |
| *Lie[4]que[1]* | Broken Sequence | 列缺 |
| *Tong[2]xuan[2]* | Child Mystery | 童玄 |
| *Wan[4]lao[2]* | Wrist Labor | 腕勞 |

FUNCTIONS

1. Exit point
2. *Luo* point

VIRTUE

Opens and clears the lung official.

In the order of *qi* circulation, the entry and exit points are generally the first and last points, respectively, on each meridian. In the metal element, however, *qi* exits the lung channel at Lu-7 to enter the large intestine channel at LI-4. Hence the normal sequence of *qi* flow is broken, yielding this point's name. Being both a *luo* and exit point, Lu-7 is particularly potent for integrating the functions of receiving and letting go. As a *luo* point, Lu-7 empowers inner clarity and openness on the deepest of levels by venting stagnation from the lungs and directing the mind inwardly toward emptiness and essence. As an exit point, Lu-7 functions to empower the lungs to let go and surrender what is of no value to the large intestine for elimination.

The opening of the lungs into the mouth and nose represent our connection to heaven through breath. The large intestine channel ends at LI-20, "welcome fragrance," located by the side of each nostril where breath begins. Hence there is a continuous circuit between *qi* entering the lungs at the nostrils, traveling the length of the lung channel to enter the large intestine channel at LI-4, and returning back to the nostrils at LI-20 where exhalation eliminates waste and the essence retained in the circulating *qi* enters the stomach channel for integration and assimilation.[8]

*Leique* is an ancient name for lightning that may refer to the sensation of the point upon being needled.[9] Note that in Chinese mythology, Gun, for failing to stop the floods, was killed by Zhongran, the yellow emperor's warrior and the god of lightning. Afterward, Gun was thrown into a "great abyss" (the name of Lu-9) to dwell for eternity. Gun, who had lost his value for failing to stop the floods, was surrendered to the abyss, making way for his son Yu to stop the flooding and unite the nation.[10]

An alternate name for Lu-7 is *tongxuan* (童玄), meaning "child mystery." Another point that makes reference to children is CV-17, "primordial child" *(yuaner)*. I consider treating Lu-7 and CV-17 for empowering breath and inspiration when these virtues are obscured by clouds of loss and longing that date to events in a patient's childhood.

### ❖ Lu-8 **Meridian Gutter**

*Jing[1]qu[2]* Meridian Gutter 經渠

FUNCTIONS

1. Metal point
2. Horary point; 3 A.M.–5 A.M., fall equinox

VIRTUE

Empowers the essential qualities of metal.

The character *jing* denotes the meridians that are like threads (糸) that cross (巠) the body like the warp of a fabric. *Jing* also refers to the classic texts, such as the *Neijing* (內經) or *Nanjing* (難經), because these texts elaborate a thread or lineage of thought as it connects the past to the present. *Jing* also denotes the notion of having experienced something in the sense of having passed through it. The character *qu* denotes a drain or gutter. The point's name imparts a sense of connecting us to the value of past experience while draining the meridians of all that is inessential.

As the metal and horary point, Lu-8 provides a strong resource for strengthening the lung official with the essential nature of metal, which is to promote emptiness, inspiration, and connection to value. As the transmitting point, Lu-8 is able to empower the receptive quality of the lungs within the other officials when it is paired with the appropriate receiving point on a *yin* meridian.

As a "meridian gutter," Lu-8 promotes purity by helping drain all that is unclear and has lost its essential worth. A gutter is a channel for carrying water away from a house. If that channel is blocked with impurities, the structure of the home is threatened because standing water can erode the foundation, walls, and roof. Similarly, a function of the lungs is to help water descend and in so doing purify all aspects of being. Failure of the lungs to descend water can be evidenced by congestion in the lungs and sinuses as well as the accumulation of impurities in any aspect of being. Phlegm can present psychospiritually as depression as viscous burden obscures the fire of the heart or inspiration of the lungs. Chronic sinusitis or diarrhea can be thought of as the body weeping tears of grief. By unblocking the meridian gutter, Lu-8 can help cleanse and renew our entire being. In this way we may restore luster and brilliance to the naturally unadorned mind and spirit.

### ❖ Lu-9 **Great Abyss**

*Tai[4]yuan[1]* Great Abyss 太淵
*Tai[4]quan[2]* Great Spring 太泉
*Gui[3]xin[1]* Ghost Heart 鬼心

FUNCTIONS

1. Earth point
2. Tonification point
3. Source point
4. Assembly point of the pulse
5. Ghost point

Dao *is a whirling emptiness (*chong*),*
*Yet in use is inexhaustible.*
*Fathomless (*yuan*),*
*It seems to be the ancestor (*zong*) of*
*ten thousand things.*
– DAODEJING, *Chapter 4*[11]

Chapter 4 of the *Daodejing*, which corresponds in number to the metal element as the fourth stage of *dao*,[12] describes the movement of *dao* as breath. The basic movement of *dao* is like a great whirlpool, rising and falling like a bellows, giving birth to all things at its periphery and receiving them back at its center. The character *yuan* (淵), translated as "abyss" in the name of Lu-9, and as "fathomless" in the verse here, depicts water flowing downward as in a whirlpool. This image evokes the function of the lungs in descending water.

Lu-9, named *taiyuan,* is associated with the whirling abyss situated between heaven and earth. Hence Lu-9 is the assembly point of the pulse whose beating is patterned on the breath of *dao*. An alternate name for Lu-9 is *taiquan* (great spring), which denotes the origin of a stream.[13] Lu-9 as both *yuan*, the abyss, and *quan*, the source, calls forth the image of the queen mother's metal gate that serves as the womb and tomb for all of creation.

*Dao*, as the origin of all origins, is termed "the ancestor of ten thousand beings." The character *zong* (宗) for ancestor is the same character used for *zongqi* (宗氣), the ancestral *qi* of the lungs in the chest.[14] The *zongqi* is what empowers rhythmic movement in every aspect of our being. It is the breath of *dao* that powers our own breath as we mirror the basic functioning of the universe. Hence Lu-9 is the assembly point of the pulse.

As the meridian's earth point, Lu-9 empowers the virtues of earth within the lung official. The life irony of the lung official is that what has the greatest value in life is least substantial. Rather than being valued, the connection to emptiness and essence empowered by the lung official is often experienced as feelings of loneliness and loss. This feeling tends to be projected externally as we attempt to accumulate worldly goods of ever increasing value, trying in vain to diminish our sense of loneliness and isolation. As the channel's earth point, Lu-9 can bring substantiality to deeply nourish the lungs. In this way we may come to value heaven as a source of nourishment, and cravings for material possessions can be mitigated. For only heaven is eternal, and all worldly goods are of transient value ultimately destined for the abyss.

The abyss denoted in the name of Lu-9 can be thought of as referencing the *dao* as the relationship of heaven (metal/father) and earth (earth/mother) as they nourish the moment of conception. The earth as mother provides substantive nourishment in the form of the food we ingest and also as the blood that nutrients are transformed into. Heaven as father provides nourishment in the form of essence and inspiration, occurring to us as sunlight internally from the heart and externally from moon, stars, and sun as heaven's luminaries. At conception the mother provides blood, created by the spleen and earth element, to nourish the fetus in the womb, and the father provides the inspiration of heaven's breath instilled within as *jing*. These same relationships are empowered by Lu-9, which unites the earth and metal elements as we are conceived by the *dao* newly in each moment. Hence Lu-9 is a powerful point to strengthen the essential nature of blood as it is embodied in both its nutrient and mineral content.

As the "ghost heart," Lu-9 can be quite effective in treating possession by surrendering all that is impure to the abyss while renewing our connection to original self through breath. People who are possessed often give the impression they are empty inside. The eyes of those so afflicted gives the impression we are staring into a great abyss of the soul, devoid of the light imparted by a healthy spirit *(shen)*.

## ROBB

***Age:*** *45*
***Diagnosis:*** *Earth, water within, spleen/kidney constitution*
***Complaint:*** *Pneumonia, phlegm in the lungs, drug-induced coma*
*C: Yellow*
*S: Sing/groan*
*O: Fragrant*
*E: Sympathy*

I knew Robb only casually as a local dance instructor in the community. Apparently Robb had treated himself for a lung infection with over-the-counter medication for one month without improvement. When he saw his doctor it was determined he had severe pneumonia in both lungs and only 10 percent lung function. He was immediately put in the hospital, intubated, and placed into a drug-induced coma with sedatives so he could be adequately treated for his condition.

Hearing the situation was life threatening, I notified his wife that I would help in anyway possible. She asked me to come to the hospital to treat Robb and I agreed, telling her we could be guaranteed of no success but I thought it was worth a try and treatment would do no harm.

*Diagnosis*

On entering Robb's room at the hospital I found him lying in bed, with a breathing tube down his throat and tubes in both his arms and stomach. He was unconscious and a machine was breathing for him. At that time he was on 90 percent oxygen and had not been able to sustain a lower percentage. It was not clear if he would live or sustain permanent brain damage from oxygen deprivation. My intuition told me, however, that he would be fine, and this was confirmed on pulse diagnosis. I had feared I would find an absent kidney pulse, suggesting his inner reserves had been wholly depleted. What I found, however, was a tense, slippery, and pounding pulse in all positions that indicated global stagnation of both *qi* and damp. I felt a true strength on Robb's left proximal kidney pulse that reinforced my feeling he would make it through this crisis.

*Treatment*

POINTS

1. Ki-1
2. Ki-24
3. Lu-1
4. Lu-9

I treated the points in the order listed here. Ki-1 was chosen to support that official in powering breath and aiding in the descent of fluids. I provided a strong stimulation to this point with no noticeable effect by any criteria I could ascertain.[15] Ki-24 was chosen to resurrect the spirit and empower breath along with Lu-1. Again, neither point had any effect at all. I informed Robb's wife that I would try one more point before giving up. Lu-9 was chosen as the assembly point of the pulse and breath. I also chose this point for its effect in stabbing the "ghost heart" and clearing this illness that possessed Robb to the point of absolute emptiness, threatening to return him to the abyss. Upon obtaining *qi* in Lu-9 on his left wrist, Robb took a huge breath and his machines started beeping loudly.

*Outcome*

The treatment of Lu-9 marked a turning point in Robb's recovery. The beeping heard after treating Lu-9 signified he was breathing on his own and against the machine that was breathing for him. By the next day his physicians were able to take him off the coma-inducing drugs and reduce his oxygen to 40 percent. Robb regained consciousness and got steadily better to the point of returning home two weeks later. He has made steady progress since coming to acupuncture weekly and is now, one year later, fully recovered.

---

### ❖ Lu-10 Fish Region
*Yu²ji⁴* Fish Region 魚際

FUNCTIONS

1. Fire point
2. Secondary tonification point

Lu-10, the fire point on the lung meridian, can help bring the warmth of fire to an overly rigid metal element. As heavenly judge, it is the lungs' job to find the highest in each of us. If the metal element becomes cold and brittle, we tend to focus on the negative, failing to acknowledge the value in others as well as in ourselves. If the presence of fire is deficient, the lungs as judge may lack compassion and exact too high a toll as we criticize ourselves and others too harshly for every perceived impurity. Cold in the lungs can manifest as asthma or any number of respiratory aliments. Heartfelt joy can melt the rigidity of metal in a way that mitigates both grief and longing. Hence Lu-10 can help empower the sun to burn away the clouds of grief that obscure the sun's (fire's) influence within the metal element.

If the presence of fire within the lungs is excessive, dryness can prevent the lungs from being able to inhale and assimilate essence effectively. Pent-up fire within the lungs can express itself as religious zealotry as we project our own inability to connect with heaven externally on that which we consider to be impure or unworthy. Mania fueled by internal heat can unconsciously propel the zealot to cut out and eliminate anything or anyone in life that he thinks will limit his ability to connect with heaven. Hence the virtue of righteousness is distorted into self-righteousness in a way that increasingly separates the fanatic from the connection to heaven he longs for.

The image of fire within metal also suggests the transformation of metal by smelting in both internal and external alchemy. In Chinese internal alchemy, the metal cinnabar represents transformation because it is the only material the ancient Chinese possessed that is stable as both a solid and liquid at room temperature. In its solid form, mercuric sulfide represents mundane consciousness that is only able to perceive the fixed nature of material reality. As a solid, mercuric sulfide is red, suggesting the influence of the fire element, which, through the application of heat, can transform it to its liquid form. As a liquid, mercury represents the flow of flexible consciousness that promotes the generation of water from metal along the *sheng* cycle as each new round of evolution is initiated.

Cinnabar also figured prominently in external alchemy's attempt to turn lead (mundane consciousness) into gold (illuminated awareness). Hence the judicious application of the fire within metal can have a profound influence in helping cut through the accretions of mundane consciousness such as obsessive grieving and longing that are often associated with the presence of phlegm and dampness within the lungs.

---

❖ **Lu-11** **Little Merchant**
*Shao[3]shang[1]* Little Merchant 少商
*Gui[3]xin[4]* Ghost Truth 鬼信

FUNCTIONS

1. Wood point
2. Secondary sedation point
3. Ghost point

In the Chinese pentatonic scale, *shang* is the sound associated with the metal element. The designation of *shao*, meaning "lesser," is appropriate because the point occurs on a *yin* channel and is the lowest note in the musical scale. The character *shang* also means "merchant," which denotes the lungs' function of connecting us to essence. A good merchant knows the value of things, how to conserve them, and when it is best to let go of something because the price paid for holding on to it is too great.

Wood can serve as a handle for metal tools so they can be of use. If the presence of wood is excessive, metal may become blunt as it is constrained by wood. If a field is overplanted, the soil will be depleted of minerals as the roots choke the essential nourishment out of the earth. In this scenario no new growth can occur because the essence that supports life has been consumed. Wood governs structure by empowering the virtues of flexibility and continuity that flows from the plant's roots to its outermost branches. These virtues must be based in our internal plan and its manifestation in the world through fluid decision making. The metal element empowers our inner structure as based on essence. This structure can be likened to the crystalline lattice of a diamond that imparts its strength and beauty. The structure provided by metal needs to be strong yet never brittle or it may crack and ultimately lose its value. Hence if wood is overly judgmental, metal can tend toward perfectionism as we see only the impurities in everything. The balance between wood and metal is imperative if our creative growth is to be inspired by heaven.

As a sedation point, Lu-11 can ease the metal's tendency to constrain wood across the *ke* cycle. Metal limits wood as pruning shears can trim a plant. If the influence of metal is excessive, we can feel as though we are continually chopped down in life as every new plan is felled like a pruned branch. As the wood point within metal, Lu-11 can engender a deep vision of essence and comprehension of its worth. In this way wood can be empowered to not overly draw on metal but to preserve it as a good merchant conserves his treasures.

### *EXERCISE*

Discuss the pairing of Lu-2 with K-27 and the following distal point combinations:

a. Ki-10 and Lu-5
b. Lu-8 and Ki-7
c. Lu-8 and Sp-5
d. Lu-9 and Ki-3
e. Lu-9 and Sp-3

## *NOTES*

1. Note that the character *shu* can be translated as "transportation," thus rendering the name *Yingzhongshu* as "center of receiving and transportation."
2. For more on the cotton quality, see Hammer, 2001.
3. Weiger, 1965, p. 125; Mathews, 1931, p. 285.
4. See *ND*, pp. 261–264.
5. *Daodejing*, Chapter 79; in Chen, 1989, p. 226.
6. Mathews, 1931, p. 144, M1045.
7. Weiger, 1965, p. 136.
8. I find this circuit fascinating as a mixed metaphor. In a sense, the circulation of *qi* in the channels and the order of physiological function of the organ systems are separate. Breath enters and leaves the nostrils in a matter of seconds, whereas nutrients take substantially more time to be abstracted by the digestive system. In reality, food passes through the stomach before entering the large intestine. Still, the relationship between breath and elimination is vitally important as a functional circuit.
9. Ellis, Wiseman, and Boss, 1989, p. 31.
10. See *ND*, pp. 17–19.
11. *Daodejing*, Chapter 4; in Chen, 1989, p. 61.
12. The Chinese character for the number four, *si* (四), is a homophone with the character *si* (死), meaning death. Hence the fourth stage of *dao* may correspond to the death of primordial *dao* and the fall to the ten thousand things. Or it may correspond to the death of the body and the end of life or of ego, signifying the rebirth of the true self.
13. *Guan* is a spring that gushes out from the ground. "In the middle the bubbles gush up from the earth; on the top, the water expanding; on the sides, the flowing." Weiger, 1965, p. 289.
14. The character *zong* refers to the building from which emanates the influence of the deceased ancestors over their posterity. Wieger, 1965, p. 101.
15. In fact, I stimulated it so strongly that, had Robb not been in a coma, I think he never would have allowed me to treat him again!

# 33

# LARGE INTESTINE

THE LARGE INTESTINE CHANNEL BEGINS AT LI-1, THE RADIAL nail point of the index finger. The channel runs along the postereolateral surface of the index finger to pass through its entry point at LI-4 in the angle of the first and second metacarpal bones. The channel continues up the radial aspect of the forearm to LI-11 at the lateral border of the elbow crease. It then rises along the lateral aspect of the biceps to the insertion of the deltoid at LI-14. From here a branch runs internally to TH-13.

The main channel continues to the shoulder, where it reaches LI-16. An internal section of the channel leaves this point to travel across the trapezius to GV-14. It returns over the shoulder to St-12, and from here the meridian bifurcates. An internal branch continues down the chest to enter the lung, penetrate through the diaphragm, and connect with the large intestine at St-25, the *mu* point of the large intestine official.

The superficial branch continues medially to LI-17 at the base of the neck and then rises up the sternocleidomastoid and across the posterior aspect of the mandible. From here it runs to GV-26 between the philtrum and the base of the nose and crosses to the opposite side of the face to reach LI-19 and then terminate at the channel's exit point, LI-20. It then travels on to meet the stomach channel at its entry point, St-1. An internal pathway leaves the main meridian in the upper jaw and encircles the mouth, passing through the gum of the lower jaw.

---

### *Thoughts on the Channel*

It is interesting that LI-20, the channel's exit point, is located at the base of the nostrils. Here the lungs inspire us with essence on each inhalation and let go of mundanity with each exhalation. Empowering us to let go of the mundane while retaining essence is the main function of the large intestine official. Hence this channel's termination by the nose speaks directly to the integration of the functions of receiving and letting go.

#### MAIN FUNCTIONS

1. Empowers the ability to retain essence while letting go of mundanity.
2. Empowers inspiration born of self-worth.
3. Creates a clear inner space to receive quality by letting go of impurities.

#### DISTAL POINT FUNCTIONS

*Water:* Regulates the balance of moisture in the large intestine, empowering the virtues of boundary, receptivity, and emptiness.

*Wood:* Empowers vision within the process of letting go.

*Fire:* Tempers self-righteousness with compassion. Allows metal to flow, burning away impurities while transforming and purifying all aspects of being.

*Earth:* Harmonizes the relationship between substantiality and emptiness, empowering nourishment while letting go of impurities.

*Metal:* Empowers the large intestine official with the essential nature of the metal element.

*Xi-cleft:* Moves stagnation manifesting as self-righteousness, grief, and longing.

*Luo:* Vents stagnation to the exterior, empowering connection to heaven and essence within and without.

---

| ❖ **LI-1** | **Merchant *Yang*** | |
|---|---|---|
| *Shang*[1]*yang*[2] | Merchant *Yang* | 商陽 |
| *Jue*[2]*yang*[2] | Extreme *Yang* | 絕陽 |

*A good merchant hides his treasures as if his store was empty and a gentleman with full virtue* (de) *appears like a stupid man. Get rid of your proud air and many desires, your overbearing manners and excessive ambitions. None of these are good for you.*
– *LAOZI*[1]

FUNCTIONS

1. Metal point
2. Horary point; 5 A.M.–7 A.M., fall equinox

VIRTUES

1. Empowers the appropriate valuation of essence.
2. Summons any and all virtues associated with the metal element to support the function of the large intestine official.

The quote here is attributed to a legendary conversation between Laozi and Confucius. It emphasizes the virtue of letting go of all that does not correspond to true self and of guarding our virtue as a treasure. The function of the large intestine official is to help create internal purity by letting go of acquired mundanity. As the horary point on the large intestine channel, LI-1 may help shake up the entire sphere of influence of this official and thus cleanse us of impure thoughts and deeds.

*Shang,* the fifth note of the Chinese scale, is associated with the metal element. The name of Lu-11 denotes *shang* as "little" *(shao)* in keeping with its *yin* designation. Here, *shang* is qualified as *yang* in keeping with the point's location on the large intestine meridian. As in the name of Lu-11 ("little merchant") there is reference made in this point name to commerce. A function of the lungs is to bring quality into life while filtering out impurity. Conversely, the large intestine must let go of impurities while allowing us to retain that which is of value in the form of minerals. A good merchant knows the value of goods that must be either bought (lungs/receptivity) or sold (large intestine/letting go).

As a transmitting point, LI-1 can help empower the virtues of the large intestine within any other official when we simultaneously treat the associated receiving point on a *yang* meridian. Hence LI-1 paired with SI-1 can empower this official's virtue of letting go within the small intestine's function of sorting. This can help move stagnation within the small intestine, thus enabling us to let go of a dysfunctional sorting process and take action instead of deliberating forever.

---

### ❖ LI-2 **Second Interval**

| | | |
|---|---|---|
| *Er⁴jian¹* | Second Interval | 二間 |
| *Jian⁴gu³* | Space Valley | 間谷 |
| *Zhou¹gu³* | Whole Valley | 周谷 |

FUNCTIONS

1. Water point
2. Sedation point

VIRTUE

Cools, soothes, and tempers metal.

Water serves as an interface, allowing the large intestine to define a boundary between us and the outside world. If the presence of water is balanced within the large intestine official, the process of letting go of waste and assimilating essence proceeds gracefully. If the presence of water within metal is excessive, diarrhea can result as we lose minerals and our electrolytes become unbalanced. Similarly, fear, the emotion associated with the water element, can lead us to let go of the things we value in life because we feel unworthy of them.

If the presence of water within is deficient, dryness can result in constipation. In the same way we can tend to cling to the people and things we value for fear of losing them even after they have lost their worth to us. If we become unable to let go of waste efficiently, toxins tend to accumulate within us. In this case we can project our internal state of impurity externally to find the worst in everything and everyone. Excessive fear can drive us to smother those we love because we are afraid to let go and give them breathing space for fear of losing them.

A dysfunctional tendency of metal is to become dry and rigid. Such rigidity can manifest physically as calcification of the joints or other problems leading to limited mobility. Psychospiritually, such rigidity can manifest as perfectionism and a holier than thou attitude. As the water point in metal, LI-2 can help "oil" the metal to help it flow more gracefully. Such lubrication can promote better range of motion in joints such as the elbow and shoulder, which are transversed by the large intestine channel. We may also experience improved digestion and bowel function as we are cleansed of impurities.

---

### ❖ LI-3 **Third Interval**

| | | |
|---|---|---|
| *San¹jian¹* | Third Interval | 三間 |
| *Xiao³gu³* | Small Valley | 小谷 |
| *Shao³gu³* | Lesser Valley | 少谷 |

FUNCTIONS

1. Wood point
2. Secondary sedation point

VIRTUE

Ensures that the function of receiving and letting go occur in harmony with heaven's plan.

As the wood point within metal, LI-3 addresses the relationship between human and heavenly justice. Fulfilling the role of judge, the metal element is the arbiter of divine justice. As a *yang* official, the large intestine is responsible for implementing the decree of heaven in the world with surgical precision, excising what must be cut out and retaining all that is of value. If the presence of wood within metal is deficient, our inner judge can be separated from heaven's guidance. In this case our actions reflect a zealotry born of our lack of healthy inspiration from heaven. As the wood point within metal, LI-3 can help empower a broader perspective than our own specific beliefs that can help temper such fanaticism.

The roots of a tree have a reciprocal relationship with the minerals in the soil. On the one hand, minerals impart an inner structure to a plant that establishes its worth. On the other hand, the roots abstract the minerals buried deep within the earth and elevate them back up toward heaven. Hence the wood element can help us manifest the metal element's virtues of inspiration and value through its own functions of planning and decision making. Empowering perspective within the metal can facilitate our ability to decisively let go of that which has lost its value. Unencumbered by the past we can stand in the present with our vision turned optimistically toward the future. However, if the presence of wood within metal is excessive, our judgments may never allow us to let go of past transgressions against us. Dispersing the presence of wood within metal can allow us to let go, forgive, and move on. For it is often only the distorted impressions and judgments of a dysfunctional mind that leave us feeling tainted by the past.

---

| ❖ **LI-4** | **Joining of the Valleys** | |
|---|---|---|
| *He$^{2}$gu$^{3}$* | Joining of the Valleys | 合谷 |
| *Hu$^{3}$kou$^{3}$* | Tiger Mouth | 虎口 |
| *Han$^{2}$kou$^{3}$* | Contained in the Mouth | 含口 |
| *He$^{2}$gu$^{2}$* | Union of Bones | 合骨 |

*Within the earth a mountain:*
*The image of modesty.*
*Thus the superior man reduces that which is too much,*
*And augments that which is too little.*
*He weighs things and makes them equal.*
– *YIJING*[2]

FUNCTIONS

1. Source point
2. Entry point

VIRTUE

Central point for empowering us to let go of impurity in all aspects of being.

Here at the entry point of the large intestine meridian, the functions of receiving (lung) and letting go (large intestine) are joined. The image of the valley in Daoism is a symbol of emptiness. The virtue of emptiness is that it empowers us to be receptive to the essential nature of life. The *Yijing* hexagram for modesty tells us, "the superior man reduces that which is too much and augments that which is too little. He weighs things and makes them equal." In her comment on the *Yijing* hexagram for modesty, Anthony states, "To equalize extremes is part of the natural law. A haughty, pretentious attitude stands like a narrow, steep mountain that is constantly being attacked by the elements; as a consequence, it erodes into the valley. The valley, likewise, because it is a depression, receives all that erodes into it"[3]—hence the name, "joining of the valleys."

LI-4 is the supreme point for empowering us to let go of all that no longer serves in every domain of being. As such this is an important point for helping patients let go who have a difficult time relaxing so treatment can be effective. The truth is that most people, even those consciously pursuing a spiritual path, are not committed to ending their suffering. For struggle is too familiar and the mind holds on to habitual patterns with an iron grip. This is even more true in people who are unwilling to confront themselves. Such people look to healers merely to provide comfort rather than helping them transcend habitual patterns. "Joining of the valleys" is a tremendous point for helping such people let down their iron mask and begin to relinquish their attachments to suffering and all aspects of self that have lost value.

As an entry point, LI-4 unites the lungs' function of receiving with the large intestine's function of letting go. Hence the large intestine must have the ability to retain *yang* in the form of minerals while surrendering all mundanity *(yin)* back to the abyss. Pairing Lu-7 with LI-4 is particularly effective for uniting these two functions because the combination serves as both an exit/entry and source/*luo* combination simultaneously. Hence the lungs may be opened and inspired to receive the new with Lu-7 while LI-4 helps create clarity by empowering us to let go of refuse from the past.

---

❖ **LI-5** ***Yang* Stream**

| | | |
|---|---|---|
| *Yang²xi¹* | *Yang* Stream | 陽谿 |
| *Zhong¹kui²* | Central Eminence | 中魁 |

FUNCTIONS

1. Fire point
2. Secondary tonification point

VIRTUE

Tempers metal to empower flow.

Physically, the relative consistency of the stool can give a clue to the balance of fire and water in the metal element. However, both excessive and deficient fire can lead to constipation or diarrhea as we indiscriminately let go of, or hold on to, what is valued in life. Hence as the fire within metal become dysfunctional we can tend to either "throw the baby out with the bath water" or hold on to mundanity for fear of losing anything that might have value.

Diarrhea manifesting from a lack of fire within metal tends to be cold and watery in nature and flow like tears. In reality a person so afflicted is weeping from his lower orifice. In this case our sense of justice tends to be overly cold as our willingness to cut out anything perceived as impure is not tempered by the heart's compassion. Hence the zealot is willing to let go of all that is perceived as being impure in a way that manifests as intolerance and self-righteousness. With our discrimination of purity so compromised, we may shut out those we have been close to for the slightest perceived indiscretion as if closing an iron door on them forever. Such friends may actually have been trying to impart to us an observation of value that we have vainly taken as an insult.

Just as valuable minerals are lost through unchecked elimination, so too are people and things of value too easily disposed of in life. As what we value slips away, our actions may be dictated by desperately trying to hold on to something, anything, of value. In so doing, our discernment may fail us as we surround ourselves with people who merely flatter us and with material goods of dubious value. People we do value may feel suffocated by our iron grip as we try obsessively to possess them. In truth all that is of value is eternal in life, and it is our own failing if we fail to contact that essence because we lose contact with our compassion in the face of life's perceived losses. In contrast, the deficient presence of fire within metal can also lead to constipation as cold constricts the intestines. The psychospiritual correlates in this case tend to be the same as described earlier as our sense of justice can become overly cold and rigid and what is valued is held on to compulsively.

If the presence of fire within metal is excessive, bowel function can still be impacted, presenting on a continuum from diarrhea to constipation. Inflammation from excessive fire can manifest as religious zealotry and intolerance as we feel a burning imperative to free the world from all we perceive as impure. Diarrhea manifesting from heat tends to be hot, thick, and foul smelling. This expression may be likened to tears of bitterness that exemplify feelings of having been burned by heaven in having lost something we valued in life. Excess fire can also manifest as constipation as the stool becomes dry.

If the presence of fire is excessive within the large intestine, a person can tend to become fanatical as internal pressure mounts and he is unable to let go of his obsession with purity. Long-term suppression of, or indulgence in, our desires and appetites can cause the gradual accumulation of heat until we feel compelled to act in a shrill and hysterical way as an outlet. This manifestation can overlap with a diagnosis in Chinese medicine known as *yangming* psychosis.

Many compulsions are based on disorders of the *po* spirits that preside over human appetite and urges. The *po* govern peristalsis in all aspects of being as we attract and draw into us what is of value from outside ourselves. If fire agitates the *po,* appetite is likely to be excessive. In this case we fail to discriminate what is of value and how much we really need to consume. But if fire within metal is deficient, peristalsis can slow as we fail to attract value into our lives and fail to eliminate what has lost its worth to us.

The cycle of binging and purging often represents an imbalance of the *po* spirit as it propagates unconscious urges. Failing to discriminate quality, the binge eater eats excessively to the point of feeling stuffed. Then, feeling unclean for having consumed a large amount of junk food, the bulimic either induces vomiting and or takes an enema to feel empty again. This cycle is often predicated on a compulsion to fill some internal void associated with feelings of worthlessness.

I often use "*yang* stream" for food stagnation because increasing the fire within metal can help burn off the accretions of mundanity that have stagnated in the large intestine. Similarly, reducing the presence of fire with LI-5 can help calm the urgency of needing to acquire value and eliminate impurities. By balancing the quality of fire within the metal element, compulsion can be let go of as the virtues of flow and grace are empowered in the way we consume life and eliminate mundanity.

---

❖ **LI-6** **Side Passage**
*Pian¹li⁴* Side Passage 偏歷

FUNCTION
*Luo* point

VIRTUE
Vents heat and pressure that stagnate in the large intestine.

The name of this point refers to the fact that the *luo* channel of the large intestine meridian leaves the main channel at this point to connect with Lu-9. Further, the location of this point and the course of the *luo* channel is along the side of the arm. The environmental condition that damages the metal element is dryness. Such dryness can present in the large intestine as a feeling of loss and having been "burned" by life. A key function of LI-6 is to "moisten dryness," to promote the movement of stagnation in the large intestine official. Note that grief and loss can manifest on either end of a physiological continuum ranging from excessive dryness to the presence of damp in the intestines.

Because of its association with Lu-9 through the channel's *luo* vessel, "side passage" is also an important point for clearing the lungs. In this sense the point can be thought of as providing an external vent through which lung stagnation, whether it be emotional (grief) or physical (phlegm), can exit one's being.

---

❖ **LI-7** **Warm Current**
*Wen¹liu⁴* Warm Current 溫溜
*Chi²tou²* Pond's Head 池頭
*Tuo²tou²* Stream's Head 沱頭
*Wen¹liu²* Restrained Warmth 溫留
*Ni⁴zhu⁴* Against the Current 逆注
*Di⁴tou²* Local 地頭
*She²tou²* Snake Head 蛇頭

FUNCTION
*Xi*-cleft point

A propensity of the metal element when it is out of balance is to become cold, piercing, and inflexible. Psychospiritually, this can manifest as perfectionism, self-righteousness, and disgust. This point helps access the "warm *yangqi*"[4] of the large intestine official to help dispel such rigidity and brittleness. Refuse carried from our past, either emotional or physical, can lead us to feel disgust and contempt for both self and others. Physiologically this can present as dampness and/or heat that stagnates in the intestines and digestive system as a whole. Hence as the *xi*-cleft point, LI-7 excels at "transforming" the damp and "clearing" the heat that can be a physiological correlate of these pathological emotions.

The emotion of disdain is the result of experiencing something as so impure and out of congruency with our internal nature that we are revolted by it. Often a patient who feels disdain as a dominant emotion is projecting his inner stagnation of impurity onto something externally. The persecution that a disdainful person inflicts on others tends to be an outer reflection of the degree to which a person persecutes himself internally. In dysfunction the large intestine can promote a vision of only the dross of life, leaving someone exceptionally negative, cold, and piercing. Cut off from compassion (fire), benevolence (wood), sympathy (earth), and wisdom (water), the hardened metal may seek surgically to remove anything and anyone perceived as impure.

The character *zhu* (注) can mean to "fix the mind" on something.[5] The name *nizhu,* "against the current," describes the process of stagnation as one in which we fix our minds in opposition to the implicit flow of *dao* as the motivating force of life. In this case counterflow (*ni:* 逆) *qi* may present as warmth fails to extend to our extremities, indicating that our actions in the world may be guided by our minds rather than our hearts.[6]

As the *xi*-cleft point, LI-7 can help move and eliminate the stagnation of hardened mundanity internally. With dross removed we are more likely to find the purity of emptiness within ourselves as well as in the world around us. Hence the first five names listed here allude to either the free flow of water or its impediment by stagnation. The phrase *ditou* means "local" or "native," as in belonging to a place, and can also mean "destination." The name *shetou,* or "snake's head," alludes to the shape of the muscle at LI-7 when the hand is made into a fist.[7]

---

| ❖ **LI-8** | **Lower Side** | |
|---|---|---|
| *Xia⁴lian²* | Lower Side | 下廉 |
| *Shou³zhi¹xia⁴lian²* | Lower Side of the Arm | 手之下廉 |

Named for its position on the arm along the radius, this point is designated as "lower side" and LI-9 is designated as "upper side." LI-8 is associated with the small intestine and stomach channel at St-39 ("lower great void"). Hence St-39 is a meeting point of these three channels and is termed a lower *he*-sea point of the small intestine channel. Because of its relationship to all three officials, LI-8 can be quite effective for moving stagnation in the intestines and digestive system. I frequently treat this point in conjunction with St-39 for bloating, undigested food in the stool, and generalized stagnation in the digestive system.

---

| ❖ **LI-9** | **Upper Side** | |
|---|---|---|
| *Shang⁴lian²* | Upper Side | 上廉 |
| *Shou³zhi¹shang⁴lian²* | Upper Side of the Arm | 手之上廉 |

Named for its position on the arm along the radius, this point is designated as "upper side," whereas LI-8 is designated as "lower side." LI-9 is associated with the stomach channel at St-37, "upper great void," that regulates the intestines and stomach and is the lower *he*-sea point of the large intestine official. When trying to clear stagnation from the large and small intestines, I often pair distal points on each meridian such as LI-4 or LI-5 with SI-4 or SI-5, respectively, and then select either LI-8 or LI-9 and pair it with its corresponding point, St-39 or St-37, on the stomach channel.

Such a strategy can help empower the elimination of waste, assimilation of nutrients, and the effective processing of food and life experience. "Upper side" and "lower side" can also be effective for pain, swelling, and reduced range of motion in the knees as these points respectively unite with St-37 and St-39 on the calf.

---

| ❖ **LI-10** | **Arm Three Miles** | |
|---|---|---|
| *Shou³san¹li³* | Arm Three Miles | 手三里 |
| *Shang⁴san¹li³* | Upper Three Miles | 上三里 |
| *Gui³xie²* | Ghost Evil | 鬼邪 |

The name of LI-10, "arm three miles," is associated with St-36, "leg three miles." Both points are found on the *yangming* channels of the large intestine and stomach officials, and both are located below the articulation of the elbow and knee joints, respectively. St-36 can help strengthen the legs and increase endurance, so LI-10 is useful for all kinds of weakness and lack of flexibility in the arms.

In congruence with its location on a *yangming* channel, and its association with St-36, I find this point useful when dysfunction of the arms and shoulders is associated with issues regarding the gathering and processing of nourishment in life. On the one hand, a person may "overharvest" as he obsessively accumulates food or material wealth. In this case, conditions of the arms tend to be excessive, related to accumulation of heat and damp. On the other hand, a patient may be too exhausted to reap the rewards of his harvest, thus evidencing an underlying functional state of deficient *qi* and/or *yang*. "Arm three miles" can help move stagnation and tonify deficiencies associated with dysfunction of the arms depending on the context of the treatment.

---

| ❖ **LI-11** | **Crooked Pond** | |
|---|---|---|
| *Qu*¹*chi*² | Crooked Pond | 曲池 |
| *Yang*²*ze*² | *Yang* Marsh | 陽澤 |
| *Gui*³*chen*² | Ghost Minister | 鬼臣 |
| *Gui*³*tui*⁴ | Ghost Leg | 鬼腿 |

FUNCTIONS

1. Earth point
2. Tonification point
3. Upper *he*-sea point of the large intestine
4. Ghost point

VIRTUE

Empowers a proper balance of connection to substance and essence.

Making reference in its name to water, this is the large intestine channel's *he*-sea point. Its location at the bend of the elbow explains its designation of being "crooked." Empowering the virtues of earth within metal, LI-11 addresses the relationship between earthly and heavenly nourishment. For the person who feels as though he has lost what has been valued in life and that his fields are barren, the earth point can bring substantial nourishment from the mother to help fill the internal void. Earth contains minerals just as a mother embraces her precious child. If the child (metal) is alone and weeping, a mother's (earth) loving embrace can provide strength and security.

If the presence of earth within metal is excessive, the large intestine's ability to sort pure from impure can be compromised. Food stagnation can be a sign that the stomach and large intestine are holding on and not processing life effectively. This can manifest as constantly chewing on the same emotional material without receiving the lesson offered, eliminating the waste, and moving on in life. Balancing the earth within the metal can empower the virtues of assimilation and letting go. Bowel movements that fluctuate between constipation and diarrhea often represents instability of the earth's relationship to metal. I find "crooked pond" to be effective for harmonizing this relationship, particularly when it is paired with St-25 and St-36.

Note that the character *tui* (腿), meaning "leg," is etymologically related to the character *tui* (褪), meaning "exorcism."[8] Hence as a ghost point LI-11 could be rendered as "ghost exorcism."

---

| ❖ **LI-12** | **Elbow Foramen** | |
|---|---|---|
| *Zhou$^3$liao$^4$* | Elbow Foramen | 肘髎 |
| *Zhou$^3$jiao$^4$* | Elbow Cavity | 肘窌 |
| *Zhou$^3$jian$^1$* | Elbow Tip | 肘尖 |

I have used this point only for elbow and arm pain and decreased range of motion. This is a perfect example of a point named solely for its anatomical location.

---

| ❖ **LI-13** | **Arm Five Miles** | |
|---|---|---|
| *Shou$^3$wu$^3$li$^3$* | Arm Five Miles | 手五里 |
| *Shou$^3$zhi$^1$wu$^3$li$^3$* | Five *Li* of the Arm | 手之五里 |
| *Chi$^3$zhi$^1$wu$^3$li$^3$* | Near Five Miles | 尺之五里 |
| *Da$^4$jin$^4$* | Great Prohibition | 大禁 |

An alternate name of this point, *dajin,* "great prohibition," can remind us that the *Lingshu* forbids needling of this point, stating that doing so can damage the *qi* of the five *zang* organs (kidney, liver, heart, spleen, and lung).[9] I have used this only for pain and decreased range of motion in the elbow and arm.

---

| ❖ **LI-14** | **Upper Arm** | |
|---|---|---|
| *Bi$^4$nao$^4$* | Upper Arm | 臂臑 |
| *Tou$^2$chong$^1$* | Head Thoroughfare | 頭衝 |
| *Jing$^3$chong$^1$* | Neck Thoroughfare | 頸衝 |

FUNCTION

Meeting point of the large intestine, small intestine, and bladder channels with the *yang* linking vessel

The *po* spirit enables our grasp to reach into the world via breath and bring what we have attained through and into us via peristalsis. To do so our arms allow us to reach into the world and grasp what may be of value to us. As a meeting point of the large intestine, small intestine, bladder, and *yang* linking channels, this is a particularly powerful point for addressing limited range of motion and pain in the shoulder. The *yang* linking channel addresses the linking of the arms and legs to the torso.

I find this point particularly effective when shoulder dysfunction is the embodiment of grief, longing, and a basic inability to grasp what is of value in life. Conversely, "upper arm" addresses the identical symptomatology when it is associated with grasping things too strongly in an unconscious attempt to avoid losing what we value in life. Hence excessive tightness in the arms and shoulders is often the embodiment of trying to hold on to what we value for fear it may slip away. People so disposed often end up suffocating those they love. The true nature of our connection with others rests in the domain of spirit, and the tighter we try to hold on to another, the more the essential nature of the connection can allude us. Ironically, loved ones can be lost if we fail to allow them sufficient breathing room. Hence what we value in life spiritually can be lost in direct proportion to the eventual weakening of our physical grip.

---

| ❖ **LI-15** | **Shoulder Bone** | |
|---|---|---|
| *Jian¹yu²* | Shoulder Bone | 肩髃 |
| *Jian¹gu²* | Shoulder Bone | 肩骨 |
| *Jian¹jian¹* | Shoulder Tip | 肩尖 |
| *Bian³jian¹* | Flat Shoulder | 扁肩 |
| *Bian³gu²* | Flat Bone | 扁骨 |
| *Zhong¹jian¹jing³* | Central Shoulder Well | 中肩井 |
| *Pian¹gu²* | Slanting Bone | 偏骨 |
| *Yu²gu²* | Shoulder Bone | 髃骨 |

FUNCTION

Meeting point of the large intestine, small intestine, and bladder channels with the *yang* motility vessel

We can think of the upper edge of the shoulders as a plateau that serves as the interface between heaven (the head) and earth (the body). Before we can let go of a particular emotional issue or past event, it must reach the mind to be processed. For the light of heaven and conscious awareness can burn away all impurities retained from past trauma. The large intestine can repress past pain dysfunctionally because the mind is unable to sort out its suffering from the lesson and light that all experience holds for us. Constriction and pain in the shoulder can be an embodiment of a generalized tightness in the functioning of the large intestine official as it suppresses painful memories from reaching consciousness. Like the previous point, LI-15 can help ease such constriction and help promote the balance between the emotional and physical spheres of the large intestine official.

---

### ❖ LI-16 **Great Bone**

*Ju⁴gu²* Great Bone 巨骨

FUNCTION

Meeting point with the *yang* motility vessel

The name of this point refers to the clavicle, which is a "great bone." I use this as a local point for shoulder and neck issues along the large intestine channel in a similar fashion to LI-14 and LI-15.

---

### ❖ LI-17 **Heavenly Vessel**

*Tian¹ding³* Heavenly Vessel 天鼎

*Tian¹ding³* Heavenly Summit 天頂

*A vessel with legs upturned furthers the removal of what has stagnated.*

– *YIJING*[10]

VIRTUES

1. Empowers the virtues of emptiness, openness, and purity.
2. Diminishes feelings of being tainted and unworthy.

The *ding* was a bronze vessel whose three legs symbolized the unity of heaven, human, and earth. It was used in banquets to hold nourishment and in the performance of rituals for making offerings to heaven and receiving spiritual influence. The function of LI-17 relates directly to *Yijing* hexagram 50 *(ding)*, "the cauldron." The essence of this hexagram's meaning is that stagnation must be removed and the vessel cleaned in order for it to be worthy to hold offerings and receive spirit during the ritual.

LI-14, LI-15, and LI-16 address issues regarding the mediation of heaven and earth from the relatively embodied perspective of pain and dysfunction in the upper surface of the shoulders. LI-17, located on the neck, represents a transition to a relatively more refined quality of *qi* associated with the psychospiritual functioning presided over by heaven.

"Heavenly vessel" fosters the state of openness and purity necessary for receiving spiritual influence and light from above. This point is not traditionally considered a "window to heaven" point. However, in my experience, LI-17 is useful for addressing issues of large intestine function as they contribute to the separation of heart and mind. Therefore, I consider "heavenly vessel" to be very similar in function to a "window" point in offering spiritual and emotional insight and resolving imbalances in these levels of being. This point is particularly potent for helping resolve issues of unworthiness or of feeling tainted by empowering the virtues of emptiness, openness, and purity.

The alternate name for this point is also pronounced *tianding* and thus a homophone of the first name. This second character *ding* implies not just a physical peak but also that something is the pinnacle of its class. As the "heavenly summit," LI-17 can help align us with the highest that heaven has placed within us and continually strives to illuminate.

---

| ❖ **LI-18** | **Support and Rush Out** | |
|---|---|---|
| *Fu²tu²* | Chimney Support | 扶突 |
| *Shui³xue²* | Water Hole | 水穴 |

FUNCTION

Heavenly window point

VIRTUES

1. Harmonizes imbalances associated with separation from one's father.
2. Empowers letting go of the inessential on the deepest of spiritual levels.

LI-18 is at the same anatomical level as CV-22, "heavenly chimney," the window of the sky point on the conception vessel meridian. The *Baiwen Bian* refers to the trachea as a tiered chimney (*zhongluo:* 重樓). The neck can be likened to a chimney, helping release heat and vapor that accumulates from the chest below. On the one hand, LI-18 supports the function of CV-22 by empowering the release of all that no longer serves so we are receptive to the influence of heaven. On the other hand, LI-18 can be effective for harmonizing lung *qi* when it counterflows to manifest as coughing or wheezing. In this sense the point can both inhibit the "rushing out" of breath as well as stimulate the reception of *qi.*

Imbalances of the large intestine are often characterized by either inappropriately clinging to the past or longing for the future. When a person has sustained a great loss in life, he often feels heaven has turned its back on him. He may ask, "If heaven is righteous and just, then how could I have lost that which I valued?" In so doing he cuts himself off from heaven and, without the inspiration of heaven's light, feels alone. As a window point, LI-18 can grant us heaven's perspective on our losses, which is that, in reality, nothing valued is lost as the essential spirit of all beings and things is eternal. Thus harmonized with life's rhythm of gain and loss we can feel complete in the moment so longing for the future and grieving for the past is resolved.

This is an important point for addressing the issue of dysfunctional separation from our father because he represents the embodiment on earth of our connection to heaven. Our father is the worldly embodiment of value originally conveying *jing* to us at conception. People have the tendency to project feelings of being separate from and not valued by their fathers onto their relationships with other men. This is particularly true with religious and authority figures who we create in our imagination to compensate perfectly for deficiencies in our own paternal relationships. Hence we set such figures up for failure and then act out our pain and disappointment in a way we were never able to at home. Feeling "betrayed" by heaven once again, we may turn our back on our spiritual beliefs and sever our connection to our place of worship.

Or we may try in vain to heal our relationship with our fathers by asking for, or by giving, forgiveness. Often people who have worked through an issue to the point of forgiveness are attached to the reestablishment of a healthy relationship with the person who has been forgiven. However, letting go of our story regarding our pain is no guarantee that a healthy relationship will ensue. It is human nature to feel resentful toward heaven for not mending the broken relationship in the face of our efforts. True forgiveness does not dictate any specific action on the part of either party involved. For example, for a woman to forgive the father who abused her sexually does not mean she needs to be in relationship with him personally. Forgiveness merely implies that the issue and its resulting pain are let go of and will no longer impede the expression of her destiny in life. The need for vengeance and earthly justice often arises simultaneously with stagnation in the wood element. When the virtues of the metal element are embraced, we are better able to "let go and let God." Thus metal no longer overcontrols wood across the *ke* cycle and the wheel of evolution represented by the *sheng* cycle can continue to spin, freeing us to progress in life untainted by the past. Hence "support and rush out" can help reestablish the quality of our connection to heaven directly so it is untainted by the quality of our relationship to our father.

---

| ❖ **LI-19** | **Grain Bone Hole** | |
|---|---|---|
| *He²liao⁴* | Grain Bone Hole | 禾髎 |
| *He²jiao⁴* | Grain Hole | 禾窌 |
| *Chang²pin²* | Long Shore | 長頻 |
| *Chang¹liao¹* | Long Foramen | 長髎 |
| *Chang³chuo⁴* | Long Cheekbone | 長出骨 |

The character *he* can be translated as rice, the grain associated with the metal element. The character *qi* (氣) depicts the steam rising off boiling rice and yields a sense of the most refined essential nourishment constituting our life force. The lungs grasp *qi* through the mouth and nostrils, and this point is located halfway between the two directly over the canine teeth in a small notch the size of a grain of rice—hence the first two names listed here.

---

| ❖ **LI-20** | **Welcome Fragrance** | |
|---|---|---|
| *Ying²xiang¹* | Welcome Fragrance | 迎香 |
| *Chong¹yang²* | *Yang* Thoroughfare | 衝陽 |
| *Chong¹yang²* | Surging *Yang* | 沖陽 |

FUNCTION

Exit point

"Welcome fragrance" is named for its function of clearing the sinuses and its location on either side of the nostrils. Here, at the place that pure *qi* is received through breath, the circulation of *qi* in the large intestine channel exits to enter the stomach channel at St-1, "receiving tears." Hence there is a close connection between breathing (lungs), letting go and receiving (large intestine), and the integration of nourishment (stomach).

The sense faculty of smell is one of the most important ways in which the reality of later heaven is transmitted into our internal world.[11] In this regard, note that the olfactory nerve terminates in the limbic system, an area of the brain directly related to human emotion. Additionally, our sense of smell contributes in a large way to the way things taste, which, in the context of Chinese medicine, relates to the reception of *qi* by the stomach official. Hence LI-20 and St-1 provide significant input into the process by which alimentation and respiration support the fires of *mingmen* by mediating the reception and integration of acquired essence. I have found LI-20 to be an important point for restoring the sense of taste when it has been lost due to illness. The name "*yang* thoroughfare" may allude to the confluence of the two *yang* channels, large intestine and stomach, at this point. Note that St-42, the source point on the stomach channel, is also named *chongyang*.

A traditional function ascribed to this point is that of opening the nasal passage and dispersing wind and heat. These pathogens can arise if we fail to digest life properly and eliminate that which has lost its essential value. When the sinuses are congested, our ability to contact essence and feel inspired is obscured. Hence we can tend toward a generally negative and pessimistic outlook as we find the worst in everything. By moving stagnation and empowering us to let go and disengage from life, LI-20 can help engender mental clarity and a corresponding positive outlook. I consider this an important point for empowering receptivity and openness in all domains of being. I find this point to be similar in function to herb formulas such as Puerreria Nasal Compound (Qingbi Tang).

## *Exercises*

1. Explain the functional relationships in the point combination of St-36, St-25, and LI-11.
   a. How could these points be used to treat a patient when grief and longing has eroded the integrity of his center?
   b. How is it possible that this point combination could be used equally well to treat diarrhea and constipation?
2. Compare LI-15 with the functioning of TH-15 and GB-21.
3. Differentiate all channel points that run through the shoulder and explain how pain, swelling, and stiffness might be the expression of psychospiritual dysfunction in each associated official.
4. Compare the function of LI-18 as it governs separation from our fathers with that of St-9, which addresses being overly merged with our mothers.
5. a. Compare the functions of LI-17 with Lu-3 inasmuch as both points can help empower connection to essence and purity as the highest that heaven has placed within us.
   b. Discuss the function of both points in relationship to the virtue of self-worth.
6. Both LI-20 and St-42 are named *chongyang*, or "surging *yang*." Discuss each point's function in helping regulate the balanced rising of *yang*.

## *NOTES*

1. Chen, 1989, p. 87.
2. Wilhelm, 1968, p. 64.
3. Anthony, 1981, p. 14.
4. DeLaney, Leonard, and Kisch, 1989, LI-7.
5. Mathews, 1931, p. 189.
6. For a discussion of the character *ni*, see *ND*, p. 317.
7. Ellis, Wiseman, and Boss, 1989, p. 43.
8. Mathews, 1931, p. 960.
9. Ellis et al., 1989, p. 49.
10. Paraphrased from Wilhelm, 1968, pp. 194–195.
11. The sense of olfaction contributes in a profound way to human emotional behavior. Current scientific understanding of this phenomenon is in its infancy.

# 34

# STOMACH

THE STOMACH CHANNEL BEGINS INTERNALLY AT LI-20, where it rises along the midline of the nose and joins Bl-1 at the medial canthus of the eye. The channel descends laterally along the inferior border of the orbit to become superficial at its entry point, St-1. The channel then runs through St-2, St-3, and St-4, descending in a straight line directly under the pupil of the eye. An internal branch leaves from St-3 and moves medially to GV-26 and then turns laterally again to join St-4 at the corner of the mouth. From here the internal branch travels medially again to join CV-24 under the center of the lower lip and rejoins the main meridian again at St-5. The meridian then ascends through St-6 and St-7, passing through Gb-3, Gb-6, Gb-5, and Gb-4 on its way to St-8. Passing through St-8 this branch terminates at GV-24 on the midline of the forehead.

The superficial pathway leaves St-5 to descend the mandible and continues down the side of the trachea to the medial end of the clavicle. The channel then runs laterally to CV-12, where it divides into superficial and internal paths. The superficial path descends the chest in line with the nipple to the fifth intercostal space, where it turns medially and continues down the abdomen to St-30. The internal path leaves St-12 to travel down the abdomen to St-30. The internal path leaves St-12 to travel through the chest, penetrate the diaphragm, and enter the organ of the stomach at the level of CV-13. A branch of the internal channel leaves from here to contact the spleen. The internal channel continues from CV-13 to reunite with the main channel at St-30.

The single path now descends the interior surface of the leg along the lateral edge of the tibia. At St-39 the channel ascends laterally to St-40 and then descends to the center of the ankle joint at St-41. It then travels along the dorsomedial aspect of the foot between the second and third metatarsal bones to terminate at St-45, the lateral nail point of the second toe. An internal branch leaves St-36 traveling laterally to the main pathway to end at the lateral nail point of the middle toe. Another internal branch leaves from St-42, the channel's exit point, and connects to the entry point of the spleen meridian at Sp-1, the medial nail point of the big toe.

---

## *Thoughts on the Channel*

Think of the top of the stomach channel, as defined by points 1 through 8, as forming the top of a funnel that collects acquired *qi* and readies it for its descent and assimilation into the body. Just as food is received via the mouth and then chewed, life experience arrives to us via the sensory orifices, where it is processed by thought *(yi),* the spirit of the earth element. Hence points St-1 through St-8, which define the cup of this "funnel," address the issues regarding the initial processing of acquired *qi.* For digestion and assimilation to proceed smoothly, only the appropriate amount of life can be processed at any given moment or the funnel will become clogged. Such stagnation is associated with dysfunction above as thought process are compromised and below as digestion and assimilation are hampered.

At St-5 the channel descends to form the neck of this funnel. The stomach and kidney channels run parallel to each other over the length of the torso. The function of acquired *qi* is to complement innate *qi* and assist in the manifestation of its potential. *Qi* acquired by the stomach is derived from the material world and later heaven. It is relatively dense in its form as compared with the essential *qi* acquired by the lungs or the innate potential that resides in *jing.* The "weight" of our acquired stomach *qi* as it descends is complementary to the ascension of kidney *jing.* As stomach *qi* descends to nourish us, kidney *jing* is elevated as the movement of our acquired and innate constitutions complement each other.

### MAIN FUNCTIONS

1. Nourishes us in the process of life.
2. Empowers the integration of life experience in a way that creates integrity.

### DISTAL POINT FUNCTIONS

*Metal:* Empowers the capacity to be nourished by essence.

*Water:* Regulates the balance of moisture in the stomach, empower ing the graceful digestion of nourishment.

*Wood:* Empowers the integration of purpose and process.

*Fire:* Empowers the stomach to cook food so potential sources of nourishment can be broken down and assimilated.

*Earth:* Empowers the essential virtues of the earth element within the stomach official.

*Xi-cleft:* Moves stagnation manifesting as undigested life experience, acquired burden, and disgust.

*Luo:* Vents stagnation to the exterior, empowering the ability to connect to what we love as nourishment rather than burden.

---

| ❖ **St-1** | **Receive Tears** | |
|---|---|---|
| *Cheng*$^{2}$*qi*$^{4}$ | Receive Tears | 承泣 |
| *Yang*$^{4}$*qi*$^{4}$ | Flowing Tears | 羕泣 |
| *Mian*$^{4}$*liao*$^{4}$ | Face Foramen | 面髎 |
| *Mian*$^{4}$*jiao*$^{4}$ | Face Hole | 面窌 |
| *Xi*$^{1}$*xue*$^{4}$ | Ravine Hole | 谿穴 |
| *Xi*$^{1}$*xue*$^{4}$ | Mouse Hole | 鼷穴 |

FUNCTIONS

1. Entry point
2. Intersection point of the stomach channel with the *yang* motility and conception vessels

VIRTUE

Empowers the processing of undigested emotional material.

The first two point names listed here refer to the ability of St-1 to empower the processing of undigested experience. The final four names refer to the point's anatomical location in a small depression in the bone of the orbit directly under the pupil when the eye is looking straight ahead.

As the entry point of the stomach official, St-1 receives *qi* from the large intestine official flowing from LI-20. The role of the stomach is to digest and integrate acquired sources of *qi*. When emotional material is not digested and integrated, it can burden us in much the same way as undigested food can impart feelings of heaviness and stuckness. If the stomach fails to process our life experience sufficiently, the large intestine will have difficulty both in abstracting the highest life has to offer us and in eliminating mundanity so we can move on. If we are so burdened by undigested life experience we may never reach the stage of letting go of the past.

St-1 can empower the receiving of tears, indicating that stagnant *qi* is moving on and we have begun integrating unprocessed experience. "Receiving tears" opens up the flow of *qi* at the source of the stomach meridian and therefore can help flush out undigested material both physiologically and emotionally. I sometimes pair St-1 with St-41, "released stream," to flush stagnation through the entire stomach channel and empower the processing of undigested life experience. The characters *chengqi* can also be translated as "containing tears," indicating the point's usefulness for someone who is habitually needy and cries frequently to win the sympathy of others. In this regard I sometimes pair "receiving tears" with St-45, "hard bargain," when a patient constantly complains and is consumed with self-pity.

Acquired sources of *qi* arriving to the stomach have *yin* and *yang* aspects. The *yin* aspect corresponds to those mundane substances that the stomach must help to descend so they can be eliminated.[1] The *yang* aspect is the healthful *qi* whose nature it is to rise. The rising of the clear *yang* helps the spleen fulfill its role of transforming and ascending the fluids to moisten the lungs, mouth, and sinuses. St-42, "*yang* rushing," initiates the rising *yang* that carries fluids upward. The inability to cry suggests this cycle of descending the mundane and rising the clear *yang* has been compromised. Tears flowing down the face from St-1 are congruent with the movement of stagnation in our digestive systems and the renewal of the stomach's function in helping us process life. "Receiving tears" can reinstitute the balanced flow of stomach *qi* so we are at once nourished by the fruits of our efforts and cleansed of past sorrow.

---

❖ **St-2** **Four Whites**
*Si⁴bai²* Four White 四白
*Gu³men²* Grain Gate 穀門

VIRTUE

Brightens the eyes.

The name of St-2 refers to the four white areas of the eye surrounding the pupil.[2] The reference to the eyes suggests the point's efficacy in treating pathology pertaining to that organ. Whereas St-1 initiates the flow of water by promoting crying, St-2 aids in the transformation of stagnant fluids that are accumulating to obscure vision or create pressure in the eye. Hence I have used this point to good advantage when the pathology involves stagnation of fluids and dampness such as conjunctivitis or the swelling associated with hyperthyroidism. I might use "four whites" in conjunction with prescribing an herbal formula such as Shigan Mingmu Tang (Cleanse Liver Brighten Eyes). In this regard, note that traditional functions ascribed to St-2 are to spread the liver *qi* and benefit the gallbladder. The point is also applicable when dampness obscuring vision is congruent with the spleen's failure to transform fluids.

The name "four whites" can also refer to the four areas around the mouth where the quality of earth *qi* can be diagnosed. Stagnation in the digestive system and the accumulation of toxicity can be evidenced by a yellow/green color around the perimeter of the mouth. The point's alternate name, "grain gate" *(gumen)*, also alludes to the mouth as the receiver of acquired sources of *qi* from alimentation. I use St-2 to address relatively physical aspects regarding the mouth and its relationship to digestion, and I use St-4 to address aspects of dysfunction that are relatively more psychospiritually based.

---

❖ **St-3** **Great Foramen**
*Ju⁴liao⁴* Great Foramen 巨髎
*Ju⁴jiao⁴* Great Hole 巨窌

FUNCTION

Intersection point of the stomach and large intestine channels with the *yang* motility vessel

St-3 is named for its location in the largest hole in the center of the cheek. I use this only as a local point when I think the stomach official is contributing to dysfunction or pain in the face. This discernment is often based on the findings of damp and heat stagnation in the *yangming* channels of the stomach and large intestine officials. Often such symptomatology is congruent with the excessive thought and worry associated with dysfunction of the *yi* and the stomach official. I have found "great hole" useful for pain and numbness in the face and lips as well as toothaches.

---

❖ **St-4** **Earth Granary**
*Di⁴cang¹* Earth Granary 地藏
*Wei⁴wei²* Stomach Link 胃維
*Hui⁴wei²* Meet and Bind 會維

FUNCTION

Intersection point of the stomach and large intestine channels with the conception and *yang* motility vessels

VIRTUES

1. Harmonizes the relationship among appetite, neediness, and nourishment in all aspects of being.
2. Addresses oral fixations and feelings of abandonment that derive from dysfunctional relationships with our mothers as they embody the earth element.

Think of the stomach as a storehouse that receives grain in the form of all material nourishment. The name of this point evokes the image of the earth as a potentially unlimited source of nourishment for those who care for it according to the virtue of reciprocity *(shu)*. A granary stores reserves of nourishment in prosperous times so we can draw on them as circumstance dictates. If our own storehouses are full we will have enough potential sources of nourishment to nourish others in the same way a successful farmer may donate grain to the community stores so those less fortunate may benefit. It is this empowered giving from abundance that is the basis of virtues such as generosity and altruism.

The earth element tends toward imbalances that vary on a continuum from selfishness to habitual giving in the form of ingratiation. Hence we may be compelled to hoard our bounty, feeling we never have enough or tend to give to others to be "nice" even though we do not have enough for ourselves. Habitual selfishness and ingratiation are often congruent with a wide range of dysfunctional eating patterns. These can include eating too quickly or irregularly, and in the extreme these can manifest as conditions such as anorexia, bulimia, and binge eating. Digestive symptoms as diverse as bloating, overpowering cravings, pain, and esophageal spasms or reflux can also accompany such dysfunctional patterns involving need and appetite.

Our mothers are the physical embodiment of the earth element during our early years. The dysfunctions for which this point is indicated often are associated with early trauma regarding having our needs met insufficiently during breastfeeding and weaning during infancy. Ideally, the mother models appropriate boundaries in life regarding the balanced identification and fulfillment of needs to both her infant and her child. Oral fixations and appetite disorders are often rooted in some aspect of dysfunction relative to the quality of care we received from our mothers early in life. Treating points on the stomach channel in the area of the mouth, nipple, and umbilicus is crucial to aiding the healing of habituated feelings of neediness and abandonment that derive from the embodiment of our relationship to our mothers. Located by the sides of the mouth, "earth granary" can help empower a balanced relationship to nourishment in all aspects of being.

---

❖ **St-5** **Great Welcome**

| | | |
|---|---|---|
| *Da⁴ying²* | Great Welcome | 大迎 |
| *Sui³kong³* | Marrow Hole | 髓孔 |

VIRTUE

Helps ease constraint and pain in the jaw that emanate from resentment and anger born of ingratiating behavior.

The character *ying* can be translated as to "welcome" or to "receive." The jaw where this point is located plays an important role in helping the stomach receive and welcome nourishment through chewing. All that we ingest materially in life must be broken down first by chewing, and all we receive psychospiritually must be digested by thought (*yi,* the spirit of earth) so it can be assimilated as nourishment. Hence when we are deliberating something we often say we are "chewing" on it.

Two interesting characters are homophones with the character *ying,* meaning "welcome." The spleen rules that aspect of blood known as *ying,* which constitutes our nutritive *qi.* The character *ying* is composed of the character for fire (火) doubled over the character *gong* (宮), meaning "palace." The character *ying* denotes an encampment of soldiers cooking their food over a fire. This imparts a sense of warmth, safety, and nourishment. Another homophone, also pronounced *ying* (盈), signifies "the abundance that comes to one when, by one's efforts, one arrived to fill with provisions one's vessels."[3] This character imparts a sense of the highest virtues empowered by nutrition.

The virtue associated with the earth element is *xin* (信), meaning integrity. *Xin* depicts a person (亻) standing by his words (言). Ingratiation is the opposite of integrity and occurs when we take care of others' needs without deference to our own. Each time we avoid confrontation by saying "yes" instead of "no," we swallow a little bit of resentment. The poison of resentment acquired by being overly welcoming (*ying:* 迎) to others compromises the quality of our own nourishment (*ying:* 營). This poison can manifest psychospiritually as feelings of bitterness and resentment and physically as a sour taste in the mouth and acid reflux.

I use St-5 for embodiments of this dynamic that manifest as pain, tension, and limited range of motion in the mouth and jaw. For the more psychospiritual aspects of this dynamic, I tend to treat St-9 (*renying,* "people welcome") relatively more.

---

❖ **St-6** **Jawbone**

| | | |
|---|---|---|
| *Jia⁴che¹* | Jawbone | 頰車 |
| *Ya²che¹* | Tooth Chariot | 牙車 |
| *Qu¹ya²* | Crooked Teeth | 曲牙 |
| *Ji¹guan¹* | Hinge | 機關 |
| *Ji¹men²* | Motion Gate | 機門 |
| *Gui³chuang²* | Ghost Bed | 鬼床 |
| *Gui³lin²* | Ghost Forest | 鬼林 |

FUNCTION

Ghost point

This point derives its name from its location on the jaw.[4] I use it for local symptoms in the face and jaw and to supplement the effects of St-5. An unbalanced relationship to nurturance can be congruent with symptoms such as decreased range of motion, numbness, and pain in the face, jaw, and mouth. Excessive chewing tends to present emotionally as mental slowness, excess deliberation, and worry. Physically, this can be congruent with such conditions as grinding of the teeth, TMJ, and trigeminal neuralgia. Deadman suggests this point may have been included as a ghost point for its efficacy in easing clenching of the jaw during epileptic seizures.[5]

---

❖ **St-7** **Lower Hinge**

| | | |
|---|---|---|
| *Xia⁴guan¹* | Lower Hinge | 下關 |

FUNCTION

Intersection point of the stomach and gallbladder channels

This point derives its name from its location on the jaw beneath the joint (hinge) of the mandible. I use it for local conditions of pain and numbness in the face and decreased range of motion in the jaw. As an intersection of the stomach and gallbladder channels, "lower hinge" can be effective when a patient clenches his jaw out of the frustration and anger that accumulates over time from ingratiating behavior. Often I pair this point (or St-5 or St-6) with Gb-4, "loathsome jaws."

---

❖ **St-8** **Head Tied**

| | | |
|---|---|---|
| *Tou²wei²* | Head Tied | 頭維 |
| *Tou²feng²* | Head Stitched | 頭縫 |
| *Sang³da⁴* | Great Forehead | 顙大 |

FUNCTION

Intersection point of the stomach and gallbladder channels with the *yang* linking vessel

VIRTUE

Unbinds the mind and eases worry.

The character *wei,* meaning to "bind" or "tie," is part of the name of the *yang* linking vessel *(yangweimaio)* that links all the *yang* channels including the governing vessel and the bladder channel which preside over the vertex of the head. These channels are conduits of *yang* that radiate as mind and spirit to govern the clarity of the interface between our inner being and the world around us. The earth spirit *yi* (意) presides over thought and ideation, facilities that hold the potential to either nourish or congest all other aspects of mind and spirit.

The emotion associated with earth is sympathy (*si:* 思), which can also be rendered as thought, concern, worry, and obsession. Wieger tells us that the etymology of the character *si* indicates that, "When one is thinking . . . the vital fluid of the heart ascends to the brain."[6] In balance, the earth element's capacity for thought directed by intention empowers the integration of the inherited and acquired constitutions in a way that promotes the virtue of integrity. Integrity manifests psychospiritually as a congruence between intention, speech, and action. Physically, integrity is embodied as a strong center cultivated by a healthy digestive system.

When the earth element is unbalanced, excessive thought manifesting as worry can drive people to cater obsessively to their own needs or to the needs of others as they feel compelled to either give or receive sympathy. Ingratiating behavior undermines both spiritual and emotional integrity as we care for others without deference to our own needs. Worry tends to be embodied as digestive disorders that undermine our physically integrity by eroding our center. In the context of Chinese medicine, obsession can be defined as repetitive thought that does not lead to the productive movement of muscles. The obsessional person either continually chews on the same thoughts without taking productive action or acts continually in a repetitive way without accomplishing anything useful.[7]

"Head tied" is an important point for easing the obsessional tendencies of the earth element. Other points on the stomach channel, such as St-24 or St-43, help move food stagnation. "Head tied" helps move congestion of thought that comes from either internally generated worry or excessive stimulation of the mind from the outside. Dysfunctional patterns of consumption mentally and emotionally often mirror our relationship to nourishment in general. For example, a patient who has the television on and reads during every meal is not likely to integrate effectively any source of nourishment. In this case, his capacity to process is overwhelmed by too many simultaneous sources of input. This phenomenon also occurs when our heads become full from excessive study such as when we cram for a test. Here the mind's capacity to integrate information meaningfully is overwhelmed in the same way as we tend to feel heavy and bloated if we eat too much or too quickly. "Head tied" can help clear the mind by unbinding all the *yang* channels to help ease worry and break repetitive patterns of thought.

---

| ❖ **St-9** | **People Welcome** | |
|---|---|---|
| *Ren²ying²* | People Welcome | 人迎 |
| *Tian¹wu³hui⁴* | Heaven Five Meetings | 天五會 |
| *Wu³hui⁴* | Five Meetings | 五會 |

FUNCTIONS

1. Window to heaven
2. Intersection point of the stomach and gallbladder channels

VIRTUES

1. Empowers the welcoming of others into our process.
2. Empowers the ability to set boundaries regarding giving to others by saying "no."
3. Helps resolve resentment that results from habitual giving.

Located on the throat over the voice box, St-9 plays an important role in engendering the virtue of integrity by empowering sincerity of intention as conveyed through speech. The virtue of the earth element *xin* (信) depicts a man (亻) standing by his words (言). Integrity is born of an alignment between speech and intention. Ingratiation erodes integrity as we hide our true intentions from others in order to avoid conflict. "People welcome" is an important point for addressing the anger and resentment that comes from people pleasing. This resentment is often evidenced as a constricted feeling in the throat at the level of this point. As *qi* stagnation ascends the digestive system to reach St-9, it becomes increasingly difficult for us to swallow and assimilate nourishment. Often patients point to St-9 when they say, "I've had it up to here." Such stagnation tends to be embodied as gas, bloating, and a general discomfort in the process of deriving nourishment from life.

In empowering speech, St-9 has a dual function. On the one hand, it can help us establish appropriate boundaries around giving by empowering us to say "no" to fulfilling the needs of others. For only if we are free to say no, can our decision to give ever come from a position of strength.

On the other hand, "people welcome" can help us welcome others into our process when we have difficulty asking for our own needs to be met.[8]

"People welcome" is an important point for patients who are overly merged with their mothers. Our entire pattern of identifying and fulfilling our needs is predicated in large part on the quality of our relationship to our mothers early and throughout life.[9] It is the mother's job to nurture the child unconditionally while simultaneously teaching it to care for its own needs. In dysfunction the mother either keeps the child overly dependent on her or pushes the child away in a vain attempt to satisfy her own needs. Either of these scenarios can impact the earth element dysfunctionally and undermine healthy patterns of nourishment throughout life.

People who are overly merged with their mothers tend to be excessively needy and may expect to be catered to in relationships. Often they are highly ambivalent in diverse realms of life because they have difficulty sorting out their own needs from the needs of others. Because the entire process of identifying and meeting needs is associated with their overbearing mother, people tend to overcompensate in creating boundaries by closing the door to nourishment indiscriminately. This behavior can have broad implications, hindering their ability to abstract nourishment from life and effectively starving them throughout diverse aspects of being. Stagnation manifesting as bitterness against our mothers who we feel have abandoned us can also negatively impact our ability to receive nourishment. "People welcome" can help us accept nourishment in life untainted by the quality of our relationship to our mothers. Hence we can differentiate from others we are overly dependent on and establish a healthy boundary relative to the giving and receiving of nourishment in relationship. In this way the *qi* of the earth element can be rectified and the virtue of integrity restored.

---

| ❖ **St-10** | **Water Rushing** | |
|---|---|---|
| *Shui³tu⁴* | Water Rushing | 水突 |
| *Shui³men²* | Water Gate | 水門 |
| *Shui³tian¹* | Water Heaven | 水天 |

"Water rushing" is named for the feeling under the finger when the pulse is taken at this point on the carotid artery. Note that the character *tu* is also used in the name of LI-18, found laterally to St-10. I generally use St-10 either before or after treating St-9 to help address similar issues. I use St-10 relatively more to address the physical manifestation of phlegm and *qi* stagnation in the throat, and I use St-9 relatively more for the psychospiritual basis of dysfunction.

---

❖ **St-11** ***Qi* Cottage**
*Qi[4]she[1]* *Qi* Cottage 氣舍

The names of St-11 through St-15 refer to parts of buildings and implements that are in a home. The earth is the home of our species, and the earth element defines and creates our physical and spiritual center as home within us. Our physical center, nourished by the *qi* and blood assimilated and generated by the digestive system, is evidenced by strong muscles and a firm *hara*. Our spiritual center is nourished by the assimilation of nonphysical forms of acquired *qi* and manifests as the virtue of integrity. These points all empower the storage and distribution of acquired *qi* as nourishment and center in all aspects of being.

St-11 and St-12 are located on the neck, which is the interface between the body (heart) and head (mind). I use these two points largely to address psychospiritual issues around nourishment that are congruent with separation between the heart and mind. When a patient grew up with divorced parents or moved continually early in life, he can have trouble ever settling down and feeling comfortable in one place. His whole life can become an unconscious search for a home that always seems to elude him. "*Qi* cottage" can benefit the person who never feels at home either in his body or in any place he resides. Our ability to feel at home in a given place wholly depends on our ability to be comfortable inside ourselves. St-11 can nourish the communication among the heart, *hara,* and spirit, allowing us to feel more secure and centered in all aspects of being. The spirit of this point evokes the image of a warm cottage for the weary traveler that welcomes him home.

---

❖ **St-12** **Broken Bowl**
*Que[1]pen[2]* Broken Bowl 缺盆
*Tian[1]gai[4]* Heaven's Cover 天蓋
*Chi[3]gai[4]* Cubit Cover 尺蓋

FUNCTION

Reunion point between stomach, small intestine, three heater, gallbladder, and large intestine channels

VIRTUES

1. Empowers the containment of nourishment.
2. Empowers self-sufficiency and decreases neediness.

St-12 is named for its location in the supraclavicular fossa, which resembles a bowl. As a reunion point for five of the *yang* officials, "broken bowl" can help us contain, and thus be nourished, by acquired resources. It is at St-12 that acquired *qi* collects before it continues its descent onto the torso and down the body. At the point that *qi* reaches St-12 it has already been broken down by chewing, the digestive enzymes inherent in saliva, and intentional thought *(yi)*. Just as a cracked bowl is unable to hold a meal, so too can we fail to be nourished by acquired sources *qi* if its flow stagnates and "spills" at this point. This imbalance can evidence as an emotional spilling, as it were, in the form of neediness, worry, and inappropriate boundaries regarding the fulfillment of our own needs and the needs of others.

An alternate name of St-12, *tiangai* (天蓋), "heaven's cover," refers to the location of this point directly over the lungs that embodies our connection to heaven through breath. Whereas the earth element governs acquired material nurturance from the mother in the form of food, the lungs preside over our connection to father, heaven, and inspiration through breath. Lu-1 can be treated in conjunction with St-12 to empower the assimilation of refined *qi* from both breath and food. In this way the virtues of inspiration and integrity can be addressed simultaneously.

---

### ❖ St-13 *Qi* Door
*Qi*[4]*hu*[4] *Qi* Door 氣戶

The clavicle, which lies between St-12 and St-13, is a kind of threshold that acquired *qi* must cross as it descends to the stomach. When this door is closed on a psychospiritual level we may have a difficult time accepting sympathy. Physically we may have difficulty swallowing, exhibiting signs of plum pit *qi* and digestive distress including tension and pressure in the esophagus. If the "*qi* door" is closed, our storehouse, as eluded to in the name of St-14, cannot be filled with the fruits of our labor. I often treat St-12 and St-13 together to help stomach *qi* bridge the clavicle and to treat psychospiritual blocks related to receiving *qi* through alimentation and breath.[10]

---

### ❖ St-14 Storehouse
*Ku*[4]*fang*[2] Storehouse 庫房

VIRTUE

Provides access to reserves of acquired *qi*.

St-14, Ki-27, and Lu-1 are all located at the level of the first intercostal space and address the assimilation and integration of acquired and inherited essence. Ki-27, *shufu*, is also named storehouse, and the name of Lu-1, "central treasury" *(zhongfu),* can also be translated as "central storehouse." These points provide access to reserves of inherited and acquired essence in keeping with the respective functions of the kidney, stomach, and lung officials.

Kidney essence dictates who we are by setting the inherited foundation for all manifestations in life. This essence is invested within us by heaven at conception as *jing*. Ki-27, at the apex of its channel, represents the highest point of our potential development. Ki-27 can help access our deepest reserves of *jing* and stimulate the rising movement of kidney essence toward the upper *jiao* to promote evolution. Acquired essence, as accessed by St-14 and governed by the stomach official, represents the possibility of which aspects of self-will be nourished and cultivated at any point during life. The earth element presides over the nutritive *qi* that forms the substantial basis of our acquired reserves.

The lungs constitute the embodiment of heaven within us. Lu-1 is the first point on the lung channel and has a dual relationship to the function of the kidneys and Ki-27. Externally, the lungs of heaven are the original inspirators of our *jing*. Heaven essentially invests the quality of our *jing* at conception by breathing original nature into us. Hence Zhuangzi tells us that heaven blows "on the ten thousand things in a different way, so each can be itself."[11] Therefore Lu-1 governs the *zongqi,* or ancestral *qi* of the chest, that binds us to ancestry and the rhythmic movements of *dao*. Internally, the lungs embody our capacity for receiving essence and light from heaven as it continues its investment in us during life. Lu-1 links the moment of conception to the present moment by empowering the synchronicity of our breath with the breath of *dao*. The *qi* of our ancestors gleaned through breath as presided over by Lu-1 inspires our highest cultivation of potential in life as presided over by Ki-27. Hence the most refined aspects of kidney *jing* accessed at Ki-27 are found just adjacent to the most refined essences acquired through breath accessed at Lu-1.

Located between Ki-27 and Lu-1, St-14 provides access to, and potentiates, our acquired stores to nourish our process of fulfilling potential. Hence blood is created as *jing* (kidney essence) meets *ying* (nutritive essence) and the essence acquired from breath at the center of the chest. I think of St-14 as empowering the offering of food to ancestors *(jing)* and heaven (breath) during ritual. St-14 can strengthen us by nourishing the integration of inherited (Ki-27) and acquired *jing* (Lu-1, St-14) as gleaned through breath and nutrition.

---

❖ **St-15** **Room Screen**
*Wu$^1$yi$^4$* Room Screen 屋翳

VIRTUES

1. Nourishes the relationship between the earth and metal elements.
2. Nourishes the lungs.

The character *yi* can be translated into English as "canopy" or "screen." St-15 is located at the top of the upper *jiao*, which covers the "room" inhabited by the heart and lungs. In turn, we can think of the lungs as a canopy or screen that covers the other organs in the middle *jiao* as heaven is a canopy that covers the earth. Physically, St-15 is often used for dysfunction and symptomatology of the lung official. Symptoms that "room screen" is indicated for include cough, wheezing, dyspnea, shortness of breath, coughing, and phlegm. "Room screen" helps resolve phlegm by activating the digestive functions of the stomach, spleen, and lungs. Accumulation of dampness can prevent the stomach and lungs from adequately assimilating nourishment. I often pair St-15 with points on the lung channel such as Lu-6 or Lu-7 to assist the digestive aspect of the lungs in transforming fluids.

The lungs are a delicate official whose vulnerability tends to be embodied when we are emotionally fragile and "thin skinned." The lungs preside over the skin, and St-15 is also indicated for generalized itching and pain of the skin to the extent that the wearing of clothes is unbearable.[12] This last indication is of interest in light of Worsley's observation that St-15 can help a patient feel at ease and secure when he feels vulnerable and exposed. He notes the importance of having empathy as healers and suggests that St-15 can provide a patient with a sense of privacy such as that afforded by a screen.[13]

---

## ❖ St-16 **Breast Window**

*Ying*[1]*chuan*[1] Breast Window 應窗

VIRTUES

1. Illuminates underlying psychospiritual issues that erode the virtues of the earth element.
2. Empowers the earth element's virtue of reciprocity (*shu*).

The production and dissemination of breast milk is based in the functional processes of the earth element as they preside over issues concerning the nourishment of self and others. St-16 can stimulate production of milk when nursing mothers experience insufficient lactation. "Breast window" can also help address the underling psychospiritual issues concerning nurturance that can be congruent with decreased milk production.

The cry of her infant can arouse lactation in a nursing mother. This response is deeply rooted in the mother's feelings for her child. Compassion, sympathy, and empathy are all related to the earth element's virtue of reciprocity. The virtue of reciprocity emerges archetypally in the balanced relationship between a mother and child. Located on the breast over the heart, St-16 can empower compassion in those who are unsympathetic to the needs of others. The function of a window is to let light in to illuminate the interior of a home and convey an accurate image of what lies externally. For people whose relationship to nourishment is obscured by feelings of abandonment and neediness, "breast window" can provide light to help illuminate and resolve these issues.

---

❖ **St-17** **Center of the Breasts**
*Ru³zhong¹* Center of the Breasts 乳中
*Dang¹ru³* Nipple 當乳

Prohibition: Forbidden to needle.

Located at the center of the nipple, this point is forbidden to treat with either needle or moxa. During the first nine months of life the fetus feeds on pure *yuanqi* through the umbilicus by the mother. After birth the umbilicus is cut and the infant takes its first breath, uniting heaven within (innate *jing*) with heaven without (acquired *jing*). The infant issues its first cry and is placed immediately to the mother's breast to reestablish its connection to *yuanqi* while ingesting the mother's colostrum. The mother's task in life is to empower the child to learn how to identify its needs and acquire appropriate sources of nourishment. While the boundaries regarding nourishment are being established the mother slowly weans the child from dependence on her.

To the degree that the relationship between mother and child is dysfunctional, the two can be overly merged with each other as the relationship is typified by inappropriate boundaries. As the child tries to establish appropriate boundaries later in life, the mother can be rejected as well as all sources of nourishment, consciously or unconsciously, identified with her. In this scenario the function of the digestive system can be slowly undermined. Adults who have failed to differentiate and establish healthy boundaries with their mothers tend to become overly dependent on others for care and nourishment. Treating points around the umbilicus, nipple, and mouth can be effective in helping heal such dysfunctional patterns.

---

### ❖ St-18 **Root of the Breasts**
*Ru²gen¹* Root of the Breasts 乳根

This point is named for its location at the base of the breast. I find it useful for treating mastitis and for promoting milk flow in nursing mothers. Generally I use St-18 to address the relatively physical aspects of milk production and flow of *qi* through the breast, and I find St-16 better for addressing the psychospiritual issues of nurturance and empowering the earth element's virtue of reciprocity.

---

### ❖ St-19 **Not at Ease**
*Bu⁴rong²* Not at Ease 不容

VIRTUE

Eases worry associated with digestive dysfunction.

The emotion associated with earth is sympathy (*si:*思).[14] St-24, "lubrication food gate," addresses relatively more physiological aspects of digestion as they impact, and are impacted by, the psychospiritual issues of the earth element such as worry and sympathy *(si)*, integrity *(xin)*, and thought *(yi)*. St-19 addresses the spiritual basis of these issues relatively more as they impact physiology. Ease of being is a metaphor for letting all things be as they are.[15] St-19 helps ease the mind when it is overengaged with life and taking everything personally. Worry and pensiveness can be embodied as a "nervous stomach" characterized by pain, burning, tightness, and distension in the region from CV-8 to CV-15.

---

### ❖ St-20 **Receiving Fullness**
*Cheng²man³* Receiving Fullness 承满

VIRTUE

Empowers the assimilation of nourishment in a way that can engender the virtue of contentment.

This point can help harmonize a continuum of unbalanced expression relative to feelings of not being or having enough in life. Receiving fullness can empower us to experience the abundance in life that emerges from connection to our source rather than wallowing in feelings of neediness or self-pity. Overeating is often a compensatory mechanism for feeling undernourished and as though we are "not enough" in life. Physically, St-20 can help ease feelings of heaviness and bloatedness that come from eating more than we can use or assimilate. In contrast, conditions such as anorexia typified by emaciation can also be the embodiment of feeling as though we are either "not enough" or "too much." The person who overeats or undereats can be equally unable to assimilate the potential sources of nourishment received. In either case, St-20 can empower us to receive the fullness of experience and nourishment that is potentially available in life.

---

❖ **St-21** **Bridge Gate**
*Liang²men²* Bridge Gate 梁門

I use both "bridge gate" (St-21) and "border gate" (St-22) for food stagnation and helping stomach *qi* descend. Whenever there is bloating and feelings of discomfort in this region, either of these points can help. I find both these points to address issues that are relatively physical in nature, whereas St-19 and St-20 address relatively more the psychospiritual issues that motivate the dysfunctional assimilation of nourishment.

---

❖ **St-22** **Border Gate**
*Guan¹men²* Border Gate 關門
*Guan¹ming²* Illuminated Gate 關明

St-22 and Ki-18 are located at the same anatomical level, and both points contain the character *guan* (關), meaning border "pass" or "gate." Stomach *qi* must descend at this point to nourish us while kidney *qi* must ascend as *jing* is transformed into wisdom. Treating both points together can integrate the influence of the inherited and acquired constitutions, helping us empower the manifestation of our potential while being nurtured in the process of fulfilling destiny. The phrase *guanmen* literally means to "shut the door."[16] Dysfunction of this door can be accompanied by a wide variety of digestive problems including constipation, diarrhea, and diminished appetite. Hence *guanmen* can help regulate the appropriate closing of this important gate to aid in the balanced assimilation of nourishment and elimination of waste. The alternate name of St-22, "illuminated gate," can refer to its role in illuminating darkness as it empowers mundanity to descend into the abyss of the intestines and supports the abstraction of the pure *yang* from acquired *qi*.

Comparing the names of St-22, St-24, Ki-21, and CV-10 yields insight into how the process of refining essence empowers life by separating the clear from mundane influences present in both innate and acquired sources of *qi*. The character *you* (幽) figures prominently in the names of

St-24, CV-10, and Ki-21. In fact, both Ki-21 and CV-10 share the name *youmen,* or "dark gate," and the name of St-24, *huayoumen* (滑幽門), can be translated as "lubrication dark gate." The character *you* (幽), translated here as "darkness," denotes the most shady (幽) recess in the hills (山) where threads (幺幺) of light barely extend and things are almost invisible.[17] Hence the character *you* has the associated meaning of subtlety, which can refer to the refinement of essence as it ascends and descends from the kidneys and stomach, respectively.

Ki-21 marks the transition of kidney *qi* as it ascends from the middle to the upper *jiao. Jing* is refined in the course of its ascent as we learn and resolve our life lessons. At Ki-21 the most refined essence cultivated from our inherited constitution enters the darkness of the burial ground where it may be illuminated by the heart.[18] Hence Ki-21 is just lateral to CV-14, the *mu* point of the heart official. With the mundanity of karma burned away, *jing* is transformed into *ling,* and, as the *yin* (*ling)* and *yang (yang)* aspects of spirit interpenetrate, the will of heaven and human become one and destiny is fulfilled.[19] In this case the darkness *(jing)* contained in the lower *jiao* has been refined in its ascent to be illuminated and empower spiritual potency in the upper *jiao.*

This process is in contrast to that mediated by St-22, St-24, and CV-10, which empower the descent of acquired mundanity into the lower heater for elimination while empowering the digestive system to abstract the clear *yang* from acquired sources of *qi.* Hence a principal use of these points is for food stagnation and its associated symptomatology.

---

❖ **St-23** **Supreme Unity**

| | | |
|---|---|---|
| *Tai⁴yi¹* | Supreme Unity | 太乙 |
| *Tai⁴yi¹* | Supreme Unity | 太一 |

VIRTUE

Empowers the integration of life experience in a way that engenders the virtue of integrity.

The character *yi* (一) denotes the number one and is identified with the influence of heaven in our lives as the single unifying principle motivating our evolution. The alternate name of St-23 refers to the unity of *dao* as a great seed from which all things arise.[20] This character *yi* 乙 represents the striving of the purpose within a seed to manifest in the world as growth.[21] Both of these characters are homophones, with the character *yi* (義) translated as "intention" or "thought" that denotes the spirit of the earth element. The healthy digestive system ensures that only those forms of acquired *qi* congruent with true self can enter the blood to form the nutritive basis of the physiological process. In fulfilling its function, the digestive system ensures that the inherited and acquired constitutions are united in a way that produces a fully integrated human being. On a physical level, this means allowing the digestive system to abstract from all sources of acquired *qi* the necessary ingredients for nourishing, building, and maintaining the body. In psychospiritual realms, the *yi* allows us to integrate our life experiences in a nourishing way that produces the virtue of integrity (*xin*: 信) as the foundation that roots all growth. This integrity is evidenced by the degree to which our actions and words reflect the intentions of our heart.

Hence the *yi* preside over the digestive functions of intentional thought that allow the processing and assimilation of our life experiences in a way that nourishes us. The name "supreme unity" relates to the function of the stomach in breaking down all influences in life into a homogeneous mixture so we can integrate acquired experience into a meaningful, unified whole. In this way, our life from birth to death in the material world can better conform to the underlying unity of early heaven. "Supreme unity" can help us integrate our life experience when our lives appear as a conglomeration of unrelated and fragmented events. In this way we may digest and integrate past experience and move on in life relatively less encumbered by undigested burden.

---

❖ **St-24** **Lubrication Food Gate**

| | | |
|---|---|---|
| *Hua²rou⁴men²* | Lubrication Food Gate | 滑肉門 |
| *Hua²you¹men²* | Gate of Darkness and Subtlety | 滑幽門 |
| *Hua²rou⁴* | Smooth Flesh | 滑肉 |

VIRTUES

1. Lubricates the process of digestion and assimilation.
2. Empowers a sense of ease and grace in receiving nourishment.

"Lubrication food gate" assists the assimilation and digestion of food to proceed smoothly by moving stagnation in the digestive system. I have found "lubrication food gate" to be helpful in conditions such as sprue or celiac disease that hamper the assimilation of nourishment. I often think of St-24 when patients report feelings of bloating, heaviness, and obstruction after eating. Reports of "feeling like a brick is in my stomach" or "food just sits" are suggestive of St-24 as a point of choice. In the psychospiritual realm, "lubrication food gate" can help ease constraint in the person who is revolted by some life circumstance, reporting he "just can't stomach it."[22] The phrase *youmen,* also the name of Ki-21, refers to both the pyloric valve as well as the underworld of lost souls. As kidney *qi* ascends through this gate at Ki-21, it passes through a stage of subtle refinement to enter the upper *jiao* and burial ground of the emperor. As stomach *qi* descends through this gate, it is also subtly refined as *yang* is abstracted as nourishment and waste moves on to the abyss, or underworld, of the intestines.

Stagnation in the digestive system can be congruent with eating too quickly so the digestive system is unable to process efficiently what has been ingested. The stomach generates excess heat as it overworks to process food not adequately broken down by chewing and the digestive enzymes present in saliva. Excess heat consumes fluid, and, eventually, the stomach suffers from *yin* deficiency and its associated pathologies. Eating too quickly is usually motivated by a restless spirit manifesting as an overactive thought *(yi)* process. Such a process is in play when we try to assimilate too much information at once. People who simultaneously eat, read, watch television, and engage in conversation can easily overwhelm their mind and spirit's *(yi)* ability to integrate information. Such excessive input and stimulation can also contribute to a condition of stomach *yin* deficiency as the mind overworks to assimilate data.

---

| ❖ **St-25** | **Heavenly Pivot** | |
|---|---|---|
| *Tian[1]shu[1]* | Heavenly Pivot | 天樞 |
| *Bu[3]yuan[2]* | Supplement the Primordial | 補元 |
| *Xun[2]yuan[2]* | Follow the Primordial | 循元 |
| *Xun[2]ji[4]* | Adhere to the Limit | 循際 |
| *Da[4]chang[2]mu[4]* | Large Intestine *Mu* | 大腸募 |
| *Chang[3]xi[1]* | Long Ravine | 長谿 |
| *Chang[3]gu[3]* | Long Valley | 長谷 |
| *Gu[3]men[2]* | Valley Gate | 谷門 |

*[The area] above the celestial pivot is ruled by celestial* qi;
*[the area] below the celestial pivot is ruled by the earthly* qi.
*The place where these* qi *intersect is the origin of man's* qi
*and the ten thousand things.*
– *Essential Questions*[23]

FUNCTIONS

1. Intersection point with large intestine channel
2. *Mu* point of the large intestine official

VIRTUE

Empowers grace through transitions by strengthening our balanced relationship to center.

The name "heavenly pivot" recalls the earth element as the central axis around which the seasons and *dao* revolve. Located on both sides of the navel, St-25 addresses the nature of our center as a fixed reference point that creates stability during transitions. "Heavenly pivot" empowers the virtue of being able to move dynamically in any direction without excessive deliberation. *Tianshu* is a name for the central star in the Big Dipper constellation, the residence of the spirits *(shen)* who preside over our destiny. The name *xunyuan,* or "follow the primordial," reminds us of the importance of orienting toward the source at our centers.

An alternate name for St-25 is *buyuan,* or "supplement the primordial." The Big Dipper circles the North Star, the life-giving heart of the heavens. The navel is the center of the human being, and it is through the umbilicus that we receive nourishment during gestation in the form of primordial *qi.* The points located directly adjacent to the navel are Ki-16 and St-25. The kidney presides over inherited essence and the stomach governs the acquired constitution. Hence these three points play an important role in the cultivation of primordial *qi* as a foundational resource in health and healing.

Located on the border between the middle and lower *jiaos,* St-25 plays a pivotal role in aiding the assimilation of nourishment and the elimination of waste. This role is emphasized in the designation of "heavenly pivot" as a reunion point between the stomach and large intestine officials. The strength of the stomach in digesting food helps empower ease in the processes of assimilation and elimination. By tonifying *qi* and moving stagnation in the stomach, the large intestine can be empowered to absorb minerals and eliminate waste more efficiently. By empowering the large intestine to let go of what no longer serves, the stomach can be empowered to aid the processes of digestion and assimilation more efficiently. St-25 is thus a pivotal point in this reciprocal relationship.

---

### ❖ St-26 **Outer Mound**

*Wai⁴ling²* Outer Mound 外陵

The character *wai* refers to a divination (卜) regarding the meaning of dreams experienced the previous evening (夕).[24] The divination must take place in the morning and certainly before sunset. For if it occurs after sunset it will have lost its proximity and relevance to the dream. Therefore this character took on the associated meanings of beyond, foreign, and extraordinary. The character *ling* (陵), meaning "mound," is a homophone with the character *ling* (靈), meaning "spirit."[25] Historically the Chinese were earth worshipers and buried their dead in mounds of earth. These burial mounds are recalled by the shape of the rectus abdominous muscles where this point is located. *Ling* is the beneficent aspect of spirit that takes care of family members after death. *Ling* as spirit is the highest emanation of kidney *jing* and reflects the potency and strength of one who has fulfilled destiny. The stomach and kidney channels run parallel with each other over the abdomen and chest, reflecting the integration of inherited and acquired forms of nourishment. "Outer mound" can help nourish our spiritual journey as the acquired constitution is summoned to complement the innate constitution.

---

❖ **St-27** **Great Might**
*Da⁴ju⁴* Great Might 大巨
*Ye⁴men²* Armpit Gate 腋門

VIRTUE

Provides access to reserves of acquired *qi* and *jing*.

"Great might" helps empower a reserve of strength emanating from the acquired constitution. Such a reserve can help complement and fuel our wills to help us reach our goals. Think of the children's story "The Little Engine That Could" to imagine the potential effects of St-27. The earth element can become exhausted from excessive work that results from the habituated desire to take care of others and to "be enough." If the "little engine" does not rest between endeavors, its heroic efforts in saving others certainly will lead to its own ruin. In cases of chronic fatigue or exhaustion after a long illness, "great might" can provide access to a reserve of *qi* and thus help get us moving again.

Patients must learn how they became exhausted in the first place. Adequate rest is necessary to allow the reserves of *qi* accessed during treatment to contribute to healing. If we practitioners merely use such points to tonify *qi,* yet fail to teach our patients how to live in harmony with nature, we will merely enable patients to exhaust themselves further instead of truly helping them heal.

---

❖ **St-28** **Waterway**
*Shui³dao⁴* Waterway 水道

"Waterway" is an important point for empowering the earth element to regulate the flow of water appropriately in the lower *jiao*. The earth element has several important functional relationships to the water element. Like a canal, earth can serve as a channel for promoting and directing the flow of water. If the presence of earth is excessive, however, it can dam water and obstruct its flow. Such obstruction can be congruent with stasis of *qi*, blood, and damp. Finally, earth, like a sponge, can absorb excess water. Hence by increasing the influence of the earth element through tonification, the stomach and spleen can better fulfill their function of transforming fluids so the tendency toward stagnation and growths is mitigated. "Waterway" is able to treat retention of urine by promoting the flow of water through the lower *jiao*.

Deficiency of water in the lower *jiao* can be congruent with constipation. The large intestine depends on an adequate balance of fluids so it can eliminate waste. If the large intestine becomes dry, the whole system can become bound up as pressure increases and mundanity is retained. By regulating the flow of water in the lower *jiao*, "waterway" can help promote smooth flow through the intestines.

Physician Sun Simiao referred to left *shuidao* as *baomen* ("gate of the uterus") and right *shuidao* as *zihu* ("child's door"), emphasizing its action on gynecological disorders typified by stasis of *qi* and blood.[26] I have found that uterine fibroids associated with stagnation of *qi*, blood, and damp can occur in women as a dysfunctional way of filling an emotional void resulting from childlessness. A child may be desired to fill an inner sense of emptiness because the woman wants someone to endlessly pour her love into. This type of giving tends to be based on the neediness congruent with a dysfunctional earth element. The fibroid itself can be the embodiment of pain and need and presents as misplaced *qi*, blood, and fluid that stagnate in the lower *jiao*.

Note that Ki-13, located between St-28 and CV-4, is also named *zihu*, "door of infants." I use St-28 and Ki-13 to nourish the processes of conception and gestation with acquired and inherited resources, respectively. I use Ki-14 to treat psychospiritual issues regarding infancy that I consider relatively karmic in nature and St-28 for issues regarding feelings of abandonment and lack of nurturance by the mother early in life. However, all three points—CV-4, Ki-13, and St-28—excel at promoting fertility and treating issues relative to infancy and childhood by treating imbalances of *qi*, blood, and fluid in the lower *jiao*.

---

❖ **St-29** **Return**

| | | |
|---|---|---|
| *Gui*[1]*lai*[2] | Return | 歸來 |
| *Xi*[1]*xue*[2] | Ravine Hole | 谿穴 |
| *Xi*[1]*gu*[3] | Ravine Valley | 谿谷 |

VIRTUE

Revives the womb by dispelling cold, thus empowering the return of new life into the world.

The character *gui* suggests that what has left this world will eventually return in some form and that what is presently here will eventually return back into the mysterious workings of *dao*. *Lai* means "to come." *Gui* evokes the cycle of life and death as it reflects the underlying process of *dao* in creating and receiving back all things. The character *gui*, meaning "return," is homophonic with the character *gui* (鬼), translated as "demon," that denotes disembodied earthbound spirits. These spirits incarnate into the body as the *hun* (魂) and *po* (魄) and then "return" (*gui:*歸) upon death as *gui* (鬼). The theme of cycles is also present in the name of St-30, *qichong* (氣沖), which recalls the whirling abyss of *qi* between heaven and earth that integrates these dual poles of the cosmos as the ten thousand things incubate in the womb of *dao*.

As a point known to be effective in treating both male and female reproductive problems, St-29 can empower the return to health of the functional processes underlying conception. A central function of *guilai* is to warm the lower *jiao* and dispel cold from either excess or deficiency. *Guilai* is particularly suited to warming the uterus in women and the genital region of both sexes. Warmth brings life to the lower *jiao* to aid the process of conception and nurture the ability to incubate the fetus during gestation. Hence St-29 has the potential to improve disorders such as irregular menstruation, amenorrhea, and infertility by returning a woman's healthy menstrual function.

---

❖ **St-30** **_Qi_ Rushing**

| | | |
|---|---|---|
| *Qi⁴chong¹* | *Qi* Rushing | 氣沖 |
| *Qi⁴chong¹* | *Qi* Thoroughfare | 氣衝 |
| *Qi⁴jie¹* | *Qi* Thoroughfare | 氣街 |

FUNCTIONS

1. Point of the penetrating vessel
2. Sea of nourishment

The character *chong* has a multiplicity of meanings in the context of this point's name. *Chongqi* (沖氣) refers to the whirling abyss of *qi* between heaven and earth that holds these two poles apart while simultaneously helping them interpenetrate to preserve the integrity and unity of *dao*. The function of the stomach is to process acquired forms of *qi* so they are effortlessly blended with *jing*, our inherited essence, to nourish the smooth unfolding of destiny. This point's designation as a "sea of nourishment" suggests the facility of stomach *qi* to integrate the inherited and acquired constitutions.

This whirling abyss of *qi* is also alluded to in the name of St-25, "heavenly pivot," and the character *chong* is present in the name of St-42, "rushing *yang*," as well. *Yang* and *qi* must rise in the body as the potential stored in *jing* evolves to manifest its virtues in the world. Hence the evolution of *jing* toward the brain as marrow and wisdom is empowered by this rising *yang*. *Yang* also helps carry nourishing fluids upward to the heart and mouth as it rises, a process addressed by St-42. This, however, is a subtle mechanism because if *yang* rises too forcefully it can damage the heart or present as rebellious stomach *qi*. Both St-42 and St-30 can help harmonize rising *yang* so it empowers rather than overwhelms life.

When *qi* does "rush" in its ascent, it can manifest as "running piglet" syndrome. According to the *Classic of Difficulties*, when the penetrating vessel is diseased, there will be upsurging *qi* and acute abdominal disturbance.[27] According to the *Essentials from the Golden Cabinet,* "Running piglet disorder arises from the lower abdomen; it rushes up to the throat with such ferocity that the patient feels he is close to death. It attacks and then remits. It is brought about by fear and fright."[28] Running piglet *qi* primarily arises when stagnant liver *qi* transforms to heat or when kidney *yang* deficiency leads to accumulation of cold in the lower *jiao*. In both cases, *qi* is violently discharged and rushes (*chong*) upward through the penetrating (*chong*) vessel, congruent with symptoms such as nausea, hot flushes, and heart palpitations. This pattern of dysfunction is often described by patients in modern times as having an "anxiety attack."

In my experience, this syndrome is often present in women who frequently feel vulnerable and exposed and possess a history of sexual abuse. The cold in the lower *jiao* associated with *yang* deficiency can be congruent with a withdrawal of *yang* from the genital area and the organs of reproduction as the patient suppresses her sexuality in response to the abuse. Reality, although suppressed, will keep asserting itself, and the anxiety attacks manifest as the patient feels exposed when she feels threatened by intimacy. *Qichong*, located on the lower abdomen at the point where the penetrating vessel emerges, can play an important role in the treatment of running piglet *qi*. By warming the womb and sexual organs and tonifying *qi* and blood, St-30 can help us integrate and heal the psychosexual issues that give rise to running piglet syndrome.

Lastly, the character *chong* is also present in the name of *chongmai* (the penetrating vessel). As the *chongqi* regulates heaven and earth, so too does *chongmai,* situated between the governor and conception vessels, regulate the generation and flow of *qi* and blood. Hence *qichong* regulates the lower *jiao* through the actions of *chongmai* in the same way that *chongqi* regulates the interaction of heaven and earth.

## Serena
## "A seed sown with clear intent will bear fruit."

**Constitution:** *Earth*
**Color:** *Yellow*
**Sound:** *Singing*
**Odor:** *Fragrant*
**Emotion:** *Sympathy*

Serena helped teach me an important lesson in my path of becoming a healer. An attractive women in her early thirties, Serena came to me for routine preventive treatment. After conducting the intake, I determined she was earth constitutionally according to her CSOE as listed here. I was struck by the general lack of brightness in her eyes and the tendency of her face to settle into a frown suggesting disgust.

In the initial treatment session I had her sit on a chair facing the treatment table with her back exposed as I sat behind her ready to place the needles to drain aggressive energy. As I leaned to touch her back and place the first needle, I could sympathetically feel a wave of nausea come over her as heat rose up her chest and her face flushed. Without hesitation I spoke the words that came to me: "You have a visceral repulsion to intimacy." Serena did not respond, and I went on to test her for AE, which proved to be present on Bl-14, Bl-18, and Bl-20, corresponding to the heart protector, liver, and spleen officials, respectively. My follow-up treatment was to have been Sp-4, HP-6, St-42, St-30, and CV-15.

To my dismay when I returned to the office the following day, Serena had canceled all her follow-up sessions. I felt abysmal, questioning myself for having the audacity to have made such a bold statement and so early in her treatment! Who was I to have presumed so much and spoken like some soothsayer?[29] This was a hard lesson to swallow, and I tried to reveal much less to patients, particularly early in their treatment, for some time. I also doubted my intuition because I had spoken words that flowed from that internal voice I believed always spoke the truth.

Occasionally I would remember Serena when I took a risk to speak frankly with a patient, and the thought would sometimes temper my communications. Six years after that initial treatment session I was curious when I received a card from Serena. I was mystified to find upon opening it that it was a wedding invitation. I went to Serena's wedding not knowing what to expect and, in fact, feeling somewhat timid. I saw her for the first time when she entered the room to walk down the aisle and be married. She was beautiful! Gone was the frown and her eyes sparkled with all the joy we would expect in a bride on her wedding day.

Upon seeing me at the reception, Serena immediately walked over to me smiling. Without hesitation she stated, "I want you to know that in large part I'm here today because of you. When you spoke the words 'visceral repulsion to intimacy,' I remembered, for the first time in my adult life, being sexually abused by my music teacher when I was a girl. I felt so exposed by the fact that someone who hardly knew me could see through me so clearly. Those words you spoke were like a homeopathic remedy that, over years, drove that sickness from me. I felt too vulnerable to be treated by a man who saw me so clearly and so I continued treatment with a female practitioner. It is because of that one session with you that lets me stand here now."

From Serena I learned several principles I consider essential to being a healer. When a communication is delivered from the heart with pure intent, it is likely to take seed and flower. The time of this flowering is in accord with heaven's plan and the patient's readiness to receive the truth. I also learned not to ever second-guess that voice inside that always tells the truth. This lesson has to do with my willingness to be a vessel for the will of heaven and to trust my ability to fulfill that role. I also learned that the most powerful medicine on earth is metaphor. Patients make themselves sick with thoughts, language, and stories that undermine their very purpose in this life. When metaphor as medicine is delivered with words, needles, and herbal formulas that are all congruent in intention, the medicine is powerful indeed.

---

### ❖ St-31 — Thigh Border

| | | |
|---|---|---|
| *Bi⁴guan¹* | Thigh Border | 髀關 |

I use St-31 as a local point for pain in the inguinal region when it is related to the earth element. Its name makes reference to its location along the border of the thigh and the torso.

---

### ❖ St-32 — Prostrate Hare

| | | |
|---|---|---|
| *Fu²tu⁴* | Prostrate Hare | 伏兔 |
| *Wai⁴qiu¹* | Outer Mound | 外丘 |
| *Wai⁴gou¹* | Outer Hook | 外勾 |

FUNCTION

Internal dragon point

St-32 is located in the center of the thigh muscle whose shape resembles a crouching rabbit. The point's name conjures for me the image of being exhausted like a rabbit that has run around in hot weather without sufficient fluids or rest. I use "prostrate hare" for leg pain and weakness associated with overexertion. Physically, a patient may be pushing himself too hard in work or exercise. Excessive worry and catering to the needs of others can also leave us exhausted. The legs provide our connection to the earth and empower our ability to manifest our motivations in our work. I find that atrophy of the muscles in the legs as our foundation can be associated with excessive neediness as presided over by the earth element.

---

### ❖ St-33 — ***Yin* Market**

| | | |
|---|---|---|
| *Yin¹shi⁴* | *Yin* Market | 陰市 |
| *Yin¹ding³* | *Yin* Vessel | 陰鼐 |

We can think of the stomach as a market where the nutritional content of food is procured. The alternate name of this point, *yinding*, can be translated as "*yin* vessel." The *ding* is a ceremonial vessel used to contain the offerings made to deities during rituals and for receiving their good tidings. Similarly, the stomach is like a cauldron that must receive the beneficent tidings of earth *(yin)* in the form of grains so we are nourished. In this regard, St-33 empowers both the production and distribution of *qi* and blood.

---

### ❖ St-34 — **Beam Mound**

| | | |
|---|---|---|
| *Liang²qiu¹* | Beam Mound | 梁丘 |
| *Kua⁴gu²* | Hipbone | 跨骨 |

FUNCTION

*Xi*-cleft point

The name "beam mound" refers to the mound of the rectus femoris muscle where this point is located. When our earth element is unbalanced, we tend to project the fulfillment of our needs externally on others. In our attempt to feel sated, we try in vain to fill our needs through excessive consumption. This can manifest as a wide variety of appetite disorders and oral fixations. When this dynamic manifests as eating too much or too quickly, food can stagnate in the stomach, leading to a bloated feeling. Acquired sources of *qi* that should have nourished us are instead transformed into dampness as the embodiment of burdens that weigh us down. Encumbered in this way by undigested experiences, we tend to feel stuck in life as our metabolism gradually slows. Resentment accumulates as we arrive at a point of no longer being able to "stomach" the needs of others and the effort that life seems to constantly acquire. "Beam mound" can help us transform this burden so we may move more freely in life and feel less encumbered. Hence functions ascribed to St-34 include harmonizing the middle burner and sedating rebellious stomach *qi*.

---

| ❖ **St-35** | **Calf's Nose** | |
|---|---|---|
| *Du*$^{2}$*bi*$^{2}$ | Calf's Nose | 犢鼻 |

St-35 is named for its location on the front of the knee, which resembles a calf's nose. I use this point for knee pain, particularly when swelling and accumulation of damp are present. When the earth element fails to transform acquired *qi* adequately into nourishment, life tends to become burdensome. Pain and dysfunction of the knee can be the embodiment of our difficulty in carrying our physical and emotional load through life. This point, as well as another nonchannel point located on the other side of the kneecap, are termed "the eyes of the knee." Treated together, I find these points useful for a wide range of pain and dysfunction affecting the knee.

---

| ❖ **St-36** | **Leg Three Miles** | |
|---|---|---|
| *Zu*$^{2}$*san*$^{1}$*li*$^{3}$ | Leg Three Miles | 足三里 |
| *San*$^{1}$*li*$^{3}$ | Three Miles | 三里 |
| *Xia*$^{4}$*san*$^{1}$*li*$^{3}$ | Lower Three Miles | 下三里 |
| *Xia*$^{4}$*ling*$^{2}$ | Lower Tomb | 下陵 |
| *Gui*$^{3}$*xie*$^{2}$ | Ghost Evil | 鬼邪 |

FUNCTIONS

1. Earth point
2. Horary point; 7 A.M.–9 A.M., late summer
3. Assembly point of the abdomen
4. Sea of nourishment

VIRTUES

1. Engenders the qualities of earth within all officials.
2. Nourishes the muscles.
3. Empowers the virtues of groundedness and center.

The designation of this point's name as "leg three miles" helps differentiate it from LI-10, named "arm three miles." In fact, the name *guixie*, "ghost evil," is shared by both points as well. The location of each point mirrors the other: each is found just distal to the major joints of the knee (St-36) and the elbow (LI-10), suggesting an anatomical metaphor in their names. Both points harmonize the *qi* and blood; LI-10 treats conditions of the arm and St-36 treats conditions of the leg relatively more.

As the earth point of the stomach official, St-36 is an archetypal point for empowering our ability to receive nourishment from the resources of later heaven. The range of functionality addressed by "leg three miles" includes empowering us to identify our needs as defined by inherited essence, seek out and acquire appropriate sources of nourishment, digest and assimilate acquired nourishment, create *qi* and blood from them, and finally to build ourselves newly out of these resources. *Zusanli* can also help resolve the burden of dampness that obscures all these processes.

As the official's horary point, St-36 strongly empowers the virtues of stability and grounding that find their foundation in a healthy earth element. The knees must bend flexibly and with strength in order for us to reap the harvest of our work. Located in the front of the knee, "leg three miles" can strengthen this foundational joint and enable us to move vigorously forward in life with intention and momentum. The virtue of balance is predicated on the earth's virtue of integrity. As our centers are made strong through the alignment of our thoughts, intentions, and deeds, our movements become guided by an unyielding center. The virtues of this center can be transferred to any *yang* official by needling the channel's earth (receiving) point alone or in conjunction with St-36.

Physically, the integrity of our center manifests as strong muscles nourished by the blood and powered by the *qi* of the earth element, processes strongly aided by the functions of *zusanli*. A strong well-functioning center is proof that our efforts in life have nourished and strengthened us. Actions that cultivate destiny by bringing heaven's intent into the world are the fruits of this entire process. Having cultivated enough for ourselves to be content in life, we have sufficient reserve to contribute good works to the betterment of others. This is the very definition of altruism and reciprocity as empowered by a healthy earth element.

If our centers become excessive due to overconsumption, we tend to feel heavy and stuck and to lack motivation. To others we can appear lethargic, stubborn, and unwilling or unable to move from our current position. When our centers are deficient we may compromise our positions too easily in order to please others. Ingratiating behavior undermines our integrity and can manifest as a lack of balance physically as our muscles fail to hold and orient us toward center.

A function ascribed to "leg three miles" is that of tonifying the kidneys and *yuanqi*. The specific quality of *jing* gleaned at conception cannot be gained by any source of *qi* acquired after the first breath. However, the entire function of the digestive system is to abstract nourishment from life to complement our specific inherited endowment. The relationship between inherited and acquired *jing* is given in the following example. Imagine your grandfather left you a large sum of money in his will. If you lost this money on the way home from the executor's office, it could be replaced in kind if I handed you another suitcase with the same amount of cash in it. You would feel no sense of loss and likely little preference between having the specific monies left by your grandfather than those I have given you. The two amounts are equivalent in their purchasing power in precisely the same way that acquired *qi* can provide physiological strength to supplement the inherited constitution. Either resource can be tapped to motivate a given amount of work in the world over the short term.

Imagine now that your grandfather has left you his pocket watch. If that watch is lost, no watch in the world can replace it, for only that specific watch is imbued with the essence of ancestry. Similarly, acquired sources of *qi* can complement innate reserves but are not imbued with destiny or life purpose as is inherited essence. As the main point for empowering the reception and distribution of acquired nourishment, St-36 can help motivate us to tap deep reserves of inherited *jing* by providing a reserve of strength so we can continue our efforts in life when exhausted by overwork and/or illness. Hence the name "leg three miles" evokes the image of providing access to a reserve of strength so a weary traveler can complete his journey. This wondrous resource must be used responsibly and in conjunction with educating the patient about efficient use of his reserves. Otherwise, by endlessly drawing on the well of resource that St-36 provides access to, we run the risk of helping the patient dysfunctionally to deplete himself further.

---

| ❖ **St-37** | **Upper Great Void** | |
|---|---|---|
| *Shang⁴ju⁴xu¹* | Upper Great Void | 上巨虛 |
| *Shang⁴lian²* | Upper Purity | 上廉 |
| *Ju⁴xu¹shang⁴lian²* | Great Void Upper Angle | 巨虛上廉 |

FUNCTIONS

1. Lower *he*-sea point of the large intestine official
2. Sea of blood

As a reunion point between the large intestine and stomach channels, St-37 excels at regulating the relationship between these two officials. The character *xu* can be interpreted to mean "empty" and suggests this point's function of moving stagnation in the digestive system. Hence St-37 can be useful in the treatment of stagnation and obstruction of the intestines. Such stagnation is often congruent with feelings of distension and pain of the abdomen, constipation, and intestinal abscess. These conditions are often the embodiment of holding on to that which has lost its value to us in life as a habitual way of avoiding the grief of loss.

*Xu* is also synonymous with the *dao* as the eternal void that receives all things once their essence has been assimilated and their form passes on. In this sense, St-37 can help empower the quality of emptiness and nonattachment that arises when we are content in life and secure enough to let go of the form of things that we have valued, choosing instead to be sustained by their essence.

*Chongmai* is known as the "sea of blood" and connects to Bl-11 in the upper regions of the body and to both St-37 and St-39 in the lower part of the body. Hence these three points all are considered part of the "sea of blood." As such, St-37 is exceptionally nourishing to all aspects of being. If this sea is empty, treating other points that access ponds, streams, and wells will often not be effective. Before calling on the resources of these other points to tonify and nourish, we must ensure the seas are full and capable of supplying our other reserves. The ultimate source of nourishment is the ocean of *dao* coidentified with the void *(xu)* that gives birth to all beings.

As the lower *he*-sea point of the large intestine channel, and a reunion point of the large intestine and stomach officials, "upper great void" can be quite effective in treating diarrhea, whether due to deficiency, cold, dampness, or damp heat. The upper and lower orifices associated with the large intestine are the nose and anus, respectively. These form a circuit so we connect to essence in life through breath and let go of waste through the anus. Diarrhea and sinusitis can be congruent with deficiency, cold, and damp. Hence both symptoms can be the embodiment of grief as we sublimate and somatasize our weeping and loss. This dynamic can be well addressed herbally with the formula Shenling Baizhu San (Ginseng and Atractylodes).

As the lower *he*-sea points of the large and small intestine officials, St-37 and St-39 are paired with these channels on the upper part of the body. Because these channels pass through the shoulder, these points can be quite effective in treating pain and limited range of motion in the shoulder region. Such conditions can be the embodiments of both difficulty in sorting and letting go in life. Utilizing St-37 and St-39 to help the shoulder can address the underlying basis of the disorder when it involves compromised digestion and assimilation due to a dysfunctional earth element.

---

### ❖ St-38 **Branch Opening**
*Tiao²kou³* Branch Opening 條口

"Branch opening" is located between the "upper great void" (St-37) associated with the large intestine and the "lower great void" (St-39) associated with the small intestine. St-39 can help empower a balanced relationship between these two officials whose charge it is to sort the pure from the impure. The small intestine must absorb sunlight *(yang)* from food in the form of amino acids while the large intestine absorbs sunlight in the form of minerals. In turn, both officials must pass on the dross so it can be eliminated effectively.

If there is a dysfunctional relationship between these two officials, the stomach can suffer due to the resulting stagnation. Any failure at sorting in either organ is likely to compromise the function of sorting in the other and result in stagnation, confusion, and a buildup of both physical and emotional toxicity. Such toxicity can be congruent with bowel problems, boils and other skin lesions, and toxic emotional states such as bitterness, disdain, and disgust.[30]

St-37 and St-39 are like branches from the stomach channel that open to the shoulders through their connection to the large and small intestine channels, respectively. The arm itself branches off the torso, and the proximity of St-37 and St-39 empowers St-38 as an important point for treating pain and dysfunction in the shoulders. Hence St-38 "opens" the shoulder as the region where the arm "branches" off the body.

---

| ❖ **St-39** | **Lower Great Void** | |
|---|---|---|
| *Xia*⁴*ju*⁴*xu*¹ | Lower Great Void | 下巨虛 |
| *Xia*⁴*lian*² | Lower Side | 下廉 |
| *Ju*⁴*xu*¹*xia*⁴*lian*² | Great Void Lower Side | 巨虛下廉 |

FUNCTIONS

1. Lower *he*-sea point of the small intestine official
2. Sea of blood

As a reunion point between the stomach and small intestine channels, "lower great void" is useful for moving stagnation in the digestive system. The stomach official must break down all acquired sources of potential nourishment, and it is the function of the small intestine to assimilate what is nourishing and pass the rest onto the large intestine. In turn the large intestine's function is to assimilate minerals and eliminate waste. Hence St-37 (large intestine), St-38 (mediation between St-37 and St-39), and St-39 (small intestine) are important points for moving stagnation in the digestive system and strengthening the digestive process.

The intimate relationship of the small intestine to the heart official accounts in part for functions ascribed to St-39 such as manic raving, sudden fright, and no pleasure in eating.[31] Heat gathering in the *yangming* channel can disturb the small intestine and the heart spirit. Mania can be understood as a result of shock to the heart and habitually clinging to peak states of awareness in life. This dynamic has been discussed in the context of GV-10 and GV-11 in *Nourishing Destiny.*[32] Such shock affects the heart directly, bypassing all layers of protection established by the three heater, heart protector, and small intestine officials.[33] Shock and fright can so agitate the heart that the small intestine is unable to sort out clearly the heart's intentions. A heart so disturbed is often congruent with the small intestine's inability to sort appropriately, resulting in both the giving and receiving of mixed messages. St-39 can help the small intestine digest experience and clear stagnation so the heart once again has a clear channel of communication with the outside world.

Conditions of the small intestine such as sprue and celiac disease tend to be congruent with massive stagnation in the digestive system. As the cilia are unable to absorb nutrients, the quality of the blood suffers and the heart is not adequately fed by the digestive process. Hence the heart can become joyless as it fails to harvest the fruits of life. In this way eating becomes a joyless experience as an expression of the degree to which hope is lost at ever tasting the fruits of our labors. "Lower great void" is therefore an important point for helping empower both digestion and assimilation.

---

## ❖ St-40 **Abundant Splendor**
*Feng[1]long[2]* Abundant Splendor 豐隆

FUNCTION

*Luo* point

VIRTUES

1. Empowers the transformation of burden into nourishment.
2. Empowers contentment.

The character *feng* depicts a vessel (豆) filled with mountainous (山) abundance (丰丰) as suggested by the presence of boughs of wheat and grain. This character represents the Chinese threshing floor at harvesttime, signifying both abundance and prosperity.[34] The character *long* also means abundance and prosperity. It denotes the totality of what descends from heaven (天) in combination with what is produced on earth (地), to yield all goods. The function of the stomach is to abstract nourishment from the earth that surrounds us with abundance and to then build the earth within us manifesting as blood and *qi,* muscle and flesh, and the virtue of integrity.

Like all acupuncture points, St-40 possesses a dual nature. On the one hand, it can help eliminate the burden of dampness. Dampness tends to be embodied as pathological abundance congruent with excessive weight, insatiable appetite, accumulation of phlegm, lipomas, neediness, selfishness, ingratiation, and feelings of being burdened. On the other hand, by resolving burden, St-40 can help us feel we are inherently enough so we can better receive and more efficiently process all the nourishment that life has to offer.

As the channel's *luo* point, St-40 harmonizes the relationship between the spleen and stomach officials. Physiologically, this point is said to transform phlegm and dampness and to calm the spirit.[35] In this context, phlegm and dampness represent the accumulation (abundance) of all unintegrated experiences. Such burdens can obscure the relationship between the stomach and spleen and thus compromise the assimilation and distribution of nourishment. Insatiable appetite based on feelings of neediness can result if burdens from the past prevent us from being nourished in the present. Neediness is often congruent with the inability to reap the harvest of our labors due to a dysfunctional earth element. Feelings of not being, or having, "enough" can motivate habitual consumption that is rarely if ever fulfilling.

"Abundant splendor" is ideal when we feel burdened rather than nourished by friends, family, and career. When a patient continually complains about those aspects of life that should nourish him to engender contentment and joy, it is often a sign of poor digestion in the psychospiritual realm. Such complaining can be evidenced explicitly by words and implicitly by a singing (earth) tone in the voice combined with weeping or lack of laughing, signifying involvement of the metal and fire elements, respectively. Such a sound intimates complaining or whining even when the words are not congruent with this message. Weak sighing can also point to this dynamic and suggest that spleen *qi* is deficient and not sufficiently nourishing our aspirations.

The function of "abundant splendor" evokes the image of a hot and humid August day where we might be content to just lie in a hammock and rest. On the one hand, such lazy activity can be deeply nourishing as we appreciate the fullness of nature and allow ourselves to let go of the motivations that usually drive us to act. On the other hand, intense humidity and heat can be overwhelming as we feel burdened and suffocated by the heaviness of the season. If we are so afflicted, transformation ceases and we can feel chronically stuck in life, unable to carry the weight of our accumulated burden.

*Fenglong* can assist in transformation and elimination of dampness and the associated feelings of being burdened in life. In this way the stomach and spleen can better cooperate in the assimilation and distribution of nourishment throughout all realms of our being. As the oppression of burden is lifted, we may begin to feel we are enough for life and that life is enough for us. Thus the virtue of contentment is engendered.

## ❖ St-41 Released Stream
*Jie*[3]*xi*[1] Released Stream 解谿

FUNCTIONS

1. Fire point
2. Tonification point

VIRTUES

1. Clears the stomach official of undigested material.
2. Empowers the assimilation of nourishment.

The name "released stream" suggests the ability of St-41 to empower the stomach to process past experience that has stagnated and become a burden. A torrent of tears may accompany such movement as we finally integrate past lessons and let go of our pain. The physical location of St-41 on the ankle in a groove between two tendons suggests a translation of the character *xi* as "ravine." A ravine is a narrow pass where a stream can stagnate and become constrained. The overall sense imparted by this point's name is of easing constraint, as we might widen a ravine to allow a stream to pass and thus reinstitute the flow of *qi* in the stomach channel. The use of the term *jie*, "to release," stands in contrast to the use of the character *wei* (維), "tied," in the name of St-8. Hence *jie* means to untie or loosen, whereas *wei* means to bind. In fact, the phrase *jiewei* (解維) refers to the process of untying a boat from its moorings imparting the sense of releasing constraint and promoting flow.[36]

The presence of fire within the earth evokes the image of an oven that nourishes us both by cooking our food and warming our home. Externally, this process occurs as warmth from the sun nourishes crops, bringing them to fruition in the fields as we prepare for the harvest. Internally, this process is embodied by the digestive system as it cooks our food so we may be nourished by life. Both the excess and deficient presence of fire within earth are typified by a lack of healthy joy in relationship to nourishment.

If the presence of fire is deficient within the earth, the process of "cooking" potential sources of nourishment is impeded. Hence the stomach will not efficiently break down acquired sources of *qi* as digestion proceeds at a less than optimal rate. In this instance our physical center (stomach) may grow as we gain fat (burden) rather than muscle *(hara)*. Or we may be overly thin due to difficulty in assimilating nourishment regardless of how much we eat. In either case we tend to lose interest in food, and eating never seems to cultivate contentment. In this instance, our internal landscape can appear barren and cold similar to a field that has been sunless for the duration of spring or summer.

When the presence of fire is deficient, fluid and cold tend to accumulate in the stomach channel and compromise any realm of functioning governed by the stomach official. Dampness can hinder digestion and extinguish the stomach's fire. Swollen and cold legs or feet can often be an embodiment of this dynamic. Strengthening the presence of fire within the earth can help balance the excessive influence of water, aid in the transformation of dampness, and diminish both fluid retention and cold. Hence by promoting increased metabolism, St-41 can be said to "release" a "stream" as damp is transformed and the presence of cold is mitigated.

In its excess presentation, appetite tends to be habitually fueled by desire to a degree that we are never sated by anything we acquire in life. Physically such a pattern is typified by hunger immediately after eating. Other signs can include bleeding gums, hypertension, toothache, and diabetes. In psychospiritual realms, we may be driven by appetite never to experience the joy that comes from contentment. In its extreme, excess fire within earth can present as mania, fits, and convulsions as the mind is affected by heat rising from the stomach. Such mania is typified by extreme self-centeredness and obsession regarding the fulfillment of our needs. Excessive talking can be likened to verbal diarrhea as heat in the stomach makes it impossible for the intestines to sort adequately. Excess fire tends to consume fluid and, in time, the stomach can become *yin* deficient.

As the fire point on the stomach channel, the issues that apply to Sp-2 also apply to the application of St-41. The spleen tends relatively more toward conditions of *qi* and *yang* deficiency, and the stomach tends relatively more toward conditions of *yin* deficiency. Excess fire within the stomach can be quelled by sedating SI-5 (fire point) in conjunction with St-41. This represents half of the four-needle technique used to sedate the earth element when it is in excess. This procedure works by draining the fire within fire and the fire within earth simultaneously to yield a strong sedation of the earth element. In essence, we have diminished the functional input to the stomach's tonification point (St-41) that comes to earth along the *sheng* cycle from fire. Similarly, the presence of fire within earth can be strengthened by tonifying these very same points. Further, by treating the influence of fire within the small intestine and stomach simultaneously, we may mitigate the degree to which digestion and assimilation are compromised by either an excess or deficiency of fire.

| ❖ **St-42** | **Rushing *Yang*** | |
|---|---|---|
| *Chong[1]yang[2]* | Rushing *Yang* | 衝陽 |
| *Hui[4]yuan[2]* | Meeting the Source | 會源 |
| *Hui[4]yuan[2]* | Meeting the Source | 會原 |
| *Hui[4]gu[2]* | Meeting of Bones | 會骨 |
| *Fu[1]yang[2]* | Bowing *Yang* | 趺陽 |
| *Hui[4]qu[1]* | Meet and Submit | 會屈 |

FUNCTION

Source point

The name *huigu*, "meeting of bones," describes the anatomical location of this point at the top of the foot where many bones converge. Our feet serve as the foundation in life, supporting our centers and imparting structural integrity to our stance. As St-42 is located in the center of the top of the foot, the stomach is located in the middle *jiao* and nourishes our center to empower the virtue of integrity. St-42 as the channel's source point can serve the function of grounding us and providing the virtues of balance, stability, and center throughout diverse aspects of being. The name "meeting the source" suggests this function as well as denoting St-42 as a source point. The names "bowing *yang*" and "meet and submit" also suggest the function of rooting ascending *yang*.

The *yangqi* of the stomach official surges *(chong)* forth at this point and can be felt as the pounding of an arterial pulse when this point is palpated. The character "*chong*" in the point's name is the same as the character denoting the *chongqi* (沖氣) that harmonizes the dual poles of heaven and earth back into primal unity.[37] Hence *chong* suggests the type of movement we might see in a whirlpool or a geyser that is shooting up toward the heavens.

The stomach and liver officials are both located in the middle *jiao* and play a crucial role in integrating the influences of the acquired and inherited constitutions as well as the influences of heaven (the upper *jiao*) and earth (the lower *jiao*). Hence it is interesting to note that the character *chong* is present in the name of Lv-3 *(taichong)* and St-42 *(chongyang)*. If *jing* is to communicate with *shen, qi* must flow freely through the middle *jiao*. Lv-3 helps fulfill this function by easing constraint in the middle *jiao* and regulating the flow of *qi* between water and fire along the *sheng* cycle. St-42 empowers the stomach to blend *(chong)* acquired sources of *qi* with the innate constitution. In fulfilling this function the virtue of integrity becomes manifest as our centers grow stronger.

The movement of acquired sources of nourishment descending through the digestive system is balanced by our innate potential rising to manifest in the world. The evolution of this innate potential is supported by a gentle rising of *yang* that carries the *yin* upward. This includes fluids to nourish the mouth, lips, and digestive tract, as well as marrow to nourish the brain and mind. The process of *yang* rising the *yin* is facilitated by the actions of St-42 in adequately governing the "surging *yang*." If *yang* does not rise with sufficient force, the digestive process may lack sufficient fluid, manifesting as dry mouth and cracked lips. If *yang* rises too forcefully, a condition known as rebellious stomach *qi* can occur. In this case food moves in the wrong direction and ascends rather than descends to manifest as nausea and vomiting. Such rising *yang* can also manifest as hypertension, heart attack, and stroke as heat generated in the stomach can rise to injure the heart and circulatory system.

The pattern of "*yangming*" (陽明) insanity is associated with stomach *yang* that surges excessively to agitate the heart and mind and thus compromise the stomach's propensity toward integrative (*xin:* 信) thought (*yi:* 意). Signs congruent with this disorder include bipolar disorder, the desires to ascend to high places and sing, and to discard clothing and run around.[38] Singing is the sound of the earth element, and the stomach empowers integrity by governing proper intention (*yi:* 意) in speaking. The desire to climb to high places is congruent with the dysfunctional influence of the rising *yang*. St-42 can be useful for bringing such rebellious *qi* "back down to earth" and is therefore said to calm the spirit.[39]

---

## ❖ St-43 **Sinking Valley**
*Xian⁴gu³* Sinking Valley 陷谷

FUNCTION

Wood point

VIRTUES

1. Empowers ease in the digestion and assimilation of life.
2. Empowers integrity by holding the center in place while allowing mundanity to descend.

Whereas St-42 governs the balanced ascension and grounding of *yang*, St-43 controls the descending tendencies of *yin*. The form *(yin)* of food must descend through the digestive tract while the essences abstracted from food are elevated in status as we assimilate them to nourish our centers. If food stagnates and does not descend properly, our assimilation of nutrients will likely be hampered. As the quantity and quality of our *qi* and blood begins to suffer, our centers may begin to drop as both our functional and structural integrity is compromised.

The name "sinking valley" suggests the quality of erosion that can undermine the stability of the earth element. The stability of our center depends in large part on the functional integrity of the relationship between the wood and earth elements. The *ke* cycle influence of wood on earth is similar to that of a plant's roots that can either hold earth in place to prevent erosion or, by growing too much, overly constrain and deplete the soil. The tendency of wood to grow toward the heavens manifests as the virtues of purpose, uprightness, and self-assertion. These are complemented by the earth's ability to "hold the center," thus engendering the virtues of stability, groundedness, and integrity. The functional relationship between wood and earth empowers our ability to strive toward goals in a centered and grounded way. In health, our innate sense of purpose never overwhelms our abilities to stay true to ourselves or be nurtured in the process of growth.

If the influence of wood within earth is deficient, our centers tend to erode as the structural organization and aspirations of wood are lost. Without the influence of wood, our centers become "valleys" and "sink." Physically, such sinking can manifest as excessive weight typified by a bulging gut. Prolapses and dropping of the lower organs, including the uterus, bladder, or anus, or hemorrhoids can all be congruent with deficient wood failing to hold our centers in place.[40] In psychospiritual realms, we may feel burdened and trapped under the weight of undigested life experiences that stagnates to smother the expression of our lost sense of purpose. Such stagnation can indefinitely hamper the assimilation of new forms of nourishment as we lie buried under a backlog of unprocessed material.

By strengthening the presence of the wood within the earth, St-43 can help control this process of erosion. This can be likened to planting shrubs on a hillside whose roots prevent the earth from washing away. As the channel's wood point, St-43 can empower vision within the earth element and help us organize and process our past experience. In this way we can digest our lives, assimilate our lessons, and pass what no longer serves onto the large intestine for elimination. Physically, increased presence of digestive enzymes within the stomach as governed by the wood officials can help us break down food stagnation to aid assimilation, increase metabolism, and help lighten our load. Hence wood within earth serves the dual function of holding our center in place to prevent the "valley" from "sinking," while at the same time promoting the "sinking" of food. As the roots of the wood element break up stagnant earth, both the digestion of food and absorption of nutrients tend to proceed more effortlessly.

If the presence of wood within earth is excessive, the expression of the earth element tends to be constrained. Physically, it is as though a tree were growing in one's stomach causing nausea, pressure, and distension. Such a presentation can be congruent with a sour stomach, pressure and tightness from CV-12 to CV-21, and a sour or bitter taste in the mouth. Other signs can include stomach, esophageal, or mouth ulcers. Excess acid poured into the stomach by the liver and gallbladder begins to slowly digest the stomach and its associated membranes. This process is similar in nature to a plant that has become root bound, slowly choking itself to death in its pot as its roots seek nutrients. Here the wood element's capacity for planning and decision making overwhelms the earth's ability to process life. Hence the drive of wood steps up metabolism to hurry the process of creation at a much faster rate than the stomach can efficiently break down and digest acquired sources of nourishment.

In psychospiritual realms, patterns of wood invading earth tend to manifest as intellectual and emotional constraint as our minds are tied in knots by overthinking. Anger tends to overwhelm our capacity for sympathy in a way that leaves us unsympathetic toward the needs of others and neglectful of our own needs as well. Hence impatience in pursuit of our goals can lead us to avoid eating on a regular schedule. We can also tend to reject sympathy offered by others yet at the same time resent others for not taking better care of us. Anger and impatience can also drive our appetites and lead us to eat too quickly for our digestive systems to process our food efficiently. Excessive wood tends to fuel fire excessively, which in turn can consume *yin* and potentiate a state of *yin* deficiency affecting the stomach official. *Yin* deficiency itself is often congruent with many of the imbalances discussed here.

Dispersion of St-43 can help diminish the expression of the wood element within the stomach official. In this way thought may proceed at a slower rate as our goals and aspirations no longer impinge our ability to efficiently process and be nourished by life.

---

❖ **St-44** **Inner Courtyard**
*Nei[4]ting[2]* Inner Courtyard 內庭

*Keeping his back still*
*So that he no longer feels his body.*
*He goes into his courtyard*
*And does not see his people.*
– YIJING, *Hexagram 52*[41]

FUNCTION

Water point

The *Yijing* hexagram for mountain consists of the trigram for earth (☷) doubled. It discusses the merits of meditation and quieting the mind. In this metaphor the solidity of the body corresponds to earth and the quietude of the mind corresponds to the water element. As the water point on the stomach channel, St-44 can empower the virtue of reflection by calming overactive thought processes that are governed by the spirit of the earth element, the *yi*. In a sense, the quality of function empowered by "inner courtyard" can be likened to that of hibernation. Hence we may be nurtured by the fruits of our previous labors during times of quietude when we are not producing in the world. This is, in fact, the balanced place of humanity during the winter months when the earth is quiet on the surface while internally incubating the seed of spring's growth. Winter, the season associated with water, is a time for quiet introspection and internal effort because it is fruitless to work in the fields during this barren season. St-44 can quiet the mind's obsessive tendency to motivate excessive production or consumption. In this way we can process and integrate what has already been achieved in a way that nourishes rather than encumbers us.

The relationship of earth to water is that of the acquired to the innate constitution. In seeking out and identifying sources of potential nourishment, the stomach must constantly make reference to the innate quality of our *jing*. In essence, the stomach is informed by the *jing* as to the daily needs of our innate nature. If the stomach loses contact with true nature, the mind is left with the task of self-fulfillment. Of course, the only thing the mind is committed to is comfort and therefore is largely incapable of nurturing true self. As the mind turns away from true nature as it establishes our internal standard of need, it looks externally into the world and dysfunctionally attempts to satisfy the habitual desires of the ego. The mind, however, can never be fulfilled unless the spirit is nourished. Contentment is fleeting as the restless mind drives us toward increased consumption as all that we crave becomes burden. "Inner courtyard" has the potential to redirect the mind back toward the center of our being where original nature, the ultimate arbiter of what truly nourishes, resides.

Excessive thought consumes *yin,* and dysfunctional emotions of the earth element *(si),* such as worry, pensiveness, and obsession, tend to create and be driven by a condition of stomach *yin* deficiency. If the presence of water within is deficient, earth tends to be parched and to yield no bounty. Fields without water cannot flourish, and a condition of barrenness tends to characterize our personal landscape. Physically we may be overly thin as fire, unregulated by water, speeds our metabolism. Such fire can raise blood pressure and contribute to conditions such as inflamed and bleeding gums, tinnitus, nosebleeds, cold sores, and thirst. Deficient fluids in the digestive system can also compromise our ability to assimilate nourishment. Constant hunger, and hunger immediately after eating, are signs of failing to be nourished by what has been consumed. These signs tend to be congruent with the digestive system's failure to abstract nourishment from life in a way that engenders contentment. Constipation can also be a sign of deficient fluids failing to lubricate the process of digestion.

For lack of water we may become infertile both in our bodies and minds as the earth within us is unable to either nourish conception or support new growth. Eating too quickly can also contribute to stomach *yin* deficiency as our minds race to consume the world and excess heat in our digestive system further consumes fluids. Insatiable appetite can be further fueled by the fear that all our attempts at nourishment will be vain. By tonifying the presence of water within the earth the mind can slow down and thus reorient itself back toward the source of our wisdom in the kidneys.

If the presence of water within is excessive, the foundations of earth tend to erode. Water mixing with earth produces mud, a dynamic embodied by the presence of phlegm and dampness. Hence St-44 is said to harmonize the intestines and clear dampness and heat and is indicated in the treatment of disorders such as diarrhea, dysentery, and abdominal pain. Fear can overwhelm the earth element's capacity for stability and balance. In this case earth can fail to control water and result in excessive urination coupled with constant worry and anxiety. If water extinguishes the fire within earth, metabolism can slow as damp and cold accumulate and *qi* stagnates. This pattern is typified by signs such as aversion to cold and cold hands and feet, indicating counterflow stagnation of *qi*.

In psychospiritual realms, excessive water within earth can manifest as slow thought processes, excess deliberation, and worry as the mind and spirit becomes bogged down by dampness and fail to embrace spirit. "Inner courtyard" can help diminish the influence of water and thereby help our center solidify, putting us back on a better footing in life. With fear quelled we may better live off our reserves and process life already consumed. As our centers grow more solid, the virtue of integrity is restored and we may better emulate the qualities attributed to the mountain by the *Yijing*.

---

## ❖ St-45 **Hard Bargain**
*Li⁴dui⁴* Hard Bargain 厲兌

FUNCTIONS

1. Metal point
2. Sedation point

VIRTUE

Empowers a functional balance in our ability to be nourished by the essential and substantial aspects of life.

Food as acquired by the stomach comprises a relatively substantive source of nourishment as compared with the quality of *qi* grasped by the lungs. Metal within the earth represents the essential nutrients that must be grasped from the potential sources of nourishment we ingest. Such essence constitutes the sunlight inherent in food in the form of minerals. These are to be absorbed by the large intestine after the food is digested in the stomach. The dysfunctional nature of earth is to fail to be nourished by available resources and therefore to both crave, consume, and cling to the material aspects of life relentlessly. Such consumption can lead to stagnation in the digestive system congruent with increased weight and bloatedness. Metal within earth represents the possibility of lightness as we surrender the form *(yin)* of food and of life, to grasp and be nourished by its essence *(yang)*.

If the metal within is deficient, earth can suffer from an inability to be nourished by quality in life. The sound of speech associated with the earth element is singing, and the sound associated with the metal element is weeping. In combination with each other, these two often present as a whining tone in the voice. Such a tone suggests that a person has failed to value what he has and is complaining about his predicament. Complaining as though his life is a "hard bargain" can be a habitual way of trying to elicit sympathy from others. Excessive weight can suggest stagnation in the digestive system associated with the failure to grasp essence. Deficient weight can also suggest that we are not deriving the essential nourishment potentially available from food. In either the case of excessive or deficient weight, the weeping/whining tone in the voice suggests the stomach's failure to grasp anything of value.

If the presence of metal within is excessive, the earth tends to become cold, rigid, and inert. Digestion can become sluggish as the stomach refuses to let go of anything it deems to have value. Here excessive weight represents a type of hoarding as the primal urges associated with the *po* spirit (metal) control our appetites. Metal coldness expressed through the earth element can manifest as self-righteousness regarding our own needs and a general lack of sympathy toward others. Excessive metal within earth can also lead to being overly thin as no essence obtained in life can be held on to. In this case what we value seems to slip through our fingers before we can even taste our success. Our bowel movements can tend to fluctuate between constipation and diarrhea and mirror our process of clinging to and then losing what we value in life.

Interestingly, St-45 is used as a symptomatic point for hangover. Its efficacy in this regard lies with its ability to help drain dampness from the stomach official. The person who tries to drink his sorrow away hoping to mitigate his losses and longings in life is certainly forging a "hard bargain." I often use this point for those who adopt the victim position in life. St-45 can help balance our valuation of essence and substance so we are better nourished, less burdened by, and more thankful for those resources available to us.

## *Exercises*

1. Compare the functional relationships between the points Lu-7, LI-4, LI-20, and St-1.
2. Discuss how the points St-4, St-9, St-16, St-18, St-20, St-25, and CV-8 differentially address the relationship between digestion, need, self-sufficiency, and the quality of our relationship with our mothers.
3. Differentiate how each of the five-element points and the *luo* and *xi*-cleft points on the stomach channel help address different aspects of food and thought stagnation as they manifest as digestive disorders and habitual worry, respectively.
4. Discuss how the earth and metal elements differentially govern our relationship to our mothers and fathers, respectively.
5. St-9 can help establish healthy boundaries in people who are overly merged with their mothers. Compare the function of St-9 with that of LI-18, the window point on the large intestine meridian, as it addresses the issue of being overly separated from one's father.
6. How do the issues in questions 4 and 5 relate to typical *yangming* (stomach and large intestine) pathology as described in Chinese medicine?
7. Discuss the point combination of Sp-3, St-40, St-15, Lu-9, and Lu-1 from the standpoint of empowering nurturance and breath and food as acquired sources of *qi*. How could this combination simultaneously address both congestion of the lung and loneliness?
8. Compare and differentiate the functions of St-19, St-20, St-25, St-23, Sp-14, Sp-16, and Sp-17 as they relate to the emotion *(si)*, spirit *(yi)*, and virtue *(xin)* of the earth element.
9. Discuss the point combination St-44, St-24, CV-12, and Sp-9. How could this combination empower the graceful assimilation

of nourishment in the physical, cognitive, and spiritual realms?

10. Compare the functions of St-25, Gb-30, Ki-1, CV-17, and GV-20 as they empower balanced orientation toward center and our ease of movement through transitions.
11. Discuss the functional relationships between Sp-4, HP-6, St-42, St-30, and CV-15 as they pertain to Serena's treatment presented in the case study.
    a. Is there an internal voice that never lies?
    b. If so, how can we cultivate our ability to hear it?
    c. What is the difference between the willingness to trust ourselves by following our inner voice and arrogance?
12. Discuss an example of a metaphor that changed your life in a positive way.
13. Discuss the point combination St-1, "receiving tears," and St-41, "released stream," as they might aid in moving stagnation in the stomach official.
14. Discuss how needling SI-5 and St-41 in conjunction with each other could be used to treat the conditions of mania, boils, halitosis, and depression.
15. Discuss the character *chong* (沖) in relation to the functions of Lv-3 and St-42.
16. Compare the functions of Lv-3, Gb-34, Sp-1, and St-43 as they each address the functional relationship of the wood and earth element.
17. Discuss the point combination St-43, St-8, Gb-34, and Gb-4 from the standpoint of easing psychic constraint.
    a. How could the addition of CV-12 and either Gb-24 or Lv-14 to the previous point combination address digestive dysfunction associated with this dynamic?
    b. What would the addition of GV-25 *(yintang)* add to this combination?
18. Discuss the point combination St-44 and St-8 from the standpoint of quieting the mind.
19. The names of St-24, "dark and subtle gate," and Ki-21, "dark gate," both allude to the pyloric valve as well as to the underworld of lost souls.
    a. Compare the function of both points as they address digestion.
    b. Compare the function of both points as they address our spiritual journey in life.

## *NOTES*

1. Clavey, 1995, p. 3.
2. Ellis, Wiseman, and Boss, 1989, p. 57.
3. Weiger, 1965, p. 62. I consider this definition to capture the essence of the highest function of the nutritive aspect of blood, also pronounced "*ying*."

4. Given the names *quya*, "crooked tooth," and *guichuang*, or "ghost bed," note that the phrase *yachuang*, or "tooth bed," refers to the jawbone. See Mathews, 1931, p. 207.
5. Deadman and Al-Khafaji, 2000, St-6.
6. Larre and Rochat, 1995, p. 189; Weiger, 1965, p. 111.
7. For an elaboration of these concepts, see *ND*, pp. 278–294.
8. The use of St-9 in this regard is discussed in the context of a case study in *ND*, pp. 406–409.
9. See the description of St-4 and St-17.
10. In this regard, see the description of St-12 and St-14.
11. Watson, 1964a, p. 32.
12. Deadman and Al-Khafaji, 2000, St-15.
13. From class notes attributed to J. R. Worsley.
14. See St-8 for more detail on this emotion and the etymology of the character *si*.
15. This notion is taught by Andrew Cohen, editor of *What Is Enlightenment?* magazine.
16. Mathews, 1931, p. 527.
17. Wieger, 1965, p. 226, L90D.
18. See my descriptions of acupuncture points Ki-21, Ki-22, and Ki-24 for further discussion.
19. See *ND*, p. 55.
20. Mathews, 1931, p. 861.
21. Wieger, 1965, p. 34, L9A.
22. I use this point in the same way I might prescribe the herb formula Baohe Wan (Citrus and Crataegus).
23. Quoted in Ellis et al., 1989, p. 79.
24. Wieger, 1965, p. 151, L56F.
25. For a discussion of the *ling* spirit, see *ND*, pp. 51–56.
26. Deadman and Al-Khafaji, 2000, St-27.
27. Ibid., St-30.
28. Ibid.
29. In reality, I hardly ever say "sooth."
30. For a discussion of these emotional states, see *ND*, pp. 145–148.
31. Deadman and Al-Khafaji, 2000, St-39.
32. See *ND*, pp. 349–350.
33. See *ND*, pp. 213–224.
34. Wieger, 1965, p. 240.
35. Bensky and O'Connor, 1981, p. 273.
36. Mathews, 1931, p. 184.
37. See *ND*, p. 8.
38. Deadman and Al-Khafaji, 2000, St-42.
39. Ibid.
40. Note that the main herbal formula used to tonify the center, Buzhong Yiqi Tang (Ginseng and Astragals), contains bupleurum, the archetypal herb for opening the liver. In fact, Buzhong can be considered the main liver *yang* tonic that integrates the upbearing nature of wood with the earth element's capacity to build center.
41. Wilhelm, 1968, p. 652.

# 35

# SPLEEN

THE SPLEEN CHANNEL BEGINS AT THE MEDIAL NAIL POINT of the big toe. It travels along the medial edge of the foot and passes in front of the medial malleolus. Then it ascends the medial surface of the leg, uniting with the liver and kidney channels at Sp-6, "three *yin* crossing." The channel continues to rise up the medial edge of the tibia and gastrocnemius to the inguinal region, passing through Sp-12 and Sp-13. Here the pathway travels internally toward the median line to CV-3 and CV-4. It then runs laterally again to emerge superficially and travel from Sp-14 to Sp-15.

Now the channel travels internally and back to the median line to join with CV-10. From here the internal branch enters the organs of the spleen, pancreas, and stomach. Another internal branch leaves from CV-10 to enter the heart and connect with its meridian. From CV-10 the channel moves laterally to become superficial again at Sp-16. The channel ascends the thorax to unite with Lv-14 and Gb-24, the *mu* points of their respective officials. The channel continues to ascend, reaching Sp-20 in the second intercostal space. From here the channel descends laterally to Sp-21, the exit point. From Sp-21 the channel travels internally to ascend the esophagus and branch throughout the tongue.

## *Thoughts on the Channel*

As stomach *qi* descends, the nutritional content abstracted from food rises to nourish the heart as well as the rest of our being. This connection is embodied as the spleen channel ends at Sp-21, the great *luo* point. This point sends collaterals to nourish our entire being as though we are held in a motherly embrace. From Sp-21, *qi* exits the spleen meridian to flow to the entry point at Ht-1. Here healthy blood and *qi* return to the heart, truly nourished by the fruits of its labors according to the earth's virtue of reciprocity. In this way the heart as our spiritual center is strengthened.

### MAIN FUNCTIONS

1. Empowers blood with acquired essence.
2. Empowers the transformation and distribution of nourishment.
3. Empowers the virtues of integrity and reciprocity to further empower the virtue of integrity.

### DISTAL POINT FUNCTIONS

***Wood:*** Empowers the earth to hold the center and diminishes constraint within the earth.

***Fire:*** Empowers the earth as oven to cook food and produce *ying*, the nutritional content of blood.

***Earth:*** Empowers all the virtues of earth within the spleen.

***Metal:*** Empowers a balance between substantial and essential nourishment.

***Water:*** Nourishes the earth to wash away burden so life may flourish.

***Xi-cleft:*** Moves the stagnation and burden of undigested experience.

***Luo:*** Drains the burden of dampness and directs the mind inwardly to recognize the true nature of need.

---

### ❖ Sp-1 Hidden White

| | | |
|---|---|---|
| *Yin³bai²* | Hidden White | 隱白 |
| *Yin¹bai²* | *Yin* White | 陰白 |
| *Gui³lei³* | Ghost Wall | 鬼壘 |
| *Gui³yan³* | Ghost Eye | 鬼眼 |

FUNCTIONS

1. Wood point
2. Secondary tonification point
3. Ghost point

VIRTUES

1. Empowers earth to hold center.
2. Diminishes constraint that comes with being "root bound."

Sp-1 is located at the medial edge of the nail on the big toe where the "white" of the toenail is "hidden." The metal element is engendered by the earth element and associated with the color white. Therefore the functional presence of metal, as symbolized by the color white, lies implicitly "hidden" within the first point of the spleen channel. Notes attributed to J. R. Worsley suggest that Sp-1 "allows the breaths of the earth to rise up to the lungs to create an equilibrium between earthly and celestial harmony." The union of *qi* abstracted from grain *(guqi)* meeting with that abstracted from air in the center of the chest is an important step in the process of creating blood.[1] If the middle *jiao* is constrained, this process can be compromised and the spleen can fail to nourish the lungs, engender the expression of metal, or create blood.

As officials of the middle *jiao,* the spleen and liver are charged with maintaining a proper balance of strength and flexibility so our centers are firm yet never overly constrained. On the one hand, earth nourishes and roots the wood element, providing a solid foundation for growth. On the other hand, the roots of the wood mobilize the earth, preventing it from stagnating, and anchor the earth to prevent erosion as well. When wood and earth are harmonious, the officials of the lower and upper *jiaos* can communicate freely through the center and be nourished in our process of manifesting potential.

The spleen's job of holding the blood within the vessels mirrors the functional relationship of the wood to the earth element. When the *qi* of the spleen is deficient, it can fail in this task with bleeding as the result. By empowering the holding of center in all aspects of being, Sp-1 can help keep the blood within the vessels where it belongs. Sp-1 can also be efficacious when bleeding is congruent with excess heat disturbing the blood. In this case excessive heat is diminished by taking a drop or two of blood from Sp-1 with a lancet.

If the presence of wood within is deficient, earth will suffer for lack of internal organization and tend to erode. Bleeding can be congruent with this erosion as the spleen fails to regulate the blood and the integrity of the center is compromised. Such lack of center can be embodied as prolapse of the bladder, anus, or uterus. The presence of hemorrhoids can also suggest the spleen is failing to hold center.

These conditions are usually considered signs of spleen *qi* deficiency. Such deficiency is often congruent with slow thought processes, lethargy, and boredom as we become bogged down by the burden of dampness. As our centers erode, the virtue of integrity is compromised and we tend to be ingratiating toward others in a dysfunctional attempt to avoid their anger, the emotion associated with the wood element. Lack of wood makes it difficult for us to assert ourselves, and we tend to feel unstable emotionally for lack of a firm center to rely on. In this case, Sp-1 can serve to anchor our roots into the earth and enable us to stand up for our own needs. Hence the functional influence of strengthening the presence of wood within earth can be likened to preventing erosion on a hillside by planting trees whose roots will serve as a stabilizing influence to the soil.

The goal-oriented facilities of decision making and planning associated with the wood element help regulate the speed of our metabolism and the quickness with which we are able to process life. Wood, in essence, is the fuel for the fire of digestion. If the presence of wood is deficient, fire cannot burn adequately and metabolic processes slow. In this case damp tends to stagnate and further slow us down as we become increasingly burdened by all we ingest. The accumulation of dampness tends to manifest as difficulty in concentration and mental fogginess as the spark of the spirit that initiates mental processes is clouded over. By increasing the presence of wood, we can empower mental clarity and vision within the earth element. The organizing influence of new root structures can soak up dampness and break up stagnation, allowing the spleen to transform potential sources of nourishment into blood and muscle rather than into burden. This process is often congruent with reduced blood sugar levels as cells are empowered to open to the nourishment present in blood. Hence, by harmonizing the functional relationship of the wood and earth elements, Sp-1 can be an important point in the treatment of diabetes.

Wood, in excess, tends to grow out of control and encroach on the function of the spleen across the *ke* cycle. If the presence of wood within is excessive, the earth element will tend to be overly constrained like a plant that is root bound. Note that the Chinese character *kun* (困), which means "constraint," depicts a tree growing inside of a box. A mind imprisoned in this way tends to obsess and ruminate as it struggles to make space for itself through fantasy. Such obsessive thoughts cover the same ground repeatedly as the mind has no new fertile soil to stretch out in. Insomnia is frequently associated with this dynamic as we lie awake at night worrying, unable to quiet our restless mind. Ultimately, this dynamic can present as stagnation and we are unable to move creatively in any direction. This stuckness can be embodied as tension, pressure, and pain across the middle of the abdomen. Acid reflux, a bitter or sour taste in the mouth, and heartburn can also accompany this pattern. "Hidden white" can help relieve such constraint in the same way that transplanting a plant into a bigger pot can allow it to once again spread out its roots and freely absorb nourishment.

## ❖ Sp-2 Great Capital
*Da*[4]*du*[1] Great Capital 大都

FUNCTIONS

1. Fire point
2. Primary tonification point

VIRTUES

1. Warms the earth so our life's harvest may flourish.
2. Helps satiate the hungry heart.

The name "great capital" suggests a busy place where people gather and affairs are transacted. The spleen is just such a meeting place where all nutrients must gather to be transformed and disseminated. The fire within the earth is a warming influence that empowers the digestion and assimilation of nutrients so health may flourish. The presence of fire is felt on the earth as the sun nourishes crops to grow, helping ensure an adequate harvest. Fire within the earth may also be likened to the heat of an oven that allows it to cook food so nourishment may readily be extracted from it. Hence the character *ying* (營), signifying the nutritional content of blood created by the spleen, depicts a campfire (火火) cooking food for an army. The phrase *dadu* literally means "on the whole" or "for the most part."[2] This usage may be taken as referring to the earth element's role in empowering integrity and embracing all things.

If the presence of fire within the earth is deficient, digestion and integration will proceed slowly in all aspects of being. Physically this can manifest as poor digestion and mentally it can occur as excessive deliberation and a too slow thought process. Deficient *qi* and *yang* impede the spleen from fulfilling its function of transforming fluids. Further, if the influence of fire is deficient, water tends to be excessive, also contributing to the stagnation of fluids. Instead of producing muscle and blood, what we ingest is turned into the burden of phlegm and dampness. Those things that should nourish us in life, such as friends, family, and hobbies, are turned into burdens and obligations to be carried through life. By tonifying the presence of fire within earth, "great capital" can help the spleen transform dampness and empower the joy of contentment that comes from being fulfilled by the fruits of our labors.

If the presence of fire within earth is excessive, our appetite tends to be insatiable as nothing we consume can sate a hungry heart. We can experience a lack of joy because we are never deeply nourished by anything attained in life and fulfillment eludes us. We can appear as though we have received bread in life but never gotten to taste the honey. Excessive fire tends to consume fluids and lead to a condition of *yin* deficiency. Hence the earth can become parched and our lives barren as nourishing fluids are depleted. Such deficiency can be congruent with signs as diverse as dry and cracked lips, constant thirst and hunger, eating too quickly, and symptoms such as constipation, diabetes, infertility, and hypertension. Geographic tongue is often a sign of earth *yin* deficiency. The cracked surface of the tongue appears like the parched earth in a desert.

Excessive weight can be the embodiment of an increased appetite fueled by a hungry heart expressing itself dysfunctionally through the earth element. Unable to fulfill itself, the heart expresses its unfulfilled desires dysfunctionally through the earth element. Longings for connection and intimacy are displaced into eating as the heart's pain and fire is sublimated in the spleen and stomach. Excessive fire pouring out of a hungry heart can infiltrate the muscles to manifest as fibromyalgia or myofibrositis. Clinically I find these conditions predominantly to affect women with a history of abuse. I interpret such burning and pain in the muscles as the heart protector's fire raging out of control within the earth element. I often sedate or disperse Sp-2 in combination with either Ht-8 or HP-8 to treat this functional dynamic.

---

### ❖ Sp-3 **Supreme White**
*Tai⁴bai²* Supreme White, Venus 太白

FUNCTIONS

1. Source point
2. Earth point
3. Horary point; 9 A.M.–11 A.M., late summer

VIRTUE

Empowers nourishment from the earth as the source of acquired *qi.*

*Taibai* is the Chinese name for the planet Venus, located in the western sky. West is the direction associated with the metal element as is the color white. Venus is associated with the seventh and eighth celestial stems, which in their *yang* aspect manifests in the world as weapons and have a martial influence,[3] hence the use of this point in sedating "uprisings" by regulating the stomach and large intestine.[4] In its *yin* aspect, the metal element is said to manifest as a kettle. A kettle's function is to contain the nourishing food that it cooks.[5] As the channel's source point, "supreme white" can powerfully stimulate earth to engender metal through the movements of the *sheng* cycle according to the principle of tonifying the mother (earth) to feed the child (metal).

As the earth point on an earth channel, Sp-3 is an horary point. Therefore treating Sp-3 at the functional high point of the official (9–11 A.M.) can provide a strong tonification to the spleen. This is particularly true during late summer, the seasonal high point of the earth element. Whereas St-42, the source point of the stomach official, can harmonize our relationship to external sources of nourishment, Sp-3 influences the internal transportation and distribution of acquired *qi* in a way that nourishes all aspects of inner being. "Supreme white" is archetypal of the spleen's function and one of the most important points for empowering the earth element's virtues of integrity and reciprocity. Integrity emerges when there is a congruence between our intentions, our speech, and our actions.

Sp-3 excels at building integrity by empowering the bountiful production of *qi* and blood to nourish our center. By facilitating the dispersion of damp, Sp-3 can help remove acquired burdens that obscure our ability to recognize the true nature of our needs and appetites. In this way our actions relative to giving and receiving nourishment can be commensurate with manifesting true nature rather than with merely attaining a certain level of fleeting comfort.

The virtue of reciprocity emerges when we derive nourishment in equal parts through balanced production and consumption.[6] In large part, this virtue is modeled early in life by the quality of our relationship to our mothers.[7] To the degree this relationship is healthy we are able to establish the integrity of our own centers in life without being excessively needy or ingratiating. Neediness and ingratiating behavior undermine the integrity of the spleen. These pathological emotions are often congruent with symptoms such as sweet cravings, excessive or diminished appetite, constipation or diarrhea, and all other patterns of dysfunction associated with the spleen official. As an archetypal earth point, Sp-3 can help rectify our relationship to our mothers as it is embodied in our dysfunctional relationship to our own center. In this way, we may become more self-reliant and less dependent on the sympathy and caretaking of others. Increasingly content and able to provide for our own needs, we may be moved to share our abundance altruistically with others.

Figure 13.3 illustrates the elements associated with the four seasons, which are shown cycling around the earth, representing the primal axis as it exists in later heaven. In a sense, we can think of Sp-3 as the source that feeds all the other *yin* source points and binds them to the center of being. All of the source points on the *yin* channels are earth points, and Sp-3 can be the anchor that centers, supports, and nourishes all these other source points with acquired *qi*. Hence Sp-3 is the transmitting point of the spleen official, capable of empowering all the virtues of the earth element within the other *yin* officials when their earth/source points are treated simultaneously. Further, as the channel's source point, Sp-3 can effectively empower any of the functions embraced by any of the other points on the channel but in a more general way. "Supreme white" can be effective in tonifying *qi* or blood or moving stagnations of *qi*, heat, or damp as well as embracing the deeper spiritual and emotional functions inherent in these other points.

---

### ❖ Sp-4 Yellow Emperor, Grandfather-Grandson[8]

*Gong*[1]*sun*[1] Yellow Emperor, Grandfather-Grandson 公孫

FUNCTIONS

1. *Luo* point
2. Master point of the penetrating vessel
3. Couple point of the *yin* linking vessel

VIRTUE

Unites the mind (stomach) and heart (spleen) of the earth element.

*Gongsun* is the family name of the mythological yellow emperor who purportedly ruled China from 2697 to 2597 B.C.E. Earth is the element associated with the period of the yellow emperor's rule. As the emperor unites the nation, so too does Sp-4, by virtue of being a *luo* point, integrate the functioning of the spleen and stomach officials. In this relationship the spleen is the grandfather and the stomach official is the grandson. The relationship between the grandfather and the grandson spans generations, forming a bridge between the wisdom of the past and our hope for the future.

In response to shock in life we can lose touch with our centers and project the fulfillment of our needs externally on others. In time our appetites come to be solely based on our drive to seek comfort with no attention paid to the quality of nourishment that our spirits truly hunger for. This dynamic can be embodied as stagnation of damp, a pathogen that obscures the connection between heart and mind in a way that compromises our ability to determine our needs appropriately. As the channel's *luo* point, Sp-4 helps dispel damp and direct the mind inwardly back toward the *jing* so it can serve as a healthy foundation for building ourselves newly from acquired *qi*. The physiological functions of Sp-4 of "invigorating" the blood and regulating the sea of blood *(chongmai)* speak to the deep levels of nourishment empowered by this point.

By draining damp and nourishing *qi* and blood, the habituated needs of the ego can be diminished while destiny and purpose are reinstituted as guiding forces in our procurement and assimilation of nourishment. By uniting the innate and acquired basis of self, Sp-4 can place us in contact with where we have come from (the *jing* of the grandfather) and where we are going (the *jing* of the grandchild). In this way we may be deeply empowered to find the strength, wisdom, and hope to continue our life's journey.

---

## ❖ Sp-5 **Merchant Mound**
*Shang*[1]*qiu*[1] Merchant Mound 商丘

FUNCTIONS

1. Metal point
2. Sedation point

VIRTUE

Empowers harmony in the process of assimilating substantial and essential nourishment.

The character *shang,* translated as "merchant," is also the musical note associated with the metal element in the pentatonic Chinese scale. Hence Sp-5 is the metal point on the spleen channel. Note that three of the first five names on the spleen channel allude to the metal element. This underscores the importance of the earth element in engendering metal. In fact, minerals and gemstones, archetypal material manifestations of the metal element, can be thought of as sunlight that is digested and concretized within the earth. Hence the term *shang* associated with metal is paired with the term *qiu,* signifying a mound of earth. On this mound two men (丅) are shown standing back to back, instead of four men whom it would have been too difficult to depict.[9]

The meaning conveyed is of a culmination or high point that provides perspective and from where we can see in all directions. Note that this same character also figures prominently in the name of Gb-40, *qiuxu* (丘虛). Sp-5 and Gb-40 are located in the depressions below the inner and outer ankle bones, respectively. The character *qiu* is etymologically related to the character *xu* (虛), depicting a high upland from where nothing can be seen and thus signifying emptiness. The function of metal within the earth is to empower the adequate assimilation of essence so as to achieve an internal state of clarity, emptiness, and lightness unburdened by our attachments to the material world. Hence Sp-5 excels at emptying the digestive system of stagnation.

The virtue of a good merchant is to recognize value and to transact affairs accordingly. The name "merchant mound" may allude to the spleen's function of distributing the nourishing essences acquired from food. If the metal within is deficient, the earth element can tend toward stagnation as essence is not assimilated or distributed and waste is not efficiently let go of. Metal within the earth represents the interpenetration of substantial (earth) and insubstantial (metal) nourishment. Substantial nourishment is gained through the material forms of the things we ingest, and insubstantial nourishment is gained through the assimilation of essence, particularly through breath. Failure to connect to our own essential worth can lead us to seek less than fulfilling sources of nourishment in the world. Hence dampness can accumulate as a result of assimilating what is not congruent with true self. Such dampness is often associated with bloating, excessive weight, constipation or diarrhea, and feelings of being stuck in life.

By increasing the presence of metal within the earth, "merchant mound" can empower the spleen's connection to quality and help it abstract the highest from life while letting go of the dross. I find this to be an excellent point for people whose self-image is tied to body weight when they continually feel worthless and heavy from overeating and bingeing on junk food. Earth in excess can lead to lethargy and an excessive center as a person gains weight from the stagnation that comes from overeating and lack of exercise. The metal point within the spleen can help empower a feeling of lightness as we are placed back in connection with essence.

If the metal within is excessive, the spleen can have a hard time holding on to nutrients. In this case diarrhea can resemble crying and be the embodiment of our grief over the value that slips away from us in life. I find the formula Shenling Baizhu San (Ginseng and Atractylodes) to address this particular dynamic well. When the presence of metal is lacking, our physique tends to be overly thin because little of value can be assimilated and incorporated into flesh and muscle. Diminishing the presence of metal within earth can help empower our ability to retain essence. Excessive metal can also congest the earth, leading again to stagnation and difficulty letting go in life. In this scenario, self-righteousness and perfectionism can so constrain our ability to be nourished that the process of assimilation through digestion and breath is obscured. In this case dispersing the influence of metal can allow the earth more breathing room.

---

### ❖ Sp-6 Three *Yin* Junction

| | | |
|---|---|---|
| *San¹yin¹jiao¹* | Three *Yin* Junction | 三陰交 |
| *Tai⁴yin¹* | Great *Yin*, The Moon | 太陰 |
| *Cheng²ming⁴* | Receiving Destiny | 承命 |
| *Xia⁴zhi¹san¹li³* | Lower Three *Li* | 下之三里 |

FUNCTION

Meeting point of the liver, kidney, and spleen channels

VIRTUE

Empowers the spleen to nourish rather than burden the process of evolution.

The name *sanyinjiao* refers to the fact that the three *yin* channels of the leg—the kidney, the liver, and the spleen—all cross at this point. The importance of these officials are such that Sp-6 excels at harmonizing a wide range of functional imbalances. The relationship of the kidney to the liver official is typified by the upward rising of innate potential into the world. The nature of the earth element is to empower the holding of center through transitions. In balance, the spleen nourishes the evolution of potential from water to wood along the left half of the *sheng* cycle so it can occur in a grounded and centered way. If the spleen becomes dysfunctional, however, it can hinder this process by smothering it with the burden of dampness.

Dampness tends to descend and frequently collects in the lower *jiao. Sanyinjiao* excels at treating damp stagnation that manifests in the urogenital tract and reproductive organs as vaginal, bladder, and prostate infections. Such stagnation of damp tends to manifest as either a white (cold) or yellow (hot) discharge. Symptoms such as uterine fibroids and leukorrhea can also indicate the presence of dampness. Damp affecting the intestines is often associated with diarrhea. In the middle *jiao* the presence of damp can be associated with food stagnation, borborygmus, abdominal pain, nausea, and other digestive distress. Such stagnation tends to smother the expression of kidney *jing,* which must rise gracefully as we assert our purpose in the world. If the lower and middle *jiao* become mired in dampness, the evolution of *jing* will be suppressed and the flower of the heart, the natural expression of innate nature, may never blossom.

This dynamic can be congruent with a wide range of dysfunctional expressions including lack of appetite, insomnia, depression, lethargy, boredom, infertility, impotence, and lack of evolutionary momentum in general. The kidney and liver provide the potency and thrust that fuel evolution. If the influence of these officials is obscured, then instead of nourishing the heart, all effort exerted in life can be transformed into a burden. Stagnation can obscure the womb in a way that undermines the process of fertilization and gestation. The process of becoming pregnant can also be compromised as worry and obsession, psychospiritual attributes associated with damp, undermine the functional integrity of the reproductive system. Through the elimination of burden and the revival of evolutionary momentum, Sp-6 can empower us to "receive destiny" as denoted by this alternate point name.

Depression can result as our spirit is smothered by our inability to fulfill our needs, real or imagined. By supporting the spleen's function of transformation and distribution of nourishment, Sp-6 can unburden the kidney and liver by dispersing damp so their influence can once again ascend to support the heart. Further, by tonifying the earth and fortifying it with inherited essence drawn from the kidney, the spleen may directly nourish the heart through the production of *qi* and blood. Hence congested earth can cease to obscure the middle and lower *jiaos* and allow for the communication among the kidney, liver, and heart officials. In this way all aspects of being may once again be nourished as original nature flourishes.

---

| ❖ **Sp-7** | **Leaky Valley** | |
|---|---|---|
| *1. Lou⁴gu³* | Leaky Valley | 漏谷 |
| *2. Tai⁴yin¹luo⁴* | *Tai Yin* Connection | 太陰絡 |

VIRTUE

Empowers the spleen to hold the center and prevent leaking.

The character *gu,* meaning "valley," is a homophone with the character *gu,* meaning grain (穀). Grains, grown in the valley, are transformed by the spleen into *ying* or nutritive *qi.*[10] *Ying* represents the spleen's contribution to blood, whose existence is evidence that we are nourished by our work in the world. The valley alluded to in the point's name can refer to the stomach, which must contain and process nourishment, or to the *hara* in the lower *jiao,* whose quality defines the integrity of our centers.

If earth *qi* is deficient, the spleen may fail to empower the center to contain nourishment adequately. Incomplete digestion can be congruent with conditions such as leaky gut syndrome in which the intestines become overly permeable. In this condition, food is broken down only partially and virus-size particles larger than amino acids are able to enter the blood. These can initiate an immune response that over the long term wears down immunity. If immunity is severely compromised, we become vulnerable to conditions such as chronic fatigue syndrome and yeast infections or the Epstein-Barr virus.

The name of St-43, "sunken valley," refers to deficient stomach *qi* failing to hold the middle and lower *jiao* in place. Hemorrhoids and prolapses are all evidence of our "valleys" sinking. Earth controls the water element across the *ke* cycle. If the controlling influence of earth is deficient, water will leak as it overflows the boundary created by the river's banks. Evidence of the valley leaking is contained in signs and symptoms associated with the stagnation of damp. Leaking of semen, urine, or vaginal discharge can all be signs indicating that earth is not supporting the center and the "valley" is "leaking." Like all points, Sp-7 harmonizes a continuum of dysfunction ranging from deficiency to excess. Hence "leaky valley" can function to prevent leaking or reduce edema and disinhibit the flow of urine when elimination is difficult.

Emotional leaking can manifest as the excessive need to give or receive sympathy. The craving of sympathy is the psychospiritual equivalent of craving sugar, and it engenders a type of dampness experienced clinically as neediness. Such dampness can also present as an overly sentimental or saccharine face that appears to others to be cloying. Cloying and neediness are the psychospiritual correlates of *ying* leaking due to erosion of our emotional center. Sp-7 can strengthen our centers and help treat such leaking in all aspects of being.

In the *Systematized Canon of Acupuncture and Moxibustion,* Sp-7 is named *taiyinluo,* possibly designating this point as a *luo* point on the spleen channel.[11] However, no other classical text makes reference to Sp-7 as a *luo* point, and my clinical experience suggests that indeed it is not.

---

| ❖ **Sp-8** | **Earth Motivator** | |
|---|---|---|
| *Di⁴ji¹* | Earth Motivator | 地機 |
| *Di⁴ji¹* | Earth Basket | 地箕 |
| *Pi²she⁴* | Spleen Residence | 脾舍 |

FUNCTION

*Xi*-cleft point

VIRTUE

Promotes integrity by moving stagnation.

Inertia and momentum define a continuum of dysfunctional expression associated with the earth element. Earth tends to remain at rest mirroring the slow process of geological change. But when earth finally does initiate movement, as in the shifting of the tectonic plates, it tends to move cataclysmically. When the earth element stagnates we tend to feel heavy and become bogged down by all our unintegrated life experiences. This is exemplified by the sultriness of a humid and hot summer day where we are content to just lie in a hammock and do nothing. Conversely, when someone's earth element is overly engaged in a process it can be impossible to get him to slow down and change course.

Either end of this spectrum, whether typified by lethargy and boredom or habitual "doing," can present as obstinacy. The function of "earth motivator" is similar to utilizing a bulldozer to come and move stuck earth. Hence tonifying Sp-8 can help motivate the earth to move, whereas sedating it can help overactive earth to relax. In this way the spleen's functions of transportation and distribution can occur in a more balanced way.

---

| ❖ **Sp-9** | ***Yin* Mound Spring** | |
|---|---|---|
| *Yin¹ling²quan²* | *Yin* Mound Spring | 陰陵泉 |

FUNCTIONS

1. Water point
2. Secondary sedation point

VIRTUES

1. Nourishes the earth to promote fertility in all aspects of being.
2. Helps engender the emotion sympathy for self and others.

Located on the inner surface of the leg, the character *yin* differentiates Sp-9 from Gb-34, "*yang* mound spring," located at the same anatomical level on the outer aspect of the leg. The character *ling* depicts a mound of earth, and the character *quan* depicts white (白) water (水) gushing out of the earth. Taken as a whole, the name *yinlingquan* denotes Sp-9 as the water point on a *yin* channel associated with the earth element. Water, sent from heaven, nourishes the earth to support the harvest. The earth embodies this loving care and transforms it into abundant splendor so life may thrive. The fruit of the earth's harvest nourishes humanity with its sweet nectar. To taste this gift and feel contentment is to reap the bounty of the earth element. Water also fulfills the function of transporting the harvest via canals and rivers to its destination. Within us the functions of transformation and distribution of nourishment are empowered in large part by the water within the earth. Hence digestive juices break down food, and our rivers of blood, created and managed by the spleen, distribute nourishment throughout our inner kingdom of being.

If the presence of water within earth is deficient, the earth can be parched as assimilation of nourishment is compromised. For lack of control by water, the fire within earth can rage. Such heat can fuel appetite and thirst although little of the potential nourishment acquired is effectively assimilated. Therefore our appetites tend to be insatiably driven by our desires, ensuring that we never reach a state of contentment. The barrenness of dry earth can be embodied as infertility as our ability to make blood and *qi* to nourish and hold a fetus is compromised. Sympathy is the emotional equivalent of sweetness. If water within is deficient, we can lack sympathy for ourselves and others as we grow hardened to the world. In response to past disappointments and feelings of abandonment we may imagine we do not need anything from anyone. "*Yin* mound spring" can increase the presence of water within earth to help the assimilation and distribution of nourishment occur more gracefully. In this way we may be more sympathetic to our own needs and to the needs of others as we open to receive nourishment in all aspects of being.

If the water within earth is excessive, the earth can turn to mud and become thick and stagnant. This dynamic can be embodied as dampness, lethargy, boredom, and a too slow thought process. Excessive water can erode the riverbanks to flood and destroy the fields. In this way fear, associated with the kidneys, can fail to be checked by the mind as our thoughts become obsessed with worry. Dampness tends to sink but can accumulate in any of the three burners. As the water point within the earth, Sp-9 excels at diminishing the presence of water within earth and therefore can be used to drain the damp pathogen wherever it accumulates. Congruent with its location, *yinlingquan* is especially adept at draining damp that accumulates at the knees to cause swelling.

When this point is tender on a woman, it can indicate dysfunction in the womb. The finding of such tenderness can be diagnostic of uterine fibroids and other types of damp stagnation that affect the reproductive organs. The ability to have a regular period and conceive and carry a fetus full term signals the embodiment of the virtues of the earth element relative to the healthy relationship between one's own needs and caring for the needs of others. A fetus is literally the fruit of the womb, and if the quality and quantity of functional water within the earth is compromised, reproductive problems are likely.

---

| ❖ **Sp-10** | **Sea of Blood** | |
|---|---|---|
| *Xue⁴hai³* | Sea of Blood | 血海 |
| *Xue⁴xi¹* | Blood Cleft | 血郄 |
| *Bai³chong²wo¹* | Hundred Insect Nest | 百蟲窩 |

FUNCTION

Sea of blood

The spleen's function is to transform all acquired influences into nurturance by empowering the nutritive content of blood *(ying)*. "Sea of blood" is an important point for tonifying and moving the blood as well as removing heat that can agitate and disturb the blood. The name "blood cleft" refers to this point's ability to move blood stasis like a *xi*-cleft point.

Sp-10 can be helpful for nourishing the blood, although I do find other points such as Ht-7, Lv-3, Sp-3, Sp-4, HP-6, Bl-14, Bl-18, Bl-20, Bl-38 (43), and Bl-17 to be more effective in this regard. Still, I often use this as a distal point to tonify and move blood when the entire right side of the pulse or the entire blood depth is thin, showing either substantial blood loss or long-term malnutrition from a variety of sources including poor diet, poor absorption, eating disorders, poverty, and vegetarianism.

Primarily Sp-10 excels at moving blood stasis and diminishing the presence of functional heat in the blood. Congruent with the spleen's association with nourishing the womb to promote fertility, Sp-10 can address a wide range of imbalances affecting the reproductive organs. These include blood stasis, blood deficiency associated with stasis, and heat in the blood congruent with excessive uterine bleeding. Note the proximity of this point to Lv-9, which addresses *qi* stagnation in the reproductive organs.

Excess heat in the blood can be a functional basis of many skin ailments characterized by hot, red, itchy lesions on the skin. Such lesions often signify that heat in the blood is venting through the skin. Although unsightly and irritating, the presence of these lesions indicates the body is attempting to dissipate the heat so it does not build up to damage an internal organ such as the liver or heart. Conventional treatments with steroids or antibiotics can have dire long-term consequences by suppressing this natural mechanism.[12] Sp-10, along with LI-11, excels at naturally reducing the presence of heat in the blood and can therefore help any condition based on the presence of such heat. The name "hundred insect nest" may refer to the point's function of removing heat from the blood to mitigate irritating skin conditions.

---

❖ **Sp-11** **Basket Gate**

| | | |
|---|---|---|
| *Ji¹men²* | Basket Gate | 箕門 |
| *Tai⁴yin¹nei⁴shi⁴* | *Taiyin* Inner Market[13] | 太陰內市 |

The name *jimen* refers to a winnower's basket that might be used to carry goods both to and from the market. The allusion to the spleen and its capacity to transform and distribute nourishment is also contained in an alternate name of this point: *taiyinneishi* ("*taiyin* inner market"). The *taiyin* meridians of spleen and lung are responsible for the abstraction and synthesis of nourishment from food and air, respectively. Traditionally Sp-11 is used for clearing dampness and heat and regulating urination.

---

❖ **Sp-12** **Rushing Gate**

| | | |
|---|---|---|
| *Chong¹men²* | Rushing Gate | 衝門 |
| *Ci¹gong¹* | Palace of Charity | 慈宮 |
| *Shang⁴ci²gong¹* | Upper Palace of Charity | 上慈宮 |
| *Qian²zhang¹men²* | Front Chapter Gate | 前章門 |

FUNCTION

Meeting point of the spleen and liver channel with the *yin* linking vessel

*Chongqi* is the whirling and surging *qi* of the center that holds heaven and earth apart while at the same time empowering the interpenetration of these two universal poles. The earth element corresponds cosmologically to the central axis that unites the other four elements. Hence the character for earth (土) denotes four directions and a center indicating the earth element. The character *chong* also appears in the name of St-30, "surging *yang*," which lies just medially to Sp-12. The inguinal region is like a gate that *qi* and blood rush through, hence the point's name. Symptoms of constipation or retention of urine can be signs of *qi* and blood not flowing freely through the inguinal region. Sp-12 can help release constraint in this area and thus improve elimination.

The character *ci*, translated as "compassion" or "mercy," is an epithet for mothers.[14] Hence the name *cigong* can be translated as "palace of motherly compassion." During pregnancy Sp-12 can be used to treat fetal *qi* that rises to disturb the mother's heart.[15] Here the relationship between mother and fetus becomes distorted in a way that pressure builds in the abdomen to unsettle the mother. If the heart *shen* is agitated, the mother will not be able to rest and can tend to worry unduly about her pregnancy. When thought becomes disordered to the point of obsession, constant worry tends to further disturb the expression of spirit. This dynamic can contribute to hypertension as the mother fails to let go and rest. Sp-12 can calm *qi* that disturbs the heart and help the mind relax, so spirit can be expressed.

The name *cigong*, "palace of charity," also evokes the virtue of altruism as it is empowered by the earth element. The presence of true altruism, as opposed to giving with a personal agenda, signifies that our abundance is flourishing to the degree we can afford to be generous with others. By calming the flow of *qi* with Sp-12, we can help empower balanced rather than compulsive giving. The name *qianzhangmen*, "front chapter gate," is similar to the name of Lv-13, *zhangmen* ("chapter gate"), the *mu* point of the spleen official.

## ❖ Sp-13 Official Residence

*Fu[3]she[4]* Official Residence 府舍

FUNCTION

Meeting point of the spleen and liver channel with the *yin* linking vessel

The character *fu* denotes a palace or the residence of an official and in the name of the Sp-13 refers to the dwelling of the intestines over which the point is located.[16] Hence Sp-13 is said to treat abdominal fullness and pain as well as constipation by empowering the transformative functions of the spleen to help the intestines move stagnation.

The earth element is particularly associated with the concept of home as the center of our being. Internally our home is our *hara*, which defines our physical center just as the home we live in is the center that our lives revolve around. The way patients relate to the concept of home is often reflected in the quality of care and nurturance they give themselves as well as the physical condition of their own bodies. The liver and spleen officials regulate the integrity and flow of *qi* through our centers. As a meeting point between these officials, "official residence" can address conditions of pain and stagnation in the abdomen, helping promote harmony in our centers.

---

❖ **Sp-14** **Abdomen Knot**

| | | |
|---|---|---|
| *Fu⁴jie²* | Abdomen Knot | 腹結 |
| *Chang²jie²* | Intestinal Knot | 腸結 |
| *Chang²ku¹* | Dwelling of the Intestines | 腸窟 |
| *Fu⁴qu¹* | Abdomen Grievance | 腹屈 |
| *Yang²ku¹* | *Yang* Dwelling | 陽窟 |

VIRTUE

Unties knots in the abdomen congruent with worry and rumination.

Sp-14 can help ease *qi* stagnation in the abdominal region that is congruent with pain and distension. Such discomfort can be the embodiment of worry, a dysfunctional emotion associated with the earth element, that ties the abdomen in knots. "Abdomen knot" is particularly useful for pain and pressure in the area around the umbilicus. The umbilicus mediates our connection to our mothers while in the womb, and the quality of this relationship can impact our ability to nourish ourselves and create a healthy center later in life. Discomfort in the umbilical region can be associated with issues regarding boundaries as they impact our assimilation of nourishment in any aspect of being.

"Head tied" (St-8) can address the obsessional tendencies of the earth element in people who constrain themselves with worry and excessive thought. This process is often congruent with pressure or pain in the head. "Abdomen knot" addresses this same dynamic as it manifests in the abdomen and impacts the healthful assimilation of nutrition.

---

❖ **Sp-15** **Great Horizontal**

| | | |
|---|---|---|
| *Da⁴heng²* | Great Horizontal | 大橫 |
| *Ren²heng²* | Human Horizontal | 人橫 |
| *Shen⁴qi⁴* | Kidney *Qi* | 腎氣 |

FUNCTION

Meeting point of the spleen channel and the *yin* linking vessel

Located just laterally to St-25, the *mu* point of the large intestine official, the "great horizontal" referred to is the transverse course of the large intestine. The end of the earth always appears to us visually as the horizontal horizon. "Great horizontal" empowers the earth element to provide support in the form of nourishment, which is the foundation of the functional ground we stand on. When spleen *qi* is massively deficient, we can be exhausted to the point of lying flat on our backs, too tired to initiate any movement. Such symptoms are present in conditions such as chronic fatigue syndrome, mononucleosis, and during convalescence from serious illness. Hence "great horizontal" is indicated for sadness, weeping, and sighing, and weakness to the point of not being able to move the limbs.[17] By tonifying spleen *qi* and moving stagnation in the large intestine, "great horizontal" can allow us to let go of our grief and help us make room for a renewed sense of vitality.

A horizontal cross section of the body passing through Sp-15 would encompass the eight points listed in Figure 35.1 (p. 674). The earth points, St-25 and Sp-15, govern postnatal *qi;* Ki-16, Bl-23, and Bl-47 (52) govern prenatal *qi.* The name "kidney *qi*" may have to do with the location of Sp-15 in front of Bl-47 (52) and the role of the acquired constitution in supplementing the innate constitution. The governor and conception vessels define the axis of heaven and earth within us. This circle of points helps comprise the belt vessel *(daimo)* that unites the first three (CV, GV, and *chongmai*) extraordinary meridians to define the functional network of the body in three-dimensional space.

---

## ❖ Sp-16 **Abdomen Sorrow**

| | | |
|---|---|---|
| 1. *Fu⁴ai¹* | Abdomen Sorrow | 腹哀 |
| 2. *Chang²ai¹* | Intestinal Sorrow | 腸哀 |
| 3. *Chang²qu¹* | Intestinal Grievance | 腸屈 |

FUNCTION

Meeting point of the spleen channel and *yin* linking channel

Sp-14, Sp-15, and Sp-16 are similar in function yet address different "levels" of imbalance relative to the depth at which they affect the body, mind, and spirit. This kind of relationship is frequently seen with points in close proximity on a given meridian or in a given anatomical region. Sp-14, "abdomen knot," addresses stagnation that compromises digestion and assimilation congruent with worry. Sp-15, "great horizontal," addresses stagnation in the intestines that can be associated with weakness, grief, and loss.

Sp-16, "abdomen sorrow," addresses sorrow in life based on the belief that our needs will never be met. In this regard longing, loneliness, and

| Front | Back |
|---|---|
| CV-8 | GV-4 |
| Ki-16 | X |
| St-25 | Bl-23 |
| Sp-15 | Bl-47 |
| Gb-26 | X |

*Figure 35.1*
DAIMAI

*I think of* daimai *(the "belt" or girdling" vessel) as including those eight points that encircle the body in a horizontal cross section passing through CV-8 and GV-4.*

sorrow present as barrenness in all realms of being. The metaphor of having eaten bread in life but never tasting honey is applicable here. The emotional emptiness felt congruent with this point's function can be associated with diarrhea that can be thought of metaphorically as a type of weeping from the lower orifice. Indigestion resulting from obstruction in the intestines can make a sound as though the abdomen were weeping, yielding yet another allusion to this point's name.

---

❖ **Sp-17** **Food Drain**
*Shi²dou⁴* Food Drain 食竇
*Ming⁴guan¹* Destiny Pass 命關

Digestive stagnation is often associated with eating too quickly or too much. Both behaviors are often predicated on feelings of not being or having enough in life. On a physical level, "food drain" can address bloating and feelings of heaviness after eating. Food stagnation is the physical embodiment of a functional deficit congruent with not processing life experience efficiently. Sp-17 can help empower the efficient processing of our life so nourishment is extracted from our experiences and mundanity can be let go. In this way, the earth element's virtue of integrity is empowered. An alternate name, *mingguan*, or "destiny pass," suggests the deeper functions of this point in nourishing destiny while empowering the letting go of mundanity. Hence we must note the location of Sp-17 at the level of the heart.

---

### ❖ Sp-18 — Heavenly Stream

*Tian[1]xi[1]* Heavenly Stream 天谿

VIRTUES

1. Empowers the earth element's virtue of reciprocity.
2. Empowers the emotions of sympathy and empathy.

The earth element is associated with the nurturance and care of the mother, and the metal element is associated with the father and the inspiration that heavenly *yang* affords us. Hence Sp-18 is indicated for shortness of breath when our "stream" from "heaven" is obstructed. Breast milk, particularly colostrum, is a way the mother imparts *yang* to the infant. "Heavenly stream" encourages the flow of milk through the breast, empowering the mother to nurture the infant adequately. Milk is a fruit of the mother's labor, and the sharing of it with her infant a perfect embodiment of the earth element's virtue of reciprocity.[18] The attentive mother is so empathetically attuned to the infant that lactation begins on hearing the infant's first cry. On an inner level, Sp-18 empowers within us the virtues of sympathy and empathy and our ability to give nurturing compassionate care to other beings in a balanced way. I have used this point to good advantage for patients who feel wounded or abandoned by their mothers and who are unable to nurture either self or others in a balanced way.

---

### ❖ Sp-19 — Chest Region

*Xiong[1]xiang[1]* Chest Region 胸鄉

I use Sp-19 only as a local point for distension and pain in the chest, often to address the embodiment of dysfunction discussed in the context of Sp-18 and Sp-20.

---

### ❖ Sp-20 — Encircling Glory

1. *Zhou[1]rong[2]* Encircling Glory 周榮
2. *Zhou[1]ying[2]* Encircling Nourishment 周營

VIRTUES

1. Empowers a balanced relationship between the spleen and lung officials.
2. Empowers a balance between earthly and heavenly nourishment.

Although the spleen meridian contains no "window" points, I consider Sp-20 to be similar in function and treat it as such. A virtue associated with the earth element is loyalty (*zhong*:忠) depicting a centered (中) heart (心). A delicate balance exists between being loyal to a person or principle in life and compromising our ideals in the service of that to which we are committed. "Encircling glory" can help empower us to experience the highest (heavenly) aspects of both giving and receiving nourishment in a way that is not obscured by neediness. Hence an alternate name for this point, *zhouying*, "encircling nourishment," speaks directly to this point's function of empowering *ying*, the nourishing aspect of blood.[19]

The presence of Sp-20 in close proximity to Lu-1 is indicative of the close functional relationship between these two officials. In the creation of blood as nourishment, the lung contributes the essential aspects of respiration while the spleen instills essence gleaned from digestion.[20] "Encircling glory" is indicated for conditions of distension and fullness of the chest and lateral costal region, cough, phlegm, shortness of breath, difficult ingestion, and the desire to drink fluids.[21] Fullness in the chest can be due to either stagnation of *qi* or the presence of damp manifesting as phlegm.

Stagnation of damp is often associated with the consumption of sweet foods as we attempt in vain to feel contented in the moment. Such behavior is based on our failure to identify and fulfill our deeper needs. The presence of dampness in our lungs, as the burden of the earth element, tends to obscure our ability to receive heaven's more essential forms of nourishment gleaned from respiration. Sp-20 can empower the spleen to transform dampness so we may integrate the highest heaven has to offer, let go of the past, and receive heaven's inspiration as breath.

---

### ❖ Sp-21 Great Enveloping
*Da⁴bao¹* Great Enveloping 大包

*This man, with this virtue of his, is about to embrace the 10,000 things and roll them into one.*
– ZHUANGZI[22]

*Therefore the sage embraces the one.*
– DAODEJING, *Chapter 22*[23]

FUNCTIONS

1. Exit point
2. Great *luo* vessel of the spleen

The character *bao* reveals in its etymology the image of a fetus surrounded by the womb. Sp-21 is the great *luo* point that sends collaterals branching around the entire torso and effectively surrounds each person with an enfolding, motherly embrace. These collaterals literally "embrace the one" as they envelop the heart. The function of these vessels is to aid the spleen in fulfilling its role of distributing *qi* and blood throughout all aspects of being. Hence a deficiency in this point's function can be as far reaching in consequence as the effects of starvation.

In Daoism the term *baoyi* (包一) refers to the virtue of the sage who is able to "embrace the one." This metaphor evokes the image of the Daoist making the spiritual journey of restoring original nature *(de)* and returning back to the womb by patterning himself on the primal *dao*. The sage who is "for the belly" and "feeds from the mother" supplements the primordial influences of *jing, qi,* and *shen* by feeding on the unconditional nourishment of *dao*. On the one hand, Sp-21 can empower us to experience life as though we are surrounded by unconditional nourishment and still in the womb. On the other hand, it can empower us to embrace life, as a mother embraces her child. In this way we may truly nourish destiny.

## *Exercises*

1. a. Discuss the functional relationship between HP-7, the earth point within fire, and Sp-2, the fire point within earth, as they relate to the issue of nourishment.
   b. Discuss a possible clinical situation in which both points could be treated in tandem.
2. Discuss how the following point names allude to their function of empowering the earth element to contain nourishment by "holding the center": St-12 ("broken bowl"), St-4 ("earth granary"), St-14 ("storehouse"), Sp-11 ("basket gate"), Sp-17 ("food drain"), and Sp-7 ("leaky valley").
3. How would the point combination Ki-3 and Sp-9 address the functional relationship between the water and the earth elements?
   a. How could this point combination be used to empower fertility?
   b. How could this point combination be used to diminish worry?
4. How does the concept of "knot" elaborated in the discussion of Sp-14 differ as expressed through the earth and wood elements?
   a. In relationship to the above, discuss the point combination Gb-34, St-36, St-8, and CV-12.
   b. How could this point combination be used to treat emotional constraint, worry, and stomachaches?
5. Compare the functions of St-1, "receiving tears," to that of Sp-16, "abdomen sorrow." How do these two points differentially address

the relationship of the emotion sorrow as it impacts our ability to integrate nourishment in life?

6. The need of the infant must be sympathetically intuited by the mother, who perfectly embodies the virtue of reciprocity in her relationship to the infant. To the degree the mother's relationship to the infant is dysfunctional, the grown child may embody a lack of care and sympathy from the mother early in life as digestive distress.
   a. Discuss the relationship among Sp-16, "abdomen sorrow," Sp-18, "heavenly stream," and the earth element's virtue of reciprocity.
   b. In what way does each point on the spleen channel help us embody a functional relationship to "mother" within ourselves?
7. Compare the name and function of Sp-20, "encircling glory," to that of Sp-21, "great enveloping."
8. Discuss the point combination Lu-8, Lu-1, Sp-5, and Sp-20 as it impacts the functional relationship between the spleen and lung officials and our ability to receive and be inspired by essence.
9. Discuss the presence of the character *chong,* meaning "insect," in the names of Sp-10 and Lv-5 as it relates to the functions of these points in treating the blood.

## *NOTES*

1. *ND*, p. 306.
2. Mathews, 1931, p. 945.
3. Mathews, 1931, p. 1176.
4. DeLaney, Leonard, and Kisch, 1989, Sp-3.
5. Mathews, 1931, p. 1176.
6. See *ND*, pp. 284–286.
7. See *ND*, pp. 278–279.
8. Both names are given in Ellis, Wiseman, and Boss, 1989, p. 103.
9. Weiger, 1965, p. 27.
10. Ellis, Wiseman, and Boss, 1989, p. 106.
11. Ibid., p. 107.
12. See *ND*, pp. 326–327.
13. This name according to Ellis et al., 1989, p. 110.
14. Mathews, 1931, p. 130.
15. According to Zhu Danxi in Deadman and Al-Khafaji, 2000, Sp-12.
16. Ellis et al., 1989, p. 112.
17. Deadman and Al-Khafaji, 2000, Sp-15.
18. See *ND*, pp. 281–283.
19. Note that the character *ying* denotes an army camp or barracks. The character depicts "huts with a fence, and two fires, for the kitchen, or to frighten away the wild beasts" (Wieger, 1965, p. 227). From this ancient imagery is derived the notion of the strength that comes from nourishment. The characters *yingyang* (營養) can be translated as "nourishment."
20. For a discussion of the creation of blood, see *ND*, pp. 299–312.
21. Deadman and Al-Khafaji, 2000, Sp-20.
22. Watson, 1964a, p. 27.
23. Chen, 1989, p. 110.

# 36

# COMBINATIONS

EVERY THERAPEUTIC INTERACTION MUST BE ASSESSED entirely on its own merits. The notion of point combinations, fixed groups of points that have a predictable effect, may seem antithetical to this idea. Nonetheless, after years of clinical practice, certain combinations of points have impressed me for their ability to empower specific virtues. In studying this material, it is relatively less important that you memorize or even utilize these specific treatments and relatively more important that you grasp the type of thinking that led to their formulation.

In some instances, I provide herbal formulas that emulate the quality of the acupuncture point combination under discussion. This further elaborates the nature of the combination and reinforces a point selection. In general, these point combinations are constitutional. That is, 99 percent of the time I use a given combination on a patient whose constitutional official is represented by one or more of the points in the treatment. For example, if I was treating Gb-40, Gb-21, SI-4, and SI-7, the patient would likely be either wood or fire constitutionally or be evidencing a strong compensatory imbalance in those functional domains.

You can utilize the treatments offered here on their own terms or modify them to better apply to a given patient. Because of the functional breadth of each official, the psychospiritual states discussed here are addressed to some degree by any point on a given meridian. For example, later I provide a point combination I use to address the issue of helping a patient discern "roots from branches" in life. However, you must appreciate that every point on the liver and gallbladder meridian has the potential to empower this virtue to the degree it is appropriate in a specific therapeutic context.

I advise you to integrate all you know from your own clinical experience and tradition of practice to each point selection I have provided in order to make it your own. The function of any given point is infinite, and its efficacy for empowering any specific virtue therapeutically depends on the overall context of a specific treatment, which always includes the quality of your own awareness and intention.

---

### *Empowering Vision Within the Heart*

| | | |
|---|---|---|
| **Lv-1** | *Dadui* | Great Esteem |
| **HP-9** | *Zhongchong* | Rushing into the Center |
| or | | |
| **Ht-9** | *Xiaochong* | Little Rushing In |

Lv-1 is the horary and transmitting point on the liver meridian. As such, it empowers the specific virtues associated with the liver such as vision, clarity, and perspective. These virtues can be empowered within the liver itself by treating Lv-1 or within any other *yin* official if its receiving point for the influence of wood is treated simultaneously with Lv-1.

The heart is said to govern through insight and understanding, yet often the clarity of the heart's vision is obscured when intimate relationships are concerned. This point combination can empower the perspective of the liver within the heart or heart protector officials. In this way we can integrate the analytic facilities of the wood element with the capacity for intuition and inner knowing that emanates from the heart. This can be ideal for the person who makes intimate connections claiming to "follow my heart" without ever affording himself a realistic perspective of who might be coming across the drawbridge into his inner domain.

By empowering a perspective that penetrates into the roots of who we are, Lv-1 can support us to enter relationships based on self-esteem rather than vainly attempting to quell the heart's desire for connection and intimacy. For only to the degree that we truly know ourselves are we capable of ever knowing another. Because both points in this combination are nail points (*jing*-well points), this treatment is very stimulating to the mind and the nervous system. A function of *jing*-well points, through their action on the nervous system, is to empower insight and to bring the effect of a specific treatment directly into conscious awareness.[1]

I pair Lv-1 with Ht-9 when my primary goal is to empower insight into matters of deep existential importance. In this scenario, the patient is grappling with issues of perspective relative to the heart's discernment of purpose in life. I treat HP-9 when the issue is a lack of perspective regarding intimacy. In this case a patient's habitual need for or avoidance of relationship is based on her response to past pain and her mind's desire for either immediate gratification or safety.

---

### *The Discernment of Roots and Branches*

**Lv-1** *Dadui* Great Esteem
**Lv-14** *Qimen* Gate of Hope

As the channel's wood and horary point, Lv-1 empowers fundamental vision of what binds us to those aspects of self that cannot be compromised for they root us into our very ground of being. The location of Lv-1 on the medial nail point of the big toe suggests its function of rooting us to the earth and providing a quality of stability for growth that is grounded in a vision of our depths.

In discussing the function of the liver meridian, think of human beings as plants. A plant may have its branches pruned so it grows tall and is able to channel its resources efficiently to attain new heights. Each branch represents a possible diversion that our minds may take en route to a goal. Certainly it can hurt to have a particular branch pruned, just as it can be difficult to let go of a possible direction our lives may take out of deference to correct action based on self-knowledge in the moment. However, by choosing actions consistent with manifesting our inner plan and not pursuing extraneous paths, we are better able to manifest our goals in life.

The name of Lv-1, "great esteem," suggests self-esteem is based on a vision of what is fundamentally important in our life. Branches can be pruned to effectively stimulate growth, but roots may never be cut without compromising the integrity of all the external manifestations that flow from them. For example, a general rule of thumb is that if a patient has one apparent genetic anomaly, it will likely have also manifested in other ways that are less apparent. For every root (gene), there are codes for many branches (physical manifestations). The effect of taking actions in life that compromise fundamental aspects of self is to erode the inner virtue of self-esteem. Having compromised our fundamental purpose, we may eventually lose all discernment regarding the true nature of self. This deficit can manifest along with poor vision, confusion, and a sense of being lost in life as though we are just a leaf blown by the wind. Lack of self-esteem internally often accompanies belligerence externally as we irrationally project our feelings of being compromised on others for the slightest perceived transgression.

In contrast to Lv-1, Lv-14 is the highest and final point on the liver meridian. Named "gate of hope," this point governs the aspect of being we call aspiration. Lv-14 is located on the rib cage directly over the diaphragm. The diaphragm is the representation within us of all walls we encounter in life that impede our progress. This wall in effect separates the middle and upper *jiaos* and offers a potential obstacle to the exit/entry flow of *qi* from Lv-14 to Lu-1, "central treasury," a point that governs the virtue of inspiration. Creative growth in life is often met with initial resistance, and the health of our wood element can in large part be assessed by how we react to the various types of walls we encounter on our journey.

The virtues of aspiration and hope as engendered by Lv-14 empower our vision of the outermost branches of our life as we strive toward heaven. Sometimes we humans use hope dysfunctionally in order to avoid taking appropriate actions in the moment that might help move us toward our goal. In fact, a powerful therapeutic tool is to suggest to the wood constitutional type that there "is no hope," and only by taking action in the world consistent with his inner vision will he ever achieve his goals in a fruitful manner.

Lv-1 empowers the vision of where we have come from, and Lv-14 grants a vision of where we are headed. By combining Lv-1 with Lv-14, we may clear the liver channel of the stagnation that obscures our innate striving to manifest our purpose in the world. In this way, a quality of vision may be granted that is grounded in our deepest roots and penetrates to our highest branches.

---

### *Nourishing the Heart*

| | | |
|---|---|---|
| **Sp-4** | *Gongsun* | Prince's Grandson |
| **HP-6** | *Neiguan* | Inner Frontier Gate |
| **Ki-16** | *Huangshu* | Vitals Correspondence |
| **CV-14** | *Juque* | Great Tower |
| or | | |
| **CV-15** | *Jiuwei* | Dovetail |

Here Sp-4 and HP-6 are used as the master and couple point of the *chongmai.* Whereas the conception and governor vessels represent the dual poles of heaven and earth, *chongmai* represents the integration of these two influences as they nourish both the *qi* and blood of humanity. *Qi* empowers us to manifest our good works in the world, and blood is that by which the fruits of our labors nourish us.[2]

The name of Ki-16, *huangshu,* refers to the area just beneath the diaphragm around the xiphoid process. This is a key reference area for the heart and heart protector, containing the *mu* points for each, CV-14 and CV-15, respectively. This area is likely to feel knotted and tight when painful separation from a loved one is accompanied by feelings of betrayal. In such circumstances we tend to feel as though we have been "shot in the heart" or "stabbed in the back." After such a heartbreak patients may report feeling a hole in the area of the heart accompanied by feelings of emptiness.

I use this combination of points to empower feelings of emotional warmth predicated on nourishment of the heart. I base the distinction of whether to utilize CV-14 or CV-15 in this treatment on pulse diagnosis, and my choice depends on my determination of which official, the heart or heart protector, is most *qi* or blood deficient. The patient who needs her heart tonified with CV-14 tends to appear to be relatively more grim and to possess a deeply ashen complexion and a sadness that is pervasive in all realms of expression. This patient's sorrow is likely to center on relatively deep existential issues regarding loss of connection to heaven itself. Patients who might benefit more from CV-15 exemplify sadness centering around the issue of lack of fulfillment in intimate relationships. Their heartbreak is relatively more likely to concern feelings of disappointment or betrayal by a lover.

---

### *Empower Speech*

| | | |
|---|---|---|
| **St-9** | *Renying* | People Welcome |
| **St-42** | *Chongyang* | Surging *Yang* |

St-9 is the heavenly window point on the stomach meridian, and St-42 is the channel's source point. Source points are used to good advantage in conjunction with window points to temper their potentially powerful psychospiritual effects by placing them under the control of nature as it governs homeostasis.

Located at the level of the voice box, St-9 empowers speech in a way that builds the virtue of integrity. The dual aspect of this point's function is that it can empower us to set limits regarding the amount of energy we are willing to give to others as well as our ability to speak up and ask for our needs to be met.[3] People who are ingratiating have the habit of swallowing resentment each time they say "yes" to fulfilling the needs of another when they should have drawn a boundary instead. Eventually they come to experience a tightness in the throat, known as "plum pit *qi*," commensurate with the degree of pressure and stagnation associated with their undelivered communication.

The character *chong* (沖) refers to the whirling abyss of *qi* that blends the dual poles of heaven and earth. It depicts a geyser shooting up toward heaven and reflects the rising nature of *yang*. As our digestive systems abstract nourishment from life, nutritive *qi (ying)* is created. *Yingqi* must rise to the heart where it is imprinted with *shen* to form blood. Speech based on personal integrity reflects the core commitments of an individual that are nourished by correct speech and action. As we take actions and speak words commensurate with our core commitments, our spirit evolves toward heaven. A function of St-42 is to ensure that our evolution is grounded, assuring our nourishment during the process of life. Together St-42 and St-9 can ground our speech into the core integrity empowered by the earth element.

The character *chong* also may be translated as "to blend" or "to mix." The formula Bianxia Houpu Tang (Pinellia and Magnolia) circulates the *qi* from CV-11 up to CV-21 located on the throat at the level of St-9. This is the premier formula for resolving plum pit *qi* and highly supportive of empowering integrity in speech. The virtue empowered by this formula is that of "tact" as we learn to speak in a way that establishes a healthy boundary without appearing selfish or imposing.[4]

---

### *Strengthen Resolve*

| | | |
|---|---|---|
| **St-36** | *Zusanli* | Leg Three Miles |
| **Bl-54 (40)** | *Weizhong* | Central Equilibrium |
| **GV-3** | *Yangguan* | Lumbar *Yang* Gate |
| **Bl-10** | *Tianzhu* | Heavenly Pillar |

The foundation of this point combination is the pairing of St-36 with Bl-54 (40), both of which are earth points on their respective meridians. St-36 is the transmitting point and thus can nourish the virtues of the earth element within any other *yang* official when its earth point is treated simultaneously. The earth and receiving point on the bladder meridian

(Bl-54) is treated simultaneously. St-36 and Bl-54 are located on the front and rear of the knee, respectively. The knee is a foundational joint in the body for empowering the virtues of strength and stability in the face of life's difficulties. Thus people who lack integrity and collapse in the face of such challenges are called "weak kneed." The pivotal role played by Bl-54 in empowering integrity and stability is alluded to in the point's name, "central equilibrium."

Earth controls water across the *ke* cycle, and this treatment utilizes this relationship to reinforce the will *(zhi)* of the water element. Overwhelming circumstances in life may be likened to a river overflowing and eroding its banks. The combination of St-36 with Bl-54 can be compared to bringing sandbags to the banks of the river in order to contain it and help it channel its life-giving resources more effectively. Note that when animals are frightened, they often urinate. In this way they embody their sense of fear and feelings of being overwhelmed as "flooding." Hence frequent urination often accompanies anxiety in response to stress.

GV-3 is selected to strengthen the lower back, a reference area for the bladder containing its *shu* point (Bl-28) and the home of the will that resides in Bl-47 (52). Bl-10, "heavenly pillar," is chosen as the heavenly window point on the bladder meridian. As the window point, it empowers inner strength and resolve and can help illuminate the inner nature of our fears. Often free-floating anxiety accompanies our projection of an unknown or repressed fear onto present events that provoke stress. Bl-10 can help us respond to present circumstances on their own terms without having our interpretation of them colored habitually by past fear.

The overall nature of this treatment empowers the type of posture in life that a martial artist might take in "ready" position. Knees locked, back straight, and head held high, the patient is ready to face life as a warrior. On occasion I may choose to needle GV-4 in circumstances where the patient is experiencing fear and hesitation in "stepping up to the plate" and taking a significant action in life. Such an action might be a proposal of marriage, filing for divorce, accepting a job, or changing careers. I may also choose to pair a conception vessel point from CV-4 to CV-7 in order to strengthen the patient's resolve and fortitude as it exists in his *hara.*

This particular combination embodies a principle that I seek in many of my point selections and herbal prescriptions. The distal points chosen—St-36 and Bl-54 (40)—root the treatment to establish its functional basis in the patient's constitutional dynamics. I then select one or more points in the center of the body (GV-3) to touch the physical and functional centers there. Finally, I treat a proximal point on the head (Bl-10) or upper part of the body to address the relatively more spirit-level aspects of the dynamic being addressed. Hence there is an integrity to the treatment from top to bottom that allows spiritual concerns to be addressed in a relatively grounded way.

---

### *Harmonize Judgment*

| | | |
|---|---|---|
| **Gb-40** | *Qiuxu* | Wilderness Mound |
| **Gb-24** | *Ri and Yue* | Sun and Moon (Illumination) |

As the source point on the gallbladder meridian, Gb-40 touches all the general qualities of function empowered by the gallbladder official. The inner function of Gb-40 is to ease constraint in a way that yields perspective. Hence its function can be likened to taking patients up a hill in the wilderness so they can see over the trees and obtain a perspective on where they have been, where they are, and where they are going. Gb-24 is the *mu* point on the gallbladder meridian. Taken together, the characters *ri* (sun) and *yue* (moon) yield the character *ming,* meaning "illumination" in the sense of enlightenment. The inner function of Gb-24 is to empower the breadth of perspective held by the sage that enables him to comprehend the unity in apparent opposites.

This combination of points is ideal for the person who values being right above all else. Able only to consider her own limited perspective, she feels torn apart by injustices perpetrated by others who fail to embrace her point of view. Such feelings of frustration and conflict may be embodied as tightness in the diaphragm and the region of CV-11 to CV-15. Pain and pressure can also be felt in the area of Gb-24 along with burning in the epigastrium that embodies her internalized resentment.

---

### *Resolve Bitterness and Resentment and Engender Forgiveness*

| | | |
|---|---|---|
| **Gb-41** | *Zulinqi* | Foot Just Before Tears |
| **Gb-16** | *Muchuang* | Eye Window |
| **SI-3** | *Houxi* | Back Ravine |
| **SI-6** | *Yanglao* | Nourishing the Old |

Here Gb-41 as wood within wood is paired with SI-3 as the receiving point for the influence of wood within fire. Gb-41 is ideal for harmonizing resentment in those who are "green with envy" because they always seem to see what others have and covet it for themselves. The grass always appears greener elsewhere as they grow increasingly frustrated to the point of tears. Failing to appreciate their own lot in life, they become resentful of others and of heaven who they view as unjustly depriving them of their due. As the gallbladder's horary point, "just before tears" can help broaden perspective and empower a quality of vision that is less constrained by jealousy.

As the wood point on the small intestine meridian, SI-3 can empower the virtues of the wood element, perspective and benevolence, within the functioning of the small intestine official. The functions of the small intestine in sorting and the gallbladder in making decisions are interdependent. If the gallbladder becomes constrained by the limited perspectives of jealousy and envy, the small intestine may not be able to convey the essence of the heart accurately into the world. Here sarcasm and bitterness can result as speech and actions that no longer clearly reflect the heart's intentions. Presenting physical signs and sensations may include a bitter taste in the mouth, cold sores, tight shoulders, limited mobility in turning the neck left to right, burning in the region of CV-15, pressure under the ribs laterally, and a bright red tongue, indicating the accumulation of heat from constraint. The pulse positions corresponding to the gallbladder and small intestine are expected to be tight (indicating constraint) and slippery. Here the slippery quality indicates damp heat, which can be the embodiment of resentment and bitterness.

Gb-16, "eye window," helps resolve judgments against self for past failures and against others for perceived past injustices that we harbor resentment over.[5] Located directly over the eyes on top of the forehead, Gb-16 empowers the highest aspects of vision that correspond to the influence of heaven in enabling us to find the highest lesson that past pain holds for us. Once we see past difficulties with a fresh perspective, we may find the clarity to forgive and move on in a way that is less burdened by the past.

SI-6, "nourishing the old," is the *xi*-cleft point on the small intestine meridian and helps move stagnation within the functional domain of that official. Hence bitterness accumulated from old heartbreaks that smothers the heart's flame can be burned away by increasing the small intestine's ability to sort pure from impure.

## *Questions*

1. Discuss how adding SI-19 and GB-4 to this combination could help address grinding of the teeth, tinnitus, and an inability to listen to another's point of view.

2. Discuss how each of these symptoms might present with the functional dynamics of the point combination discussed here.

---

### *Mania and Depression: Ascent to the Summit, Return from the Mountain*

| | | |
|---|---|---|
| **GV-10** | *Lingtai* | Spiritual Tower |
| **GV-11** | *Shendao* | Spirit Path |
| **Ht-7** | *Shenmen* | Spirit Gate |

This point combination represents a functional core that points could be added to depending on the patient's presentation during a given treatment. I use Ht-7 here as a distal point to stabilize the heart and moderate the effects of the other two governor vessel points. Think of mania and depression as existing on a continuum of heart dysfunction. "Spirit gate" helps create stability so the opening and closing of the heart's gate occurs relatively effortlessly as presided over by the virtue of *wuwei* and is relatively less driven by the mind's habituated desires.

In Daoism, *lingtai*, as present in the name of GV-10, is a term that refers to the heart. Mencius recounts the tale of how the multitudes flocked to wise King Wan as if they were his children and built his "spiritual tower" *(lingtai)* in one day. This is a prime example of the effectiveness of the role of the sage. The people "rejoiced" to do this work because the sage empowered the people so they took pleasure in aligning themselves with his purpose. Thus by empowering the people, the emperor's own heart was in turn rectified.

This tale of the *lingtai* brings to mind the Daoist folktale of the forlorn governor who could not see over the trees surrounding his residence. So he built a tower to enable him to gain perspective on his kingdom.[6] Like the tower, GV-10 is a point that facilitates the perspective and "penetrating insight" of the heart.

We can become addicted to the insight afforded by peak states of awareness. If we do not come down "off the mountain" (see GV-10 earlier) and make use of our knowledge in the world, what use is the wisdom acquired there? Hence GV-11 helps ground peak states of awareness and place our spirit back in the world on a path of action. The shock of divorce, the loss of a loved one, or receiving a terminal diagnosis are all occurrences that may shake up our view of reality and provide a glimpse of original nature. This glimpse occasionally produces a "high," or, in other words, a manic reaction. This reaction may be characterized by the momentary experience of an all-empowering vision of the significance and interrelationships of the events in our life. The vision may be experienced in a way that had previously been hidden by our mistaken interpretation of reality.

Consider the nature of a significant intimate relationship. The plot of the relationship consists of all the individual events from the moment the two parties meet until they part ways. The theme of the relationship is the nature of the lesson to be learned from the connection. While engaged in the relationship, both parties are so involved in the events of the plot that the theme often eludes them. Imagine that one party in this relationship becomes dissatisfied and, over time, grows apart from the other party. Eventually, the dissatisfied partner will feel ready to leave the relationship and notify the other person of the decision to do so. By definition, the theme of the relationship is what ties together every event from the first moment to the last. Presented with the end of the relationship, the partner being left may be shocked out of involvement with the plot. Now that the relationship is over, an all-embracing comprehension of the theme may occur in one instant. The implications of all the subtle communications and meanings that previously signaled the other partner's dissatisfaction become painfully clear.

Generally, the individual experiencing this vision appears inappropriately happy, given the seriousness of the life events in which he or she is engaged. This can be interpreted as denial. The source of this "empty joy" results from the all-embracing vision of past events coupled with feelings of unlimited potential for the future. Initially, this artificial feeling of joy fluctuates with depression, and, as the person heals, these fluctuations diminish. I have often used GV-11 with GV-10 for quieting the heart and sedating tendencies toward mania as well as for uplifting the heart during depression. Note that these are both important points on the governor vessel meridian for addressing the functional relationship between the heart's *ling* and *shen* spirits. These points are located on the dorsal aspect of the body directly behind Ki-23, Ki-24, and Ki-25, whose importance in addressing the balance between *ling* and *shen* I discuss later.

Patients may experience pain and muscle spasms around these points, which are all referred from a tightly held heart. The area around the points can feel either warmer or cooler than the surrounding flesh. Excessive warmth can be interpreted as the result of unexpressed desires repressed within the heart that generate heat. Coolness can reflect a heart fire that is extinguished and weary from past sorrow. In this regard it is often beneficial to treat these points with moxa, having the effect of warming a cold heart by increasing the functional presence and influence of heart *yang*. These two points can be beneficial when treating any change in stability on the pulse as indicated by the parameters of rate, rhythm, amplitude, or intensity. In this case stability is supported by aligning the heart with the governor vessel, the central axis of *yang* in the body and a foundational pillar between the axis of heaven and earth.

---

*Return Fire to Depths of Self*

| | | |
|---|---|---|
| **TH-4** | *Yangqi* | *Yang* Pond |
| **TH-23** | *Sizhukong* | Silk Bamboo Hollow |
| **HP-6** | *Neiguan* | Inner Frontier Gate |

TH-4 and HP-6 are the source and *luo* points on their respective meridians. Together they integrate the function of the fire element as it concerns the appropriate balance of boundaries in social and intimate relationships. By treating TH-4, we are stimulating the function of the three heater to regulate our internal balance of fire in a way that empowers an appropriate relationship to our environment. "Inner frontier gate" is a point that opens the gate to the heart, allowing for intimacy based on compassion toward ourselves and others.

The three heater governs the body's thermostat, ensuring that for every change outside of us there is a corresponding change inside. Ideally, boundaries in relationships, like all homeostatic mechanisms, should function beneath the level of our conscious awareness. As we encounter people who are safe to engage with, our hearts should open accordingly without us having to figure out with our minds how close we want to be. Instead we merely acknowledge the reality of how open our hearts are in the presence of another and accept the quality of the relationship for what it is.

When the three heater official becomes dysfunctional, it can compel us to try to make contact with others in an attempt to be liked. In this circumstance, a false face is worn in the world as we grow weary trying in vain to win the affections of others. The three heater is the outermost official in the fire element, and TH-23 is the last point on the three heater meridian. We can interpret its name, "silk bamboo hollow," metaphorically as referring to the relationship between the flowers (silk) of the bamboo plant that attract attention to its outside (face) and the inside of the plant that is hollow and therefore without ego.

Together these three points may nourish the heart of those who are weary expending all their *qi* socially in an attempt to be liked or to avoid intimate contact. TH-4 is used to ground TH-23, which returns the superficial and external expression of fire back into the interior aided by the actions of HP-6, the "inner frontier gate."

### *Soothing the Mediator*

| | | |
|---|---|---|
| **St-36** | *Zusanli* | Leg Three Miles |
| **Gb-34** | *Yanglingquan* | *Yang* Mound Spring |
| **Gb-24** | *Ri* and *Yue* | Sun and Moon, Illumination |
| **Lv-13** | *Zhangmen* | Chapter Gate |
| **Lv-14** | *Qimen* | Gate of Hope |
| **CV-11** | *Jianli* | Inner Strength[7] |

ALTERNATE POINTS

| | | |
|---|---|---|
| **CV-12** | *Zhongwan* | Middle Duct |
| **CV-15** | *Jiuwei* | Dovetail |
| **HP-6** | *Neiguan* | Inner Frontier Gate |

The strategy of this point selection is to harmonize the relationship between wood and earth so the process of growth is nurturing and we feel less inclined to take on the position of mediator in other people's conflicts. This pattern is often found in adults who, as children, were in the position of being trapped between fighting parents. In order to preserve the harmony and the integrity of the family, the child attempted to mediate the parents' conflict. Over time, the child absorbed the parents' angst, and the functional dynamic of the conflict eventually comes to be embodied as a disharmony between the wood and earth elements. Although they have left their family situation, these children as adults retain the tendency to play the role of mediator between conflicting parties.

I consider the appendix to be a functional ancillary to the gallbladder. The appendix is said to absorb anger, resentment, and undigested pain. Patients who lose their appendix early in life often do so because of stress that was internalized from familial conflicts. Generally, I find that once the appendix is removed, the gallbladder takes over its function of absorbing the resentment that comes from mediating conflicts. Eventually, it too may become ill and need to be removed. Once the gallbladder is removed, if there is no change in awareness and behavior, resentment moves deeper into the liver official, and serious illness is often the result.

In this point combination, St-36 and Gb-34 are chosen as the transmitting and receiving points for the influence of the earth element. Think of these points as harmonizing the natural relationship between earth (St-36) as it nurtures growth and wood (Gb-34) as it aspires continually toward its goals. In this way constraint in the process of growth can be eased so the earth is better able to support the height the tree aspires to. The wood element empowers the virtues of clarity and decisiveness as it implements our inner plan. Hence wood must be able to hold the vision of a goal during our entire journey from inception to end. Contrast this to the nature of earth, which empowers the process that takes place between the moments of conception and completion. These two elements, both necessary for healthy growth, often conflict with each other if one predominates.

The name of Gb-24, "sun and moon," alludes to the function of wood in empowering the ability to discern between choices. Trapped between warring parties, the wood element can embody conflict in the region of Gb-24. This "tearing apart" can present as a knotted feeling from CV-11 to CV-15, with tightness ascending through the chest, a burning feeling in this area, and a sour taste in the mouth evidencing esophageal reflux. These conditions often accompany the obsessive need to be right and justify our point of view and can become embodied sympathetically by the mediator in response to the stress of the situation. This pattern is similar to, and can overlap with, the dynamic discussed earlier for empowering speech (St-42 and St-9). The mediation of a conflict can require a fair amount of ingratiation if we do not have the inner strength to stand our ground.

Lv-13 and Lv-14 are the *mu* points on their respective meridians. The meeting point of the liver and spleen officials, Lv-13, "chapter gate," helps relieve feelings of stuckness that constrain the free-flowing nature of creativity. Lv-14, "gate of hope," relieves frustration by helping empower a higher perspective that can help us see past our current dilemma and better receive the influence of heaven. Receiving heaven is the goal of all growth, symbolized by the journey of our *qi* past the diaphragm to reach Lu-1 as it represents the portal to heaven as embodied within us.

You can choose either CV-11 or CV-12 to further open the center and ease constraint. Generally I choose CV-11 if I think *qi* stagnation and excess heat are the central physiological issue, and I choose CV-12 if I think *yin* deficiency predominates. I may also decide to utilize CV-15 and HP-6 with this point combination. Often, when conflict is internalized, a person's heart can feel battered. Burning at the area of CV-15 and tightness in the chest can indicate that bitterness accumulated from conflict is attacking the heart. Treating CV-15, the heart protector's *mu* point, can help fortify the heart protector and thus relax the heart. HP-6, the "inner frontier gate," can help bring the heart's insight and compassion to self and others in resolving life's conflicts. It is also highly effective for easing constraint in the region from CV-14 to CV-17 that defines our "inner frontier."

### *Ease Judgment and Broaden Perspective*

| | | |
|---|---|---|
| **Gb-40** | *Qiuxu* | Wilderness Mound |
| **Gb-21** | *Jianjing* | Shoulder Well |
| **SI-4** | *Wangu* | Wrist Bone |
| **SI-7** | *Zhizheng* | Upright Branch |
| **GV-14** | *Dazhui* | Great Hammer |

This combination overlaps the previous one in intention. Healthy growth must occur in a way that is unconstrained by excess striving. If growth is motivated by reaction to anger, we can feel compelled to fight against every perceived impediment to our chosen direction in life as though it was an injustice being perpetrated against us. In this way the mind of the wood element can become habitually concerned with being right. Such a limited perspective can manifest as tightness along the gallbladder and small intestine channels as they pass through the shoulder and neck. If the gallbladder's facility of decision making is compromised, the small intestine official's ability to sort in a healthy way is also likely to suffer. Bitterness, resentment, sarcasm, and spite can present as emotional toxicity accrued from the gallbladder and small intestine's failure to clarify the *qi.* These emotions tend to fester poisoning, both in thought and verbal expression, in the ways I discussed in Chapter 2.

If wood is constrained by feelings of jealousy, envy, and belligerence, growth tends to be driven in a way that causes conflict internally and externally in life. If we attempt to use force to break through obstacles, rather than finding creative ways around them, the *qi* of the wood element tends to become constrained as it rises through the neck and shoulder region. The flexibility of our neck embodies our ability to turn our head in a way that yields perspective and the consideration of different viewpoints.

Both Gb-40 and SI-4 are the source points on their respective meridians, and I use them here to empower a broad spectrum of virtues associated with the wood and fire elements. The pairing of Gb-40 with Gb-21 helps provide perspective (Gb-40) in a way that relaxes the shoulders and neck (Gb-21). One function of Gb-21 is to direct rising gallbladder *qi* downward, which can help relieve strain in the neck muscles that results from excessive striving. The pairing of SI-4 with SI-7 helps the small intestine to clarify issues while venting pressure accumulated in the sorting process to the outside. As the *luo* point on the small intestine meridian, SI-7 helps eliminate such functional heat and pressure by venting stagnant heat and *qi* to the exterior.

I find GV-14, "great hammer," to be an excellent point for opening up the shoulders and upper spine. It can be useful whenever there is a sense that pains in the arm radiating along the small intestine meridian are coming from impingement in the cervical area. As the meeting point of the *yang* channels, sedating GV-14 can help slow the rising of wood *qi* so it does not overwhelm and constrict the muscles of the shoulders and neck to limit our perspective.

---

### *Get* Hun *Moving: Kidney Stones*

| | | |
|---|---|---|
| **Ki-1** | *Yongquan* | Bubbling Spring |
| **Lv-8** | *Ququan* | Crooked Spring |
| **Ht-9** | *Shaochong* | Little Rushing In |
| **HP-9** | *Zhongchong* | Rushing into the Middle |

The left half of the *ke* cycle represents the evolutionary journey of the *hun* spirit as it rises from the primordial depths and ascends toward heaven. The *hun* is an expression of our *jing, qi,* and *shen,* which reside in the kidney, liver, and heart, respectively. The inherent strength of each individual's will *(zhi)* to persevere in the face of life's challenges is set at conception. If a person becomes resigned and suppresses his evolutionary instinct, the *zhi* will eventually collapse. This dynamic typifies the husband/wife imbalance, as previously discussed.[8] I have found this selection of points to be effective in resurrecting the will and initiating its ascent upward along the *ke* cycle through wood and fire. This movement is synonymous with resurrecting a person's will to live and to strive without compromise to manifest her innate potential.

Ki-1, "bubbling spring," is the wood point on the kidney meridian. Its inner function may be likened to pulling the roots of a tree down into the depths where fresh resources can be tapped to renew growth. "Bubbling spring" is a strongly tonifying point that initiates a rising movement in *qi* from the bottom of the foot up toward the head. This movement can be enhanced by Lv-8, the tonification point on the liver channel, which pulls potential up and out of our depths. Water imparts flexibility to wood, and "crooked spring" helps impart the virtue of flexibility while simultaneously keeping us focused on our goals. In this way we may avoid resignation.

If we liken water to the seed, and wood to the flourishing growth of spring, the fire element can be likened to the blossoming of a flower during the summer. This treatment is completed by choosing either the tonification point on either the heart (Ht-9) or heart protector (HP-9) meridian. The appropriate wood point draws the rising *qi* from wood to fire and helps empower the opening of the heart. My selection of either Ht-9 or Hp-9 depends both on pulse diagnosis as well as my sense of the patient. If I am strictly trying to resurrect the left-hand pulses, I choose Ht-9. If I am trying to resurrect the will relative to the establishment of intimacy, I choose HP-9. This choice may be appropriate when the will has collapsed after remaining in a abusive relationship. In this case a patient may have lost his ability to trust his own judgment or to risk intimacy again.

When performing this treatment I generally expect the pulses of the left hand to be deep and feeble, indicating a deficiency of *qi* and *yang* on the entire left half of the *sheng* cycle. In this case each of the points would be tonified in the order Ki-1, Lv-8, and then Ht-9. On several occasions, however, I have performed this treatment on patients evidencing an excess kidney pulse when the left middle (liver) and distal positions (heart) have been either deficient or just as excessive. In such a scenario the left proximal pulse corresponding to the kidney meridian is tense, indicating stagnation, and pounding, indicating heat. Interestingly, I have had three different patients pass kidney stones within twenty-four hours of this treatment. In each case, after the patient returned for treatment the kidney pulse lost its intensity and the middle and distal positions filled out nicely. Here the kidney stones represented an internalized block that effectively prevented the water from generating wood and ultimately fire.[9]

---

## *Healing Damaged Goods*

LUNG OFFICIAL

| | | |
|---|---|---|
| **Lu-9** | *Taiyuan* | Very Great Abyss |
| **Lu-6** | *Kongzui* | Greatest Hole |
| **Lu-3** | *Tianfu* | Heavenly Palace |

LARGE INTESTINE OFFICIAL

| | | |
|---|---|---|
| **LI-1** | *Shangyang* | Merchant *Yang* |
| or | | |
| **LI-4** | *Hegu* | Joining of the Valleys |
| **LI-7** | *Wenliu* | Warm Current |
| **LI-17** | *Tianding* | Heavenly Vessel |
| or | | |
| **LI-18** | *Shuixue* | Support and Rush Out |

In dysfunction, the metal element's virtue of empowering purity can become distorted into perfectionism. Each of us inevitably experiences pain in life, but the perfectionist interprets her pain as proof she is worthless. Her mind is always able to find and focus on a fatal flaw that renders her inner value worthless. Such lack of self-worth tends to be projected externally as she feels unacknowledged by others in life, which is then interpreted as further proof that her spirit is somehow soiled. Obsession with purity can lead the perfectionist to suppress any aspects of self that are considered unclean. Self-righteousness is the result as her suppression is projected externally on others and she wages a holy war against their real or imagined faults.

In truth, no life event is able to do more than obscure the diamond of constitution placed within at conception. The following points can empower us to appreciate the inherent perfection within that no life event can ever touch. In this way we may stay receptive to beauty in this perfectly imperfect world. Generally, I treat these dynamics through the officials of the metal element. As a *yin* official, the lung is more likely to be concerned with issues of self-worth, and the large intestine, as a *yang* official, is more likely to project feelings of unworthiness externally on others.

### *Treating the Lung Official*

Lu-9 is the source point on the lung meridian and connects each of us to the abyss of *dao* that resides at our center. The infinite nature of this abyss is that in receiving all things it is never filled. Cut off from the nature of both self and *dao,* the habituated metal element compels us to mistake that essence which is most precious in life as vacuity. Lu-9 as the assembly point of the pulse can empower us to surrender our grief to the void and, in being truly empty, to be reinspired by the breath of *dao*. The name of Lu-6, "greatest hole," also alludes to the *dao* as the abyss that receives all things. As the channel's *xi*-cleft point, Lu-6 moves stagnation from the past that does not correspond to true self. In this way feelings of sulliedness that tarnish the virtue of self-worth can be let go of and surrendered to the abyss. "Heavenly palace," as the heavenly window point on the lung meridian, can empower us to embrace the wisdom that heaven, through its grace, only sees the highest within us. So inspired we may find the strength to accept our failings and pain and abstract the highest value they impart to our lives.

### *Treating the Large Intestine Official*

The nature of metal when it is habituated is to become rigid and break. The intention of this point combination is to empower metal to embrace the fluidity of mercury, the Daoist symbol of flexible consciousness. Hence the utilization of moxa during this protocol can be particularly effective in helping warm metal so it may flow. In this case, I ground the treatment of the large intestine with either LI-1, the channel's metal point, or with LI-4, the source point. Metal is associated with the fall season when the weights and measures were adjusted in the marketplace to ensure that transactions were conducted fairly. LI-1, "merchant *yang,*" addresses the metal element's virtue of understanding the essential worth of things as any good merchant must. In this way those concepts that we hold regarding self and others which do not hold value can be let go of because the price we pay for holding on to them is too dear.

In accordance with *Yijing* hexagram 15, "modesty," LI-4 helps harmonize feelings of pretentiousness and helps us to nourish those lower aspects of self that are not sufficiently valued. As the channel's source point, LI-4 empowers us to let go of all that no longer serves in life while retaining everything that still holds value. Hence we may have an easier time finding quality both within ourselves and in others. In accordance with its name, LI-7, "warm current," helps thaw frozen metal so it may flow and give rise to the water element. As the channel's *xi*-cleft point, LI-7 supports us in letting go of stagnation that obscures our diamond of original nature.

LI-17 and LI-18 are located on the neck, a region that mediates the relationship between the head (mind) and the heart. The inner function of "heavenly vessel" (LI-17) is related to the text of *Yijing* hexagram 50, "the cauldron." Here we are told that in order to receive the spirits during ritual, the vessel must be cleaned of all past stagnation. LI-18, as a heavenly window point, can empower us to find the highest that past experience has to offer us so we can let go of mundanity that has been carried along and move on feeling both lighter and cleaner within ourselves.

---

### *Releasing Primordial Fear*[10]

| | | |
|---|---|---|
| **Ki-6** | *Zhaohai* | Illuminated Sea |
| **Ki-27** | *Shufu* | Storehouse |
| **Ki-13** | *Zihu* | Door of Infants |

I have found this combination to be effective for both existential terror arising from the unconscious past as well as for alleviating shock from recent physical or emotional traumas such as a car accident or loss of a relationship as occurs in divorce.

Ki-6 is the master point of the *yin* motility vessel and the conception vessel. The eight extra meridians represent the primordial depths on which the structural foundations of our life are built. The name of Ki-6, "illuminated sea," makes reference to the virtue of the sage who is capable of self-reflection in a way that engenders illumination. Like a perfectly still lake, the mind of the sage comprehends with perfect fidelity all that is reflected in it. Hence Ki-6 can quiet the mind by removing the surface ripples caused by fear and anxiety that emanate from our depths. Ki-6 lies over Ki-2, "blazing valley," the fire point on the kidney meridian. It is the insight of the heart as empowered by fire that illuminates our unconscious depths in a way that assuages fear.

Ki-27 is the highest and final point on the kidney meridian. The destiny of the water element is the transformation of fear into wisdom. The *jing*'s ascent up the spine toward the head where it empowers wisdom through the production or marrow can be frozen by the presence of fear. The names of the kidney points from Ki-18 through Ki-27 evoke an entry into our spiritual depths that reminds me of the river journey taken in Joseph Conrad's novel, *Heart of Darkness* (1901). *Qi* exits the kidney meridian at Ki-22 where it leaves to enter the heart protector meridian at HP-1. The remaining seven points on the kidney channel may be likened to the statues on either side of the spirit road *(lingdao)* that approaches the emperor's mausoleum.[11] The pairing of Ki-6 with Ki-27 can help guide us through these different stages and clear the entire kidney channel of fear, helping empower the graceful and fluid realization of our life's purpose. The treasure stored in Ki-27 is the highest ascent of this purpose before it is channeled through the throat to reach our brains and minds to engender the wisdom we have gained in our journey.

When I think a patient's fear involves variables regarding infancy, I include Ki-13, "door of infants," with the points cited earlier. Cases in which this might be appropriate include the mother suffering a near death experience while carrying her child or the patient himself having such an experience during delivery or in early life. Any of the proximal points along the kidney channel can be included with this protocol or substituted for Ki-13, depending on the nature of the fear that is blocking the patient's progress in life and the functional level at which it is manifesting.

---

### *Annoyance over Details*

| | | |
|---|---|---|
| **Gb-40** | *Qiuxu* | Wilderness Mound |
| **Lv-5** | *Ligou* | Insect Drain |

The function of a healthy wood element is to empower a perspective broad enough to encompass both the details of our life plan as well as a vision of the overall direction of our journey. The habituated mind of the wood element tends to focus on details in a way that constrains our overall progress toward our destination. Gb-40, "wilderness mound," helps ease constraint that arises from feelings of not being able to see the forest for the trees. Lv-5, "insect drain," supports us to grow gracefully around annoying details that can hinder us from effectively implementing our plan. I think of this point as ideal for the person whose picnic is always ruined by ants.

The *yin* and *yang* officials of the wood element separate as the integrity of their connection is undermined by habitual response to the emotion anger. In this case the mind represented by the function of the gallbladder official turns outward as its functional connection to the inner plan of the liver is obscured by its reaction to anger. A dysfunctional gallbladder official can compel us to project our anger onto external circumstances rather than looking to ourselves for the cause of the conflicts we encounter in life. Making decisions based on our response to anger instead of taking actions commensurate with our plans, we lose perspective and lose our life's journey.

Lv-5, as the channel's *luo* point, opens the liver channel and simultaneously allows the liver to vent stagnation externally. Treating Gb-40 and Lv-5 together, the mind of the gallbladder is directed back to the depths of liver so functions of decision making and planning are reintegrated. In this way we may be afforded a quality of vision that is grounded in our life's plan and embraces the elevated perspective of benevolence.

---

### *Open Loins, Ease Constraint*

| | | |
|---|---|---|
| **Ki-10** | *Yingu* | *Yin* Valley |
| **Lv-8** | *Ququan* | Crooked Spring |
| **Lv-9** | *Yinbao* | *Yin* Wrapping |

The liver meridian is the only channel that runs through the genitals. Anger can be a call to vision and creativity when our growth in life is blocked. The natural tendency of anger is to rise forcefully in a way that can help carry us past such obstacles. If the rising of anger is suppressed, *qi* stagnation is a result. Every point on the liver meridian represents a different aspect of "wall" as it may be embodied within us or projected externally onto life's circumstances.

If we liken a human being to a tree, we can see that the effects of *qi* stagnation over the long term tend to appear like knots in a tree that grows in on itself rather than freely outward. Hence we can see the expressions of liver *qi* stagnation at chief nodal points such as the ankles, knees, hips, xiphoid process, the center of the chest, the throat, and the temples. Each of these regions represents a discrete level of suppression relative to the expression of anger. The knees and hips particularly are related to the expression of sexuality. Anger regarding sexual abuse or perceived betrayals can be repressed in a way that locks the knees and closes the groin in a defensive posture. This closing may also be evident in psychospiritual realms as the patient behaves like she is being attacked whenever asked to compromise.

Ki-10 is the horary point on the kidney meridian. Water always follows its nature by flowing downward, arriving at the ocean regardless of the obstacles it encounters on its journey. Ki-10 is also an accumulation point for *yin* that is acquired during life. In alchemy, acquired *yin* represents all aspects of being held on to that do not correspond to true self. Hence Ki-10, like a mighty river, can help wash away impurities and impart the virtue of flow throughout being.

Lv-8 as the water point on the liver meridian is the receiving point for the influence of water when paired with Ki-10. Here the virtues of water in its ability to flow around obstacles are empowered within the wood element. The name of Lv-8, "crooked spring," suggests the image of a small winding stream that flows around all obstacles to reach its goal. The *Daodejing* alludes to the virtue of flexibility when it says of the *dao,* "it is bent yet preserved whole."[12] Both Ki-10 and Lv-8 are located on the medial surface of the knee and can help empower the qualities of flow and openness that the *Daodejing* imparts to the *dao.* As water points, this combination can help fortify *yin* and thereby soften the quality of anger we direct toward ourselves and others who have transgressed against us both in the past and the present.

The name of Lv-9, *yinbao* (陰包), depicts a fetus (巳) within the womb (勹). This is an important point for treating *qi* stagnation in the reproductive organs that presents as fibroids, endometriosis, scar tissue from ectopic pregnancies, blood stasis, menstrual cramps and associated mood swings, as well as anger and defensiveness that is projected on anyone who approaches us in a way that requires us to open ourselves to the possibility of intimacy. Pairing Lv-9 with Lv-8 and Ki-10 can help empower the virtues of softness and flow resulting in an openness of the knees and loins as well as a softening of our judgments held against ourselves and others. Flowing past the suppression that blocks it, anger now has the opportunity to enter consciousness and be expressed. In this way we may gain a perspective on unconscious forces that limit our capacity for sexual connection and intimacy.

### *Insatiable Appetite*

| | | |
|---|---|---|
| **St-44** | *Neiting* | Inner Courtyard |
| **St-25** | *Tianshu* | Heavenly Pivot |
| **Ki-3** | *Taixi* | Great Mountain Stream |

The spirit of the earth element is the *yi,* which translates into English as "thought" or "ideation." Thought is the digestive aspect of the mind that helps us assimilate and be nurtured by our life experience. If the mind is habitually driven by need, we tend to think unproductively in a way that manifests as worry, *si* (思), the emotion of the earth element. When earth is dysfunctional, our minds can tend to seek comfort through immediate gratification and lead us to consume too quickly in all realms of life. If our quest for nourishment in life is habitually driven by worry and neediness, our quest for deep nourishment may be fruitless.

Food eaten quickly does not have the advantage of having been broken down by chewing or by the enzymes present in saliva. Arriving in the stomach in large pieces, the stomach now has to work forcefully to break down and "cook" the food so it may be assimilated. Extra work produces excessive heat, which consumes the fluids of the stomach and ultimately leads to a condition of stomach *yin* deficiency. Similarly, excessive thought, predicated on overwork of the nervous system, also consumes *yin.* Stomach *yin* deficiency can manifest as sugar cravings, insatiable appetite, and excessive worry. Eating too quickly can also result in bloating and gas in the short term and high blood pressure and diabetes in the long term as kidney *yin* is ultimately consumed. St-44 empowers the virtue of quietude and reflection associated with the water element. As the water point on the stomach meridian, St-44 can help increase the influence of water within the stomach official to help mitigate the effects of stomach *yin* deficiency.

The name "inner courtyard" and the function of St-44 is congruent with the text of *Yijing* hexagram 52. The name of this hexagram is "mountain," and it counsels us on the virtue of building a solid center through disciplined self-reflection. The function of the earth element is to empower the virtue of integrity by building strength in our center physically as well as emotionally. The text of the hexagram extols the virtues of meditation, which may slow the mind and ease worry as we disengage from the world to travel inward. Such a journey can help satiate the mind and quiet the overwrought nervous system. The fifth line of the hexagram states, "keeping his jaws still the words have order and remorse disappears."[13] Here the virtue of integrity *xin* (信) associated with the earth element is engendered through cessation of idle chatter. The character *xin* depicts a man standing upright by his words so integrity is created through the alignment of proper thought and action.

St-25, "heavenly pivot," is the *mu* point of the stomach and its meeting point with the large intestine official. Traditional functions ascribed to St-25 include dispersing heat in the *yangming* channels (stomach and large intestine). Such heat often accompanies symptoms such as excessive appetite and neediness. Sharing its name with the central star in the Big Dipper, St-25 empowers balanced and centered movement that is not burdened by overthinking. Note that St-24, "lubrication food gate," can be a good alternative selection here because it helps empower graceful assimilation of nourishment.

As stomach *yin* is consumed over a long period of time, the kidney provides *yin* to the stomach official and eventually becomes *yin* deficient itself. The relationship between the stomach and kidney dysfunction often presents as alternating cravings for sweet and salty foods. Sweet and salty are the favors associated with the earth and water elements, respectively. In this instance, the function of the kidney tends to be undermined by fear, the disordered emotion of the water element, that potentiates the earth element's obsessive tendencies. Thus I pair Ki-3, the earth point on the kidney meridian, with the other two points discussed earlier. Ki-3 helps restore the earth's control of the water element across the *ke* cycle in a way that calms feelings of being overwhelmed and nervousness.

---

### *Uniting Heaven and Earth*

| | | |
|---|---|---|
| **Ki-1** | *Yongquan* | Bubbling Spring |
| **GV-20** | *Baihui* | Hundred Meetings |

The image of a human being standing upright to mediate the interpenetration of heaven and earth is central to the notion of fulfilling destiny. When human will *(zhi)* is perfectly aligned with the will of heaven *(ming)*, humanity becomes a conduit for the authentic *(zhen)* divine *qi* of heaven and earth. *Zhenqi* is the *qi* that is present when a person manifests destiny by being true to his authentic self.[14] According to Porkert, the *zhenqi* sustains the integrity of an individual and protects and defends him against exogenous and endogenous attacks and disturbances.[15] Hence the term *zhenqi* contains the notion that our very source of health, integrity, and immunity spring from the fulfillment of destiny. Health flowing from original nature and virtue *(de)* creates, and is in turn created by, the ability to perceive life with absolute fidelity. Receiving life intuitively into his heart without deviation is the very basis of the sage's spontaneity *(ziran)* that the *Daodejing* defines as ideal health.

A central effect of shock is to disorder one's relationship to both heaven and earth. If pressed, it becomes clear that most patients who project their pain onto a particular event in life ultimately blame heaven. Patients may attribute the source of their pain to a rape, loss of a child, or some other traumatic event. However, there is always an innate knowing that all pain in life comes to us as a matter of destiny. Unconsciously, humans tend to blame heaven for their trauma. The fire constitutional type assumes "if God loved me, I wouldn't have been raped." The wood type assumes "If heaven was just, I wouldn't have lost my child." And so on.

When this dynamic is most explicitly present, I expect to see signs of chaos and shock ranging from constant changes on the pulse of rate, rhythm, amplitude, intensity, and qualities to conditions that might typically receive a biomedical diagnosis of mental illness. In its subtler forms, patients may evidence depression, lack of faith, feelings of persecution, and give the general impression that they cannot find a comfortable place in this world.

The pairing of Ki-1 and GV-20 is a powerful way to reestablish the flow of *qi* through the patient by realigning her to the dual poles of heaven and earth. In this way purpose may flow more effortlessly from its innate source in our unknown depths to its destination in heaven to engender the enlightened perspective granted by wisdom. Ki-1, "bubbling spring," located on the ventral surface of the foot, is the central point that provides our connection to the cosmological pole of earth as *yin* (as opposed to the earth element). As the wood point on a water meridian, we can think of Ki-1 as embodying the greatest depth to which the liver as our tree of life can send its roots in order to anchor us, create stability, and receive nourishment. The kidney meridian can be conceived of as a mighty river. "Bubbling spring" is the very source of that river as it percolates up from the earth. As compared with Ki-1, the lowest point on the body, GV-20, "hundred meetings," is the body's highest point. Whereas Ki-1 represents our lowest root, GV-20 represents the very top of the liver meridian and our uppermost branches as they extend toward the North Star, the heart of heaven, as it is embodied within us.

It is interesting to compare this treatment to that of the CV/GV block presented in Chapter 6. Treatment of the CV/GV block addresses a patient's connection to *yin* and *yang*. These are the dual poles on which the entire functional edifice of the six other extraordinary meridians and the twelve main meridians are based. The conception and governor vessels are the foundation for the expression of the blood and *qi* that supports the function of the organ systems. The connection to *yin* and *yang* mediated by conception and governor vessels is not personal and has more to do with the forces of *yin* and *yang* as they act thermodynamically within the universe. In contrast, the inner functions of GV-20 and Ki-1 are intimately tied to the quality of our personal connection to heaven and earth in all domains of being as we as humans mediate the flow of *qi* between these two poles.

Anyone who has ever had Ki-1 needled knows it can be a shocking experience. There are times when it is appropriate to use shock as a device to restore original nature. In these cases needling Ki-1 can be appropriate. Some patients are so sensitive, however, that treating Ki-1 with a needle might be upsetting to them in a way that does not further the intention of this particular treatment. In these cases I would use moxa at Ki-1 and GV-20 rather than a needle.

---

### *Writer's Block: Psychic Indigestion*

| | | |
|---|---|---|
| **Lv-8** | *Ququan* | Crooked Spring |
| **Lv-13** | *Zhangmen* | Chapter Gate |
| **Sp-8** | *Diji* | Earth Motivator |
| **Sp-9** | *Yinlingquan* | *Yin* Mound Spring |
| **CV-11** | *Jianli* | Inner Strength |

The creative process requires functional harmony between the liver and spleen officials. Although wood governs the creative process itself, all growth must be nourished by and rooted in the earth. Traditionally, all Chinese arts, from the practice of calligraphy to the martial arts, emphasize a broad technical knowledge as well as the physical grounding of all technique in one's center (*hara*/earth). Mastery of a given art involves transcending technique to achieve the virtue of spontaneity. At this level of performance the art lives dynamically in the very being of the artist and transcends all form as it emerges through the artist spontaneously in each moment.

The impulse of the wood element toward spontaneous growth must be balanced with the capability of the earth to sustain a given rate of development. All creative acts, whether they be painting, writing a book, or choreographing a dance, must reflect the integrity of the art as it is embodied within the artist. The nature of the wood element is to want whatever the mind conceives to be realized immediately on the physical plane. The sapling can conceive of being an oak tree and may not want to wait the hundred years it may take to realize its form. Wood can conceive of so many ways to create that it often grows impatient with the process of bringing a plan to fruition.

Such impatience can lead to frustration and psychic blockage because the earth element cannot effectively process all that the wood is trying to assimilate. Such a blockage between the wood and earth element can leave a person feeling psychically congested with no vision of what direction further growth is to take. Such congestion may manifest physically as abdominal bloating, tenderness under the ribs, esophageal reflux, and pressure in the abdomen and chest. Emotionally, patients may present frustration, depression, and anger as their progress grinds to a halt. This treatment is similar in intention to that discussed here under the heading of "Soothing the Mediator." Generally, I would do this treatment in an earlier session and that treatment at a later date.

This point combination can harmonize psychic congestion and help empower a greater sense of flow in the creative process. Lv-8 and Sp-9 as the water points on their respective meridians help move stagnation and empower flow in the functional domain of the liver and spleen, respectively. I find this point combination ideal when the middle position of the pulse is bilaterally tense and pounding, indicating the presence of stagnant *qi* and excess heat, or when both positions are tight, indicating *yin* deficiency.

Sp-8, "earth motivator," is the *xi*-cleft point on the spleen meridian and, as such, helps move stagnation. It is a tendency of creative people who push too hard to become weighed down under all they are trying to accomplish. Consequently, that which should nourish them in the creative process instead becomes a burden as they lose the joy of their endeavor. Think of "earth motivator" as a bulldozer summoned to move accumulated burden and help get a person moving again.

The name of Lv-13, "chapter gate," precisely describes the functional dynamics of this point in helping move writer's block. A meeting point between the liver and spleen officials, "chapter gate" can help a patient move past his current feelings of being stuck and back into the creative process. Note that the next point on the liver channel is Lv-14, "gate of hope," a central point for rekindling the virtue of aspiration. I include CV-11 as a harmonizing point that moves *qi* stagnation in the middle *jiao*. Hence we see the spleen and liver officials united below in the combination of Sp-9 with Lv-8 and above with the selection of Lv-13, the meeting point of both officials. The inclusion of CV-11 unites the upper and lower point selections by helping to both nourish and move the center.

Often when my intention is specifically to move the psychic blockages contributing to writer's block, I include the points St-8 ("head tied") for overthinking and Gb-4 ("loathsome jaws") for dysfunctional frustration and anger that impede the creative process.

### *The Restoration of Intuition*

| | | |
|---|---|---|
| **SI-4** | *Wangu* | Wrist Bone |
| **SI-19** | *Tinggong* | Listening Palace |
| **Ht-5** | *Tongli* | Penetrating Inside |

### EXERCISES

1. How could this last point combination help restore intuition?
2. What *is* intuition?
3. What is the relationship between a person's health and his or her intuitive capacity?
4. What is the relationship of intuition to one's capacity to listen?
5. To what extent should intuition be trusted?

## NOTES

1. This notion was introduced to me by Jeffrey Yuen.
2. For a discussion of *qi* and blood in accordance with the inner tradition, see *ND*, Chapter 11, pp. 299–312.
3. An example of this dynamic is discussed in a case study in *ND*, pp. 406–407.
4. Arrived at in conversation with Thea Elijah.
5. My pairing of this point with Gb-41 is discussed in the context of a case study presented in *ND*, p. 255.
6. Van Over, 1973, pp. 179–180.
7. My translation of this point follows that of Ellis, Wiseman, and Boss, 1989, pp. 313–314.
8. Chapter 4 of this text and Chapter 7 in *ND*.
9. One such case study is presented in *ND*, pp. 191–192.
10. The pairing of Ki-6 with Ki-27 for treating terror was taught to me by a student who attributed the combination to her studies with Kikko Matsumato.
11. See Paludan, 1991.
12. Chen, 1989, Chapter 22.
13. Wilhelm, 1968, p. 656.
14. Larre and Rochat de la Vallee, 1985, p. 63.
15. Porkert, 1982, p. 171.

# PART V

# PERSPECTIVE

# 37

# COGNITIVE STYLES IN THE PRACTICE OF CHINESE MEDICINE

*"No indeed!" said Jo of the North Sea. "There is no end to the weighing of things, no stop to time, no constancy to the division of lots, no fixed rule to beginning and end."*
– *ZHUANGZI*[1]

THE MAIN FOCUS OF MY WRITING HAS BEEN ON FIVE-ELEMENT constitutional medicine as it pertains to nourishing the fulfillment of destiny.[2] However, in practice, Chinese medicine is based on several paradigms, each having their specific application. Mastery entails cultivating the ability to touch each patient therapeutically at precisely the level of being that will most efficiently further his evolution in that moment. Knowledge of each method and its appropriate use is essential if you are to be able to treat the widest possible range of patients effectively.

Individual traditions of Chinese medicine are a composite of several traditions reflecting the ongoing synthesis of material by each practitioner as well as that assimilated by her lineage of teachers. My own practice brings together two distinct, although complementary, traditions. The first is five-element constitutional diagnosis, and the second is centered around a pre-TCM tradition of pulse diagnosis based largely on eight-principle physiology.[3] The interplay of these two orientations as they inform my practice is present in the case studies I have published.[4]

As Chinese medicine has become established in the West, practitioners from traditions that rely more explicitly on either the five-element or eight-principle systems have made claims of superiority. I have come to believe that the attempt to make ultimate distinctions between the two systems is tantamount to Western science's futile attempts at trying to separate the relative contributions of genetics and environment to a specific human attribute. All systems of thought have their relative weaknesses and strengths that are determined a priori by the assumptions on which they are based. The practice of Chinese medicine often entails being able to hold several diagnostic models simultaneously and knowing when it is appropriate to apply each. Over time I have come to form an integrated view of these two systems and understand the five elements and eight principles as complementing each other in a way that allows me to form an integrated diagnosis based on the assessment of a patient's constitutional and acquired patterns of function.

Here I examine the relationships that exist between the five-element and eight-principle systems as they occur to me theoretically and in my clinical practice. I am clear that the two ways of knowing are inextricably linked and my discernments of differences between the two are limited by my own experience and orientation toward the subject matter. In comparing these two systems, when I refer to the perspective of the "eight-principle" or the "five-element" practitioner, I am actually discussing different cognitive styles and value systems that are simultaneously present in degrees in each of us, regardless of our tradition of practice.

I examine the cognitive styles inherent in each system with an eye toward discerning a possible explanation for why the eight-principle system has predominated Chinese medicine in recent times. I also look at the consequences of the foundational differences between the two systems as they impact social policy toward the practice and development of our medicine. The importance of embracing and then transcending both systems of thought for the greater good is also discussed. Lastly, I present the spiral dynamics model of the evolution of consciousness and its bearing on the development, present state, and future of Chinese medicine.

## *The Enumeration of Healing*

The sages who formulated our medicine recognized that no single model could explain all observed phenomena. In view of life's functional intricacies, they devised different ways of ordering the world, each with its own unique application, weakness, and strength. Each diagnostic and therapeutic model is based on a number from one through twelve and defines a way of knowing about the world and human beings' place in it (see Figure 37.1).

| NUMBER | MODEL |
|---|---|
| *1* | *To look and know* |
| *2* | Yin/Yang *theory* |
| *3* | *Three heater diagnosis* |
| *4* | *Four divisions* |
| *5* | *Five elements* |
| *6* | *Six stages* |
| *7* | *Seven pathogens* |
| *8* | *Eight principles* |
| *9* | *Nine stars/divisions of the pulse* |
| *10* | *Ten stems* |
| *11* | *Eleven* zang |
| *12* | *Twelve branches/officials* |

*Figure 37.1*
ENUMERATING DIAGNOSIS

In Figure 37.1 I have denoted the highest form of diagnoses, corresponding to the number one, as "to look and know."[5] This capacity is predicated on the flowering of intuition in the open heart of the sage. At this level of attainment, you are in direct contact with the patient at the level of his primordial influences of *jing, qi,* and *shen.* You are not practicing Chinese medicine per se, but practicing in communion with the sole immutable principle of all healing modalities. This principle may be stated succinctly as "do what is right."

Each model has a relatively different emphasis on the role played by innate and acquired influences and their contribution to illness. For example, the four-division and six-stage paradigms describe the progression toward the interior of hot and cold acquired influences, respectively. In contrast, the five-element model focuses on the precise dynamics of constitution as they predispose us to illness. In order to attain a mastery of Chinese medicine, you must be conversant with each available model and aware of the context in which to apply it. It behooves our generation to update these models so they remain relevant to birthing and caring for the new emerging being of humanity. Here I discuss the natural hierarchical relationship, and its current distortions, between the five-element and eight-principle models.

---

## *The Imagined Dichotomy*

Historically, five-element (5E) thought and *yin/yang* thinking existed side by side in the classic texts. Together these approaches yield an integrated approach to medicine and life that draws equally on the cognitive styles inherent in the left and right brain. The eight-principle (8P) system represents a relatively late simplification of *yin/yang* thinking. In fact, the term *bagang* (八綱), denoting the eight principles as a formal system of pattern differentiation, did not emerge until 1947.[6] Due to historical circumstances, the 5E and 8P systems have grown apart as they have been adopted by specific traditions of practice. The five-element method, as I elaborate it in my work, has come to be identified with the tradition of J. R. Worsley, who has inevitably impressed on the approach his own value system. Similarly, the eight-principle system has been adopted as the core approach by the modern Chinese state, which has impressed its own value system on it as well.

*Yin/yang* thinking itself is inclined toward holistic thought because it empowers us to always see the presence of an opposite within any thing or phenomenon we are observing. For example, this type of thought is inherent in the constitutional notion that a person's greatest strength externally in the world tends to be mirrored as an internal weakness. The reduction of the infinite pairings of *yin* and *yang* to eight guiding criteria, under the influence of a materialistic core value system, has led to an objectification of physiology that is relatively more congruent with causal and linear modes of inquiry that have predominated the world since the industrial revolution. This trend is apparent in the formulation of TCM under the auspices of the Chinese state and its subsequent assimilation into materialistic American culture during the "me" decades (the 1970s and 1980s) by the baby boomers.

Reacting to the challenge of bringing China into the modern world, the Marxists sought to eliminate the ingrained superstition that they identified as a basis of their cultural stagnation. In fact, one of their greatest philosophical imperatives was to argue against the notion of destiny.[7] In so doing they tried to eliminate the influence of all doctrines deemed to be at odds with dialectical materialism. Chief among these were the spiritual orientations of Daoism and Buddhism. As the state sought to modernize the country, the mechanistic views of the Western sciences became prominent as Social Darwinism replaced so-called superstitious religious concepts related to spiritual evolution. In formulating TCM according to the principles of Marxism, the eight principles gained ascendancy as the primary model of medicine. As we shall see, the cognitive style implicit in the eight-principle model is a relatively closer fit for the causal and linear style of mechanistic thought adopted by the dialectical materialists than are the "planet as organism" holistic theories of five-element medicine.

Reacting to the materialism of the modern world and its influence in the practice of Chinese medicine, J. R. Worsley and his followers looked to the spirit of Daoism inherent in the classical texts to form the core value system of their medicine. These core values focus on the preservation of original nature in the world as the guiding influence in the evolution and expression of the human spirit. As I have pointed out earlier, much of this tradition has nothing to do with the five-element system itself. However, the core approach of diagnosing according to elemental type and of prioritizing the element points in treatment has led Worsley and his followers to think of themselves as "five-element" practitioners. Hence it is the core value system inherent in the five-element model that motivates their approach to the medicine in general.

The archetypal criticism by the detractors of the five-element model and its practitioners is that treatment appears to focus on some imagined depth of the patient and may entirely miss the reason the patient says he is seeking treatment in the first place. Further, treatment of so-called esoteric conditions such as possession seem naive and superstitious to the "Doctor of TCM." "I know someone who went to a five-element practitioner for three years and her arm still hurts," a critic might say. From the standpoint of the doctor of TCM, the five-element tradition has thrown out the intellectual rigor of the scientific approach in favor of a belief in magic and spiritualism. What this physician may be missing is the extraordinary rigor exercised in honing the diagnostic and treatment skills of the five-element tradition. Learning to face a patient as a health care professional is one thing; choosing to face one's self is entirely another. The importance of the five-element tradition's orientation toward the practice of medicine as a cultivational art and science can not be overestimated.

The archetypal criticism of the eight-principle model and its practitioners from the perspective of the five-element practitioner is that patients seem to be objectified in a way similar to the practice of Western medicine. As a physician might relate exclusively to a patient's illness, the TCM physician is criticized for focusing on syndrome patterns as if they were concrete entities separate from the patient. This tendency is in evidence when the physician tends to focus on the external plot that emerges during diagnosis and ignores the constitutional and elemental theme that emerges from the interior. The five-element practitioner might say, "Sure the patient's symptoms got better, but he learned nothing. You can run but you can't hide from the will of heaven. The symptoms will find some other way to manifest because the constitutional basis of all manifestations has not been addressed." From the standpoint of the five-element practitioner, the TCM physician has lost touch with the spirit and heart of the medicine as well as the patient. What might be missed by this critique is the compassion exercised by the TCM physician who seeks to make substantive changes in the organic basis of the patient's illness. Note that here I am disregarding those who do practice straightforward symptomatic medicine and lauding those who apply the rigors of TCM in aspiring toward a truly preventive physical medicine.[8]

---

### *Preventive Medicine: What Is It We Are Preventing?*

Both camps see the patient as metaphorically standing on a train track. The eight-principle practitioner is concerned that the five-element practitioner will merely help the patient feel very good about standing on the train track while the train of serious illness is steadily approaching. The eight-principle practitioner strives concretely to get the patient off this track to help mitigate any tendencies toward the manifestation of serious pathology. However, the five-element practitioner knows one train is ultimately coming for us all that cannot be avoided. Her concern is that the patient not die in a state of ignorance, having never recognized the innate purpose of his life or even that such a purpose existed. If you practice in a tradition with a materialist core value system, diagnosis and prognoses will always be based on the patient's physical health. Ultimately, there will never be any good clinical news because everybody is dying. In fact, after every treatment session, our patients are one hour closer to death. If you are in a tradition whose core value system is based on spiritual evolution, there is only good clinical news because every soul is moving toward heaven. Ultimately, I consider that the highest virtue of medicine resides in assisting the evolution of the human spirit. This intention must inform each and every clinical choice we make in the practice of our art.

I have heard these concerns expressed since the beginning of my involvement with Chinese medicine. My experience in teaching, however, is that upon running into the limitations of their own tradition, most practitioners seek out material of a complementary nature to what they learned in school. Graduates of five-element traditions often seek to advance their understanding of the medicine by integrating the eight principles into their practices, and the graduates of TCM schools hunger for knowledge of the deeper, more spiritual nature of Chinese medicine. Hence a growing body of practitioners are sophisticated enough to understand the importance of integrating both systems.

Although the five-element and eight-principle traditions are inextricably linked, and they both are necessary for the integrated practice of medicine, it is a fact that the core values of each do not equally inform policy making within the profession. The academic, credentialing, and licensing structures in place in America have concretized enough to now weigh on, rather than advance, this necessary stage of integration so critical to the evolution of our medicine. And, as we shall see, the very concept of standardization itself as an ultimate principle is antithetical to the core value system that lies at the heart of Chinese medicine. The materialist core values at the heart of TCM and American culture prevent the five-element and eight-principle systems from taking their rightful places according to natural hierarchy as relatively internal *(nei)* and external *(wai)* models, respectively.

In modern times, the eight-principle paradigm has gained ascendancy, and the five-element tradition has played a minority role to the point of never having been seriously addressed in any modern TCM text I am aware of. Whereas the five-element schools teach the eight-principle approach as dictated by standardized testing, most TCM curriculums do little more than pay lip service to the five-element system or its core values. In fact, even in relation to the eight principles, current licensing exams better test a student's knowledge of medical anthropology than they assess any real aptitude for practicing Chinese medicine in the context of the struggles we humans face at this point in history. Finally, the new clinical doctorate, with its exaggerated emphasis on research and biomedicine, offers little hope that the art and science of Chinese medicine will be cultivated on its own terms.

As the practice of Chinese medicine in America is increasingly influenced by this country's educational, accreditation, and managed health care models, its very foundations as a complementary and holistic form of medicine are being eroded. Because eight-principle thought has attributes innately similar to the linear and causal thought prevalent in the West, the cognitive style that lies at the heart of the medicine is failing to be embraced. In short, the analytic mind sees something in the eight-principle approach that looks familiar and then extrapolates the approach into a physical medicine rather than accepting the depth of *yin/yang* thinking on its own terms. Of course, it misses the cognitive style inherent in the five-element tradition entirely because the values inherent in the system are not even on the radar screen of the materialist mind. Even when the techniques of the five-element system are integrated into practice, the core values of the method are often missed because they conflict with the practitioner's bottom line.

Only if the five-element tradition is reintegrated to assume its natural hierarchical position within Chinese medicine is there any real hope that the medicine will fulfill its potential of becoming an integrated and sophisticated science of healing and health care relevant to the struggles that face us in the new millennia.[9] Now let us compare the differences in cognitive styles inherent in both models with an eye toward illuminating their natural relationship to each other.

## *The Absolute Nature of Being*

*Dao gives birth to one,*
*One gives birth to two,*
*Two gives birth to three,*
*Three gives birth to the ten thousand things.*
– DAODEJING[10]

The absolute nature of the unnamed *dao* is of nonarising.[11] This absolute state is one where neither space nor time exist. The *dao* named has the dual property of both nonarising and arising. The primary attribute of named *dao* is a state of nonarising in which all things are wholly implicit within each other to form a single, integral being. In this state, there is time that is present as an endless cycling as *dao* moves away from and returns forever to itself. In fact, this cycling of time presides over the period during which "being" is incubating. The form of this being exists in space, which has eight directions.[12] Hence the form of the incubating human is structured around the eight extra meridians. Although space and time do exist in the named *dao,* they exist implicitly, and only one thing, which the Daoists liken to a chicken egg, can be comprehended.

In the moment of being named, a "big bang" occurs in which the *dao* explodes to give rise to the material universe of the ten thousand things. The force of this explosion is a giant "yes!" that changes the quality of time from being an endless cycle into an upward spiral. The outward momentum of this arising is the undercurrent of evolution itself, in which the passing of time is marked by changes in the forms of all things.

## *The Geometry of Heaven and Earth*

*I do not know its proper name but will call it* Dao.
*If forced to give it a name, I shall call it great.*
*Great means "moving away."*
*"Moving away" means "far away"* (yuan),
*And "far away" means ultimately to return.*
– DAODEJING[13]

In considering the relationship of the five elements (5E) to the eight principles (8P), it is helpful to conceive of them diagrammatically. Here I examine the five elements and eight principles as complementary modes of inquiry that utilize circular and linear modes of thinking, respectively.

### *The Currency of Being and Nonbeing*

The ancient Chinese conception of heaven and earth is represented in the structure of their coins (see Figure 37.2). Here the circumference of the coin represents heaven as the canopy that surrounds earth. Earth is represented by the inner square. The space at the center of the square represents the absolute position of the eternal unnamed *dao* that lies at the heart of all beings to which it gives birth.

The nature of heaven as round is that, like the chicken egg of eternal *dao,* it comprises a unity that encompasses all things implicitly. As practitioners of Chinese medicine, we are used to seeing diagrams of the five elements arranged in the *sheng* (creative) cycle. Therefore it is natural to conceive of the five elements as a circle. In fact, you can think of the five elements as the face of a clock denoting the passing of time as *dao* cycles away from and returns to itself endlessly. We may think of the five elements appearing in three-dimensional space as a sphere comprised of smaller spheres (Figure 37.3, p. 718). In this way the officials are depicted as "orbs" of function as defined by Porkert, which is a more accurate representation of their complex natures than the simple two-dimensional picture depicted on most acupuncture charts (see Figure 12.2).[14]

By contrast, earth is relatively linear possessing four directions and a center. The endless cycling of heaven is the basis of time and function, whereas earth is the basis of structure as defined in three dimensions. In contrast to the circular five-element model, the eight-principle model is a relatively linear way of knowing. When mapped onto a square, the eight principles define a three-dimensional space (see Figure 37.4, p. 719).

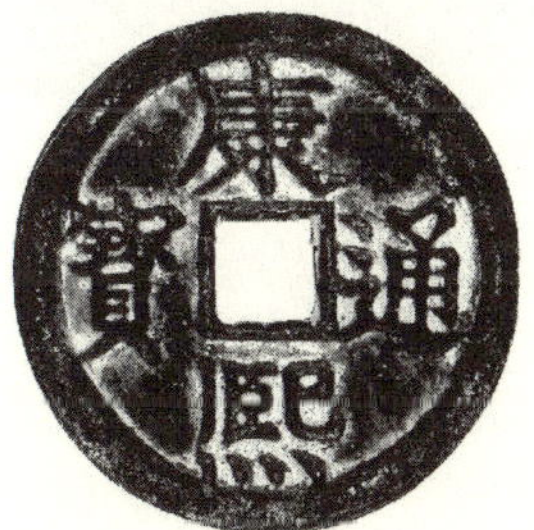


*Figure 37.2*
THE CURRENCY OF CHANGE

*Here a Chinese coin depicts heaven, the circle, enveloping earth, the square. The circle represents the unity of the primal* dao *in which the manifestation of all things on earth is implicit. In this sphere there is only function as the "ten thousand things" interpenetrate each other to exist only as potential. The square, as earth, represents directionality as the "ten thousand things" implicit in heaven become individually manifest with their structures defined by the eight directions. The space at the center of the square represents the absolute position of eternal* dao *relative to both space and time.*

In Figure 37.4 the continuums of hot and cold, external and internal, and excess and deficiency are shown as a three-dimensional axis that defines a cube. The front, top, and right side of this cube are relatively *yang,* and the rear, bottom, and left side of this cube are relatively *yin.* By moving a point within this three-dimensional space, any of the eight-principle syndrome patterns are defined by a particular quadrant. Hence the front lower left quadrant defines a pattern of external, cold, and deficiency, whereas the rear upper right quadrant defines a pattern of interior, excess, and heat.[15]

The eight principles define the space/time coordinates of physical phenomena. The continuum of internal to external defines the location of a

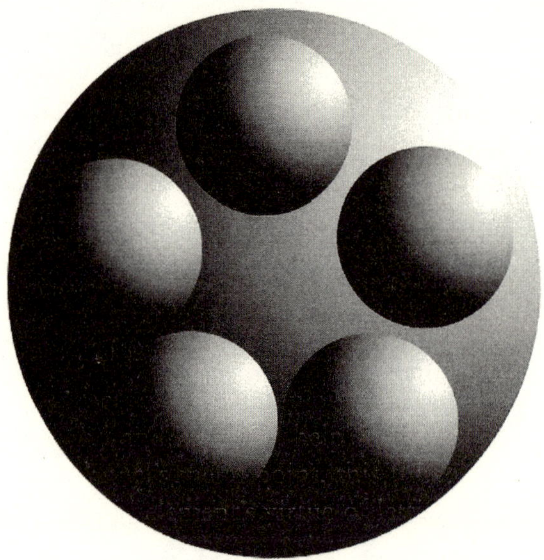

*Figure 37.3*
SPHERES OF TRANSFORMATION

*It occurs to me that the typical five-element chart would more accurately convey the holographic nature of the five elements if it depicted the elements in three dimensions. Here the five elements are shown mapped onto a sphere that imparts the sense of the officials as "orbs" of function as described by Porkert.*[16] *Think of this picture as representative of the holographic nature of* dao *in which every thing retains its unique function yet is implicit in every other thing. Like a diamond, our entrance in through any facet takes us inwardly toward the same central and absolute reality. Each element, although discrete in function, contains within it the implicit image of the other five elements. In acupuncture, this representation exists as the five-element point on each meridian. The absolute perspective is represented by the center of the circle where we have the same relative view of all positions.*

phenomena in physical space. For instance, a pathological condition may be said to be in the organs, in the sinews, or in the muscle layer. These are all physical locations. The continuum of deficiency to excess defines pathology according to relative quantity. The continuum of hot to cold is understood to precisely follow thermodynamic principles. The continuum of *yin* to *yang* is used to qualify the overall quality of interaction among the other three continuums. In essence, the modern use of the eight-principle system characterizes the functional processes of the human body according to a thermodynamic model that follows the laws of physics.[17]

### *The Reality of Structure and Function*

From the standpoint of early heaven, function (time) is real, and structure is an illusion contained implicitly within it. If we could stand in early heaven, we would experience time as ultimate reality, and the existence of structure would have to be taken on faith. For in primal *dao* all things exist only as potential and are interpenetrating to a degree of wholeness that no discrete thing can be perceived. In later heaven, however, structure defines reality and function lies implicitly within form. Here the passing of time can only be known by the change perceived in physical structures. In the material world where we live, function is able to be sensed qualitatively but can never be touched.

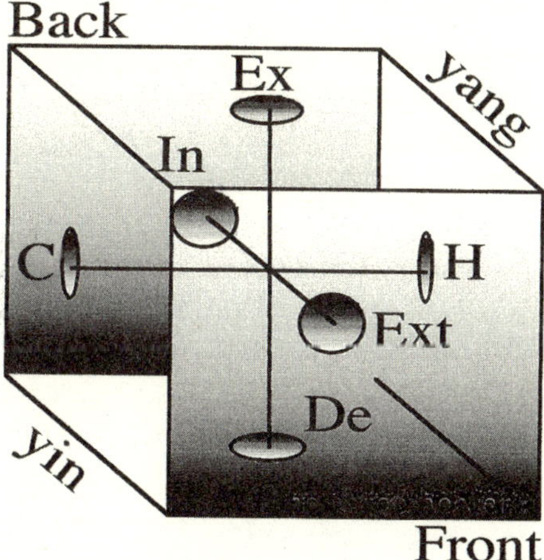


*Figure 37.4*

THE EIGHT PRINCIPLES AS A CUBE

*Here the eight principles are shown as defining a three-dimensional space. The absolute perspective is represented by the central point of the x, y, and z axis. Ex = excess, De = deficient, H = hot, C = cold, Ext = external, In = internal.*

For example, in Western science, mind and spirit (heaven, *yang*) are thought of as secondary emanations of the physical substrate (earth, *yin*). Mind is seen as the by-product of the physiological functioning of the nervous system. From the perspective of traditional Chinese science, physical reality (earth, structure) is deemed to be an outer manifestation of an underlying functional process that finds its basis in heaven. Hence function is considered to be "real," whereas structures (the ten thousand things) are thought to be an impermanent illusion. From this perspective, the structure of the nervous system can be seen as a transient manifestation of universal consciousness (spirit).

Gravity is the most pervasive physical force, and ignorance is the most pervasive nonphysical force. From the perspective of the inner tradition, the highest purpose of medicine is to free the expression of spirit from the bondage of ego so that we may transcend the illusions of our conditioning that lead us to identify the material world and its happenings as constituting ultimate reality. In this way ignorance is dispelled, and, in the parlance of the Daoist texts, the body becomes light both in the sense of radiant and in the sense of having overcome gravity.

---

## *The Eight Principles as Chinese Thermodynamics*

*He who comprehends the greater destiny becomes himself a part of it. He who comprehends the lesser destiny resigns himself to the inevitable.*
– ZHUANGZI[18]

When I was young, I used to sit and watch the wind blow the trees. Up to a certain age I remember thinking that the trees moved of their own accord. Eventually I realized the wind, although invisible, was influencing the direction the trees moved. Soon I began to wonder, "What moves the wind?" I see the eight-principle system as describing the nature of the mechanical forces in life that interact in a causal way with the body. I see the five-element system as addressing relatively more the issue of what motivates these forces. How does who I am being direct the flow of *qi* in my life?

What karmic issue attracts a given wind into a person's life is a question that deals more ostensibly with a patient's quality of mind as seen through the five-element model. However, once that wind arrives, although it is ephemeral in nature, it still is a physical force that can be understood in a linear and causal way according to the eight-principle system.

We may liken the physical substrate of the body to the tree. From the conformation of proteins on a cell's surface all the way to the shape of a person's tongue, the eight principles allow us to assess the directionality of the physical forces that, like the wind, blow to influence physiological structure and functioning. For example, a typical eight-principle statement might sound like this: An individual was exposed to wind that entered the *taiyang* meridians. In response to this cold, the body raised a fever that created excess heat. This heat pushed most, but not all, of the cold out of the body. The cold stagnated in the meridians, and the body continued to produce excess heat while trying to move the cold. This heat consumed fluids over a long period of time, which lead to a state of *yin* deficiency in the lungs. The kidney supplied *yin* to supplement the lungs and itself became *yin* and ultimately *jing* deficient.

In describing a patient's bladder infection, we might say that heat from the heart traveled to the small intestine, where it in turn proceeded to the bladder. Therefore the patient's urine is burning as the heat is dispelled. This excess heat is causing inflammation in the urethra, and therefore urination is difficult. These examples illustrate a cause-and-effect, linear quality of thought quite similar to the type we are familiar with in Western biomedicine. These statements are quite different in nature from those that might be made from a five-element perspective relative to the elemental quality of *qi* that motivates a patient's choices in life. Despite the linear and causal nature of this type of deductive thinking, it is necessary, to a degree, if we are to be modern practitioners of an integrated medicine.

---

## *Inner/Outer and the Enumeration of Being*

In the Chinese enumeration of being, odd numbers are *yang,* corresponding in nature to heaven, and even numbers are *yin,* corresponding to earth. The numbers five and one are both odd and *yang* and therefore correspond in nature to heaven. The number eight is further from one *(dao)* than the number five and is even in nature, therefore corresponding to earth. Hence the five-element system is a relatively internal (closer to heaven) system, addressing the pure *yang* motivational nature of *dao* as it is evident in the qualities of mind, spirit, and internal constitutional dynamics (early heaven: *xiantian qi*).[19] In contrast, the eight-principle system is a relatively outer system that addresses phenomena of a more *yin* and physical nature at the level of thermodynamics. Therefore it is relatively more facile in assessing acquired characteristics (later heaven: *houtian qi*). Although it is imperative to acknowledge that both types of thought are integral to the practice of our medicine, it is also imperative to acknowledge their natural hierarchical relationship as relatively internal and external theories.

## *Ways of Knowing*[20]

*To see the small is called illumination (*ming*).*
*To abide by the soft is called strength.*
*Use the bright light (*guang*),*
*But return to the dim light.*

– DAODEJING[21]

The cognitive style of Western biomedicine can be designated as being ultimate *yang* in nature. As a hard science, it studies the form of things *(yin)* with a *yang* approach (active, analytic, linear, causal, reductionist, left brained, and deductive) that is necessary to illuminate the nature of form. Therefore we can designate Western medicine as ultimately *yang* in nature. The *yin* within this cognitive *yang* is constituted of the soft sciences such as social science and psychology. Often these misapply the quantitative method to the study of nonphysical *(yang)* phenomena such as culture and mind. Practitioners of such methods seem to be yearning for the holistic, spiritual, and integrated approach of a form such as Chinese medicine, but because their core value system is rooted in the hard sciences, they fail to ever truly make the necessary leap to a truly integral perspective.

The quality of thought inherent in Chinese medicine may be designated as *yin* (soft, receptive, intuitive, right brained, inductive, synthetic) relative to the *yang* modes of inquiry inherent in Western science and medicine. The five-element system represents a form of inquiry that may be considered absolute *yin* in quality. Because the spirit and mind have no form and are purely functional *(yang)* in nature, it takes a *yin* approach to reflect their movements. As a relatively circular and right-brained style of thought, the five-element system allows us to discern the nature of *yang* through the process of reflection as it animates the functioning of mind and spirit. The five-element system, in reflecting the qualitative nature of constitution, addresses that which is ultimately intangible, the purpose of life itself.

The quality of thought inherent in the eight-principle system of diagnoses constitutes the *yang* within the *yin* of Chinese medical thought. As a relatively *yang* mode of inquiry, the eight-principle system focuses more on the *yin* and static aspects of structure and physiology. Although clearly a functional, as opposed to a structurally based model, the eight-principle model entails a relatively linear mode of thinking that involves analytic thought. This linearity is expressed in each of the paired guiding criteria. For example, think of the parameters of cold and heat as existing as extremes at either end of a linear continuum of temperature. The eight-principle model assesses the relative nature of one's physical template and how it interacts with the environment as predicted by the principles of thermodynamics. The syndrome patterns themselves are fixed entities superimposed over an infinitely complex and dynamic system to impose a sense of order.[22]

In short, the eight-principle system addresses a given manifestation at a moment in time. The five-element system addresses the conscious or unconscious motivation of that manifestation. Whereas the eight-principle system tends to differentiate symptoms or "what's manifesting now," the five-element system differentiates the context of who the person was made spiritually at conception and how his consciousness has guided him to this point through the making of choices. The eight-principle system is relatively more useful for determining who the person was made physically at conception and how each choice made has become embodied physically.

In this world, our bodies and conditioned minds are bound by time and space. As we see later, the five-element and eight-principle systems are inextricably linked to each other, and it is sheer delusion for any practitioner to think otherwise. Although the conversation occurs in the context of the five-element versus the eight-principle systems, we must understand that, in actuality, both cognitive process are occurring simultaneously during the diagnosis and treatment of a patient. In fact, we can think of the five-element and eight-principle systems as describing relatively right- and left-brained approaches to our medicine, respectively.[23] To deny either source of input to the diagnostic and treatment process is to deny a significant part of one's capability as an integrated human being.

---

## *The Five and the Eight*

Let me illustrate the differences in cognitive style between the five-element and eight-principle systems of thought by comparing the process of diagnosis and prognosis utilized in each. When treating a patient in an integrated way, you are faced with two tasks. The first is to identify the quality of the patient's constitution. This is the deepest view of the patient, which corresponds to the nature of the inborn influences that will most effectively support the patient's healthy functioning. The quality of this endowment may be likened to a diamond buried in the patient's depths. Constitutional diagnosis allows you to access these influences and, in essence, to turn up the fires from within that support the patient's evolutionary path.

Your second task is to determine the ways that these primordial influences have been tarnished in life. In other words, what is the nature of the trash that lies on top of and obscures the nature of this inner diamond? The five-element and eight-principle systems empower complementary views of both innate and acquired influences. Here I elaborate these as they pertain both to theory and clinical practice.

---

## *Early Heaven: Views of Constitution*

In the Western sciences, the study of constitution limits its inquiry to the physical mode of transmission from our ancestry. The biomedical concept of genetics focuses on DNA, RNA, and the physical, causal mechanisms that produce specific manifestations from the genetic code. As a science focused equally on mind, body, and spirit, the notion of constitution in Chinese medicine encompasses both physical and nonphysical transmission from ancestry.[24] Our nonphysical transmission from ancestry is present as the concept of karma, which includes the inheritance of both our physical form as well as the lessons we bring to this life.[25] Our karmic endowment contains the fixed aspect of who we are that can never change, which I refer to as "fate." This fixed aspect of self constitutes the template of all we can possibly become, given the best environment and most conscious effort exerted on our own behalf. The ability to fulfill this potential depends primarily on our willingness to acknowledge who we are fundamentally, take appropriate actions in the world based on our choice to always manifest virtue, and to make the most of life whatever it may offer us. Living in this way is the path to fulfilling destiny.

---

## *The Five-Element View of Constitution*

In the five-element system, all observations are referenced to the functional relationships inherent in the *sheng* and *ke* cycles. The five-element model empowers the discernment of individual destiny because it is the motivating force behind each human life. The inborn constitutional influences are seen as a patient's deepest source of strength. The five-element constitutional treatment focuses on reestablishing the *jing, qi,* and *shen* as the guiding influences in a patient's life and eliminating the dysfunctional *qi* that supports the life of the created self. For example, a patient who habitually responds to the emotion fear by squandering resources may be determined to be water constitutionally. Therapeutic action is then taken to harmonize the patient's relationship to fear by choosing acupuncture points and herb formulas that aid in cultivating the virtue of wisdom.[26] The emergence of each element's virtue is seen as the fulfillment of its highest innate potential.

A statement about five-element constitutional type is a definitive statement about the quality of a patient's consciousness and experience of life. The five-element system allows us to discern how the qualitative nature of a patient's consciousness impacts both the expression of his virtues as well as the embodiment of his vices. In the five-element system, the quality of the patient's constitution is the central focus of every treatment. Any specific manifestation is always interpreted in the context of the quality of his constitutional dynamics.

---

## *The Eight-Principle View of Constitution*

The notion of inherited constitution in the practice of eight-principle traditions is quite different than that just described. The eight-principle system is used to assess a patient's physiology according to patterns of imbalance, which are referenced to a system of eight criteria rather than the five elements and twelve officials. These "eight guiding criteria" are used to qualify an imbalance according to whether it is relatively *yin* or *yang*, internal or external, excess or deficient, and hot or cold.

The focus of eight-principle practice with regard to constitution is on aiding a patient to compensate for inherited deficiencies or on supplementing resources that have been squandered during life. Functional imbalances that are described as being constitutional in the eight-principle system generally refer to a deficiency of kidney *yang* or *jing*. This often presents on the pulse as a deep and/or feeble kidney pulse in a younger person, indicating the deficiency occurred prenatally and not from overwork during life. Symptoms that might appear in such an instance include physical deformities such as cleft lip, mental retardation, kidney-deficient asthma, or a weak nervous system such as might be found in attention deficient disorder.

In the eight-principle tradition, when a statement is made regarding the constitutional nature of a symptom or illness, it refers to weakness in an organ system that has been inherited in a genetic and physical sense. There is no implication that this weakness corresponds to an individual's life lesson or purpose. Note here that, in fact, the five-element tradition recognizes that the constitutional official can be either the weakest or the strongest organ as determined by pulse diagnosis.

## *Summing Up Views of Constitution*

The five-element system emphasizes the relative quality of a patient's constitutional endowment. The eight-principle system, however, in assessing one's innate endowment of *yin* and *yang*, places emphasis on the relative quantity of one's constitutional resources. Quality of constitution relates relatively more to the intangible qualities of a patient's consciousness and to the choices he makes in embracing or rejecting destiny. Focus on the relative quantity of the constitution relates more to the causal structure of the human body and the physical forces that impinge on it. Hence the eight-principle model addresses relatively more the aspect of inheritance I have termed fate. To say it another way, the five-element system is relatively concerned with considerations of consciousness and how it impacts our physical substrate. The eight-principle model focuses relatively more on the body's form and how it impacts functioning.

For example, the ultimate *yin/yang* designation of a human being might be considered his or her genetic sex. Men are designated *yang* and women *yin*. Our physical sex is genetically determined or "fated" from conception and manifests in the physical substrate. Human will alone cannot change it, and the form of our sex certainly impacts our consciousness in life. However, whereas our sex is fixed, our sexuality and our relationship to it is variable depending on the quality of our spirit and mind. Any life event that impacts our experience of sexuality will be interpreted according to the dictates of our constitutional type. The choices we make in life can seal our fate if they are unconscious or, to the degree they are conscious, forge our destiny.

## *Views Toward the Acquired Constitution*

From the perspective of Chinese physiology, sunlight constitutes the only source of nourishment from our first breath onward. The five-element model specifically focuses on the way constitutional variables "color" the quality of all *qi* that arrives to us. Hence we may understand that the earth element is innately prone to generating damp and to suffering in the presence of damp. Regardless of the specific physical manifestation, the five-element model informs us of the innate variables that motivate its existence.

In contrast, the eight-principle model elaborates the nature and functional location of the pathology itself. Hence the eight principles in conjunction with the four-division and six-stage models deal eminently better with the nature of acquired characteristics themselves. Is the wind (a five-element consideration) internal or external, hot or cold? The five-element system informs us the liver is prone to wind, but it is the eight-principle system that addresses the detailed nature of the specific manifestation.

To sum up, the five-element system elaborates the nature of inborn constitution as the theme of life, whereas the eight-principle system elaborates its relative *yin* or *yang* nature. The five-element system discerns the motivating theme of life, whereas the eight-principle system discerns the nuances of the plot.

---

## *The Two Models Are Implicit Within Each Other*

Here I advance the notion that the five-element and eight principle modes of inquiry are complementary in nature and lie implicitly within each other. The difference between traditions that emphasize either the five elements or eight principles over the other lies only in which model is primary. The other form of diagnosis often lies implicitly within the primary diagnosis. In fact, it is not possible to be absolutely a "five-element" or "eight-principle" practitioner in the way many of us like to think of ourselves.

For example, a practitioner of a tradition based on the eight principles may discern that a patient's skin condition emanates from a relative excess of heat in the patient's blood. However, as soon as this condition is attributed to a specific organ system, considerations of the five elements must implicitly inform both the diagnosis and treatment plan. If it is discerned that excessive heat from the liver is affecting the blood, a treatment strategy may be chosen that focuses on draining heat and cooling the liver by sedating acupuncture point Lv-2, the fire point on the liver meridian. This treatment may be performed for the explicit reason of draining excess fire from the liver, and there may be no consideration given to the patient's constitutional type. However, implicitly, a five-element needle technique of sedation is implemented that possesses a broad array of psychological and spiritual effects. That is, Lv-2 may help the patient relax enough to gain perspective in life, ultimately helping transform the disordered emotion of belligerence into the virtue of benevolence. Of course, if the practitioner's awareness is not focused on the possibility of this transformation, its occurrence may be lost on the patient as well.

However, a practitioner of a five-element constitutional tradition may discern that a given patient's constitutional type is wood. This discernment alone, however, is not specific enough to constitute a framework for treatment. In order to refine the diagnosis, you must discern whether the patient's constitution is governed by the gallbladder or liver official, which is to have made a *yin/yang*, internal/external, distinction. Further, once you note the official of the constitutional type, you must use the eight guiding criteria to inform decisions regarding whether a sedating or tonifying needle technique is to be used, suggesting, respectively, that the patient is relatively excess or deficient. You must also decide to use moxa or not, which implies having to make distinctions relative to the continuum of cold and heat. Lastly, the discernment of what level of being the illness is obscuring—body, mind, or spirit—involves a distinction according to the continuum of internal (spirit) to external (body).

---

## *The Integrated Diagnosis*

The internal syndrome patterns are indicative of the way one's entire functional system is compensating for, as well as manifesting, an underlying constitutional imbalance. The eight-principle syndrome pattern is, in every instance, a compensation for the constitutional imbalance that may or may not be involved explicitly in the pattern. For example, an individual may have a pattern diagnosed as deficient *yin* of the liver with heat rising to disturb the heart. This pattern may correspond to a Western medical diagnosis of essential hypertension. However, the presence of this pattern does not suggest in any way that the individual's constitution is either wood or fire.

A person of any constitutional type may evidence this pattern, and having a constitutional type of either wood or fire does not suggest a person is prone to this syndrome pattern or to hypertension. Treatment that tonifies *yin* and drains heat may yield an improvement in symptomatology depending on the syndrome pattern involved. However, from a five-element constitutional point of view, if the syndrome pattern was merely a secondary compensation for the dysfunction of the constitutional official, nothing of lasting value has been accomplished therapeutically. It is expected that either the previous symptom or a more serious one will return because the underlying constitutional basis of the illness and pattern has not been addressed. Hence it is imperative to address constitutional dynamics simultaneously with those of the syndrome pattern itself.

However, an individual's constitutional official and element may well be involved in their predominant syndrome pattern. For instance, in the previous example, the patient evidencing liver fire disturbing the heart might possibly be a liver or heart constitutional type. In this scenario, five-element and eight-principle treatment strategies are more likely to overlap because both therapies focus on the same issues. A constitutional herbal formula may be chosen that drains liver fire and addresses liver *yin* deficiency, helping cool the fire and lessen its tendency to rise and disturb the heart. Further acupuncture points that cool and calm the liver and heart may be chosen so both therapies address both the underlying imbalance (the constitutional weakness) as well as the secondary manifestation named by the specific syndrome pattern.

Through the course of my clinical practice, I have evolved an integrated understanding of the five elements and eight principles. In formulating an integrated diagnosis of a patient, I observe the five-element constitutional type and note habituated patterns of thought that ultimately drive the patient to overwork either physically, which leads ultimately to *jing* deficiency through a path of *qi* and *yang* deficiency, or emotionally, which leads ultimately to *jing* deficiency based on a path of stagnation and *yin* deficiency. In this way I am able to comprehend the entire gamut of internal syndromes as they exist in Chinese medicine. For example, an earth constitutional type who habitually overworks mentally will tend toward patterns of deficient stomach *yin* because overwork of the nervous system depletes *yin*. In this scenario the overworking of the mind is related to the spirit *(shen)* associated with the earth element, which is the *yi* or thought. In contrast, an earth type who is more inclined toward overworking physically will tend more toward patterns of deficient spleen *qi* or *yang*.

---

### *The Inner and Outer Aspects of Diagnosis: Theme vs. Plot*

A primary distinction between the diagnostic processes utilized in the five-element and the eight-principle traditions is that the former tends to focus on the theme that emerges, whereas the latter tends to focus on the plot. The theme is the meaning implicit in what happens; the plot is the form of what happens. In essence, the five-element system focuses on the meaning implicit in life's events and then proceeds to understand how that created meaning has been embodied over time to yield who the patient is in the moment. The eight-principle system focuses on the current momentary manifestation and then attributes meaning to it in order to discern the functional basis.

For example, the five-element practitioner, in asking a question about the quality of a patient's digestion, places primary emphasis on the purely functional qualities of the patient's response. Changes in the patient's color, sound, odor, and emotion while discussing his digestion give clues as to the constitutional basis of the imbalance, which is the underlying elemental theme of the individual's life. Emphasis is also placed on the degree of conscious awareness the patient displays while discussing the topic. A primary interest here is the degree to which the patient's answer conforms to clinical reality. A patient whose pulse and tongue confirm weak digestion and who states that digestion is poor is demonstrating awareness of his condition. A patient whose answer conflicts with other clinical findings often is out of touch with his own internal state, and this corresponds to a diagnosis of ignorance. All things being equal, the degree to which a patient is consciously aware of his own state of being, the better the prognosis from the standpoint of constitutional medicine.

In contrast, from an eight-principle viewpoint, one tends to focus on the informational content of the answer to a diagnostic question. Considerations of the presence of gas, bloating, sensations of heat or burning, cravings, and the quality of the stool are of central importance. This type of information is identified with the plot of the patient's story or "what happens." Our life theme stretches from conception to death and, perhaps, beyond. The plot of life consists of all the individual events that occur between our first breath and the moment of death. Although the plot may change, and any individual manifestation may improve or worsen, the theme that corresponds to our life lesson never does.

---

## *Diagnosis*

*Anybody who looks and knows it is to be called a spirit;*
*Anybody who listens and knows it is to be called a sage;*
*Anybody who asks and knows it is to be called an artisan;*
*Anybody who feels the vessels and knows it is to be called a skilled workman.*

– *NANJING*[27]

Practitioners in the five-element tradition of J. R. Worsley diagnose based on considerations of color, sound, odor, and emotion (CSOE). These parameters are thought of as being as relatively more "energetic" in nature as compared with other traditions of Chinese medicine that focus relatively more on the parameters of physical symptomatology.[28] Responding to such a statement, Giovanni Maciocia wrote, "Why are color, sound, emotion, and smell 'energetic' and the pulse and tongue are not? In my view all manifestations are energetic, whether it is thirst, a red face, anger, or constipation. Certainly some symptoms, such as tongue and pulse, are more meaningful than others."[29] Of course, all manifestations are based on *qi* ("energy") for their existence.[30] The discernment of "energetic" and nonenergetic or "physical" diagnosis is invalid as an ultimate principle. Yet Chinese medicine is a science based largely on discernment of increasingly fine shades of quality, and distinctions can be made between relatively "fast" moving waveforms such as a patient's psychospiritual state and more "slowly" moving waveforms such as those that support the manifestation of the coating on the tongue.

The Sixty-First Difficult Issue in the *Nanjing* compares the abilities of those who diagnose by looking (color) to that of the spirits *(shen),* by sound to that of the sages, by asking to that of the artisans, and by pulse to the ability of the skilled workman. I take this as a hierarchy, indicating that even using physical indicators such as the pulse are not as "deep" (revealing of spirit) a diagnostic method as the others mentioned. I believe this author's meaning is that just to look at the patient and know his diagnosis, in essence his quality of destiny, is the highest form of practice. To one who can immediately discern the theme of a life, learning the plot becomes a technical detail. Technical though as they may be, discerning the qualities of the specific manifestations of symptoms and signs are vital in the practice of medicine.

In the five-element tradition, determining constitutional type is premised on the most subtle and rapidly changing (fast) waveforms that emanate from the patient's being. These are the patient's CSOE. Using these as diagnostic methods ensures that you are perceiving the whole of the patient with your entire sensory apparatus. Hence you become a finely tuned instrument for reception of data as you are able to discern finer and finer shades of human functional expression. By attending to CSOE moment to moment over many years, your senses are renewed as the conditioning effect of ego is gradually removed and the constitutional tint on your window of consciousness is removed. It is diagnosis by CSOE that plays a central role in the practice of the five-element tradition as a cultivational art. That the waveforms underlying CSOE change so quickly reflects that they are synchronous with the momentary functional state of the patient because his life is based in spirit. The process of being in communication with these subtle shifts during diagnosis and treatment affords you the deepest possible contact with the patient's motivating force in life. This brings you into the proximity of the patient's ground of being itself.

Unlike CSOE, which are waveforms that can be sensed at a distance, the pulse is the most subtle and rapidly changing waveform that can accessed by physically touching the body. The amount of information gleaned from the pulse is limited only by your ability and the sophistication of the system you are using. Nonetheless, because pulse information is conveyed through physical touch, I feel it is skewed toward providing information about relatively more physical levels of being than CSOE.

Tongue diagnosis, although not conducted through physical touch, also yields diagnostic information of a more physically substantive nature. Inasmuch as the tongue and its coating change relatively slowly, we can say it reflects the functional change of a relatively slow waveform. Diagnostic indicators that change instantaneously, such as CSOE or pulse, perfectly reflect the momentary state of the patient. In so doing, they precisely contain the implicit image of the individual's past, present, and future. They also, therefore, give a qualitative appraisal of the aspects of being that may most rapidly change to support the evolution of the individual. Of course, the fastest moving waveform is that of evolution itself, and the slowest is that corresponding to the stagnation of mundanity (ego) that thwarts evolution. Waveforms that change more slowly and support the manifestation of diagnostic indicators such as the tongue or *hara* tend to represent aspects of self that are more embodied and less likely to change in the short term.

Knowing a patient's constitutional type yields a deep view of the themes that lay at the heart of each patient's life. Our life theme is synonymous with our destiny and purpose for having entered into this incarnation. All ill health results from a suppression of the true self, and pulse diagnosis may help determine precisely how the theme of life, if not expressed virtuously, presents as functional and ultimately physical pathology.[31] The diagnosis obtained from such an assessment is generally expressed in terms of eight-principle physiology.

---

## *The Relationship Between Herbal Medicine and Acupuncture*

In my practice I tend to use acupuncture in large part to address functional imbalances emanating from the patient's constitution, and I tend to use herbs more frequently to address the attendant eight-principle pattern. When the constitutional organ is directly involved in the syndrome pattern, both strategies tend to overlap. In this case I am likely to choose a constitutional herbal formula that will reinforce the intention of my acupuncture point selection and other therapeutic suggestions.

Acupuncture and herbal medicine both make reference to the same systems of thought, namely the five elements and eight principles. However, there are fundamental differences in the practices of these two disciplines both theoretically and practically. For the most part, I find acupuncture to be largely a homeostatic form of therapy. Which is to say that, within wide parameters, the use of acupuncture will either help balance an individual's functional system, aiding all physiological processes to move toward a median point of harmony based in the absolute, or do nothing at all.[32] Hence it is quite difficult to harm an individual with acupuncture, short of either gross neglect or incompetence.

Because acupuncture points function by harmonizing the excesses and deficiencies that lie at the heart of any given therapeutic issue, it is difficult to move an individual in a pathological direction. For example, if Lu-5, the water point associated with the lung official, is treated, its functional effect will tailor itself to the needs of the patient. If the patient's lungs are too moist, it will disperse the excess moisture, and if the patient's lungs are too dry, it will lubricate the lungs.

Herbs, however, can be relatively more directional in nature and do not always balance physiological processes in the same way as acupuncture.[33] An herb with a specific function of drying the lungs (for instance, pinellia) will only have a drying effect. In this case if it is prescribed and the dosage is too high, or it is given for too long a time, the individual's lung function may be compromised. Further, if the diagnosis is wrong and the patient's lungs were not damp to begin with, there exists a real potential for injuring the normal physiological process of the official.

A concept such as "drying" or "moistening" the lungs has implications on many levels of being. For example, the presence of the emotion grief, which affects the lungs, may obscure the heart spirit in much the same way that clouds obscure the sun. The presence of phlegm in the lungs either chronically or acutely may also be compared to clouds that cause obscurity. Both grief and phlegm may be considered to exist on a continuum of dampness in the lungs as it expresses itself in relatively less to relatively more materially manifest aspects of being.[34] Therefore, treating either of these conditions could involve a therapeutic strategy of drying or resolving dampness. In my experience acupuncture and herbal medicine possess different domains of efficacy when it comes to addressing the psychospiritual or physiologically based aspects of such a condition.

In a scenario where an emotional or spiritual imbalance is the basis of the primary obfuscation in the lungs, acupuncture will most readily enable the patient to experience that which is being obscured, namely the virtue of inspiration empowered by balanced lung function. Acupuncture may instantly restore the memory of a pure aspect of being (a virtue) by accessing the primordial *qi*, that aspect of heaven within us that remains untouched by life. An acupuncture treatment such as Lu-5 (the water point on the lung meridian) and Lu-2 ("cloud gate") might be chosen to eliminate the damp condition and resolve the grief. However, because in this case no clinical evidence indicates dampness manifesting in the lungs physically as mucus, it is unlikely an herbal formula would be prescribed that is drying. If, however, the dampness in the lungs presents as phlegm, then herbal treatment will resolve it more readily in the short term.

Herbs have relatively more directionality on the material plane, and their functions do not vary as widely as do the functions of acupuncture points. For this reason, I consider acupuncture more purely functional in nature relative to herbal medicine, which I perceive as relatively more materially based. Acupuncture points do not exist as discrete anatomical structures. They exist solely as the functional relationships among many anatomical structures (like nerves, blood vessels, muscles, etc.) as well as nonmaterial aspects of being like emotions, virtues, spirits, and belief systems.

As opposed to an acupuncture point, an herb is an entity that possesses a discrete structure and can be weighed. Its effects are mediated by the digestive system through which it materially enters the body. For this reason I tend to think of herbs as acting through and being most closely associated with blood. The effects of acupuncture, in contrast, are mediated physically more by the nervous system, which represents a significantly faster mode of transmission than the digestive system. For this reason I consider acupuncture to act through, and be more closely related to, *qi*.

An acupuncture treatment is performed in a moment, and its effect can be instantaneous. Therefore you must be greatly in synch with the momentary functional dynamics that emanate continuously from the patient such as CSOE and pulse. Herbs, however, are prescribed over a much longer period of time. It is not unusual for a patient to take a given formula for months or perhaps even years. Therefore, the herbal prescription occurs with less emphasis on the moment and relatively more on a greater expanse of time.

Acupuncture being more aligned with *qi* is therefore a relatively more *yang* form of therapy as compared with herbal medicine, which is more affiliated with blood and by extension more associated with *yin*. Thus you may think of acupuncture as being associated with the qualitative way in which *shen* (the *yang* aspect of spirit) acts as a configurative force. The action of the acupuncturist in creating the context for a particular treatment may be likened to the performance of a ritual. The potency of this ritual creates a great receptivity on the part of the patient to the particular treatment chosen.

Needling a point in precisely the right place and moment may be likened to that of a lightning bolt from heaven striking the primordial sea to initiate evolutionary change. This impulse allows the *qi* to harmonize the functional basis of separation that lies between the mind and the heart of each patient's being. Each acupuncture point is unique in its ability to touch some aspect of being to which an individual patient has lost access. In "touching" this aspect of being, the memory of original nature encoded within the point's function may be restored to the patient. Acupuncture points work by harmonizing continuums of unbalanced expression precisely in the way that the *chongqi* is said to harmonize the dualities of heaven and earth back into a state of primal unity.[35]

Herbal medicine, associated more with blood, may be considered a relatively *yin* form of therapy compared to acupuncture. Thus you can think of herbal medicine as being more aligned with the function of the *ling*, the *yin* aspect of heart spirit.[36] The acupuncturist performs a ritual externally to the patient in creating the context for each treatment. However, in herbal medicine it is the patient who performs the ritual of preparing and taking the herbs on a regular basis. Compared with the momentary effect of an acupuncture treatment, herbs slowly evoke change over time by altering the form of the substrate through which our *qi* moves. Acupuncture may be said to change the direction and quality of the wind (the nature of our consciousness) that blows through and thus alters the conformation of the trees or the substance of the body. Herbal medicine may be said to change the conformation and the quality of the trees (the protein conformations on cell surfaces, for example) in order to attract a different quality of wind (consciousness).

In acupuncture, you act on the patient from the outside and initiate a change within. In herbal medicine, the patient is acted on from the inside, and the change occurs from without as the physical structure on the body is altered. Acupuncture ultimately causes our belief system to realign with the truth that corresponds to our innate purpose in life, and this alignment can occur in one instant because it is predicated on consciousness, which is the fastest moving form of physiological *qi*. Herbs work over a longer period by changing the actual structure of the body, which may also alter our experience of life.

Note that both acupuncture and herbs do seem to have components of action that are faster than can be accounted for by purely physical processes. For example, I have seen cases where the placement of one needle in a patient's knee (St-36) during an initial treatment resulted in immediate and long lasting relief from crippling arthritis in her hands. This example of healing occurred faster than could be explained by any known source of information transmission. In a similar way, I have had the direct experience of being able to discern the effects of an herb the moment it touched my tongue and long before it had a chance to be digested and enter my bloodstream.

Taken together, both acupuncture and herbal medicine complement each other to yield an integrated therapeutic regimen in precisely the same way that the five-element and eight-principle systems complement each other to offer an integrated diagnostic and treatment method. Acupuncture, dealing relatively more with the instantaneous movements of *qi*, consciousness, and spirit, lends itself naturally to the five-element approach. Herbal medicine, addressing relatively more the *yin* of the body's structure, lends itself relatively more to the eight-principle approach.

However, these findings are generalizations. Constitutional formulas are prescribed from the perspective of a five-element constitutional approach. Thea Elijah has formulated a sophisticated practice of Chinese herbal medicine that elaborates harmonizing the variables of conscious awareness and spirit even in the use of formulas that are not generally considered constitutional in nature.[37] And, as we all know, the eight-principle model has been applied to the practice of acupuncture. Regardless of the technique or method of healing, it is clear that considerations of spirit are the foundation of meaningful healing and must always inform any therapeutic action we take.

---

## *Obtaining the Absolute*

If a patient's endowment of *yin* and *yang* were perfectly integrated, it would be theoretically impossible to perform a five-element or eight-principle diagnosis on that individual. In such an imaginary case, one would not be able to discern any pathological tendency toward a functional expression that was relatively more external or internal, excessive or deficient, warm as compared with cold, or *yin* as compared to *yang*. Further, the five elements would be so integrated that none could be said to dominate the patient's functional dynamic. Of course, the only individuals conceivably possessing such a configuration are the idealized infant and sage as portrayed in the *Daodejing*.[38]

The five-element and eight-principle systems, representing time and space, respectively, offer a dualistic view of material existence. Both models posit a central point that represents the absolute position in which all influences are in harmony and no pathology can be discerned. The relationship of each system to the absolute is instructive as to the relevance of each model to a person in different phases of his life.

Before we embrace an absolute perspective in life, the five-element model is relatively more important for helping a patient transcend his egoic view of the world. By diminishing the dysfunctional *qi* that supports the created self, the five-element system can help deflate the stories about who we are, and how life is, that delude us. This is because the five-element model can help us reorient to the three fundamental relationships on which the created self is based: the arising of thought, the presence of feeling, and the passage of time.[39] The five-element system can evoke an experience of true self, prior to the moment of the false self's birth, that can return our connection to, and identification with, our innate ground of being. In short, the five-element system nourishes the fulfillment of destiny.

Before we embrace an absolute perspective in life, the eight-principle model is efficacious in helping us refine a constitutional diagnosis and address specific symptoms while we are treating the underlying constitutional dynamics. The eight-principle system also empowers the possibility of practicing a truly preventive medicine. It can help us determine the likelihood that a specific manifestation will arise so we can direct the underlying functional dynamic toward a more benevolent outcome. This is an important aspect of eight-principle practice because it is compassionate. While ignorant, people take actions that negatively impact their bodies and subvert healthy physiological practice. Helping mitigate the effects of such *past* practices (of course you will educate and empower patients to stop such behaviors) can help ensure that patients will have less to regret after they wake up to a new, absolute perspective in life (I am optimistic). Further, our bodies do appear to be subject to the laws of thermodynamics as well as the principles of genetics, and the eight-principle system can help mitigate these influences in perpetuating illness.

The absolute position in the five-element model as represented by the relationships of the *sheng* and *ke* cycles is only ever one moment, and one step away, toward the center of the circle. Attaining the absolute perspective relative to the five elements is within the grasp of anyone who sets his will upon it single-mindedly. Standing in this place, we no longer personalize thoughts or feelings and now perceive the cycling of the elements as a wheel of ignorance *(samsara)*. At the center of this circle all virtues become one, and the constitutional element now expresses innate virtue instead of narcissistic self-concern. This positive momentum born of identifying with and expressing the authentic self resolves karma as we become increasingly bright and clear.

Because earth can be considered to define the central position among the elements, integrity becomes the core virtue from which all others arise and strengthen by their presence. Although, from a five-element perspective, the absolute is attainable psychospiritually, it is not attainable physically. That is to say that, theoretically, one must always have a weakest organ. Hence I have always been able to identify a constitutional type in the most enlightened sages I have met. However, it is certainly a matter of choice whether or not we choose to identify with or express the pathological thoughts and feelings associated with our constitutional official.

The central position of the eight-principle model, although it exists theoretically, does not appear to be attainable by human beings. For this is a position where *yin* and *yang* are in absolute balance. To suppose a living human, as we now know humanity, could obtain such a position is to posit that gravity would have no effect on his body. Consciousness and spirit can certainly transcend matter to obtain the absolute perspective available at the center of the five-element circle. But the body does not appear able to absolutely transcend the laws of thermodynamics.

By the time people have their awakening in their 30s and 40s, or later, their momentum of ignorance will have become embodied past what a change in perspective can fully rectify. The spirit can change direction and gain full enlightenment in one heartbeat, but change in the body takes time.[40] Certainly miracles occur every day and I have seen rapid great improvement in, and even disappearances of, medical conditions after a person has gained a radically new perspective in life. However, I have always been able to discern fundamental imbalances in *yin* and *yang* in every person regardless of the degree of their spiritual attainment or physical health. Note that, from a spiritual perspective, absolute physical balance is not a pressing consideration. That is to say, it is through spirit alone that we are able to transcend the limitations of the body specifically and the material world in general.

After we embrace an absolute perspective in life, the importance of the five-element and eight-principle systems reverses to a degree. From an absolute perspective, our problems, emotions, and thoughts become trivial and uninteresting, especially when considered in the context of the challenges facing humanity today. If a patient is not personalizing his thoughts or feelings, the constitutional element no longer creates a compelling source of disharmony and the natural hierarchy inherent in the *sheng* and *ke* cycles reemerge to establish homeostasis based on the Daoist ideal of *ziran* (spontaneity).[41] At this point, five-element treatment becomes rather simple as the psychospiritual thrust of the practice falls into the background. The sine qua non of five-element treatment is alignment with the absolute and, once it occurs and a patient has the single-minded commitment not to move from there, the application of the five-element system changes.[42]

However, the patient will still evidence ingrained physical symptoms and syndrome patterns that are well addressed with an eight-principle approach. I noticed when I first started treating people who had adopted an enlightened perspective in life that they rarely complained about anything and never adopted the position of being a victim. Yes, they mentioned their physical problems, but they did not complain about them. In other words, the problems were in no way impeding them from fulfilling their purposes in life. In this case the eight-principle approach was beneficial for addressing their concerns. In fact, their moment-to-moment commitment to not moving from the absolute rectified their *qi* sufficiently that the psychospiritual aspects of the five-element system now played less of a role in my treatment approach.

Of course, ego is our supreme opponent and does not give up the fight for its life so easily. Habits tend to reassert themselves, and the five-element model plays an important role in keeping at bay the dysfunctional *qi* that supports the ego. From an absolute perspective, the five-element approach is still quite useful for seasonal treatments and for helping *qi* continue to flow in its evolutionary direction when obstacles arise in the spiritual path. Together the two approaches can address the embodied aspects of ignorance that maintain the momentum of the created self (eight principles) as well as mitigate the degree to which the mind chooses the bondage of ego over original nature (five elements) once the availability of such a choice is known.

---

## *Deductive and Inductive Reasoning*

*Chinese medicine, like the other Chinese sciences, defines data on the basis of the inductive and synthetic mode of cognition.*
– MANFRED PORKERT[43]

Deductive and inductive reasoning are complementary modes of inquiry. The process of deduction lies at the core of the Western sciences and seeks to infer from established theory the properties or behavior of an object. Inductive reasoning, foundational in Chinese medicine, seeks to formulate generally applicable theories based on specific findings. Hence deductive reasoning applies principles ("hard facts") to specific cases, whereas inductive reasoning is used to formulate generally applicable principles themselves.

### *Deductive Reasoning*

*In being enlightened and comprehending all,*
*Can you do it without knowledge?*
– DAODEJING[44]

Deductive reasoning is a top-down approach that proceeds from a general theory to observations about a particular case. In deductive reasoning, the premises, or so-called facts, guarantee the conclusion. If the premises are true, the conclusion must also be true. For example, theory states that a mole of any element contains $6.022 \times 10^{23}$ molecules of that element. A mole of any substance is the molecular weight of that substance in grams. For example, water ($H_2O$) has a molecular weight of 18.0 (16.0 for the oxygen atom and 1.0 for each of the hydrogen atoms), so the mole-to-gram relation for water is 1 mole water = 18 grams of water. It would be impossible to count the number of $H_2O$ molecules in every 18 grams of water on earth to ultimately prove this theory. Yet theory allows me to predict accurately that if I take precisely 18 grams of water from the tap, it will contain exactly $6.022 \times 10^{23}$ molecules of water.

An example of this type of thought in TCM is the formulation of the principle that a fast pulse indicates the presence of heat. Therefore, if an individual patient's pulse is fast, the patient must have heat. This "if X then Y" type of thought is linear in nature and proceeds from fixed expression such as "a fast pulse" to fixed conclusions, such as the presence of "heat."

### *Inductive Reasoning*

Inductive reasoning is a "bottom-up" approach that proceeds by observing an actual phenomenon and extrapolating the principles that account for it. For example, we may note the patient's myriad patterns of functioning and then formulate a principle that fits this unique case. Hence in Chinese medicine theory can always be manipulated to fit a given functional dynamic. For example, if two people are getting married we may say, "Of course, he's metal and she's wood. They complement each other perfectly!" Here we have used the reality of the two people loving each other to confirm a general theory that metal and wood are complementary. However, three years later when the couple is getting divorced, we may say, "Of course, his metal overcontrols her wood; she can never grow in the relationship!" In inductive reasoning, the application of theory is flexible, and it is the individual case or "what is" that constitutes "reality."

Whereas the conclusions of a deductive argument are always determined by the premise, the conclusions of an inductive argument may or may not be correct when applied to any individual case. For example, if I tell you that everyone I have met with red hair has had a temper, and you notice that Carol has red hair, it may or may not be true she has a temper. Because an individual case may not conform to the general principles, theory must always be flexible enough to account continually for each new observation.

---

## *Induction and Deduction in Chinese and Western Medicine*

*From knowing to not knowing,*
*This is superior,*
*From not knowing to knowing,*
*This is sickness.*

– *DAODEJING*[45]

Although deductive reasoning is used, it plays a relatively minor role in the development and practice of Chinese medicine as a holistic science that is complementary in nature to Western medicine. Chinese medicine is not a science of fixed manifestations and inflexible rules but rather a science of tendencies and therefore always basically inductive in nature. In Chinese medicine, the application of principles allows us to discern the pathological momentum and direction of physiological processes and of determining what action is likely, but never guaranteed, to influence them in a positive direction. Our clinical skills allow us to infer, given any current manifestation, the process that generated it and the likely future outcome if nothing changes. As an inductive science, every new observation we make modifies our collection of theories, which continues to grow and expand flexibly in proportion to our quality of attention and experience.[46] In diagnosing the functional dynamics of any individual, we are free to draw on any of the diverse theories of Chinese medicine, to the degree we have an intellectual and cognitive grasp of them, and to modify them as needed to fit each specific case.

In Chinese medicine, all observations are context sensitive. Therefore a fast pulse can indicate the presence of heat in one person, yet indicate shock and disruption of the heart/kidney axis in another. A tight pulse in the liver position can indicate a state of *yin* deficiency in one case and in another suggest the presence of pain in the flanks. The right proximal pulse can indicate the functional state of the heart protector, three heater, bladder, small intestine, large intestine, lower *jiao,* or kidney *yang* depending on the context of the individual and moment in which that pulse is taken. From the perspective of one who is looking from the absolute heart of the matter, there are no statements of "fact" in Chinese medicine.[47] Hence the *Daodejing*'s emphasis on "not knowing" quoted earlier.

Western medicine, in contrast, is largely deductive in nature because general theories are applied to specific cases. This works well in the context of the physical sciences where the laws of thermodynamics do not vary from one carbon atom to the next. It also works well in treating trauma where the import of the physical variables of health loom large. However, in the practice of preventive medicine or health maintenance, where considerations of mind and spirit are paramount, the lack of flexibility evidenced by the hard facts of theory undermine the medicine's clinical relevance. This shortcoming is evidenced in the commonly made observation that symptoms rather than patients tend to be diagnosed. "Patients with liver problems have elevated liver enzymes" is a theoretical statement of fact. If a given patient has a one-sided headache, a sour taste in the mouth, right flank pain, and is angry all the time, but his enzymes show no statistical deviation from normal, he is deemed to have a healthy liver. Regardless of the functional findings to the contrary, the context of the individual case is ignored as the specific physical manifestation of "liver enzymes" is focused on. In this case the patient is likely to be diagnosed with a "psychosomatic" problem manifesting as a cluster of "unrelated" symptoms.

Or consider this reasoning process: "Hypertension is caused by a constriction of the circulatory system. George has hypertension; therefore his circulatory system is constricted. If we apply a drug that relaxes the circulatory system we will have addressed the cause of the disorder, and the hypertension will be automatically cured." Here the functional basis of the hypertension as might be differentiated according to the principles of Chinese medicine has been ignored in deference to the physical attributes of the specific manifestation. In fact, "George" and the millions of other unique individuals having the similar manifestation of hypertension are missing from the picture entirely as the reality of the symptom they all share in common is diagnosed and treated according to a mechanistic "this manifestation equals that cause which gets this response" value system.

---

## *Deductive and Inductive Thought in Chinese Medicine*

*Somehow a way was always found in China to reconcile opposing views and to build bridges—fragile as they appear to the outside observer—permitting thinkers and practitioners to employ liberally all the concepts available.*
– PAUL UNSCHULD[48]

An important hallmark of one who has grasped the theoretical heart of Chinese medicine is the ability to hold two apparently contradictory statements as being simultaneously true. To such a person, the notion that any specific functional theory could have a one-to-one correspondence with any specific physical manifestation, its interpretation, or therapeutic response would appear ludicrous. Such a person would feel free to interpret every clinical finding entirely on its own merits given the always unique context in which it was observed. With every new observation it is theory that is modified to account flexibly for any perceived phenomena. Reality is always right, and theories bend accordingly.[49] This inductive process lay at the heart of the synthesis of Chinese medicine from its inception up until the arrival of the Jesuits to China in the 1600s.[50]

It is clear that the cognitive process at the heart of Chinese medicine is inductive in nature. Yet it is also clear that with the rise of materialism in modern times, there has been an increasing trend toward the use of deductive reasoning, ultimately to the exclusion of the inductive process, in both the teaching and practice of Chinese medicine. The domination of TCM by a materialistic core value system and the deductive thought process has moved it away from its theoretical foundations and increasingly into the realm of Western biomedicine. This movement is potentiated by a willingness to compromise the core values of Chinese medicine in order to integrate its form into Western medical, educational, and economic models, which themselves are predicated on a materialistic ideology.

When confronted with two statements that apparently contradict each other, the Western analytic and deductive mind requires only one possibility to be true and asserted as fact. Hence each individual manifestation is focused on, and the overall context of health and healing is lost. Thus we see the trend to standardize every conceivable aspect of the language, teaching, testing, and practice of Chinese medicine. This has gone so far as the suggestion for the standardization of Chinese pulse diagnosis through the application of computer technology so students can be tested objectively.[51] This in the name of integrating Chinese medicine into Western cultures on the terms of deductive, reductionist, mechanistic thinking itself. This movement away from the heart of the medicine is not exclusive to those practicing in the TCM paradigm either.[52]

It is important to discern the difference between TCM proper, as a state-run medicine based on the core values of dialectical materialism and its use of the eight principles, and the eight-principle system itself. For example, I witnessed Leon Hammer working in a pre-TCM eight-principle tradition of Chinese pulse diagnosis that afforded huge vistas onto the ever-evolving panorama that is human physiology. It is the core value system (transcendent or materialist) of an individual interacting with her balance of cognitive processes (inductive/deductive, holistic/reductionist) that will determine the decisions she makes both relative to how she practices medicine and how she legislates that others should practice.

Under the influence of those with a materialistic core value system and a deductive thought process, Chinese medicine is growing increasingly similar in nature to that of Western biomedicine. Now syndrome patterns (symptoms) are diagnosed instead of patients, and herbs and needles are prescribed, as the equivalent of drugs and surgery, for specific manifestations in a "this equals that" manner. Now pattern discrimination, rather than being infinitely variable and arrived at as the end result of a diagnosis, has been turned into a set of immutable theories that are equated to specific treatments. Rather than differentiating each patient to arrive at a statement that defines his unique physiological state, all findings are referenced to a limited and unchanging set of syndrome patterns that fail to account for the diverse presentations of evolving humanity. In this regard, note the failure of TCM to acknowledge the existence of deficient liver *yang* or kidney excess as functional disharmonies or of shock as the central etiology of a fast pulse in modern times.[53] Note also the tendency to reduce every functional metaphor in the language of Chinese medicine to its most external *(wai)* physical equivalent.[54]

It is largely the conscious, or unconscious, reliance on the deductive thought process that allows for the acceptance of reduced iconographies of the pulse and reliance on a limited number of diagnostic patterns. In turn, these reduced theory sets fail to capture the breadth and depth of the ever-evolving beings that we humans are. Linear and causal thinking becomes the norm as long lists of symptomatic indications for herbs and acupuncture points appear in texts and product literature, ignoring pattern differentiation all together. Standards in translation that offer a one-to-one correspondence between Chinese characters and English words are also strong evidence for the rise of the deductive thought process in Chinese medicine. The "this character is the equivalent of that word" philosophy mirrors the "this point for that symptom" treatment approach and denies the rich metaphorical spirit of the Chinese language. It also reinforces the deductive thought process in students to the detriment of the heart of our medicine as a whole.

---

## *Summary*

Despite the movement toward deductive reasoning in TCM, it is clear that the five-element system, as delineated in my work, has preserved the inductive style of thought at the heart of its approach. Viewed from the center of the *sheng* and *ke* cycle, every patient is diagnosed uniquely according to the infinite array of five-element expressions possible. Standing in the absolute perspective, the practitioner recognizes the natural hierarchical relationships of the various diagnostic models and is free to apply them all flexibly as they are relevant to any specific diagnosis. All symptoms and syndrome patterns are viewed as secondary emanations of constitutional dynamics that, in conjunction with ever-changing life circumstance, yield a continually variable and flexible array of diagnostic and treatment options. With every diagnosis and treatment, the practitioner's set of available theories expands in number and complexity. If this inductive and synthetic approach constitutes one's core value system, than she is likely to support legislation that allows for a broad diversity of tradition in teaching, testing, licensing, and clinical practice.

The point here is not that the process of deduction should play no role in Chinese medicine. The point is that, unless the method of inductive synthesis is full grasped and embodied, the heart of the medicine will never be available to the practitioner and is likely to disappear in the medicine itself. Inductive reasoning is the inner *(nei)* aspect of the medicine, and the deductive process is a relatively external *(wai)* process. In

Figure 37.5 (pp. 746–747), I categorize different cognitive processes and value systems according to their *yin/yang* and internal/external designations. Of course, due to the complementary natures of *yin* and *yang*, the presence of each quality will always be apparent in its opposite. We must be clear that the limitation here is not inherent in either *yin/yang* thinking or in the eight-principle system. The problem, rather, lies in our unwillingness to grasp the cognitive style of inductive thought and to embrace an integral core value system based on transcendent principles.

---

## *Beyond Chinese Medicine*[55]

*Problems cannot be solved by the same*
*level of thinking that created them.*
– *Albert Einstein*

The five-element and the eight-principle models are complementary in nature, allowing us to describe the motivation generating a specific manifestation (5E) and to characterize the specific attributes of the manifestation (8P) itself. The fundamental dualities of time and space addressed by these two systems characterize the material world perceived by the conditioned senses. It is interesting to observe how, even today, people practicing Chinese medicine tend to see the five-element and eight-principle systems as discrete entities. In part this is due to different cognitive styles of thought and core value systems that are culturally ingrained and chosen by practitioners of each system. Cultural distortions not withstanding, both qualities of thought are implicit within each other, and any separation between the two represents a lack of integration on the part of the practitioner.

So many of us upon first encountering Chinese medicine recognized an innate beauty that complements the analytic and causal approach to life. Yet the materialist worldview inherent in TCM can be transmitted like a virus that reinforces the already-knowing of the conditioned Western mind. This virus can make it either difficult or impossible for us to ever achieve the fruit of the longing sparked in our hearts when we are first touched by Chinese medicine. For some of us, this recognition has led to a rejection of deductive thought in favor of the softer cognitive style we find in the five-element tradition. However, just as the body serves as an anchor for the spirit, the deductive thought process is a necessity in the balanced practice of our medicine.

Another important source of input contributes to the separation between the 5E and 8P models and a lack of integration in their associated thought processes. This has to do with a genuine lack at the theoretical root of Chinese medical, and cosmological, theory itself. Fundamentally, the ancient view of time, present in all perennial religions and philosophies, is two dimensional. That is, if we look at the five-element model as depicted, it becomes abundantly clear that the classical Chinese view of time was circular. Season followed season, year followed year, and dynasty followed dynasty, and nothing ever changed. It was water, wood, fire, earth, metal, and then water again, eternally reflecting the nonarising of *dao* on which the movement of the elements are patterned.

True, forms changed, and such changes could be qualified elementally, but only ever in terms of a functional process that itself was cyclical and unchanging. *Yin/yang* thinking could also describe the transformation of one thing into another, but all states arrived at were considered equivalent.

BASIC ASSOCIATIONS

| ***Yang*** | ***Yin*** |
|---|---|
| Heaven | Earth |
| Function | Form |
| Spirit | Body |
| Round | Square |
| Time | Space |
| True *qi* | Mundanity |
| Authentic self | Ego |
| Acupuncture | Herbs |

COGNITIVE MODE

| ***Yin*** | ***Yang*** |
|---|---|
| Five element | Eight principle |
| Right brain | Left brain |
| Reflect | Illuminate |
| Circular | Linear |
| Soft | Hard |
| Inductive | Deductive |
| Ever-expanding theory sets | Reduced iconographies |
| Intuition | Data |
| Holistic | Reductionist |
| Metaphor | Literal |
| Art | Science |
| Theme | Plot |
| Not knowing | Already knowing |
| Chinese | English |
| Cultivation | Research |
| Humility | Arrogance |
| Faceless | Face |
| Who am I? | Self-image |
| I feel, therefore I am | I think, therefore I am |

*Figure 37.5*

DIFFERENTIATING CLINICAL PRACTICE

When Zhuangzi, for example, informs us that he does not know if he is Zhuangzi dreaming he is a butterfly or a butterfly dreaming he is Zhuangzi, we are alerted to the notion that transformation is the nature of life itself.[56] However, each reality, the butterfly and Zhuangzi, are equivalent in that they are each just one of the ten thousand things, each representing an illusion relative to the absolute that is unnamed *dao*. True, fear transforms into wisdom and *jing* into *ling*, but there was historically no perspective that what was called fear, wisdom, *jing*, and *ling* were themselves evolving.[57] Time was thought to be circular and form linear, and they existed in static relationship to each other. There was, in short, no notion of evolution motivating change. In fact, if any directional movement of transformation was discerned by the Daoists, it was one of devolution as

VALUE SYSTEMS

| *Yang* | *Yin* |
|---|---|
| Practitioner | Physician |
| Apprenticeship | Standardized tests |
| More substance in education | More hours in education |
| Selfless service | Service of self |
| Evolution | Status quo |
| Radical transformation | Conservatism |
| Fee for service | Insurance reimbursement |
| Diversity | Standardization |

*Figure 37.5 (continued)*
DIFFERENTIATING CLINICAL PRACTICE

*Note that my inclusion of the eight-principle system in the right column represents only a specific distortion of* yin/yang *thinking as it occurs in modern TCM under the influence of materialism and deductive thought processes. It is clear that* yin/yang *thinking itself can be practiced relatively holistically and inductively if there is a shift in core values toward the heart of Chinese medicine. Because* yin *and* yang *always exist implicitly within each other, all categorizations here are negotiable. For example, herbal medicine can certainly be practiced in a way that liberates the spirit, and acupuncture, as we all know, can be practiced symptomatically. Note that in the* yin *cognitive mode, the ego introduces distortions by personalizing feelings (I feel, therefore I am), and in the* yang *cognitive mode, distortions are introduced by personalizing thoughts (I think, therefore I am). In balance, the* yin *approach presided over by the heart is typified by having no self-image yet being interested in self-discovery as apparent in the question of "who am I?" The* yang *approach, presided over by the conditioned mind, generates a fixed self-image defined by ego that tends to end inquiry into true nature.*

humanity was thought to move increasingly away from the pristine state of *dao* as it existed in the longed for, and imagined, golden age.

Now, however, we know that time and space are integrally related and inextricably linked through the process of evolution. The form of our bodies and the structures of our consciousness evolve over time. The linearity of eight-principle thought and the circular nature of the five-element model unite as one in the helix. The helix depicts time as not strictly circular but as a spiral staircase, like a molecule of DNA, winding ever upward. The position of humanity relative to evolution is unique among all life-forms on earth. For we humans are in the position to play a conscious role in our own evolution both literally now in terms of directing it with technology and by consciously engaging with it through our willingness to change, now.[58]

---

## *An Evolutionary Model*

As the quotation from Albert Einstein suggests, the qualities of thought that produce a problem will never be able to solve that problem. In this regard, I thought it might be interesting to look at Chinese medicine, both the forces that have shaped it historically and its current status, from an emerging perspective on the evolution of human consciousness. Spiral dynamics (SD) is a model of the evolution of human consciousness that is complementary in nature to the orientation of Chinese medicine generally and to the five-element constitutional approach specifically.[59] I am hoping that this model, holographic in nature and Western in origin, might objectively reflect for us what steps will be necessary for us to take as the caretakers of our medicine for present and future generations.

### *The Model*

From the perspective of SD, the potential for all states of consciousness that humanity can embrace lie as dormant within us. These unique qualities of consciousness, or core value systems, are termed *memes*. A meme is a "basic stage of development that can be expressed in any activity."[60] Like the Chinese five elements, the memes are not conceived as static fixed stages of development but as flowing waves (similar to the orbs in Porkert's terminology) that transform into and interact with each other. Individual memes are activated as the challenges that face us, and our species, evolve over time. Each meme describes an innate and emergent core value system that is inherent to meeting life's evolving challenges.

As each official in Chinese medicine contains an implicit representation of the whole, each new meme that arises incorporates all previous memes. Each meme describes a core value system possessing a specific set of potential virtues. To the degree that ego is the motivating force of human behavior, the value system inherent in a meme is distorted in a way that is self-serving to either an individual or a culture. Each meme is associated with a specific color, which, in the context of this model, has no inherent significance other than providing an expedient way to talk about each quality of consciousness.

Graves predicted that each tier would contain six memes with each successive tier representing higher and more refined states of the lower tier memes. However, this model is very much in flux, as is the evolution of consciousness itself, and for the sake of this discussion I have divided the currently identified memes into three tiers (see Figure 37.6, p. 753). The first-tier memes, beige through green, describe the various states of the evolution of human consciousness beginning with the appearance of humans on earth some fifty thousand years ago up to the present. These are grouped together because a primary characteristic shared by these states is that each has only its own perspective dominating its outlook on life. In other words, a first-tier individual or culture tends to have one meme that dominates both belief and behavior to the relative exclusion or denial of the others.

The second-tier memes are newly emergent states of consciousness that are now in evidence. They possess the unique trait of having perspective on all previous states of consciousness (memes). Hence they are potentially able to recognize the innate importance of each, as well as the ways in which their manifestation has become distorted by the egoic mind. It is recognized that, in order for these new emergent states of consciousness and their core value systems to flower, a harmonious balance of first-tier memes must first occur. As we proceed up the spiral through the third tier, each meme, yellow through teal, is characterized by greater integration and wholeness with a corresponding decrease in the influence of ego.

The egoless states that spiritual seekers associate with enlightenment begin to occur in the third tier with the emergence of the coral and teal memes.[61] These are now experienced by those deep in meditation and lived by those who are truly enlightened.[62] The current wave supporting this evolutionary step is in its infancy but does represent the collective destiny of the human race should we survive. In fact, as discussed in Chapter 1, it is only through mitigation of the ego that the human race appears to have any chance of survival at all.[63]

## *A Comparison of Models*[64]

A human being is the sum total of all inherited and acquired sources of input acting together in a way that is inextricably linked. Inheritance can be divided into two types. The first, physical transmission from ancestry, is recognized in the West as the genetic code. The second, nonphysical transmittance, is recognized by the Eastern sciences as karma. Acquired experience can also, perhaps, be divided into two sources of input. The first are the physical events of one's life or what actually happens. The second are the nonphysical aspects of life experience or the *memetic* (existential) nature of what happens.

The five-element model discerns the constitutional tint inherent from conception that will color a person's unconscious interpretation of his life experience. It tells us how a person is inherently prone to interpreting the meaning of life events and how he comes to embody that meaning as either health or pathology. In other words, the model helps us discern the *innate* tint on the window that an individual looks at life through. This is a model that excels at assessing the individual but can be extended to describe the functional dynamics of any system culturally or globally. Hence we see the five-element model applied historically in fields as diverse as alchemy, spirituality, medicine, architecture, military strategy, and politics.

Spiral dynamics, in contrast, is a model that excels at discerning the core value systems of cultures that can also be applied to individuals. According to SD, it is the quality of the external events of our life that activate certain innate capacities known as memes. The memes then provide a tint to consciousness that colors our experience of who we are and how life is in a way that defines our core value system. To state the relationship between the models succinctly, the 5E system discerns the inborn constitutional variables that define our core value system (constitutional type) in a way that is destined to emerge *regardless* of what happens in life. The SD model discerns the quality of innate potential activated by our life circumstances *regardless* of who we are. The five-element system describes the configuring forces that arise innately from within, and the SD model describes the configuring forces of acquired experience. Both models emphasize the nature of the tint on the window that we see life through.

From a 5E perspective, what happens in life is the plot, and one's constitutional tint defines the theme of how we will interpret the meaning of those occurrences. If the tint on your window is destined to be blue (water) at conception, everything that happens in life will look blue regardless of its nature. From a SD perspective, if a green (meme) set of problems arises in life, it will activate a green core value system within us as our innate cognitive capacity rises to meet the qualitative nature of the challenges we face. Both models endeavor to describe the quality of the tint that an individual (5E) or culture (SD) experience self and life through. We might say the 5E model describes how we project ourselves into the world, whereas the SD model describes how the cultural context of our world projects itself onto us. And both models hold the potential to educate humanity about the tints on our window of perception so we can see more clearly the motivations and assumptions that influence our actions, and then change.

---

## *The Spiral Dynamics Model*

The SD model describes different states in the evolution of consciousness that have occurred in humanity for the last fifty thousand years. These have been verified by research to exist across a broad spectrum of humanity.[65] Think of the cool- and warm-colored memes as representing the dual influences of *yin* and *yang,* respectively. The dual threads of the spiral suggest the various waves of evolution rise back and forth between self- (warm memes) and social- (cool memes) oriented phases. In other words, a warm meme such as beige arises where the core value system is self-centered on the individual's survival. As this approach reaches its limits, a new set of problems present themselves, and a new cognitive state (purple) emerges that is more socially oriented, to solve the problems the previous meme created. Then, eventually as a rebellion to the forces of socialization, the red meme emerges as individuals reassert their own authority and power. This pattern is repeated throughout the first tier.

### *The Memes*

Here I give some metaphors to impart a sense of the core values inherent in each meme.[66] Think of these as imparting a tint to the window we see life through in the same way as the five-element constitutional type. The key difference between the two is that constitution arrives from within (early heaven), and the memes are activated from without (later heaven). Memes, like constitution, are a functional concept that, in this case, denote the relationship between core value systems and behaviors.

#### *First Tier*

***Beige:*** *Archaic-instinctual.* Relates to basic survival; prioritizes food, water, warmth, sex, and safety. Survival is based on the use of habits and instincts. Sense of a distinct self is negligible. Humans are the smartest of animals but are not much different from animals. Life is perpetuated by forming into survival bands that hunt in packs.

In ancient China, think of Huntun, the emperor of Chaos from Zhuangzi, and the depiction of Shennong, the Spiritual Farmer, appearing with long claws like a wild animal.[67] This depiction actually represents the next stage of development, purple, under the auspices of Daoism looking back at beige and idealizing it as representing a time of perfect harmony or to quote Laozi, "the wilderness before the dawn."[68]

***Purple:*** *Magical-animistic.* Belief in magical spirits, shamanism. Curses, spells, and portents determine events. Forms into ethnic tribes bonded by the spirits of ancestors. Political status determined by kinship and lineage.

Evidenced in: tribes and gangs, and present in ritualistic practices and superstition. The New Age values that lead to use of crystals, rituals, and the wearing of purple. In Chinese medicine this meme is inherent in the notions of *ling, gui, gu* illness, and possession. Also present in the notion of healer as shaman and of treatment as ritual.

***Red:*** *Power gods.* Represents the initial emergence of a self that is distinct from the tribe. This self is asserted based on strength and impulsivity. It seeks immediate gratification, taking what it can with no concern for the consequences. Gods and goddesses are almighty forces that play with humankind and are to be both feared and respected. Warlords protect the community in exchange for obedience and labor.

Evidenced in: temper tantrums in two-year-old children, punk rock, teenage rebellion, the gunfighter in the "Old West," soldier of fortune, New Age narcissism,[69] football, Genghis Khan, feudal empires. To understand the virtue associated with the red meme, think of the heroism of the police and firefighters on 9/11. In China, think of the "Warring States" period (1027–220 B.C.E.) and warlords feuding prior to the communist revolution in 1949.

***Blue:*** *Mythic order.* This stage brings order and structure to the egocentrism and impulsivity of red. Life has meaning and a purpose with outcomes determined by an omnipotent god or order. Destiny is appointed by heaven. The righteous order enforces a code of ethics and conduct according to the absolute and unvarying principles of "right" and "wrong." Those who act righteously are rewarded, and those who act wrongly suffer severe consequences in life and perhaps even eternal damnation. Rigid social hierarchies; law and order; impulses controlled by guilt; fundamentalism; conformist and conservative. A sense of absolutism that can be either religious or atheistic in nature.

Evidenced in: Puritan America, Confucian and Marxist China, totalitarian states, the "moral" majority, patriotism, nationalism. The assertion by certain leaders of Chinese medical traditions that their tradition is the "One right way."

***Orange:** Scientific achievement.* Here the self, born in the red meme, reasserts itself to break free from the "herd mentality" of the blue meme. Meaning is sought on the terms of the individual. Cognitive style is mechanistic and deductive, relying on "objective" data arrived at experimentally. The world is viewed as a machine with natural laws that can be mastered and rationally manipulated toward one's own ends. Materialistic

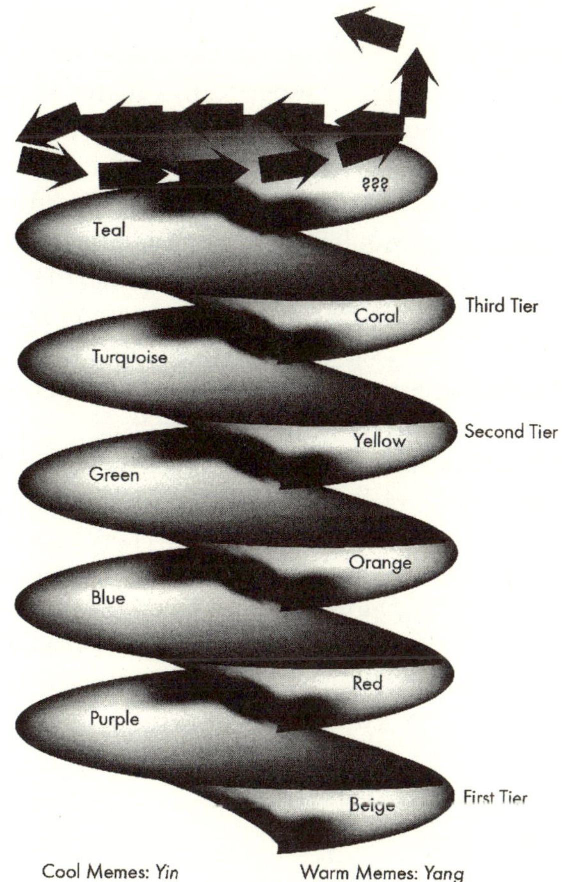


*Figure 37.6*

THE EVOLUTIONARY SPIRAL

*Here the SD model is presented as a single-coiled helix depicting the ongoing cyclical transformation of warm into cool memes and back again. If a line was drawn vertically between each of the cool and warm memes and these coils were twisted, we would arrive at a double helical model similar to DNA. Here I have designated the warm memes that are self oriented as being* yang *in nature and the cool memes that are socially oriented as being* yin *in nature.*

gains motivate individual and group achievement. The laws of science, particularly Newtonian physics and Social Darwinism, govern political, economic, and social arenas.[70] The earth's resources are manipulated by corporate states for strategic gain.

Evidenced in: Wall Street, colonialism, materialism, capitalism, entrepreneurship, multilevel marketing. In Chinese medicine, those who see how the "game" of success is played in America and want to win it on the game's own terms; evidenced-based studies, the "status" of accredited degrees and professional titles, the desire to get insurance reimbursement and "use" the system to one's own advantage.

***Green:*** *The sensitive self.*[71] Emerges as a reaction to the "uptight" conservatism of blue and the "superficial" materialism of orange. Communes, egalitarianism evidenced in the civil rights movement (and women's rights, gay rights, children's rights, rights for gun owners, rights for people who smoke, rights for loggers, etc.), environmentalism. Feelings, subjectivity, and nonlinear thinking take precedence over cold objectivity and rationality. Rejects hierarchical thinking as the basis of prejudice. All viewpoints are considered relative, and therefore all have equal merit. Wait for consensus before taking action that can lead to endless processing and indecisiveness. The human potential movement; self-actualization. Pluralism, diversity, multiculturalism.

Evidenced in: the Green Party and Greenpeace. Amsterdam; socialized health care, humanistic psychology, consciousness raising (CR) groups, civil rights, feminism, political correctness, diversity as a political stance, Gaia. In Chinese medicine, the emphasis placed on feelings and the relativistic viewpoint emphasized by the five-element tradition (each official is the "most" important). The movement to protect diversity of tradition from the absolute outlook of blue (TCM) and the materialistic outlook of orange (the doctors of TCM). The orientation of practitioners toward "unconditional love" that makes it OK (I'm OK, you're OK) for their patients not to change.

### *Second Tier*

With the flowering of the green meme in the 1960s and its descent into the narcissism of the 1970s, human consciousness stands ready for a jump to second-tier states of awareness. The second-tier memes are characterized by having a perspective that both includes and transcends all first-tier memes. Hence the second-tier memes can think both laterally (within a given meme) and horizontally, using the cognitive approach of each meme as it fits any specific context.[72] This perspective also affords a view of the virtues and distortions of each previous meme. Distortions are eliminated as the ego's influence of behavior is mitigated, and the virtue of each meme is incorporated for the health of the overall spiral or "for the sake of the whole."[73] Note that the second-tier memes can be thought of as "harmonics" of the first-tier memes. Hence yellow is a higher order harmonic of beige and turquoise of purple. This is similar to the notion in Chinese medicine that the *ling* spirit is a higher order expression of *jing* or that virtue *(de)* itself is a higher order expression of original nature *(de)*. The second tier is the collective leading edge in the evolution of human consciousness.

***Yellow:*** *Integrative.* Life is an ever-changing rainbow of natural hierarchies (holarchies: the *sheng* and the *ke* cycles),[74] forms, and systems. The highest priority is given to functionality, spontaneity, and flexibility. Natural degrees of ranking and excellence are recognized to complement egalitarianism. Hence each official can be thought of as being the "most" important, but we all know the Heart is the Most Important. Knowledge and ability supplant power, status, or group sensitivity. Good governance facilitates the emergence of individual entities through the levels of increasing complexity or nested hierarchies.[75] Understands that chaos and change are natural phenomena.

***Turquoise:*** *Holistic.* Universal holistic systems. Here a "unified field theory" of all of existence becomes possible theoretically and in actuality. Uses the entire spiral to detect harmonics, mystical forces, and the "pervasive flow states" that penetrate any organization.[76] The world is viewed as a unified, dynamic organism possessing a collective mind. Self exists both autonomously and in communion with a larger whole.

Theoretically the second tier has six stages that can be thought of as harmonics of the first-tier memes. However, the emergence of memes above the first tier is a relatively new phenomenon, and not a lot of data has been collected on these newer types of consciousness. For the sake of this discussion, I am designating yellow and turquoise as second-tier memes and coral and teal as belonging to the third tier of consciousness. The second tier memes appear to be characterized by a fundamental integration of cognitive processes that empowers the understanding of holistic and integral models. In contrast, the third-tier memes appear to represent a deeper spiritual integration that is increasingly characterized by the transcendence of ego.

Second tier is evidenced in integral holistic systems thinking as illustrated in Wilber's theory of everything (TOE).[77] In Chinese medicine, such thinking recognizes the natural hierarchy of the *sheng* and the *ke* cycle as a universal theory. Don Beck describes the yellow meme as "left brain with feelings" and the turquoise meme as "right brain with data."[78] This represents to me the ability for the practitioner of Chinese medicine to fully integrate the cognitive styles inherent in the five-element and eight-principle systems as discussed earlier. Such an integration would include being able to utilize both inductive and deductive thinking and to understand as well as transcend the traditional uses of the different diagnostic models presented in Figure 37.1. Hence the ability emerges to apply the numeric systems of Chinese medicine "out of the box" so they become universally relevant. For example, the six-division model of cold-induced illness has the potential to be universally applicable as a way of describing how life events impress themselves on us to extract emergent cognitive states.

*Third Tier*

***Coral and Teal.*** These represent transpersonal waves of consciousness where the influence of ego has been mitigated. Beck does not discuss these in detail, although Wilber does name coral as the "psychic wave."[79] These are also the stages in which Kimura postulates that cosmic consciousness emerges.[80]

The coral and teal memes are experienced in enlightened states and represent a transpersonal realm of functioning. Throughout history there have been individuals, such as the icons of the world's religious traditions, who have evidenced this type of awareness. This wave of consciousness is in its infancy but represents the collective destiny of humanity if we survive and choose to fulfill our calling. Here the dual principles of autonomy and communion are realized to the degree that unity with the first cause (*yuan:* 元) is obtained and sustained. Each part of the whole functions autonomously to fulfill its own destiny, not for itself, but for the sake of the whole. Thus we may gain an absolute perspective on the different, relative, and illusory states of consciousness inherent in the *sheng* cycle. In such a state the input of ego to behavior is mitigated, and the heart takes its rightful place as emperor as natural hierarchy, intuition, and the integrity of the heart/kidney axis are restored.

### *The Elements and the Memes*

Complementary in nature, both the five-element and SD models describe the internal and external tints on the window we see life through. The elements and memes can be viewed as being functionally related in some interesting ways I discuss here. It is possible to differentiate the memes according to their elemental associations, and these thoughts represent only my initial speculation on the matter. Note in this regard that the first five memes can be thought of as arising in the order of elemental generation. Remember that the elements are generated cosmologically in the order of water, fire, wood, metal, and earth.[81] Here I offer some initial observations on the relationship between the memes and the elements. Do not take these to indicate that a person with a given predominant meme will have that specific elemental constitution. I am merely noting functional similarities between the two models.

The beige meme can be thought of as corresponding to the water element. Here "fight or flight" responses govern survival as the individual is undifferentiated from his surroundings. Hence the kidney official and water element is the basis of all internal syndrome patterns just as beige is the basis of the spiral.

The purple meme can be thought of as corresponding to the fire element. Here the heart spirits, *shen* and *ling*, and fire and water mix as awareness of a distinct self is born. Here magical ritual is empowered and embodied, respectively, by the heart spirits *shen* and *ling* and the virtue of the fire element(禮: ritual).

The red meme can be thought of as corresponding to the wood element. Planning and decision making are negligible as the dominant ego emerges to assert itself impulsively regardless of the consequences. Hence the strong presence of red can be thought of as corresponding to conditions of liver heat entering the blood and the rising of liver *yang*. Conversely, the suppression of healthy red in an individual can be thought of as corresponding to deficient liver *qi* or *yang* and the associated expressions of lack of self-confidence, self-esteem, and an inability to forcefully assert one's self.

The blue meme can be thought of as corresponding to the metal element. Just as the blue meme arises evolutionarily to "civilize" the impulsiveness of red, so too does metal (blue) control wood (red) across the *ke* cycle. Hence the metal element's virtue of "righteousness" and of being in touch with heaven regulates the self-oriented impulsivity of wood.

The orange meme can be thought of as corresponding to the earth element. Here the earth is seen as an endless resource to be utilized according to one's own ends. The scientific method, corresponding to the capacity for thought *(si)* and intention *(yi)*, are applied to mining the earth's bounty. Unbalanced earth is driven by the narcissistic self-concern focused on this question: "What can I get for myself?" Hence unbalanced orange expresses itself as materialism, consumerism, and overexploitation of the earth's resources.

The green meme can be thought of as corresponding to the wood element. Here we have a break with the order of elemental generation, which is purely cyclical in nature. Chinese cosmology would therefore predict that the next stage would be a return to water where the cycle would begin again. Whereas the red meme seems to correspond to a state of liver excess typified by aggression, the green meme seems to be typified by passive aggression associated with conditions of liver *yang* and *qi* deficiency. This is evident in the reticence of the baby boomers to judge anything in the name of rejecting hierarchies. In fact, the only thing the green meme will always judge are those who are deemed to be "uptight" and therefore "judgmental" themselves. The 1960s were typified by a passive aggression against the government and culture at large ("Hell, no, we won't go" paired with "Peace, love, freedom, happiness"). Marijuana (green) was the drug of choice, and it is interesting to note that it undermines liver *yang* and harms the processes of decision making, planning, and, ironically, creativity in general.

The yellow meme falls under the auspices of the fire element and the three heater official, specifically. Here an integration occurs as consciousness recognizes and integrates all previous stages of consciousness and development. This is present outwardly as humanity replicates its nervous system externally as the Internet and information technology promotes communication between all peoples and ideas on earth. In yellow the entire organism of society and self is brought under the integrated control of the heart.

The turquoise meme can be thought of as corresponding to a deep integration of all the elements and a rectification of the heart/kidney axis. Here planetary, group, and self concerns assume their proper hierarchical order, respectively. The concern for self drops away as survival of the species and self now depend on selflessness. As we move on toward the third-tier memes, the human species is liberated from ego as the kidneys and heart are liberated from the bondage of fear and desire, respectively.

Memes are socially conditioned forms of consciousness, whereas the elements arise internally. It is interesting to note in patients their "memetic" makeup, and I do so now regularly. The five-element system offers a way to decrease the presence of dominant memes and increase the presence of those that have not manifested fully. This area offers a new frontier for Chinese medicine that shifts its emphasis from a mere medicine of "self" toward a true planetary medicine.

I have noticed that people of any memetic composition can have any relative elemental balance. For example, a person in whom the red meme figures prominently will act impulsively and forcefully to fulfill desires with no concern for consequences. In a water type this will manifest as excessive ambition; in a wood type this will manifest as belligerence; a fire type will tend toward sexual aggression; an earth type will consume excessively; and a metal type will tend toward idealistic fanaticism. These patterns could also be considered indicative of an excessive wood elemental overacting on various elements and officials. Conversely a given elemental constitution can express itself uniquely in each meme. In other words, a person of any memetic quality of consciousness can still grieve inappropriately (metal) or have poor sexual boundaries (fire). I have found that anything—acupuncture, herbs, homeopathy, or spiritual experience—that rectifies *qi* harmonizes both the elements and memes simultaneously.

## JAMES

***Constitution:*** *Heart Protector: Fire/Wood within*
***Dominant Memes:*** *Purple, red, and green*
***Deficient Memes:*** *Blue and orange*
***Symptom:*** *Asthma*

James is 32 years old and works in whatever construction jobs he can find. He's exceptionally talented as a singer/songwriter, sculptor, and painter. Having been front man for a punk rock band, his arms and torso are covered by self-inflicted tribal tattoos of his own design. All the lyrics of his songs were directed against the hypocrisy he perceived in the "establishment." Extremely impulsive in nature, James would "follow his heart," staying up late and pushing himself hard in the pursuit of life's "pleasures." He wore a Bowie knife in a sheath on his right hip. James had recently gotten a bad cold that went deeply into his chest and left him with difficulty in breathing that was not resolving. He had also hurt his back while lifting on a construction job. His pulse was tense and pounding at all positions, and his tongue was bright red.

### *Analysis*

From the perspective of Chinese medicine, James was a heart protector constitution with secondary liver involvement. His liver was pouring heat into his blood, which in turn agitated his heart. This heat fueled the emotional content of James's art, ultimately leaving him with unfulfilled desires because his hunger could never be sated. The heat and *qi* stagnation in his upper *jiao* was responsible for the feelings of oppression in his chest and his difficulty in breathing. This dynamic was potentiated by numerous breakups with lovers that resulted in the generation of *qi* stagnation in his diaphragm.[82]

From the perspective of SD, James's configuration was dominated by the expression of the purple, red, and green memes. The purple was evident in his tribal markings and the fantasy nature of his art. The red meme was evident in his burning passion, impulsivity, and the aggression in his music and lifestyle. His Indian-style tattoos and the Bowie knife also suggested his identification with the tribal and frontier lifestyles. A strong man, James's heroic (red) spirit drove him to lift large rocks, way past his physical capacity.

His green core value system lead him to reject his own expression of the blue and orange memes, which he associated with the dominating influences of conservative religion and corporate greed. In so doing, however, he failed to embody the virtues of discipline (blue) and entrepreneurship (orange). The dynamic of green rejecting blue can be thought of as paralleling his condition in which his liver (green) overacted on his lungs (blue according to SD).

*Treatment*

Treatment focused on diminishing the functional heat in James's blood so he would be less impulsive and driven by passion. Constitutional acupuncture focused on points such as Lv-2, Lv-14, HP-2, HP-8, Bl-14, Bl-18, and CV-15. I also treated the "four gates" (LI-4 with Lv-3 bilaterally) to promote functional harmony between the liver and metal elements. Lv-4 and Lu-8 were also frequently chosen to root treatments and for their cooling effect on the liver. Here the influence of metal is empowered within the liver in a way that can be said to empower the core value system of the lungs (righteousness) within the wood (belligerence).

*Result*

As the functional heat in James's liver and blood diminished, he was afforded a new perspective in life. His lifestyle of smoking, drinking, using drugs, staying up late, and living and loving hard grew increasingly less appealing. Arriving for a treatment, James discussed with me how he could now see that the actions he had taken in life had undesirable consequences and the way he had lived was not in his best interest or, for that matter, for the good of anyone else either. "I'm searching for something, Lonny, but I don't know what. Can you give me your perspective?" he asked.

Because we had talked before about elements and officials, I thought I'd answer James's question from a different perspective. I discussed with him the spiral of life and pointed out that his quality of conscious awareness was actually stuck at a level (purple and red) that had emerged and matured fully in many cultures thousands of years ago. We discussed the different memes and how purple and red, their virtues and vices, were both expressed in his life. I pointed out that the very nature of his question itself evidenced the emergence of the blue meme within him as he was becoming increasingly concerned with the effects of his actions on self and other.

I pointed out how his green core value system prevented him from embracing the states of blue and orange and that this would be necessary if he was ever to move on in life. After all, it is one thing to write a protest song asking others to change; it is another thing entirely to change one's self.

James was attentive and protested, "But I work hard, so I have a lot of orange, right?" I pointed out that he did work hard, but in a red and not an orange way. Just as a frontiersman might hunt when he was hungry, James worked at a subsistence level. When he needed money, he would work, then spend it. Orange has ambitions that are motivated by the high hopes of a bright future. Orange has investments and a retirement fund. I pointed out to James that he had nothing to show for his work but what he had earned this week and a bad back. James was really listening.

His lungs were unable to bear the heat from his liver and heart and were suffering. Their suffering was born of a longing for righteousness, that moral structure of metal that controls the wood across the *ke* cycle. Similarly, I knew the presence of the blue meme would help civilize James's fire and impulsivity and pull both his purple and red further up the spiral. "James, what you need is the perspective afforded by a spiritual discipline in life," I told him. "Yes, I know that's true. You are so right. What would you recommend?"

I suggested some books for him to read so the choice would be his. James was very touched by this discussion and it inspired in him a new seriousness in guiding his life. His actions became increasingly consequence oriented as the influence of his blue meme strengthened. James was able to quit smoking and drinking and, with his newfound discipline, was able to get enough rest and care for himself properly. I expect that as he continues to grow, the virtues of inspiration and discipline inherent in the blue meme will strengthen and the virtues of striving and aspiration inherent in the orange meme will begin to emerge.

---

## *Spiral Dynamics and the Evolution of Chinese Medicine*

We can use the SD model to describe how Chinese medicine has evolved over its four thousand years of practice as well as understand the unique forces that are impacting its evolution today. Dating the history of Chinese medicine to the beginning of the Shang dynasty (1766 B.C.E), it is clear it was formulated by a purple culture. Hence demonology, magic, and spirits played an important role in the conceptualization of the medicine.[83] The cultural ideal, innate in Daoism, of a golden age where people lived like wild animals in their natural state represents the perspective of a purple magical culture looking back at the beige meme and the dawn of humanity as a paradise state. The constant warring of feudal states and warlords persisted from the dawn of the warring states period up until the communist revolution unified the country under the totalitarian state in 1949.

Early on, the impulsivity of the red meme (warring states) evolved into the blue consciousness of Confucianism, which emerged as a socializing force at the time the *Neijing Suwen* and other great medical and philosophical texts were written. It is both interesting and ironic that the communists rejected the specific doctrines of Confucianism while fully embracing its blue quality of consciousness in espousing "the one right way." The classic medical and philosophical texts were written at a time that the purple (Daoist) and blue (Confucian) perspectives dominated the culture as forces of social consciousness. Hence these texts evidence magical thinking (the idea of resonance, for example) wholly integrated with absolutism (thou shalt follow the laws of *yin* and *yang*).

By the 1940s, though, much of the Western world had long since moved on to the orange meme, and the Chinese culture as a whole was still largely dominated by the purple (superstition), red (warlords), and blue (Confucianism) memes. It is remarkable to realize that only recently has China begun to evidence the orange meme, a state being advanced with China's reintegration of Hong Kong and a move to a free market economy. When a hint of the green meme arrived during the Tiananmen Square incident, the Chinese government rode over it with a tank. Faced with needing to unify China and bring the country into the twentieth century, it is only natural that the blue meme would arrive to be reinstated (after Confucianism) in the form of communism. Seeking to create a cultural model based on "the one right way," the factional influence of red was controlled. Seeking to free the masses from the grip of myth and mysticism, anything that smacked of purple was eradicated by the blue atheistic Marxists. Hence the spirit and beauty of all arts and sciences suffered as the baby (spirit, depth, inductive thought) was thrown out with the bath water (myth and superstition).

In the name of "elevating standards,"[84] any aspect of the medicine related to spirituality was eradicated by the atheists. Hence the Daoist five-element system was relegated to an inferior position in clinical practice, and the eight principles, more in line with the materialistic precepts of Newtonian physics and Darwinism, became dominant. As Chinese medicine came to America in the early 1970s, it arrived when the green meme was reaching its peak as a new stage of human conscious evolution. We recognized Chinese medicine as something very unique and wholly different from any form of medicine that had arisen or was being practiced within Western culture. The arrival of Chinese medicine was received with one of two responses depending on chance, or on karma if you will, what kind of Chinese medicine a person was first exposed to.

On the one hand, those exposed to TCM proper as represented by the Chinese state assimilated the blue meme influence in the medicine. It is ironic that the modern Chinese vision of medicine was accepted, given the counterculture values generally espoused by those who assimilated it. I posit that those who assimilated TCM proper were able to do so because the cognitive style of the medicine appeared to be different to that of Western thought. The Western movement to expand consciousness assimilated the Eastern philosophical teachings, and it was assumed these were somehow still present in China's medical thought and technology. In effect, though, the blue conservatism of the West was merely exchanged for the blue conservatism of the East.

On the other hand, those influenced by J. R. Worsley were exposed to the purple meme influence in the medicine as it is present in the core value system of Daoism. Ironically, they too fully assimilated the blue meme under the auspices of "classical" five-element acupuncture. As *yin* and *yang* are always implicit within each other, we must note that those who embraced TCM were at least intuitively aware of the purple nature of the medicine. Because they were working with *qi* as an invisible force, it satisfied some longing for a spiritual influence in the Western materialistic lifestyle. Conversely, many exposed to Worsley's teachings, having forsaken orthodox religion, implicitly longed for the influence of the blue meme as his approach was itself represented as "the one right way."

We must note that despite significant differences in the fundamental orientation of the two approaches, TCM and 5E, both groups adopting those approaches were orienting from the same place, that of reaching for an alternate worldview that was revolutionary to the Western mind and its wholly materialistic concept of medicine and humanity's place on earth. To a degree, both groups were duped as the TCM crowd wound up embracing a materialistic core value system and the 5E crowd generally renounced intellectualism, scholarship, and a disciplined thought process.

Blue eventually evolves into orange, and both groups, the purple and the blue, developed a very strong orange value system. In order to grow and survive in America in the face of resistance from the blue/orange-dominant culture of modern medicine, it became necessary for those practicing Chinese medicine to develop a strong orange bias. Hence entrepreneurship became imperative as schools needed to be formed and state legislatures needed to be sold on the idea of Chinese medicine as an independent entity. However, the core value systems of the purple and blue camps differed in how they approached the implementation of the orange meme. Those practicing TCM proper sought to integrate Chinese medicine into America on the terms of the prevalent blue/orange ethic of America itself. Because materialism was at the basis of this approach anyway, the structure of American educational, credentialing, and medical models were a natural fit. Greatly outnumbered, those practicing from a purple 5E perspective not only had to fight for the acceptance of Chinese medicine in America but for the existence of their own traditions, which were discriminated against by their colleagues with a TCM/blue perspective in formulating educational, licensing, examination, and credentialing requirements.

Now that Chinese medicine is established, a new set of challenges face us in the evolution of our medicine. Our medicine cannot be complete unless all the memes are active and making positive contributions. We can see that in relation to the prevalent influence of the blue and orange memes in the culture of Chinese medicine, a huge lack of purple has been felt by practitioners who continue to seek for the original heart of the medicine so absent in their training. Remember, it is the integrated presence of the purple meme that allows for the emergence "one octave up" for the expression of turquoise. And it is here that the promise of Chinese medicine as a truly holistic and integral science is fulfilled.

The green meme is shared in the West by almost all those who practice Chinese medicine. In fact, the arrival of Eastern philosophy en masse in the United States corresponded to the flowering of green consciousness in the 1960s. Certainly the green value system of that era was greatly influential in my own approach to Chinese medicine as a tool for promoting the evolution of consciousness. However, the egalitarianism of the green meme has a fundamental downside when it is applied therapeutically that negatively impacts virtually all New Age healing modalities. The notion that reality is a matter of perspective and that everybody's reality has equal merit denies the absolute nature of reality itself. Everyone wants to be healed, but no one wants to change because there is no discrimination regarding any human state as being higher than any other. Nowhere is this dynamic more apparent than in the notion of "unconditional love" foisted by green practitioners on their patients. Because all perspectives are deemed to be relative, the practitioner, in validating her own view, must also validate that of her patients, the very perspective that must change for the better if the patient is to heal. Healing can only be judged as such to the degree that it fosters meaningful change.

At this point in the evolution of Chinese medicine in America, the entrepreneurship of the orange meme and "morality" of the blue meme are threatening to squeeze the last drop of life out of our medicine. Overregulation and a licensing and credentialing apparatus that overly constrain the free and easy development of the medicine and art threaten to limit its ability to meet the new emerging needs of humanity. Those whose primary motivation is influenced by the orange meme relate to the medicine primarily as a way to obtain wealth and status. Unfortunately, these are the types of people who often are innately most interested in working in the political arena of a profession as opposed, say, to practicing the art of healing.

We now have the perspective to look back over the evolution of our medicine and see the different core value systems that have emerged as Chinese medicine has faced different challenges. With the advent of modern medicine, systems of sanitation, and the general availability of shelter and food, the emphasis of Chinese medicine on externally contracted illness shifted to the importance of differentiation of internal patterns of disease largely predicated on the personalization of thoughts and feelings. As the human race moves toward yellow and turquoise realms of consciousness, Chinese medicine will have to meet the needs of those realms and cannot accomplish this without an integration of all the previous ways of thinking that have come before.

Only if we as practitioners can embrace a larger view of our medicine, which transcends the personal, is Chinese medicine likely to fulfill its potential as the ascendant holistic medicine of the new millennium. This movement will require the integration of Chinese and Western medicine in a way that they take their natural hierarchical relationship to each other. That is, except in cases of lifesaving intervention, Chinese medicine should always take precedence over the application of drugs or surgery. Further, the natural hierarchical relationship among all systems of Chinese medicine must be restored so each is applied appropriately. Hence constitutional medicine must assume its rightful place as the foundation of medical treatment. Finally, all human potentials, left and right brained, inductive and deductive, must merge into one as we reach the second and third tiers to become fully integrated human beings.

And only if the five-element model and its core value system are reintegrated back into the heart of our practices will we possess a medicine, born of heaven and earth, that can attend to the new being that is emerging even now. The fact is, Chinese culture as a whole has not evolved significantly past the blue meme. The incorporation of Hong Kong and initial forays into capitalism suggest the development of orange is now in its infancy. The Tiananmen Square incident also suggests there is a small beginning of the green wave in China. However, China is far from fully embracing the orange or green memes, a step that would be signaled by the institution of an open democratic system of government.

The fact is that most practitioners of Chinese medicine in the West have a fully developed first-tier consciousness and, if the back of the green meme can be broken, we can be among the first to move into second-tier consciousness. Hence it is our position in the West, if we take it, to lead the vanguard of Chinese medicine as a modern evolving science and art. Given the rapid and never-ending evolution of human consciousness, if Chinese medicine is to remain relevant, it must adapt to the changing human condition that it purports to treat. Burdened by four thousand years of classical tradition, or "mess" in the terminology of Bruce Lee, Chinese medicine must be reinvented according to an entirely new core value system that begins today and rapidly grows to embrace the new emerging being of humanity. And, of course, if the medicine is to embrace the new evolving structures of human consciousness, we practitioners must work tirelessly to embody them ourselves.

## *Exercises*

In Figure 37.5 I have given several *yin/yang* pairs of associations relative to the practice and culture of Chinese medicine.

a. Discuss the relative merit of each pair of associations.
b. In what way are "already knowing" and arrogance related?
c. What is the difference between "already knowing" and wanting to know?
d. Discuss the relative merits of basing one's assessment of reality on thinking versus feeling. Are either relevant? Why?
e. I have stated that the number five is odd and therefore *yang* in nature and the number eight is even and therefore *yin* in nature. Yet I have also stated that the five-element system is relatively *yin* in nature as compared with the eight-principle system, which is *yang*. Discuss the significance and merit of my differentiation.
f. I have stated that the five-element and eight-principle methods are based on different cognitive modes. Is this true?
g. Discuss why the popular notion of unconditional love can actually thwart a patient's healing.
h. In the first tier of consciousness, which of the memes do you most identify with and which do you reject?
i. Can Chinese medicine be any more of a holistic science and art than the degree to which the practitioner's own mind is integrated?
j. What are you doing to change, now?

# *NOTES*

1. Watson, 1964, p. 98.
2. *ND*, 1998.
3. I have studied five-element constitutional diagnosis since 1980. The foundation of this study is based on the teachings of Dr. J. R. Worsley and the TAI-Sophia Institute in Laurel, Maryland. Subsequently I spent ten years studying pulse diagnosis with Dr.

Leon Hammer. When I refer to Traditional Chinese Medicine, or TCM, I am referring to state-run medicine as formulated in modern China under the auspices of dialectical materialism.

4. See *ND*, pp. 387–434, as well as Jarrett, 2000, pp. 152–166.
5. See the Nanjing, Difficult Issue Number 61, in Unschuld, 1986, p. 539.
6. Eight-principle thought emerged in the late Ming era (1368–1628 C.E.). See Scheid, 2002, pp. 344–345.
7. See *ND*, pp. 36–37.
8. The term *TCM* can be applied to any and all systems and techniques that fall under the auspices of Chinese medicine. It can also be applied to Chinese state-run medicine as a political expression.
9. Note that the emphasis here is placed on the importance of the core values and cognitive style inherent in the five-element system and not on any specific technical knowledge including that contained in this book.
10. Chapter 42; see Girardot, 1983, p. 56.
11. For an exposition of these concepts, see *ND*, Chapter 1.
12. These directions are south, southwest, west, northwest, north, northeast, east, and southeast.
13. Girardot, 1983, p. 49.
14. Porkert, 1982, pp. 107–196.
15. Note that the theoretical slots of external/deficient/heat (external deficiency with the presence of heat) and external/deficient/cold (external deficiency with the presence of cold) are not generally discussed in Chinese medicine. Nonetheless, two herb formulas may be considered to address these syndromes. Bupleurum and Puerreria may be used for an external deficiency and the presence of heat. This formula tonifies *qi* and releases heat to the exterior. Guizhi Tang (Cinnamon Twig Soup) may be used for an external deficiency of *weiqi* with the presence of cold. This formula tonifies *weiqi* and drives out external cold. Special thanks to Subhuti Dharmananda for helping refine my understanding of these categories and the application of these formulas.
16. Porkert, 1982, p. 18.
17. Note that the potentially deeper uses of a system of healing based on the number eight based on the trigrams of the *Yijing* are virtually absent from any modern text on TCM.
18. Morgan, 1920, p. 28.
19. For a discussion of the hierarchy of internal and external, see Thea Elijah's discussion in Chapter 10 as well as Chapter 12 in Larre, Schatz, and de la Vallee, 1986, p. 67.
20. For a greater elaboration of the theoretical differences between Eastern and Western sciences, see *ND*, Appendix, pp. 435–453.
21. Chapter 52 in Chen, 1989, p. 178.
22. Of course, all models and ways of knowing are maps superimposed on reality to allow us to navigate through chaos.
23. Neuroscience research has discerned cognitive difference between how the left and right brains operate to know the world. The left brain, controlling the dominant right hand, approaches life from a relatively linear and causal perspective. The right brain approaches life more holistically and synthetically.
24. This observation illustrates an important concept. Because Chinese medicine recognizes the body, it can accommodate all the findings of Western biomedicine. However, because biomedicine can never quantify the mind and spirit, it cannot accommodate the 66 percent of Chinese medicine that addresses nonphysical phenomena.
25. Karma: From the Sanskrit *kri*, to do; literally, "deed"; may be taken to signify all that we bring to this life from our past lives and ancestors. Karma can be understood to be the momentum that conditions us in life that is born of all past actions. This has implications in every realm of life from our physical attributes to our spiritual lessons. The modern concept of genetics refers solely to physical transmission from our ancestry. The notion of karma includes nonphysical transmission from ancestry as well.

26. The basic associations of the five elements are listed here.

| Element | Color | Sound | Odor | Emotion | Virtue |
|---|---|---|---|---|---|
| Water | Blue | Groan | Putrid | Fear | Wisdom |
| Wood | Green | Shout | Rancid | Anger | Benevolence |
| Fire | Red | Laugh | Scorched | Joy | Propriety |
| Earth | Yellow | Sing | Sweet | Sympathy | Integrity |
| Metal | White | Weep | Rotten | Grief | Righteousness |

27. Sixty-First Difficult Issue; Unschuld, 1986, p. 539.
28. See Mole, 1992, pp. 3–10.
29. Maciocia, 1992, pp. 39–41.
30. For a discussion of why I do not like the term *energetic* as applied to Chinese medicine, see my discussion in *ND*, pp. 300–302.
31. Keep in mind that pulse diagnosis does not exist in a vacuum and is informed by all other available diagnostic information. In my own practice, the pulse is taken only after a comprehensive 45-minute interview. Hence all information gleaned from the pulse is interpreted within the context of all previously gathered and simultaneously arising data.
32. I think of the virtue of *ziran* (spontaneity) as being the Daoist ideal of homeostasis. For a discussion of *ziran*, see *ND*, pp. 316–317.
33. The upper class of herbs as listed in the *Shennong Bencao Jing* may, however, harmonize psychospiritual issues when prescribed in relatively low doses appropriate for emotional- or spirit-level treatment. For instance, an herb like Schizandra (Wuweizi) may be used to treat insomnia or to "wake" a person up in the sense of helping inspire him. This insight according to Thea Elijah.
34. Of course, grief can also present as dryness in the lungs.
35. See my discussion of acupuncture point function in Chapter 23.
36. For a discussion of *ling*, see *ND*, pp. 51–55.
37. See Thea's description of two formulas in Chapter 10.
38. Hence the *Daodejing* tells us in Chapter 55 that "One who contains *de* (virtue or original nature) in fullness, is to be compared to an infant. . . . Such is the perfection of its life-force (*jing*)." See Chapter 55; in Chen, 1989, p. 185.
39. Andrew Cohen discusses the importance of having a proper relationship to thought, feelings, and time in his book *Embracing Heaven and Earth*.
40. For elaboration, see *ND*, pp. 323–325.
41. For a discussion of spontaneity (*ziran*), see *ND*, pp. 316–317. I would sum up the concept by saying that a spontaneous person assesses each moment of life entirely on its own merits unencumbered by the past. This is the vision of health proffered in the *Daodejing* and the writings of Zhuangzi.
42. At this point, psychotherapy becomes irrelevant altogether.
43. Porkert, 1982, p. 1.
44. Chapter 10; in Chen, 1989, p. 78.
45. Chapter 71; in Chen, 1989, p. 215.
46. Hence Porkert (1982) has termed the cognitive mode at the heart of Chinese medicine "inductive synthesis."
47. The closest I have ever come to an absolute principle in the practice of Chinese medicine is "do what's right."
48. Unschuld, 1985, p. 57.

49. For Thea Elijah's point of view on such open awareness, see her discussion in Chapter 10.
50. For an interesting discussion of this topic, see Henderson, 1984.
51. Birch, 1992, pp. 2–13.
52. It is ironic that the author who proposed standardizing pulse diagnosis is coauthor of a text on a five-element tradition. See Matsumoto and Birch, 1983.
53. For example, deficient liver *yang* is ubiquitous in cases of chronic fatigue, Lyme disease, and marijuana abuse. Certainly these conditions figure largely in the modern practice of medicine.
54. In this regard, compare the description of Ki-7 in *Grasping the Wind* (Ellis et al., 1989) to my description in *ND*, Chapters 7 and 13. The former book reduces one of the deepest philosophical concepts made in the history of Chinese philosophy to a statement like this (I am paraphrasing here): Ki-7 is named "returning current" because the kidney channel completes a circle around the ankle at that point. Hence the "cause" of the point's name is deemed by the authors to have a physical basis rather than synthetically realizing that the circle made by the channel, the name, and the functional basis of that circle inherent in the idea of "return" are all simultaneous manifestations of the same principle.
55. I recommend you review Beck and Cowan, 1995, and Wilber, 2000.
56. Watson, 1964a, p. 45.
57. This is another reason that lexicons that offer a one-to-one correspondence between Chinese characters and English words are not generally useful. They have the effect of reinforcing an already-knowing approach to something that is, like reality, continually changing.
58. Recombinant DNA technology represents an objectification of our capacity to play a role in our own evolution. "With great power comes great responsibility" (from the film *Spider Man*), and if the choices we make are not motivated by the absolute, but rather by the egoic quest for physical immortality, the consequences will not be benevolent, and our best intent will come to naught.
59. This model was conceived by Clare Graves and has been championed recently by Don Beck and Ken Wilber. See Beck and Cowan, 1995; Wilber, 2000.
60. Wilber, 2000, p. 7.
61. From a lecture by Andrew Cohen, 2003.
62. Andrew Cohen points out that, from a certain perspective, there is not much difference between an enlightened human and one who fully embraces an enlightened perspective in life, consciously choosing never to express ego. See Cohen, 2002.
63. See my discussion of the nature of shock in Chapter 1.
64. This speculation on the relationship between the five-element system and spiral dynamics is entirely my own. It represents my initial impressions of a vast topic and my attempt to help create a much larger context in which to consider the practice of Chinese medicine.
65. Wilber, 2000, p. 6 and p. 145, note 6.
66. These are derived in large part from Wilber's nomenclature. Wilber, 2000, p. 9.
67. For a discussion of Huntun, see *ND*, p. 14.
68. Quote from *Daodejing*, Chapter 20; in Chen, 1989, p. 103.
69. In this regard, read Ken Wilber's book, *Boomeritis* (2002), which should be considered essential reading for our entire generation.
70. See Capra, 1975, 1983.
71. This stage, and the importance of transcending it, is discussed at length in Wilber, 2000.
72. See *ND*, Figure A.1, p. 440, for a representation of this type of thinking.
73. See my discussion in Chapter 1 on the nature of shock.

74. See Figure 12.3. The *sheng* and *ke* cycles can be thought of as imaging an hierarchical living organism.
75. Wilber, 2000, p. 13.
76. Ibid.
77. For example, see Wilber, 2000, p. 13.
78. In Beck, 2002, p. 126.
79. Wilber, 2000, p. 146, note 6.
80. Kimura, 2002, p. 28.
81. See *ND*, p. 11.
82. See my description of this dynamic in Chapter 5 on exit and entry points.
83. See Chapter 3 on possession for an elaboration of the role played by belief in spirits in the formulation of Chinese medicine.
84. A phrase still widely popular among those ringing the life force out of the medicine in the name of professionalization.

# APPENDIX A

# *Starting a Practice*

New practitioners often ask me for advice on the best way to start a practice. Here I offer tips on building and conducting a practice culled from my years of clinical experience. I begin by discussing some foundational concepts for establishing a deeply rewarding and successful practice.

## *Right Work*

The primary consideration in building a practice is the same required for success in any career. Your choice to pursue a career must derive from an innate sense that it is the correct work for you to be doing. There must be room within the work for you to manifest your core commitments and express a broad range of talents. If our choice of work is based largely on considerations of money, status, or power, the work is not likely ever to be really successful or spiritually fulfilling.

When I made the decision to pursue a career in Chinese medicine in 1980, the profession really did not exist in the United States. In fact, Chinese medicine was only legal in four states at that time. When I entered school, none of us had any idea if we would be able to support ourselves after graduating. To a person, we had committed ourselves to practice solely for the love of the medicine. Today, when prospective students ask me about their decision to pursue a career in Chinese medicine, their first question often involves potential income. Although there are many considerations in entering any career, the nature of your destined work must take precedence over any other consideration. Therefore, if you have determined that your choice to practice Chinese medicine flows from your deepest knowledge of self, the following advice may help build a successful and rewarding practice.

## *Confidence, Intention, and Mastery*

At the outset you must be on a path of attaining mastery, not just in your clinical practice, but in life generally. Like the fulfillment of destiny, mastery is only ever achieved relatively, yet it is the center of the bull's-eye we strive for with each needle placed and herb prescribed. Bow in and out of your practice, and while there, conduct yourself with clear intention and a confidence that comes from knowing you are committed to doing your absolute best with the tools and knowledge at hand. Having confidence in yourself and your commitment to your art forms the foundation of your patients' ability to believe they can heal.

Mastery to me implies that your own internal alignment, coupled with the respect, awe, and grace with which you conduct your art, is able to initiate healing within the patient. Attaining mastery to me suggests you are no longer practicing Chinese medicine. Instead, all therapeutic actions flow spontaneously as natural expressions of self rather than emanating from conscious theory. Only on an off day do I consider that I am practicing Chinese medicine. When I am confused about a clinical choice, only then must I resort to theories of *yin* and *yang* or considerations of the five elements. When I am practicing with mastery, I just do what is right and never resort to figuring things out. I consider that listening, as I have defined it in *Nourishing Destiny,* is the key to attaining mastery.[1]

## *You Get the Practice You Build*

You have the right and the ability to build exactly the type of practice you want. Hold an image in your mind and create a picture of what you and your practice will become. Years from now, when your practice has been established, you will have built the form of that practice with each clinical interaction and every decision. Will you have a practice with a high turnover rate of patients who terminate after several treatments if their expectations of quick symptomatic relief are not met or who show up only occasionally for a few treatments each time they have a pain somewhere or a crisis to manage?

Or will you build the kind of practice that helps you cultivate the clinical expertise to treat patients through every stage of life from birth to death? The decisions you make early on will form the foundations of the practice you eventually build. Take care at the outset because you are likely to get what you ask for.

---

## *Pain Clinics and Health Spas*

In the beginning of your career it may be tempting to accept work in pain clinics or at health spas to support yourself. But these types of settings rarely help cultivate the type of experience you will need to manage a patient's long-term health care needs. The economic imperatives of insurance companies and the feel-good agendas of health spas have little to do with the depth of healing potentially available through Chinese medicine.

Health spas do not afford the opportunity to treat patients over the long term. Often their aim is to provide the patient with a relaxing experience (draining AE is an ideal strategy in such settings) and has little to do with healing. But health spas do introduce patients to acupuncture with a pleasant experience and give the practitioner the possibility to refer them for continuing work with someone in their own area. Only accept such positions if they allow sufficient time and freedom to cultivate building your own practice where patients can be managed independently and treated according to your own commitments. If you do take such a job, I strongly encourage you to also cultivate an independent practice at the same time.

---

## *Choosing a Place to Practice*

Students or newly graduated practitioners often call me and ask where I think they should practice. Often they are concerned about a perceived oversupply of practitioners where they live or would like to move, and they beseech me to suggest some place with less "competition." My advice is always to find the place they would be happiest living without regarding other practitioners as competition. No other practitioner can offer what you have to offer, and your success is assured if you stay true to yourself while building your practice.

When I first moved to the Berkshires in western Massachusetts, no other practitioners were working full time in professional office space. The one or two other practitioners in the area worked out of their homes. Chinese medicine was not yet established in the county, and physicians were, at best, indifferent and, at worst, openly hostile to my practice. In fact, one physician wrote two lengthy letters to the local newspaper denouncing Chinese medicine as quackery as soon as I opened my practice. I am forever in his debt because the publicity jump-started my career! Thus I had no so-called competition from other practitioners, but few people were educated about the potential benefits of Chinese medicine. It took three years of lecturing, writing, and communicating at every opportunity about Chinese medicine to slowly build a practice that began to support me.

Today Chinese medicine has entered the general culture and many people are aware of its successes. Now new practitioners can expect relatively more discourse with, and referrals from, physicians and allied health care personnel as well as from established practitioners whose practices are full. I can see only one to two new patients each week, which amounts to, at best, a hundred new patients each year. With 240 million people in America, clearly there is room for many new practitioners to support themselves. Ultimately our only competition are the debilitating messages we receive from the conditioned mind. There is great suffering in this world and there will never be too many practitioners to attend to it. If you love Chinese medicine, acquire sufficient training in a deep tradition, and work hard, you will be successful.

## *Practice Building*

### *Altruism*

Treat every patient who seeks treatment regardless of what he or she can afford to pay. The cultivation of mastery requires immersion in your art. The point is to practice. Give freely and openly, and the return will be a thousandfold both in goodwill and in the development of compassion, which is the foundation of clinical practice.

I have a sliding scale that ranges from $50 to $70 per treatment session. I let patients pay what they can afford and trust them to make that determination based solely on self-inquiry. If a patient's treatment is successful, I raise the rate, assuming it is not at full scale, as the time between treatments increases. This helps the patient afford the early treatments, which are spaced closer together.

Donating time to work with those in need can help provide clinical experience until your practice generates momentum. I started a free AIDS treatment program in the county and treated people with HIV for five years. I can think of no more rewarding work that I have done. I believe relatively too much emphasis is placed on obtaining insurance reimbursement. What is really needed to ensure our medicine is available to a broad spectrum of people is sixty thousand practitioners with generous hearts.

### *First Impressions*

In the initial stage of practice, your reputation has not yet been established in the community. Be vigilant in taking every opportunity to display your commitment to your work. Check your phone messages with neurotic frequency, and try to answer every incoming call within an hour of receiving it. This lets patients know from the moment they call that you are available and committed to helping them. I initiate every return call by first introducing myself and then asking, "How can I help you?" This reinforces the notion that help is available from the moment of first contact.

Schedule patients so they see each other coming and going. If you have two patients in a day, try and schedule them back to back. This uses your time more efficiently and helps build confidence in your new patients. Perceived success breeds success.

### *Be on Time*

Timeliness is the single greatest way to assess the quality of the heart's intention. Patients are used to sitting for long periods in the waiting rooms of other health care practitioners, which is inconsiderate. If you wish to build a practice in which patients respect your time, be sure to respect theirs. I have two treatment rooms running concurrently and a third available should I need it. Patients are scheduled for 45-minute appointments, but my extra room allows me the luxury of permitting patients up to one and a half hours for a session if necessary. I rarely ever run more than 15 minutes late for any given session, and most of the time I am either on time or early. Cultivating timeliness is of the utmost importance if we are to cultivate stability and strength in our patients' hearts.

## *Teaching*

Learning to speak precisely and with intention about the medicine hones therapeutic skills and helps clarify the nature of your practice. A significant part of a successful practice involves gaining rapport with patients through the spoken word. As soon as I graduated from school, I started teaching classes on Chinese medicine. These classes consisted of weekly two-hour sessions for eight to ten weeks. I advertised them both to the general public as well as to bodyworkers and psychotherapists. As a result, almost all the students came for treatment, and the professionals referred patients to me who they thought could benefit from my approach.

Here I provide the course outline I used, but I suggest you tailor it to your own tradition, interests, and needs. Maintain a good balance between theory and experiential exercises so the new student feels engaged.

**Class 1.** Introduction

a. History and orientation of the medicine

b. Differences between Chinese and Western medicine (see appendix in *ND*, p. 435)

c. Brief introduction to the five elements

**Classes 2–6.** The Five Elements

Discuss the general associations of each element including how that element presents in nature both internally and externally. Conduct exercises to experience the color, sound, odor, and emotion (CSOE) of each element. Finally, present the names and inner functions of points on each meridian within the context of their elemental natures.

Class 2. Water

Class 3. Wood

Class 4. Fire

Class 5. Earth

Class 6. Metal

**Classes 7–10.** Clinical practice

Class 7. Oral intake (*ND*, Chapter 14)

Class 8. The physical (pulse, tongue, *hara* diagnosis, etc.)

Class 9. Students bring patients and I do an intake in front of the class with full analysis.

Class 10. Exercises in CSOE with the whole class.

---

## *Writing*

Like teaching, writing formalizes our thoughts about what we are doing and why, and it helps us hone our intentionality in clinical practice. I began writing a regular column in a local holistic healing magazine that publishes quarterly. I did this for five years, and it helped people learn about me and my orientation toward healing and Chinese medicine. These articles served in part as the basis of my first text.

### *Public Speaking*

Appropriate forums for speaking include high schools and local colleges, visiting nurses associations, hospitals, and local businesses. The national Area Health Education Council (AHEC) organizes CEU (continuing education units) events for health care professionals. They pay a reasonable hourly fee for speaking and provide an audience that is interested in receiving treatment and referring patients.

Ideally, a lecture on Chinese medicine offers the audience an experience similar to receiving a treatment. With properly honed intention in speaking, you will be able to inspire the audience with your love of the material. To hear someone so moved by his or her work often touches something within the audience that inspires them to initiate their own healing.

### *Socializing*

Take every opportunity to discuss the medicine you love in a way that inspires people with your heartfelt connection to the path you have chosen. But do not be overbearing. When a patient approaches me for treatment, my inclination is to travel with him as deeply toward the heart of healing as the patient is willing. If a patient withdraws his interest in working with me, my policy is to never pursue him or try to convince him to continue.

Similarly, if a person asks me about Chinese medicine, I talk to him as long as I sense his interest is held. I never have mentioned to a person of my own accord that I practice Chinese medicine or think he should come for treatment. The other person must initiate the conversation about his health. Going to parties, taking classes, or joining clubs are all excellent ways to meet people.

### *The Rules of Engagement*

When you are self-employed, your worst scenario is failure. However, mark my words, the second worst scenario is success. Here I share several principles to help ensure that your growing practice does not become a burden. The clearer you are about the conditions you need to practice at your best, the easier it will be to create a practice that supports you both spiritually and financially. I consider the following rules inviolable. If they are compromised, the patient's quality of treatment and your enjoyment of the work will suffer.

1. Never accept a patient who will not call to make his own appointment. In all my years of clinical practice, no patient has ever shown up for a session that someone else booked. On occasion I let a family member who is already a patient make an appointment for someone else in order to secure an initial consultation sooner. But I always require a new patient to call within forty-eight hours to confirm the appointment. If a prospective patient is too busy to call for his own appointment, you can be sure he does not have much of a commitment to healing and will continually miss and reschedule appointments.

2. Never continue working with a patient you find abusive because you need the money. Patients should be allowed fairly wide latitude in their behavior. After all, we are in a health care profession, and much of any given patient's illness is predicated on inappropriate behavior. Further, it is easy in the initial stages of a career to feel that as healers we should be able to find whatever resource is called for within ourselves no matter how difficult the patient.

Nevertheless, we each must have certain rules. If a patient violates these rules in a way that compromises our enjoyment of our work, we will naturally come to resent him. It is impossible to help a patient heal once resentment toward him begins to grow. As you gain clinical experience, you will learn to identify such problem patients earlier in treatment. Once identified, refer such patients to other practitioners both for the patient's well-being as well as your own. One problem patient can negatively impact your experience in treating all your patients.

3. Charge patients for missed appointments. The first time a patient misses an appointment I charge half my fee. From then on, each patient is charged the full amount of the missed session. Place your policy in a highly visible place in the office. Of course I take each case into consideration based on its unique merits. However, I do find that, in general, if I do not charge a patient who misses his appointments regularly, I will harbor resentment that my time is not valued sufficiently.

---

## *Expenditure of Resources*

Think of each patient as having spent a certain number of years digging his or her way into a hole. It can be tempting to want to climb down into each hole and lift each patient out of it on your back. But to expend your resources in this way is not the most efficient use of your talents. Recall the Chinese proverb that if you feed a hungry person a fish you have given him a meal, but if you teach him to fish you have helped feed him for a lifetime.

If we use all our resources emotionally to help our patients, clinical practice may become a joyless burden. If we are to pull each patient out of the hole he is trapped in, how many people can we really treat effectively before our own backs are broken? Rather than climb down into our patients' holes (that is, predicaments), it is more fruitful to walk around the tops of such holes and throw down a rope long enough to touch each individual patient. It is much easier to encourage motivated people to climb out of their own predicaments on their own than it is to build a practice of people who expect us to make them better.

---

## *Charlatan Attacks*

In the course of clinical practice you will likely occasionally experience what Thea Elijah has termed *charlatan attacks*. These come regularly as you begin your practice and then generally with decreasing intervals as your clinical experience increases. However, even after eighteen years of practice, I still occasionally experience times when I feel I have merely hypnotized myself into believing Chinese medicine is real, that I know anything about it, or that I am capable of applying its principles to help my patients. In part this has to do with my experience of awe when faced with the depth of Chinese medicine itself.

These episodes of self-doubt are a healthy phase in the practice of any discipline. I am always suspicious of people who express complete confidence in the veracity of what they already know. Such an attitude is generally compelled by the ego's desperate attempt to maintain its hold over the person by imparting a false sense of security. However, I am generally comfortable when a person's stand in life imparts an absolute comfort with the unknown. After all, like all science, the practice of Chinese medicine is based on a highly concretized mythology. It is useful over a specific range of life experience for empowering specific virtues. No medical or scientific paradigm holds all the answers, and it is healthy for our worldview to collapse occasionally. Then it can re-form, less hindered by learned material that proves to be inconsistent with our authentic clinical experience.

I believe new practitioners experience charlatan attacks because they lack confidence and have not yet embodied the theory they have learned through the discipline of clinical practice. In the experienced practitioner, such periods of self-doubt often stem from the realization that the ultimate truth of what occurs in our treatment rooms lies beyond our intellectual grasp despite years of acquired knowledge and clinical experience. In any case, I find such periods of confusion and self-doubt necessary on the path to mastery. They indicate that our clinical abilities are integrating and being embodied in deeper realms of being. When clarity returns after such an experience, our practice and abilities have often improved dramatically.

So do not let such experiences hinder you on the path to mastery through clinical practice. Rather, learn to practice with clear intention when you are in this fluid place of not knowing. For it is in not knowing where we find mastery of this and all arts.

## *Conclusion*

Every acupuncture practice differs to the extent you have truly made your chosen tradition of practice your own. The preceding is knowledge gained from my own years of clinical experience, and I hope it will help you build your practice in a way that is consistent with the values that flow from the heart of your own connection to the beauty of Chinese medicine.

# *NOTES*

1. See *ND*, pp. 358–359.

APPENDIX B

# Needle Techniques

My emphasis clinically lies in the quality of my diagnosis, understanding the depth of point function, finding the point precisely, and in obtaining *qi*. There is relatively little complexity in terms of actual needle technique. In my practice, I use three main methods of needling.

## *Tonification*

In cases of clear *yang* or *qi* deficiency, as suggested by the finding of deep, spreading, feeble, or absent pulses, I use a technique I call tonification. I insert the needle in the direction of *qi* flow and turn it 180 degrees clockwise or until I feel the arrival of *qi*. Then I quickly withdraw the needle and cover the point with a finger for a moment to assist the retention of *qi*. When tonifying points on the twelve main meridians, I always treat the point on the left side of the body first. I insert the needle as the patient begins to inhale and try to attain *qi* and remove the needle as the inhalation reaches its peak. I expect this technique to increase the amount of *qi* or *yang* supporting the official's function as assessed by an increased volume and amplitude of the pulse corresponding to the official in question.

Other pulse positions whose underlying deficiency is based dysfunctionally on the primary official being treated can also show increases of *qi* and *yang*.

## *Sedation*

I use a technique of sedation when I determine a clear excess is present by pulse diagnosis. Qualities suggesting such excess can include pulses that are tense, overflowing, inflated, or pounding. In this case, the pulse is expected to have a larger than normal volume and to be pounding, indicating the presence of both excess heat and stagnant *qi*. Here I insert the needle against the flow of *qi* in the meridian and turn it 180 degrees counterclockwise until I feel the arrival of *qi*. Needles are retained up to forty minutes or when I have determined that the pulse has relaxed sufficiently. When sedating points on the twelve main meridians, I always treat the point on the right side of the body first. Then I remove the needles slowly and do not cover the point. A positive pulse change is indicated by decreased volume and pounding on the pulse.

## *Tonification and Dispersion*

The preceding techniques, which involve treating clear excesses and deficiencies, account for perhaps 20 percent of the treatments I perform. The other 80 percent of the time I use a technique I consider to tonify relative deficiency and to disperse relative excess as opposed to sedating a true excess. With this technique, I insert the needle in the direction of *qi* flow and turn it 180 degrees clockwise or until *qi* is obtained. I then retain needles for up to fifteen minutes and remove them slowly.

I conceive of this technique as allowing the patient's functional dynamics to sort out the relative balance of tonification and dispersal needed to attain harmony. Here I am commanding the *qi* relatively less and drawing on the innate homeostatic functions of the points relatively more. This technique is appropriate for patients who are not at the extremes of excess or deficiency as indicated by pulse diagnosis. Many people who do exhibit *qi* and *yang* deficiency are in need of tonification, but they also have minds and nervous systems that need to relax. I find the tonification treatment discussed earlier to be too stimulating for this large percentage of people. The technique described here allows the patient's mind to relax while receiving a gentle tonification.

## *Ancillary Methods*

Other than these three main techniques, I use two other methods. With superficial needling, I tap the needle perpendicularly into the skin through an insertion tube without pushing it any deeper. I use this technique for superficial draining of pernicious *qi* as in the method for clearing aggressive energy. Lastly, a neutral needle technique involves placing the needle perpendicularly into the meridian neither with or against the flow of *qi*. This technique figures prominently in transferring *qi* around the *sheng* or across the *ke* cycle as discussed in Chapter 12.

APPENDIX C

# The Meeting Points

Here I've provided tables of the meeting points for the twelve main channels and the eight extra meridians.[1]

## NOTE

1. The meeting points on the twelve main channels are according to Worsley, 1982, p. 308, and those of the eight extra meridians are according to Deadman and Al-Khafaji, 2000.

| | Heart | Small Intestine | Bladder | Kidney | Heart Protector | Three Heater | Gallbladder | Liver | Lung | Large Intestine | Stomach | Spleen | Conception v. | Governing v. |
|---|---|---|---|---|---|---|---|---|---|---|---|---|---|---|
| Ht-1 | ● | | | | | | | | | | | ● | | |
| Ht-5 | ● | ● | | | | | | | | | | | | |
| Ht-9 | ● | ● | | | | | | | | | | | | |
| SI-1 | ● | ● | | | | | | | | | | | | |
| SI-7 | ● | ● | | | | | | | | | | | | |
| SI-12 | | ● | | | | ● | ● | | | | | | | |
| SI-18 | | ● | | | | ● | ● | | | | | | | |
| SI-19 | | ● | ● | | | ● | ● | | | | | | | |
| Bl-1 | | ● | ● | | | ● | ● | | | | ● | | | |
| Bl-11 | | | ● | | | | ● | | | | | | | |
| Bl-12 | | | ● | | | | | | | | | | | ● |
| Bl-31 | | | ● | | | | ● | | | | | | | |
| Bl-33 | | | ● | | | | ● | | | | | | | |
| Bl-58 | | | ● | ● | | | | | | | | | | |
| Bl-67 | | | ● | ● | | | | | | | | | | |
| Ki-1 | | | ● | ● | | | | | | | | | | |
| Ki-4 | | | ● | ● | | | | | | | | | | |
| Ki-22 | | | | ● | ● | | | | | | | | | |
| HP-1 | | | | ● | ● | | | | | | | | | |
| HP-5 | ● | | | | ● | | | | ● | | | | | |
| HP-6 | | | | | ● | ● | | | | | | | | |
| HP-8 | | | | | ● | ● | | | | | | | | |
| TH-1 | | | | | ● | ● | | | | | | | | |
| TH-5 | | | | | ● | ● | | | | | | | | |
| TH-8 | | ● | | | | ● | | | | ● | | | | |
| TH-13 | | | | | | ● | | | | ● | | | | |
| TH-17 | | | | | | ● | ● | | | | | | | |
| TH-20 | | | | | | ● | ● | | | | | | | |
| TH-22 | | | | | | ● | ● | | | | | | | |
| Gb-1 | | ● | | | | ● | ● | | | | | | | |
| Gb-3 | | | | | | | ● | | | | ● | | | |

| | Heart | Small Intestine | Bladder | Kidney | Heart Protector | Three Heater | Gallbladder | Liver | Lung | Large Intestine | Stomach | Spleen | Conception v. | Governing v. |
|---|---|---|---|---|---|---|---|---|---|---|---|---|---|---|
| Gb-4 | | | | | | • | • | | | | • | | | |
| Gb-5 | | | | | | • | • | | | | • | | | |
| Gb-6 | | | | | | | • | | | | • | | | |
| Gb-8 | | | • | | | | • | | | | | | | |
| Gb-9 | | | • | | | | • | | | | | | | |
| Gb-10 | | | • | | | | • | | | | | | | |
| Gb-11 | | | • | | | | • | | | | | | | |
| Gb-12 | | | • | | | | • | | | | | | | |
| Gb-14 | | | | | | • | • | | | | | | | |
| Gb-21 | | | | | | • | • | | | | | | | |
| Gb-24 | | | | | | | • | | | | | • | | |
| Gb-30 | | | • | | | | • | | | | | | | |
| Gb-37 | | | | | | | • | • | | | | | | |
| Gb-39 | | | • | | | | • | | | | • | | | |
| Gb-41 | | | | | | | • | • | | | | | | |
| Lv-1 | | | | | | | • | • | | | | | | |
| Lv-5 | | | | | | | • | • | | | | | | |
| Lv-13 | • | | | • | | | • | • | • | | | • | | |
| Lv-14 | | | | | | | | • | • | | | • | | |
| Lu-1 | | | | | | | | • | • | | | • | | |
| Lu-7 | | | | | | | | | • | • | | | | |
| LI-4 | | | | | | | | | • | • | | | | |
| LI-6 | | | | | | | | | • | • | | | | |
| LI-20 | | | | | | | | | | • | • | | | |
| St-1 | | | | | | | | | | • | • | | • | |
| St-5 | | | | | | | • | | | | • | | | |
| St-6 | | | | | | | • | | | | • | | | |
| St-12 | | • | | | | • | • | | | • | • | | | |
| St-25 | | | | | | | | | | • | • | | | |
| St-30 | | | | | | | • | | | | • | | | |
| St-40 | | | | | | | | | | | • | • | | |

| | Heart | Small Intestine | Bladder | Kidney | Heart Protector | Three Heater | Gallbladder | Liver | Lung | Large Intestine | Stomach | Spleen | Conception v. | Governing v. |
|---|---|---|---|---|---|---|---|---|---|---|---|---|---|---|
| St-42 | | | | | | | | | | | • | • | | |
| Sp-1 | | | | | | | | | | | • | • | | |
| Sp-4 | | | | | | | | | | | • | • | | |
| Sp-6 | | | | • | | | | • | | | | • | | |
| Sp-12 | | | | | | | | • | | | | • | | |
| Sp-13 | | | | | | | | • | | | | • | | |
| Sp-21 | • | | | | | | | | | | | • | | |
| CV-1 | | | | | | | | | | | | | • | • |
| CV-2 | | | | | | | | • | | | | | • | |
| CV-3 | | | • | • | | | | • | | | | • | • | |
| CV-4 | | • | | • | | | | • | | | • | • | • | |
| CV-5 | | | | | | • | | | | | | | • | |
| CV-7 | | | | • | • | • | | | | | | | • | |
| CV-9 | | | | | | | | | • | | | | • | |
| CV-10 | | | | | | | | | | | | • | • | |
| CV-11 | | • | | | | | | | • | | • | • | • | |
| CV-12 | | • | • | | • | • | • | | • | • | • | | • | |
| CV-13 | | • | | | | | | | • | | • | | • | |
| CV-14 | • | | | | | | | | | | | | • | |
| CV-15 | | | | | • | | | | | | | | • | |
| CV-17 | • | • | | • | • | • | | | | | | | • | |
| CV-24 | | | | | | | | | | | • | | • | • |
| GV-1 | | | | • | | | • | • | | | | | • | • |
| GV-13 | | | • | | | | | | | | | | | • |
| GV-14 | | • | • | | | • | • | | | • | • | | | • |
| GV-17 | | | • | | | | | | | | | | | • |
| GV-20 | | • | • | | | | • | • | | • | • | | | • |
| GV-23 | | | • | | | | • | | | | | | | • |
| GV-24 | | | • | | | | | | | | • | | | • |
| GV-26 | | | | | | | | | | • | • | | | • |
| GV-28 | | | | | | | | | | | • | | • | • |

| | Conception v. | Governing v. | *Yang* Linking v. | *Yin* Linking v. | *Yang* Motility v. | *Yin* Motility v. | Penetrating v. | Girdling v. |
|---|---|---|---|---|---|---|---|---|
| SI-10 | | | • | | • | | | |
| Bl-1 | | • | | | • | • | | |
| Bl-11 | | • | | | | | | |
| Bl-12 | | • | | | | | | |
| Bl-59 | | | | | • | | | |
| Bl-61 | | | | | • | | | |
| Bl-62 | | | | | • | | | |
| Bl-63 | | | • | | | | | |
| Ki-9 | | | | | | • | | |
| Ki-11 | | | | | | | • | |
| Ki-12 | | | | | | | • | |
| Ki-13 | | | | | | | • | |
| Ki-14 | | | | | | | • | |
| Ki-15 | | | | | | | • | |
| Ki-16 | | | | | | | • | |
| Ki-17 | | | | | | | • | |
| Ki-18 | | | | | | | • | |
| Ki-19 | | | | | | | • | |
| Ki-20 | | | | | | | • | |
| Ki-21 | | | | | | | • | |
| Th-13 | | | • | | | | | |
| Th-15 | | | • | | | | | |
| Gb-13 | | | • | | | | | |
| Gb-14 | | | • | | | | | |
| Gb-15 | | | • | | | | | |
| Gb-16 | | | • | | | | | |
| Gb-17 | | | • | | | | | |
| Gb-18 | | | • | | | | | |
| Gb-19 | | | • | | | | | |
| Gb-20 | | | • | | | | | |
| Gb-21 | | | • | | | | | |
| Gb-26 | | | | | | | | • |
| Gb-27 | | | | | | | | • |
| Gb-28 | | | | | | | | • |
| Gb-29 | | | | | • | | | |
| Gb-35 | | | • | | | | | |

| | Conception v. | Governing v. | *Yang* Linking v. | *Yin* Linking v. | *Yang* Motility v. | *Yin* Motility v. | Penetrating v. | Girdling v. |
|---|---|---|---|---|---|---|---|---|
| Lv-14 | | | | ● | | | | |
| LI-15 | | | | | ● | | | |
| LI-16 | | | | | ● | | | |
| St-1 | ● | | | | ● | | | |
| St-3 | | | | | ● | | | |
| St-4 | ● | | | | ● | | | |
| St-8 | | | ● | | | | | |
| St-30 | | | | | | | ● | |
| Sp-12 | | | | ● | | | | |
| Sp-13 | | | | ● | | | | |
| Sp-15 | | | | ● | | | | |
| Sp-16 | | | | ● | | | | |
| GV-1 | ● | | | | | | | |
| GV-15 | | | ● | | | | | |
| GV-16 | | | ● | | | | | |
| GV-28 | ● | | | | | | | |
| CV-1 | | ● | | | | | ● | |
| CV-7 | | | | | | | ● | |
| CV-22 | | | | ● | | | | |
| CV-23 | | | | ● | | | | |
| CV-24 | | ● | | | | | | |

APPENDIX D

# Resources

## Resources

1. Contact: I can be reached via e-mail at Lonny@nourishingdestiny.com. All questions regarding my writing should be directed to my discussion group, listed in number 2. My publishing company, Spirit Path Press, can be reached at 413-298-4221.

2. Online discussion: I moderate an online discussion forum on Chinese medicine. Members may ask questions or open a discussion on any aspect of Chinese medicine that interests them. To join, register at Nourishingdestiny.com. I also moderate the "Chinese Medicine: Scholar Physicians" page on Facebook.

3. Lectures: I teach at various schools and conferences of Chinese medicine throughout the year. My teaching schedule can be viewed at Shenmingseminars.blogspot.com.

4. Courses: I teach a two-year Clinical Integration course on my approach to Chinese medicine. The class focuses on integrating constitutional medicine with pulse diagnosis while looking at healing through an integral, evolutionary, and spiritual perspective. The course is twelve weekends over two years and begins every September. For information, e-mail me or visit my Web site listed in 3 above.

*Other Resources*

KEN WILBER: Ken's work has been inspirational to me for over thirty years. His, "*A Theory of Everything*" should be read by anyone wishing to consider a perspective broad enough to help ensure the relevance of Chinese medicine in the twenty-first century. See information at: https://www.integrallife.com/

## *Schools*

Those wishing to pursue a career based on a five-element tradition of Chinese medicine should investigate these two schools:

The Academy of Five Element Acupuncture
305 SE 2nd Ave,
Gainesville, FL 32601
(352) 335-2332
www.acupuncturist.edu

The Maryland University of Intergrative Health
7750 Montpelier Road
Laurel, MD 20723
(800) 735-2968
www.muih.edu

# REFERENCES

ANTHONY, C. K. (1981). *The Philosophy of the I Ching.* Stow, Mass.: Anthony Publishing.

AYSCOUGH, F. (1930). "Notes on the symbolism of the purple forbidden city." *Journal of the North China Branch of the Royal Asiatic Society* 52: 51–78.

BECK, D. (2002). "An Interview with Don Beck: The Never-Ending Upward Quest." *What Is Enlightenment?* (Fall/Winter): 126.

BECK, D., AND COWAN, C. (1995). *Spiral Dynamics, Mastering Values, Leadership, and Change.* Cambridge, Mass.: Blackwell.

BENSKY, D., AND GAMBLE, A. (1986). *Chinese Herbal Medicine: Materia Medica.* Seattle: Eastland Press.

BIRCH, S. (1992). "Naming the unnameable: A historical study of radial pulse six position diagnosis." *Traditional Acupuncture Society Journal* 12: 2–13.

BISHOP, C. W. (1933). "The worship of earth in ancient China." *Journal of the North China Branch of the Royal Asiatic Society* 64: 24–43.

CAPRA, F. (1975). *The Tao of Physics.* Berkeley: Shambala.

———. (1983).*The Turning Point: Science, Society and the Rising Culture.* New York: Bantam.

CHEN, E. M. (1989). *The Tao Te Ching.* New York: Paragon House.

CLAVEY, S. (1995). *Fluid Physiology and Pathology in Traditional Chinese Medicine.* South Melbourne, Australia: Churchill Livingstone.

CLEARY, T. (1986a). *The Inner Teachings of Taoism.* Boston: Shambhala.

————. (1986b). *The Taoist I-Ching.* Boston: Shambhala.

————. (1989). *The Book of Balance and Harmony.* San Francisco: North Point Press.

COHEN, A. (2001). *Embracing Heaven and Earth.* Lenox, Mass.: Moksha Press.

DALE, R. A. (1993). "The demystification of Chinese pulse diagnosis: An overview of the validations, holograms, and systemics for learning the principles and techniques." *American Journal of Acupuncture* 21, no. 1: 63–80.

DEADMAN, P., AND AL-KHAFAJI, M. (2000). *A Manual of Acupuncture.* CD-ROM. East Sussex, U.K.: Journal of Chinese Medicine Publications.

DEADMAN, P., MAZIN, A., & BAKER, K. (2000). *A Manual of Acupuncture.* East Sussex, U.K.: Journal of Chinese Medicine Publications.

DELANEY, C., LEONARD, D., AND KISCH, L. (1989). *The Acupuncture Point Book.* Makawao, Hawaii: Roast Duck Productions.

ECKMAN, P. (1996). *In the Footsteps of the Yellow Emperor: Tracing the History of Traditional Acupuncture.* San Francisco: Cypress.

ELLIS, A., WISEMAN, N., AND BOSS, K. (1989). *Grasping the Wind.* Brookline, Mass.: Paradigm.

FINGARETTE, H. (1972). *Confucius—The Secular as Sacred.* New York: Harper & Row.

FISCHER, E. S. (1930). "A journey to the Tung Ling and a visit to the desecrated Eastern mausolea of the Ta Tsing dynasty in 1929." *Journal of the North China Branch of the Royal Asiatic Society* 61: 20–39.

GIRARDOT, N. J. (1983). *Myth and Meaning in Early Taoism.* Berkeley: University of California Press.

GRAHAM, A. C. (trans.). (1990). *The Book of Lieh-tzu: A Classic of Tao.* New York: Columbia University Press.

HAMMER, L. (1990). *Dragon Rises, Red Bird Flies.* Barrytown, N.Y.: Station Hill Press.

————. (2001). *Chinese Pulse Diagnosis: A Contemporary Approach.* Seattle: Eastland Press.

HENDERSON, J. B. (1984). *The Development and Decline of Chinese Cosmology.* New York: Columbia University Press.

HICKS, S. (1985). *Catalogue of Acupuncture Point Translations.* Columbia, Md.: Traditional Acupuncture Institute.

HOMANN, R. (trans.). (1976). *Pai Wen Pien or The Hundred Questions: A Dialogue Between Two Taoists on the Macrocosmic and Microcosmic System of Correspondence.* Leiden: E. J. Brill.

HUMPHREYS, C. (1984). *A Popular Dictionary of Buddhism.* London: Curzon Press.

JARRETT, L. S. (1983). *A Neural Interpretation of Acupuncture.* Tape W210. Available through Creative Audio, 8751 Osborne, Highland, IN 46322.

————. (1985, Autumn). "The holographic paradigm and acupuncture." *Journal of Traditional Acupuncture* 8, no. 2: 36–41.

————. (1992a, April). "Myth and meaning in Chinese medicine." *Traditional Acupuncture Society Journal,* no. 11: 45–48.

————. (1992b, October). "The returned spirit *(gui ling)* of traditional Chinese medicine." *Traditional Acupuncture Society Journal,* no. 12: 19–31.

————. (1992c). "The role of human will *(zhi),* and the spirit of Bladder-52." *American Journal of Acupuncture* 20, no. 4: 349–358.

————. (1993a). "Constitutional type and the internal tradition of Chinese medicine—Part I: The ever present cause." *American Journal of Acupuncture* 21, no. 1: 19–32.

————. (1993b). "Constitutional type and the internal tradition of Chinese medicine—Part II: The ontogeny of life." *American Journal of Acupuncture* 21, no. 2: 141–158.

————. (1994a). "The loss and return of original nature: The law of husband/wife." *American Journal of Acupuncture* 22, no. 1: 29–45.

————. (1994b, Fall). "The use of entry and exit points in traditional acupuncture." *Journal of the National Academy of Acupuncture and Oriental Medicine* 1, no. 1: 19–30.

————. (1995a). "Chinese medicine and the betrayal of intimacy: The theory and treatment of abuse, incest, rape and divorce with acupuncture and herbs—Part I." *American Journal of Acupuncture* 23, no. 1: 35–51.

————. (1995b). "Chinese medicine and the betrayal of intimacy: The theory and treatment of abuse, incest, rape and divorce with acupuncture and herbs—Part II." *American Journal of Acupuncture* 23, no. 2: 123–151.

————. (1995c). "Chinese medicine and the betrayal of intimacy: The theory and treatment of abuse, incest, rape and divorce with acupuncture and herbs—Part III: Case study." *American Journal of Acupuncture* 23, no. 3: 241–267.

————. (1996). *"Niu Huang Qing Xin Wan."* http://www.infinite.org/innertraditions/articles.html.

————. (1998). *Nourishing Destiny: The Inner Tradition of Chinese Medicine.* Stockbridge, Mass.: Spirit Path Press.

————. (2002). "Recovery from chronic fatigue: The transformation of ingratiation into integrity." In *Contemporary Chinese Medicine and Acupuncture,* edited by C. M. Cassidy. Philadelphia: Churchill Livingstone.

JUNFAN, LI (Bruce Lee). (1979). *The Tao of Jeet Kune Do.* Burbank, Calif.: Ohara Publications.

KIMURA,Y. (2002). "An Interview with Yasuhiko Kimura: A Philosopher of Change." *What Is Enlightenment?* (Fall/Winter): 28.

KOHN, L. (1992). *Early Chinese Mysticism: Philosophy and Soteriology in the Taoist Tradition.* Princeton, N.J.: Princeton University Press.

————. (2002). *Living with the Dao: Conceptual Issues in Daoist Practice.* Cambridge: Three Pines Press (e-book available at Threepinespress.com).

LAGERWEY, J. (1987). *Taoist Ritual in Chinese Society and History.* New York: Macmillan.

LARRE, C., AND ROCHAT DE LA VALLEE, E. (1985). *The Secret Treatise of the Spiritual Orchard.* East Grinstead, U.K.: International Register of Oriental Medicine.

————. (1993). *Rooted in Spirit: The Heart of Chinese Medicine.* Barrytown, N.Y.: Station Hill Press.

————. (1997). *The Eight Extraordinary Meridians.* Cambridge: Monkey Press.

LARRE, C., SCHATZ, J., AND ROCHAT DE LA VALLEE, E. (1986). *Survey of Traditional Chinese Medicine.* Columbia, Md.: Traditional Acupuncture Institute.

LEGGE, J. (trans.). (1962). *The Texts of Taoism: The T'ai Shang Tractate, The Writings of Chuang Tzu: Part II. The Sacred Books of China.* New York: Dover.

————. (1971). *Confucius: Confucian Analects, The Great Learning and the Doctrine of the Mean.* New York: Dover.

LOW, R. (1985). *The Secondary Vessels of Acupuncture.* New York: Thorsons.

LU GWEI-DJEN, AND NEEDHAM, J. (1980). *Celestial Lancets: A History and Rationale of Acupuncture and Moxa.* Cambridge: Cambridge University Press.

MACIOCIA, G. (1992, November). Letter to the editor. *Traditional Acupuncture Society Journal* 12: 39–41.

MATHEWS, R. H. (1931). *Mathews' Chinese-English Dictionary.* Cambridge, Mass.: Harvard University Press.

MATSUMOTO, K., AND BIRCH, S. (1983). *Five Elements and Ten Stems,* Nan Jing *Theory, Diagnostics, and Practice.* Brookline, Mass.: Paradigm Publications.

MING, OU. (1982). *Chinese-English Glossary of Common Terms in Traditional Chinese Medicine.* Hong Kong: Joint Publishing.

MOLE, P. (1992, April). "Further down the road: A personal view of the strengths and weaknesses of Leamington acupuncture." *Traditional Acupuncture Society Journal* 11: 3–10.

MORGAN, F. (1920). "Destiny, fate." *Journal of the North China Branch of the Royal Asiatic Society* 51: 25.

MUNRO, D. J. (ed.). (1985). *Individualism and Holism: Studies in Confucian and Taoist Values.* Ann Arbor: Center for Chinese Studies, University of Michigan.

O'CONNOR, J., AND BENSKY, D. (trans.). (1987). *Acupuncture: A Comprehensive Text.* Shanghai College of Traditional Medicine. Seattle: Eastland Press.

OMURA, Y. (1982). *Acupuncture Medicine.* Tokyo: Japan Publications.

PALUDAN, A. (1991). *The Chinese Spirit Road: The Classical Tradition of Stone Tomb Statuary.* New Haven, Conn.: Yale University Press.

PORKERT, M. (1982). *The Theoretical Foundations of Chinese Medicine.* Cambridge, Mass.: MIT Press.

————. (1983). "The essentials of Chinese diagnostics." *Acta Medicinae*

*Sinensis*. Zurich, Switzerland: Chinese Medicine Publications.

SCHEID,V. (2002). *Chinese Medicine in Contemporary China, Plurality and Synthesis*. Durham, N.C.: Duke University Press.

SCHIPPER, K. (1975). *Concordance du Tao Tsang: Titres des ouvrages*. Paris: Publications de l'Ecole Française d'Extrême Orient.

SMITH, F. F. (1986). *Inner Bridges: A Guide to Energy Movement and Body Structure*. Atlanta: Humanics Ltd. Partners.

SMITH, S. (1998). *The Five Element Acupuncture Handbook*. Columbia, Md.: TAI-Sophia Institute. Available through TAIS at (800) 735-2968.

SUN TZU. (1973). *The Art of War*. Hong Kong: Grand Cultural Service Company.

UNSCHULD, P. U. (1985). *Medicine in China: A History of Ideas*. Berkeley: University of California Press.

————. (1986). *Nan-Ching: The Classic of Difficult Issues*. Berkeley: University of California Press.

————. (1988). *Introductory Readings in Classical Chinese Medicine*. Boston: Kluwer Academic.

VAN OVER, R. (1973). *Taoist Tales*. New York: Meridian.

VEITH, I. (1949). *The Yellow Emperor's Classic of Internal Medicine*. Berkeley: University of California Press.

WARE, J. R.(1966). *Alchemy, Medicine, and Religion in the China of A.D. 320*. Mineola, N.Y.: Dover.

WATSON, B. (trans.). (1964a). *Chuang Tzu: Basic Writings*. New York: Columbia University Press.

————. (1964b). *Han Fei Tzu, Basic Writings*. New York: Columbia University Press.

————. (1968). *The Complete Works of Chuang Tzu*. New York: Columbia University Press.

WIEGER, L. (1965). *Chinese Characters*. New York: Paragon Book Reprint.

WILBER, K. (2000). *A Theory of Everything: An Integral Vision for Business, Politics, Science, and Spirituality*. Boston: Shambala.

————. *Boomeritis*. (2002). Boston: Shambala.

WILHELM, R. (1962). *The Secret of the Golden Flower*. New York: Harcourt, Brace & World.

————. (1968). *The I-Ching or Book of Changes*. Princeton, N.J.: Princeton University Press.

WILLIAMS, C. A. S. (1974). *Chinese Symbolism and Art Motifs*. North Clarendon, Vt.: Charles E. Tuttle.

WORSLEY, J. R. (1979). *The Meridians of Ch'i Energy: Point Reference Guide*. Columbia, Md.: Traditional Acupuncture Institute.

————. (1982). *Traditional Chinese Acupuncture: Vol. 1. Meridians and Points*. Tisbury, U.K.: Element Books.

ZEITLIN, JUDITH T. (1993). *Historian of the Strange: Pu Songling and the Chinese Classic Tale*. Stanford: Stanford University Press.

# ENGLISH INDEX

# PINYIN INDEX

# CHINESE HERB INDEX

# ACUPUNCTURE POINT INDEX

# CHARACTER INDEX

## *Acupuncture Point Names*

Here I've listed alphabetically, by their pinyin spelling, each of the characters used in the acupuncture point names. Each character is cross-referenced to the appropriate lesson in Wieger's (W) etymological text *Chinese Characters* as well as to *Mathews' Chinese-English Dictionary* (M). Lack of an appropriate entry in either is indicated by an "X". For example, a designation of WX or MX indicates that a specific character is not listed in that source. The appearance of an asterisk next to a lesson number (for example, W54B*) indicates it is related to, but does not cover, the exact character in question. I have also included one, or several, simple definitions for each character as they relate to my most common translation in the point names. It is my hope that this index will facilitate your own research into the meaning of the point names making you less dependent on any author's rendering of the characters.

*AI*$^{1}$ 哀 sorrow, W16C, M3
*AN*$^{1}$ 安 peaceful, quiet, W67G, M26
*BAI*$^{2}$ 白 white, W88A, M4975
*BAI*$^{3}$ 百 hundred, W88B, M4976
*BAO*$^{1}$ 胞 womb, bladder, W54B*, M4940
*BAO*$^{1}$ 包 envelope, wrapping, W54B, M4937
*BEI*$^{4}$ 背 back, WX, M4989
*BEN*$^{3}$ 本 root, W120A, M5025
*BI*$^{2}$ 鼻 nose, W40C, M5100

*BI*[4] 髀 hip, thigh, WX, M5073
*BI*[4] 臂 arm, WX, M5107
*BIAN*[1] 邊 limit, W34K, M5243
*BIAN*[3] 扁 flat, W156D, M5228
*BIE*[2] 別 separate, W118B, M5208
*BIN*[1] 賓 guest, W112L, M5259
*BIN*[1] 濱 embankment, WX, M5265
*BIN*[4] 臏 knee, WX, M5268
*BIN*[4] 鬢 hair on the temples, WX, M5271
*BING*[3] 秉 grasp, W44I, M5291
*BO*[2] 佰 respect, WX, M4977
*BO*[2] 膊 shoulder, WX, M5324
*BU*[3] 補 supplement, WX, M5372
*BU*[4] 步 walking, W112G, M5363
*BU*[4] 部 class, division, section, WX, M5376

*CAN*[1] 參 aid, W62C, M6685
*CANG*[1] 倉 granary, W26M, M6707
*CHA*[1] 差 servant, WX, M105
*CHANG*[1] 昌 glorious, W73A, M206
*CHANG*[2] 長 long, W113A, M213
*CHANG*[2] 腸 intestine, WX, M220
*CHE*[1] 車 a cart, a chariot, W167A, M280
*CHEN*[2] 臣 official, W82E, M327
*CHENG*[2] 承 receive, W47W, M386
*CHI*[2] 池 pond, WX, M1032
*CHI*[3] 尺 cubit, W32F, M1045
*CHONG*[1] 沖 rushing, WX, M1523
*CHONG*[1] 衝 thoroughfare, WX, M1532
*CHONG*[2] 蟲 insect, W110D, M1519
*CHU*[3] 處 to dwell, resting place, WX, M1407
CHUAI[4] 踹 heel, WX, M1423
*CHUANG*[1] 窗 window, WX, M1461
*CHUANG*[2] 床 bed, WX, M1459
*CHUO*[4] 䪼 cheekbone, W p. 803, MX
*CI*[1] 慈 charity, WX, M6965
*CI*[4] 刺 thorn, W120H, M6985
*CI*[4] 次 second, W99B, M6980
*CUAN*[4] 攢 collect, WX, M6845
*DA*[4] 大 big, great, W60A, 60G; M5943
*DAI*[4] 帶 belt, girdle, W24Q, M6005
*DAN*[3] 膽 gallbladder, WX, M6047
*DANG*[1] 當 at, on, W36E, M6087

*DAO*[4] 道 path, W160A, M6136
*DOU*[4] 竇 drain, WX, M6485
*DI*[4] 地 earth, WX, M6198
*DING*[3] 鼎 vessel, tripod, W127D, M6392
*DING*[3] 頂 summit, WX, M6390
*DU*[1] 都 capital, WX, M6500
*DU*[1] 督 governor, WX, M6508
*DU*[2] 瀆 ditch, river, WX, M6518
*DU*[2] 犢 calf, a victim for sacrifice, WX, M6519
*DUI*[4] 兑 open, W29D, M6560
*DUN*[1] 敦 esteem, W75E, M6571
*DUO*[1] 多 enough, much, W64E, M6416

*ER*[3] 耳 ear, W146A, M1744

*FA*[3] 髮 hair, WX, M1770
*FANG*[2] 房 chariot, WX, M1806
*FEI*[1] 飛 fly, W11A, M1850
*FEI*[4] 肺 the lungs, W79G*, M1843
*FEN*[1] 分 branch, division, W18B, M1851
*FENG*[1] 風 wind, W21B, M1890
*FENG*[1] 封 seal, W79E, M1887
*FENG*[1] 豐 abundant, W97B, M1897
*FENG*[2] 縫 stich, WX, M1882
*FU*[1] 趺 bowing, WX, 1913
*FU*[1] 跗 instep, WX, M1923
*FU*[2] 扶 support, WX, M1909
*FU*[2] 浮 superficial, W94B, M1906
*FU*[2] 浮 rising, W94A, M1906
*FU*[3] 府 palace, storehouse, treasury, W45C, M1928
*FU*[4] 付 transfer, W45C, M1917
*FU*[4] 附 attach, WX, M1924
*FU*[4] 腹 belly, WX, M1994
*FU*[4] 復 return, W75I, M1992
*FU*[4] 伏 hidden, humble, prostrate, W25E, M1964

*GAI*[4] 蓋 cover, W38G, M3199
*GAN*[1] 肝 liver, WX, M3217
*GANG*[1] 綱 net, WX, M3271
*GAO*[1] 高 tall, high, tower, W75B, M3290
*GAO*[1] 膏 fat, the area below the heart, WX, M3296
*GE*[2] 膈 diaphragm, WX, M3318
*GEN*[1] 根 root, WX, M3328

| | | |
|---|---|---|
| *Gong*[1] | 宮 | palace, W90G, M3705 |
| *Gong*[1] | 公 | nobility, W18C, M3701 |
| *Gou*[1] | 溝 | ditch, drain, WX, M3429 |
| *Gou*[1] | 勾 | hook, W54F, M3409 |
| *Gu*[3] | 骨 | bone, W118A, M3486 |
| *Gu*[3] | 谷 | valley, W18E, M3483 |
| *Gu*[3] | 穀 | grain, WX, M3490 |
| *Guan*[1] | 關 | pass, barrier, W92G, M3571 |
| *Guang*[1] | 光 | illumination, W24J, M3583 |
| *Guang*[1] | 胱 | bladder, WX, M3586 |
| *Gui*[1] | 歸 | return, W86B, M3617 |
| *Gui*[3] | 鬼 | ghost, demon, W40C, M3634 |
| | | |
| *Hai*[3] | 海 | sea, WX, M2014 |
| *Han*[2] | 寒 | cold, W47U, M2048 |
| *Han*[2] | 含 | contain, W14L, M2017 |
| *Han*[4] | 頷 | the jaws, WX, M2022 |
| *He*[1] | 呵 | laughter, WX, M2110 |
| *He*[2] | 合 | joining, unite, W14B, M2117 |
| *He*[2] | 和 | harmony, W121E, M2115 |
| *He*[4] | 赫 | brightness, W126B, M2091 |
| *Heng*[2] | 橫 | horizontal, transverse, WX, M2106 |
| *Hou*[4] | 後 | back, later, W90A, M2143 |
| *Hu*[3] | 虎 | tiger, W135B, M2161 |
| *Hu*[4] | 戶 | door, W129A, M2180 |
| *Hua*[2] | 滑 | lubrication, WX, M2227 |
| *Huan*[2] | 環 | a ring, bracelet, encircle, WX, M2258 |
| *Huang*[1] | 肓 | area between the heart and diaphragm, WX, M2274 |
| *Hui*[4] | 會 | meeting, W14D, M2345 |
| *Hun*[2] | 魂 | spirit of the liver official, WX, M2365 |
| *Huo*[4] | 或 | possible, W71J, M2402 |
| | | |
| *Ji*[1] | 機 | motion, WX, M411 |
| *Ji*[1] | 箕 | basket, WX, M402 |
| *Ji*[2] | 急 | urgent, W19D, M480 |
| *Ji*[2] | 吉 | happiness, W24C, M476 |
| *Ji*[2] | 極 | utmost, extreme, WX, M484 |
| *Ji*[2] | 脊 | spine, W13I, M489 |
| *Ji*[4] | 際 | region, W65H*, M467 |
| *Ji*[4] | 季 | last, WX, M435 |
| *Ji*[4] | 瘈 | spasm, WX, MX |
| *Jia*[1] | 夾 | pressed, W27F, M611 |

*JIA*[4] 頰 jaw, WX, M614
*JIAN*[1] 肩 shoulder, W65F, M824
*JIAN*[1] 間 space, intermediary, interval, WX, M835
*JIAN*[1] 尖 tip, W18I, M865
*JIAO*[1] 焦 burning space, heater, W126A, M721
*JIAO*[1] 交 exchange, W61D, M702
*JIAO*[3] 角 angle, W142B, M1174
*JIAO*[4] 窌 hole, WX, M718
*JIE*[1] 街 thoroughfare, WX, M619
*JIE*[2] 結 knot, WX, M782
*JIE*[2] 節 joint, W26M, M795
*JIE*[3] 解 released, W142B, M626
*JIN*[1] 筋 muscle, sinew, WX, M1058
*JIN*[1] 金 metal gold, W14T, M1057
*JIN*[4] 禁 prohibition, W119M, M1077
*JING*[1] 經 meridian, the classics, WX, M1123
*JING*[1] 睛 the eyes, WX, M1147
*JING*[1] 精 essence, WX, M1149
*JING*[1] 京 capital, W75C, M1127
*JING*[3] 頸 neck, WX, M1126
*JING*[3] 井 well, W115A, M1143
*JIU*[3] 九 nine, W23A, M1198
*JIU*[4] 臼 mortar, W139A, M1202
*JU*[1] 居 dwelling, W32C, M1535
*JU*[4] 巨 great, very, W82D, M1544
*JUE*[2] 厥 *jue*, W102D, M1680
*JUE*[2] 絕 broken, extreme, W55G, M1703

*KE*[4] 客 guest, W31B, M3324
*KONG*[1] 空 hole, W82A, M3722
*KONG*[3] 孔 opening, hole, WX, M3720
*KOU*[3] 口 mouth, W72A, M3434
*KU*[1] 窟 dwelling, WX, M3503
*KU*[4] 庫 treasury, storehouse, W58I, M3496
*KUA*[4] 跨 to straddle, WX, M3531
*KUAN*[1] 髖 hip, WX, MX
*KUI*[2] 魁 eminence, WX, M3655
*KUN*[1] 崑 in the name of Kunlun Mountain, WX, M3679

*LAI*[2] 來 to come, W13C, M3768
*LANG*[2] 廊 verandah, WX, M3822
*LANG*[2] 郎 gentleman, W75F, M3820

| | | |
|---|---|---|
| *LAO*$^{2}$ | 勞 | labor, toil, weary, W126F, M3826 |
| *LAO*$^{3}$ | 老 | old, W30E, M3833 |
| *LEI*$^{3}$ | 壘 | wall, W149F, M4228 |
| *LEI*$^{4}$ | 肋 | rib, WX, M3840 |
| *LEI*$^{4}$ | 淚 | tears, WX, M4243 |
| *LENG*$^{3}$ | 冷 | cold, WX, M3844 |
| *LI*$^{2}$ | 釐 | tuft, WX, M3883 |
| *LI*$^{3}$ | 蠡 | insect, WX, M3894 |
| *LI*$^{3}$ | 里 | a measure of distance, W149D, M3857 |
| *LI*$^{3}$ | 理 | reason, principle, to regulate, WX, M3864 |
| *LI*$^{4}$ | 歷 | passage, W121L, M3931 |
| *LI*$^{4}$ | 厲 | hard, W23H, M3906 |
| *LI*$^{4}$ | 瀝 | trickle, WX, M3934 |
| *LI*$^{4}$ | 利 | advantage, profit, gain, W52F, M3867 |
| *LIAN*$^{2}$ | 廉 | angle, W121I, M4003 |
| *LIANG*$^{2}$ | 梁 | beam, bridge, W52B, M3951 |
| *LIAO*$^{2}$ | 髎 | foramen, bone hole, WX; M3486, 3962 |
| *LIE*$^{4}$ | 列 | sequence, W12F, 52D; M3984 |
| *LIN*$^{2}$ | 臨 | before, near to, W82F, M4027 |
| *LIN*$^{2}$ | 林 | forest, W119L, M4022 |
| *LING*$^{2}$ | 陵 | mound, tomb, WX, M4067 |
| *LING*$^{2}$ | 靈 | spirit, potency, W72K, M4071 |
| *LIU*$^{1}$ | 溜 | current, WX, M4085 |
| *LIU*$^{2}$ | 留 | to restrain, W129E, M4083 |
| *LONG*$^{2}$ | 蘢 | basket, WX, M4271 |
| *LONG*$^{2}$ | 聾 | deafness, WX, M4272 |
| *LONG*$^{2}$ | 龍 | dragon, W140A, M4258 |
| *LONG*$^{2}$ | 隆 | splendor, W79F, M4255 |
| *LOU*$^{4}$ | 漏 | to leak, W32G, M4152 |
| *LU*$^{2}$ | 盧 | skull, WX, M4171 |
| *LU*$^{2}$ | 膂 | backbone, spine, WX, M4287 |
| *LU*$^{3}$ | 呂 | tube, W90F, M4280 |
| *LU*$^{4}$ | 路 | road, W31B, M4181 |
| *LUN*$^{2}$ | 崙 | in the name of Kunlun Mountain, WX, M4249 |
| *LUO*$^{4}$ | 絡 | connect, blood vessels, meridians, WX, M4125 |
| *LUO*$^{4}$ | 濼 | river, WX, M4130 |
| *MAI*$^{4}$ | 脈 | vessel, meridian, W125E, M4382 |
| *MAN*$^{3}$ | 滿 | full, W35M*, M4326 |
| *MEI*$^{2}$ | 眉 | eyebrow, W7A, M4391 |
| *MEN*$^{2}$ | 門 | gate, W129C, M4418 |
| *MI*$^{3}$ | 米 | rice, W122A, M4446 |
| *MIAN*$^{4}$ | 面 | face, W160B, M4497 |

*MING*$^{2}$ 明 illumination, bright, enlightenment, WX, M4534
*MING*$^{4}$ 命 destiny, W14I, M4537
*MU*$^{4}$ 募 to summon, to raise, WX, M4585
*MU*$^{4}$ 目 eye, W158A, M4596

*NAO*$^{3}$ 腦 brain, WX, M4638
*NAO*$^{4}$ 臑 shoulder blade, WX, M4647
*NI*$^{4}$ 逆 to go against, counterflow, WX, M4677
*NIE*$^{4}$ 嚙 chew, WX, M4704
*NIE*$^{4}$ 顳 the temporal bones, W146G, M4709
*NEI*$^{4}$ 內 internal, inner, WX, M4766

*PANG*$^{2}$ 膀 groin, loins, bladder, WX, M4931
*PEN*$^{2}$ 盆 bowl, WX, M5034
*PI*$^{2}$ 脾 spleen, WX, M5164
*PI*$^{2}$ 皮 skin, W43H, M5142
*PIAN*$^{1}$ 偏 side, WX, M5246
*PIN*$^{2}$ 頻 shore, W112G, M5275
*PING*$^{2}$ 平 tranquility, W58F, M5303
*PO*$^{4}$ 魄 spirit of the lung official, WX, M4988
*PU*$^{2}$ 僕 servant, W102I*, M5401

*QI*$^{1}$ 七 seven, W33A, M579
*QI*$^{2}$ 期 hope, WX, M526
*QI*$^{4}$ 氣 *qi*, W98A, M554
*QI*$^{4}$ 泣 tears, WX, M563
*QIAN*$^{2}$ 前 forward, W66D, M919
*QIANG*$^{2}$ 強 strong, W110B, M668
*QIANG*$^{2}$ 墻 wall, WX, M674
*QIAO*$^{1}$ 蹻 motility, W75B*, M750
*QIAO*$^{4}$ 竅 hole, WX, M751
*QING*$^{1}$ 青 cyan, W115D, M1168
*QING*$^{1}$ 清 pure, WX, M1171
*QIU*$^{1}$ 秋 autumn, harvest, W121C*, M1227
*QIU*$^{1}$ 丘 mound, W27H, M1213
*QU*$^{1}$ 曲 crooked, W51B, M1623
*QU*$^{1}$ 胠 opening, WX, M1597
*QU*$^{1}$ 屈 grievance, submit, W78E, M1621
*QU*$^{2}$ 渠 gutter, WX, M1603
*QU*$^{2}$ 衢 thoroughfare, WX, M1611
*QUAN*$^{2}$ 泉 spring, W125F, M1674
*QUAN*$^{2}$ 顴 cheek, WX, M1664

| | | |
|---|---|---|
| *Que*[1] | 缺 | broken, WX, M1708 |
| *Que*[4] | 闕 | tower gate, WX, M1712 |
| *Que*[4] | 卻 | decline, W17H, M 1183 |
| | | |
| *Ran*[2] | 然 | blazing, W65G, M3072 |
| *Re*[4] | 熱 | heat, WX, M3095 |
| *Ri*[4] | 日 | sun, W143A, M3124 |
| *Rong*[2] | 容 | easy, glory, W18E, M7560 |
| *Rong*[2] | 榮 | bright, WX, M7582 |
| *Rou*[4] | 肉 | flesh, W65AQ, M3153 |
| *Ru*[2] | 顬 | the temporal bone, WX, M3151 |
| *Ru*[3] | 乳 | breast, milk, WX, M3144 |
| *Rui*[4] | 銳 | valiant, WX, M3174 |
| | | |
| *San*[1] | 三 | three, W3A, M5415 |
| *Sang*[3] | 顙 | forehead, WX, M5428 |
| *Shan*[1] | 山 | mountain, W80A, M5630 |
| *Shang*[1] | 商 | merchant, W15D, M5673 |
| *Shang*[1] | 傷 | harm, injury, W101B, M5666 |
| *Shang*[4] | 上 | upper, W5A, M5669 |
| *Shao*[4] | 少 | little, lesser, W18M, M5675 |
| *She*[2] | 蛇 | snake, WX, M5698 |
| *She*[4] | 舍 | abode, dwelling, W14C, M5699 |
| *Shen*[1] | 申 | extend, W50C, M5712 |
| *Shen*[2] | 神 | spirit, WX, M5716 |
| *Shen*[4] | 腎 | kidney, WX, M5736 |
| *Shi*[1] | 濕 | damp, W92E, M5823 |
| *Shi*[2] | 十 | ten, W24A, M5807 |
| *Shi*[2] | 使 | messenger, WX, M5770 |
| *Shi*[2] | 石 | stone, W59D, M5813 |
| *Shi*[2] | 食 | food, W26M, M5810 |
| *Shi*[3] | 始 | beginning, WX, M5772 |
| *Shi*[4] | 室 | room, W133B, M5820 |
| *Shi*[4] | 市 | market, W34D, M5792 |
| *Shou*[3] | 手 | hand, W48A, M5838 |
| *Shou*[4] | 受 | receive, W49E, M5840 |
| *Shu*[1] | 俞 | transport, W14F, M7628 |
| *Shu*[1] | 輸 | tribute, WX, M5864 |
| *Shu*[1] | 樞 | pivot, WX, M5859 |
| *Shu*[4] | 束 | bind, W120I, M5891 |
| *Shuai*[4] | 率 | leading, net, W91D, M5910 |
| *Shuai*[4] | 蟀 | cricket, WX, MX |

*SHUI*[3] 水 water, W12B, M5922

*SHUN*[4] 順 comply, follow, W160C, M5935

*SHUO*[4] 鑠 shining, WX, M5835

*SHUO*[4] 爍 brilliance, WX, M5834

*SI*[1] 絲 silk, WX, M5571

*SI*[4] 四 four, W42A, M5598

*SUI*[3] 髓 marrow, WX, M5525

*SUI*[2] 隋 Sui dynasty, WX, M5522

*SUN*[1] 孫 grandson, W92B, M5541

*SUO*[3] 所 a place, that, who, what, W128A, M5465

*TAI*[4] 太 very, great, WX, M6020

*TANG*[2] 堂 hall, W36E, M6107

*TI*[4] 體 body, WX, M6246

*TIAN*[1] 天 heaven, W1C & 60C, M6361

*TIAO*[2] 條 branch, WX, M6300

*TIAO*[2] 銚 spear, WX, M6289

*TIAO*[4] 跳 jump, WX, M6287

*TING*[1] 聽 listen, W10O, M6402

*TING*[2] 庭 courtyard, W81F*, M6405

*TONG*[1] 通 penetrating, communication, WX, M6638

*TONG*[2] 瞳 pupil, WX, M6633

*TONG*[2] 童 child, W19K, M6626

*TOU*[2] 頭 head, WX, M6489

*TU*[2] 突 chimney, rush out, W37B, M6540

*TU*[4] 兔 hare, WX, M6534

*TUI*[3] 腿 leg, W31C*, M6569

*TUO*[2] 沱 water diverging into streams, WX, M6442

*WA*[1] 凹 hollow, concave, W177, M7268

*WAI*[4] 外 beyond, external, outer, W56F, M7001

*WAN*[2] 完 final, W29H, M7008

*WAN*[4] 腕 wrist, WX, M7023

*WEI*[2] 維 bind, link, WX, M7067

*WEI*[3] 委 servant, W121F, M7098

*WEI*[4] 胃 stomach, W122C, M7075

*WEN*[1] 溫 warmth, WX, M7125

*WEN*[2] 聞 to hear, W129C, M7142

*WO*[1] 窩 nest, WX, M7155

*WU*[1] 屋 room, W32G, M7212

*WU*[3] 五 five, W39A, M7187

*XI*$^{1}$ 谿 mountain stream, ravine, WX, M511
*XI*$^{1}$ 鼷 mouse, W139B*, M2430
*XI*$^{1}$ 郄 cleft, WX, M2474
*XI*$^{1}$ 譆 exclamation, WX, M2436
*XI*$^{2}$ 息 breath, W159A, M2495
*XI*$^{4}$ 細 thin, WX, M2467
*XIA*$^{2}$ 俠 valiant, WX, M2631
*XIA*$^{4}$ 下 lower, W5B, M2520
*XIAN*$^{4}$ 陷 to sink, WX, M2694
*XIANG*$^{1}$ 香 fragrance, W73B, M2547
*XIANG*$^{1}$ 鄉 region, W26M, M2556
*XIAO*$^{1}$ 消 thaw, melt, WX, M2607
*XIAO*$^{3}$ 小 little, W18H, M2605
*XIE*$^{2}$ 邪 evil, W147B, M2625
*XIE*$^{2}$ 脅 rib, WX, M2641
*XIN*$^{1}$ 心 heart, W107A, M2735
*XIN*$^{4}$ 囟 skull, WX, M2752
*XIN*$^{4}$ 信 integrity, trust, faith, pledge, W25H, M2748
*XING*$^{2}$ 行 move, walk, W63C, M2754
*XIONG*$^{1}$ 胸 chest, W38D, M2812
*XU*$^{1}$ 虛 mound, void, W27H*, M2823
*XU*$^{1}$ 墟 burial ground, WX, M2823
*XUAN*$^{2}$ 玄 mysterious, W91A, M2881
*XUAN*$^{2}$ 旋 revolve, W112C, M2894
*XUAN*$^{2}$ 懸 suspend, WX, M2887
*XUE*$^{4}$ 穴 cave, W37A, M2899
*XUE*$^{4}$ 血 blood, W1J, M2901
*XUN*$^{2}$ 循 adhere, follow, WX, M2926

*YA*$^{2}$ 牙 tooth, W147A, M7214
*YAN*$^{3}$ 眼 eye, WX, M7400
*YAN*$^{4}$ 厭 loathsome, to detest, W65G, M7387
*YANG*$^{2}$ 揚 flourish, scatter, WX, M7259
*YANG*$^{2}$ 陽 sunny side of a hill, complement to *yin*, W86A, 101B; M7265
*YANG*$^{3}$ 養 nourish, W103A, M7254
*YANG*$^{4}$ 羕 flowing, W103A, MX
*YAO*$^{1}$ 腰 loins, W50N*, M7302
*YE*$^{4}$ 液 fluid, WX, M3033
*YE*$^{4}$ 腋 armpit, WX, M3034
*YE*$^{4}$ 掖 armpit, WX, M3032
*YE*$^{4}$ 夜 darkness, W60I, M7315
*YI*$^{1}$ 一 one, W1A, M3016

*Yi*$^{1}$ 乙 one, unity, second of the ten stems, W9A, M3017

*Yi*$^{2}$ 儀 apparatus, WX, M3003

*Yi*$^{4}$ 意 thought, the spirit of the spleen, W73E, M2960

Yi$^{4}$ 譩 exclamation, WX, M2961

*Yi*$^{4}$ 益 benefit, W125C, M3052

*Yi*$^{4}$ 翳 screen, WX, M2977

*Yin*$^{1}$ 陰 shady side of a hill, complementary to *yang*, W14P, M7444

*Yin*$^{1}$ 殷 prosperous, WX, M7423

*Yin*$^{3}$ 隱 hidden, mysterious, WX, M7448

*Ying*$^{1}$ 膺 breast, W168J*, M7478

*Ying*$^{2}$ 營 living, an army encampment, nutritive *qi*, WX, M7467

*Ying*$^{2}$ 迎 welcome, WX, M7473

*Yong*$^{3}$ 湧 bubbling, WX, M7572

*You*$^{1}$ 幽 dark, W90D, M7505

*You*$^{3}$ 牖 window, WX, M7507

*Yu*$^{2}$ 魚 fish, W142A, M7668

*Yu*$^{4}$ 玉 jade, W83A, M7666

*Yu*$^{4}$ 彧 elegance, WX, M7677

*Yu*$^{4}$ 域 frontier, WX, M7676

*Yuan*$^{1}$ 淵 abyss, whirlpool, W125C, M7723

*Yuan*$^{2}$ 垣 wall, WX, M7724

*Yuan*$^{2}$ 元 primordial, W29H, M7707

*Yuan*$^{2}$ 員 official, W161B, M7721

*Yuan*$^{2}$ 原 source, W125F, M7725

*Yuan*$^{2}$ 源 source, WX, M7728

*Yue*$^{4}$ 月 moon, W64G, M7696

*Yun*$^{2}$ 雲 cloud, W93B, M7750

*Zai*$^{4}$ 在 at, in, on, to be alive, W96D, M6657

*Ze*$^{2}$ 澤 marsh, WX, M277

*Zhang*$^{1}$ 章 chapter, law, W73E, M182

*Zhang*$^{3}$ 掌 palm of the hand, sole of the foot, W36E, M203

*Zhao*$^{4}$ 照 illuminated, shining, WX, M238

*Zhe*$^{2}$ 輒 attach, WX, M284

*Zhen*$^{1}$ 貞 upright, W56C, M346

*Zhen*$^{3}$ 枕 pillow, WX, M308

*Zheng*$^{4}$ 正 upright, W112I, M351

*Zhi*$^{1}$ 支 branch, support, W43C, M937

*Zhi*$^{1}$ 之 he, she, it, W79B, M935

*Zhi*$^{2}$ 直 straight, upright, direct, W10K, M1006

*Zhi*$^{4}$ 室 great, W133B, M982

*Zhi*$^{4}$ 至 extremity, W133B, M982

*ZHI*[4] 秩 sequence, WX, M1011
*ZHI*[4] 志 will, ambition, spirit of the kidney official, W79B, M971
*ZHONG*[1] 中 center, middle, W109A, M1504
*ZHONG*[1] 鍾 bell, cup, WX, M1514
*ZHOU*[1] 周 whole, W109C, M1293
*ZHOU*[1] 周 encircle, W109C, M1293
*ZHOU*[3] 肘 elbow, W45G, M1301
*ZHU*[2] 竹 bamboo, W77B, M1373
*ZHU*[2] 築 building, WX, M1376
*ZHU*[3] 渚 islet, WX, M1355
*ZHU*[3] 主 host, WX, M1336
*ZHU*[3] 主 master, W83D, M1336
*ZHU*[4] 柱 pillar, WX, M1339
*ZHU*[4] 杼 shuttle, WX, M1369
*ZHU*[4] 注 flow, WX, M1340
*ZI*[3] 子 infant, W94A, M6939
*ZI*[3] 資 assist, WX, M6927
*ZI*[4] 眦 canthus of the eye, WX, M6953
*ZONG*[1] 宗 ancestor, W36B, M6896
*ZU*[2] 足 leg, W112B, M6824
*ZUI*[4] 最 great, W34J, M6858

LONNY S. JARRETT, M.AC., author of *Nourishing Destiny, The Inner Tradition of Chinese Medicine*, has been a student of Chinese medicine since 1980. He is a graduate of the Traditional Acupuncture Institute and a fellow of the National Academy of Acupuncture and Oriental Medicine. He holds a master's degree in neurobiology and a fourth-degree black belt in Tae Kwon Do. Lonny maintains his clinical practice in Stockbridge, Massachusetts.